Federal
Aviation
Regulations

Includes
Parts 1, 61, 91, 119, 135, 141,
HMR 175, and NTSB 830

FAR Study Guide with
Questions and Answers

JEPPESEN®
Sanderson Training Products

ii

JS314703R

PREFACE _____

The Federal Aviation Regulations are an integral part of your private, instrument, and commercial training. This book contains applicable portions of Parts 1, 61, 91, 119, 135, 141, and NTSB 830. It also contains a summary of Hazardous Materials Regulation (HMR) 175. Rather than being bound into your pilot training manual, these regulations are printed separately so they can be updated frequently.

The FARs are presented in numerical sequence, and each is preceded by a table of contents for that Part. To help you tailor your studies, a list of recommended regulations for private, instrument, and commercial pilots is provided at the front of this book. You should study the recommended regulations thoroughly, making notes in the wide margins provided on each page. To check your understanding, work the exercises presented at the back of the book. They are divided into private, instrument, and commercial exercises. Check your answers against the answer section, then review the regulations, as needed.

Other pertinent regulations include Parts 67, 71, and 97. They are not reprinted here because the information they contain is covered elsewhere in the Jeppesen Sanderson materials. For example, Part 67 spells out medical standards, but Part 61 also includes the information you will need. Part 71 gives information on designation of Federal airways and airspace; however, this is covered thoroughly in your manual in the airspace discussion. Part 97 pertains to standard instrument approach procedures. Again, this is contained in the *Instrument/Commercial Manual*. There are many other regulations which apply to particular aviation segments, such as Part 133, "Rotorcraft External-Load Operations" and Part 137, "Agricultural Aircraft Operations." As you move into more specific areas, you should investigate these other FARs. You should also seek out and review current regulations periodically, since they undergo frequent revisions.

TABLE OF CONTENTS

RECOMMENDED STUDY LISTS

PRIVATE PILOT

✓1.1	61.102	91.155
✓1.2	61.103	91.157
✓1.3	61.105	91.159
✓61.1	61.107	91.169
✓61.3	61.109	91.203
✓61.5	61.111	91.205
61.6	61.118	91.207
61.11	61.120	91.209
61.13	91.1	91.211
61.15	91.3	91.213
61.16	91.7	91.215
61.17	91.9	91.217
61.19	91.11	91.303
61.23	91.13	91.305
61.25	91.15	91.307
61.27	91.17	91.309
61.29	91.19	91.311
61.31	91.25	91.313
61.33	91.101	91.315
61.35	91.103	91.401
61.37	91.105	91.403
61.39	91.107	91.405
61.41	91.109	91.407
61.43	91.111	91.409
61.45	91.113	91.411
61.47	91.115	91.413
61.49	91.117	91.417
61.51	91.119	91.421
61.53	91.121	91.703
61.56	91.123	91.707
61.57	91.125	91.903
61.59	91.126	830.1
61.60	91.127	830.2
61.61	91.129	830.5
61.63	91.130	830.6
61.69	91.131	830.10
61.71	91.133	830.15
61.81	91.135	
61.83	91.137	
61.85	91.139	
61.87	91.141	
61.89	91.143	
61.91	91.144	
61.93	91.151	
61.95	91.153	

INSTRUMENT RATING

1.1	91.103	91.217
1.2	91.105	91.313
1.3	91.107	91.315
61.1	91.109	91.401
61.3	91.111	91.403
61.5	91.113	91.411
61.6	91.115	91.413
61.11	91.117	91.703
61.13	91.119	91.707
61.15	91.121	91.903
61.16	91.123	830.1
61.17	91.125	830.2
61.23	91.126	830.5
61.25	91.127	830.6
61.29	91.129	830.10
61.33	91.130	830.15
61.35	91.131	
61.37	91.133	
61.39	91.135	
61.41	91.137	
61.43	91.139	
61.45	91.144	
61.47	91.151	
61.49	91.153	
61.51	91.155	
61.53	91.157	
61.56	91.159	
61.57	91.167	
61.59	91.169	
61.60	91.171	
61.61	91.173	
61.65	91.175	
61.71	91.177	
61.129	91.179	
91.1	91.181	
91.3	91.183	
91.7	91.185	
91.9	91.187	
91.11	91.203	
91.13	91.205	
91.17	91.207	
91.19	91.209	
91.21	91.211	
91.25	91.213	
91.101	91.215	

COMMERCIAL PILOT

1.1	91.3	91.209	135.99
1.2	91.7	91.211	135.101
1.3	91.9	91.213	135.103
61.1	91.11	91.215	135.105
61.3	91.13	91.217	135.107
61.5	91.15	91.303	135.117
61.6	91.17	91.305	135.127
61.11	91.19	91.307	135.128
61.13	91.21	91.309	135.141
61.14	91.23	91.311	135.143
61.15	91.25	91.313	135.149
61.16	91.101	91.315	135.151
61.17	91.103	91.401	135.153
61.19	91.105	91.403	135.171
61.23	91.107	91.405	135.201
61.25	91.109	91.407	135.203
61.29	91.111	91.409	135.205
61.31	91.113	91.411	135.209
61.33	91.115	91.413	135.211
61.35	91.117	91.417	135.213
61.37	91.119	91.421	135.215
61.39	91.121	91.703	135.217
61.41	91.123	91.707	135.219
61.43	91.125	91.903	135.221
61.45	91.126	91.905	135.223
61.47	91.127	119.1	135.225
61.49	91.129	119.2	135.227
61.51	91.130	119.3	135.229
61.53	91.131	119.5	135.241
61.55	91.133	119.7	135.243
61.56	91.135	135.1	135.245
61.57	91.137	135.3	135.247
61.59	91.139	135.5	135.249
61.60	91.141	135.10	135.251
61.61	91.143	135.11	135.341
61.63	91.144	135.19	830.1
61.69	91.151	135.21	830.2
61.71	91.153	135.23	830.5
61.121	91.155	135.25	830.6
61.123	91.157	135.33	830.10
61.125	91.159	135.61	830.15
61.127	91.169	135.85	
61.129	91.203	135.87	
61.139	91.205	135.89	
91.1	91.207	135.93	

FEDERAL AVIATION REGULATIONS

FARs

R

INTENTIONALLY

LEFT

BLANK

FEDERAL AVIATION REGULATIONS

PART 1 — DEFINITIONS AND ABBREVIATIONS

➤ This part contains all effective amendments through #45 effective 1 August 1996.

TABLE OF CONTENTS

INTENTIONALLY

LEFT

BLANK

1.1 GENERAL DEFINITIONS

As used in Subchapters A through K of this chapter unless the context requires otherwise:

"Administrator" means the Federal Aviation Administrator or any person to whom he has delegated his authority in the matter concerned.

"Aerodynamic coefficients" means nondimensional coefficients for aerodynamic forces and moments.

"Air carrier" means a person who undertakes directly by lease, or other arrangement, to engage in air transportation.

"Air commerce" means interstate, overseas, or foreign air commerce or the transportation of mail by aircraft or any operation or navigation of aircraft within the limits of any Federal airway or any operation or navigation of aircraft which directly affects, or which may endanger safety in, interstate, overseas, or foreign air commerce.

"Aircraft" means a device that is used or intended to be used for flight in the air.

"Aircraft engine" means an engine that is used or intended to be used for propelling aircraft. It includes turbosuperchargers, appurtenances, and accessories necessary for its functioning, but does not include propellers.

"Airframe" means the fuselage, booms, nacelles, cowlings, fairings, airfoil surfaces (including rotors but excluding propellers and rotating airfoils of engines), and landing gear of an aircraft and their accessories and controls.

"Airplane" means an engine-driven fixed-wing aircraft heavier than air, that is supported in flight by the dynamic reaction of the air against its wings.

"Airport" means an area of land or water that is used or intended to be used for the landing and takeoff of aircraft, and includes its buildings and facilities, if any.

"Airship" means an engine-driven lighter-than-air aircraft that can be steered.

"Air traffic" means aircraft operating in the air or on an airport surface, exclusive of loading ramps and parking areas.

"Air traffic clearance" means an authorization by air traffic control, for the purpose of preventing collision between known aircraft, for an aircraft to proceed under specified traffic conditions within controlled airspace.

"Air traffic control" means a service operated by appropriate authority to promote the safe, orderly, and expeditious flow of air traffic.

"Air transportation" means interstate, overseas, or foreign air transportation or the transportation of mail by aircraft.

"Alert Area" means an established area in which a high volume of pilot training or an unusual type of aeronautical activity is conducted.

"Alternate airport" means an airport at which an aircraft may land if a landing at the intended airport becomes inadvisable.

"Altitude engine" means a reciprocating aircraft engine having a rated takeoff power that is producible from sea level to an established higher altitude.

"Appliance" means any instrument, mechanism, equipment, part, apparatus, appurtenance, or accessory, including communications equipment, that is used or intended to be used in operating or controlling an aircraft in flight, is installed in or attached to the aircraft, and is not part of an airframe, engine, or propeller.

"Approved," unless used with reference to another person, means approved by the Administrator.

"Area navigation (RNAV)" means a method of navigation that permits aircraft operations on any desired course within the coverage of station-referenced navigation signals or within the limits of self-contained system capability.

"Area navigation high route" means an area navigation route within the airspace extending upward from, and including, 18,000 feet MSL to flight level 450.

"Area navigation low route" means an area navigation route within the airspace extending upward from 1,200 feet above the surface of the earth to, but not including, 18,000 feet MSL.

"Armed Forces" means the Army, Navy, Air Force, Marine Corps, and Coast Guard, including their regular and reserve components and members serving without component status.

"Autorotation" means a rotorcraft flight condition in which the lifting rotor is driven entirely by action of the air when the rotorcraft is in motion.

"Auxiliary rotor" means a rotor that serves either to counteract the effect of the main rotor torque on a rotorcraft or to maneuver the rotorcraft about one or more of its three principal axes.

"Balloon" means a lighter-than-air aircraft that is not engine-driven.

"Brake horsepower" means the power delivered at the propeller shaft (main drive or main output) of an aircraft engine.

"Calibrated airspeed" means indicated airspeed of an aircraft, corrected for position and instrument error. Calibrated airspeed is equal to true airspeed in standard atmosphere at sea level.

"Canard" means the forward wing of a canard configuration and may be a fixed, movable, or variable geometry surface, with or without control surfaces.

1.1 GENERAL DEFINITIONS (Cont)

"Canard configuration" means a configuration in which the span of the forward wing is substantially less than that of the main wing.

"Category" —
   (1) As used with respect to the certification, ratings, privileges, and limitations of airmen, means a broad classification of aircraft. Examples include: airplane; rotorcraft; glider; and lighter-than-air; and
   (2) As used with respect to the certification of aircraft, means a grouping of aircraft based upon intended use or operating limitations. Examples include: transport; normal; utility; acrobatic; limited; restricted; and provisional.

"Category A," with respect to transport category rotorcraft, means multiengine rotorcraft designed with engine and system isolation features specified in Part 29 and utilizing scheduled takeoff and landing operations under a critical engine failure concept which assures adequate designated surface area and adequate performance capability for continued safe flight in the event of engine failure.

"Category B," with respect to transport category rotorcraft, means single-engine or multiengine rotorcraft which do not fully meet all Category A standards. Category B rotorcraft have no guaranteed stay-up ability in the event of engine failure and unscheduled landing is assumed.

"Category II operations," with respect to the operation of aircraft, means a straight-in ILS approach to the runway of an airport under a Category II ILS instrument approach procedure issued by the Administrator or other appropriate authority.

"Category III operations," with respect to the operation of aircraft, means an ILS approach to, and landing on, the runway of an airport using a Category III ILS instrument approach procedure issued by the Administrator or other appropriate authority.

Category IIIa operations, an ILS approach and landing with no decision height (DH), or a DH below 100 feet (30 meters), and controlling runway visual range not less than 700 feet (200 meters).

Ⓐ

Category IIIb operations, an ILS approach and landing with no DH, or with a DH below 50 feet (15 meters), and controlling runway visual range less than 700 feet (200 meters), but not less than 150 feet (50 meters).

Category IIIc operations, an ILS approach and **Ⓐ** landing with no DH and no runway visual range limitation.

"Ceiling" means the height above the earth's surface of the lowest layer of clouds or obscuring phenomena that is reported as "broken," "overcast," or "obscuration" and not classified as "thin" or "partial."

"Civil aircraft" means aircraft other than public aircraft.

"Class" —
   (1) As used with respect to the certification, ratings, privileges, and limitations of airmen, means a classification of aircraft within a category having similar operating characteristics. Examples include: single engine; multiengine; land; water; gyroplane; helicopter; airship; and free balloon; and
   (2) As used with respect to the certification of aircraft, means a broad grouping of aircraft having similar characteristics of propulsion, flight or landing. Examples include: airplane; rotorcraft; glider; balloon; landplane and seaplane.

"Clearway" means:
   (1) For turbine engine powered airplanes certificated after August 29, 1959, an area beyond the runway, not less than 500 feet wide, centrally located about the extended centerline of the runway, and under the control of the airport authorities. The clearway is expressed in terms of a clearway plane, extending from the end of the runway with an upward slope not exceeding 1.25 percent, above which no object nor any terrain protrudes. However, threshold lights may protrude above the plane if their height above the end of the runway is 26 inches or less and if they are located to each side of the runway.
   (2) For turbine engine powered airplanes certificated after September 30, 1958, but before August 30, 1959, an area beyond the takeoff runway extending no less than 300 feet on either side of the extended centerline of the runway, at an elevation no higher than the elevation of the end of the runway, clear of all fixed obstacles, and under the control of the airport authorities.

Ⓐ *Amend #45 eff 8-1-96*

"Climbout speed," with respect to rotorcraft, means a referenced airspeed which results in a flight path clear of the height-velocity envelope during initial climbout.

"Commercial operator" means a person who, for compensation or hire, engages in the carriage by aircraft in air commerce of persons or property, other than as an air carrier or foreign air carrier or under the authority of *Part 375 of this Title. Where it is doubtful that an operation is for "compensation or hire," the test applied is whether the carriage by air is merely incidental to the person's other business or is, in itself, a major enterprise for profit.

"Controlled airspace" means an airspace of defined dimensions within which air traffic control service is provided to IFR flights and to VFR flights in accordance with the airspace classification.

Note— Controlled airspace is a generic term that covers Class A, Class B, Class C, Class D, and Class E airspace.

"Controlled Firing Area" means an area that is established to contain activities, which if not conducted in a controlled environment, would be hazardous to nonparticipating aircraft.

"Crewmember" means a person assigned to perform duty in an aircraft during flight time.

"Critical altitude" means the maximum altitude at which, in standard atmosphere, it is possible to maintain, at a specified rotational speed, a specified power or a specified manifold pressure. Unless otherwise stated, the critical altitude is the maximum altitude at which it is possible to maintain, at the maximum continuous rotational speed, one of the following:
 (1) The maximum continuous power, in the case of engines for which this power rating is the same at sea level and at the rated altitude.
 (2) The maximum continuous rated manifold pressure, in the case of engines, the maximum continuous power of which is governed by a constant manifold pressure.

"Critical engine" means the engine whose failure would most adversely affect the performance or handling qualities of an aircraft.

"Decision height," with respect to the operation of aircraft, means the height at which a decision must be made, during an ILS or PAR instrument approach, to either continue the approach or to execute a missed approach.

"Equivalent airspeed" means the calibrated airspeed of an aircraft corrected for adiabatic compressible flow for the particular altitude. Equivalent airspeed is equal to calibrated airspeed in standard atmosphere at sea level.

"Extended over-water operation" means —
 (1) With respect to aircraft other than helicopters, an operation over water at a horizontal distance of more than 50 nautical miles from the nearest shoreline; and
 (2) With respect to helicopters, an operation over water at a horizontal distance of more than 50 nautical miles from the nearest shoreline and more than 50 nautical miles from an off-shore heliport structure.

"External load" means a load that is carried, or extends, outside of the aircraft fuselage.

"External-load attaching means" means the structural components used to attach an external load to an aircraft, including external-load containers, the backup structure at the attachment points, and any quick-release device used to jettison the external load.

"Fireproof" —
 (1) With respect to materials and parts used to confine fire in a designated fire zone, means the capacity to withstand at least as well as steel in dimensions appropriate for the purpose for which they are used, the heat produced when there is a severe fire of extended duration in that zone; and
 (2) With respect to other materials and parts, means the capacity to withstand the heat associated with fire at least as well as steel in dimensions appropriate for the purpose for which they are used.

"Fire resistant" —
 (1) With respect to sheet or structural members means the capacity to withstand the heat associated with fire at least as well as aluminum alloy in dimensions appropriate for the purpose for which they are used; and
 (2) With respect to fluid-carrying lines, fluid system parts, wiring, air ducts, fittings, and powerplant controls, means the capacity to perform the intended functions under the heat and other conditions likely to occur when there is a fire at the place concerned.

"Flame resistant" means not susceptible to combustion to the point of propagating a flame, beyond safe limits, after the ignition source is removed.

"Flammable", with respect to a fluid or gas, means susceptible to igniting readily or to exploding.

"Flap extended speed" means the highest speed permissible with wing flaps in a prescribed extended position.

"Flash resistant" means not susceptible to burning violently when ignited.

"Flight crewmember" means a pilot, flight engineer, or flight navigator assigned to duty in an aircraft during flight time.

"Flight level" means a level of constant atmospheric pressure related to a reference datum of 29.92 inches of mercury. Each is stated in three digits that represent hundreds of feet. For example, flight level 250 represents a barometric altimeter indication of 25,000 feet; flight level 255, an indication of 25,500 feet.

"Flight plan" means specified information, relating to the intended flight of an aircraft, that is filed orally or in writing with air traffic control.

"Flight time" means the time from the moment the aircraft first moves under its own power for the purpose of flight until the moment it comes to rest at the next point of landing. ("Block-to-block" time.)

"Flight visibility" means the average forward horizontal distance, from the cockpit of an aircraft in flight, at which prominent unlighted objects may be seen and identified by day and prominent lighted objects may be seen and identified by night.

"Foreign air carrier" means any person other than a citizen of the United States, who undertakes directly, by lease or other arrangement, to engage in air transportation.

"Foreign air commerce" means the carriage by aircraft of persons or property for compensation or hire, or the carriage of mail by aircraft, or the operation or navigation of aircraft in the conduct or furtherance of a business or vocation, in commerce between a place in the United States and any place outside thereof; whether such commerce moves wholly by aircraft or partly by aircraft and partly by other forms of transportation.

"Foreign air transportation" means the carriage by aircraft of persons or property as a common carrier for compensation or hire, or the carriage of mail by aircraft, in commerce between a place in the United States and any place outside of the United States, whether that commerce moves wholly by aircraft or partly by aircraft and partly by other forms of transportation.

"Forward wing" means a forward lifting surface of a canard configuration or tandem-wing configuration airplane. The surface may be a fixed, movable, or variable geometry surface, with or without control surfaces.

"Glider" means a heavier-than-air aircraft that is supported in flight by the dynamic reaction of the air against its lifting surfaces and whose free flight does not depend principally on an engine.

"Go-around power or thrust setting" means the maximum allowable in-flight power or thrust setting identified in the performance data.

"Ground visibility" means prevailing horizontal visibility near the earth's surface as reported by the United States National Weather Service or an accredited observer.

"Gyrodyne" means a rotorcraft whose rotors are normally engine-driven for takeoff, hovering, and landing, and for forward flight through part of its speed range, and whose means of propulsion, consisting usually of conventional propellers, is independent of the rotor system.

"Gyroplane" means a rotorcraft whose rotors are not engine-driven except for initial starting, but are made to rotate by action of the air when the rotorcraft is moving; and whose means of propulsion, consisting usually of conventional propellers, is independent of the rotor system.

"Helicopter" means a rotorcraft that, for its horizontal motion, depends principally on its engine-driven rotors.

"Heliport" means an area of land, water, or structure used or intended to be used for the landing and takeoff of helicopters.

"Idle thrust" means the jet thrust obtained with the engine power control lever set at the stop for the least thrust position at which it can be placed.

"IFR conditions" means weather conditions below the minimum for flight under visual flight rules.

"IFR over-the-top," with respect to the operation of aircraft, means the operation of an aircraft over-the-top on an IFR flight plan when cleared by air traffic control to maintain "VFR conditions" or "VFR conditions on top."

"Indicated airspeed" means the speed of an aircraft as shown on its pitot static airspeed indicator calibrated to reflect standard atmosphere adiabatic compressible flow at sea level uncorrected for airspeed system errors.

"Instrument" means a device using an internal mechanism to show visually or aurally the attitude, altitude, or operation of an aircraft or aircraft part. It includes electronic devices for automatically controlling an aircraft in flight.

"Interstate air commerce" means the carriage by aircraft of persons or property for compensation or hire, or the carriage of mail by aircraft, or the operation or navigation of aircraft in the conduct or furtherance of a business or vocation, in commerce between a place in any State of the United States, or the District of Columbia, and a place in any other State of the United States, or the District of Columbia; or between places in the same State of the United States through the airspace over any place outside thereof; or between places in the same territory or possession of the United States, or the District of Columbia.

"Interstate air transportation" means the carriage by aircraft of persons or property as a common carrier for compensation or hire, or the carriage of mail by aircraft, in commerce —
(1) Between a place in a State or the District of Columbia and another place in another State or the District of Columbia;
(2) Between places in the same State through the airspace of any place outside that State; or
(3) Between places in the same possession of the United States; whether that commerce moves wholly by aircraft or partly by aircraft and partly by other forms of transportation.

"Intrastate air transportation" means the carriage of persons or property as a common carrier for compensation or hire, by turbojet-powered aircraft capable of carrying thirty or more persons, wholly within the same State of the United States.

"Kite" means a framework, covered with paper, cloth, metal, or other material, intended to be flown at the end of a rope or cable, and having as its only support the force of the wind moving past its surfaces.

"Landing gear extended speed" means the maximum speed at which an aircraft can be safely flown with the landing gear extended.

"Landing gear operating speed" means the maximum speed at which the landing gear can be safely extended or retracted.

"Large aircraft" means aircraft of more than 12,500 pounds maximum certificated takeoff weight.

"Lighter-than-air aircraft" means aircraft that can rise and remain suspended by using contained gas weighing less than the air that is displaced by the gas.

"Load factor" means the ratio of a specified load to the total weight of the aircraft. The specified load is expressed in terms of any of the following: aerodynamic forces, inertia forces, or ground or water reactions.

"Long-range communication system (LRCS)" means a system that uses satellite relay, data link, high frequency, or another approved communication system which extends beyond line of sight.

Ⓐ "Long-range navigation system (LRNS)" means an electronic navigation unit that is approved for use under instrument flight rules as a primary means of navigation, and has at least one source of navigational input, such as inertial navigation system, global positioning system, Omega/very low frequency, or Loran C.

"Mach number" means the ratio of true airspeed to the speed of sound.

"Main rotor" means the rotor that supplies the principal lift to a rotorcraft.

"Maintenance" means inspection, overhaul, repair, preservation, and the replacement of parts, but excludes preventive maintenance.

"Major alteration" means an alteration not listed in the aircraft, aircraft engine, or propeller specifications —
(1) That might appreciably affect weight, balance, structural strength, performance, powerplant operation, flight characteristics, or other qualities affecting airworthiness; or
(2) That is not done according to accepted practices or cannot be done by elementary operations.

"Major repair" means a repair —
(1) That, if improperly done, might appreciably affect weight, balance, structural strength, performance, powerplant operation, flight characteristics, or other qualities affecting airworthiness; or
(2) That is not done according to accepted practices or cannot be done by elementary operations.

Ⓐ *Amend #44 eff 2-26-96*

"Manifold pressure" means absolute pressure as measured at the appropriate point in the induction system and usually expressed in inches of mercury.

"Maximum speed for stability characteristics, V_{FC}/M_{FC}" means a speed that may not be less than a speed midway between maximum operating limit speed (V_{MO}/M_{MO}) and demonstrated flight diving speed (V_{DF}/M_{DF}), except that, for altitudes where the Mach number is the limiting factor, M_{FC} need not exceed the Mach number at which effective speed warning occurs.

"Medical certificate" means acceptable evidence of physical fitness on a form prescribed by the Administrator.

"Military operations area" (MOA) means an airspace that is established outside Class A airspace to seperate or segregate certain nonhazardous military activities from IFR Traffic and to identify for VFR traffic where theses activities are conducted.

"Minimum descent altitude" means the lowest altitude, expressed in feet above mean sea level, to which descent is authorized on final approach or during circle-to-land maneuvering in execution of a standard instrument approach procedure, where no electronic glide slope is provided.

"Minor alteration" means an alteration other than a major alteration.

"Minor repair" means a repair other than a major repair.

"Navigable airspace" means airspace at and above the minimum flight altitudes prescribed by or under this chapter, including airspace needed for safe takeoff and landing.

"Night" means the time between the end of evening civil twilight and the beginning of morning civil twilight, as published in the American Air Almanac, converted to local time.

"Nonprecision approach procedure" means a standard instrument approach procedure in which no electronic glide slope is provided.

"Operate," with respect to aircraft, means use, cause to use or authorize to use aircraft, for the purpose (except as provided in §91.13 of this chapter) of air navigation including the piloting of aircraft, with or without the right of legal control (as owner, lessee, or otherwise).

"Operational control," with respect to a flight, means the exercise of authority over initiating, conducting, or terminating a flight.

"Overseas air commerce" means the carriage by aircraft of persons or property for compensation or hire, or the carriage of mail by aircraft, or the operation or navigation of aircraft in the conduct of furtherance of a business or vocation, in commerce between a place in any State of the United States, or the District of Columbia, and any place in a territory or possession of the United States; or between a place in a territory or possession of the United States, and a place in any other territory or possession of the United States.

"Overseas air transportation" means the carriage by aircraft of persons or property as a common carrier for compensation or hire, or the carriage of mail by aircraft, in commerce —
(1) Between a place in a State or the District of Columbia and a place in a possession of the United States; or
(2) Between a place in a possession of the United States and a place in another possession of the United States;
whether that commerce moves wholly by aircraft or partly by aircraft and partly by other forms of transportation.

"Over-the-top" means above the layer of clouds or other obscuring phenomena forming the ceiling.

"Parachute" means a device used or intended to be used to retard the fall of a body or object through the air.

"Person" means an individual, firm, partnership, corporation, company, association, joint-stock association, or governmental entity. It includes a trustee, receiver, assignee, or similar representative of any of them.

"Pilotage" means navigation by visual reference to landmarks.

"Pilot in command" means the pilot responsible for the operation and safety of an aircraft during flight time.

"Pitch setting" means the propeller blade setting as determined by the blade angle measured in a manner, and at a radius, specified by the instruction manual for the propeller.

"Positive control" means control of all air traffic, within designated airspace, by air traffic control.

"Precision approach procedure" means a standard instrument approach procedure in which an electronic glide slope is provided, such as ILS and PAR.

"Preventive maintenance" means simple or minor preservation operations and the replacement of small standard parts not involving complex assembly operations.

"Prohibited area" means an airspace that is designated under Part 73 within which no person may operate an aircraft without the permission of the using agency.

"Propeller" means a device for propelling an aircraft that has blades on an engine- driven shaft and that, when rotated, produces by its action on the air, a thrust approximately perpendicular to its plane of rotation. It includes control components normally supplied by its manufacturer, but does not include main and auxiliary rotors or rotating airfoils of engines.

"Public aircraft" means an aircraft used only for the United States Government, or owned and operated (except for commercial purposes), or exclusively leased for at least 90 continuous days, by a government (except the United States Government), including a State, the District of Columbia, or a territory or possession of the United States, or political subdivision of that government; but does not include a government-owned aircraft transporting property for commercial purposes, or transporting passengers other than transporting (for other than commercial purposes) crewmembers or other persons aboard the aircraft whose presence is required to perform, or is associated with the performance of, a governmental function such as firefighting, search and rescue, law enforcement, aeronautical research, or biological or geological resource management; or transporting (for other than commercial purposes) persons aboard the aircraft if the aircraft is operated by the Armed Forces or an intelligence agency of the United States. An aircraft described in the preceding sentence shall, notwithstanding any limitation relating to use of the aircraft for commercial purposes, be considered to be a public aircraft for the purposes of this Chapter without regard to whether the aircraft is operated by a unit of government on behalf of another unit of government, pursuant to a cost reimbursement agreement between such units of government, if the unit of government on whose behalf the operation is conducted certifies to the Administrator of the Federal Aviation Administration that the operation was necessary to respond to a significant and imminent threat to life or property (including natural resources) and that no service by a private operator was reasonably available to meet the threat.

"Rated continuous OEI power," with respect to rotorcraft turbine engines, means the approved brake horsepower developed under static conditions at specified altitudes and temperatures within the operating limitations established for the engine under Part 33 of this chapter, and limited in use to the time required to complete the flight after the failure of one engine of a multiengine rotorcraft.

"Rated maximum continuous augmented thrust," with respect to turbojet engine type certification, means the approved jet thrust that is developed statically or in flight, in standard atmosphere at a specified altitude, with fluid injection or with the burning of fuel in a separate combustion chamber, within the engine operating limitations established under Part 33, and approved for unrestricted periods of use.

"Rated maximum continuous power," with respect to reciprocating, turbopropeller, and turboshaft engines, means the approved brake horsepower that is developed statically or in flight, in standard atmosphere at a specified altitude, within the engine operating limitations established under Part 33, and approved for unrestricted periods of use.

"Rated maximum continuous thrust," with respect to turbojet engine type certification, means the approved jet thrust that is developed statically or in flight, in standard atmosphere at a specified altitude, without fluid injection and without the burning of fuel in a separate combustion chamber, within the engine operating limitations established under Part 33 of this chapter, and approved for unrestricted periods of use.

"Rated takeoff augmented thrust," with respect to turbojet engine type certification, means the approved jet thrust that is developed statically under standard sea level conditions, with fluid injection or with the burning of fuel in a separate combustion chamber, within the engine operating limitations established under Part 33 of this chapter, and limited in use to periods of not over 5 minutes for takeoff operation.

"Rated takeoff power," with respect to reciprocating, turbopropeller, and turboshaft engine type certification, means the approved brake horsepower that is developed statically under standard sea level conditions, within the engine operating limitations established under Part 33, and limited in use to periods of not over 5 minutes for takeoff operation.

"Rated takeoff thrust," with respect to turbojet engine type certification, means the approved jet thrust that is developed statically under standard sea level conditions, without fluid injection and without the burning of fuel in a separate combustion chamber, within the engine operating limitations established under Part 33 of this chapter, and limited in use to periods of not over 5 minutes for takeoff operation.

"Rated 30-minute OEI power", with respect to rotorcraft turbine engines, means the approved brake horsepower developed under static conditions at specified altitudes and temperatures within the operating limitations established for the engine under Part 33 of this chapter, and limited in use to a period of not more than 30 minutes after the failure of one engine of a multiengine rotorcraft.

"Rated 2 1/2-minute OEI power", with respect to rotorcraft turbine engines, means the brake horsepower developed under static conditions at specified altitudes and temperatures within the operating limitations established for the engine under Part 33 of this chapter, and limited in use to a period of not more than 2 1/2 minutes after the failure of one engine of a multiengine rotorcraft.

"Rating" means a statement that, as a part of a certificate, sets forth special conditions, privileges, or limitations.

"Reporting point" means a geographical location in relation to which the position of an aircraft is reported.

"Restricted area" means airspace designated under Part 73 within which the flight of aircraft, while not wholly prohibited, is subject to restriction.

"RNAV waypoint (W/P)" means a predetermined geographical position used for route or instrument approach definition or progress reporting purposes that is defined relative to a VORTAC station position.

"Rocket" means an aircraft propelled by ejected expanding gases generated in the engine from self-contained propellants and not dependent on the intake of outside substances. It includes any part which becomes separated during the operation.

"Rotorcraft" means a heavier-than-air aircraft that depends principally for its support in flight on the lift generated by one or more rotors.

"Rotorcraft-load combination" means the combination of a rotorcraft and an external load, including the external load attaching means. Rotorcraft-load combinations are designated as Class A, Class B, Class C, and Class D, as follows:
(1) "Class A rotorcraft-load combination" means one in which the external load cannot move freely, cannot be jettisoned, and does not extend below the landing gear.
(2) "Class B rotorcraft-load combination" means one in which the external load is jettisonable and is lifted free of land or water during the rotorcraft operations.
(3) "Class C rotorcraft-load combination" means one in which the external load is jettisonable and remains in contact with land or water during the rotorcraft operation.
(4) "Class D rotorcraft-load combination" means one in which the external load is other than a Class A, B, or C and has been specifically approved by the Administrator for that operation.

"Route segment" means a part of a route. Each end of that part is identified by —
(1) a continental or insular geographical location; or
(2) a point at which a definite radio fix can be established.

"Sea level engine" means a reciprocating aircraft engine having a rated takeoff power that is producible only at sea level.

"Second in command" means a pilot who is designated to be second in command of an aircraft during flight time.

"Show," unless the context otherwise requires, means to show to the satisfaction of the Administrator.

"Small aircraft" means aircraft of 12,500 pounds or less, maximum certificated takeoff weight.

"Special VFR conditions" mean meteorological conditions that are less than those required for basic VFR flight in controlled airspace and in which some aircraft are permitted flight under visual flight rules.

"Special VFR operations" means aircraft operating in accordance with clearances within controlled airspace in meteorological conditions less than the basic VFR weather minima. Such operations must be requested by the pilot and approved by ATC.

1.1 GENERAL DEFINITIONS (Cont)

"Standard atmosphere" means the atmosphere defined in *U.S. Standard Atmosphere, 1962* (Geopotential altitude tables).

"Stopway" means an area beyond the takeoff runway, no less wide than the runway and centered upon the extended centerline of the runway, able to support the airplane during an aborted takeoff, without causing structural damage to the airplane, and designated by the airport authorities for use in decelerating the airplane during an aborted takeoff.

"Takeoff power" —
  (1) With respect to reciprocating engines, means the brake horsepower that is developed under standard sea level conditions, and under the maximum conditions of crankshaft rotational speed and engine manifold pressure approved for the normal takeoff, and limited in continuous use to the period of time shown in the approved engine specification; and
  (2) With respect to turbine engines, means the brake horsepower that is developed under static conditions at a specified altitude and atmospheric temperature, and under the maximum conditions of rotorshaft rotational speed and gas temperature approved for the normal takeoff, and limited in continuous use to the period of time shown in the approved engine specification.

"Takeoff safety speed" means a referenced airspeed obtained after lift-off at which the required one-engine-inoperative climb performance can be achieved.

"Takeoff thrust," with respect to turbine engines, means the jet thrust that is developed under static conditions at a specific altitude and atmospheric temperature under the maximum conditions of rotorshaft rotational speed and gas temperature approved for the normal takeoff, and limited in continuous use to the period of time shown in the approved engine specification.

"Tandem wing configuration" means a configuration having two wings of similar span, mounted in tandem.

"TCAS I" means a TCAS that utilizes interrogations of, and replies from, airborne radar beacon transponders and provides traffic advisories to the pilot.

"TCAS II" means a TCAS that utilizes interrogations of, and replies from airborne radar beacon transponders and provides traffic advisories and resolution advisories in the vertical plane.

"TCAS III" means a TCAS that utilizes interrogation of, and replies from, airborne radar beacon transponders and provides traffic advisories and resolution advisories in the vertical and horizontal planes to the pilot.

"Time in service," with respect to maintenance time records, means the time from the moment an aircraft leaves the surface of the earth until it touches it at the next point of landing.

"Traffic pattern" means the traffic flow that is prescribed for aircraft landing at, taxiing on, or taking off from, an airport.

"True airspeed" means the airspeed of an aircraft relative to undisturbed air. True airspeed is equal to equivalent airspeed multiplied by $(po/p)^{1/2}$.

"Type" —
  (1) As used with respect to the certification, ratings, privileges, and limitations of airmen, means a specific make and basic model of aircraft, including modifications thereto that do not change its handling or flight characteristics. Examples include: DC-7, 1049, and F-27; and
  (2) As used with respect to the certification of aircraft, means those aircraft which are similar in design. Examples include: DC-7 and DC-7C; 1049G and 1049H; and F-27 and F-27F.
  (3) As used with respect to the certification of aircraft engines, means those engines which are similar in design. For example, JT8D and JT8D-7 are engines of the same type, and JT9D-3A and JT9D-7 are engines of the same type.

"United States," in a geographical sense, means (1) the States, the District of Columbia, Puerto Rico, and the possessions, including the territorial waters, and (2) the airspace of those areas.

"United States air carrier" means a citizen of the United States who undertakes directly by lease, or other arrangement, to engage in air transportation.

1.1 GENERAL DEFINITIONS (Cont)

"VFR over-the-top," with respect to the operation of aircraft, means the operation of an aircraft over-the-top under VFR when it is not being operated on an IFR flight plan.

"Warning area" means airspace of defined dimensions, extending from 3 nautical miles outward from the coast of the United States, that contains activity that may be hazardous to nonparticipating aircraft. The purpose of such warning areas is to warn nonparticipating pilots of the potential danger. A warning area may be located over domestic or international waters or both.

"Winglet or tip fin" means an out-of-plane surface extending from a lifting surface. The surface may or may not have control surfaces.

🅐 *Amend #42 eff 1-15-96*

1.2 ABBREVIATIONS AND SYMBOLS

In Subchapters A through K of this chapter:

AGL means above ground level.

ALS means approach light system.

ASR means airport surveillance radar.

ATC means air traffic control.

CAS means calibrated airspeed.

CAT II means Category II.

CONSOL or CONSOLAN means a kind of low or medium frequency long range navigational aid.

DH means decision height.

DME means distance measuring equipment compatible with TACAN.

EAS means equivalent airspeed.

FAA means Federal Aviation Administration.

FM means fan marker.

GS means glide slope.

HIRL means high-intensity runway light system.

IAS means indicated airspeed.

ICAO means International Civil Aviation Organization.

IFR means instrument flight rules.

ILS means instrument landing system.

IM means ILS inner marker.

INT means intersection.

LDA means localizer-type directional aid.

LFR means low-frequency radio range.

LMM means compass locator at middle marker.

LOC means ILS localizer.

LOM means compass locator at outer marker.

M means mach number.

MAA means maximum authorized IFR altitude.

MALS means medium intensity approach light system.

MALSR means medium intensity approach light system with runway alignment indicator lights.

MCA means minimum crossing altitude.

MDA means minimum descent altitude.

MEA means minimum enroute IFR altitude.

MM means ILS middle marker.

MOCA means minimum obstruction clearance altitude.

MRA means minimum reception altitude.

MSL means mean sea level.

NDB(ADF) means nondirectional beacon (automatic direction finder).

NOPT means no procedure turn required.

OEI means one engine inoperative.

OM means ILS outer marker.

PAR means precision approach radar.

RAIL means runway alignment indicator light system.

RBN means radio beacon.

RCLM means runway centerline marking.

RCLS means runway centerline light system.

REIL means runway end identification lights.

RR means low or medium frequency radio range station.

RVR means runway visual range as measured in the touchdown zone area.

SALS means short approach light system.

SSALS means simplified short approach light system.

SSALSR means simplified short approach light system with runway alignment indicator lights.

TACAN means ultra-high frequency tactical air navigational aid.

TAS means true airspeed.

TCAS means a traffic alert and collision avoidance system.

TDZL means touchdown zone lights.

TVOR means very high frequency terminal omnirange station.

V_A means design maneuvering speed.

V_B means design speed for maximum gust intensity.

V_C means design cruising speed.

V_D means design diving speed.

V_{DF}/M_{DF} means demonstrated flight diving speed.

V_F means design flap speed.

V_{FC}/M_{FC} means maximum speed for stability characteristics.

V_{FE} means maximum flap extended speed.

V_H means maximum speed in level flight with maximum continuous power.

V_{LE} means maximum landing gear extended speed.

V_{LO} means maximum landing gear operating speed.

V_{LOF} means lift-off speed.

V_{MC} means minimum control speed with the critical engine inoperative.

V_{MO}/M_{MO} means maximum operating limit speed.

V_{MU} means minimum unstick speed.

V_{NE} means never-exceed speed.

V_{NO} means maximum structural cruising speed.

V_R means rotation speed.

V_S means the stalling speed or the minimum steady flight speed at which the airplane is controllable.

V_{S_0} means the stalling speed or the minimum steady flight speed in the landing configuration.

V_{S_1} means the stalling speed or the minimum steady flight speed obtained in a specified configuration.

V_{TOSS} means takeoff safety speed for Category A rotorcraft.

V_X means speed for best angle of climb.

V_Y means speed for best rate of climb.

V_1 means takeoff decision speed (formerly denoted as critical engine failure speed).

V_2 means takeoff safety speed.

$V_{2\ min}$ means minimum takeoff safety speed.

VFR means visual flight rules.

VHF means very high frequency.

VOR means very high frequency omnirange station.

VORTAC means collocated VOR and TACAN.

1.3 RULES OF CONSTRUCTION

(a) In Subchapter A through K of this chapter, unless the context requires otherwise:
    (1) Words importing the singular include the plural;
    (2) Words importing the plural include the singular; and
    (3) Words importing the masculine gender include the feminine.

(b) In Subchapters A through K of this chapter, the word:
    (1) "Shall" is used in an imperative sense:
    (2) "May" is used in a permissive sense to state authority or permission to do the act prescribed, and the words "no person may . . ." or "a person may not . . ." mean that no person is required, authorized, or permitted to do the act prescribed; and
    (3) "includes" means "includes but is not limited to."

FEDERAL AVIATION REGULATIONS

PART 61 — CERTIFICATION: PILOTS AND FLIGHT INSTRUCTORS

This part contains all effective amendments through #100. This revision incorporates amendment #98 (not published herein) and amendment #99 effective 16 September 1996 and #100 effective 1 August 1996.

TABLE OF CONTENTS

SUBPART A — GENERAL

TABLE OF CONTENTS

SUBPART B — AIRCRAFT RATINGS AND SPECIAL CERTIFICATES

SUBPART C — STUDENT AND RECREATIONAL PILOTS

SUBPART D — PRIVATE PILOTS

SUBPART E — COMMERCIAL PILOTS

TABLE OF CONTENTS

SUBPART F — AIRLINE TRANSPORT PILOTS

SUBPART G — FLIGHT INSTRUCTORS

INTENTIONALLY

LEFT

BLANK

SUBPART A — GENERAL

61.1 APPLICABILITY

(a) This Part prescribes the requirements for issuing pilot and flight instructor certificates and ratings, the conditions under which those certificates and ratings are necessary, and the privileges and limitations of those certificates and ratings.

(b) Except as provided in § 61.71, an applicant for a certificate or rating must meet the requirements of this part.

61.2 DEFINITION OF TERMS

For the purpose of this part:

(a) *Authorized Instructor* means —
  (1) An instructor who has a valid ground instructor certificate or current flight instructor certificate with appropriate ratings issued by the Administrator;
  (2) An instructor authorized under Part 121 (SFAR 58), Part 135, or Part 142 of this chapter to give instruction under those parts; or
  (3) Any other person authorized by the Administrator to give instruction under this part.

(b) *Flight Simulator, Airplane* means a device that —
  (1) Is a full-sized airplane cockpit replica of a specific type of airplane, or make, model, and series of airplane;
  (2) Includes the hardware and software necessary to represent the airplane in ground operations and flight operations;
  (3) Utilizes a force cueing system that provides cues at least equivalent to those cues provided by a 3 degree freedom of motion system;
  (4) Utilizes a visual system that provides at least a 45° horizontal field of view and a 30° vertical field of view simultaneously for each pilot; and
  (5) Has been evaluated, qualified, and approved by the Administrator.

(c) *Flight Simulator, Helicopter* means a device that —
  (1) Is a full-sized helicopter cockpit replica of a specific type of aircraft, or make, model, and series of helicopter;
  (2) Includes the hardware and software necessary to represent the helicopter in ground operations and flight operations;
  (3) Utilizes a force cueing system that provides cues at least equivalent to those cues provided by a 3 degree freedom of motion system;
  (4) Utilizes a visual system that provides at least a 45° horizontal field of view and a 30° vertical field of view simultaneously for each pilot; and
  (5) Has been evaluated, qualified, and approved by the Administrator.

(d) *Flight Training Device* means a device that —
  (1) Is a full-sized replica of instruments, equipment, panels, and controls of an airplane or rotorcraft, or set of airplanes or rotorcraft, in an open flight deck area or in an enclosed cockpit, including the hardware and software for systems installed, necessary to simulate the airplane or rotorcraft in ground operations and flight operations;
  (2) Need not have a force (motion) cueing or visual system; and
  (3) Has been evaluated, qualified, and approved by the Administrator.

(e) *Set of Airplanes or Rotorcraft* means airplanes or rotorcraft which all share similar performance characteristics, such as similar airspeed and altitude operating envelope, similar handling characteristics, and the same number and type of propulsion systems.

61.3 CERTIFICATION OF FOREIGN PILOTS AND FLIGHT INSTRUCTORS

(a) A person who is neither a U.S citizen nor a resident alien may be issued a pilot certificate or flight instructor certificate under this part (other than under § 61.75 or 61.77), outside the United States, only when the Administrator finds that —
  (1) The pilot certificate is needed for the operation of a U.S. registered civil aircraft or;
  (2) The flight instructor certificate is needed for the training of students who are citizens of the United States.

Ⓐ *Amend #100 eff 8-1-96*

(b) Training centers, and their satellite training centers certificated under Part 142 of this chapter, may, outside the United States —

(1) Prepare and recommend applicants for additional ratings and endorsements to certificates issued by the Administrator under the provisions of this part, and award additional ratings and endorsements with in the authority granted to that training center by the Administrator; and

(2) Prepare and recommend U.S. citizen applicants for airman certificates, and issue certificates to U.S. citizens within the authority granted to that training center by the Administrator.

61.4 QUALIFICATION AND APPROVAL OF FLIGHT SIMULATORS AND FLIGHT TRAINING DEVICES

Each flight simulator and each flight training device used for training, for which an airman is to receive credit to satisfy any training, testing, or checking requirement under this chapter, must be qualified and approved by the Administrator for —

(a) The training, testing, and checking for which it is used;

(b) Each particular maneuver, procedure, or crewmember function performed; and

(c) The representation of the specific category and class of aircraft, type of aircraft, particular variation within type of aircraft, or set of aircraft in the case of some flight training devices.

61.5 REQUIREMENT FOR CERTIFICATES, RATING, AND AUTHORIZATIONS

(a) *Pilot Certificate.* No person may act as pilot-in-command or in any other capacity as a required pilot flight crewmember of a civil aircraft of United States registry unless he has in his personal possession a current pilot certificate issued to him under this Part. However, when the aircraft is operated within a foreign country a current pilot license issued by the country in which the aircraft is operated may be used.

(b) *Pilot Certificate: Foreign Aircraft.* No person may, within the United States, act as a pilot-in-command or in any other capacity as a required pilot flight crewmember of a civil aircraft of foreign registry unless he has in his personal possession a current pilot certificate issued to him under this Part, or a pilot license issued to him or validated for him by the country in which the aircraft is registered.

(c) *Medical Certificate.* Except for free balloon pilots piloting balloons and glider pilots piloting gliders, no person may act as pilot-in-command or in any other capacity as a required pilot flight crewmember of an aircraft under a certificate issued to him under this Part, unless he has in his personal possession an appropriate current medical certificate issued under Part 67 of this chapter. However, when the aircraft is operated within a foreign country with a current pilot license issued by that country, evidence of current medical qualification for that license, issued by that country may be used. In the case of a pilot certificate issued on the basis of a foreign pilot license under 61.75, evidence of current medical qualification accepted for the issue of that license is used in place of a medical certificate.

(d) *Flight Instructor Certificate.* Unless otherwise authorized by the Administrator, and except for lighter-than-air instruction in lighter-than-air aircraft, no person other than the holder of a flight instructor certificate issued in accordance with subpart G of this part, with an appropriate rating on that certificate may —

(1) Give any of the flight instruction required to qualify for a solo flight, solo cross-country flight, or for the issue of a pilot or flight instructor certificate or rating;

(2) Endorse a pilot logbook to show that he has given any flight instruction; or

(3) Endorse a student pilot certificate or logbook for solo operating privileges.

(e) *Instrument Rating.* No person may act as pilot-in-command of a civil aircraft under instrument flight rules, or in weather conditions less than the minimums prescribed for VFR flight unless —

(1) In the case of an airplane, he holds an instrument rating or an airline transport pilot certificate with an airplane category rating on it;

(2) In the case of a helicopter, he holds a helicopter instrument rating or an airline transport pilot certificate with a rotorcraft category and helicopter class rating not limited to VFR;

(3) In the case of a glider, he holds an instrument rating (airplane) or an airline transport pilot certificate with an airplane category rating; or

(4) In the case of an airship, he holds a commercial pilot certificate with lighter-than-air category and airship class ratings.

Amend #100 eff 8-1-96

(f) *Category II Pilot Authorization.*

   (1) No person may act as pilot-in-command of a civil aircraft during Category II operations unless—

      (i) That person holds a current Category II pilot authorization for that category or class of aircraft, and the type of aircraft, if applicable; or

      (ii) In the case of a civil aircraft of foreign registry, that person is authorized by the country of registry to act as pilot-in-command of that aircraft in Category II operations.

   (2) No person may act as second-in-command of a civil aircraft during Category II operations unless that person—

      (i) Holds a valid pilot certificate with category and class ratings for that aircraft and a current instrument rating for that category aircraft;

      (ii) Holds an airline transport pilot certificate with category and class ratings for that aircraft; or

      (iii) In the case of a civil aircraft of foreign registry, is authorized by the country of registry to act as second-in-command of that aircraft during Category II operations.

(g) *Category A Aircraft Pilot Authorization.* The Administrator may issue a certificate of authorization to the pilot of a small aircraft identified as a Category A aircraft in §97.3(b)(1) of this chapter to use that aircraft in a Category II operation, if he finds that the proposed operation can be safely conducted under the terms of the certificate. Such authorization does not permit operation of the aircraft carrying persons or property for compensation or hire.

(h) *Inspection of Certificate.* Each person who holds a pilot certificate, flight instructor certificate, medical certificate, authorization, or license required by this Part shall present it for inspection upon the request of the Administrator, an authorized representative of the National Transportation Safety Board, or any Federal, State, or local law enforcement officer.

(i) *Category III Pilot Authorization.*

   (1) No person may act as pilot-in-command of a civil aircraft during Category III operations unless —

      (i) That person holds a current Category III pilot authorization for that category or class of aircraft, and the type of aircraft, if applicable; or

      (ii) In the case of a civil aircraft of foreign registry, that person is authorized by the country of registry to act as pilot-in-command of that aircraft in Category III operations.

   (2) No person may act as second-in-command of a civil aircraft during Category III operations unless that person —

      (i) Holds a valid pilot certificate with category and class ratings for that aircraft and a current instrument rating for that category aircraft;

      (ii) Holds an airline transport pilot certificate with category and class ratings for that aircraft; or

      (iii) In the case of a civil aircraft of foreign registry, is authorized by the country of registry to act as second-in-command of that aircraft during Category III operations.

(j) *Exceptions.* Paragraphs (f) and (i) of this section do not apply to operations conducted by the holder of a certificate issued under Part 121 or Part 135 of this chapter.

61.6 CERTIFICATES AND RATINGS ISSUED UNDER THIS PART

(a) The following certificates are issued under this Part:

   (1) Pilot certificates:

      (i) Student pilot.

      (ii) Recreational pilot.

      (iii) Private pilot.

      (iv) Commercial pilot.

      (v) Airline transport pilot.

   (2) Flight instructor certificates.

(b) The following ratings are placed on pilot certificates (other than student pilot) where applicable:

(1) Aircraft category ratings:
   (i) Airplane.
   (ii) Rotorcraft.
   (iii) Glider.
   (iv) Lighter-than-air.

(2) Airplane class ratings:
   (i) Single-engine land.
   (ii) Multiengine land.
   (iii) Single-engine sea.
   (iv) Multiengine sea.

(3) Rotorcraft class ratings:
   (i) Helicopter.
   (ii) Gyroplane.

(4) Lighter-than-air class ratings:
   (i) Airship.
   (ii) Free balloon.

(5) Aircraft type ratings are listed in Advisory Circular 61-1 entitled "Aircraft Type Ratings." This list includes ratings for the following:
   (i) Large aircraft, other than lighter-than-air.
   (ii) Small turbojet-powered airplanes.
   (iii) Small helicopters for operations requiring an airline transport pilot certificate.
   (iv) Other aircraft type ratings specified by the Administrator through aircraft type certificate procedures.

(6) Instrument ratings (on private and commercial pilot certificates only):
   (i) Instrument — airplanes.
   (ii) Instrument — helicopter.

(c) The following ratings are placed on flight instructor certificates where applicable:

(1) Aircraft category ratings:
   (i) Airplane.
   (ii) Rotorcraft.
   (iii) Glider.

(2) Airplane class ratings:
   (i) Single-engine.
   (ii) Multiengine.

(3) Rotorcraft class ratings:
   (i) Helicopter.
   (ii) Gyroplane.

(4) Instrument ratings:
   (i) Instrument — airplane.
   (ii) Instrument — helicopter.

61.7 OBSOLETE CERTIFICATES AND RATINGS

(a) The holder of a free balloon pilot certificate issued before November 1, 1973, may not exercise the privileges of that certificate.

(b) The holder of a pilot certificate that bears any of the following category ratings without an associated class rating, may not exercise the privileges of that category rating:

(1) Rotorcraft.
(2) Lighter-than-air.
(3) Helicopter.
(4) Autogiro.

61.9 EXCHANGE OF OBSOLETE CERTIFICATES AND RATINGS FOR CURRENT CERTIFICATES AND RATINGS

(a) The holder of an unexpired free balloon pilot certificate, or an unexpired pilot certificate with an obsolete category rating listed in 61.7(b) of this Part may exchange that certificate for a certificate with the following applicable category and class rating, without a further showing of competency, until October 31, 1975. After that date, a free balloon pilot certificate or certificate with an obsolete rating expires.

(b) *Private or Commercial Pilot Certificate with Rotorcraft Category Rating.* The holder of a private or commercial pilot certificate with a rotorcraft category rating is issued that certificate with a rotorcraft category rating, and a helicopter or gyroplane class rating, depending upon whether a helicopter or a gyroplane is used to qualify for the rotorcraft category rating.

(c) *Private or Commercial Pilot Certificate with Helicopter or Autogiro Category Rating.* The holder of a private or commercial pilot certificate with a helicopter or autogiro category rating is issued that certificate with a rotorcraft category rating and a helicopter class rating (in the case of a helicopter category rating), or a gyroplane class rating (in the case of an autogiro rating).

(d) *Airline Transport Pilot Certificate with Helicopter or Autogiro Category Rating.* The holder of an airline transport pilot certificate with a helicopter or autogiro category rating is issued that certificate with a rotorcraft category rating (limited to VFR) and a helicopter class and type rating (in the case of a helicopter category rating), or a gyroplane class rating (in the case of an autogiro category rating).

(e) *Airline Transport Pilot Certificate with a Rotorcraft Category Rating (Without a Class Rating).* The holder of an airline transport pilot certificate with a rotorcraft category rating (without a class rating) is issued that certificate with a rotorcraft category rating limited to VFR, and a helicopter and type rating or a gyroplane class rating, depending upon whether a helicopter or gyroplane is used to qualify for the rotorcraft category rating.

(f) *Free Balloon Pilot Certificate.* The holder of a free balloon pilot certificate is issued a commercial pilot certificate with a lighter-than-air category rating and a free balloon class rating. However, a free balloon class rating may be issued with the limitations provided in §61.141.

(g) *Lighter-than-air Pilot Certificate or Pilot Certificate with Lighter-than-air Category (Without a Class Rating).*

     (1) In the case of an application made before November 1, 1975, the holder of a lighter-than-air pilot certificate or a pilot certificate with a lighter- than-air category rating (without a class rating) is issued a private or commercial pilot certificate, as appropriate, with a lighter-than-air category rating and airship and free balloon class ratings.

     (2) In the case of an application made after October 31, 1975, the holder of a lighter-than-air pilot certificate with an airship rating issued prior to November 1, 1973, may be issued a free balloon class rating upon passing the appropriate flight test in a free balloon.

61.11 EXPIRED PILOT CERTIFICATES AND REISSUANCE

(a) No person who holds an expired pilot certificate or rating may exercise the privileges of that pilot certificate, or rating.

(b) Except as provided, the following certificates and ratings have expired and are not reissued:

     (1) An airline transport pilot certificate issued before May 1, 1949, or containing a horsepower rating. However, an airline transport pilot certificate bearing an expiration date and issued after April 30, 1949, may be reissued without an expiration date if it does not contain a horsepower rating.

     (2) A private or commercial pilot certificate, or a lighter-than-air or free balloon pilot certificate, issued before July 1, 1945. However, each of those certificates issued after June 30, 1945, and bearing an expiration date, may be reissued without an expiration date.

(c) A private or commercial pilot certificate or a special purpose pilot certificate, issued on the basis of a foreign pilot license, expires on the expiration date stated thereon. A certificate without an expiration date is issued to he holder of the expired certificate only if he meets the requirements of §61.75 for the issue of a pilot certificate based on a foreign pilot license.

61.13 APPLICATION AND QUALIFICATION

(a) An application for a certificate and rating or for an additional rating under this Part is made on a form and in a manner prescribed by the Administrator. Each person who is neither a United States citizen nor a resident alien must show evidence that the fee prescribed by Appendix A of Part 187 of this chapter has been paid if that person —

     (1) Applies for a student pilot certificate to be issued outside the United States; or

     (2) Applies for a written or practical test to be administered outside the United States for any certificate or rating issued under this Part.

(b) An applicant who meets the requirements of this Part is entitled to an appropriate pilot certificate with aircraft ratings. Additional aircraft category, class, type and other ratings, for which the applicant is qualified, are added to his certificate. However, the Administrator may refuse to issue certificates to persons who are not citizens of the United States and who do not reside in the United States.

(c) An applicant who cannot comply with all of the flight proficiency requirements prescribed by this Part because the aircraft used by him for his flight training or flight test is characteristically incapable of performing a required pilot operation, but who meets all other requirements for the certificate or rating sought, is issued the certificate or rating with appropriate limitations.

(d) An applicant for a pilot certificate who holds a medical certificate under §67.19 of this chapter with special limitations on it, but who meets all other requirements for that pilot certificate, is issued a pilot certificate containing such operating limitations as the Administrator determines are necessary because of the applicant's medical deficiency.

(e) The following requirements apply to a Category II pilot authorization and to a Category III pilot authorization:

  (1) The authorization is issued by a letter of authorization as a part of the applicant's instrument rating or airline transport pilot certificate.

  (2) Upon original issue the authorization contains a visibility limitation —
    (i) For Category II operations, the limitation is 1600 feet RVR and a 150-foot decision height; and
    (ii) For Category III operations, each initial limitation is specified in the authorization document.

  (3) Limitations on an authorization may be removed as follows:
    (i) In the case of Category II limitations, a limitation is removed when the holder shows that, since the beginning of the sixth preceding month, the holder has made three Category II ILS approaches with a 150-foot decision height to a landing under actual or simulated instrument conditions.
    (ii) In the case of Category III limitations, a limitation is removed as specified in the authorization.

  (4) To meet the experience requirement of paragraph (e)(3) of this section, and for the practical test required by this part for a Category II or a Category III authorization, a flight simulator or flight training device may be used if it is approved by the Administrator for such use.

(f) Unless authorized by the Administrator —
  (1) A person whose pilot certificate is suspended may not apply for any pilot or flight instructor certificate or rating during the period of suspension; and
  (2) A person whose flight instructor certificate only is suspended may not apply for any rating to be added to that certificate during the period of suspension.

(g) Unless the order of revocation provides otherwise —
  (1) A person whose pilot certificate is revoked may not apply for any pilot or flight instructor certificate or rating for 1 year after the date of revocation; and
  (2) A person whose flight instructor certificate only is revoked may not apply for any flight instructor certificate for 1 year after the date of revocation.

61.14 REFUSAL TO SUBMIT TO A DRUG OR ALCOHOL TEST.

(a) This section applies to an employee who performs a function listed in appendix I or appendix J to part 121 of this chapter directly or by contract for a part 121 certificate holder, a part 135 certificate holder, or an operator as defined in §135.1(c) of this chapter.

(b) Refusal by the holder of a certificate issued under this part to take a drug test required under the provisions of appendix I to part 121 or an alcohol test required under the provisions of appendix J to part 121 is grounds for—
  (1) Denial of an application for any certificate or rating issued under this part for a period of up to 1 year after the date of such refusal; and
  (2) Suspension or revocation of any certificate or rating issued under this part.

61.15 OFFENSES INVOLVING ALCOHOL OR DRUGS

(a) A conviction for the violation of any Federal or state statute relating to the growing, processing, manufacture, sale, disposition, possession, transportation, or importation of narcotic drugs, marihuana, or depressant or stimulant drugs or substances is grounds for —

A *Amend #100 eff 8-1-96*

(1)   Denial of an application for any certificate or rating issued under this part for a period of up to 1 year after the date of final conviction; or

(2)   Suspension or revocation of any certificate or rating issued under this part.

(b)   The commission of an act prohibited by §91.17(a) or §91.19(a) of this chapter is grounds for —

(1)   Denial of an application for a certificate or rating issued under this part for a period of up to 1 year after the date of that act; or

(2)   Suspension or revocation of any certificate or rating issued under this part.

(c)   For the purposes of paragraphs (d) and (e) of this section, a motor vehicle action means—

(1)   A conviction after November 29, 1990, for the violation of any Federal or state statute relating to the operation of a motor vehicle while intoxicated by alcohol or a drug, while impaired by alcohol or a drug, or while under the influence of alcohol or a drug;

(2)   The cancellation, suspension, or revocation of a license to operate a motor vehicle by a state after November 29, 1990, for a cause related to the operation of a motor vehicle while intoxicated by alcohol or a drug, while impaired by alcohol or a drug, or while under the influence of alcohol or a drug; or

(3)   The denial after November 29, 1990, of an application for a license to operate a motor vehicle by a state for a cause related to the operation of a motor vehicle while intoxicated by alcohol or a drug, while impaired by alcohol or a drug, or while under the influence of alcohol or a drug.

(d)   Except in the case of a motor vehicle action that results from the same incident or arises out of the same factual circumstances, a motor vehicle action occurring within 3 years of a previous motor vehicle action is grounds for—

(1)   Denial of an application for any certificate or rating issued under this part for a period of up to 1 year after the date of the last motor vehicle action; or

(2)   Suspension or revocation of any certificate or rating issued under this part.

(e)   Each person holding a certificate issued under this part shall provide a written report of each motor vehicle action to the FAA, Civil Aviation Security Division (AAC-700), P.O. Box 25810, Oklahoma City, OK 73125, not later than 60 days after the motor vehicle action. The report must include—

(1)   The person's name, address, date of birth, and airman certificate number;

(2)   The type of violation that resulted in the conviction or the administrative action;

(3)   The date of the conviction or administrative action;

(4)   The state that holds the record of conviction or administrative action; and

(5)   A statement of whether the motor vehicle action resulted from the same incident or arose out of the same factual circumstances related to a previously-reported motor vehicle action.

(f)   Failure to comply with paragraph (e) of this section is grounds for—

(1)   Denial of an application for any certificate or rating issued under this part for a period of up to 1 year after the date of the motor vehicle action; or

(2)   Suspension or revocation of any certificate or rating issued under this part.

61.16   REFUSAL TO SUBMIT TO AN ALCOHOL TEST OR TO FURNISH TEST RESULTS

A refusal to submit to a test to indicate the percentage by weight of alcohol in the blood, when requested by a law enforcement officer in accordance with §91.17(c) of this chapter, or a refusal to furnish or authorize the release of the test results requested by the Administrator in accordance with §91.17(c) or (d) of this chapter, is grounds for —

(a)   Denial of an application for any certificate or rating issued under this part for a period of up to 1 year after the date of that refusal; or

(b)   Suspension or revocation of any certificate or rating issued under this part.

61.17   TEMPORARY CERTIFICATE

(a)   A temporary pilot or flight instructor certificate, or a rating, effective for a period of not more than 120 days, is issued to a qualified applicant pending a review of his qualifications and the issuance of a permanent certificate or rating by the Administrator. The permanent certificate or rating is issued to an applicant found qualified and a denial thereof is issued to an applicant found not qualified.

(b)   A temporary certificate issued under paragraph (a) of this section expires —

(1)   At the end of the expiration date stated thereon; or

(2)   Upon receipt by the applicant of —

(i)   The certificate or rating sought; or

(ii)   Notice that the certificate or rating sought is denied.

61.19   **DURATION OF PILOT AND FLIGHT INSTRUCTOR CERTIFICATES**

(a)   *General*. The holder of a certificate with an expiration date may not, after that date, exercise the privileges of that certificate.

(b)   *Student Pilot Certificate*. A student pilot certificate expires at the end of the 24th month after the month in which it is issued.

(c)   *Other Pilot Certificates*. Any pilot certificate (other than a student pilot certificate) issued under this Part is issued without a specific expiration date. However, the holder of a pilot certificate issued on the basis of a foreign pilot license may exercise the privileges of that certificate only while the foreign pilot license on which that certificate is based is effective.

(d)   *Flight Instructor Certificate*. A flight instructor certificate —

    (1)   Is effective only while the holder has a current pilot certificate and a medical certificate appropriate to the pilot privileges being exercised; and

    (2)   Expires at the end of the 24th month after the month in which it was last issued or renewed.

(e)   *Surrender, Suspension, or Revocation*. Any pilot certificate or flight instructor certificate issued under this Part ceases to be effective if it is surrendered, suspended, or revoked.

(f)   *Return of Certificate*. The holder of any certificate issued under this Part that is suspended or revoked shall, upon the Administrator's request, return it to the Administrator.

61.21   **DURATION OF CATEGORY II AND CATEGORY III PILOT AUTHORIZATION**
(For other than Part 121 and Part 135 use.)

A Category II pilot authorization and a Category III pilot authorization expire on the last day of the sixth month after the month last issued or renewed. Upon passing a practical test it is renewed for each type aircraft for which an authorization is held. However, an authorization for any particular type aircraft for which an authorization is held will not be renewed to extend beyond the end of the 12th month after the practical test was passed in that type aircraft. If the holder of the authorization passes the practical test for a renewal in the month before the authorization expires, he is considered to have passed it during the month the authorization expired.

61.23   **DURATION OF MEDICAL CERTIFICATES**

(a)   A first-class medical certificate expires at the end of the last day of —

    (1)   The sixth month after the month of the date of examination shown on the certificate, for operations requiring an airline transport pilot certificate;

    (2)   The 12th month after the month of the date of examination shown on the certificate, for operations requiring only a commercial pilot certificate; and

    (3)   The period specified in paragraph (c) of this section for operations requiring only a private, recreational, or student pilot certificate.

(b)   A second-class medical certificate expires at the end of the last day of—

    (1)   The 12th month after the month of the date of examination shown on the certificate, for operations requiring a commercial pilot certificate or an air traffic control tower operator certificate; and

    (2)   The period specified in paragraph (c) of this section for operations requiring only a private, recreational, or student pilot certificate.

(c)   A third-class medical certificate for operations requiring a private, recreational, or student pilot certificate issued—

    (1)   Before September 16, 1996, expires at the end of the 24th month after the month of the date of examination shown on the certificate.

    (2)   On or after September 16, 1996, expires at the end of the:

       (i)   36th month after the month of the date of the examination shown on the certificate if the person has not reached his or her 40th birthday on or before the date of the examination; or

       (ii)   24th month after the month of the date of the examination shown on the certificate if the person has reached his or her 40th birthday on or before the date of the examination.

Ⓐ *Amend #100 eff 8-1-96*
Ⓑ *Amend #99 eff 9-16-96*

61.25 CHANGE OF NAME

An application for the change of a name on a certificate issued under this Part must be accompanied by the applicant's current certificate and a copy of the marriage license, court order, or other document verifying the change. The documents are returned to the applicant after inspection.

61.27 VOLUNTARY SURRENDER OR EXCHANGE OF CERTIFICATE

The holder of a certificate issued under this Part may voluntarily surrender it for cancellation, or for the issue of a certificate of lower grade, or another certificate with specific ratings deleted. If he so requests, he must include the following signed statement or its equivalent:

"This request is made for my own reasons, with full knowledge that my (insert name of certificate or rating, as appropriate) may not be reissued to me unless I again pass the tests prescribed for its issue."

61.29 REPLACEMENT OF LOST OR DESTROYED CERTIFICATE

(a) An application for the replacement of a lost or destroyed airman certificate issued under this Part is made by letter to the Department of Transportation, Federal Aviation Administration, Airman Certification Branch, Post Office Box 25082, Oklahoma City, OK 73125. The letter must —
    (1) State the name of the person to whom the certificate was issued, the permanent mailing address (including zip code), social security number (if any), date and place of birth of the certificate holder, and any available information regarding the grade, number, and date of issue of the certificate, and the ratings on it; and
    (2) Be accompanied by a check or money order for $2.00, payable to the Federal Aviation Administration.

(b) An application for the replacement of a lost or destroyed medical certificate is made by letter to the Department of Transportation, Federal Aviation Administration, Aeromedical Certification Branch, Post Office Box 25082, Oklahoma City, OK 73125, accompanied by a check or money order for $2.00.

(c) A person who has lost a certificate issued under this Part, or a medical certificate issued under Part 67 of this chapter, or both, may obtain a telegram from the FAA confirming that it was issued. The telegram may be carried as a certificate for a period not to exceed 60 days pending his receipt of a duplicate certificate under paragraph (a) or (b) of this section, unless he has been notified that the certificate has been suspended or revoked. The request for such a telegram may be made by letter or prepaid telegram, including the date upon which a duplicate certificate was previously requested, if a request had been made, and a money order for the cost of the duplicate certificate. The request for a telegraphic certificate is sent to the office listed in paragraph (a) or (b) of this section, as appropriate. However, a request for both airman and medical certificates at the same time must be sent to the office prescribed in paragraph (a) of this section.

61.31   GENERAL LIMITATIONS

(a)   *Type Ratings Required.* A person may not act as pilot-in-command of any of the following aircraft unless he holds a type rating for that aircraft:

    (1)   A large aircraft (except lighter-than-air).

    (2)   A helicopter, for operations requiring an airline transport pilot certificate.

    (3)   A turbojet powered airplane.

    (4)   Other aircraft specified by the Administrator through aircraft type certificate procedures.

(b)   *Authorization in Lieu of a Type Rating.*

    (1)   In lieu of a type rating required under paragraphs (a) (1), (3), and (4) of this section, an aircraft may be operated under an authorization issued by the Administrator, for a flight or series of flights within the United States, if —

        (i)   The particular operation for which the authorization is requested involves a ferry flight, a practice or training flight, a flight test for a pilot type rating, or a test flight of an aircraft, for a period that does not exceed 60 days;

        (ii)   The applicant shows that compliance with paragraph (a) of this section is impracticable for the particular operation; and

        (iii)   The Administrator finds that an equivalent level of safety may be achieved through operating limitations on the authorization.

    (2)   Aircraft operated under an authorization issued under this paragraph —

        (i)   May not be operated for compensation or hire; and

        (ii)   May carry only flight crewmembers necessary for the flight.

    (3)   An authorization issued under this paragraph may be reissued for an additional 60-day period for the same operation if the applicant shows that he was prevented from carrying out the purpose of the particular operation before his authorization expired.

The prohibition of paragraph (b)(2)(i) of this section does not prohibit compensation for the use of an aircraft by a pilot solely to prepare for or take a flight test for a type rating.

(c)   *Category and Class Rating: Carrying Another Person or Operating for Compensation or Hire.* Unless he holds a category and class rating for that aircraft, a person may not act as pilot-in-command of an aircraft that is carrying another person or is operated for compensation or hire. In addition, he may not act as pilot-in-command of that aircraft for compensation or hire.

(d)   *Category and Class Rating; Other Operations.* No person may act as pilot-in-command of an aircraft in solo flight in operations not subject to paragraph (c) of this section, unless he meets at least one of the following:

    (1)   He holds a category and class rating appropriate to that aircraft.

    (2)   He has received flight instruction in the pilot operations required by this Part, appropriate to the category and class of aircraft for first solo, given to him by a certificated flight instructor who found him competent to solo that category and class of aircraft and has so endorsed his pilot logbook.

    (3)   He has soloed and logged pilot-in-command time in that category and class of aircraft before November 1, 1973.

(e)   *High Performance Airplanes.* A person holding a private or commercial pilot certificate may not act as pilot-in-command of an airplane that has more than 200 horsepower, or that has a retractable landing gear, flaps, and a controllable propeller, unless he has received flight instruction from an authorized flight instructor who has certified in his logbook that he is competent to pilot an airplane that has more than 200 horsepower, or that has a retractable landing gear, flaps, and a controllable propeller, as the case may be. However, this instruction is not required if he has logged flight time as pilot-in-command in high performance airplanes before November 1, 1973.

(f)   *High Altitude Airplanes.*

    (1)   Except as provided in paragraph (f)(2) of this section, no person may act as pilot-in-command of a pressurized airplane that has a service ceiling or maximum operating altitude, whichever is lower, above 25,000 feet MSL unless that person has completed the ground and flight training specified in paragraphs (f)(1)(i) and (ii) of this section and has received a logbook or training record endorsement from an authorized instructor certifying satisfactory completion of the training. The training shall consist of:

(i) Ground training that includes instruction on high altitude aerodynamics and meteorology; respiration; effects, symptoms, and causes of hypoxia and any other high altitude sicknesses; duration of consciousness without supplemental oxygen; effects of prolonged usage of supplemental oxygen; causes and effects of gas expansion and gas bubble formations; preventive measures for eliminating gas expansion, gas bubble formations, and high altitude sicknesses; physical phenomena and incidents of decompression; and any other physiological aspects of high altitude flight; and

(ii) Flight training in an airplane, or in a simulator that meets the requirements of § 121.407 of this chapter, and which is representative of an airplane as described in paragraph (f)(1) of this section. This training shall include normal cruise flight operations while operating above 25,000 feet MSL; the proper emergency procedures for simulated rapid decompression without actually depressurizing the airplane; and emergency descent procedures.

(2) The training required in paragraph (f)(1) of this section is not required if a person can document accomplishment of any of the following in an airplane, or in a simulator that meets the requirements of § 121.407 of this section, and that is representative of an airplane described in paragraph (f)(1) of this section:

(i) Served as pilot-in-command prior to April 15, 1991;

(ii) Completed a pilot proficiency check for a pilot certificate or rating conducted by the FAA prior to April 15, 1991;

(iii) Completed an official pilot-in-command check by the military services of the United States; or

(iv) Completed a pilot-in-command proficiency check under parts 121, 125, or 135 conducted by the FAA or by an approved pilot check airman.

(g) *Tailwheel Airplanes.* No person may act as pilot-in-command of a tailwheel airplane unless that pilot has received flight instruction from an authorized flight instructor who has found the pilot competent to operate a tailwheel airplane and has made a one time endorsement so stating in the pilot's logbook. The endorsement must certify that the pilot is competent in normal and crosswind takeoffs and landings, wheel landings unless the manufacturer has recommended against such landings, and go-around procedures. This endorsement is not required if a pilot has logged flight time as pilot-in-command of tailwheel airplanes prior to April 15, 1991.

(h) *Exception.* This section does not require a class rating for gliders, or category and class ratings for aircraft that are not type certificated as airplanes, rotorcraft, or lighter-than-air aircraft. In addition, the rating limitations of this section do not apply to —

(1) The holder of a student pilot certificate;

(2) The holder of a recreational pilot certificate when operating under the provisions of §61.101(f), (g), and (h).

(3) The holder of a pilot certificate when operating an aircraft under the authority of an experimental or provisional type certificate;

(4) An applicant when taking a flight test given by the Administrator; or

(5) The holder of a pilot certificate with a lighter-than-air category rating when operating a hot air balloon without an airborne heater.

61.33 TESTS: GENERAL PROCEDURE

Tests prescribed by or under this part are given at times and places, and by persons, designated by the Administrator.

61.35 WRITTEN TEST: PREREQUISITES AND PASSING GRADES

(a) An applicant for a written test must—

(1) Show that he has satisfactorily completed the ground instruction or home study course required by this part for the certificate or rating sought;

(2) Present as personal identification an airman certificate, driver's license, or other official document; and

(3) Present a birth certificate or other official document showing that he meets the age requirement prescribed in this Part for the certificate sought not later than 2 years from the date of application for the test.

(b) The minimum passing grade is specified by the Administrator on each written test sheet or booklet furnished to the applicant.

This section does not apply to the written test for an airline transport pilot certificate or a rating associated with that certificate.

61.37   WRITTEN TESTS: CHEATING OR OTHER UNAUTHORIZED CONDUCT

(a)   Except as authorized by the Administrator, no person may —

(1)   Copy, or intentionally remove, a written test under this part;

(2)   Give to another, or receive from another, any part or copy of that test;

(3)   Give help on that test to, or receive help on that test from, any person during the period that test is being given;

(4)   Take any part of that test in behalf of another person;

(5)   Use any material or aid during the period that test is being given; or

(6)   Intentionally cause, assist, or participate in any act prohibited by this paragraph.

(b)   No person whom the Administrator finds to have committed an act prohibited by paragraph (a) of this section is eligible for any airman or ground instructor certificate or rating, or to take any test therefor, under this chapter for a period of 1 year after the date of that act. In addition, the commission of that act is a basis for suspending or revoking any airman or ground instructor certificate or rating held by that person.

61.39   PREREQUISITES FOR FLIGHT TESTS

(a)   To be eligible for a flight test for a certificate, or an aircraft or instrument rating issued under this Part, the applicant must —

(1)   Have passed any required written test since the beginning of the 24th month before the month in which he takes the flight test;

(2)   Have the applicable instruction and aeronautical experience prescribed in this part;

(3)   Hold a current medical certificate appropriate to the certificate the applicant seeks or, in the case of a rating to be added to the applicant's pilot certificate, at least a current third-class medical certificate issued under Part 67 of this chapter;

(4)   Except for a flight test for an airline transport pilot certificate, meet the age requirement for the issuance of the certificate or rating he seeks; and

(5)   Have a written statement from an appropriately certificated flight instructor certifying that he has given the applicant flight instruction in preparation for the flight test within 60 days preceding the date of application, and finds him competent to pass the test and to have satisfactory knowledge of the subject areas in which he is shown to be deficient by his FAA airman written test report. However, an applicant need not have this written statement if he —

(i)   Holds a foreign pilot license issued by a contracting State to the Convention on International Civil Aviation that authorizes at least the pilot privileges of the airman certificate sought by him;

(ii)   Is applying for a type rating only, or a class rating with an associated type rating; or

(iii)   Is applying for an airline transport pilot certificate or an additional aircraft rating on that certificate.

(6)   If all increments of the practical test for a certificate or rating are not completed on one date, all remaining increments of the test must be satisfactorily completed not more than 60 calendar days after the date on which the applicant begins the test.

(7)   If all increments of the practical test are not satisfactorily completed within 60 calendar days as required by paragraph (a)(6) of this section, the applicant must retake the entire practical test, including those increments satisfactorily completed.

(b)   Notwithstanding paragraph (a)(1) of this section, an applicant for an airline transport pilot certificate or rating may take the flight test for that certificate or rating if —

(1)   The applicant —

(i)   Within the period ending 24 calendar months after the month in which the applicant passed the first of any required written tests, was employed as a flight crewmember by a U.S. air carrier or commercial operator operating either under Part 121 or as a commuter air carrier under Part 135 (as defined in Part 298 of this title) and is employed by such a certificate holder at the time of the flight test;

(ii)   Has completed initial training, and, if appropriate, transition or upgrade training; and

(iii)   Meets the recurrent training requirements of the applicable part; or

(2)   Within the period ending 24 calendar months after the month in which the applicant passed the first of any required written tests, the applicant participated as a pilot in a pilot training program of a U.S. scheduled military air transportation service and is currently participating in that program.

Ⓐ *Amend #100 eff 8-1-96*
Ⓑ *Amend #99 eff 9-16-96*

61.41 FLIGHT INSTRUCTION RECEIVED FROM FLIGHT INSTRUCTORS NOT CERTIFICATED BY FAA

Flight instruction may be credited toward the requirements for a pilot certificate or rating issued under this part if it is received from —

(a) An Armed Force of either the United States or a foreign contracting State to the Convention on International Civil Aviation in a program for training military pilots; or

(b) A flight instructor who is authorized to give that flight instruction by the licensing authority of a foreign contracting State to the Convention on International Civil Aviation and the flight instruction is given outside the United States.

61.43 FLIGHT TESTS: GENERAL PROCEDURES

(a) The ability of an applicant for a private or commercial pilot certificate, or for an aircraft or instrument rating on that certificate to perform the required pilot operations is based on the following:

   (1) Executing procedures and maneuvers within the aircraft's performance capabilities and limitations, including use of the aircraft's systems.

   (2) Executing emergency procedures and maneuvers appropriate to the aircraft.

   (3) Piloting the aircraft with smoothness and accuracy.

   (4) Exercising judgment.

   (5) Applying his aeronautical knowledge.

   (6) Showing that he is the master of the aircraft, with the successful outcome of a procedure or maneuver never seriously in doubt.

(b) If the applicant fails any of the required pilot operations in accordance with the applicable provisions of paragraph (a) of this section, the applicant fails the flight test. The applicant is not eligible for the certificate or rating sought unless he passes any pilot operations he has failed.

(c) The examiner or the applicant may discontinue the test at any time when the failure of a required pilot operation makes the applicant ineligible for the certificate or rating sought. If the test is discontinued the applicant is entitled to credit for only those entire pilot operations that he has successfully performed.

61.45 PRACTICAL TESTS: REQUIRED AIRCRAFT AND EQUIPMENT

(a) *General.* Except when an applicant for a certificate or rating under this part is permitted to accomplish the entire flight increment of the practical test in a qualified and approved flight simulator or in a qualified and approved flight training device:

   (1) The applicant must furnish for each required test, except as provided by paragraph (a)(2) of this section, an aircraft of U.S. registry—

     (i) Of the category and class aircraft, and type aircraft, if applicable, for which the applicant is applying for a certificate or rating; and

     (ii) That has a current standard or limited airworthiness certificate.

   (2) At the discretion of the person authorized by the Administrator to conduct the test, the applicant may furnish—

     (i) An aircraft that has a current airworthiness certificate other than standard or limited, but that otherwise meets the requirement of paragraph (a)(1) of this section;

     (ii) An aircraft of the category and class, and type aircraft, if applicable, of foreign registry that is certificated by the country of registry; or

     (iii) A military aircraft of the category and class aircraft, and type aircraft, if applicable, for which the applicant is applying for a certificate or rating.

(b) *Required Equipment (Other Than Controls).* Aircraft furnished for a flight test must have —

   (1) The equipment for each pilot operation required for the flight test;

   (2) No prescribed operating limitations that prohibit its use in any pilot operation required on the test;

   (3) Pilot seats with adequate visibility for each pilot to operate the aircraft safely, except as provided in paragraph (d) of this section; and

   (4) Cockpit and outside visibility adequate to evaluate the performance of the applicant, where an additional jump seat is provided for the examiner.

Ⓐ *Amend #100 eff 8-1-96*

(c) *Required Controls.* An applicant must furnish for each practical test an aircraft—
 (1) (Other than lighter-than-air) listed in paragraph (a) of this section.
 (2) That has engine controls and flight controls—
  (i) That are easily reached; and
  (ii) Unless the evaluator conducting the test accepts otherwise, that can be operated in a conventional manner by the applicant, other required crewmembers, and the evaluator if the evaluator occupies a pilot's seat.

(d) *Simulated Instrument Flight Equipment.* An applicant for any practical test involving flight maneuvers and flight procedures accomplished solely by reference to instruments, must furnish equipment that—
 (1) Excludes the applicant's visual reference to objects outside the aircraft; and
 (2) Is otherwise acceptable to the Administrator.

(e) *Aircraft With Single Controls.* At the discretion of the examiner, an aircraft furnished under paragraph (a) of this section for a flight test may, in the cases listed herein, have a single set of controls. In such case, the examiner determines the competence of the applicant by observation from the ground or from another aircraft.
 (1) A flight test for addition of a class or type rating, not involving demonstration of instrument skills, to a private or commercial pilot certificate.
 (2) A flight test in a single-place gyroplane for —
  (i) A private pilot certificate with a rotorcraft category rating and gyroplane class rating, in which case the certificate bears the limitation "rotorcraft single-place gyroplane only"; or
  (ii) Addition of a rotorcraft category rating and gyroplane class rating to a pilot certificate, in which case a certificate higher than a private pilot certificate bears the limitation "rotorcraft single-place gyroplane, private pilot privileges, only".

The limitations prescribed by this subparagraph may be removed if the holder of the certificate passes the appropriate flight test in a gyroplane with two pilot stations or otherwise passes the appropriate flight test for a rotorcraft category rating.

61.47 FLIGHT TESTS: STATUS OF FAA INSPECTORS AND OTHER AUTHORIZED FLIGHT EXAMINERS

An FAA inspector or other authorized flight examiner conducts the flight test of an applicant for a pilot certificate or rating for the purpose of observing the applicant's ability to perform satisfactorily the procedures and maneuvers on the flight test. The inspector or other examiner is not pilot-in-command of the aircraft during the flight test unless he acts in that capacity for the flight, or portion of the flight, by prior arrangement with the applicant or other person who would otherwise act as pilot-in-command of the flight, or portion of the flight. Notwithstanding the type of aircraft used during a flight test, the applicant and the inspector or other examiner are not, with respect to each other (or other occupants authorized by the inspector or other examiner), subject to the requirements or limitations for the carriage of passengers specified in this chapter.

61.49 RETESTING AFTER FAILURE

(a) An applicant for a written or practical test who fails that test may not apply for retesting until 30 days after the date the test was failed. However, in the case of a first failure, the applicant may apply for retesting before the 30 days have expired provided the applicant presents a logbook or training record endorsement from an authorized instructor who has given the applicant remedial instruction and finds the applicant competent to pass the test.

(b) An applicant for a flight instructor certificate with an airplane category rating, or for a flight instructor certificate with a glider category rating, who has failed the practical test due to deficiencies of knowledge or skill relating to stall awareness, spin entry, spins, or spin recovery techniques must, during the retest, satisfactorily demonstrate both knowledge and skill in these areas in an aircraft of the appropriate category that is certificated for spins.

A *Amend #100 eff 8-1-96*

61.51   PILOT LOGBOOKS

(a)   The aeronautical training and experience used to meet the requirements for a certificate or rating, or the recent flight experience requirements of this part must be shown by a reliable record. The logging of other flight time is not required.

(b)   *Logbook Entries.* Each pilot shall enter the following information for each flight or lesson logged:

    (1)   *General.*
       (i)   Date.
       (ii)   Total time of flight or flight lesson.
       (iii)   Except for simulated flight, the place, or points of departure and arrival.
       (iv)   Type and identification of aircraft, flight simulator, or flight training device.

    (2)   *Type of Pilot Experience or Training*
       (i)   Pilot-in-command or solo.
       (ii)   Second-in-command.
       (iii)   Flight instruction received from an authorized flight instructor.
       (iv)   Instrument flight instruction from an authorized flight instructor.
       (v)   Pilot ground trainer instruction.
       (vi)   Participating crew (lighter-than-air).
       (vii)   Other pilot time.
       (viii)   Instruction in a flight simulator or instruction in a flight training device.

    (3)   *Conditions of Flight.*
       (i)   Day or night.
       (ii)   Actual instrument.
       (iii)   Simulated instrument conditions in actual flight, in a flight simulator, or in a flight training device.

(c)   *Logging of Pilot Time.*

    (1)   *Solo Flight Time.* A pilot may log as solo flight time only that flight time when he is the sole occupant of the aircraft. However, a student pilot may also log as solo flight time that time during which he acts as the pilot-in-command of an airship requiring more than one flight crewmember.

    (2)   *Pilot-in-Command Flight Time.*
       (i)   A private or commercial pilot may log as pilot-in-command time that flight time when the pilot is—
           (A)   The sole manipulator of the controls of an aircraft for which the pilot is rated; or
           (B)   Acting as pilot-in-command of an aircraft on which more than one pilot is required under type certification of the aircraft or the regulation under which the flight is conducted.
       (ii)   An airline transport pilot may log as pilot-in-command time all of the flight time during which he acts as pilot-in-command.
       (iii)   A certificated flight instructor may log as pilot-in-command time all flight time during which he acts as a flight instructor.
       (iv)   A recreational pilot may log as pilot-in-command time only that time when the pilot is the sole manipulator of the controls of an aircraft for which the pilot is rated.

    (3)   *Second-in-Command Flight Time.* A pilot may log as second-in-command time all flight time during which he acts as second-in-command of an aircraft on which more than one pilot is required under the type certification of the aircraft, or the regulations under which the flight is conducted.

    (4)   *Instrument Flight Time.*
       (i)   Except as provided in paragraph (c)(4)(iv) of this section, a pilot may log as instrument flight time only that time when the pilot operates an aircraft solely by reference to instruments under actual or simulated instrument flight conditions.
       (ii)   For simulated instrument conditions a qualified and approved flight simulator or qualified and approved flight training device may be used, provided an authorized instructor is present during the simulated flight.
       (iii)   Each entry in the pilot logbook must include—
           (A)   The place and type of each instrument approach completed; and
           (B)   The name of the safety pilot for each simulated instrument flight conducted in flight.
       (iv)   An instrument flight instructor conducting instrument flight instruction in actual instrument weather conditions may log instrument time.

    (5)   *Instruction Time.* All time logged as instruction time must be certified by the authorized instructor from whom it was received.

Ⓐ *Amend #100 eff 8-1-96*

(d) *Presentation of Logbook.*

   (1) A pilot must present his logbook (or other record required by this section) for inspection upon reasonable request by the Administrator, an authorized representative of the National Transportation Safety Board, or any State or local law enforcement officer.

   (2) A student pilot must carry his logbook (or other record required by this section) with him on all solo cross-country flights, as evidence of the required instructor clearances and endorsements.

   (3) A recreational pilot must carry his or her logbook that has the required instructor endorsements on all solo flights—

     (i) In excess of 50 nautical miles from an airport at which instruction was received;

     (ii) In airspace in which communication with air traffic control is required;

     (iii) Between sunset and sunrise; and

     (iv) In an aircraft for which the pilot is not rated.

61.53 OPERATIONS DURING MEDICAL DEFICIENCY

No person may act as pilot-in-command, or in any other capacity as a required pilot flight crewmember while he has a known medical deficiency, or increase of a known medical deficiency, that would make him unable to meet the requirements for his current medical certificate.

61.55 SECOND-IN-COMMAND QUALIFICATIONS

(a) Except as provided in paragraph (d) of this section, no person may serve as second-in-command of an aircraft type certificated for more than one required pilot flight crewmember, unless that person holds—

   (1) At least a current private pilot certificate with appropriate category and class ratings; and

   (2) An appropriate instrument rating in the case of flight under IFR.

(b) Except as provided in paragraph (d) of this section, no person may serve as second-in-command of an aircraft type certificated for more than one required pilot flight crewmember unless, since the beginning of the 12th calendar month before the month in which the pilot serves, the pilot has, with respect to that type of aircraft —

   (1) Become familiar with all information concerning the aircraft's power plant, major components and systems, major appliances, performance and limitations, standard and emergency operating procedures and the contents of the approved aircraft flight manual or approved flight manual material, placards, and markings.

   (2) Except as provided in paragraph (e) of this section, performed and logged —

     (i) Three takeoffs and three landings to a full stop in the aircraft as the sole manipulator of the flight controls; and

     (ii) Engine-out procedures and maneuvering with an engine out while executing the duties of a pilot-in-command.

   (3) Except as provided in paragraph (b)(4) of this section, the requirements of this paragraph (b)(3) may be accomplished in a flight simulator that is—

     (i) Qualified and approved by the Administrator for such purposes; and

     (ii) Used in accordance with an approved course conducted by a training center certificated under Part 142 of this chapter.

   (4) An applicant for an initial second-in-command qualification for a particular type of aircraft who is qualifying under the terms of paragraph (b)(3) of this section shall satisfactorily complete a minimum of one takeoff and one landing in an aircraft of the same type for which the qualification is sought.

(c) If a pilot complies with the requirements in paragraph (b) of this section in the calendar month before, or the calendar month after, the month in which compliance with those requirements is due, he is considered to have complied with them in the month they are due.

(d) This section does not apply to a pilot who —

   (1) Meets the pilot-in-command proficiency check requirements of Part 121, 125, 127, or 135 of this chapter;

   (2) Is designated as the second-in-command of an aircraft operated under the provisions of Part 121, 125, 127, or 135 of this chapter; or

   (3) Is designated as the second-in-command of an aircraft for the purpose of receiving flight training required by this section and no passengers or cargo are carried on that aircraft.

Ⓐ *Amend #100 eff 8-1-96*

(e) The holder of a commercial or airline transport pilot certificate with appropriate category and class ratings need not meet the requirements of paragraph (b)(2) of this section for the conduct of ferry flights, aircraft flight tests, or airborne equipment evaluation, if no persons or property other than as necessary for the operation are carried.

61.56　FLIGHT REVIEW

(a) A flight review consists of a minimum of 1 hour of flight instruction and 1 hour of ground instruction. The review must include-
　(1) A review of the current general operating and flight rules of part 91 of this chapter; and
　(2) A review of those maneuvers and procedures which, at the discretion of the person giving the review, are necessary for the pilot to demonstrate the safe exercise of the privileges of the pilot certificate.
(b) Glider pilots may substitute a minimum of three instructional flights in a glider, each of which includes a 360-degree turn, in lieu of the 1 hour of flight instruction required in paragraph (a) of this section.
(c) Except as provided in paragraphs (d) and (e) of this section, no person may act as pilot-in-command of an aircraft unless, since the beginning of the 24th calendar month before the month in which that pilot acts as pilot-in-command, that person has—
　(1) Accomplished a flight review given in an aircraft for which that pilot is rated by an appropriately rated instructor certificated under this part or other person designated by the Administrator; and
　(2) A logbook endorsed by the person who gave the review certifying that the person has satisfactorily completed the review.
(d) A person who has, within the period specified in paragraph (c) of this section, satisfactorily completed a pilot proficiency check conducted by the FAA, an approved pilot check airman, or a U.S. Armed Force, for a pilot certificate, rating, or operating privilege, need not accomplish the flight review required by this section.
(e) An applicant who has, within the period specified in paragraphs (c) and (d) of this section, satisfactorily completed a test for a pilot certificate, rating, or operating privilege, need not accomplish the flight review required by this section if the test was conducted by a person authorized by the Administrator, or authorized by a U.S. Armed Force, to conduct the test.
(f) A person who holds a current flight instructor certificate who has, within the period specified in paragraph (c) of this section, satisfactorily completed a renewal of a flight instructor certificate under the provisions on §61.197(c), need not accomplish the 1 hour of ground instruction specified in subparagraph (a)(1) of this section.
(g) The requirements of this section may be accomplished in combination with the requirements of §61.57 and other applicable recency requirements at the discretion of the instructor.
(h) A flight simulator or flight training device may be used to meet the flight review requirements of this section subject to the following conditions:
　(1) The flight simulator or flight training device must be approved by the Administrator for that purpose.
　(2) The flight simulator or flight training device must be used in accordance with an approved course conducted by a training center certificated under Part 142 of this chapter.
　(3) Unless the review is undertaken in a flight simulator that is approved for landings, the applicant must meet the takeoff and landing requirements of § 61.57 (c) or (d).
　(4) The flight simulator or flight training device used must represent an aircraft, or set of aircraft, for which the pilot is rated.

61.57　RECENT FLIGHT EXPERIENCE: PILOT-IN-COMMAND

(a) Reserved.
(b) Reserved.

Ⓐ Amend #100 eff 8-1-96

(c) *General experience.*
   (1) Except as otherwise provided in paragraph (f) of this section, no person may act as pilot-in-command of an aircraft carrying passengers, or of an aircraft certificated for more than one required pilot flight crewmember, unless that person meets the following requirements—
      (i) Within the preceding 90 calendar days, that person must have made three takeoffs and three landings as the sole manipulator of the flight controls in an aircraft of the same category and class and, if a type rating is required, of the same type of aircraft.
      (ii) If the aircraft operated under paragraph (c)(1)(i) of this section is a tailwheel airplane, that person must have made to a full stop the landings required by that paragraph.
   (2) For the purposes of meeting the requirements of this section, a person may act as pilot-in-command of a flight under day visual flight rules (VFR) or day instrument flight rules (IFR) if no persons or property are carried other than as necessary for compliance with this part.
   (3) The takeoffs and landings required by paragraph (c)(1) of this section may be accomplished in a flight simulator or flight training device—
      (i) Qualified and approved by the Administrator for landings; and
      (ii) Used in accordance with an approved course conducted by a training center certificated under Part 142 of this chapter.

(d) *Night experience.*
   (1) Except as provided in paragraph (f) of this section, no person may act as pilot-in-command of an aircraft carrying passengers at night (the period beginning 1 hour after sunset and ending 1 hour before sunrise (as published in the American Air Almanac)) unless, within the preceding 90 days, that person has made not fewer than three takeoffs and three landings to a full stop, at night, as the sole manipulator of the flight controls in the same category and class of aircraft.
   (2) The takeoffs and landings required by paragraph (d)(1) of this section may be accomplished in a flight simulator that is—
      (i) Qualified and approved by the Administrator for takeoffs and landings, if the visual system is adjusted to represent the time of day described in paragraph (d)(1) of this section; and
      (ii) Used in accordance with an approved course conducted by a training center certificated under part 142 of this chapter.

(e) *Instrument currency.*
   (1) Except as provided by paragraph (f) of this section, no person may act as pilot-in-command under IFR, or in weather conditions less than the minimums prescribed for VFR, unless, within the preceding 6 calendar months, that person has—
      (i) In the case of an aircraft other than a glider—
         (A) Logged at least 6 hours of instrument time including at least six instrument approaches under actual or simulated instrument conditions, not more than 3 hours of which may be in approved simulation representing aircraft other than gliders; or
         (B) Passed an instrument competency test as described in paragraphs (e)(2) and (e)(3) of this section; or
      (ii) In the case of a glider, the person must have logged at least 3 hours of instrument time, at least half of which was in a glider or an airplane, except that the person may not carry a passenger in the glider until that person has completed at least 3 hours of instrument flight time in a glider.
   (2) A person who does not meet the recent instrument experience requirements of paragraph (e)(1) of this section during the prescribed time, or within 6 calendar months thereafter, may not serve as pilot-in-command under IFR, or in weather conditions less than the minimums prescribed for VFR, until that person passes an instrument competency test in the category and class of aircraft involved, given by a person authorized by the Administrator to conduct the test.
   (3) The Administrator may authorize the conduct of all or part of the test required by paragraph (e)(2) of this section in a qualified and approved flight simulator or flight training device.

🅐 *Amend #100 eff 8-1-96*

(f)   *Exceptions.* This section does not apply to a pilot in command, employed by a part 121 or 135 air carrier, engaged in a flight operation under part 91, 121, or 135 for the air carrier, if the pilot is in compliance with §§121.437 and 121.439 or §§135.243 and 135.247 respectively.

61.58   PILOT-IN-COMMAND PROFICIENCY CHECK: OPERATION OF AIRCRAFT REQUIRING MORE THAN ONE REQUIRED PILOT

(a)   Except as otherwise provided in this section, to serve as pilot-in-command of an aircraft that is type certificated for more than one required pilot crewmember, a person must—
  (1)   Within the preceding 12 calendar months, complete a pilot-in-command check in an aircraft that is type certificated for more than one required pilot crewmember; and
  (2)   Within the preceding 24 calendar months, complete a pilot-in-command check in the particular type of aircraft in which that person will serve as pilot-in-command.

(b)   This section does not apply to persons conducting operations under Part 121, Part 125, Part 127, Part 133, Part 135 or Part 137 of this chapter.

(c)   The pilot-in-command check given in accordance with the provisions of Part 121, Part 125, Part 127, or Part 135 of this chapter may be used to satisfy the requirements of this section.

(d)   The pilot-in-command check required by paragraph (a) of this section may be accomplished by satisfactory completion of one of the following—
  (1)   A pilot-in-command proficiency check conducted by a person authorized by the Administrator, consisting of the maneuvers and procedures required for a type rating;
  (2)   The practical test required for a type rating;
  (3)   The initial or periodic practical test required for the issuance of a pilot examiner or a check airman designation; or
  (4)   A military flight check required for a pilot-in-command with instrument privileges, in an aircraft that the military requires to be operated by more than one pilot.

(e)   A check or a test described in paragraphs (d)(1) through (d)(4) of this section may be accomplished in a flight simulator qualified and approved under Part 142 of this chapter subject to the following:
  (1)   Except as allowed in paragraphs (e)(2) and (e)(3) of this section, if an otherwise qualified and approved flight simulator used for a pilot-in-command proficiency check is not qualified and approved for a specific required maneuver—
    (i)   The training center shall annotate, in the applicant's training record, the maneuver or maneuvers omitted; and
    (ii)   Prior to acting as pilot-in-command, the pilot shall demonstrate proficiency in each omitted maneuver in an aircraft or flight simulator qualified and approved for each omitted maneuver.
  (2)   If the flight simulator used pursuant to this paragraph (e) is not qualified and approved for circling approaches—
    (i)   The applicant's record shall be annotated with the statement, "Proficiency in circling approaches not demonstrated"; and
    (ii)   The applicant may not perform circling approaches as pilot-in-command when weather conditions are less than the basic VFR conditions described in § 91.155 of this chapter, until proficiency in circling approaches has been successfully demonstrated in an approved simulator or aircraft to a person authorized by the Administrator to conduct the check required by this section.
  (3)   If the flight simulator used pursuant to this paragraph (e) is not qualified and approved for landings the applicant must—
    (i)   Hold a type rating in the airplane represented by the simulator; and
    (ii)   Have completed, within the preceding 90 days, at least three takeoffs and three landings (one to a full stop) as the sole manipulator of the flight controls in the type airplane for which the pilot-in-command proficiency check is sought.

(f)   For the purpose of meeting the check requirements of paragraph (a) of this section, a person may act as pilot-in-command of a flight under day VFR conditions or day IFR conditions if no person or property is carried, other than as necessary to demonstrate compliance with this part.

(g)   If a pilot takes the check required by this section in the calendar month before, or the calendar month after, the month in which it is due, the pilot is considered to have taken it in the month in which it was due for the purpose of computing when the next check is due.

61.59   FALSIFICATION, REPRODUCTION, OR ALTERATION OF APPLICATIONS, CERTIFICATES, LOGBOOKS, REPORTS, OR RECORDS

(a)   No person may make or cause to be made —
  (1)   Any fraudulent or intentionally false statement on any application for a certificate, rating, or duplicate thereof, issued under this part;
  (2)   Any fraudulent or intentionally false entry in any logbook, record, or report that is required to be kept, made, or used, to show compliance with any requirement for the issuance, or exercise of the privileges, or any certificate or rating under this part;
  (3)   Any reproduction, for fraudulent purpose, of any certificate or rating under this part; or
  (4)   Any alteration of any certificate or rating under this part.

(b)   The commission by any person of an act prohibited under paragraph (a) of this section is a basis for suspending or revoking any airman or ground instructor certificate or rating held by that person.

61.60   CHANGE OF ADDRESS

The holder of a pilot or flight instructor certificate who has made a change in his permanent mailing address may not after 30 days from the date he moved, exercise the privileges of his certificate unless he has notified in writing the Department of Transportation, Federal Aviation Administration, Airman Certification Branch, Box 25082, Oklahoma City, OK 73125, of his new address.

SUBPART B — AIRCRAFT RATINGS AND SPECIAL CERTIFICATES

61.61 APPLICABILITY

This subpart prescribes the requirements for the issuance of additional aircraft ratings after a pilot or instructor certificate is issued, and the requirements and limitations for special pilot certificates and ratings issued by the Administrator.

61.63 ADDITIONAL AIRCRAFT RATINGS (OTHER THAN AIRLINE TRANSPORT PILOT)

(a) *General.* To be eligible for an additional aircraft rating to a pilot certificate, an applicant who is a pilot crewmember employee of a Part 121 certificate holder or a Part 135 certificate holder must meet the requirements of paragraphs (b) through (d) of this section, as applicable to the rating sought.

(b) *Category Rating.* An applicant for a category rating to be added on his pilot certificate must meet the requirements of this Part for the issue of the pilot certificate appropriate to the privileges for which the category rating is sought. However, the holder of a category rating for powered aircraft is not required to take a written test for the addition of a category rating on his pilot certificate.

(c) *Class Rating.* An applicant for an aircraft class rating to be added on his pilot certificate must —

    (1) Present a logbook record certified by an authorized flight instructor showing that the applicant has received flight instruction in the class of aircraft for which a rating is sought and has been found competent in the pilot operations appropriate to the pilot certificate to which his category rating applies; and

    (2) Pass a flight test appropriate to his pilot certificate and applicable to the aircraft category and class rating sought.

A person who holds a lighter-than-air category rating with a free balloon class rating, who seeks an airship class rating, must meet the requirements of paragraph (b) of this section as though seeking a lighter-than-air category rating.

(d) *Type Rating.* An applicant for a type rating to be added on his pilot certificate must meet the following requirements:

    (1) He must hold, or concurrently obtain, an instrument rating appropriate to the aircraft for which a type rating is sought.

    (2) He must pass a flight test showing competence in pilot operations appropriate to the pilot certificate he holds and to the type rating sought.

    (3) He must pass a flight test showing competence in pilot operations under instrument flight rules in an aircraft of the type for which the type rating is sought or, in the case of a single pilot station airplane, meet the requirements of paragraph (d)(3)(i) or (ii) of this section, whichever is applicable.

        (i) The applicant must have met the requirements of this paragraph in a multi-engine airplane for which a type rating is required.

        (ii) If he does not meet the requirements of paragraph (d)(3)(i) of this section and he seeks a type rating for a single-engine airplane, he must meet the requirements of this subparagraph in either a single or multiengine airplane, and have the recent instrument experience set forth in §61.57(e) when he applies for the flight test under paragraph (d)(2) of this section.

    (4) An applicant who does not meet the requirements of paragraphs (d)(1) and (3) of this section may obtain a type rating limited to "VFR only". Upon meeting these instrument requirements or the requirements of §61.73(e)(2), the "VFR only" limitation may be removed for the particular type of aircraft in which competence is shown.

    (5) When an instrument rating is issued to the holder of one or more type ratings, the type ratings on the amended certificate bear the limitation described in paragraph (d)(4) of this section for each airplane type rating for which he has not shown his instrument competency under this paragraph.

    (6) On and after April 15, 1991, an applicant for a type rating to be added to a pilot certificate must —

        (i) Have completed ground and flight training on the maneuvers and procedures of Appendix A of this part that is appropriate to the airplane for which a type rating is sought, and received an endorsement from an authorized instructor in the person's logbook or training records certifying satisfactory completion of the training; or

Ⓐ Amend #100 eff 8-1-96

      (ii)   For a pilot employee of a part 121 or part 135 certificate holder, have completed the certificate holder's approved ground and flight training that is appropriate to the airplane for which a type rating is sought.

61.64   **ADDITIONAL AIRCRAFT RATINGS FOR OTHER-THAN-AIRLINE TRANSPORT PILOT CERTIFICATES**
(For other than Parts 121 and 135 use.)

(a)   *General.* To be eligible for an additional aircraft rating to a pilot certificate, an applicant who is not a crewmember employee applicant of a Part 121 training program or a Part 135 training program must meet the requirements of paragraphs (b) through (i) of this section, applicable to the rating sought.

(b)   *Category Rating.* An applicant who holds a pilot certificate and applies to add a category rating must meet the following requirements:
   (1)   Present a record of training certified by an authorized instructor showing that the applicant has—
      (i)   Received ground training on the aeronautical knowledge areas applicable to the pilot certificate and aircraft category and class rating sought;
      (ii)   Received flight training in the category and class of aircraft on the areas of operation applicable to the pilot certificate and aircraft category and class rating sought;
      (iii) Been found competent by the certifying flight instructor in the aeronautical knowledge areas required for the pilot certificate to which the added aircraft category rating would apply; and
      (iv) Been found competent by the certifying flight instructor in the areas of operation required for the pilot certificate to which the added aircraft category rating would apply;
   (2)   Pass the knowledge test applicable to the pilot certificate and aircraft category and class rating sought; and
   (3)   Pass the practical test required for the pilot certificate held, and category and class rating sought.

Ⓐ

(c)   *Class Rating.* An applicant who holds a pilot certificate and applies to add a class rating must meet the following requirements:
   (1)   The applicant must present a record certified by an authorized instructor showing that the applicant has—
      (i)   Received flight instruction in the class of aircraft on the areas of operation applicable to the pilot certificate and aircraft class rating sought;
      (ii)   Received ground training on the aeronautical knowledge areas applicable to the pilot certificate and aircraft class rating sought;
      (iii) Been found competent by the certifying flight instructor in the aeronautical knowledge areas applicable to the pilot certificate to which the category and class rating would apply; and
      (iv) Been found competent by the certifying flight instructor in the areas of operation applicable to the pilot certificate to which the aircraft class rating would apply;
   (2)   Pass a knowledge test applicable to the pilot certificate and aircraft class rating sought; and
   (3)   Pass a practical test required for the pilot certificate held, and required for the category and class rating sought.

(d)   *Type Rating.* An applicant who holds a pilot certificate and applies to add a type rating must meet the following requirements—
   (1)   Present a record of training certified by an authorized instructor that shows that the applicant has—
      (i)   Received ground training on the aeronautical knowledge areas applicable to the type rating sought;
      (ii)   Received flight training on the areas of operation applicable to the type rating sought; and
      (iii) Been found competent by the certifying flight instructor in the areas of operation required for the issue of the pilot certificate for which the aircraft type rating is sought.
   (2)   Passed a required practical test on the areas of operation listed in § 61.158 or 61.163, as applicable, for the aircraft type rating sought.

Ⓐ *Amend #100 eff 8-1-96*

    (3)   If the applicant does not hold an instrument rating, in addition to the tasks required by paragraph (d)(2) of this section, the applicant must also demonstrate competency in the operations required by § 61.65(9).

(e)   The tasks required by paragraphs (b), (c), and (d) of this section shall be performed as follows:

   (1)   Except as provided in paragraph (e)(2) of this section, the tasks must be performed in an aircraft of the same category, class, and type, if applicable, as the aircraft for which the added rating is sought.

   (2)   Subject to the limitations of paragraph (e)(3) through (e)(12) of this section, the tasks may be performed in a flight simulator or a flight training device that represents the aircraft for which the added rating is sought.

   (3)   The flight simulator or flight training device use permitted by paragraph (e)(2) of this section shall be conducted in accordance with an approved course at a training center certificated under Part 142 of this chapter.

   (4)   To complete all training and testing (except preflight inspection) for an unlimited added rating in a flight simulator—

     (i)   The flight simulator must be qualified as Level C or Level D; and

     (ii)   The applicant must meet at least one of the following:

       (A)   Hold a type rating for a turbojet airplane of the same class as the class of airplane for which the type rating is sought, or have been appointed by a military service as a pilot-in-command of an airplane of the same class as the class of airplane for which the type rating is sought, if a turbojet type rating is sought.

       (B)   Hold a type rating for a turbo propeller airplane of the same class as the class of airplane for which the type rating is sought, or have been designated by a military service as a pilot-in-command of an airplane of the same class as the class of airplane for which the type rating is sought, if a turbo propeller airplane type rating is sought.

       (C)   Have at least 2,000 hours of actual flight time, of which 500 hours must be in turbine-powered airplanes of the same class as the class of airplane for which the type rating is sought.

       (D)   Have at least 500 hours of actual flight time in the same type airplane as the airplane for which the rating is sought.

       (E)   Have at least 1,000 hours of flight time in at least two different airplanes requiring a type rating.

   (5)   Subject to the limitation of paragraph (e)(6) of this section, an applicant who does not meet the requirements of paragraph (e)(4) of this section may complete all training and testing (except for preflight inspection) for an added rating in a flight simulator if—

     (i)   The flight simulator is qualified as Level C or Level D; and

     (ii)   The applicant meets at least one of the following:

       (A)   Holds a type rating in a propeller-driven airplane if a type rating in a turbojet airplane is sought, or holds a type rating in a turbojet airplane if a type rating in a propeller-driven airplane is sought.

       (B)   Since the beginning of the 12th calendar month before the month in which the applicant completes the practical test for the added rating, has logged—

         (1)   At least 100 hours of flight time in airplanes in the same class of airplane for which the type rating is sought and which require a type rating; and

         (2)   At least 25 hours of flight time in airplanes in the same type of airplane for which the rating is sought.

   (6)   An applicant meeting only the requirements of paragraph (e)(5) of this section will be issued an added rating with a limitation.

   (7)   The limitation on certificates issued under the provisions of paragraph (e)(6) of this section shall state, "This certificate is subject to pilot-in-command limitations for the added rating."

   (8)   An applicant gaining a certificate with the limitation specified in paragraph (e)(7) of this section—

     (i)   May not act as pilot-in-command of the aircraft for which an added rating was obtained under the provisions of this section until he or she has had the limitation removed from the certificate; and

Ⓐ *Amend #100 eff 8-1-96*

    (ii)   May have the limitation removed by serving 15 hours of supervised operating experience as pilot-in-command under the supervision of a qualified and current pilot-in-command, in the seat normally occupied by the pilot-in-command, in an aircraft of the same type as the airplane to which the limitation applies.

(9)   An applicant who does not meet the requirements of paragraph (e)(4) or (e)(5) of this section may be awarded an added rating after successful completion of one of the following requirements:

    (i)   Compliance with paragraph (e)(2) and (e)(3) of this section and the following tasks, applicable to airplane ratings only, which must be successfully completed on a static airplane or in flight, as appropriate:

        (A)   Preflight inspection;
        (B)   Normal takeoff;
        (C)   Normal ILS approach;
        (D)   Missed approach; and
        (E)   Normal landing.

    (ii)   Compliance with paragraphs (e)(2), (e)(3), and (e)(10) through (e)(12) of this section.

(10)   An applicant meeting only the requirements of paragraph (e)(9) of this section will be issued an added rating with a limitation.

(11)   The limitation on certificates issued under the provisions of paragraph (e)(10) of this section shall state, "This certificate is subject to pilot-in-command limitations for the added rating."

(12)   An applicant gaining a certificate with the limitation specified in paragraph (e)(11) of this section—

    (i)   May not act as pilot-in-command of the aircraft for which an added rating was obtained under the provisions of this section until he or she has had the limitation removed from the certificate; and

    (ii)   May have the limitation removed by serving 25 hours of supervised operating experience as pilot-in-command under the supervision of a qualified and current pilot-in-command, in the seat normally occupied by the pilot-in-command, in an aircraft of the same type as the airplane to which the limitation applies.

(f)   An applicant for a type rating who provides an aircraft not capable of the instrument maneuvers and procedures required by § 61.158 or 61.163 for the practical test may—

(1)   Obtain a type rating limited to "VFR only"; and

(2)   Remove the "VFR only" limitation for each aircraft type in which the applicant demonstrates compliance with the instrument requirements of § 61.158 or 61.163 or the requirements of § 61.73 (e)(2).

(g)   An applicant for a type rating may be issued a certificate with the limitation "VFR only" for each aircraft type not equipped for the applicant to show instrument competency.

(h)   An applicant for a type rating in a multiengine, single-pilot station airplane may meet the requirements of this part in another multiengine airplane.

(i)   An applicant for a type rating in a single-engine, single pilot-station airplane may meet the requirements of this part in another single-engine or multiengine airplane if the applicant meets the instrument currency requirements of § 61.57 (e).

61.65   INSTRUMENT RATING REQUIREMENTS

(a)   *General.* To be eligible for an instrument rating (airplane) or an instrument rating (helicopter), an applicant must —

(1)   Hold at least a current private pilot certificate with an aircraft rating appropriate to the instrument rating sought;

(2)   Be able to read, speak, and understand the English language; and

(3)   Comply with the applicable requirements of this section.

(b)   *Ground Instruction and Written Test.* An applicant for the written test for an instrument rating must have received ground instruction or have logged home study in, and passed a written test on, at least the following areas of aeronautical knowledge applicable to the rating sought:

(1)   The regulations of this chapter that apply to flight under IFR conditions, the Airman's Information Manual, and the IFR air traffic system and procedures;

Ⓐ Amend #100 eff 8-1-96

    (2) Dead reckoning appropriate to IFR navigation, IFR navigation by radio aids using the VOR, ADF, and ILS systems, and the use of IFR charts and instrument approach plates;

    (3) The procurement and use of aviation weather reports and forecasts, and the elements of forecasting weather trends on the basis of that information and personal observation of weather conditions; and

    (4) The safe and efficient operation of airplanes or helicopters, as appropriate, under instrument weather conditions.

(c) *Flight Instruction.* Except as otherwise provided in this paragraph, an applicant for the practical test for an instrument rating must present a record certified by an authorized instructor showing instrument flight instruction and competency in an aircraft of the same category for which the instrument rating is sought, in each of the following areas of operations:

    (1) Control and accurate maneuvering of the aircraft solely by reference to instruments.

    (2) IFR navigation by the use of the VOR and ADF systems, including compliance with air traffic control instructions and procedures.

    (3) Instrument approaches to published minimums using two different nonprecision approach systems and one precision approach system.

    (4) Cross-country flight in an aircraft in simulated or actual IFR conditions, on Federal airways or as routed by air traffic control, subject to the following:

        (i) The flight must be at least 250 nautical miles (100 nautical miles for helicopters) including a minimum of one precision instrument approach and two nonprecision instrument approaches.

        (ii) Each instrument approach must be accomplished at a different airport.

        (iii) If the departure and final destination airports are the same airport, the destination airport may be considered as the third airport.

        (iv) No approach need be done more than once.

    (5) Simulated emergencies involving equipment or instrument malfunctions, missed approach procedures, deviations to unplanned alternates, recovery from unusual attitudes, loss of communications, and simulated loss of power on at least one-half of the engines if a multiengine aircraft is used.

    (6) Flight instruction required by paragraphs (c)(1), (c)(2), (c)(3), and (c)(5) of this section may be accomplished in a qualified and approved flight simulator or in a qualified and approved flight training device.

(d) [Reserved]

(e) *Flight Experience.* Except as provided in paragraph (h) of this section, an applicant for an instrument rating must have at least the following flight time as a pilot:

    (1) A total of 125 hours of pilot flight time, of which 50 hours are as pilot-in-command in cross-country flight in a powered aircraft with other than a student pilot certificate. Each cross-country flight must have a landing at a point more than 50 nautical miles from the original departure point.

    (2) 40 hours of simulated or actual instrument time, which may include—

        (i) Not more than a combined total of 20 hours of instrument instruction by an authorized instructor in a qualified and approved flight simulator or in a qualified and approved flight training device; or

        (ii) Not more than 30 hours of instrument instruction accomplished in an approved course conducted by a training center certificated under Part 142 of this chapter.

    (3) 15 hours of instrument flight instruction by an authorized flight instructor, including at least 5 hours in an airplane or a helicopter, as appropriate.

(f) [Reserved]

(g) *Practical Test.* An applicant for an instrument rating must pass a practical test consisting of an oral increment and a flight increment, as follows:

    (1) The flight increment required by this paragraph (g)(1) may be accomplished in any category, class, and type aircraft that is certificated for flight in instrument conditions, or in a qualified and approved flight simulator or qualified and approved flight training device.

    (2) The practical test required by this paragraph (g)(2) must include instrument flight procedures, selected by the person authorized by the Administrator to conduct the practical test, to determine the applicant's ability to perform competently the IFR operations described in paragraph (c) of this section.

Ⓐ *Amend #100 eff 8-1-96*

  (3) The following requirements of the practical test must be accomplished in an aircraft or in a qualified and approved flight simulator:

    (i) At least one published precision, nonprecision, and circling approach.

    (ii) At least one landing.

    (iii) At least one cross-country flight.

(h) *Training Qualifications.* An applicant for the instrument rating who has satisfactorily completed an approved curriculum conducted at a training center certificated under Part 142 of this chapter must have—

  (1) A total of at least 95 hours of pilot flight time, including at least 35 hours of simulated or actual instrument flight time; or

  (2) Satisfactorily completed the requirements of an approved instrument rating course at a Part 142 certified training center that has received approval from the Administrator to conduct a curriculum satisfying the requirements of the instrument rating in—

    (i) Fewer than 95 hours of pilot flight time; or

    (ii) Fewer than 35 hours of simulated instrument time or actual instrument time.

61.67 CATEGORY II PILOT AUTHORIZATION REQUIREMENTS

(a) *General.* An applicant for a Category II pilot authorization must hold —

  (1) A pilot certificate with an instrument rating or an aircraft transport pilot certificate; and

  (2) A type rating for the aircraft for which the authorization is sought if that aircraft requires a type rating.

(b) *Experience Requirements.* An applicant for a Category II authorization must have at least—

  (1) 50 hours of night flight time as pilot-in-command;

  (2) 75 hours of instrument time under actual or simulated instrument conditions that may include not more than—

    (i) A combination of 25 hours of simulated instrument flight time in qualified and approved flight simulators or qualified and approved flight training devices; or

    (ii) 40 hours of simulated instrument flight time if accomplished in an approved course conducted by an appropriately rated training center certificated under Part 142 of this chapter.

  (3) 250 hours of cross-country flight time as pilot-in-command.

Night flight and instrument flight time used to meet the requirements of paragraphs (b)(1) and (2) of this section may also be used to meet the requirements of paragraph (b)(3) of this section.

(c) *Practical Test Required*

  (1) The practical test must be passed by —

    (i) An applicant for issue or renewal of an authorization; and

    (ii) An applicant for the addition of another type aircraft to his authorization.

  (2) To be eligible for the practical test, an applicant must—

    (i) Meet the requirements of paragraphs (a) and (b) of this section;

    (ii) Hold the appropriate class rating; and

    (iii) If the applicant has not passed a practical test for this authorization since the beginning of the twelfth calendar month, meet the following recent experience requirements—

      (A) The requirements of § 61.57 (e); and

      (B) At least six ILS approaches since the beginning of the sixth month before the practical test, subject to the following:

        (1) The approaches must be conducted under actual or simulated instrument flight conditions.

        (2) The approaches must be conducted down to the minimum decision height for the ILS approach in the type aircraft in which the practical test is to be conducted.

        (3) Except as provided in paragraph (c)(4) of this section, the approaches must be accomplished in an aircraft of the same category and class, and type, as applicable, as the aircraft in which the practical test is to be conducted.

Ⓐ *Amend #100 eff 8-1-96*

(4) The approaches may be accomplished in a flight simulator that—
    (i) Represents an aircraft of the same category and class, and type, as applicable, as the aircraft in which the authorization is sought; and
    (ii) Is used in accordance with an approved course conducted by a training center certificated under Part 142 of this chapter.

(5) The approaches need not be conducted down to the decision height authorized for Category II operations if conducted in a qualified and approved flight simulator or qualified and approved flight training device.

(6) At least three of the approaches required by paragraph (c)(2)(iii)(B) of this section must be conducted manually, without the use of an approach coupler.

(7) The flight time acquired in meeting the requirements of paragraph (c)(2)(iii)(B) of this section may be used to meet the requirements of paragraph (c)(2)(iii)(A) of this section.

(d) *Practical Test Procedures.* Oral questioning may be conducted at any time during the practical test. The practical test consists of two increments:

(1) *Oral Increment.* The applicant must demonstrate knowledge of the following:
    (i) Required landing distance.
    (ii) Recognition of the decision height.
    (iii) Missed approach procedures and techniques utilizing computed or fixed attitude guidance displays.
    (iv) RVR, its use and limitations.
    (v) Use of visual clues, their availability or limitations, and altitude at which they are normally discernible at reduced RVR readings.
    (vi) Procedures and techniques related to transition from nonvisual to visual flight during a final approach under reduced RVR.
    (vii) Effects of vertical and horizontal wind shear.
    (viii) Characteristics and limitations of the ILS and runway lighting system.
    (ix) Characteristics and limitations of the flight director system, auto approach coupler (including split axis type if equipped), auto throttle system (if equipped), and other required Category II equipment.
    (x) Assigned duties of the second-in-command during Category II approaches.
    (xi) Instrument and equipment failure warning systems.

(2) *Flight Increment.* The following requirements apply to the flight increment of a practical test:
    (i) The flight increment may be conducted in an aircraft of the same category and class and type, as applicable, as the aircraft in which the authorization is sought or in a flight simulator that—
      (A) Represents an aircraft of the same category and class, and type, as applicable, as the aircraft in which the authorization is sought; and
      (B) Is used in accordance with an approved course conducted by a training center certificated under Part 142 of this chapter.
    (ii) At least two ILS approaches to 100 feet AGL including at least one landing and one missed approach.
    (iii) All approaches must be made with the approved flight control guidance system, except that if an approved automatic approach coupler is installed, at least one approach must be hand flown using flight director commands.
    (iv) If a multiengine airplane with the performance capability to execute a missed approach with one engine inoperative is used, one missed approach must be executed with an engine, which shall be the most critical engine, if applicable, set at idle or zero thrust before reaching the middle marker.
    (v) If a flight simulator is used, the missed approach must be executed with an engine, which shall be the most critical engine, if applicable, failed.
    (vi) For authorizations for aircraft that require a type rating, the test must be performed in coordination with a second-in-command who holds a type rating in the aircraft in which the authorization is sought.

61.68   CATEGORY III PILOT AUTHORIZATION REQUIREMENTS

(a)   *General.* An applicant for a Category III pilot authorization must hold—

    (1)   A pilot certificate with an instrument rating or airline transport pilot certificate;

    (2)   A valid medical certificate;

    (3)   A category and class rating for the aircraft for which the authorization is sought; and

    (4)   A type rating for the aircraft for which the authorization is sought, if that aircraft requires a type rating.

(b)   *Experience Requirements.* An applicant for a Category III authorization must have at least—

    (1)   50 hours of night flight time as pilot-in-command;

    (2)   Except as provided in paragraph (c) of this section, 75 hours of instrument flight time during actual or simulated instrument conditions that may include not more than a combination of 25 hours of simulated instrument flight time in qualified and approved flight simulators or qualified and approved flight training devices; and

    (3)   250 hours of cross-country flight time as pilot-in-command.

(c)   *Increasing Instrument Flight Time Hours.* The instrument flight time allowed in flight simulators or flight training devices under paragraph (b)(2) of this section may be increased to not more than 40 hours if accomplished in an approved course conducted by a training center certificated under Part 142 of this chapter.

(d)   *Practical Test Required.*

    (1)   An applicant for the issuance or renewal of a Category III authorization or for the addition of another type aircraft to an authorization must pass a practical test.

    (2)   If the applicant has not passed a practical test for this authorization since the beginning of the twelfth calendar month, the applicant must meet the following recency of experience requirements:

        (i)   The requirements of § 61.57 (e).

        (ii)   At least six ILS approaches since the beginning of the sixth month before the practical test, subject to the following:

            (A)   The approaches must be conducted under actual or simulated instrument flight conditions and flown down to the minimum altitude for the ILS approach.

            (B)   Except as provided in paragraph (d)(2)(ii)(C) of this section, the approaches must be accomplished in an aircraft of the same category and class, and type, as applicable, as the aircraft in which the practical test is to be conducted.

            (C)   The approaches may be accomplished in a flight simulator or flight training device that—

                (1)   Represents an aircraft of the same category and class, and type, as applicable, as the aircraft for which the authorization is sought; and

                (2)   Is used in accordance with an approved course conducted by a training center certificated under Part 142 of this chapter.

            (D)   Conducted down to the alert height or decision height, as applicable, authorized for Category III operations only if conducted in a qualified and approved flight simulator or qualified and approved flight training device.

(e)   *Practical Test Procedures.* Oral questioning may be conducted at any time during the practical test. The practical test consists of two increments:

    (1)   *Oral Increment.* The applicant must demonstrate knowledge of the following:

        (i)   Required landing distance.

        (ii)   Determination and recognition of the alert height or decision height, as applicable, including use of a radar altimeter.

        (iii)   Recognition of and proper reaction to significant failures encountered prior to and after reaching the alert height or decision height, as applicable.

        (iv)   Missed approach procedures and techniques using computed or fixed attitude guidance displays and expected height loss as they relate to manual go-around or automatic go-around and initiation altitude, as applicable.

        (v)   The use and limitations of RVR, including determination of controlling RVR and required transmissometers.

Ⓐ *Amend #100 eff 8-1-96*

(vi) The use, availability, or limitations of visual cues and the altitude at which they are normally discernible at reduced RVR readings including—
  (A) Unexpected deterioration of conditions to less than minimum RVR during approach, flare, and rollout;
  (B) Demonstration of expected visual references with weather at minimum conditions; and
  (C) The expected sequence of visual cues during an approach in which visibility is at or above landing minima.
(vii) Procedures and techniques for making a transition from instrument reference flight to visual flight during a final approach under reduced RVR.
(viii) Effects of vertical and horizontal wind shear.
(ix) Characteristics and limitations of the ILS and runway lighting system.
(x) Characteristics and limitations of the flight director system auto approach coupler (including split axis type if so equipped), auto throttle system, if applicable, and other Category III equipment, as applicable.
(xi) Assigned duties of the second-in-command during Category III operations, unless the aircraft for which authorization is sought does not require a second-in-command.
(xii) Recognition of the limits of acceptable aircraft position and flight path tracking during approach, flare, and, if applicable, rollout.
(xiii) Recognition of, and reaction to, airborne or ground system faults or abnormalities, particularly after passing alert height or decision height, as applicable.

(2) *Flight Increment.* The following requirements apply to the flight increment of the practical test:
(i) The flight increment may be conducted in an aircraft of the same category and class, and type, as applicable, as the aircraft in which the authorization is sought, or in a flight simulator that—
  (A) Represents an aircraft of the same category and class, and type, as applicable, as the aircraft in which the authorization is sought; and
  (B) Is used in accordance with an approved course conducted by a training center certificated under Part 142 of this chapter.
(ii) All approaches must be made with the approved automatic landing system or an equivalent landing system approved by the Administrator and must consist of the following:
  (A) At least two ILS approaches to 100 feet AGL, including one landing and one missed approach initiated from a very low altitude that may result in a touchdown during the go-around maneuver.
  (B) If a multiengine aircraft with the performance capability to execute a missed approach with one engine inoperative is used, a missed approach shall be executed with an engine, which shall be the most critical engine, if applicable, set at idle or zero thrust before reaching the middle or outer marker.
  (C) If a flight simulator or flight training device is used, a missed approach must be executed with an engine, which shall be the most critical engine, if applicable, failed.
  (D) Subject to the limitations of paragraph (e)(2)(ii)(E) of this section, for Category IIIb operations predicated on the use of a fail-passive rollout control system, at least one manual rollout using visual reference or a combination of visual and instrument references.
  (E) The maneuver required by paragraph (e)(2)(ii)(D) of this section shall be initiated by a fail-passive disconnect of the rollout control system—
    (1) After main gear touchdown;
    (2) Prior to nose gear touchdown;
    (3) In conditions representative of the most adverse lateral touchdown displacement allowing a safe landing on the runway; and
    (4) In weather conditions anticipated in Category IIIb operations.
(iii) For authorizations for aircraft that require a type rating, the practical test must be performed in coordination with a second-in-command who holds a type rating in the aircraft in which the authorization is sought.

61.69　GLIDER TOWING: EXPERIENCE AND INSTRUCTION REQUIREMENTS

No person may act as pilot-in-command of an aircraft towing a glider unless he meets the following requirements:

(a)　He holds a current pilot certificate (other than a student or recreational pilot certificate) issued under this part.

(b)　He has an endorsement in his pilot logbook from a person authorized to give flight instruction in gliders, certifying that he has received ground and flight instruction in gliders and is familiar with the techniques and procedures essential to the safe towing of gliders, including airspeed limitations, emergency procedures, signals used, and maximum angles of bank.

(c)　He has made and entered in his pilot logbook —
　(1)　At least three flights as sole manipulator of the controls of an aircraft towing a glider while accompanied by a pilot who has met the requirements of this section and made and logged at least 10 flights as pilot-in-command of an aircraft towing a glider; or
　(2)　At least three flights as sole manipulator of the controls of an aircraft simulating glider towing flight procedures (while accompanied by a pilot who meets the requirements of this section), and at least three flights as pilot or observer in a glider being towed by an aircraft.
　However, any person who, before May 17, 1967, made, and entered in his pilot logbook, 10 or more flights as pilot-in-command of an aircraft towing a glider in accordance with a certificate of waiver need not comply with paragraphs (c)(1) and (2) of this section.

(d)　If he holds only a private pilot certificate he must have had, and entered in his pilot logbook at least—
　(1)　100 hours of pilot flight time in powered aircraft; or
　(2)　200 total hours of pilot flight time in powered or other aircraft.

(e)　Within the preceding 12 months he has—
　(1)　Made at least 3 actual or simulated glider tows while accompanied by a qualified pilot who meets the requirements of this section; or
　(2)　Made at least 3 flights as pilot-in-command of a glider towed by an aircraft.

61.71　GRADUATES OF CERTIFICATED FLYING SCHOOLS: SPECIAL RULES

(a)　A graduate of a flying school that is certificated under Part 141 of this chapter is considered to meet the applicable aeronautical experience requirements of this Part if he presents an appropriate graduation certificate within 60 days after the date he is graduated. However, if he applies for a flight test for an instrument rating he must hold a commercial pilot certificate, or hold a private pilot certificate and meet the requirements of §§61.65(e)(1) and 61.123 (except paragraphs (d) and (e) thereof). In addition, if he applies for a flight instructor certificate he must hold a commercial pilot certificate.

(b)　An applicant for a certificate or rating under this part is considered to meet the aeronautical knowledge and skill requirements, or both, applicable to that certificate or rating if the applicant applies within 90 days after graduation from an appropriate course given by a pilot school that is certificated under Part 141 of this chapter and is authorized to test applicants on aeronautical knowledge or skill, or both.

61.73　MILITARY PILOTS OR FORMER MILITARY PILOTS: SPECIAL RULES

(a)　*General.* A rated military pilot or former rated military pilot who applies for a private or commercial pilot certificate, or an aircraft or instrument rating, is entitled to that certificate with appropriate ratings or to the addition of a rating on the pilot certificate he holds, if he meets the applicable requirements of this section. This section does not apply to a military pilot or former military pilot who has been removed from flying status for lack of proficiency or because of disciplinary action involving aircraft operations.

(b)　*Military Pilots on Active Flying Status Within 12 Months.* A rated military pilot or former rated military pilot who has been on active flying status within the 12 months before he applies must pass a written test on the parts of this chapter relating to pilot privileges and limitations, air traffic and general operating rules, and accident reporting rules. In addition, he must present documents showing that he meets the requirements of paragraph (d) of this section for at least one aircraft rating, and that he is, or was at any time since the beginning of the twelfth month before the month in which he applies —

    (1)   A rated military pilot on active flying status in an armed force of the United States; or

    (2)   A rated military pilot of an armed force of a foreign contracting State to the Convention on International Civil Aviation, assigned to pilot duties (other than flight training) with an armed force of the United States who holds, at the time he applies, a current civil pilot license issued by that foreign State authorizing at least the privileges of the pilot certificate he seeks.

(c)   *Military Pilots Not on Active Flying Status Within Previous 12 Months.* A rated military pilot or former military pilot who has not been on active flying status within the 12 months before he applies must pass the appropriate written and flight tests prescribed in this part for the certificate or rating he seeks. In addition, he must show that he holds an FAA medical certificate appropriate to the pilot certificate he seeks and present documents showing that he was, before the beginning of the twelfth month before the month in which he applies, a rated military pilot as prescribed by either paragraph (b)(1) or (2) of this section.

(d)   *Aircraft Ratings: Other Than Airplane Category and Type.* An applicant for a category, class, or type rating (other than airplane category and type rating) to be added on the pilot certificate he holds, or for which he has applied, is issued that rating if he presents documentary evidence showing one of the following:

    (1)   That he has passed an official United States military checkout as pilot-in-command of aircraft of the category, class, or type for which he seeks a rating since the beginning of the twelfth month before the month in which he applies.

    (2)   That he has had at least 10 hours of flight time serving as pilot-in-command of aircraft of the category, class, or type for which he seeks a rating since the beginning of the twelfth month before the month in which he applies and previously has had an official United States military checkout as pilot-in-command of that aircraft.

    (3)   That he has met the requirements of paragraph (b)(1) or (2) of this section, has had an official United States military checkout in the category of aircraft for which he seeks a rating, and that he passes an FAA flight test appropriate to that category and the class or type rating he seeks. To be eligible for that flight test, he must have a written statement from an authorized flight instructor, made not more than 60 days before he applies for the flight test, certifying that he is competent to pass the test.

A type rating is issued only for aircraft types that the Administrator has certificated for civil operations. Any rating placed on an airline transport pilot certificate is limited to commercial pilot privileges.

(e)   *Airplane Category and Type Ratings.*

    (1)   An applicant for a commercial pilot certificate with an airplane category rating, or an applicant for the addition of an airplane category rating on his commercial pilot certificate, must hold an airplane instrument rating, or his certificate is endorsed with the following limitation: "not valid for the carriage of passengers or property for hire in airplanes on cross-country flights of more than 50 nautical miles, or at night."

    (2)   An applicant for a private or commercial pilot certificate with an airplane type rating, or for the addition of an airplane type rating on his private or commercial pilot certificate who holds an instrument rating (airplane), must present documentary evidence showing that he has demonstrated instrument competency in the type of airplane for which the type rating is sought, or his certificate is endorsed with the following limitation: "VFR only."

(f)   *Instrument Rating.* An applicant for an airplane instrument rating or a helicopter instrument rating to be added on the pilot certificate he holds, or for which he has applied, is entitled to that rating if he has, within the 12 months preceding the month in which he applies, satisfactorily accomplished an instrument flight check of a U.S. Armed Force in an aircraft of the category for which he seeks the instrument rating and is authorized to conduct IFR flights on Federal airways. A helicopter instrument rating added on an airline transport pilot certificate is limited to commercial pilot privileges.

(g)   *Evidentiary Documents.* The following documents are satisfactory evidence for the purposes indicated:

    (1)   To show that the applicant is a member of the armed forces, an official identification card issued to the applicant by an armed force may be used.

    (2)   To show the applicant's discharge or release from an armed force, or his former membership therein, an original or a copy of a certificate of discharge or release may be used.

    (3)   To show current or previous status as a rated military pilot on flying status with a U.S. Armed Force, one of the following may be used:

        (i)   An official U.S. Armed Force order to flight duty as a military pilot.

        (ii)   An official U.S. Armed Force form or logbook showing military pilot status.

        (iii)   An official order showing that the applicant graduated from a U.S. military pilot school and is rated as a military pilot.

    (4)   To show flight time in military aircraft as a member of a U.S. Armed Force, an appropriate U.S. Armed Force form or summary of it, or a certificated United States military logbook may be used.

    (5)   To show pilot-in-command status, an official U.S. Armed Force record of a military checkout as pilot-in-command, may be used.

    (6)   To show instrument pilot qualification, a current instrument card issued by a U.S. Armed Force, or an official record of the satisfactory completion of an instrument flight check within the 12 months preceding the month of the application may be used. However, a Tactical (Pink) instrument card issued by the U.S. Army is not acceptable.

61.75   PILOT CERTIFICATE ISSUED ON BASIS OF A FOREIGN PILOT LICENSE

(a)   *Purpose.* The holder of a current private, commercial, senior commercial, or airline transport pilot license issued by a foreign contracting State to the Convention on International Civil Aviation may apply for a pilot certificate under this section authorizing him to act as pilot of a civil aircraft of U.S. registry.

(b)   *Certificate Issued.* A pilot certificate is issued to an applicant under this section, specifying the number and State of issuance of the foreign pilot license on which it is based. An applicant who holds a foreign private pilot license is issued a private pilot certificate, and an applicant who holds a foreign commercial, senior commercial, or airline transport pilot license is issued a commercial pilot certificate, if —

    (1)   He meets the requirements of this section;

    (2)   His foreign pilot license does not contain an endorsement that he has not met all the standards of ICAO for that license; and

    (3)   He does not hold a U.S. pilot certificate of private pilot grade or higher.

(c)   *Limitation on Licenses Used as Basis for U.S. Certificate.* Only one foreign pilot license may be used as a basis for issuing a pilot certificate under this section.

(d)   *Aircraft Ratings Issued.* Aircraft ratings listed on the applicant's foreign pilot license, in addition to any issued after testing under the provisions of this part, are placed on the applicant's pilot certificate.

(e)   *Instrument Rating Issued.* An instrument rating is issued to an applicant if —

    (1)   His foreign pilot license authorizes instrument privileges; and

    (2)   Within 24 months preceding the month in which he makes application for a certificate, he passed a test on the instrument flight rules in Subpart B of Part 91 of this chapter, including the related procedures for the operation of the aircraft under instrument flight rules.

(f)   *Medical Standards and Certification.* An applicant must submit evidence that he currently meets the medical standards for the foreign pilot license on which the application for a certificate under this section is based. A current medical certificate issued under Part 67 of this chapter is accepted as evidence that the applicant meets those standards. However, a medical certificate issued under Part 67 of this chapter is not evidence that the applicant meets those standards outside the United States, unless the State that issued the applicant's foreign pilot license also accepts that medical certificate as evidence of meeting the medical standards for his foreign pilot license.

(g)   *Limitations Placed on Pilot Certificate.*

    (1)   If the applicant cannot read, speak, and understand the English language, the Administrator places any limitation on the certificate that he considers necessary for safety.

    (2)   A certificate issued under this section is not valid for agricultural aircraft operations, or the operation of an aircraft in which persons or property are carried for compensation or hire. This limitation is also placed on the certificate.

(h)   *Operating Privileges and Limitations.* The holder of a pilot certificate issued under this section may act as a pilot of a civil aircraft of U.S. registry in accordance with the pilot privileges authorized by the foreign pilot license on which that certificate is based, subject to the limitations of this part and any additional limitations placed on his certificate by the Administrator. He is subject to these limitations while he is acting as a pilot of the aircraft within or outside the United States. However, he may not act as pilot-in-command, or in any other capacity as a required pilot flight crewmember, of a civil aircraft of U.S. registry that is carrying persons or property for compensation or hire.

(i)   *Flight Instructor Certificate.* A pilot certificate issued under this section does not satisfy any of the requirements of this part for the issuance of a flight instructor certificate.

61.77   SPECIAL PURPOSE PILOT CERTIFICATE: OPERATION OF U.S. REGISTERED CIVIL AIRPLANES LEASED BY A PERSON NOT A U.S. CITIZEN

(a)   *General.* The holder of a current foreign pilot certificate or license issued by a foreign contracting State to the Convention on International Civil Aviation, who meets the requirements of this section, may hold a special purpose pilot certificate authorizing the holder to perform pilot duties on a civil airplane of U.S. registry, leased to a person not a citizen of the United States, carrying persons or property for compensation or hire. Special purpose pilot certificates are issued under this section only for airplane types that can have a maximum passenger seating configuration, excluding any flight crewmember seat, of more than 30 seats or a maximum payload capacity (as defined in §135.2(e) of this chapter) of more than 7,500 pounds.

(b)   *Eligibility.* To be eligible for the issuance or renewal of a certificate under this section, an applicant or a representative of the applicant must present the following to the Administrator:

    (1)   A current foreign pilot certificate or license, issued by the aeronautical authority of a foreign contracting State to the Convention on International Civil Aviation, or a facsimile acceptable to the Administrator. The certificate or license must authorize the applicant to perform the pilot duties to be authorized by a certificate issued under this section on the same airplane type as the leased airplane.

    (2)   A current certification by the lessee of the airplane —
        (i)   Stating that the applicant is employed by the lessee;
        (ii)   Specifying the airplane type on which the applicant will perform pilot duties; and
        (iii)   Stating that the applicant has received ground and flight instruction which qualifies the applicant to perform the duties to be assigned on the airplane.

    (3)   Documentation showing that the applicant has not reached the age of 60 and that the applicant currently meets the medical standards for the foreign pilot certificate or license required by paragraph (b)(1) of this section, except that a U.S. medical certificate issued under *Part 67 of this chapter is not evidence that the applicant meets those standards unless the State which issued the applicant's foreign pilot certificate or license accepts a U.S. medical certificate as evidence of medical fitness for a pilot certificate or license.

(c)   *Privileges.* The holder of a special purpose pilot certificate issued under this section may exercise the same privileges as those shown on the certificate or license specified in paragraph (b)(1), subject to the limitations specified in this section. The certificate holder is not subject to the requirements of §§ 61.55, 61.57, and 61.58 of this part.

(d)   *Limitations.* Each certificate issued under this section is subject to the following limitations:

    (1)   It is valid only —
        (i)   For flights between foreign countries or for flights in foreign air commerce;
        (ii)   While it and the foreign pilot certificate or license required by paragraph (b)(1) of this section are in the certificate holder's personal possession and are current;
        (iii)   While the certificate holder is employed by the person to whom the airplane described in the certification required by paragraph (b)(2) of this section is leased;
        (iv)   While the certificate holder is performing pilot duties on the U.S. registered civil airplane described in the certification required by paragraph (b)(2) of this section;
        (v)   While the medical documentation required by paragraph (b)(3) of this section is in the certificate holder's personal possession and is currently valid; and
        (vi)   While the certificate holder is under 60 years of age.

    (2)   Each certificate issued under this section contains the following:
        (i)   The name of the person to whom the U.S. registered civil aircraft is leased.
        (ii)   The type of aircraft.
        (iii)   The limitation: "Issued under, and subject to, §61.77 of the Federal Aviation Regulations."
        (iv)   The limitation; "Subject to the privileges and limitations shown on the holder's foreign pilot certificate or license."

    (3)   Any additional limitations placed on the certificate which the Administrator considers necessary.

(e)   *Termination.* Each special purpose pilot certificate issued under this section terminates—

    (1)   When the lease agreement for the airplane described in the certification required by paragraph (b)(2) of this section terminates;

    (2)   When the foreign pilot certificate or license, or the medical documentation, required by paragraph (b) of this section is suspended, revoked, or no longer valid;

    (3)   When the certificate holder reaches the age of 60; or

    (4)   After 24 months after the month in which the special purpose pilot certificate was issued.

(f)   *Surrender of certificate.* The certificate holder shall surrender the special purpose pilot certificate to the Administrator within 7 days after the date it terminates.

(g)   *Renewal.* The certificate holder may have the certificate renewed by complying with the requirements of paragraph (b) of this section at the time of application for renewal.

SUBPART C — STUDENT AND RECREATIONAL PILOTS

61.81   APPLICABILITY

This subpart prescribes the requirements for the issuance of student pilot certificates and recreational pilot certificates and ratings, the conditions under which those certificates and ratings are necessary, and the general operating rules and limitations for the holders of those certificates and ratings.

61.83   ELIGIBILITY REQUIREMENTS: STUDENT PILOTS

To be eligible for a student pilot certificate, a person must —
(a)   Be at least 16 years of age, or at least 14 years of age for a student pilot certificate limited to the operation of a glider or free balloon;
(b)   Be able to read, speak, and understand the English language, or have such operating limitations placed on his pilot certificate as are necessary for the safe operation of aircraft, to be removed when he shows that he can read, speak, and understand the English language; and
(c)   Hold at least a current third-class medical certificate issued under Part 67 of this chapter, or, in the case of glider or free balloon operations, certify that he has no known medical defect that makes him unable to pilot a glider or a free balloon.

61.85   APPLICATION

An application for a student pilot certificate is made on a form and in a manner provided by the Administrator and is submitted to —
(a)   A designated aviation medical examiner when applying for an FAA medical certificate; or
(b)   An FAA operations inspector or designated pilot examiner, accompanied by a current FAA medical certificate, or in the case of an application for a glider or free balloon pilot certificate it may be accompanied by a certification by the applicant that he has no known medical defect that makes him unable to pilot a glider or free balloon.

61.87   SOLO FLIGHT REQUIREMENTS FOR STUDENT PILOTS

(a)   *General.* A student pilot may not operate an aircraft in solo flight unless that student meets the requirements of this section. The term "solo flight," as used in this subpart, means that flight time during which a student pilot is the sole occupant of the aircraft, or that flight time during which the student acts as pilot-in-command of an airship requiring more than one flight crewmember.
(b)   *Aeronautical knowledge.* A student pilot must have demonstrated satisfactory knowledge to an authorized instructor, of the appropriate portions of Parts 61 and 91 of the Federal Aviation Regulations that are applicable to student pilots. This demonstration must include the satisfactory completion of a written examination to be administered and graded by the instructor who endorses the student's pilot certificate for solo flight. The written examination must include questions on the applicable regulations and the flight characteristics and operational limitations for the make and model aircraft to be flown.
(c)   *Pre-solo flight training.* Prior to being authorized to conduct a solo flight, a student pilot must have received and logged instruction in at least the applicable maneuvers and procedures listed in paragraphs (d) through (j) of this section for the make and model of aircraft to be flown in solo flight, and must have demonstrated proficiency to an acceptable performance level as judged by the instructor who endorses the student's pilot certificate.
(d)   For all aircraft (as appropriate to the aircraft to be flown in solo flight), the student pilot must have received pre-solo flight training in —
    (1)   Flight preparation procedures, including preflight inspections, power plant operation, and aircraft systems;
    (2)   Taxiing or surface operations, including run-ups;
    (3)   Takeoffs and landings, including normal and crosswind;
    (4)   Straight and level flight, shallow, medium, and steep banked turns in both directions;
    (5)   Climbs and climbing turns;
    (6)   Airport traffic patterns including entry and departure procedures, and collision and wake turbulence avoidance;
    (7)   Descents with and without turns using high and low drag configurations;

(8) Flight at various airspeeds from cruising to minimum controllable airspeed;
(9) Emergency procedures and equipment malfunctions; and
(10) Ground reference maneuvers.

(e) For airplanes, in addition to the maneuvers and procedures in paragraph (d) of this section, the student pilot must have received pre-solo flight training in —
(1) Approaches to the landing area with engine power at idle and with partial power;
(2) Slips to a landing;
(3) Go-arounds from final approach and from the landing flare in various flight configurations including turns;
(4) Forced landing procedures initiated on takeoff, during initial climb, cruise, descent, and in the landing pattern; and
(5) Stall entries from various flight attitudes and power combinations with recovery initiated at the first indication of a stall, and recovery from a full stall.

(f) For rotorcraft (other than single-place gyroplanes), in addition to the maneuvers and procedures in paragraph (d) of this section and as allowed by the aircraft's performance and maneuver limitations, the student pilot must have received pre-solo flight training in —
(1) Approaches to the landing area;
(2) Hovering turns and air taxiing (for helicopters only) and ground maneuvers;
(3) Go-arounds from landing hover and from final approach;
(4) Simulated emergency procedures, including autorotational descents with a power recovery or running landing in gyroplanes, a power recovery to a hover in a single engine helicopter, or approaches to a hover or landing with one engine inoperative in multiengine helicopters; and
(5) Rapid decelerations (helicopters only).

(g) For single-place gyroplanes, in addition to the appropriate maneuvers and procedures in paragraph (d) of this section, the student pilot must have received pre-solo flight training in —
(1) Simulated emergency procedures, including autorotational descents with a lower recovery or a running landing;
(2) At least three successful flights in gyroplanes under the observation of a qualified instructor; and
(3) For nonpowered single-place gyroplanes only, at least three successful flights in a gyroplane towed from the ground under the observation of the flight instructor who endorses the student's pilot certificate.

(h) For gliders, in addition to the appropriate maneuvers and procedures in paragraph (d) of this section, the student pilot must have received pre-solo flight training in —
(1) Preflight inspection of towline rigging, review of signals, and release procedures to be used;
(2) Aerotows, ground tows, or self-launch;
(3) Principles of glider disassembly and assembly;
(4) Stall entries from various flight attitudes with recovery initiated at the first indication of a stall, and recovery from a full stall;
(5) Straight glides, turns, and spirals;
(6) Slips to a landing;
(7) Procedures and techniques for thermalling in convergence lift or ridge lift as appropriate to the training area; and
(8) Emergency operations including towline break procedures.

(i) In airships, in addition to the appropriate maneuvers and procedures in paragraph (d) of this section, the student pilot must have received pre-solo flight training in —
(1) Rigging, ballasting, controlling pressure in the ballonets, and superheating; and
(2) Landings with positive and with negative static balance.

(j) In free balloons, in addition to the appropriate maneuvers and procedures in paragraph (d) of this section, the student pilot must have received pre-solo flight training in —
(1) Operation of hot air or gas source, ballast, valves, and rip panels, as appropriate;
(2) Emergency use of rip panel (may be simulated);
(3) The effects of wind on climb and approach angles; and
(4) Obstruction detection and avoidance techniques.

(k) The instruction required by this section must be given by an authorized flight instructor who is certificated —
(1) In the category and class of airplanes, for airplanes;
(2) Except as provided in paragraph (k)(3) of this section, in helicopters or gyroplanes, as appropriate, for rotorcraft;
(3) In airplanes or gyroplanes, for single-place gyroplanes; and
(4) In gliders for gliders.

(l)   The holder of a commercial pilot certificate with a lighter-than-air category rating may give the instruction required by this section in —
- (1)   Airships, if that commercial pilot holds an airship class rating; and
- (2)   Free balloons, if that commercial pilot holds a free balloon class rating.

(m)   Flight instructor endorsements. No student pilot may operate an aircraft in solo flight unless that student's pilot certificate and logbook have been endorsed for the specific make and model aircraft to be flown by an authorized flight instructor certificated under this part, and the student's logbook has been endorsed, within the 90 days prior to the student operating in solo flight, by an authorized flight instructor certificated under this part who has flown with the student. No flight instructor may authorize solo flight without endorsing the student's logbook. The instructor's endorsement must certify that the instructor —
- (1)   Has given the student instruction in the make and model aircraft in which the solo flight is to be made;
- (2)   Finds that the student has met the flight training requirements of this section; and
- (3)   Finds that the student is competent to make a safe solo flight in that aircraft.

(n)   Notwithstanding the requirements of paragraphs (a) through (m) of this section, each student pilot, whose student pilot certificate and logbook are endorsed for solo flight by an authorized flight instructor on or before August 30, 1989, may operate an aircraft in solo flight until the 90th day after the date on which the logbook was endorsed for solo flight.

61.89   GENERAL LIMITATIONS

(a)   A student pilot may not act as pilot-in-command of an aircraft —
- (1)   That is carrying a passenger;
- (2)   That is carrying property for compensation or hire;
- (3)   For compensation or hire;
- (4)   In furtherance of a business;
- (5)   On an international flight, except that a student pilot may make solo training flights from Haines, Gustavus, or Juneau, Alaska, to White Horse, Yukon, Canada, and return, over the province of British Columbia;
- (6)   With a flight or surface visibility of less than 3 statute miles during daylight hours or 5 statute miles at night;
- (7)   When the flight cannot be made with visual reference to the surface; or
- (8)   In a manner contrary to any limitations placed in the pilot's logbook by the instructor.

(b)   A student pilot may not act as a required pilot flight crewmember on any aircraft for which more than one pilot is required by the type certificate of the aircraft or regulations under which the flight is conducted, except when receiving flight instruction from an authorized flight instructor on board an airship and no person other than a required flight crewmember is carried on the aircraft.

61.91   AIRCRAFT LIMITATIONS: PILOT-IN-COMMAND

A student pilot may not serve as pilot-in-command of any airship requiring more than one flight crewmember unless he has met the pertinent requirements prescribed in §61.87.

61.93   CROSS-COUNTRY FLIGHT REQUIREMENTS (FOR STUDENT AND RECREATIONAL PILOTS SEEKING PRIVATE PILOT CERTIFICATION)

(a)   *General.* No student pilot may operate an aircraft in solo cross-country flight, nor may that student, except in an emergency, make a solo flight landing at any point other than the airport of takeoff, unless the student has met the requirements of this section. The term cross-country flight, as used in this section, means a flight beyond a radius of 25 nautical miles from the point of departure.

(b)   Notwithstanding paragraph (a) of this section, an authorized flight instructor, certificated under this part, may permit the student to practice solo takeoffs and landings at another airport within 25 nautical miles from the airport at which the student receives instruction if the flight instructor —
- (1)   Determines that the student pilot is competent and proficient to make those landings and takeoffs;
- (2)   Has flown with that student prior to authorizing those takeoffs and landings; and
- (3)   Endorses the student pilot's logbook with an authorization to make those landings and takeoffs.

(c) *Flight training.* A student pilot, in addition to the pre-solo flight training maneuvers and procedures required by §61.87(c), must have received and logged instruction from an authorized flight instructor in the appropriate pilot maneuvers and procedures of this section. Additionally, a student pilot must have demonstrated an acceptable standard of performance, as judged by the authorized flight instructor certificated under this part, who endorses the student's pilot certificate in the appropriate pilot maneuvers and procedures of this section.

(1) For all aircraft —

(i) The use of aeronautical charts for VFR navigation using pilotage and dead reckoning with the aid of a magnetic compass;

(ii) Aircraft cross-country performance, and procurement and analysis of aeronautical weather reports and forecasts, including recognition of critical weather situations and estimating visibility while in flight;

(iii) Cross-country emergency conditions including lost procedures, adverse weather conditions, and simulated precautionary off-airport approaches and landing procedures;

(iv) Traffic pattern procedures, including normal area arrival and departure, collision avoidance, and wake turbulence precautions;

(v) Recognition of operational problems associated with the different terrain features in the geographical area in which the cross-country flight is to be flown; and

(vi) Proper operation of the instruments and equipment installed in the aircraft to be flown.

(2) For airplanes, in addition to paragraph (c)(1) of this section —

(i) Short and soft field takeoff, approach, and landing procedures, including crosswind takeoffs and landings;

(ii) Takeoffs at best angle and rate of climb;

(iii) Control and maneuvering solely by reference to flight instruments including straight and level flight, turns, descents, climbs, and the use of radio aids and radar directives;

(iv) The use of radios for VFR navigation and for two-way communication; and

(v) For those student pilots seeking night flying privileges, night flying procedures including takeoffs, landings, go-arounds, and VFR navigation.

(3) For rotorcraft, in addition to paragraph (c)(1) of this section and as appropriate to the aircraft being flown —

(i) High altitude takeoff and landing procedures;

(ii) Steep and shallow approaches to a landing hover;

(iii) Rapid decelerations (helicopters only); and

(iv) The use of radios for VFR navigation and two-way communication.

(4) For gliders, in addition to the appropriate maneuvers and procedures in paragraph (c)(1) of this section —

(i) Landings accomplished without the use of the altimeter from at least 2,000 feet above the surface;

(ii) Recognition of weather conditions and conditions favorable for cross-country soaring; and

(iii) The use of radios for two-way radio communications.

(5) For airships, in addition to the appropriate maneuvers and procedures in paragraph (c)(1) of this section —

(i) Control of gas pressure with regard to superheating and altitude; and

(ii) Control of the airship solely by reference to flight instruments.

(6) For free balloons, the appropriate maneuvers and procedures in paragraph (c)(1) of this section.

(d) No student pilot may operate an aircraft in solo cross-country flight, unless —

(1) The instructor is an authorized instructor certificated under this part and the student's certificate has been endorsed by the instructor attesting that the student has received the instruction and demonstrated an acceptable level of competency and proficiency in the maneuvers and procedures of this section for the category of aircraft to be flown; and

(2) The instructor has endorsed the student's logbook —

(i) For each solo cross-country flight, after reviewing the student's preflight planning and preparation, attesting that the student is prepared to make the flight safely under the known circumstances and subject to any conditions listed in the logbook by the instructor; and

(ii) For repeated specific solo cross-country flights that are not greater than 50 nautical miles from the point of departure, after giving that student flight instruction in both directions over the route, including takeoffs and landings at the airports to be used, and has specified the conditions for which the flights can be made.

61.95   OPERATIONS IN CLASS B AIRSPACE AND AT AIRPORTS LOCATED WITHIN CLASS B AIRSPACE

(a) A student pilot may not operate an aircraft on a solo flight in Class B airspace unless —
   (1) The pilot has received both ground and flight instruction from an authorized instructor on that Class B airspace area and the flight instruction was received in the specific Class B airspace area for which solo flight is authorized;
   (2) The logbook of that pilot has been endorsed within the preceding 90 days for conducting solo flight in that specific Class B airspace area by the instructor who gave the flight training; and
   (3) The logbook endorsement specifies that the pilot has received the required ground and flight instruction and has been found competent to conduct solo flight in that specific Class B airspace area.
(b) Pursuant to §91.131(b), a student pilot may not operate an aircraft on a solo flight to, from, or at an airport located within a Class B airspace unless —
   (1) That student pilot has received both ground and flight instruction from an authorized instructor to operate at that airport and the flight and ground instruction has been received at the specific airport for which the solo flight is authorized;
   (2) The logbook of that student pilot has been endorsed within the preceding 90 days for conducting solo flight at that specific airport by the instructor who gave the flight training; and
   (3) The logbook endorsement specifies that the student pilot has received the required ground and flight instruction and has been found competent to conduct solo flight operations at that specific airport.

61.96   ELIGIBILITY REQUIREMENTS: RECREATIONAL PILOTS

To be eligible for a recreational pilot certificate, a person must —
(a) Be at least 17 years of age;
(b) Be able to read, speak, and understand the English language, or have such operating limitations placed on the pilot certificate as are necessary for the safe operation of aircraft, to be removed when the recreational pilot shows the ability to read, speak, and understand the English language;
(c) Hold at least a current third-class medical certificate issued under Part 67 of this chapter;
(d) Pass a written test on the subject areas on which instruction or home study is required by §61.97;
(e) Pass an oral and flight test on maneuvers and procedures selected by an FAA inspector or designated pilot examiner to determine the applicant's competency in the appropriate flight operations listed in §61.98; and
(f) Comply with the sections of this part that apply to the rating sought.

61.97   AERONAUTICAL KNOWLEDGE

An applicant for a recreational pilot certificate must have logged ground instruction from an authorized instructor, or must present evidence showing satisfactory completion of a course of instruction or home study in at least the following areas of aeronautical knowledge appropriate to the category and class of aircraft for which a rating is sought:
(a) The Federal Aviation Regulations applicable to recreational pilot privileges, limitations, and flight operations, the accident reporting requirements of the National Transportation Safety Board, and the use of the applicable portions of the "Airman's Information Manual" and the FAA advisory circulars;
(b) The use of aeronautical charts for VFR navigation using piloting with the aid of a magnetic compass;
(c) The recognition of critical weather situations from the ground and in flight and the procurement and use of aeronautical weather reports and forecasts;
(d) The safe and efficient operation of aircraft including collision and wake turbulence avoidance;
(e) The effects of density altitude on takeoff and climb performance;
(f) Weight and balance computations;

(g)   Principles of aerodynamics, powerplants, and aircraft systems; and

(h)   Stall awareness, spin entry, spins, and spin recovery techniques.

61.98   FLIGHT PROFICIENCY

The applicant for a recreational pilot certificate must have logged instruction from an authorized flight instructor in at least the pilot operations listed in this section. In addition, the applicant's logbook must contain an endorsement by an authorized flight instructor who has found the applicant competent to perform each of those operations safely as a recreational pilot.

(a)   *In airplanes.*

   (1)   Preflight operations, including weight and balance determination, line inspection, airplane servicing, power plant operations, and aircraft systems;

   (2)   Airport and traffic pattern operations, collision and wake turbulence avoidance;

   (3)   Flight maneuvering by reference to ground objects;

   (4)   Pilotage with the aid of magnetic compass;

   (5)   Flight at slow airspeeds with realistic distractions and the recognition of and recovery from stalls entered from straight flight and from turns;

   (6)   Emergency operations, including simulated aircraft and equipment malfunctions;

   (7)   Maximum performance takeoffs and landings; and

   (8)   Normal and crosswind takeoffs and landings.

(b)   *In helicopters.* (1) Preflight operations including weight and balance determination, line inspection, helicopter servicing, power plant operations, and aircraft systems;

   (2)   Airport and traffic pattern operations, collision and wake turbulence avoidance;

   (3)   Hovering, air taxiing, and maneuvering by reference to ground objects;

   (4)   Pilotage with the aid of magnetic compass;

   (5)   High altitude takeoffs and roll-on landings, and rapid decelerations; and

   (6)   Emergency operations, including auto-rotative descents.

(c)   *In gyroplanes.* (1) Preflight operations including weight and balance determination, line inspection, gyroplane servicing, power plant operations, and aircraft systems;

   (2)   Airport and traffic pattern operations, collision and wake turbulence avoidance;

   (3)   Flight maneuvering by reference to ground objects;

   (4)   Pilotage with the aid of a magnetic compass;

   (5)   Maneuvering at critically slow airspeeds, and the recognition of and recovery from high rates of descent at low airspeeds; and

   (6)   Emergency procedures, including maximum performance takeoffs and landings.

61.99   AIRPLANE RATING: AERONAUTICAL EXPERIENCE

(a)   An applicant for a recreational pilot certificate with an airplane rating must have had at least a total of 30 hours of flight instruction and solo flight time which must include the following:

   (1)   Fifteen hours of flight instruction from an authorized flight instructor, including at least —

      (i)   Except as provided for in paragraph (b), 2 hours outside of the vicinity of the airport at which instruction is given, including at least three landings at another airport that is located more than 25 nautical miles from the airport of departure; and

      (ii)   Two hours in airplanes in preparation for the recreational pilot flight test within the 60-day period before the test.

   (2)   Fifteen hours of solo flight time in airplanes.

(b)   Pilots based on small islands.

   (1)   An applicant who is located on an island from which the flight required in §61.99(a)(1)(i) cannot be accomplished without flying over water more than 10 nautical miles from the nearest shoreline need not comply with §61.99(a)(1)(i). However, if other airports that permit civil operations are available to which a flight may be made without flying over water more than 10 nautical miles from the nearest shoreline, the applicant must show completion of a dual flight between those two airports which must include three landings at the other airport.

   (2)   The pilot certificate issued to a person under paragraph (b)(1) of this section contains an endorsement with the following limitation which may subsequently be amended to include another island if the applicant complies with paragraph (b)(1) of this section with respect to that island:

Passenger carrying prohibited in flights more than 10 nautical miles from (appropriate island).

(3) The holder of a recreational pilot certificate with an endorsement described in paragraph (b)(2) of this section is entitled to removal of the endorsement if the holder presents satisfactory evidence of compliance with the applicable flight requirements of § 61.93 (c) to an FAA inspector or designated pilot examiner.

61.100 ROTORCRAFT RATING: AERONAUTICAL EXPERIENCE

An applicant for a recreational pilot certificate with a rotorcraft category rating must have at least the following aeronautical experience:
(a) For a helicopter rating, an applicant must have a minimum of 30 hours of flight instruction and solo flight time in aircraft, which must include the following:
  (1) Fifteen hours of flight instruction from an authorized flight instructor including at least —
    (i) Two hours of flight instruction in helicopters from an authorized flight instructor outside the vicinity of the airport at which instruction is given, including at least three landings at another airport that is located more than 25 nautical miles from the airport of departure; and
    (ii) Two hours of flight instruction in preparation for the flight test within the 60-day period preceding the test.
  (2) Fifteen hours of solo time in helicopters including —
    (i) A takeoff and landing at an airport that serves both airplanes and helicopters; and
    (ii) A flight with a landing at a point other than an airport.
(b) For a gyroplane rating, an applicant must have a minimum of 30 hours of flight instruction and solo flight time in aircraft, which must include the following:
  (1) Fifteen hours of flight instruction from an authorized flight instructor including at least —
    (i) Two hours of flight instruction in gyroplanes from an authorized flight instructor outside the vicinity of the airport at which instruction is given, including at least three landings at another airport that is located more than 25 nautical miles from the airport of departure; and
    (ii) Two hours of flight instruction in preparation for the flight test within the 60-day period preceding the test.
  (2) Ten hours of solo flight time in a gyroplane, including flights with takeoffs and landings at paved and unpaved airports.

61.101 RECREATIONAL PILOT PRIVILEGES AND LIMITATIONS

(a) A recreational pilot may —
  (1) Carry not more than one passenger; and
  (2) Share the operating expenses of the flight with the passenger.
  (3) Act as pilot-in-command of an aircraft only when —
    (i) The flight is within 50 nautical miles of an airport at which the pilot has received ground and flight instruction from an authorized instructor certificated under this part;
    (ii) The flight lands at an airport within 50 nautical miles of the departure airport; and
    (iii) The pilot carries, in that pilot's personal possession, a logbook that has been endorsed by the instructor attesting to the instruction required by paragraph (a)(3)(i) of this section.
(b) Except as provided in paragraphs (f) and (g) of this section, a recreational pilot may not act as pilot-in-command of an aircraft —
  (1) That is certificated —
    (i) For more than four occupants;
    (ii) With more than one power plant;
    (iii) With a power plant of more than 180 horsepower; or
    (iv) With retractable landing gear.
  (2) That is classified as a glider, airship, or balloon;
  (3) That is carrying a passenger or property for compensation or hire;
  (4) For compensation or hire;
  (5) In furtherance of a business;
  (6) Between sunset and sunrise;
  (7) In airspace in which communication with air traffic control is required;
  (8) At an altitude of more than 10,000 feet MSL or 2,000 feet AGL, whichever is higher;

(9)   When the flight or surface visibility is less than 3 statute miles;

(10)   Without visual reference to the surface;

(11)   On a flight outside the United States;

(12)   To demonstrate that aircraft in flight to a prospective buyer;

(13)   That is used in a passenger-carrying airlift and sponsored by a charitable organization; and

(14)   That is towing any object.

(c)   A recreational pilot may not act as a required pilot flight crewmember on any aircraft for which more than one pilot is required by the type certificate of the aircraft or the regulations under which the flight is conducted, except when receiving flight instruction from an authorized flight instructor on board an airship and no person other than a required flight crewmember is carried on the aircraft.

(d)   A recreational pilot who has logged fewer than 400 flight hours and who has not logged pilot-in-command time in an aircraft within the preceding 180 days may not act as pilot-in-command of an aircraft until the pilot has received flight instruction from an authorized flight instructor who certifies in the pilot's logbook that the pilot is competent to act as pilot-in-command of the aircraft. This requirement can be met in combination with the requirements of §§61.56 and 61.57 at the discretion of the instructor.

(e)   The recreational pilot certificate issued under this subpart carries the notation "Holder does not meet ICAO requirements."

(f)   For the purpose of obtaining additional certificates or ratings, while under the supervision of an authorized flight instructor, a recreational pilot may fly as sole occupant of an aircraft —

(1)   For which the pilot does not hold an appropriate category or class rating;

(2)   Within airspace that requires communication with air traffic control; or

(3)   Between sunset and sunrise, provided the flight or surface visibility is at least 5 statute miles.

(g)   In order to fly solo as provided in paragraph (f) of this section, the recreational pilot must meet the appropriate aeronautical knowledge and flight training requirements of §61.87 for that aircraft. When operating an aircraft under the conditions specified in paragraph (f) of this section, the recreational pilot shall carry the logbook that has been endorsed for each flight by an authorized pilot instructor who —

(1)   Has given the recreational pilot instruction in the make and model of aircraft in which the solo flight is to be made;

(2)   Has found that the recreational pilot has met the applicable requirements of §61.87; and

(3)   Has found that the recreational pilot is competent to make solo flights in accordance with the logbook endorsement.

(h)   Notwithstanding paragraph 61.101 (a)(3), a recreational pilot may, for the purpose of obtaining an additional certificate or rating, while under the supervision of an authorized flight instructor, act as pilot-in-command of an aircraft on a flight in excess of 50 nautical miles from an airport at which flight instruction is received if the pilot meets the flight training requirements of §61.93 and in that pilot's personal possession is the logbook that has been endorsed by an authorized instructor attesting that:

(1)   The recreational pilot has received instruction in solo cross-country flight and the training described in §61.93 applicable to the aircraft to be operated, and is competent to make solo cross-country flights in the make and model of aircraft to be flown; and

(2)   The instructor has reviewed the student's preflight planning and preparation for the specific solo cross-country flight and that the recreational pilot is prepared to make the flight safely under the known circumstances and subject to any conditions listed in the logbook by the instructor.

SUBPART D — PRIVATE PILOTS

61.102 APPLICABILITY

This subpart prescribes the requirements for the issuance of private pilot certificates and ratings, the conditions under which those certificates and ratings are necessary, and the general operating rules for the holders of those certificates and ratings.

61.103 ELIGIBILITY REQUIREMENTS: GENERAL

To be eligible for a private pilot certificate, a person must —
(a) Be at least 17 years of age, except that a private pilot certificate with a free balloon or a glider rating only may be issued to a qualified applicant who is at least 16 years of age;
(b) Be able to read, speak, and understand the English language, or have such operating limitations placed on his pilot certificate as are necessary for the safe operation of aircraft, to be removed when he shows that he can read, speak, and understand the English language;
(c) Hold at least a current third-class medical certificate issued under Part 67 of this chapter, or, in the case of a glider or free balloon rating, certify that he has no known medical defect that makes him unable to pilot a glider or free balloon, as appropriate;
(d) Pass a written test on the subject areas on which instruction or home study is required by §61.105;
(e) Pass an oral and flight test on procedures and maneuvers selected by an FAA inspector or examiner to determine the applicant's competency in the flight operations on which instruction is required by the flight proficiency provisions of §61.107; and
(f) Comply with the sections of this part that apply to the rating he seeks.

61.105 AERONAUTICAL KNOWLEDGE

An applicant for a private pilot certificate must have logged ground instruction from an authorized instructor, or must present evidence showing that he has satisfactorily completed a course of instruction or home study in at least the following areas of aeronautical knowledge appropriate to the category of aircraft for which a rating is sought.
(a) *Airplanes and Rotorcraft.*
    (1) The accident reporting requirements of the National Transportation Safety Board and the Federal Aviation Regulations applicable to private pilot privileges, limitations, and flight operations for airplanes or rotorcraft, as appropriate, the use of the "Airman's Information Manual," and FAA advisory circulars;
    (2) VFR navigation, using pilotage, dead reckoning, and radio aids;
    (3) The recognition of critical weather situations from the ground and in flight, the procurement and use of aeronautical weather reports and forecasts;
    (4) The safe and efficient operation of airplanes or rotorcraft, as appropriate, including high density airport operations, collision avoidance precautions, and radio communication procedures;
    (5) Basic aerodynamics and the principles of flight which apply to airplanes or rotorcraft, as appropriate; and
    (6) Stall awareness, spin entry, spins, and spin recovery techniques for airplanes.
(b) *Gliders.*
    (1) The accident reporting requirements of the National Transportation Safety Board and the Federal Aviation Regulations applicable to glider pilot privileges, limitations, and flight operations;
    (2) Glider navigation, including the use of aeronautical charts and the magnetic compass;
    (3) Recognition of weather situations of concern to the glider pilot, and the procurement and use of aeronautical weather reports and forecasts;
    (4) The safe and efficient operation of gliders, including ground and/or aero tow procedures, as appropriate, signals, and safety precautions; and
    (5) Stall awareness, spin entry, spins, and spin recovery techniques for gliders.
(c) *Airships.*
    (1) The Federal Aviation Regulations applicable to private lighter-than-air pilot privileges, limitations, and airship flight operations;
    (2) Airship navigation, including pilotage, dead reckoning, and the use of radio aids;
    (3) The recognition of weather conditions of concern to the airship pilot, and the procurement and use of aeronautical weather reports and forecasts; and
    (4) Airship operations, including free ballooning, the effects of superheating, and positive and negative lift.

   (d)   *Free Balloons.*
- (1) The Federal Aviation Regulations applicable to private free balloon pilot privileges, limitations, and flight operations;
- (2) The use of aeronautical charts and the magnetic compass for free balloon navigation;
- (3) The recognition of weather conditions of concern to the free balloon pilot, and the procurement and use of aeronautical weather reports and forecasts appropriate to free balloon operations; and
- (4) Operating principles and procedures of free balloons, including gas and hot air inflation systems.

61.107   FLIGHT PROFICIENCY

The applicant for a private pilot certificate must have logged instruction from an authorized flight instructor in at least the following pilot operations. In addition, his logbook must contain an endorsement by an authorized flight instructor who has found him competent to perform each of those operations safely as a private pilot.

   (a)   *In Airplanes.*
- (1) Preflight operations, including weight and balance determination, line inspection, and airplane servicing;
- (2) Airport and traffic pattern operations, including operations at controlled airports, radio communications, and collision avoidance precautions;
- (3) Flight maneuvering by reference to ground objects;
- (4) Flight at slow airspeeds with realistic distractions, and the recognition of and recovery from stalls entered from straight flight and from turns;
- (5) Normal and crosswind takeoffs and landings;
- (6) Control and maneuvering an airplane solely by reference to instruments, including descents and climbs using radio aids or radar directives;
- (7) Cross-country flying, using pilotage, dead reckoning, and radio aids, including one 2-hour flight;
- (8) Maximum performance takeoffs and landings;
- (9) Night flying, including takeoffs, landings, and VFR navigation; and
- (10) Emergency operations, including simulated aircraft and equipment malfunctions.

   (b)   *In Helicopters.*
- (1) Preflight operations, including the line inspection and servicing of helicopters;
- (2) Hovering, air taxiing, and maneuvering by ground references;
- (3) Airport and traffic pattern operations, including collision avoidance precautions;
- (4) Cross-country flying, using pilotage, dead reckoning, and radio aids, including one 1-hour flight;
- (5) Operations in confined areas and on pinnacles, rapid decelerations, landings on slopes, high-altitude takeoffs, and run-on landings;
- (6) Night flying, including takeoffs, landings, and VFR navigation; and
- (7) Simulated emergency procedures, including aircraft and equipment malfunctions, approaches to a hover or landing with an engine inoperative in a multiengine helicopter, or autorotational descents with a power recovery to a hover in single-engine helicopters.

   (c)   *In Gyroplanes.*
- (1) Preflight operations, including the line inspection and servicing of gyroplanes;
- (2) Flight maneuvering by ground references;
- (3) Maneuvering at critically slow airspeeds, and the recognition of and recovery from high rates of descent at low airspeeds;
- (4) Airport and traffic pattern operations, including collision avoidance precautions and radio communication procedures;
- (5) Cross-country flying by pilotage, dead reckoning, and the use of radio aids; and
- (6) Emergency procedures, including maximum performance takeoffs and landings.

   (d)   *In Gliders.*
- (1) Preflight operation, including the installation of wings and tail surfaces specifically designed for quick removal and installation by pilots, and line inspection.
- (2) Ground (auto or winch) tow or aero tow (the applicant's certificate is limited to the kind of tow selected);
- (3) Precision maneuvering, including steep turns and spirals in both directions;
- (4) The correct use of critical sailplane performance speeds;
- (5) Flight at slow airspeeds with realistic distractions, and the recognition of and recovery from stalls entered from straight flight and from turns; and
- (6) Accuracy approaches and landings with the nose of the glider stopping short of and within 200 feet of a line or mark.

(e) *In Airships.*
    (1)   Ground handling, mooring, rigging, and preflight operations;
    (2)   Takeoffs and landing with static lift, and with negative and positive lift, and the use of two-way radio;
    (3)   Straight and level flight, climbs, turns, and descents;
    (4)   Precision flight maneuvering;
    (5)   Navigation, using pilotage, dead reckoning, and radio aids; and
    (6)   Simulated emergencies, including equipment malfunction, the valving of gas, and the loss of power on one engine.

(f) *In Free Balloons.*
    (1)   Rigging and tethering, including the installation of baskets and burners specifically designed for quick removal or installation by a pilot; and the interchange of baskets or burners, when provided for in the type certificate data, classified as preventive maintenance, and subject to the recording requirements of *§43.9 of this chapter.
    (2)   Operation of burner, if airborne heater used;
    (3)   Ascents and descents;
    (4)   Landing; and
    (5)   Emergencies, including the use of the ripcord (may be simulated).

61.109   AIRPLANE RATING: AERONAUTICAL EXPERIENCE

(a) Except as provided in paragraph (h) of this section, an applicant for a private pilot certificate with an airplane category rating must have at least the following aeronautical experience:
    (1)   At least 20 hours of flight instruction from an authorized instructor, including at least—
        (i)   3 hours of cross-country flight.
        (ii)   3 hours of flight at night, including ten takeoffs and ten landings for applicants seeking night flying privileges.
        (iii)   3 hours in airplanes in preparation for the private pilot practical test within 60 calendar days prior to that test.
    (2)   At least 20 hours of solo flight time, including at least—
        (i)   10 hours of flight in airplanes;
        (ii)   10 hours of cross-country flight; and
        (iii)   Three solo takeoffs and landings to a full stop at an airport with an operating control tower.

(b) Each flight required by paragraph (a)(2)(ii) of this section must include—
    (1)   A landing at a point more than 50 nautical miles from the original departure point; and
    (2)   One flight of at least 300 nautical miles with landings at a minimum of three points, one of which is at least 100 nautical miles from the original departure point.

(c) An applicant who does not meet the night flying requirement of paragraph (a)(l)(ii) of this section may be issued a private pilot certificate bearing the limitation "night flying prohibited." The limitation may be removed if the holder of the certificate shows that he or she has met the requirements of paragraph (a)(1)(ii) of this section.

(d) Except as provided in paragraph (e) of this section, a maximum of 2.5 hours of instruction in a flight simulator or flight training device representing an airplane from an authorized instructor may be credited toward the total hours required by paragraph (a) of this section.

(e) A maximum of 5 hours of instruction in a flight simulator or flight training device representing an airplane may be credited toward the total hours required by paragraph (a) of this section if the instruction is accomplished in a course conducted by a training center certificated under Part 142 of this chapter.

(f) Except where fewer hours are approved by the Administrator, an applicant for a private pilot certificate with an airplane rating who has satisfactorily completed an approved private pilot course conducted by a training center certificated under Part 142 of this chapter need have only a total of at least 35 hours of pilot flight time in aircraft, flight simulators, or flight training devices.

61.111   CROSS-COUNTRY FLIGHTS: PILOTS BASED ON SMALL ISLANDS

(a)   An applicant who shows that he is located on an island from which the required flights cannot be accomplished without flying over water more than 10 nautical miles from the nearest shoreline need not comply with paragraph (b)(2) of §61.109. However, if other airports that permit civil operations are available to which a flight may be made without flying over water more than 10 nautical miles from the nearest shoreline, he must show that he has completed two round trip solo flights between those two airports that are farthest apart, including a landing at each airport on both flights.

(b)   The pilot certificate issued to a person under paragraph (a) of this section contains an endorsement with the following limitation which may be subsequently amended to include another island if the applicant complies with paragraph (a) of this section with respect to that island:
Passenger carrying prohibited on flights more than 10 nautical miles from (appropriate island).

(c)   If an applicant for a private pilot certificate under paragraph (a) of this section does not have at least 3 hours of solo cross-country flight time, including a round trip flight to an airport at least 50 nautical miles from the place of departure with at least two full stop landings at different points along the route, his pilot certificate is also endorsed as follows:
Holder does not meet the cross-country flight requirements of ICAO.

(d)   The holder of a private pilot certificate with an endorsement described in paragraph (b) or (c) of this section, is entitled to a removal of the endorsement, if he presents satisfactory evidence to an FAA inspector or designated pilot examiner that he has complied with the applicable solo cross-country flight requirements and has passed a practical test on cross-country flying.

61.113   ROTORCRAFT RATING: AERONAUTICAL EXPERIENCE

(a)   Except as provided in paragraph (g) of this section, an applicant for a private pilot certificate with a rotorcraft category rating must have at least the following aeronautical experience:

(1)   For a helicopter class rating, 40 hours of flight instruction and solo flight time including at least—

(i)   20 hours of flight instruction from an authorized flight instructor, 15 hours of which must be in a helicopter, including—

(A)   3 hours of cross-country flying in helicopters; and

(B)   3 hours of night flying in helicopters, including 10 takeoffs and 10 landings, each of which must be separated by an enroute phase of flight;

(ii)   3 hours in helicopters in preparation for the private pilot practical test within 60 calendar days before that test;

(iii)   A flight in a helicopter with a landing at a point other than an airport; and

(2)   20 hours of solo flight time, 15 hours of which must be in a helicopter, including at least—

(i)   3 hours of cross-country flying in helicopters, including one flight with a landing at three or more points, each of which must be more than 25 nautical miles from each of the other landing points; and

(ii)   Three takeoffs and three landings in helicopters at airports or heliports with operating control towers, each separated by an enroute phase of flight.

(b)   Except as provided in paragraph (c) of this section, a maximum of 2.5 hours of instruction in a flight simulator or flight training device representing a helicopter from an authorized instructor may be credited toward the total hour requirement of paragraph (a) of this section.

(c)   A maximum of 5 hours of instruction in a flight simulator or flight training device representing a helicopter may be credited toward the total hours required by paragraph (a) of this section if the instruction is accomplished in a course conducted by a training center certificated under Part 142 of this chapter.

(d)   The applicant for a gyroplane class rating must have a total of at least—

(1)   20 hours of flight instruction from an authorized flight instructor, 15 hours of which must be in a gyroplane, including at least the following—

(i)   3 hours of cross-country flying in gyroplanes;

(ii)   3 hours of night flying in gyroplanes, including ten takeoffs and ten landings; and

A *Amend #100 eff 8-1-96*

           (iii)   3 hours in gyroplanes in preparation for the private pilot flight test within 60 calendar days before that test.

    (2)   20 hours of solo flight time, 10 hours of which must be in a gyroplane, including—

        (i)   3 hours of cross-country flying in gyroplanes, including one flight with a landing at three or more points, each of which must be more than 25 nautical miles from each of the other two points; and

        (ii)   Three takeoffs and three landings in gyroplanes at an airport with an operating control tower.

    (3)   Except as provided in paragraph (d)(4) of this section, a maximum of 2.5 hours of instruction in a flight simulator or flight training device representing a gyroplane may be credited toward the total hours required by paragraph (d)(1) of this section.

    (4)   A maximum of 5 hours of instruction in a flight simulator or flight training device representing a gyroplane may be credited toward the total hours required by paragraph (d)(1) of this section if the instruction is accomplished in an approved course conducted by a training center certificated under Part 142 of this chapter.

(e)   An applicant who does not meet the night flying requirements of paragraph (a)(1)(i)(B) or paragraph (d)(1)(ii) of this section will be issued a private pilot certificate bearing the limitation "night flying prohibited."

(f)   The limitation required by paragraph (e) of this section may be removed if the holder of the certificate demonstrates compliance with the requirements of paragraph (a)(1)(i)(B) or paragraph (d)(1)(ii) of this section, as applicable.

(g)   Except where fewer hours are approved by the Administrator, an applicant for a private pilot certificate with a rotorcraft category rating who has satisfactorily completed an approved private pilot course conducted by a training center certificated under Part 142 of this chapter need have only a total of at least 35 hours of pilot flight time in aircraft, flight simulators, or flight training devices.

61.115   GLIDER RATING: AERONAUTICAL EXPERIENCE

An applicant for a private pilot certificate with a glider rating must have logged at least one of the following:

(a)   Seventy solo glider flights, including 20 flights during which 360° turns were made.

(b)   Seven hours of solo flight in gliders, including 35 glider flights launched by ground tows, or 20 glider flights launched by aero tows.

(c)   Forty hours of flight time in gliders and single-engine airplanes, including 10 solo glider flights during which 360° turns were made.

61.117   LIGHTER-THAN-AIR RATING: AERONAUTICAL EXPERIENCE

An applicant for a private pilot certificate with a lighter-than-air category rating must have at least the aeronautical experience prescribed in paragraph (a) or (b) of this section, appropriate to the rating sought.

(a)   *Airships.* A total of 50 hours of flight time as pilot with at least 25 hours in airships, which must include 5 hours of solo flight time in airships, or time performing the functions of pilot-in-command of an airship for which more than one pilot is required.

(b)   *Free Balloons.*

    (1)   If a gas balloon or a hot air balloon with an airborne heater is used, a total of 10 hours in free balloons with at least six flights under the supervision of a person holding a commercial pilot certificate with a free balloon rating. These flights must include —

        (i)   Two flights each of at least 1 hour's duration, if a gas balloon is used, or of 30 minute's duration, if a hot air balloon with an airborne heater is used;

        (ii)   One ascent under control to 5,000 feet above the point of takeoff, if a gas balloon is used, or 3,000 feet above the point of takeoff, if a hot air balloon with an airborne heater is used; and

        (iii)   One solo flight in a free balloon.

    (2)   If a hot air balloon without an airborne heater is used, six flights in a free balloon under the supervision of a commercial balloon pilot, including at least one solo flight.

61.118   **PRIVATE PILOT PRIVILEGES AND LIMITATIONS: PILOT-IN-COMMAND**

Except as provided in paragraphs (a) through (d) of this section, a private pilot may not act as pilot-in-command of an aircraft that is carrying passengers or property for compensation or hire; nor may he, for compensation or hire, act as pilot-in-command of an aircraft.

(a)   A private pilot may, for compensation or hire, act as pilot-in-command of an aircraft in connection with any business or employment if the flight is only incidental to that business or employment and the aircraft does not carry passengers or property for compensation or hire.

(b)   A private pilot may share the operating expenses of a flight with his passengers.

(c)   A private pilot who is an aircraft salesman and who has at least 200 hours of logged flight time may demonstrate an aircraft in flight to a prospective buyer.

(d)   A private pilot may act as pilot-in-command of an aircraft used in a passenger- carrying airlift sponsored by a charitable organization, and for which the passengers make a donation to the organization, if —

     (1)   The sponsor of the airlift notifies the FAA Flight Standards District Office having jurisdiction over the area concerned, at least 7 days before the flight, and furnishes any essential information that the office requests;

     (2)   The flight is conducted from a public airport adequate for the aircraft used, or from another airport that has been approved for the operation by an FAA inspector;

     (3)   He has logged at least 200 hours of flight time;

     (4)   No acrobatic or formation flights are conducted;

     (5)   Each aircraft used is certificated in the standard category and complies with the 100-hour inspection requirement of §91.409 of this chapter; and

     (6)   The flight is made under VFR during the day.

For the purpose of paragraph (d) of this section, a "charitable organization" means an organization listed in Publication No. 78 of the Department of the Treasury called the Cumulative List of Organizations described in section 170(c) of the Internal Revenue Code of 1954, as amended from time to time by published supplemental lists.

61.119   **FREE BALLOON RATINGS: LIMITATIONS**

(a)   If the applicant for a free balloon rating takes his flight test in a hot air balloon with an airborne heater, his pilot certificate contains an endorsement restricting the exercise of the privilege of that rating to hot air balloons with airborne heaters. The restriction may be deleted when the holder of the certificate obtains the pilot experience required for a rating on a gas balloon.

(b)   If the applicant for a free balloon rating takes his flight test in a hot air balloon without an airborne heater, his pilot certificate contains an endorsement restricting the exercise of the privileges of that rating to hot air balloons without airborne heaters. The restriction may be deleted when the holder of the certificate obtains the pilot experience and passes the tests required for a rating on a free balloon with an airborne heater or a gas balloon.

61.120   **PRIVATE PILOT PRIVILEGES AND LIMITATIONS: SECOND IN COMMAND OF AIRCRAFT REQUIRING MORE THAN ONE REQUIRED PILOT**

Except as provided in paragraphs (a) through (d) of §61.118 a private pilot may not, for compensation or hire, act as second-in-command of an aircraft that is type certificated for more than one required pilot, nor may he act as second-in-command of such an aircraft that is carrying passengers or property for compensation or hire.

SUBPART E — COMMERCIAL PILOTS

61.121   APPLICABILITY

This subpart prescribes the requirements for the issuance of commercial pilot certificates and ratings, the conditions under which those certificates and ratings are necessary, and the limitations upon those certificates and ratings.

61.123   ELIGIBILITY REQUIREMENTS: GENERAL

To be eligible for a commercial pilot certificate, a person must —
(a)   Be at least 18 years of age;
(b)   Be able to read, speak, and understand the English language, or have such operating limitations placed on his pilot certificate as are necessary for safety, to be removed when he shows that he can read, speak, and understand the English language;
(c)   Hold at least a valid second-class medical certificate issued under Part 67 of this chapter, or, in the case of a glider or free balloon rating, certify that he has no known medical deficiency that makes him unable to pilot a glider or a free balloon, as appropriate;
(d)   Pass a written examination appropriate to the aircraft rating sought on the subjects in which ground instruction is required by §61.125;
(e)   Pass an oral and flight test appropriate to the rating he seeks, covering items selected by the inspector or examiner from those on which training is required by §61.127; and
(f)   Comply with the provisions of this subpart which apply to the rating he seeks.

61.125   AERONAUTICAL KNOWLEDGE

An applicant for a commercial pilot certificate must have logged ground instruction from an authorized instructor, or must present evidence showing that he has satisfactorily completed a course of instruction or home study, in at least the following areas of aeronautical knowledge appropriate to the category of aircraft for which a rating is sought.
(a)   *Airplanes.*
　　(1)   The regulations of this chapter governing the operations, privileges, and limitations of a commercial pilot, and the accident reporting requirements of the National Transportation Safety Board;
　　(2)   Basic aerodynamics and the principles of flight which apply to airplanes;
　　(3)   Airplane operations, including the use of flaps, retractable landing gears, controllable propellers, high altitude operation with and without pressurization, loading and balance computations, and the significance and use of airplane performance speeds; and
　　(4)   Stall awareness, spin entry, spins, and spin recovery techniques for airplanes.
(b)   *Rotorcraft.*
　　(1)   The regulations of this chapter which apply to the operations, privileges, and limitations of a commercial rotorcraft pilot, and the accident reporting requirements of the National Transportation Safety Board;
　　(2)   Meteorology, including the characteristics of air masses and fronts, elements of weather forecasting, and the procurement and use of aeronautical weather reports and forecasts;
　　(3)   The use of aeronautical charts and the magnetic compass for pilotage and dead reckoning, and the use of radio aids for VFR navigation;
　　(4)   The safe and efficient operation of helicopters or gyroplanes, as appropriate to the rating sought; and
　　　　(5)   Basic aerodynamics and principles of flight which apply to rotorcraft and the significance and use of performance charts.
(c)   *Gliders.*
　　(1)   The regulations of this chapter pertinent to commercial glider pilot operations, privileges, and limitations, and the accident reporting requirements of the National Transportation Safety Board;
　　(2)   Glider navigation, including the use of aeronautical charts and the magnetic compass, and radio orientation;
　　(3)   The recognition of weather situations of concern to the glider pilot from the ground and in flight, and the procurement and use of aeronautical weather reports and forecasts;
　　(4)   The safe and efficient operation of gliders, including ground and/or aero tow procedures, as appropriate, signals, critical glider performance speeds, and safety precautions; and

     (5)   Stall awareness, spin entry, spins, and spin recovery techniques for gliders.

(d)   *Airships.*

     (1)   The regulations of this chapter pertinent to airship operations, VFR and IFR, including the privileges and limitations of a commercial airship pilot;

     (2)   Airship navigation, including pilotage, dead reckoning, and the use of radio aids for VFR and IFR navigation, and IFR approaches;

     (3)   The use and limitations of the required flight instruments;

     (4)   ATC procedures for VFR and IFR operations, and the use of IFR charts and approach plates;

     (5)   Meteorology, including the characteristics of air masses and fronts, and the procurement and use of aeronautical weather reports and forecasts;

     (6)   Airship ground and flight instruction procedures; and

     (7)   Airship operating procedures and emergency operations, including free ballooning procedures.

(e)   *Free Balloons.*

     (1)   The regulations of this chapter pertinent to commercial free balloon piloting privileges, limitations, and flight operations;

     (2)   The use of aeronautical charts and the magnetic compass for free balloon navigation;

     (3)   The recognition of weather conditions significant to free balloon flight operations, and the procurement and use of aeronautical weather reports and forecasts appropriate to free ballooning;

     (4)   Free balloon flight and ground instruction procedures; and

     (5)   Operating principles and procedures for free balloons, including emergency procedures such as crowd control and protection, high wind and water landings, and operations in proximity to buildings and power lines.

61.127   FLIGHT PROFICIENCY

The applicant for a commercial pilot certificate must have logged instruction from an authorized flight instructor in at least the following pilot operations. In addition, his logbook must contain an endorsement by an authorized flight instructor who has given him the instruction certifying that he has found the applicant prepared to perform each of those operations competently as a commercial pilot.

(a)   *Airplanes.*

     (1)   Preflight duties, including load and balance determination, line inspection, and aircraft servicing;

     (2)   Flight at slow airspeeds with realistic distractions, and the recognition of and recovery from stalls entered from straight flight and from turns.

     (3)   Normal and crosswind takeoffs and landings, using precision approaches, flaps, power as appropriate, and specified approach speeds;

     (4)   Maximum performance takeoffs and landings, climbs, and descents;

     (5)   Operation of an airplane equipped with a retractable landing gear, flaps, and controllable propeller(s), including normal and emergency operations; and

     (6)   Emergency procedures, such as coping with power loss or equipment malfunctions, fire in flight, collision avoidance precautions, and engine-out procedures if a multiengine airplane is used.

(b)   *Helicopters.*

     (1)   Preflight duties, including line inspection and helicopter servicing;

     (2)   Straight and level flight, climbs, turns, and descents;

     (3)   Air taxiing, hovering, and maneuvering by ground references;

     (4)   Normal and crosswind takeoffs and landings;

     (5)   Recognition of and recovery from imminent flight at critical/rapid descent with power (settling with power);

     (6)   Airport and traffic pattern operations, including collision avoidance precautions and radio communications;

     (7)   Cross-country flight operations;

     (8)   Operations in confined areas and on pinnacles, rapid decelerations, landing on slopes, high-altitude takeoffs, and run-on landings; and

     (9)   Simulated emergency procedures, including failure of an engine or other component or system, and approaches to a hover or landing with one engine inoperative in multiengine helicopters, or autorotational descents with a power recovery to a hover in single-engine helicopters.

(c) *Gyroplanes.*
    (1) Preflight operations, including line inspection and gyroplane servicing;
    (2) Straight and level flight, turns, climbs, and descents;
    (3) Flight maneuvering by ground references;
    (4) Maneuvering at critically slow airspeeds, and the recognition of and recovery from high rates of descent at slow airspeeds;
    (5) Normal and crosswind takeoffs and landings;
    (6) Airport and traffic pattern operations, including collision avoidance precautions and radio communications;
    (7) Cross-country flight operations; and
    (8) Emergency procedures, such as power failures, equipment malfunctions, maximum performance takeoffs and landings and simulated liftoffs at low airspeed and high angles of attack.

(d) *Gliders.*
    (1) Preflight duties, including glider assembly and preflight inspection;
    (2) Glider launches by ground (auto or winch) or by aero tows (the applicant's certificate is limited to the kind of tow selected);
    (3) Precision maneuvering, including straight glides, turns to headings, steep turns and spirals in both directions;
    (4) The correct use of the glider's performance speeds, flight at slow airspeeds with realistic distractions, and the recognition of and recovery from stalls entered from straight flight and from turns; and
    (5) Accuracy approaches and landings, with the nose of the glider coming to rest short of and within 100 feet of a line or mark.

(e) *Airships.*
    (1) Ground handling, mooring, and preflight operations;
    (2) Straight and level flight, turns, climbs, and descents, under VFR and simulated IFR conditions;
    (3) Takeoffs and landings with positive and with negative static lift;
    (4) Turns and figure eights;
    (5) Precision turns to headings under simulated IFR conditions;
    (6) Preparing and filing IFR flight plans, and complying with IFR clearances;
    (7) IFR radio navigation and instrument approach procedures;
    (8) Cross-country flight operations, using pilotage, dead reckoning, and radio aids; and
    (9) Emergency operations, including engine-out operations, free ballooning an airship, and ripcord procedures (may be simulated).

(f) *Free Balloons.*
    (1) Assembly of basket and burner to the envelope, and rigging, inflating, and tethering of a free balloon;
    (2) Ground and flight crew briefing;
    (3) Ascents;
    (4) Descents;
    (5) Landings;
    (6) Operation of airborne heater, if balloon is so equipped; and
    (7) Emergency operations, including the use of the ripcord (may be simulated), and recovery from a terminal velocity descent if a balloon with an airborne heater is used.

61.129   AIRPLANE RATING: AERONAUTICAL EXPERIENCE

(a) *General.* An applicant for a commercial pilot certificate with an airplane rating must hold a private pilot certificate with an airplane rating. If he does not hold that certificate and rating he must meet the flight experience requirements for a private pilot certificate and airplane rating and pass the applicable written and practical test prescribed in Subpart D of this Part. In addition, the applicant must hold an instrument rating (airplane), or the commercial pilot certificate that is issued is endorsed with a limitation prohibiting the carriage of passengers for hire in airplanes on cross-country flights of more than 50 nautical miles, or at night.

(b) *Flight Time As Pilot.* Except as provided in paragraph (c) of this section, an applicant for a commercial pilot certificate with an airplane rating must have at least the following aeronautical experience:

  (1) A total of at least 250 hours of flight time as a pilot that may include not more than—

    (i) Except as provided in paragraph (b)(1)(ii) of this section, 50 hours of flight simulator instruction or flight training device instruction from an authorized instructor; or

    (ii) 100 hours of flight simulator instruction or flight training device instruction, if the instruction is accomplished in an approved course conducted by a training center certificated under Part 142 of this chapter.

  (2) The flight time required by paragraph (b)(1) of this section must include—

    (i) 10 hours of instrument instruction, of which at least 5 hours must be in flight in airplanes, and

    (ii) 10 hours of instruction in preparation for the commercial pilot flight test; and

  (3) 100 hours of pilot-in-command time, including at least —

    (i) 50 hours in airplanes;

    (ii) 50 hours of cross-country flights, each flight with a landing at a point more than 50 nautical miles from the original departure point. One flight must have landings at a minimum of three points, one of which is at least 150 nautical miles from the original departure point if the flight is conducted in Hawaii, or at least 250 nautical miles from the original departure point if it is conducted elsewhere; and

    (iii) 5 hours of night flying including at least 10 takeoffs and landings as sole manipulator of the controls.

  (4) Flight simulator instruction and flight training device instruction must be accomplished in a qualified and approved flight simulator or in a qualified and approved flight training device representing an airplane.

(c) Except where fewer hours are approved by the Administrator, an applicant for a commercial pilot certificate with an airplane rating who has satisfactorily completed an approved commercial pilot course conducted by a training center certificated under part 142 of this chapter must have a total of at least 190 hours of pilot flight time in aircraft, flight simulators, or flight training devices.

61.131 ROTORCRAFT RATINGS: AERONAUTICAL EXPERIENCE

Except as provided in paragraph (c) of this section, an applicant for a commercial pilot certificate with a rotorcraft category rating must have at least the following aeronautical experience:

(a) *Helicopter Class Rating.* A total of 150 hours of flight time, including at least 100 hours in powered aircraft, 50 hours of which must be in a helicopter, including at least —

  (1) 40 hours of flight instruction from an authorized flight instructor, 15 hours of which must be in a helicopter, including —

    (i) 3 hours of cross-country flying in helicopters;

    (ii) 3 hours of night flying in helicopters, including 10 takeoffs and landings, each of which must be separated by an enroute phase of flight;

    (iii) 3 hours in helicopters preparing for the commercial pilot flight test within 60 days before that test; and

    (iv) Takeoffs and landings at three points other than airports; and

  (2) 100 hours of pilot-in-command flight time, 35 hours of which must be in a helicopter, including at least —

    (i) 10 hours of cross-country flying in helicopters, including one flight with a landing at three or more points, each of which must be more than 50 nautical miles from each of the other two points; and

    (ii) Three takeoffs and landings in helicopters, each of which must be separated by an enroute phase of flight, at an airport with an operating control tower.

  (3) Except as provided in paragraph (a)(4) of this section, a maximum of 35 hours of flight simulator instruction or flight training device instruction from an authorized instructor may be credited toward the total hour requirement for a pilot certificate.

  (4) A maximum of 50 hours of flight simulator instruction or flight training device instruction may be credited toward the total hours required by paragraph (a)(1) of this section if the instruction is accomplished in an approved course conducted by a training center certificated under Part 142 of this chapter.

A *Amend #100 eff 8-1-96*

(b) *Gyroplane Class Rating.* For a gyroplane class rating:
    (1) An applicant must have at least 150 hours of flight time in aircraft, including at least 100 hours in powered aircraft, 25 hours of which must be in a gyroplane, including at least—
      (i)   3 hours of cross-country flying in gyroplanes;
      (ii) 3 hours of night flying in gyroplanes, including 10 takeoffs and landings; and
      (iii) 3 hours in gyroplanes preparing for the commercial pilot flight test within 60 days before that test; and
    (2) 100 hours of pilot-in-command flight time, 15 hours of which must be in a gyroplane, including at least —
      (i)   10 hours of cross-country flying in gyroplanes, including one flight with a landing at three or more points, each of which is more than 50 nautical miles from each of the other two points; and
      (ii) Three takeoffs and landings in gyroplanes at an airport with an operating control tower.
    (3) Except as provided in paragraph (b)(4) of this section, a maximum of 35 hours of flight simulator instruction or flight training device instruction from an authorized instructor may be credited toward the total requirement for a pilot certificate if the instruction is accomplished in a flight simulator or in a flight training device representing a gyroplane.
    (4) A maximum of 50 hours of flight simulator instruction or flight training device instruction may be credited toward the total hours required by paragraph (b)(1) of this section if the instruction is accomplished in an approved course conducted by a training center certificated under Part 142 of this chapter.
(c) Except as otherwise approved by the Administrator, an applicant for a commercial pilot certificate with a rotorcraft rating and a helicopter class rating who has satisfactorily completed an approved commercial pilot course conducted by a training center certificated under Part 142 of this chapter must have a total of at least 150 hours of pilot flight time in aircraft, flight simulators, or flight training devices.

61.133 GLIDER RATING: AERONAUTICAL EXPERIENCE

An applicant for a commercial pilot certificate with a glider rating must meet either of the following aeronautical experience requirements;
(a) A total of at least 25 hours of pilot time in aircraft, including 20 hours in gliders, and a total of 100 glider flights as pilot-in-command, including 25 flights during which 360° turns were made; or
(b) A total of 200 hours of pilot time in heavier-than-air aircraft, including 20 glider flights as pilot-in-command during which 360° turns were made.

61.135 AIRSHIP RATING: AERONAUTICAL EXPERIENCE

An applicant for a commercial pilot certificate with an airship rating must have a total of at least 200 hours of flight time as pilot, including —
(a) 50 hours of flight time as pilot in airships;
(b) 30 hours of flight time, performing the duties of pilot-in-command in airships, including—
    (1) 10 hours of cross-country flight; and
    (2) 10 hours of night flight; and
(c) 40 hours of instrument time, of which at least 20 hours must be in flight with 10 hours of that flight time in airships.

61.137 FREE BALLOON RATING: AERONAUTICAL EXPERIENCE

An applicant for a commercial pilot certificate with a free balloon rating must have the following flight time as pilot:
(a) If a gas balloon or a hot air balloon with an airborne heater is used, a total of at least 35 hours of flight time as pilot, including —
    (1) 20 hours in free balloons; and
    (2) 10 flights in free balloons, including —
      (i)   Six flights under the supervision of a commercial free balloon pilot;
      (ii) Two solo flights;
      (iii) Two flights of at least 2 hours duration if a gas balloon is used, or at least 1 hour duration if a hot air balloon with an airborne heater is used; and

Amend #100 eff 8-1-96

   (iv) One ascent under control to more than 10,000 feet above the takeoff point if a gas balloon is used or 5,000 feet above the takeoff point if a hot air balloon with an airborne heater is used.

(b) If a hot air balloon without an airborne heater is used, ten flights in free balloons, including —

  (1) Six flights under the supervision of a commercial free balloon pilot; and

  (2) Two solo flights.

61.139 COMMERCIAL PILOT PRIVILEGES AND LIMITATIONS: GENERAL

The holder of a commercial pilot certificate may:

(a) Act as pilot-in-command of an aircraft carrying persons or property for compensation or hire;

(b) Act as pilot-in-command of an aircraft for compensation or hire; and

(c) Give flight instruction in an airship if he holds a lighter-than-air category and an airship class rating, or in a free balloon if he holds a free balloon class rating.

61.141 AIRSHIP AND FREE BALLOON RATINGS: LIMITATIONS

(a) If the applicant for a free balloon class rating takes his flight test in a hot air balloon without an airborne heater, his pilot certificate contains an endorsement restricting the exercise of the privileges of that rating to hot air balloons without airborne heaters. The restriction may be deleted when the holder of the certificate obtains the pilot experience and passes the test required for a rating on a free balloon with an airborne heater or a gas balloon.

(b) If the applicant for a free balloon class rating takes his flight test in a hot air balloon with an airborne heater, his pilot certificate contains an endorsement restricting the exercise of the privileges of that rating to hot air balloons with airborne heaters. The restriction may be deleted when the holder of the certificate obtains the pilot experience required for a rating on a gas balloon.

SUBPART F — AIRLINE TRANSPORT PILOTS

61.151 ELIGIBILITY REQUIREMENTS: GENERAL

To be eligible for an airline transport pilot certificate, a person must —
(a) Be at least 23 years of age;
(b) Be of good moral character;
(c) Be able to read, write, and understand the English language and speak it without accent or impediment of speech that would interfere with two-way radio conversation;
(d) Be a high school graduate, or its equivalent in the Administrator's opinion, based on the applicant's general experience and aeronautical experience, knowledge, and skill;
(e) Have a first-class medical certificate issued under Part 67 of this chapter within the 6 months before the date he applies; and
(f) Comply with the sections of this Part that apply to the rating he seeks.

61.153 AIRPLANE RATING: AERONAUTICAL KNOWLEDGE

An applicant for an airline transport pilot certificate with an airplane rating must, after meeting the requirements of §§61.151 (except paragraph (a) thereof) and 61.155, pass a written test on —
(a) The sections of this Part relating to airline transport pilots and Part 121, Subpart C of Part 65, and §§91.1 through 91.13 and Subpart B of Part 91 of this chapter, and so much of Parts 21 and 25 of this chapter as relate to the operations of air carrier aircraft;
(b) The fundamentals of air navigation and use of formulas, instruments, and other navigational aids, both in aircraft and on the ground, that are necessary for navigating aircraft by instruments;
(c) The general system of weather collection and dissemination;
(d) Weather maps, weather forecasting, and weather sequence abbreviations, symbols, and nomenclature;
(e) Elementary meteorology, including knowledge of cyclones as associated with fronts;
(f) Cloud forms;
(g) National Weather Service Federal Meteorology Handbook No. 1, as amended;
(h) Weather conditions, including icing conditions and upper-air winds, that affect aeronautical activities;
(i) Air navigation facilities used on Federal airways, including rotating beacons, course lights, radio ranges, and radio marker beacons;
(j) Information from airplane weather observations and meteorological data reported from observations made by pilots on air carrier flights;
(k) The influence of terrain on meteorological conditions and developments, and their relation to air carrier flight operations;
(l) Radio communication procedure in aircraft operations; and
(m) Basic principles of loading and weight distribution and their effect on flight characteristics.

61.155 AIRPLANE RATING: AERONAUTICAL EXPERIENCE

(a) Except as provided in paragraph (d) of this section, for an applicant for an airline transport pilot certificate with an airplane category and class rating, the following requirements apply:
(1) The applicant must hold a commercial pilot certificate, a foreign airline transport pilot, or commercial pilot license without limitations issued by a member state of ICAO, or meet the requirements of § 61.73 that would qualify the applicant for a commercial pilot certificate;
(2) The applicant must have at least 1500 hours of total time as a pilot that includes at least—
(i) 500 hours of cross-country flight time;
(ii) 100 hours of night flight time;
(iii) 75 hours of instrument flight time, in actual or simulated instrument conditions, subject to the following:
(A) Except as provided in paragraph (a)(2)(iii)(B) of this section, an applicant may not receive more than 25 hours of simulated instrument time in flight simulators and flight training devices.

     (B) A maximum of 50 hours of instruction in a flight simulator or flight training device may be credited toward the total hours required by paragraph (a)(2) of this section if the instruction is accomplished in a course conducted by a training center certificated under Part 142 of this chapter.

     (C) Instruction in a flight simulator or flight training device must be accomplished in a qualified and approved flight simulator or in a qualified and approved flight training device, representing an airplane; and

   (iv) 250 hours of flight time in an airplane as a pilot-in-command or as a second-in-command performing the duties and functions of a pilot-in-command under the supervision of a pilot-in-command, or any combination thereof, which includes at least—

     (A) 100 hours of cross-country flight time; and

     (B) 25 hours of night flight time; and

(3) Not more than 100 hours of total pilot experience may be obtained in a flight simulator or flight training device, provided the pilot experience is accomplished in an approved course conducted by a training center certificated under Part 142 of this chapter.

(b) An applicant who has performed at least 20 night takeoffs and landings to a full stop may substitute each additional night takeoff and landing to a full stop in excess of the minimum 20 takeoffs for 1 hour of night flight time to satisfy the requirements of paragraph (a)(2) of this section, for a total credited time of no more than 25 hours.

(c) If an applicant with less than 150 hours of pilot-in-command time otherwise meets the requirements of paragraph (a)(2)(iv) of this section, the applicant's certificate will be endorsed "Holder does not meet the pilot-in-command flight experience requirement of ICAO", as prescribed by article 39 of the "Convention on International Civil Aviation." Whenever the pilot presents satisfactory written evidence that 150 hours of pilot-in-command time has been accumulated, the applicant is entitled to a new certificate without the endorsement.

(d) A commercial pilot may credit the following second-in-command and flight engineer flight time (or a combination of either crewmember position flight time) toward the 1500 hours of total time as a pilot required by paragraph (a) of this section:

(1) All second-in-command time acquired in an airplane required to have more than one pilot by the airplane's flight manual or type certificate or by the regulations under which the flight is conducted.

(2) Flight engineer time, provided the time—

   (i) Is acquired in an airplane that is required to have a flight engineer by the airplane's flight manual, the type certificate, or the regulations under which the flight is conducted;

   (ii) Is acquired while the applicant is participating in a pilot training program approved under Part 121 of this chapter; and

   (iii) Is credited at a rate of 1 hour of flight time for each 3 hours of flight engineer time, for a total credited time of no more than 500 hours.

(e) If an applicant who credits second-in-command or flight engineer time under paragraph (d) of this section toward the 1500 hours total flight time requirement of paragraph (a)(2) of this section—

(1) Does not have at least 1200 hours of flight time as a pilot including not more than 50 percent of the second-in-command time and none of the flight engineer time; but

(2) Otherwise meets the requirements of paragraph (a)(2) of this section, the applicant's certificate will be endorsed "Holder does not meet the pilot flight experience requirements of ICAO," as prescribed by article 39 of the "Convention on International Civil Aviation." Whenever the applicant presents satisfactory evidence of having accumulated 1200 hours of flight time as a pilot including no more than 50 percent of the second-in-command time and none of the flight engineer time, the applicant is entitled to a new certificate without the endorsement.

Ⓐ *Amend #100 eff 8-1-96*

A ➤ **61.157   AIRPLANE RATING: AERONAUTICAL SKILL**
(For Parts 121 and 135 use only)

(a) An applicant for an airline transport pilot certificate with a single-engine or multi-engine class rating or an additional type rating must pass a practical test that includes the items set forth in Appendix A of this Part. The FAA inspector or designated examiner may modify any required maneuver where necessary for the reasonable and safe operation of the airplane being used and, unless specifically prohibited in Appendix A, may combine any required maneuvers and may permit their performance in any convenient sequence.

(b) Whenever an applicant for an airline transport pilot certificate does not already have an instrument rating he shall, as part of the oral part of the practical test, comply with §61.65(g) and, as part of the flight part, perform each additional maneuver required by §61.65(g) that is appropriate to the airplane type and not required in Appendix A of this Part.

(c) Unless the Administrator requires certain or all maneuvers to be performed, the person giving a flight test for an airline transport pilot certificate or additional airplane class or type rating may, in his discretion, waive any of the maneuvers for which a specific waiver authority is contained in Appendix A of this part if a pilot being checked —

(1) Is employed as a pilot by a Part 121 certificate holder; and

(2) Within the preceding 6 calendar months, has successfully completed that certificate holder's approved training program for the airplane type involved.

(d) The items specified in paragraph (a) of this section may be performed in the airplane simulator or other training device specified in Appendix A to this part for the particular item if —

(1) The airplane simulator or other training device meets the requirements of §121.407 of this chapter; and

(2) In the case of the items preceded by an asterisk (*) in Appendix A, the applicant has successfully completed the training set forth in §121.424(d) of this chapter. However, the FAA inspector or designated examiner may require Items II(d), V(f), or V(g) of Appendix A to this part to be performed in the airplane if he determines that action is necessary to determine the applicant's competence with respect to that maneuver.

(e) An approved simulator may be used instead of the airplane to satisfy the inflight requirements of Appendix A of this Part, if the simulator—

(1) Is approved under §121.407 of this chapter and meets the appropriate simulator requirements of Appendix H of Part 121; and

(2) Is used as part of an approved program that meets the training requirements of §121.424 (a) and (c) and Appendix H of Part 121 of this chapter.

(f) On and after April 15, 1991, an applicant for a type rating to be added to an airline transport pilot certificate, or for issuance of an airline transport pilot certificate in an airplane requiring a type rating, must —

(1) Have completed ground and flight training on the maneuvers and procedures of Appendix A of this part that is appropriate to the airplane for which a type rating is sought and received an endorsement from an authorized instructor in the person's logbook or training records certifying satisfactory completion of the training; or

(2) For a pilot employee of a Part 121 or Part 135 certificate holder, have completed ground and flight training that is appropriate to the airplane for which a type rating is sought and is approved under Parts 121 and 135.

(g) Successful completion of a proficiency check under § 121.441 of this chapter or successful completion of both a competency check, under § 135.293 of this chapter, and a pilot-in-command instrument proficiency check, under § 135.297 of this chapter, satisfies the requirements of this section for the appropriate aircraft rating.

61.158   AIRPLANE RATING: AERONAUTICAL SKILL
(For other than Parts 121 and 135)

A

(a) An applicant for an airline transport pilot certificate with a single engine or multiengine class rating or type rating, must—

(1) Pass a practical test based on the following areas of operation:

(i) Preflight procedures.

(ii) Ground operations.

(iii) Takeoff and departure maneuvers.

(iv) Inflight maneuvers.

A *Amend #100 eff 8-1-96*

         (v)   Instrument procedures.

         (vi)   Landings and approaches to landings.

         (vii)   Normal and abnormal procedures.

         (viii)   Emergency procedures.

         (ix)   Postflight procedures.

    (2)   If seeking an airplane type rating, present a record of training certified by an authorized instructor showing that the applicant has—

         (i)   Received ground training on the aeronautical knowledge areas required by this section applicable to the airplane type rating sought; and

         (ii)   Received flight training on the areas of operation applicable to the airplane type rating sought.

(b)   If the applicant does not hold an instrument rating, in addition to the areas specified in paragraph (a)(1) of this section, the applicant must also demonstrate competency in the operations referenced in § 61.65 (g).

(c)   The demonstrations required by paragraphs (a) and (b) of this section must be performed in—

    (1)   An airplane of the same class, and, if applicable, an airplane of the same type, for which the class rating or type rating is sought;

    (2)   Subject to the requirements of paragraphs (d)(1) through (d)(8) of this section, as applicable, a flight simulator or a flight training device that represents the airplane type for which the type rating is sought, or set of airplanes if the airplane for which the class rating is sought, does not require a type rating.

(d)   The following requirements apply to a demonstration of competency under this section in a flight simulator or a flight training device;

    (1)   The flight simulator or flight training device use permitted by paragraph (c)(2) of this section must be in accordance with an approved course at a training center certificated under Part 142 of this chapter;

    (2)   To complete all training and testing (except preflight inspection) for an unlimited added rating in a flight simulator—

         (i)   The flight simulator must be qualified as Level C or Level D; and

         (ii)   The applicant must meet the aeronautical experience requirements of §61.155 and at least one of the following:

             (A)   Hold a type rating for a turbojet airplane of the same class as the class of airplane for which the type rating is sought or have been designated by a military service as a pilot-in-command of an airplane of the same class as the class of airplane for which the type rating is sought, if a turbojet type rating is sought.

             (B)   Hold a type rating for a turbopropeller airplane of the same class as the class of airplane for which the type rating is sought, or have been appointed by a military service as a pilot-in-command of an airplane of the same class as the class of airplane for which the type rating is sought, if a turbopropeller airplane type rating is sought.

             (C)   Have at least 2000 hours of actual flight time, of which 500 hours must be in turbine-powered airplanes of the same class as the class of airplane for which the type rating is sought.

             (D)   Have at least 500 hours of actual flight time in the same type airplane as the type of airplane for which the type rating is sought.

             (E)   Have at least 1000 hours of flight time in at least two different airplanes requiring a type rating.

    (3)   Subject to the limitation of paragraph (d)(4) of this section an applicant who does not meet the requirements of paragraph (d)(2) of this section may complete all training and testing (except for preflight inspection) for an added rating if—

         (i)   The flight simulator is qualified as Level C or Level D; and

         (ii)   The applicant meets the aeronautical experience requirements of § 61.155 and at least one of the following:

             (A)   Holds a type rating in a propeller-driven airplane if a type rating in a turbojet airplane is sought, or holds a type rating in a turbojet airplane if a type rating in a propeller-driven airplane is sought.

             (B)   Since the beginning of the 12th calendar month before the month in which the applicant completes the practical test for the added rating, has logged—

                 (1) At least 100 hours of flight time in airplanes in the same class as the class of airplane for which the type rating is sought and which require a type rating; and

A *Amend #100 eff 8-1-96*

(2) At least 25 hours of flight time in airplanes of the same type as the type of airplane for which the type rating is sought.

(4) An applicant meeting only the requirements of paragraph (d)(3)(ii)(A) and (B) of this section will be issued an added rating, or an airline transport pilot certificate with an added rating, as applicable, with a limitation. The limitation shall state: "This certificate is subject to pilot-in-command limitations for the added rating."

(5) An applicant gaining a certificate with the limitation specified in paragraph (d)(4) of this section—
   (i)   May not act as pilot-in-command of the aircraft for which an added rating was obtained under the provisions of this section until he or she has had the limitation removed from the certificate; and
   (ii) May have the limitation removed by serving 15 hours of supervised operating experience as pilot-in-command under the supervision of a qualified and current pilot-in-command, in the seat normally occupied by the pilot-in-command, in an airplane of the same type as the type of airplane to which the limitation applies.

(6) An applicant who does not meet the requirements of paragraph (d)(2)(ii)(A) through (E) or (d)(3)(ii)(A) and (B) of this section may be awarded an airline transport pilot certificate or an added rating to that certificate after successful completion of one of the following requirements:
   (i)   An approved course at a training center which includes all training and testing for that certificate or rating followed by training and testing on the following tasks, which must be successfully completed on a static airplane or in flight, as appropriate:
         (A) Preflight inspection;
         (B) Normal takeoff;
         (C) Normal ILS approach;
         (D) Missed approach; and
         (E) Normal landing.
   (ii) An approved course at a training center which includes all training and testing for that certificate or rating and compliance with paragraphs (d)(7) and (d)(8) of this section.

(7) An applicant meeting only the requirements of paragraph (d)(6) of this section will be issued an added rating, or an airline transport pilot certificate with an added rating, as applicable, with a limitation. The limitation shall state: "This certificate is subject to pilot-in-command limitations for the added rating."

(8) An applicant gaining a certificate with the limitation specified in paragraph (d)(7) of this section—
   (i)   May not act as pilot-in-command of the aircraft for which an added rating was obtained under the provisions of this section until he or she has had the limitation removed from the certificate; and
   (ii) May have the limitation removed by serving 25 hours of supervised operating experience as pilot-in-command under the supervision of a qualified and current pilot-in-command, in the seat normally occupied by the pilot-in-command, in an airplane of the same type as the type of airplane to which the limitation applies.

(e) Unless the Administrator requires certain or all tasks to be performed, the person authorized by the Administrator to conduct the practical test for an airline transport pilot certificate may waive any of the tasks for which the Administrator approves waiver authority.

Ⓐ *Amend #100 eff 8-1-96*

61.159   ROTORCRAFT RATING: AERONAUTICAL KNOWLEDGE

An applicant for an airline transport pilot certificate with a rotorcraft category and a helicopter class rating must pass a written test on —
(a)   So much of this chapter as relates to air carrier rotorcraft operations;
(b)   Rotorcraft design, components, systems and performance limitations;
(c)   Basic principles of loading and weight distribution and their effect on rotorcraft flight characteristics;
(d)   Air traffic control systems and procedures relating to rotorcraft;
(e)   Procedures for operating rotorcraft in potentially hazardous meteorological conditions;
(f)   Flight theory as applicable to rotorcraft; and
(g)   The items listed under paragraphs (b) through (m) of §61.153.

61.161   ROTORCRAFT RATING: AERONAUTICAL EXPERIENCE

(a)   An applicant for an airline transport pilot certificate with a rotorcraft category and helicopter class rating must hold a commercial pilot certificate, or a foreign airline transport pilot or commercial pilot certificate with a rotorcraft category and helicopter class rating issued by a member of ICAO, or be a pilot in an armed force of the United States whose military experience qualifies that pilot for the issuance of a commercial pilot certificate under §61.73.
(b)   An applicant must have had at least 1,200 hours of flight time as a pilot, including at least —
(1)   500 hours of cross-country flight time;
(2)   100 hours of night flight time, of which at least 15 hours are in helicopters;
(3)   200 hours in helicopters, including at least 75 hours as pilot-in-command, or as second-in-command performing the duties and functions of a pilot-in-command under the supervision of a pilot-in-command, or any combination thereof; and
(4)   75 hours of actual or simulated instrument time under actual or simulated conditions. At least 50 hours of this time must be completed in flight with at least—
(i)   25 hours in helicopters as pilot-in-command;
(ii)   25 hours in helicopters as second-in-command performing the duties of a pilot-in-command under the supervision of a pilot-in-command; or
(iii)   Any combination of paragraph (b)(4)(i) and (b)(4)(ii) of this section that totals 25 hours in helicopters.
(5)   Flight simulator or flight training device instruction may be credited toward the total hour requirement of paragraph (b)(4) of this section subject to the following:
(i)   Flight simulator and flight training device instruction must be accomplished in a qualified and approved flight simulator or in a qualified and approved flight training device, representing a rotorcraft.
(ii)   Except as provided in paragraph (b)(5)(iii) of this section, an applicant may receive credit for not more than a combined total of 25 hours of simulated instrument time in flight simulators and flight training devices.
(iii)   A maximum of 50 hours of flight simulator instruction or flight training device instruction may be credited toward the total hours required by paragraph (b)(4) of this section if the instruction is accomplished in an approved course conducted by a training center certificated under Part 142 of this chapter.

61.163   ROTORCRAFT RATING: AERONAUTICAL SKILL

(a)   An applicant for an airline transport pilot certificate with a rotorcraft category and helicopter class rating or a type rating must pass a practical test based on the following areas of operation:
(1)   Preflight procedures.
(2)   Ground operations.
(3)   Takeoff and departure procedures.
(4)   In-flight maneuvers
(5)   Instrument procedures.
(6)   Landings and approaches to landings.
(7)   Normal and abnormal procedures.
(8)   Emergency procedures.
(9)   Postflight procedures.

Ⓐ *Amend #100 eff 8-1-96*

(b) If the applicant does not hold an instrument rating, in addition to the areas specified in paragraph (a) of this section, the applicant must also demonstrate competency in the operations required by § 61.65 (g).

(c) The demonstrations required by paragraphs (a) and (b) of this section must be performed in—

  (1) The helicopter for which the class rating or type rating is sought; or

  (2) Subject to the requirements of paragraphs (d)(1) through (d)(8) of this section, as applicable, a flight simulator or flight training device that represents the helicopter for which the class rating or type rating is sought.

(d) The following requirements apply to a demonstration of competency under this section in a flight simulator or a flight training device:

  (1) The flight simulator or flight training device use permitted by paragraph (c)(2) of this section must be in accordance with an approved course at a training center certificated under Part 142 of this chapter.

  (2) To complete all training and testing (except preflight inspection) for an unlimited added rating in a flight simulator—

    (i) The flight simulator must be qualified as Level C or Level D; and

    (ii) The applicant must meet the aeronautical experience requirements of § 61.161 and at least one of the following:

      (A) Hold a type rating for a turbine-powered helicopter, or have been designated by a military service as a pilot-in-command of an a turbine-powered helicopter, if a turbine-powered helicopter type rating is sought.

      (B) Have at least 1200 hours of actual flight time, of which 500 hours must be in turbine-powered helicopters.

      (C) Have at least 500 hours of actual flight time in the same type helicopter as the helicopter for which the type rating is sought.

      (D) Have at least 1000 hours of flight time in at least two different helicopters requiring a type rating.

  (3) Subject to the limitation of paragraph (d)(4) of this section, an applicant who does not meet the requirements of paragraph (d)(2) of this section may complete all training and testing (except for preflight inspection) for an added rating if—

    (i) The flight simulator is qualified as Level C or Level D; and

    (ii) The applicant meets the aeronautical experience requirements of § 61.161 and, since the beginning of the 12th calendar month before the month in which the applicant completes the practical test for the added rating, has logged—

      (A) At least 100 hours of flight time in helicopters; and

      (B) At least 15 hours of flight time in helicopters of the same type as the helicopter for which the type rating is sought.

  (4) An applicant meeting only the requirements of paragraph (d)(3)(ii)(A) and (B) of this section will be issued an added rating, or an airline transport pilot certificate with a limitation. The limitation shall state: "This certificate is subject to pilot-in-command limitations for the added rating."

  (5) An applicant gaining a certificate with the limitation specified in paragraph (d)(4) of this section—

    (i) May not act as pilot-in-command of the aircraft for which an added rating was obtained under the provisions of this section until he or she has had the limitation removed from the certificate; and

    (ii) May have the limitation removed by serving 15 hours of supervised operating experience as pilot-in-command under the supervision of a qualified and current pilot-in-command, in the seat normally occupied by the pilot-in-command, in an aircraft of the same type as the type of aircraft to which the limitation applies.

  (6) An applicant who does not meet the requirements of paragraph (d)(2)(ii) (A) through (D) or (d)(3)(ii)(A) and (B) of this section may be awarded an airline transport pilot certificate or an added rating to that certificate after successful completion of one of the following requirements:

    (i) An approved course at a training center which includes all training and testing for that certificate or rating followed by training and testing on the following tasks, which must be successfully completed on a static aircraft or in flight, as appropriate:

      (A) Preflight inspection;

      (B) Normal takeoff from a hover;

         (C)   Manually flown precision approach; and
         (D)   Steep approach and landing to an off-airport heliport;
     (ii)   An approved course at a training center which includes all training and testing for that certificate or rating and compliance with paragraphs (d)(7) and (d)(8) of this section.
   (7)   An applicant meeting only the requirements of paragraph (d)(6) of this section will be issued an added rating or an airline transport pilot certificate with an added rating, as applicable, with a limitation. The limitation shall state: "This certificate is subject to pilot-in-command limitations for the added rating."
   (8)   An applicant gaining a certificate with the limitation specified in paragraph (d)(7) of this section—
     (i)   May not act as pilot-in-command of the aircraft for which an added rating was obtained under the provisions of this section until he or she has had the limitation removed from the certificate; and
     (ii)   May have the limitation removed by serving 25 hours of supervised operating experience as pilot-in-command under the supervision of a qualified and current pilot-in-command, in the seat normally occupied by the pilot-in-command, in an aircraft of the same type as the type of aircraft to which the limitation applies.
(e)   Unless the Administrator requires certain or all tasks to be performed, the person authorized by the Administrator to conduct the practical test for an airline transport pilot certificate may waive any of the tasks for which the Administrator approves waiver authority.

61.165   ADDITIONAL CATEGORY RATINGS

(a)   *Rotorcraft category with a helicopter class rating.* The holder of an airline transport pilot certificate (airplane category) who applies for a rotorcraft category with a helicopter class rating must meet the applicable requirements of §§61.159, 61.161, and 61.163 and —
   (1)   Have at least 100 hours, including at least 15 hours at night, of rotorcraft flight time as pilot-in-command or as second-in-command performing the duties and functions of a pilot-in-command under the supervision of a pilot-in-command who holds an airline transport pilot certificate with an appropriate rotorcraft rating, or any combination thereof; or
   (2)   Complete a training program conducted by a certificated air carrier or other approved agency requiring at least 75 hours of rotorcraft flight time as pilot-in-command, second-in-command, or as flight instruction from an appropriately rated FAA certificated flight instructor or an airline transport pilot, or any combination thereof, including at least 15 hours of night flight time.
(b)   *Airplane rating.* The holder of an airline transport pilot certificate (rotorcraft category) who applies for an airplane category must comply with §§61.153, 61.155 (except §61.155(b)(1)), and 61.157 and —
   (1)   Have at least 100 hours, including at least 15 hours at night, of airplane flight time as pilot-in-command or as second-in-command performing the duties and functions of a pilot-in-command under the supervision of a pilot-in-command who holds an airline transport pilot certificate with an appropriate airplane rating, or any combination thereof; or
   (2)   Complete a training program conducted by a certificated air carrier or other approved agency requiring at least 75 hours of airplane flight time as pilot-in-command, second-in-command, or as flight instruction from an appropriately rated FAA certificated flight instructor or an airline transport pilot, or any combination thereof, including at least 15 hours of night flight time.

61.167   TESTS

(a)   Each applicant for an airline transport pilot certificate must pass each practical and theoretical test to the satisfaction of the Administrator. The minimum passing grade in each subject is 70 percent. Each flight maneuver is graded separately. Other tests are graded as a whole.
(b)   Information collected incidentally to such a test shall be treated as a confidential matter by the persons giving the test and by employees of the FAA.

Ⓐ Amend #100 eff 8-1-96

61.169   **INSTRUCTION IN AIR TRANSPORTATION SERVICE**

   (a)   An airline transport pilot may instruct—

      (1)   Other pilots in air transportation service in aircraft of the category, class, and type, as applicable, for which the airline transport pilot is rated;

      (2)   In flight simulators and flight training devices representing the aircraft referenced in paragraph (a)(1) of this section, when instructing under the provisions of this section;

      (3)   Only as provided in this section, unless the airline transport pilot also holds a flight instructor certificate, in which case he or she may exercise the instructor privileges of subpart G of Part 61 for which he or she is rated; and

      (4)   When instructing under the provisions of this section in an actual aircraft, only if the aircraft has functioning dual controls, when instructing under the provisions of this section.

   (b)   Excluding briefings and debriefings, an airline transport pilot may not instruct in aircraft, flight simulators, and flight training devices under this section—

      (1)   For more than 8 hours in any 24-consecutive-hour period; or

      (2)   For more than 36 hours in any 7-consecutive-day period.

   (c)   An airline transport pilot may not instruct in Category II or Category III operations unless he or she has been trained and successfully tested under Category II or Category III operations, as applicable.

61.171   **GENERAL PRIVILEGES AND LIMITATIONS**

An airline transport pilot has the privileges of a commercial pilot with an instrument rating. The holder of a commercial pilot certificate who qualifies for an airline transport pilot certificate retains the ratings on his commercial pilot certificate, but he may exercise only the privileges of a commercial pilot with respect to them.

SUBPART G — FLIGHT INSTRUCTORS

61.181 APPLICABILITY

This subpart prescribes the requirements for the issuance of flight instructor certificates and ratings, the conditions under which those certificates and ratings are necessary, and the limitations upon these certificates and ratings.

61.183 ELIGIBILITY REQUIREMENTS: GENERAL

To be eligible for a flight instructor certificate a person must —

(a) Be at least 18 years of age;

(b) Read, write, and converse fluently in English;

(c) Hold —
   (1) A commercial or airline transport pilot certificate with an aircraft rating appropriate to the flight instructor rating sought, and
   (2) An instrument rating, if the person is applying for an airplane or an instrument instructor rating;

(d) Pass a written test on the subjects in which ground instruction is required by § 61.185; and

(e) Pass a practical test on all items in which instruction is required by § 61.187 and, in the case of an applicant for a flight instructor-airplane or flight instructor-glider rating, present a logbook endorsement from an appropriately certificated and rated flight instructor who has provided the applicant with spin entry, spin, and spin recovery training in an aircraft of the appropriate category that is certificated for spins, and has found that applicant competent and proficient in those training areas. Except in the case of a retest after a failure for the deficiencies stated in § 61.49(b), the person conducting the practical test may either accept the spin training logbook endorsement or require demonstration of the spin entry, spin, and spin recovery maneuver on the flight portion of the practical test.

61.185 AERONAUTICAL KNOWLEDGE

(a) Present evidence showing that he has satisfactorily completed a course of instruction in at least the following subjects:
   (1) The learning process.
   (2) Elements of effective teaching.
   (3) Student evaluation, quizzing, and testing.
   (4) Course development.
   (5) Lesson planning.
   (6) Classroom instructing techniques.

(b) Have logged ground instruction from an authorized ground or flight instructor in all of the subjects in which ground instruction is required for a private and commercial pilot certificate, and for an instrument rating, if an airplane or instrument instructor rating is sought.

61.187 FLIGHT PROFICIENCY

(a) An applicant for a flight instructor certificate must have received flight instruction, appropriate to the instructor rating sought in the subjects listed in this paragraph by a person authorized in paragraph (b) of this section. In addition, his logbook must contain an endorsement by the person who has given him the instruction certifying that he has found the applicant competent to pass a practical test on the following subjects:
   (1) Preparation and conduct of lesson plans for students with varying backgrounds and levels of experience and ability.
   (2) The evaluation of student flight performance.
   (3) Effective preflight and postflight instruction.
   (4) Flight instructor responsibilities and certifying procedures.
   (5) Effective analysis and correction of common student pilot flight errors.
   (6) Performance and analysis of standard flight training procedures and maneuvers appropriate to the flight instructor rating sought. For flight instructor-airplane and flight instructor-glider applicants, this shall include the satisfactory demonstration of stall awareness, spin entry, spins, and spin recovery techniques in an aircraft of the appropriate category that is certificated for spins.

(b)   The flight instruction required by paragraph (a) of this section must be given by a person who has held a flight instructor certificate during the 24 months immediately preceding the date the instruction is given, who meets the general requirements for a flight instructor certificate prescribed in §61.183, and who has given at least 200 hours of flight instruction, or 80 hours in the case of glider instruction, as a certificated flight instructor.

(c)   The flight instruction required by this section may be accomplished—
     (1)   In an aircraft; and
     (2)   In a flight simulator or in a flight training device used in accordance with an approved course at a training center certificated under Part 142 of this chapter.

61.189   FLIGHT INSTRUCTOR RECORDS

(a)   Each certificated flight instructor shall sign the logbook of each person to whom he has given flight or ground instruction and specify in that book the amount of time and the date on which it was given. In addition, he shall maintain a record in his flight instructor logbook, or in a separate document containing the following:
     (1)   The name of each person whose logbook or student pilot certificate he has endorsed for solo flight privileges. The record must include the type and date of each endorsement.
     (2)   The name of each person for whom he has signed a certification for a written, flight, or practical test, including the kind of test, date of his certification, and the result of the test.

(b)   The record required by this section shall be retained by the flight instructor separately or in his logbook for at least 3 years.

61.191   ADDITIONAL FLIGHT INSTRUCTOR RATINGS

The holder of a flight instructor certificate who applies for an additional rating on that certificate must —

(a)   Hold an effective pilot certificate with ratings appropriate to the flight instructor rating sought;

(b)   Have had at least 15 hours as pilot-in-command in the category and class of aircraft appropriate to the rating sought; and

(c)   Pass the written and practical test prescribed in this subpart for the rating sought.

(d)   If accomplished in accordance with an approved course conducted by a training center certificated under Part 142 of this chapter, the practical test may be conducted in a flight simulator, or a flight training device.

61.193   FLIGHT INSTRUCTOR AUTHORIZATIONS

(a)   The holder of a flight instructor certificate is authorized, within the limitations of that person's flight instructor certificate and ratings, to give the —
     (1)   Flight instruction required by this part for a pilot certificate or rating;
     (2)   Ground instruction or a home study course required by this part for a pilot certificate and rating;
     (3)   Ground and flight instruction required by this subpart for a flight instructor certificate and rating, if that person meets the requirements prescribed in § 61.187(b);
     (4)   Flight instruction required for an initial solo or cross-country flight;
     (5)   Flight review required in § 61.56 in a manner acceptable to the Administrator;
     (6)   Instrument competency check required in § 61.57(e)(2);
     (7)   Pilot-in-command flight instruction required under § 61.101(d); and
     (8)   Ground and flight instruction required by this part for the issuance of the endorsements specified in paragraph (b) of this section.

(b)   The holder of a flight instructor certificate is authorized within the limitations of that person's flight instructor certificate and rating, to endorse —
     (1)   In accordance with §§ 61.87(m) and 61.93(c) and (d), the pilot certificate of a student pilot the instructor has instructed authorizing the student to conduct solo or solo cross-country flights, or to act as pilot-in-command of an airship requiring more than one flight crew member;
     (2)   In accordance with §§ 61.87(m) and 61.93(b) and (d), the logbook of a student pilot the flight instructor has instructed, authorizing single or repeated solo flights;
     (3)   In accordance with § 61.93(d), the logbook of a student pilot whose preparation and preflight planning for a solo cross-country flight the flight instructor has reviewed and found adequate for a safe flight under the conditions the flight instructor has listed in the logbook;

(4) In accordance with § 61.95, the logbook of a student pilot the flight instructor has instructed authorizing solo flights in a Class B airspace area or at an airport within a Class B airspace area;

(5) The logbook of a pilot or another flight instructor who has been trained by the person described in paragraph (b) of this section, certifying that the pilot or other flight instructor is prepared for an operating privilege, a written test, or practical test required by this part;

(6) In accordance with §§ 61.57(e)(2) and 61.101(d), the logbook of a pilot the flight instructor has instructed authorizing the pilot to act as pilot-in-command;

(7) [Reserved]; and

(8) In accordance with §§ 61.101(g) and (h), the logbook of a recreational pilot the flight instructor has instructed authorizing solo flight.

61.195 FLIGHT INSTRUCTOR LIMITATIONS

The holder of a flight instructor certificate is subject to the following limitations:

(a) *Hours of Instruction.* He may not conduct more than eight hours of flight instruction in any period of 24 consecutive hours.

(b) *Ratings.* Flight instruction may not be conducted in any aircraft for which the flight instructor does not hold a category, class, and if appropriate, a type rating, on the flight instructor's pilot and flight instructor certificates.

(c) *Endorsement of Student Pilot Certificate.* He may not endorse a student pilot certificate for initial solo or solo cross-country flight privileges, unless he has given that student pilot flight instruction required by this Part for the endorsement, and considers that the student is prepared to conduct the flight safely with the aircraft involved.

(d) *Logbook Endorsement.* He may not endorse a student pilot's logbook—

(1) For solo flight unless he has given that student flight instruction and found that student pilot prepared for solo flight in the type of aircraft involved;

(2) For a cross-country flight, unless he has reviewed the student's flight preparation, planning, equipment, and proposed procedures and found them to be adequate for the flight proposed under existing circumstances; or

(3) For solo flights in a Class B airspace area or at an airport within a Class B airspace area unless the flight instructor has given that student ground and flight instruction and has found that student prepared and competent to conduct the operations authorized.

(e) *Solo Flights.* He may not authorize any student pilot to make a solo flight unless he possesses a valid student pilot certificate endorsed for solo in the make and model aircraft to be flown. In addition, he may not authorize any student pilot to make a solo cross-country flight unless he possesses a valid student pilot certificate endorsed for solo cross-country flight in the category of aircraft to be flown.

(f) *Instruction in Multiengine Airplane or Helicopter.* He may not give flight instruction required for the issuance of a certificate or a category, or class rating, in a multiengine airplane or a helicopter, unless he has at least 5 hours of experience as pilot-in-command in the make and model of that airplane or helicopter, as the case may be.

(g) *Recreational Pilot Endorsements.* The flight instructor may not endorse a recreational pilot's logbook unless the instructor has given that pilot the ground and flight instruction required under this Part for the endorsement and found that pilot competent to pilot the aircraft safely.

(h) A flight instructor may not give instruction in Category II or Category III operations unless the flight instructor has been trained and tested in Category II or Category III operations, pursuant to § 61.67 or 61.68, as applicable.

61.197 RENEWAL OF FLIGHT INSTRUCTOR CERTIFICATES

(a) Except as provided in paragraph (b) of this section, the holder of a flight instructor certificate may renew that certificate for an additional period of 24 calendar months if that individual satisfactorily completes a practical test for—

(1) Renewal of the flight instructor certificate and rating sought; or

(2) An additional flight instructor rating.

(b) The holder of a flight instructor certificate may renew that certificate and its ratings without accomplishing a practical test, by presenting to a FAA Flight Standards District Office evidence of one of the following:

Ⓐ *Amend #100 eff 8-1-96*

(1) A record showing that, during the preceding 24 calendar months, the instructor has served—

    (i) As a company check pilot;

    (ii) As a chief flight instructor;

    (iii) As a company check airman or flight instructor in a Part 121 or Part 135 operation; or

    (iv) In a comparable position involving the regular evaluation of pilots.

(2) A graduation certificate from an approved flight instructor refresher course, provided that—

    (i) The course was completed prior to the expiration date of the flight instructor certificate; and

    (ii) The course consists of not less than 24 hours of ground training, flight training, or a combination of ground training and flight training.

(c) If an instructor satisfactorily completes the requirements of this section within 90 calendar days prior to the expiration date of the flight instructor certificate, the instructor is considered to have completed the requirements of this section prior to the expiration date, and the certificate will be renewed for an additional 24 calendar months beyond the expiration date.

(d) Except as allowed by paragraph (e) of this section, the practical test required by paragraph (a) of this section must be conducted in an aircraft.

(e) The practical test required by paragraph (a) of this section may be accomplished in a flight simulator or in a flight training device if the test is accomplished pursuant to an approved course conducted by a training center certificated under Part 142 of this chapter.

61.199 EXPIRED FLIGHT INSTRUCTOR CERTIFICATES AND RATINGS

(a) *Flight Instructor Certificates.* The holder of an expired flight instructor certificate may exchange that certificate for a new certificate by passing the practical test prescribed in §61.187.

(b) *Flight Instructor Ratings.* A flight instructor rating or a limited flight instructor rating on a pilot certificate is no longer valid and may not be exchanged for a similar rating or a flight instructor certificate. The holder of either of those ratings is issued a flight instructor certificate only if he passes the written and practical test prescribed in this subpart for the issue of that certificate.

61.201 CONVERSION TO NEW SYSTEM OF FLIGHT INSTRUCTOR RATINGS

General. The holder of a flight instructor certificate that does not bear any of the new class or instrument ratings listed in §61.5(c)(2), (3), or (4) for a flight instructor certificate, may not exercise the privileges of that certificate. The holder of a flight instructor certificate with a glider rating need not convert that rating to a new class rating to exercise the privileges of that certificate and rating.

INTENTIONALLY

LEFT

BLANK

APPENDIX A

**PRACTICAL TEST REQUIREMENTS FOR AIRPLANE AIRLINE TRANSPORT PILOT
CERTIFICATES AND ASSOCIATED CLASS AND TYPE RATINGS**
(For Parts 121 and 135 use only)

Throughout the maneuvers prescribed in this appendix, good judgment commensurate with a high level of safety must be demonstrated. In determining whether such judgment has been shown, the FAA inspector or designated examiner who conducts the check considers adherence to approved procedures, actions based on analysis of situations for which there is no prescribed procedure or recommended practice, and qualities of prudence and care in selecting a course of action.

Each maneuver or procedure must be performed in flight except to the extent that certain maneuvers or procedures may be performed in an airplane simulator with a visual system (visual simulator) or an airplane simulator without a visual system (non-visual simulator) or may be waived as indicated by an X in the appropriate columns. A maneuver authorized to be performed in a non-visual simulator may be performed in a visual simulator, and a maneuver authorized to be performed in a training device may be performed in a non-visual or a visual simulator.

An asterisk (*) preceding a maneuver or procedure indicates that the maneuver or procedure may be performed in an airplane simulator or other training device as indicated, provided the applicant has successfully completed the training set forth in §121.424(d) of this chapter.

When a maneuver or procedure is preceded by this symbol (#), it indicates that the FAA inspector or designated examiner may require the maneuver or procedure to be performed in the airplane if he determines such action is necessary to determine the applicant's competence with respect to that maneuver.

An X and asterisk (X*) indicates that a particular condition is specified in connection with the maneuver, procedure, or waiver provisions.

Maneuvers/Procedures	Required		Permitted			
	Simulated Instrument Conditions	Inflight	Visual Simulator	Non-visual Simulator	Training Device	Waiver Provisions of 61.157(c)
The procedures and maneuvers set forth in this appendix must be performed in a manner that satisfactorily demonstrates knowledge and skill with respect to— (1) The airplane, its systems and components; (2) Proper control of airspeed, configuration, direction altitude, and attitude in accordance with procedures and limitations contained in the approved Airplane Flight Manual, check lists, or other approved material appropriate to the airplane type; and (3) Compliance with approved enroute, instrument approach, missed approach, ATC, or other applicable procedures.						
I. *Preflight.* (a) Equipment examination (oral). As part of the practical test the equipment examination must be closely coordinated with, and related to, the flight maneuvers portion but may not be given during the flight maneuvers portion. Notwithstanding 61.21 the equipment examination may be given to an applicant who has completed a ground school that is part of an approved training program under Federal Aviation Regulations Part 121 for the airplane type involved and who is recommended by his instructor. The equipment examination must be repeated if the flight maneuvers portion is not satisfactorily completed within 60 days. The equipment examination must cover —					X	

Maneuvers/Procedures	Required		Permitted			
	Simulated Instrument Conditions	Inflight	Visual Simulator	Non-visual Simulator	Training Device	Waiver Provisions of 61.157(c)
(1) Subjects requiring a practical knowledge of the airplane, its power plants, systems, components, operational, and performance factors;						
(2) Normal, abnormal, and emergency procedures, and the operations and limitations relating thereto; and						
(3) The appropriate provisions of the approved Airplane Flight Manual.						
(b) Preflight Inspection. The pilot must—						
(1) Conduct an actual visual inspection of the exterior and interior of the airplane, locating each item and explaining briefly the purpose of inspecting it; and					X	X*
(2) Demonstrate the use of the prestart check list, appropriate control system checks, starting procedures, radio and electronic equipment checks, and the selection of proper navigation and communications radio facilities and frequencies prior to flight.				X		

If a flight engineer is a required crewmember for the particular type airplane, the actual visual inspection may either be waived or it may be replaced by using an approved pictorial means that realistically portrays the location and detail of inspection items.

Maneuvers/Procedures	Required		Permitted			
	Simulated Instrument Conditions	Inflight	Visual Simulator	Non-visual Simulator	Training Device	Waiver Provisions of 61.157(c)
(c) Taxiing. This maneuver includes taxiing, sailing, or docking procedures in compliance with instructions issued by the appropriate traffic control authority or by the FAA inspector or designated examiner.						
(d) Powerplant checks. As appropriate to the airplane type.						
II. Takeoffs.						
(a) Normal. One normal takeoff which, for the purpose of this maneuver, begins when the airplane is taxied into position on the runway to be used.		X				
* (b) Instrument. One takeoff with instrument conditions simulated at or before reaching an altitude of 100 feet above the airport elevation.	X	X	X			
(c) Crosswind. One crosswind takeoff, if practicable under the existing meteorological, airport, and traffic conditions.		X*				
*# (d) Power plant failure. One takeoff with a simulated failure of the most critical powerplant—			X	X		
(1) At a point after V_1 and before V_2 that in the judgment of the person conducting the check is appropriate to the airplane type under the prevailing conditions; or						
(2) At a point as close as possible after V_1 when V_1 and V_2 or V_1 and V_R are identical; or						
(3) At the appropriate speed for non-transport category airplanes.						
For additional type rating in an airplane group with engines mounted in similar positions or from wing-mounted engines to aft fuselage-mounted engines this maneuver may be performed in a nonvisual simulator.						

Maneuvers/Procedures	Required		Permitted			
	Simulated Instrument Conditions	Inflight	Visual Simulator	Non-visual Simulator	Training Device	Waiver Provisions of 61.157(c)
(e) Rejected. A rejected takeoff performed in an airplane during a normal takeoff run after reaching a reasonable speed determined by giving due consideration to aircraft characteristics, runway length, surface conditions, wind direction and velocity, brake heat energy, and any other pertinent factors that may adversely affect safety or the airplane.						
III. *Instrument Procedures.*						
* (a) Area departure and area arrival. During each of these maneuvers the applicant must—	X			X		X*
(1) Adhere to actual or simulated ATC clearances (including assigned radials); and						
(2) Properly use available navigation facilities. Either area arrival or area departure, but not both, may be waived under §61.157(c).						
* (b) Holding. This maneuver includes entering, maintaining, and leaving holding patterns. It may be performed under either area departure or area arrival.	X			X		X*
(c) ILS and other instrument approaches. There must be the following:						
* (1) At least one normal ILS approach	X		X			
# (2) At least 1 manually controlled ILS approach with a simulated failure of 1 power plant. The simulated failure should occur before initiating the final approach course and must continue to touchdown or through the missed approach procedure.	X		X	X		X*
However, either the normal ILS approach or the manually controlled ILS approach must be performed in flight.						

Maneuvers/Procedures	Required		Permitted			
	Simulated Instrument Conditions	Inflight	Visual Simulator	Non-visual Simulator	Training Device	Waiver Provisions of 61.157(c)
(3) At least one nonprecision approach procedure that is representative of the non-precision approach procedures that the applicant is likely to use.	X		X			
(4) Demonstration of at least one nonprecision approach procedure on a letdown aid other than the approach procedure performed under subparagraph (3) of this paragraph that the applicant is likely to use. If performed in a synthetic instrument trainer, the procedures must be observed by the FAA inspector or designated examiner, or if the applicant has completed an approved training course under Part 121 of this chapter for the airplane type involved, the procedures may be observed by a person qualified to act as an instructor or check airman under that approved training program.	X				X	

Each instrument approach must be performed according to any procedures and limitations approved for the approach facility used. The instrument approach begins when the airplane is over the initial approach fix for the approach procedure being used (or turned over to the final approach controller in the case of GCA approach) and ends when the airplane touches down on the runway or when transition to a missed approach configuration is completed. Instrument conditions need not be simulated below 100 feet above touchdown zone elevation.

Maneuvers/Procedures	Required		Permitted			
	Simulated Instrument Conditions	Inflight	Visual Simulator	Non-visual Simulator	Training Device	Waiver Provisions of 61.157(c)
(d) Circling approaches. At least one circling approach must be made under the following conditions: (1) The portion of the circling approach to the authorized minimum circling approach altitude must be made under simulated instrument conditions. (2) The approach must be made to the authorized minimum circling approach altitude followed by a change in heading and the necessary maneuvering (by visual reference) to maintain a flight path that permits a normal landing on a runway at least 90 degrees from the final approach course of the simulated instrument portion of the approach. (3) The circling approach must be performed without excessive maneuvering, and without exceeding the normal operating limits of the airplane. The angle of bank should not exceed 30 degrees. When the maneuver is performed in an airplane, it may be waived as provided in §61.157(c) if local conditions beyond the control of the pilot prohibit the maneuver or prevent it from being performed as required. The circling approach maneuver is not required for a pilot employed by a certificate holder subject to the operating rules of Part 121 of this chapter, if the certificate holder's manual prohibits a circling approach in weather conditions below 1000-3 (ceiling and visibility).	X		X			X*

Maneuvers/Procedures	Required		Permitted			
	Simulated Instrument Conditions	Inflight	Visual Simulator	Non-visual Simulator	Training Device	Waiver Provisions of 61.157(c)
* (e) Missed approaches. Each applicant must perform at least two missed approaches, with at least one missed approach from an ILS approach. A complete approved missed approach procedure must be accomplished at least once and, at the discretion of the FAA inspector or designated examiner, a simulated power plant failure may be required during any of the missed approaches. These maneuvers maybe performed either independently or in conjunction with maneuvers required under Sections III or V of this appendix. At least one must be performed inflight.	X	X*	X*			
IV. *Inflight Maneuvers.*						
* (a) Steep turns. At least one steep turn in each direction must be performed. Each steep turn must involve a bank angle of 45 degrees with a heading change of at least 180 degrees but not more than 360 degrees.	X			X		X
* (b) Approaches to stalls. For the purpose of this maneuver the required approach to a stall is reached when there is a perceptible buffet or other response to the initial stall entry. Except as provided below, there must be at least three approaches to stalls as follows: (1) One must be in the takeoff configuration (except where the airplane uses only a zero-flap takeoff configuration). (2) One in a clean configuration. (3) One in a landing configuration. At the discretion of the FAA inspector or designated examiner, one approach to a stall must be performed in one of the above configurations while in a turn with a bank angle between 15 and 30 degrees. Two out of the three approaches required by this paragraph may be waived as provided in 61.157(c).	X			X		X*

Maneuvers/Procedures	Required — Simulated Instrument Conditions	Required — Inflight	Permitted — Visual Simulator	Permitted — Non-visual Simulator	Permitted — Training Device	Permitted — Waiver Provisions of 61.157(c)
* (c) Specific flight characteristics. Recovery from specific flight characteristics that are peculiar to the airplane type.				X		X
(d) Powerplant failures. In addition to the specific requirements for maneuvers with simulated power plant failures, the FAA inspector or designated examiner may require a simulated power plant failure at any time during the check.		X				
V. Landings and Approaches to Landings. Notwithstanding the authorizations for combining of maneuvers and for waiver of maneuvers, at least three actual landings (one to a full stop) must be made. These landings must include the types listed below but more than one type can be combined where appropriate:						
(a) Normal landing						
# (b) Landing in sequence from an ILS instrument approach except that if circumstances beyond the control of the pilot prevent an actual landing, the person conducting the check may accept an approach to a point where in his judgment a landing to a full stop could have been made. In addition, where a simulator approved for the landing maneuver out of an ILS approach is used, the approach may be continued through the landing and credit given for 1 of the 3 landings required by this section.		X	X*			
(c) Crosswind landing, if practical under existing meteorological, airport, and traffic conditions.		X*				
# (d) Maneuvering to a landing with simulated power plant failure, as follows: (1) In the case of 3-engine airplanes, maneuvering to a landing with an approved procedure that approximates the loss of 2 power plants (center and 1 outboard engine); or		X*	X*			

Maneuvers/Procedures	Required		Permitted			
	Simulated Instrument Conditions	Inflight	Visual Simulator	Non-visual Simulator	Training Device	Waiver Provisions of 61.157(c)
(2) In the case of other multiengine airplanes, maneuvering to a landing with a simulated failure of 50 percent of available power plants, with the simulated loss of power on the side of the airplane. However, before Jan. 1, 1975, in the case of a 4-engine turbojet-powered airplane, maneuvering to a landing with a simulated failure of the most critical power plant may be substituted therefore, if a flight instructor in an approved training program under Part 121 of this chapter certifies to the Administrator that he has observed the applicant satisfactorily perform a landing in that type airplane with a simulated failure of 50 percent of the available power plants. The substitute maneuver may not be used if the Administrator determines that training in the 2-engine out landing maneuver provided in the training program is unsatisfactory.						
If an applicant performs this maneuver in a visual simulator, he must, in addition, maneuver in flight to a landing with a simulated failure of the most critical powerplant.			X*			
* (e) Except as provided in paragraph (f), landing under simulated circling approach conditions except that if circumstances beyond the control of the pilot prevent a landing, the person conducting the check may accept an approach to a point where, in his judgment, a landing to a full stop could have been made. The circling approach maneuver is not required for a pilot employed by a certificate holder subject to the operating rules of Part 121 of this chapter, if the certificate holder's manual prohibits a circling approach in weather conditions below 1000-3 (ceiling and visibility).						

Maneuvers/Procedures	Required		Permitted			Waiver Provisions of 61.157(c)
	Simulated Instrument Conditions	Inflight	Visual Simulator	Non-visual Simulator	Training Device	
*# (f) A rejected landing, including a normal missed approach procedure, that is rejected approximately 50 feet over the runway and approximately over the runway threshold. This maneuver may be combined with instrument, circling, or missed approach procedures, but instrument conditions need not be simulated below 100 feet above the runway.	X*		X*			
# (g) A zero-flap visual approach to a point where, in the judgment of the person conducting the check, a landing to a full stop on the appropriate runway could be made. This maneuver is not required for a particular airplane type if the Administrator has determined that the probability of flap extension failure on that type is extremely remote due to system design. In making this determination, the Adminstrator determines whether checking on slats only and partial flap approaches is necessary.			X*			
(h) For a single power plant rating only, unless the applicant holds a commercial pilot certificate, he must accomplish accuracy approaches and spot landings that include a series of three landings from an altitude of 1000 feet or less, with the engine throttled and 180 degrees change in direction. The airplane must touch the ground in a normal landing attitude beyond and within 200 feet from a designated line. At least one landing must be from a forward slip. One hundred eighty degree approaches using two 90 degree turns with a straight base leg are preferred although circular approaches are acceptable.		X				

Maneuvers/Procedures	Required		Permitted			
	Simulated Instrument Conditions	Inflight	Visual Simulator	Non-visual Simulator	Training Device	Waiver Provisions of 61.157(c)
VI. *Normal and Abnormal Procedures.* Each applicant must demonstrate the proper use of as many of the systems and devices listed below as the FAA inspector or designated examiner finds are necessary to determine that the person being checked has a practical knowledge of the use of the systems and devices appropriate to the aircraft type:						
(a) Anti-icing and deicing systems;				X		
(b) Auto-pilot systems;				X		
(c) Automatic or other approach aid systems;				X		
(d) Stall warning devices, stall avoidance devices, and stability augmentation devices;						
(e) Airborne radar devices;				X		
(f) Any other systems, devices, or aids available;				X		
(g) Hydraulic and electrical system failures and malfunctions;					X	
(h) Landing gear and flap systems failures or malfunctions; and					X	
(i) Failure of navigation or communications equipment.				X		
VII. *Emergency Procedures.* Each applicant must demonstrate the proper emergency procedures for as many of the emergency situations listed below as the FAA inspector or designated examiner finds are necessary to determine that the person being checked has an adequate knowledge of, and ability to perform, such procedures:						
(a) Fire inflight;				X		
(b) Smoke control;				X		
(c) Rapid decompression;				X		
(d) Emergency descent; and				X		
(e) Any other emergency procedures outlined in the appropriate approved airplane flight manual.						

FEDERAL AVIATION REGULATIONS

PART 91 — GENERAL OPERATING AND FLIGHT RULES

This part contains all effective amendments through #251 effective 1 August 1996. Amendment #243 and #250 have not yet been issued.

TABLE OF CONTENTS

SUBPART A — GENERAL

SUBPART B — FLIGHT RULES
GENERAL

TABLE OF CONTENTS

SUBPART B — FLIGHT RULES (Cont)

VISUAL FLIGHT RULES

INSTRUMENT FLIGHT RULES

SUBPART C — EQUIPMENT, INSTRUMENT, AND CERTIFICATE REQUIREMENTS

SUBPART D — SPECIAL FLIGHT OPERATIONS

TABLE OF CONTENTS

SUBPART D — SPECIAL FLIGHT OPERATIONS (Cont)

TABLE OF CONTENTS

SUBPART G — ADDITIONAL EQUIPMENT AND OPERATING REQUIREMENTS FOR LARGE AND TRANSPORT CATEGORY AIRCRAFT

SUBPART H - FOREIGN AIRCRAFT OPERATIONS AND OPERATIONS OF U.S.-REGISTERED CIVIL AIRCRAFT OUTSIDE OF THE UNITED STATES

SUBPART I - OPERATING NOISE LIMITS

TABLE OF CONTENTS

SUBPART J - WAIVERS

INTENTIONALLY

LEFT

BLANK

SUBPART A — GENERAL

91.1 APPLICABILITY

(a) Except as provided in paragraph (b) of this section and §91.703, this part prescribes rules governing the operation of aircraft (other than moored balloons, kites, unmanned rockets, and unmanned free balloons, which are governed by part 101 of this chapter, and ultralight vehicles operated in accordance with part 103 of this chapter) within the United States, including the waters within 3 nautical miles of the U.S. coast.

(b) Each person operating an aircraft in the airspace overlying the waters between 3 and 12 nautical miles from the coast of the United States shall comply with §§91.1 through 91.21; §§91.101 through 91.143; §§91.151 through 91.159; §§91.167 through 91.193; §91.203; §91.205; §§91.209 through 91.217; §91.221; §§91.303 through 91.319; §91.323; §91.605; §91.609; §§91.703 through 91.715; and 91.903.

91.3 RESPONSIBILITY AND AUTHORITY OF THE PILOT IN COMMAND

(a) The pilot in command of an aircraft is directly responsible for, and is the final authority as to, the operation of that aircraft.

(b) In an in-flight emergency requiring immediate action, the pilot in command may deviate from any rule of this part to the extent required to meet that emergency.

(c) Each pilot in command who deviates from a rule under paragraph (b) of this section shall, upon the request of the Administrator, send a written report of that deviation to the Administrator.

(Approved by the Office of Management and Budget under OMB control number 2120-005)

91.5 PILOT IN COMMAND OF AIRCRAFT REQUIRING MORE THAN ONE REQUIRED PILOT

No person may operate an aircraft that is type certificated for more than one required pilot flight crewmember unless the pilot in command meets the requirements of §61.58 of this chapter.

91.7 CIVIL AIRCRAFT AIRWORTHINESS

(a) No person may operate a civil aircraft unless it is in an airworthy condition.

(b) The pilot in command of a civil aircraft is responsible for determining whether that aircraft is in condition for safe flight. The pilot in command shall discontinue the flight when unairworthy mechanical, electrical, or structural conditions occur.

91.9 CIVIL AIRCRAFT FLIGHT MANUAL, MARKING, AND PLACARD REQUIREMENTS

(a) Except as provided in paragraph (d) of this section, no person may operate a civil aircraft without complying with the operating limitations specified in the approved Airplane or Rotorcraft Flight Manual, markings, and placards, or as otherwise prescribed by the certificating authority of the country of registry.

(b) No person may operate a U.S. registered civil aircraft —
   (1) For which an Airplane or Rotorcraft Flight Manual is required by *§21.5 of this chapter unless there is available in the aircraft a current, approved Airplane or Rotorcraft Flight Manual or the manual provided for in §121.141(b); and
   (2) For which an Airplane or Rotorcraft Flight Manual is not required by *§21.5 of this chapter, unless there is available in the aircraft a current approved Airplane or Rotorcraft Flight Manual, approved manual material, markings, and placards, or any combination thereof.

(c) No person may operate a U.S. registered civil aircraft unless that aircraft is identified in accordance with *part 45 of this chapter.

*(Not published herein — Ed.)

(d) Any person taking off or landing a helicopter certificated under *part 29 of this chapter at a heliport constructed over water may make such momentary flight as is necessary for takeoff or landing through the prohibited range of the limiting height-speed envelope established for that helicopter if that flight through the prohibited range takes place over water on which a safe ditching can be accomplished and if the helicopter is amphibious or is equipped with floats or other emergency flotation gear adequate to accomplish a safe emergency ditching on open water.

91.11   PROHIBITION AGAINST INTERFERENCE WITH CREWMEMBERS

No person may assault, threaten, intimidate, or interfere with a crewmember in the performance of the crewmember's duties aboard an aircraft being operated.

91.13   CARELESS OR RECKLESS OPERATION

(a) *Aircraft operations for the purpose of air navigation.* No person may operate an aircraft in a careless or reckless manner so as to endanger the life or property of another.

(b) *Aircraft operations other than for the purpose of air navigation.* No person may operate an aircraft, other than for the purpose of air navigation, on any part of the surface of an airport used by aircraft for air commerce (including areas used by those aircraft for receiving or discharging persons or cargo), in a careless or reckless manner so as to endanger the life or property of another.

91.15   DROPPING OBJECTS

No pilot in command of a civil aircraft may allow any object to be dropped from that aircraft in flight that creates a hazard to persons or property. However, this section does not prohibit the dropping of any object if reasonable precautions are taken to avoid injury or damage to persons or property.

91.17   ALCOHOL OR DRUGS

(a) No person may act or attempt to act as a crewmember of a civil aircraft —
  (1) Within 8 hours after the consumption of any alcoholic beverage;
  (2) While under the influence of alcohol;
  (3) While using any drug that affects the person's faculties in any way contrary to safety; or
  (4) While having .04 percent by weight or more alcohol in the blood.

(b) Except in an emergency, no pilot of a civil aircraft may allow a person who appears to be intoxicated or who demonstrates by manner or physical indications that the individual is under the influence of drugs (except a medical patient under proper care) to be carried in that aircraft.

(c) A crewmember shall do the following:
  (1) On request of a law enforcement officer, submit to a test to indicate the percentage by weight of alcohol in the blood, when —
    (i) The law enforcement officer is authorized under State or local law to conduct the test or to have the test conducted; and
    (ii) The law enforcement officer is requesting submission to the test to investigate a suspected violation of State or local law governing the same or substantially similar conduct prohibited by paragraph (a)(1), (a)(2), or (a)(4) of this section.
  (2) Whenever the Administrator has a reasonable basis to believe that a person may have violated paragraph (a)(1), (a)(2), or (a)(4) of this section, that person shall, upon request by the Administrator, furnish the Administrator, or authorize any clinic, hospital, doctor, or other person to release to the Administrator, the results of each test taken within 4 hours after acting or attempting to act as a crewmember that indicates percentage by weight of alcohol in the blood.

*(Not published herein — Ed.)

(d)   Whenever the Administrator has a reasonable basis to believe that a person may have violated paragraph (a)(3) of this section, that person shall, upon request by the Administrator, furnish the Administrator, or authorize any clinic, hospital, doctor, or other person to release to the Administrator, the results of each test taken within 4 hours after acting or attempting to act as a crewmember that indicates the presence of any drugs in the body.

(e)   Any test information obtained by the Administrator under paragraph (c) or (d) of this section may be evaluated in determining a person's qualifications for any airman certificate or possible violations of this chapter and may be used as evidence in any legal proceeding under *section 602, 609, or 901 of the Federal Aviation Act of 1958.

91.19   CARRIAGE OF NARCOTIC DRUGS, MARIHUANA, AND DEPRESSANT OR STIMULANT DRUGS OR SUBSTANCES

(a)   Except as provided in paragraph (b) of this section, no person may operate a civil aircraft within the United States with knowledge that narcotic drugs, marihuana, and depressant or stimulant drugs or substances as defined in Federal or State statutes are carried in the aircraft.

(b)   Paragraph (a) of this section does not apply to any carriage of narcotic drugs, marihuana, and depressant or stimulant drugs or substances authorized by or under any Federal or State statute or by any Federal or State agency.

91.21   PORTABLE ELECTRONIC DEVICES

(a)   Except as provided in paragraph (b) of this section, no person may operate, nor may any operator or pilot in command of an aircraft allow the operation of, any portable electronic device on any of the following U.S.—registered civil aircraft:
(1)   Aircraft operated by a holder of an air carrier operating certificate or an operating certificate; or
(2)   Any other aircraft while it is operated under IFR.

(b)   Paragraph (a) of this section does not apply to —
(1)   Portable voice recorders;
(2)   Hearing aids;
(3)   Heart pacemakers;
(4)   Electric shavers; or
(5)   Any other portable electronic device that the operator of the aircraft has determined will not cause interference with the navigation or communication system of the aircraft on which it is to be used.

(c)   In the case of an aircraft operated by a holder of an air carrier operating certificate or an operating certificate, the determination required by paragraph (b) (5) of this section shall be made by that operator of the aircraft on which the particular device is to be used. In the case of other aircraft, the determination may be made by the pilot in command or other operator of the aircraft.

91.23   TRUTH—IN—LEASING CLAUSE REQUIREMENT IN LEASES AND CONDITIONAL SALES CONTRACTS

(a)   Except as provided in paragraph (b) of this section, the parties to a lease or contract of conditional sale involving a U.S.-registered large civil aircraft and entered into after January 2, 1973, shall execute a written lease or contract and include therein a written truth-in-leasing clause as a concluding paragraph in large print, immediately preceding the space for the signature of the parties, which contains the following with respect to each such aircraft:
(1)   Identification of the Federal Aviation Regulations under which the aircraft has been maintained and inspected during the 12 months preceding the execution of the lease or contract of conditional sale, and certification by the parties thereto regarding the aircraft's status of compliance with applicable maintenance and inspection requirements in this part for the operation to be conducted under the lease or contract of conditional sale.

---

*(Not published herein — Ed.)

      (2)   The name and address (printed or typed) and the signature of the person responsible for operational control of the aircraft under the lease or contract of conditional sale, and certification that each person understands that person's responsibilities for compliance with applicable Federal Aviation Regulations.

      (3)   A statement that an explanation of factors bearing on operational control and pertinent Federal Aviation Regulations can be obtained from the nearest FAA Flight Standards district office.

  (b)   The requirements of paragraph (a) of this section do not apply —

      (1)   To a lease or contract of conditional sale when —

          (i)   The party to whom the aircraft is furnished is a foreign air carrier or certificate holder under Part 121, 125, *127, 135, or 141 of this chapter; or

          (ii)   The party furnishing the aircraft is a foreign air carrier, certificate holder under Part 121, 125, *127, or 141 of this chapter, or a certificate holder under part 135 of this chapter having appropriate authority to engage in air taxi operations with large aircraft.

      (2)   To a contract of conditional sale, when the aircraft involved has not been registered anywhere prior to the execution of the contract, except as a new aircraft under a dealer's aircraft registration certificate issued in accordance with *§47.61 of this chapter.

  (c)   No person may operate a large civil aircraft of U.S. registry that is subject to a lease or contract of conditional sale to which paragraph (a) of this section applies, unless —

      (1)   The lessee or conditional buyer, or the registered owner if the lessee is not a citizen of the United States, has mailed a copy of the lease or contract that complies with the requirements of paragraph (a) of this section, within 24 hours of its execution, to the Aircraft Registration Branch, Attn: Technical Section, P.O. Box 25724, Oklahoma City, Oklahoma 73125;

      (2)   A copy of the lease or contract that complies with the requirements of paragraph (a) of this section is carried in the aircraft. The copy of the lease or contract shall be made available for review upon request by the Administrator; and

      (3)   The lessee or conditional buyer, or the registered owner if the lessee is not a citizen of the United States, has notified by telephone or in person, the FAA Flight Standards district office nearest the airport where the flight will originate. Unless otherwise authorized by that office, the notification shall be given at least 48 hours before takeoff in the case of the first flight of that aircraft under that lease or contract and inform the FAA of —

          (i)   The location of the airport of departure;

          (ii)   The departure time; and

          (iii)   The registration number of the aircraft involved.

  (d)   The copy of the lease or contract furnished to the FAA under paragraph (c) of this section is commercial or financial information obtained from a person. It is, therefore, privileged and confidential and will not be made available by the FAA for public inspection or copying under *5 U.S.C. 552(b)(4), unless recorded with the FAA under *part 49 of this chapter.

  (e)   For the purpose of this section, a lease means any agreement by a person to furnish an aircraft to another person for compensation or hire, whether with or without flight crewmembers, other than an agreement for the sale of an aircraft and a contract of conditional sale under *section 101 of the Federal Aviation Act of 1958. The person furnishing the aircraft is referred to as the lessor, and the person to whom it is furnished is the lessee.

(Approved by the Office of Management and Budget under OMB control number 2120-0005)

---

*(Not published herein — Ed.)

91.25   AVIATION SAFETY REPORTING PROGRAM: PROHIBITION AGAINST USE OF REPORTS FOR ENFORCEMENT PURPOSES

The Administrator of the FAA will not use reports submitted to the National Aeronautics and Space Administration under the Aviation Safety Reporting Program (or information derived therefrom) in any enforcement action, except information concerning accidents or criminal offenses which are wholly excluded from the program.

91.27 — 91.99 [Reserved]

INTENTIONALLY

LEFT

BLANK

SUBPART B — FLIGHT RULES

GENERAL

91.101 APPLICABILITY

This subpart prescribes flight rules governing the operation of aircraft within the United States and within 12 nautical miles from the coast of the United States.

91.103 PREFLIGHT ACTION

Each pilot in command shall, before beginning a flight, become familiar with all available information concerning that flight. This information must include —
(a) For a flight under IFR or a flight not in the vicinity of an airport, weather reports and forecasts, fuel requirements, alternatives available if the planned flight cannot be completed, and any known traffic delays of which the pilot in command has been advised by ATC;
(b) For any flight, runway lengths at airports of intended use, and the following takeoff and landing distance information:
(1) For civil aircraft for which an approved airplane or Rotorcraft Flight Manual containing takeoff and landing distance data is required, the takeoff and landing distance data contained therein; and
(2) For civil aircraft other than those specified in paragraph (b)(1) of this section, other reliable information appropriate to the aircraft, relating to aircraft performance under expected values of airport elevation and runway slope, aircraft gross weight, and wind and temperature.

91.105 FLIGHT CREWMEMBERS AT STATIONS

(a) During takeoff and landing, and while en route, each required flight crewmember shall —
(1) Be at the crewmember station unless the absence is necessary to perform duties in connection with the operation of the aircraft or in connection with physiological needs; and
(2) Keep the safety belt fastened while at the crewmember station.
(b) Each required flight crewmember of a U.S.-registered civil aircraft shall, during takeoff and landing, keep his or her shoulder harness fastened while at his or her assigned duty station. This paragraph does not apply if—
(1) The seat at the crewmember's station is not equipped with a shoulder harness; or
(2) The crewmember would be unable to perform required duties with the shoulder harness fastened.

91.107 USE OF SAFETY BELTS, SHOULDER HARNESSES, AND CHILD RESTRAINT SYSTEMS

(a) Unless otherwise authorized by the Administrator—
(1) No pilot may take off a U.S.-registered civil aircraft (except a free balloon that incorporates a basket or gondola, or an airship type certificated before November 2, 1987) unless the pilot in command of that aircraft ensures that each person on board is briefed on how to fasten and unfasten that person's safety belt and, if installed, shoulder harness.
(2) No pilot may cause to be moved on the surface, take off, or land a U.S.-registered civil aircraft (except a free balloon that incorporates a basket or gondola, or an airship type certificated before November 2, 1987) unless the pilot in command of that aircraft ensures that each person on board has been notified to fasten his or her safety belt and, if installed, his or her shoulder harness.

(3)   Except as provided in this paragraph, each person on board a U.S.-registered civil aircraft (except a free balloon that incorporates a basket or gondola or an airship type certificated before November 2, 1987) must occupy an approved seat or berth with a safety belt and, if installed, shoulder harness, properly secured about him or her during movement on the surface, takeoff, and landing. For seaplane and float equipped rotorcraft operations during movement on the surface, the person pushing off the seaplane or rotorcraft from the dock and the person mooring the seaplane or rotorcraft at the dock are excepted from the preceding seating and safety belt requirements. Notwithstanding the preceding requirements of this paragraph, a person may:

(i)   Be held by an adult who is occupying a seat or berth if that person has not reached his or her second birthday;

(ii)   Use the floor of the aircraft as a seat, provided that the person is on board for the purpose of engaging in sport parachuting; or

(iii)   Notwithstanding any other requirement of this chapter, occupy an approved child restraint system furnished by the operator or one of the persons described in paragraph (a)(3)(iii)(A) of this section provided that:

    (A)   The child is accompanied by a parent, guardian, or attendant designated by the child's parent or guardian to attend to the safety of the child during the flight;

    (B)   The approved child restraint system bears one or more labels as follows:

       (1)   Seats manufactured to U.S. standards between January 1, 1981, and February 25, 1985, must bear the label: "This child restraint system conforms to all applicable Federal motor vehicle safety standards." Vest- and harness-type child restraint systems manufactured before February 26, 1985, bearing such a label are not approved for the purposes of this section;

       (2)   Seats manufactured to U.S. standards on or after February 26, 1985, must bear two labels:

          (i)   "This child restraint system conforms to all applicable Federal motor vehicle safety standards"; and

          (ii)   "THIS RESTRAINT IS CERTIFIED FOR USE IN MOTOR VEHICLES AND AIRCRAFT" in red lettering;

       (3)   Seats that do not qualify under paragraphs (a)(3)(iii)(B)(1) and (a)(3)(iii)(B)(2) of this section must bear either a label showing approval of a foreign government or a label showing that the seat was manufactured under the standards of the United Nations; and

    (C)   The operator complies with the following requirements:

       (1)   The restraint system must be properly secured to an approved forward-facing seat or berth;

       (2)   The child must be properly secured in the restraint system and must not exceed the specified weight limit for the restraint system; and

       (3)   The restraint system must bear the appropriate label(s).

(b)   Unless otherwise stated, this section does not apply to operations conducted under Part 121, 125, or 135 of this chapter. Paragraph (a)(3) of this section does not apply to persons subject to §91.105.

91.109   **FLIGHT INSTRUCTION; SIMULATED INSTRUMENT FLIGHT AND CERTAIN FLIGHT TESTS**

(a) No person may operate a civil aircraft (except a manned free balloon) that is being used for flight instruction unless that aircraft has fully functioning dual controls. However, instrument flight instruction may be given in a single-engine airplane equipped with a single, functioning throwover control wheel in place of fixed, dual controls of the elevator and ailerons, when —

    (1) The instructor has determined that the flight can be conducted safely; and

    (2) The person manipulating the controls has at least a private pilot certificate with appropriate category and class ratings.

(b) No person may operate a civil aircraft in simulated instrument flight unless —

    (1) The other control seat is occupied by a safety pilot who possesses at least a private pilot certificate with category and class ratings appropriate to the aircraft being flown.

    (2) The safety pilot has adequate vision forward and to each side of the aircraft, or a competent observer in the aircraft adequately supplements the vision of the safety pilot; and

    (3) Except in the case of lighter-than-air aircraft, that aircraft is equipped with fully functioning dual controls. However, simulated instrument flight may be conducted in a single-engine airplane, equipped with a single, functioning, throwover control wheel, in place of fixed, dual controls of the elevator and ailerons, when —

        (i) The safety pilot has determined that the flight can be conducted safely; and

        (ii) The person manipulating the controls has at least a private pilot certificate with appropriate category and class ratings.

(c) No person may operate a civil aircraft that is being used for a flight test for an airline transport pilot certificate or a class or type rating on that certificate, or for a part 121 proficiency flight test, unless the pilot seated at the controls, other than the pilot being checked, is fully qualified to act as pilot in command of the aircraft.

91.111   **OPERATING NEAR OTHER AIRCRAFT**

(a) No person may operate an aircraft so close to another aircraft as to create a collision hazard.

(b) No person may operate an aircraft in formation flight except by arrangement with the pilot in command of each aircraft in the formation.

(c) No person may operate an aircraft, carrying passengers for hire, in formation flight.

91.113   **RIGHT-OF-WAY RULES: EXCEPT WATER OPERATIONS**

(a) *Inapplicability*. This section does not apply to the operation of an aircraft on water.

(b) *General*. When weather conditions permit, regardless of whether an operation is conducted under instrument flight rules or visual flight rules, vigilance shall be maintained by each person operating an aircraft so as to see and avoid other aircraft. When a rule of this section gives another aircraft the right-of-way, the pilot shall give way to that aircraft and may not pass over, under, or ahead of it unless well clear.

(c) *In distress*. An aircraft in distress has the right-of-way over all other air traffic.

(d) *Converging*. When aircraft of the same category are converging at approximately the same altitude (except head-on, or nearly so) the aircraft to the other's right has the right-of-way. If the aircraft are of different categories —

    (1) A balloon has the right-of-way over any other category of aircraft;

    (2) A glider has the right-of-way over an airship, airplane or rotorcraft; and

    (3) An airship has the right-of-way over an airplane or rotorcraft.

However, an aircraft towing or refueling other aircraft has the right-of-way over all other engine-driven aircraft.

INTENTIONALLY

LEFT

BLANK

(e) *Approaching head-on.* When aircraft are approaching each other head-on, or nearly so, each pilot of each aircraft shall alter course to the right.

(f) *Overtaking.* Each aircraft that is being overtaken has the right-of-way and each pilot of an overtaking aircraft shall alter course to the right to pass well clear.

(g) *Landing.* Aircraft, while on final approach to land or while landing, have the right-of-way over other aircraft in flight or operating on the surface, except that they shall not take advantage of this rule to force an aircraft off the runway surface which has already landed and is attempting to make way for an aircraft on final approach. When two or more aircraft are approaching an airport for the purpose of landing, the aircraft at the lower altitude has the right-of-way, but it shall not take advantage of this rule to cut in front of another which is on final approach to land or to overtake that aircraft.

91.115   RIGHT-OF-WAY RULES: WATER OPERATIONS

(a) *General.* Each person operating an aircraft on the water shall, insofar as possible, keep clear of all vessels and avoid impeding their navigation, and shall give way to any vessel or other aircraft that is given the right-of-way by any rule of this section.

(b) *Crossing.* When aircraft, or an aircraft and a vessel, are on crossing courses, the aircraft or vessel to the other's right has the right-of-way.

(c) *Approaching head-on.* When aircraft, or an aircraft and a vessel, are approaching head-on, or nearly so, each shall alter its course to the right to keep well clear.

(d) *Overtaking.* Each aircraft or vessel that is being overtaken has the right-of-way, and the one overtaking shall alter course to keep well clear.

(e) *Special circumstances.* When aircraft, or an aircraft and a vessel, approach so as to involve risk of collision, each aircraft or vessel shall proceed with careful regard to existing circumstances, including the limitations of the respective craft.

91.117   AIRCRAFT SPEED

(a) Unless otherwise authorized by the Administrator, no person may operate an aircraft below 10,000 feet MSL at an indicated airspeed of more than 250 knots (288 m.p.h.).

(b) Unless otherwise authorized or required by ATC, no person may operate an aircraft at or below 2,500 feet above the surface within 4 nautical miles of the primary airport of a Class C or Class D airspace area at an indicated airspeed of more than 200 knots (230 mph.). This paragraph (b) does not apply to any operations within a Class B airspace area. Such operations shall comply with paragraph (a) of this section.

(c) No person may operate an aircraft in the airspace underlying a Class B airspace area designated for an airport or in a VFR corridor designated through such a Class B airspace area, at an indicated airspeed of more than 200 knots (230 mph.).

(d) If the minimum safe airspeed for any particular operation is greater than the maximum speed prescribed in this section, the aircraft may be operated at that minimum speed.

91.119   MINIMUM SAFE ALTITUDES: GENERAL

Except when necessary for takeoff or landing, no person may operate an aircraft below the following altitudes:

(a) *Anywhere.* An altitude allowing, if a power unit fails, an emergency landing without undue hazard to persons or property on the surface.

(b) *Over congested areas.* Over any congested area of a city, town, or settlement, or over any open air assembly of persons, an altitude of 1,000 feet above the highest obstacle within a horizontal radius of 2,000 feet of the aircraft.

(c) *Over other than congested areas.* An altitude of 500 feet above the surface, except over open water or sparsely populated areas. In those cases, the aircraft may not be operated closer than 500 feet to any person, vessel, vehicle, or structure.

(d) *Helicopters.* Helicopters may be operated at less than the minimums prescribed in paragraph (b) or (c) of this section if the operation is conducted without hazard to persons or property on the surface. In addition, each person operating a helicopter shall comply with any routes or altitudes specifically prescribed for helicopters by the Administrator.

91.121 ALTIMETER SETTINGS

(a) Each person operating an aircraft shall maintain the cruising altitude or flight level of that aircraft, as the case may be, by reference to an altimeter that is set, when operating —

  (1) Below 18,000 feet MSL, to —

    (i) The current reported altimeter setting of a station along the route and within 100 nautical miles of the aircraft;

    (ii) If there is no station within the area prescribed in paragraph (a)(1)(i) of this section, the current reported altimeter setting of an appropriate available station; or

    (iii) In the case of an aircraft not equipped with a radio, the elevation of the departure airport or an appropriate altimeter setting available before departure; or

  (2) At or above 18,000 feet MSL, to 29.92" Hg.

(b) The lowest usable flight level is determined by the atmospheric pressure in the area of operation, as shown in the following table:

Current altimeter setting	Lowest usable flight level
29.92 (or higher)	180
29.91 through 29.42	185
29.41 through 28.92	190
28.91 through 28.42	195
28.41 through 27.92	200
27.91 through 27.42	205
27.41 through 26.92	210

(c) To convert minimum altitude prescribed under §§91.119 and 91.177 to the minimum flight level, the pilot shall take the flight level equivalent of the minimum altitude in feet and add the appropriate number of feet specified below, according to the current reported altimeter setting:

Current altimeter setting	Adjustable factor
29.92 (or higher)	None
29.91 through 29.42	500
29.41 through 28.92	1,000
28.91 through 28.42	1,500
28.41 through 27.92	2,000
27.91 through 27.42	2,500
27.41 through 26.92	3,000

91.123 COMPLIANCE WITH ATC CLEARANCES AND INSTRUCTIONS

(a) When an ATC clearance has been obtained, no pilot in command may deviate from that clearance unless an amended clearance is obtained, an emergency exists, or the deviation is in response to a traffic alert and collision avoidance system resolution advisory. However, except in Class A airspace, a pilot may cancel an IFR flight plan if the operation is being conducted in VFR weather conditions. When a pilot is uncertain of an ATC clearance, that pilot shall immediately request clarification from ATC.

Ⓐ *Amend #244 eff 10/30/95*

(b) Except in an emergency, no person may operate an aircraft contrary to an ATC instruction in an area in which air traffic control is exercised.

(c) Each pilot in command who, in an emergency, or in response to a traffic alert and collision avoidance system resolution advisory, deviates from an ATC clearance or instruction shall notify ATC of that deviation as soon as possible.

(d) Each pilot in command who (though not deviating from a rule of this subpart) is given priority by ATC in an emergency, shall submit a detailed report of that emergency within 48 hours to the manager of that ATC facility, if requested by ATC.

(e) Unless otherwise authorized by ATC, no person operating an aircraft may operate that aircraft according to any clearance or instruction that has been issued to the pilot of another aircraft for radar air traffic control purposes.

91.125   ATC LIGHT SIGNALS

ATC light signals have the meaning shown in the following table.

Color and type of signal	Meaning with respect to aircraft on the surface	Meaning with respect to aircraft in flight
Steady green.....	Cleared for takeoff	Clear to land.
Flashing green...	Cleared to taxi.......	Return for landing (to be followed by steady green at proper time).
Steady red.........	Stop.......................	Give way to other aircraft and continue circling.
Flashing red.......	Taxi clear of runway in use.	Airport unsafe—do not land.
Flashing white....	Return to starting point on airport.	Not applicable
Alternating red and green	Exercise extreme caution	Exercise extreme caution

91.126   OPERATING ON OR IN THE VICINITY OF AN AIRPORT IN CLASS G AIRSPACE

(a) *General.* Unless otherwise authorized or required, each person operating an aircraft on or in the vicinity of an airport in a Class G airspace area must comply with the requirements of this section.

(b) *Direction of turns.* When approaching to land at an airport without an operating control tower in Class G airspace —
    (1) Each pilot of an airplane must make all turns of that airplane to the left unless the airport displays approved light signals or visual markings indicating that turns should be made to the right, in which case the pilot must make all turns to the right; and
    (2) Each pilot of a helicopter must avoid the flow of fixed-wing aircraft.

(c) *Flap settings.* Except when necessary for training or certification, the pilot in command of a civil turbojet-powered aircraft must use, as a final flap setting, the minimum certificated landing flap setting set forth in the approved performance information in the Airplane Flight Manual for the applicable conditions. However, each pilot in command has the final authority and responsibility for the safe operation of the pilot's airplane, and may use a different flap setting for that airplane if the pilot determines that it is necessary in the interest of safety.

(d) *Communications with control towers.* Unless otherwise authorized or required by ATC, no person may operate an aircraft to, from, through, or on an airport having an operational control tower unless two-way radio communications are maintained between that aircraft and the control tower. Communications must be established prior to 4 nautical miles from the airport, up to and including 2,500 feet AGL. However, if the aircraft radio fails in flight, the pilot in command may operate that aircraft and land if weather conditions are at or above basic VFR weather minimums, visual contact with the tower is maintained, and a clearance to land is received. If the aircraft radio fails while in flight under IFR, the pilot must comply with §91.185.

Ⓐ *Amend #244 eff 10/30/95*

91.127   **OPERATING ON OR IN THE VICINITY OF AN AIRPORT IN CLASS E AIRSPACE**

(a)   Unless otherwise required by Part 93 of this chapter or unless otherwise authorized or required by the ATC facility having jurisdiction over the Class E airspace area, each person operating an aircraft on or in the vicinity of an airport in a Class E airspace area must comply with the requirements of §91.126.

(b)   *Departures.* Each pilot of an aircraft must comply with any traffic patterns established for that airport in Part 93 of this chapter.

(c)   *Communications with control towers.* Unless otherwise authorized or required by ATC, no person may operate an aircraft to, from, through, or on an airport having an operational control tower unless two-way radio communications are maintained between that aircraft and the control tower. Communications must be established prior to 4 nautical miles from the airport, up to and including 2,500 feet AGL. However, if the aircraft radio fails in flight, the pilot in command may operate that aircraft and land if weather conditions are at or above basic VFR weather minimums, visual contact with the tower is maintained, and a clearance to land is received. If the aircraft radio fails while in flight under IFR, the pilot must comply with §91.185.

91.129   **OPERATIONS IN CLASS D AIRSPACE**

(a)   *General.* Unless otherwise authorized or required by the ATC having jurisdiction over the Class D airspace area, each person operating an aircraft in Class D airspace must comply with the applicable provisions of this section. In addition, each person must comply with §§91.126 and 91.127. For the purpose of this section, the primary airport is the airport for which the Class D airspace area is designated. A satellite airport is any other airport within the Class D airspace area.

(b)   *Deviations.* An operator may deviate from any provision of this section under the provisions of an ATC authorization issued by the ATC facility having jurisdiction over the airspace concerned. ATC may authorize a deviation on a continuing basis or for an individual flight, as appropriate.

(c)   *Communications.* Each person operating an aircraft in Class D airspace must meet the following two-way radio communications requirements:

     (1)   *Arrival or through flight.* Each person must establish two-way radio communications with the ATC facility (including foreign ATC in the case of foreign airspace designated in the United States) providing air traffic services prior to entering that airspace and thereafter maintain those communications while within that airspace.

     (2)   *Departing flight.* Each person —

         (i)   From the primary airport or satellite airport with an operating control tower must establish and maintain two-way radio communications with the control tower, and thereafter as instructed by ATC while operating in the Class D airspace area; or

         (ii)   From a satellite airport without an operating control tower, must establish and maintain two-way radio communications with the ATC facility having jurisdiction over the Class D airspace area as soon as practicable after departing.

(d)   *Communications failure.* Each person who operates an aircraft in a Class D airspace area must maintain two-way radio communications with the ATC facility having jurisdiction over that area.

     (1)   If the aircraft radio fails in flight under IFR, the pilot must comply with §91.185 of this part.

     (2)   If the aircraft radio fails in flight under VFR, the pilot in command may operate that aircraft and land if —

         (i)   Weather conditions are at or above basic VFR weather minimums;

         (ii)   Visual contact with the tower is maintained; and

         (iii)   A clearance to land is received.

(e)   *Minimum altitudes.* When operating to an airport in Class D airspace, each pilot of—

     (1)   A large or turbine-powered airplane shall, unless otherwise required by the applicable distance from cloud criteria, enter the traffic pattern at an altitude of at least 1,500 feet above the elevation of the airport and maintain at least 1,500 feet until further descent is required for a safe landing;

     (2)   A large or turbine-powered airplane approaching to land on a runway served by an instrument landing system (ILS), if the airplane is ILS equipped, shall fly that airplane at an altitude at or above the glide slope between the outer marker (or point of interception of glide slope, if compliance with the applicable distance from cloud criteria requires interception closer in) and the middle marker; and

     (3)   An airplane approaching to land on a runway served by a visual approach slope indicator shall maintain an altitude at or above the glide slope until a lower altitude is necessary for a safe landing.

Paragraphs (e)(2) and (e)(3) of this section do not prohibit normal bracketing maneuvers above or below the glide slope that are conducted for the purpose of remaining on the glide slope.

(f) *Approaches.* Except when conducting a circling approach under Part 97 of this chapter or unless otherwise required by ATC, each pilot must —
   (1) Circle the airport to the left, if operating an airplane; or
   (2) Avoid the flow of fixed-wing aircraft, if operating a helicopter.

(g) *Departures.* No person may operate an aircraft departing from an airport except in compliance with the following:
   (1) Each pilot must comply with any departure procedures established for that airport by the FAA.
   (2) Unless otherwise required by the prescribed departure for that airport or the applicable distance from clouds criteria, each pilot of a turbine-powered airplane and each pilot of a large airplane must climb to an altitude of 1,500 feet above the surface as rapidly as practicable.

(h) *Noise abatement.* Where a formal runway use program has been established by the FAA, each pilot of a large or turbine-powered airplane assigned a noise abatement runway by ATC must use that runway. However, consistent with the final authority of the pilot in command concerning the safe operation of the aircraft as prescribed in §91.3(a), ATC may assign a different runway if requested by the pilot in the interest of safety.

(i) *Takeoff, landing, taxi clearance.* No person may, at any airport with an operating control tower, operate an aircraft on a runway or taxiway, or take off or land an aircraft, unless an appropriate clearance is received from ATC. A clearance to "taxi to" the takeoff runway assigned to the aircraft is not a clearance to cross that assigned takeoff runway, or to taxi on that runway at any point, but is a clearance to cross other runways that intersect the taxi route to that assigned takeoff runway. A clearance to "taxi to" any point other than an assigned takeoff runway is clearance to cross all runways that intersect the taxi route to that point.

91.130   OPERATIONS IN CLASS C AIRSPACE

(a) *General.* Unless otherwise authorized by ATC, each aircraft operation in Class C airspace must be conducted in compliance with this section and §91.129. For the purpose of this section, the primary airport is the airport for which the Class C airspace area is designated. A satellite airport is any other airport within the Class C airspace area.

(b) *Traffic patterns.* No person may take off or land an aircraft at a satellite airport within a Class C airspace area except in compliance with FAA arrival and departure traffic patterns.

(c) *Communications.* Each person operating an aircraft in Class C airspace must meet the following two-way radio communications requirements:
   (1) *Arrival or through flight.* Each person must establish two-way radio communications with the ATC facility (including foreign ATC in the case of foreign airspace designated in the United States) providing air traffic services prior to entering that airspace and thereafter maintain those communications while within that airspace.
   (2) *Departing flight.* Each person —
     (i) From the primary airport or satellite airport with an operating control tower, must establish and maintain two-way radio communications with the control tower, and thereafter as instructed by ATC while operating in the Class C airspace area; or
     (ii) From a satellite airport without an operating control tower, must establish and maintain two-way radio communications with the ATC facility having jurisdiction over the Class C airspace area as soon as practicable after departing.

(d) *Equipment requirements.* Unless otherwise authorized by the ATC having jurisdiction over the Class C airspace area, no person may operate an aircraft within a Class C airspace area designated for an airport unless that aircraft is equipped with the applicable equipment specified in §91.215.

(e) *Deviations.* An operator may deviate from any provision of this section under the provisions of an ATC authorization issued by the ATC facility having jurisdiction over the airspace concerned. ATC may authorize a deviation on a continuing basis for an individual flight, as appropriate.

Amend #239
eff 3-11-94

91.131 OPERATIONS IN CLASS B AIRSPACE

(a) *Operating rules.* No person may operate an aircraft within a Class B airspace area except in compliance with §91.129 and the following rules:

(1) The operator must receive an ATC clearance from the ATC facility having jurisdiction for that area before operating an aircraft in that area.

(2) Unless otherwise authorized by ATC, each person operating a large turbine engine-powered airplane to or from a primary airport for which a Class B airspace area is designated must operate at or above the designated floors of the Class B airspace area while within the lateral limits of that area.

(3) Any person conducting pilot training operations at an airport within a Class B airspace area must comply with any procedures established by ATC for such operations in that area.

(b) *Pilot requirements.*

(1) No person may take off or land a civil aircraft at an airport within a Class B airspace area or operate a civil aircraft within a Class B airspace area unless —

(i) The pilot in command holds at least a private pilot certificate; or

(ii) The aircraft is operated by a student pilot or recreational pilot who seeks private pilot certification and has met the requirements of §61.95 of this chapter.

(2) Notwithstanding the provisions of paragraph (b)(1)(ii) of this section, no person may take off or land a civil aircraft at those airports listed in section 4 of appendix D of this part unless the pilot in command holds at least a private pilot certificate.

(c) *Communications and navigation equipment requirements.* Unless otherwise authorized by ATC, no person may operate an aircraft within a Class B airspace area unless that aircraft is equipped with —

(1) *For IFR operation.* An operable VOR or TACAN receiver; and

(2) *For all operations.* An operable two-way radio capable of communications with ATC on appropriate frequencies for that Class B airspace area.

(d) *Transponder requirements.* No person may operate an aircraft in a Class B airspace area unless the aircraft is equipped with the applicable operating transponder and automatic altitude reporting equipment specified in paragraph (a) of §91.215, except as provided in paragraph (d) of that section.

91.133 RESTRICTED AND PROHIBITED AREAS

(a) No person may operate an aircraft within a restricted area (designated in Part 73) contrary to the restrictions imposed, or within a prohibited area, unless that person has the permission of the using or controlling agency, as appropriate.

(b) Each person conducting, within a restricted area, an aircraft operation (approved by the using agency) that creates the same hazards as the operations for which the restricted area was designated may deviate from the rules of this subpart that are not compatible with his operation of the aircraft.

91.135 OPERATIONS IN CLASS A AIRSPACE

Except as provided in paragraph (d) of this section, each person operating an aircraft in Class A airspace must conduct that operation under instrument flight rules (IFR) and in compliance with the following:

(a) *Clearance.* Operations may be conducted only under an ATC clearance received prior to entering the airspace.

(b) *Communications.* Unless otherwise authorized by ATC, each aircraft operating in Class A airspace must be equipped with a two-way radio capable of communicating with ATC on a frequency assigned by ATC. Each pilot must maintain two-way radio communications with ATC while operating in Class A airspace.

(c) *Transponder requirement.* Unless otherwise authorized by ATC, no person may operate an aircraft within Class A airspace unless that aircraft is equipped with the applicable equipment specified in §91.215.

(d) *ATC authorizations.* An operator may deviate from any provision of this section under the provisions of an ATC authorization issued by the ATC facility having jurisdiction of the airspace concerned. In the case of an inoperative transponder, ATC may immediately approve an operation within a Class A airspace area allowing flight to continue, if desired, to the airport of ultimate destination, including any intermediate stops, or to proceed to a place where suitable repairs can be made, or both. Requests for deviation from any provision of this section must be submitted in writing, at least 4 days before the proposed operation. ATC may authorize a deviation on a continuing basis or for an individual flight.

91.137 TEMPORARY FLIGHT RESTRICTIONS

(a) The Administrator will issue a Notice to Airmen (NOTAM) designating an area within which temporary flight restrictions apply and specifying the hazard or condition requiring their imposition, whenever he determines it is necessary in order to —

    (1) Protect persons and property on the surface or in the air from a hazard associated with an incident on the surface;

    (2) Provide a safe environment for the operation of disaster relief aircraft; or

    (3) Prevent an unsafe congestion of sightseeing and other aircraft above an incident or event which may generate a high degree of public interest.

The Notice to Airmen will specify the hazard or condition that requires the imposition of temporary flight restrictions.

(b) When a NOTAM has been issued under paragraph (a)(1) of this section, no person may operate an aircraft within the designated area unless that aircraft is participating in the hazard relief activities and is being operated under the direction of the official in charge of on scene emergency response activities.

(c) When a NOTAM has been issued under paragraph (a)(2) of this section, no person may operate an aircraft within the designated area unless at least one of the following conditions are met:

    (1) The aircraft is participating in hazard relief activities and is being operated under the direction of the official in charge of on scene emergency response activities.

    (2) The aircraft is carrying law enforcement officials.

    (3) The aircraft is operating under the ATC approved IFR flight plan.

    (4) The operation is conducted directly to or from an airport within the area, or is necessitated by the impracticability of VFR flight above or around the area due to weather, or terrain; notification is given to the Flight Service Station (FSS) or ATC facility specified in the NOTAM to receive advisories concerning disaster relief aircraft operations; and the operation does not hamper or endanger relief activities and is not conducted for the purpose of observing the disaster.

    (5) The aircraft is carrying properly accredited news representatives, and, prior to entering the area, a flight plan is filed with the appropriate FAA or ATC facility specified in the Notice to Airmen and the operation is conducted above the altitude used by the disaster relief aircraft, unless otherwise authorized by the official in charge of on scene emergency response activities.

(d) When a NOTAM has been issued under paragraph (a)(3) of this section, no person may operate an aircraft within the designated area unless at least one of the following conditions is met:

    (1) The operation is conducted directly to or from an airport within the area, or is necessitated by the impracticability of VFR flight above or around the area due to weather or terrain, and the operation is not conducted for the purpose of observing the incident or event.

    (2) The aircraft is operating under an ATC approved IFR flight plan.

    (3) The aircraft is carrying incident or event personnel, or law enforcement officials.

    (4) The aircraft is carrying properly accredited news representatives and, prior to entering that area, a flight plan is filed with the appropriate FSS or ATC facility specified in the NOTAM.

(e) Flight plans filed and notifications made with an FSS or ATC facility under this section shall include the following information:

    (1) Aircraft identification, type and color.

    (2) Radio communications frequencies to be used.

    (3) Proposed times of entry of, and exit from, the designated area.

    (4) Name of news media or organization and purpose of flight.

    (5) Any other information requested by ATC.

91.138 TEMPORARY FLIGHT RESTRICTIONS IN NATIONAL DISASTER AREAS IN THE STATE OF HAWAII

(a) When the Administrator has determined, pursuant to a request and justification provided by the Governor of the State of Hawaii, or the Governor's designee, that an inhabited area within a declared national disaster area in the State of Hawaii is in need of protection for humanitarian reasons, the Administrator will issue a Notice to Airmen (NOTAM) designating an area within which temporary flight restrictions apply. The Administrator will designate the extent and duration of the temporary flight restrictions necessary to provide for the protection of persons and property on the surface.

(b) When a NOTAM has been issued in accordance with this section, no person may operate an aircraft within the designated airspace unless:
(1) That person has obtained authorization from the official in charge of associated emergency or disaster relief response activities, and is operating the aircraft under the conditions of that authorization;
(2) The aircraft is carrying law enforcement officials;
(3) The aircraft is carrying persons involved in an emergency or a legitimate scientific purpose;
(4) The aircraft is carrying properly accredited newspersons, and that prior to entering the area, a flight plan is filed with the appropriate FAA or ATC facility specified in the NOTAM and the operation is conducted in compliance with the conditions and restrictions established by the official in charge of on-scene emergency response activities; or,
(5) The aircraft is operating in accordance with an ATC clearance or instruction.
(c) A NOTAM issued under this section is effective for 90 days or until the national disaster area designation is terminated, whichever comes first, unless terminated by notice or extended by the Administrator at the request of the Governor of the State of Hawaii or the Governor's designee.

91.139 EMERGENCY AIR TRAFFIC RULES
(a) This section prescribes a process for utilizing Notices to Airmen (NOTAMs) to advise of the issuance and operations under emergency air traffic rules and regulations and designates the official who is authorized to issue NOTAMs on behalf of the Administrator in certain matters under this section.
(b) Whenever the Administrator determines that an emergency condition exists, or will exist, relating to the FAA's ability to operate the air traffic control system and during which normal flight operations under this chapter cannot be conducted consistent with the required levels of safety and efficiency —
(1) The Administrator issues an immediately effective air traffic rule or regulation in response to that emergency condition, and
(2) The Administrator or the Associate Administrator for Air Traffic may utilize the NOTAM system to provide notification of the issuance of the rule or regulation. Those NOTAMs communicate information concerning the rules and regulations that govern flight operations, the use of navigation facilities, and designation of that airspace in which the rules and regulations apply.
(c) When a NOTAM has been issued under this section, no person may operate an aircraft, or other device governed by the regulation concerned, within the designated airspace except in accordance with the authorizations, terms, and conditions prescribed in the regulation covered by the NOTAM.

91.141 FLIGHT RESTRICTIONS IN THE PROXIMITY OF THE PRESIDENTIAL AND OTHER PARTIES

No person may operate an aircraft over or in the vicinity of any area to be visited or traveled by the President, the Vice President, or other public figures contrary to the restrictions established by the Administrator and published in a Notice to Airmen (NOTAM).

91.143 FLIGHT LIMITATION IN THE PROXIMITY OF SPACE FLIGHT OPERATIONS

No person may operate any aircraft of U.S. registry, or pilot any aircraft under the authority of an airman certificate issued by the Federal Aviation Administration within areas designated in a Notice to Airmen (NOTAM) for space flight operations except when authorized by ATC, or operated under the control of the Department of Defense Manager for Space Transportation System Contingency Support Operations.

91.144 TEMPORARY RESTRICTION ON FLIGHT OPERATIONS DURING ABNORMALLY HIGH BAROMETRIC PRESSURE CONDITIONS

(a) *Special flight restrictions.* When any information indicates that barometric pressure on the route of flight currently exceeds or will exceed 31 inches of mercury, no person may operate an aircraft or initiate a flight contrary to the requirements established by the Administrator and published in a Notice to Airmen issued under this section.

Amend #240 eff 5-12-94 (b) *Waivers.* The Administrator is authorized to waive any restriction issued under paragraph (a) of this section to permit emergency supply, transport, or medical services to be delivered to isolated communities, where the operation can be conducted with an acceptable level of safety.

91.145 — 91.149 [Reserved]

VISUAL FLIGHT RULES

91.151   FUEL REQUIREMENTS FOR FLIGHT IN VFR CONDITIONS

(a)   No person may begin a flight in an airplane under VFR conditions unless (considering wind and forecast weather conditions) there is enough fuel to fly to the first point of intended landing and, assuming normal cruising speed —
(1)   During the day, to fly after that for at least 30 minutes; or
(2)   At night, to fly after that for at least 45 minutes.
(b)   No person may begin a flight in a rotorcraft under VFR conditions unless (considering wind and forecast weather conditions) there is enough fuel to fly to the first point of intended landing and, assuming normal cruising speed, to fly after that for at least 20 minutes.

91.153   VFR FLIGHT PLAN: INFORMATION REQUIRED

(a)   *Information Required.* Unless otherwise authorized by ATC, each person filing a VFR flight plan shall include in it the following information:
(1)   The aircraft identification number and, if necessary, its radio call sign.
(2)   The type of the aircraft or, in the case of a formation flight, the type of each aircraft and the number of aircraft in the formation.
(3)   The full name and address of the pilot in command or, in the case of a formation flight, the formation commander.
(4)   The point and proposed time of departure.
(5)   The proposed route, cruising altitude (or flight level), and true airspeed at that altitude.
(6)   The point of first intended landing and the estimated elapsed time until over that point.
(7)   The amount of fuel on board (in hours).
(8)   The number of persons in the aircraft, except where that information is otherwise readily available to the FAA.
(9)   Any other information the pilot in command or ATC believes is necessary for ATC purposes.
(b)   *Cancellation.* When a flight plan has been activated, the pilot in command, upon canceling or completing the flight under the flight plan, shall notify an FAA Flight Service Station or ATC facility.

91.155   BASIC VFR WEATHER MINIMUMS

(a)   Except as provided in paragraph (b) of this section and §91.157, no person may operate an aircraft under VFR when the flight visibility is less, or at a distance from clouds that is less, than that prescribed for the corresponding altitude and class of airspace in the following table:

Altitude	Flight visibility	Distance from clouds
Class A	Not applicable	Not Applicable.
Class B	3 statute miles . . .	Clear of Clouds.
Class C	3 statute miles . . .	500 feet below. 1,000 feet above. 2,000 feet horizontal.
Class D	3 statute miles . . .	500 feet below. 1,000 feet above. 2,000 feet horizontal.
Class E: Less than 10,000 feet MSL	3 statute miles . . .	500 feet below. 1,000 feet above. 2,000 feet horizontal.
At or above 10,000 feet MSL	5 statute miles . . .	1,000 feet below. 1,000 feet above. 1 statute mile horizontal.

Altitude	Flight visibility	Distance from clouds
Class G: 1,200 feet or less above the surface (regardless of MSL altitude).		
Day, except as provided in §91.155(b) . . .	1 statute mile	Clear of clouds.
Night, except as provided in §91.155(b) . .	3 statute miles . . .	500 feet below. 1,000 feet above. 2,000 feet horizontal.
More than 1,200 feet above the surface but less than 10,000 feet MSL		
Day	1 statute mile	500 feet below. 1,000 feet above. 2,000 feet horizontal.
Night	3 statute miles . . .	500 feet below. 1,000 feet above. 2,000 feet horizontal.
More than 1,200 feet above the surface and at or above 10,000 feet MSL	5 statute miles . . .	1,000 feet below. 1,000 feet above. 1 statute mile horizontal.

(b)   *Class G Airspace.* Notwithstanding the provisions of paragraph (a) of this section, the following operations may be conducted in Class G airspace below 1,200 feet above the surface:

     (1)   *Helicopter.* A helicopter may be operated clear of clouds if operated at a speed that allows the pilot adequate opportunity to see any air traffic or obstruction in time to avoid a collision.

     (2)   *Airplane.* When the visibility is less than 3 statute miles but not less than 1 statute mile during night hours, an airplane may be operated clear of clouds if operated in an airport traffic pattern within one-half mile of the runway.

(c)   Except as provided in §91.157, no person may operate an aircraft beneath the ceiling under VFR within the lateral boundaries of controlled airspace designated to the surface for an airport when the ceiling is less than 1,000 feet.

(d)   Except as provided in §91.157 of this part, no person may take off or land an aircraft, or enter the traffic pattern of an airport, under VFR, within the lateral boundaries of the surface areas of Class B, Class C, Class D, or Class E airspace designated for an airport —

     (1)   Unless ground visibility at that airport is at least 3 statute miles; or

     (2)   If ground visibility is not reported at that airport, unless flight visibility during landing or takeoff, or while operating in the traffic pattern is at least 3 statute miles.

(e)   For the purpose of this section, an aircraft operating at the base altitude of a Class E airspace area is considered to be within the airspace directly below that area.

91.157   **SPECIAL VFR WEATHER MINIMUMS**

  (a)   Except as provided in appendix D, section 3, of this part, special VFR operations may be conducted under the weather minimums and requirements of this section, instead of those contained in §91.155, below 10,000 feet MSL within the airspace contained by the upward extension of the lateral boundaries of the controlled airspace designated to the surface for an airport.

  (b)   Special VFR operations may only be conducted—
    (1)   With an ATC clearance;
    (2)   Clear of clouds;
    (3)   Except for helicopters, when flight visibility is at least 1 statute mile; and

Ⓐ ➤   (4)   Except for helicopters, between sunrise and sunset (or in Alaska, when the sun is 6° or more below the horizon) unless—
      (i)   The person being granted the ATC clearance meets the applicable requirements for instrument flight under part 61 of this chapter; and
      (ii)   The aircraft is equipped as required in §91.205(d).

  (c)   No person may take off or land an aircraft (other than a helicopter) under special VFR—
    (1)   Unless ground visibility is at least 1 statute mile; or
    (2)   If ground visibility is not reported, unless flight visibility is at least 1 statute mile.

91.159   **VFR CRUISING ALTITUDE OR FLIGHT LEVEL**

Except while holding in a holding pattern of 2 minutes or less, or while turning, each person operating an aircraft under VFR in level cruising flight more than 3,000 feet above the surface shall maintain the appropriate altitude or flight level prescribed below, unless otherwise authorized by ATC:

  (a)   When operating below 18,000 feet MSL and —
    (1)   On a magnetic course of zero degrees through 179 degrees, any odd thousand foot MSL altitude + 500 feet (such as 3,500, 5,500, or 7,500); or
    (2)   On a magnetic course of 180 degrees through 359 degrees, any even thousand foot MSL altitude + 500 feet (such as 4,500, 6,500 or 8,500).

  (b)   When operating above 18,000 feet MSL to flight level 290 (inclusive), and —
    (1)   On a magnetic course of zero degrees through 179 degrees, any odd flight level + 500 feet (such as 195, 215 or 235); or
    (2)   On a magnetic course of 180 degrees through 359 degrees, any even flight level + 500 feet (such as 185, 205, or 225).

  (c)   When operating above flight level 290 and —
    (1)   On a magnetic course of zero degrees through 179 degrees, any flight level, at 4,000-foot intervals, beginning at and including flight level 300 (such as flight level 300, 340, or 380); or
    (2)   On a magnetic course of 180 degrees through 359 degrees, any flight level at 4,000 foot intervals, beginning at and including flight level 320 (such as flight level 320, 360, or 400).

91.161 — 91.165 **[Reserved]**

Ⓐ *Amend #247 eff 12-27-95*

INTENTIONALLY

LEFT

BLANK

INSTRUMENT FLIGHT RULES

91.167   FUEL REQUIREMENTS FOR FLIGHT IN IFR CONDITIONS

(a)   Except as provided in paragraph (b) of this section, no person may operate a civil aircraft in IFR conditions unless it carries enough fuel (considering weather reports and forecasts and weather conditions) to —
(1)   Complete the flight to the first airport of intended landing;
(2)   Fly from that airport to the alternate airport; and
(3)   Fly after that for 45 minutes at normal cruising speed or, for helicopters, fly after that for 30 minutes at normal cruising speed.

(b)   Paragraph (a)(2) of this section does not apply if —
(1)   *Part 97 of this chapter prescribes a standard instrument approach procedure for the first airport of intended landing; and
(2)   For at least 1 hour before and 1 hour after the estimated time of arrival at the airport, the weather reports or forecasts or any combination of them indicate —
(i)   The ceiling will be at least 2,000 feet above the airport elevation; and
(ii)   Visibility will be at least 3 statute miles.

91.169   IFR FLIGHT PLAN: INFORMATION REQUIRED

(a)   *Information required.* Unless otherwise authorized by ATC, each person filing an IFR flight plan shall include in it the following information:
(1)   Information required under §91.153(a).
(2)   An alternate airport, except as provided in paragraph (b) of this section.

(b)   *Exceptions to applicability of paragraph (a)(2) of this section.* Paragraph (a)(2) of this section does not apply if *part 97 of this chapter prescribes a standard instrument approach procedure for the first airport of intended landing and, for at least 1 hour before and 1 hour after the estimated time of arrival, the weather reports or forecasts, or any combination of them, indicate —
(1)   The ceiling will be at least 2,000 feet above the airport elevation; and
(2)   The visibility will be at least 3 statute miles.

(c)   *IFR alternate airport weather minimums.* Unless otherwise authorized by the Administrator, no person may include an alternate airport in an IFR flight plan unless current weather forecasts indicate that, at the estimated time of arrival at the alternate airport, the ceiling and visibility at that airport will be at or above the following alternate airport weather minimums:
(1)   If an instrument approach procedure has been published in *part 97 of this chapter for that airport, the alternate airport minimums specified in that procedure or, if none are so specified, the following minimums:
(i)   Precision approach procedure: Ceiling 600 feet and visibility 2 statute miles.
(ii)   Nonprecision approach procedure: Ceiling 800 feet and visibility 2 statute miles.
(2)   If no instrument approach procedure has been published in *part 97 of this chapter for that airport, the ceiling and visibility minimums are those allowing descent from the MEA, approach, and landing under basic VFR.

(d)   *Cancellation.* When a flight plan has been activated, the pilot in command, upon canceling or completing the flight under the flight plan, shall notify an FAA Flight Service Station or ATC facility.

91.171   VOR EQUIPMENT CHECK FOR IFR OPERATIONS

(a)   No person may operate a civil aircraft under IFR using the VOR system of radio navigation unless the VOR equipment of that aircraft —
(1)   Is maintained, checked, and inspected under an approved procedure; or
(2)   Has been operationally checked within the preceding 30 days, and was found to be within the limits of the permissible indicated bearing error set forth in paragraph (b) or (c) of this section.

*(Not published herein — Ed.)

(b)   Except as provided in paragraph (c) of this section, each person conducting a VOR check under paragraph (a)(2) of this section shall —
    (1)   Use, at the airport of intended departure, an FAA-operated or approved test signal or a test signal radiated by a certificated and appropriately rated radio repair station or, outside the United States, a test signal operated or approved by an appropriate authority to check the VOR equipment (the maximum permissible indicated bearing error is plus or minus 4 degrees); or
    (2)   Use, at the airport of intended departure, a point on the airport surface designated as a VOR system checkpoint by the Administrator, or, outside the United States, by an appropriate authority (the maximum permissible bearing error is plus or minus 4 degrees);
    (3)   If neither a test signal nor a designated checkpoint on the surface is available, use an airborne checkpoint designated by the Administrator or, outside the United States, by an appropriate authority (the maximum permissible bearing error is plus or minus 6 degrees); or
    (4)   If no check signal or point is available, while in flight —
        (i)   Select a VOR radial that lies along the centerline of an established VOR airway;
        (ii)   Select a prominent ground point along the selected radial preferably more than 20 nautical miles from the VOR ground facility and maneuver the aircraft directly over the point at a reasonably low altitude; and
        (iii) Note the VOR bearing indicated by the receiver when over the ground point (the maximum permissible variation between the published radial and the indicated bearing is 6 degrees).

(c)   If dual system VOR (units independent of each other except for the antenna) is installed in the aircraft, the person checking the equipment may check one system against the other in place of the check procedures specified in paragraph (b) of this section. Both systems shall be tuned to the same VOR ground facility and note the indicated bearings to that station. The maximum permissible variation between the two indicated bearings is 4 degrees.

(d)   Each person making the VOR operational check, as specified in paragraph (b) or (c) of this section, shall enter the date, place, bearing error, and sign the aircraft log or other record. In addition, if a test signal radiated by a repair station, as specified in paragraph (b)(1) of this section, is used, an entry must be made in the aircraft log or other record by the repair station certificate holder or the certificate holder's representative certifying to the bearing transmitted by the repair station for the check and the date of transmission.

(Approved by the Office of Management and Budget under OMB control number 2120-0005)

91.173   ATC CLEARANCE AND FLIGHT PLAN REQUIRED

No person may operate an aircraft in controlled airspace under IFR unless that person has —
(a)   Filed an IFR flight plan; and
(b)   Received an appropriate ATC clearance.

91.175   TAKEOFF AND LANDING UNDER IFR

(a)   *Instrument approaches to civil airports.* Unless otherwise authorized by the Administrator, when an instrument letdown to a civil airport is necessary, each person operating an aircraft, except a military aircraft of the United States, shall use a standard instrument approach procedure prescribed for the airport in *part 97 of this chapter.

---

*(Not published herein — Ed.)

(b) *Authorized DH or MDA.* For the purpose of this section, when the approach procedure being used provides for and requires the use of a DH or MDA, the authorized DH or MDA is the highest of the following:
  (1) The DH or MDA prescribed by the approach procedure.
  (2) The DH or MDA prescribed for the pilot in command.
  (3) The DH or MDA for which the aircraft is equipped.
(c) *Operation below DH or MDA.* Where a DH or MDA is applicable, no pilot may operate an aircraft, except a military aircraft of the United States, at any airport below the authorized MDA or continue an approach below the authorized DH unless —
  (1) The aircraft is continuously in a position from which a descent to a landing on the intended runway can be made at a normal rate of descent using normal maneuvers, and for operations conducted under part 121 or part 135 unless that descent rate will allow touchdown to occur within the touchdown zone of the runway of intended landing.
  (2) The flight visibility is not less than the visibility prescribed in the standard instrument approach procedure being used; and
  (3) Except for a Category II or Category III approach where any necessary visual reference requirements are specified by the Administrator, at least one of the following visual references for the intended runway is distinctly visible and identifiable to the pilot:
    (i) The approach light system, except that the pilot may not descend below 100 feet above the touchdown zone elevation using the approach lights as a reference unless the red terminating bars or the red side row bars are also distinctly visible and identifiable.
    (ii) The threshold.
    (iii) The threshold markings.
    (iv) The threshold lights.
    (v) The runway end identifier lights.
    (vi) The visual approach slope indicator.
    (vii) The touchdown zone or touchdown zone markings.
    (viii) The touchdown zone lights.
    (ix) The runway or runway markings.
    (x) The runway lights.
(d) *Landing.* No pilot operating an aircraft, except a military aircraft of the United States, may land that aircraft when the flight visibility is less than the visibility prescribed in the standard instrument approach procedure being used.
(e) *Missed approach procedures.* Each pilot operating an aircraft, except a military aircraft of the United States, shall immediately execute an appropriate missed approach procedure when either of the following conditions exist:
  (1) Whenever the requirements of paragraph (c) of this section are not met at either of the following times:
    (i) When the aircraft is being operated below MDA; or
    (ii) Upon arrival at the missed approach point, including a DH where a DH is specified and its use is required, and at any time after that until touchdown.
  (2) Whenever an identifiable part of the airport is not distinctly visible to the pilot during a circling maneuver at or above MDA, unless the inability to see an identifiable part of the airport results only from a normal bank of the aircraft during the circling approach.
(f) *Civil airport takeoff minimums.* Unless otherwise authorized by the Administrator, no pilot operating an aircraft under parts 121, 125, *127, 129, or 135 of this chapter may take off from a civil airport under IFR unless weather conditions are at or above the weather minimums for IFR takeoff prescribed for that airport under *part 97 of this chapter. If takeoff minimums are not prescribed under *part 97 of this chapter for a particular airport, the following minimums apply to takeoffs under IFR for aircraft operating under those parts:
  (1) For aircraft, other than helicopters, having two engines or less — 1 statute mile visibility.
  (2) For aircraft having more than two engines — 1/2 statute mile visibility.
  (3) For helicopters — 1/2 statute mile visibility.

*(Not published herein)

(g) *Military airports.* Unless otherwise prescribed by the Administrator, each person operating a civil aircraft under IFR into or out of a military airport shall comply with the instrument approach procedures and the takeoff and landing minimum prescribed by the military authority having jurisdiction of that airport.

(h) *Comparable values of RVR and ground visibility.*

(1) Except for Category II or Category III minimums, if RVR minimums for takeoff or landing are prescribed in an instrument approach procedure, but RVR is not reported for the runway of intended operation, the RVR minimum shall be converted to ground visibility in accordance with the table in paragraph (h)(2) of this section and shall be the visibility minimum for takeoff or landing on that runway.

(2) RVR Table:

RVR (feet)	Visibility (statute miles)
1,600	1/4
2,400	1/2
3,200	5/8
4,000	3/4
4,500	7/8
5,000	1
6,000	1 1/4

(i) *Operations on unpublished routes and use of radar in instrument approach procedures.* When radar is approved at certain locations for ATC purposes, it may be used not only for surveillance and precision radar approaches, as applicable, but also may be used in conjunction with instrument approach procedures predicated on other types of radio navigational aids. Radar vectors may be authorized to provide course guidance through the segments of an approach to the final course or fix. When operating on an unpublished route or while being radar vectored, the pilot, when an approach clearance is received, shall, in addition to complying with §91.177, maintain the last altitude assigned to that pilot until the aircraft is established on a segment of a published route or instrument approach procedure unless a different altitude is assigned by ATC. After the aircraft is so established, published altitudes apply to descent within each succeeding route or approach segment unless a different altitude is assigned by ATC. Upon reaching the final approach course or fix, the pilot may either complete the instrument approach in accordance with a procedure approved for the facility or continue a surveillance or precision radar approach to a landing.

(j) *Limitation on procedure turns.* In the case of a radar vector to a final approach course or fix, a timed approach from a holding fix, or an approach for which the procedure specifies "No PT," no pilot may make a procedure turn unless cleared to do so by ATC.

(k) *ILS components.* The basic ground components of an ILS are the localizer, glide slope, outer marker, middle marker, and, when installed for use with Category II or Category III instrument approach procedures, an inner marker. A compass locator or precision radar may be substituted for the outer or middle marker. DME, VOR, or nondirectional beacon fixes authorized in the standard instrument approach procedure or surveillance radar may be substituted for the outer marker. Applicability of, and substitution for, the inner marker for Category II or III approaches is determined by the appropriate *part 97 approach procedure, letter of authorization, or operations specification pertinent to the operation.

*(Not published herein)

91.177   MINIMUM ALTITUDES FOR IFR OPERATIONS

(a)   *Operation of aircraft at minimum altitudes.* Except when necessary for takeoff or landing, no person may operate an aircraft under IFR below —
   (1)   The applicable minimum altitudes prescribed in *parts 95 and 97 of this chapter; or
   (2)   If no applicable minimum altitude is prescribed in those parts —
      (i)   In the case of operations over an area designated as a mountainous area in *part 95, an altitude of 2,000 feet above the highest obstacle within a horizontal distance of 4 nautical miles from the course to be flown; or
      (ii)   In any other case, an altitude of 1,000 feet above the highest obstacle within a horizontal distance of 4 nautical miles from the course to be flown.
   However, if both a MEA and a MOCA are prescribed for a particular route or route segment, a person may operate an aircraft below the MEA down to, but not below, the MOCA, when within 22 nautical miles of the VOR concerned (based on the pilot's reasonable estimate of that distance).

(b)   *Climb.* Climb to a higher minimum IFR altitude shall begin immediately after passing the point beyond which that minimum altitude applies, except that when ground obstructions intervene, the point beyond which that higher minimum altitude applies shall be crossed at or above the applicable MCA.

91.179   IFR CRUISING ALTITUDE OR FLIGHT LEVEL

(a)   *In controlled airspace.* Each person operating an aircraft under IFR in level cruising flight in controlled airspace shall maintain the altitude or flight level assigned that aircraft by ATC. However, if the ATC clearance assigns "VFR conditions on-top," that person shall maintain an altitude or flight level as prescribed by §91.159.

(b)   *In uncontrolled airspace.* Except while holding in a holding pattern of 2 minutes or less or while turning, each person operating an aircraft under IFR in level cruising flight in uncontrolled airspace shall maintain an appropriate altitude as follows:
   (1)   When operating below 18,000 feet MSL and —
      (i)   On a magnetic course of zero degrees through 179 degrees, any odd thousand foot MSL altitude (such as 3,000, 5,000, or 7,000); or
      (ii)   On a magnetic course of 180 degrees through 359 degrees, any even thousand foot MSL altitude (such as 2,000, 4,000, or 6,000).
   (2)   When operating at or above 18,000 feet MSL but below flight level 290, and —
      (i)   On a magnetic course of zero degrees through 179 degrees, any odd flight level (such as 190, 210, or 230); or
      (ii)   On a magnetic course of 180 degrees through 359 degrees, any even flight level (such as 180, 200, or 220).
   (3)   When operating at flight level 290 and above, and —
      (i)   On a magnetic course of zero degrees through 179 degrees, any flight level, at 4,000-foot intervals, beginning at and including flight level 290 (such as flight level 290, 330, or 370); or
      (ii)   On a magnetic course of 180 degrees through 359 degrees, any flight level, at 4,000-foot intervals, beginning at and including flight level 310 (such as flight level 310, 350, or 390).

91.181   COURSE TO BE FLOWN

Unless otherwise authorized by ATC, no person may operate an aircraft within controlled airspace under IFR except as follows:
(a)   On a Federal airway, along the centerline of that airway.
(b)   On any other route, along the direct course between the navigational aids or fixes defining that route.
However, this section does not prohibit maneuvering the aircraft to pass well clear of other air traffic or the maneuvering of the aircraft in VFR conditions to clear the intended flight path both before and during climb or descent.

*(Not published herein — Ed.)

91.183   IFR RADIO COMMUNICATIONS

The pilot in command of each aircraft operated under IFR in controlled airspace shall have a continuous watch maintained on the appropriate frequency and shall report by radio as soon as possible —

(a) The time and altitude of passing each designated reporting point, or the reporting points specified by ATC, except that while the aircraft is under radar control, only the passing of those reporting points specifically requested by ATC need be reported;

(b) Any unforecast weather conditions encountered; and

(c) Any other information relating to the safety of flight.

91.185   IFR OPERATIONS: TWO-WAY RADIO COMMUNICATIONS FAILURE

(a) *General.* Unless otherwise authorized by ATC, each pilot who has two-way radio communications failure when operating under IFR shall comply with the rules of this section.

(b) *VFR conditions.* If the failure occurs in VFR conditions, or if VFR conditions are encountered after the failure, each pilot shall continue the flight under VFR and land as soon as practicable.

(c) *IFR conditions.* If the failure occurs in IFR conditions, or if paragraph (b) of this section cannot be complied with, each pilot shall continue the flight according to the following:

(1) *Route.*

  (i) By the route assigned in the last ATC clearance received;

  (ii) If being radar vectored, by the direct route from the point of radio failure to the fix, route, or airway specified in the vector clearance;

  (iii) In the absence of an assigned route, by the route that ATC has advised may be expected in a further clearance, or

  (iv) In the absence of an assigned route or a route that ATC has advised may be expected in a further clearance, by the route filed in the flight plan.

(2) *Altitude.*

At the highest of the following altitudes or flight levels for the route segment being flown:

  (i) The altitude or flight level assigned in the last ATC clearance received;

  (ii) The minimum altitude (converted, if appropriate, to minimum flight level as prescribed in §91.121(c)) for IFR operations; or

  (iii) The altitude or flight level ATC has advised may be expected in a further clearance.

(3) *Leave clearance limit.*

  (i) When the clearance limit is a fix from which an approach begins, commence descent or descent and approach as close as possible to the expect-further-clearance time if one has been received, or if one has not been received, as close as possible to the estimated time of arrival as calculated from the filed or amended (with ATC) estimated time en route.

  (ii) If the clearance limit is not a fix from which an approach begins, leave the clearance limit at the expect-further-clearance time if one has been received, or if none has been received, upon arrival over the clearance limit, and proceed to a fix from which an approach begins and commence descent or descent and approach as close as possible to the estimated time of arrival as calculated from the filed or amended (with ATC) estimated time en route.

91.187   OPERATION UNDER IFR IN CONTROLLED AIRSPACE: MALFUNCTION REPORTS

(a)   The pilot in command of each aircraft operated in controlled airspace under IFR shall report as soon as practical to ATC any malfunctions of navigational, approach, or communication equipment occurring in flight;

(b)   In each report required by paragraph (a) of this section, the pilot in command shall include the —
   (1)   Aircraft identification;
   (2)   Equipment affected;
   (3)   Degree to which the capability of the pilot to operate under IFR in the ATC system is impaired; and
   (4)   Nature and extent of assistance desired from ATC.

91.189   CATEGORY II AND III OPERATIONS: GENERAL OPERATING RULES

(a)   No person may operate a civil aircraft in a Category II or Category III operation unless:
   (1)   The flight crew of the aircraft consists of a pilot in command and a second in command who hold the appropriate authorizations and ratings prescribed in §61.3 of this chapter;
   (2)   Each flight crewmember has adequate knowledge of, and familiarity with, the aircraft and the procedures to be used; and
   (3)   The instrument panel in front of the pilot who is controlling the aircraft has appropriate instrumentation for the type of flight control guidance system that is being used.

(b)   Unless otherwise authorized by the Administrator, no person may operate a civil aircraft in a Category II or Category III operation unless each ground component required for that operation and the related airborne equipment is installed and operating.

(c)   *Authroized DH.* For the purpose of this section, when the approach procedure being used provides for and requires the use of a DH, the authorized DH is the highest of the following:
   (1)   The DH prescribed by the approach procedure.
   (2)   The DH prescribed for the pilot in command.
   (3)   The DH for which the aircraft is equipped.

(d)   Unless otherwise authorized by the Administrator, no pilot operating an aircraft in a Category II or Category III approach that provides and requires use of a DH may continue the approach below the authorized decision height unless the following conditions are met:
   (1)   The aircraft is in a position from which a descent to a landing on the intended runway can be made at a normal rate of descent using normal maneuvers, and where that descent rate will allow touchdown to occur within the touchdown zone of the runway of intended landing.
   (2)   At least one of the following visual references for the intended runway is distinctly visible and identifiable to the pilot:
      (i)   The approach light system, except that the pilot may not descend below 100 feet above the touchdown zone elevation using the approach lights as a reference unless the red terminating bars or the red side row bars are also distinctly visible and identifiable.
      (ii)   The threshold.
      (iii)   The threshold markings.
      (iv)   The threshold lights.
      (v)   The touchdown zone or touchdown zone markings.
      (vi)   The touchdown zone lights.

(e)   Unless otherwise authorized by the Administrator, each pilot operating an aircraft shall immediately execute an appropriate missed approach whenever prior to touchdown, the requirements of paragraph (d) of this section are not met.

(f)   No person operating an aircraft using a Category III approach without decision height may land that aircraft except in accordance with the provisions of the letter of authorization issued by the Administrator.

(g)   Paragraphs (a) through (f) of this section do not apply to operations conducted by the holders of certificates issued under parts 121, 125, 129, or 135 of this chapter. No person may operate a civil aircraft in a Category II or Category III operation conducted by the holder of a certificate issued under parts 121, 125, 129, or 135 of this chapter unless the operation is conducted in accordance with that certificate holder's operations specifications.

91.191   CATEGORY II AND CAATEGORY III MANUAL

(a)   Except as provided in paragraph (c) of this section, after August 4, 1997, no person may operate a U.S.-registered civil aircraft in a Category II or a Category III operation unless —

   (1)   There is available in the aircraft a current, approved Category II or Category III manual, as appropriate, for that aircraft;

   (2)   The operation is conducted in accordance with the procedures, instructions, and limitations in the appropriate manual; and

   (3)   The instruments and equipment listed in the manual that are required for a particular Category II or Category III operation have been inspected and maintained in accordance with the maintenance program contained in the manual.

(b)   Each operator must keep a current copy of each approved manual at its principal base of operations and must make each manual available for inspection upon request by the Administrator.

(c)   This section does not apply to operations conducted by the holder of a certificate issued under part 121 or part 135 of this chapter.

(Approved by the Office of Management and Budget under OMB control number 2120-0005)

91.193   CERTIFICATE OF AUTHORIZATION FOR CERTAIN CATEGORY II OPERATIONS

The Administrator may issue a certificate of authorization authorizing deviations from the requirements of §§91.189, 91.191, and 91.205(f) for the operation of small aircraft identified as Category A aircraft in *§97.3 of this chapter in Category II operations if the Administrator finds that the proposed operation can be safely conducted under the terms of the certificate. Such authorization does no permit operation of the aircraft carrying persons or property for compensation or hire.

91.195 — 91.199 [Reserved]

Ⓐ *Amend #251 eff 8-1-96*

SUBPART C — EQUIPMENT, INSTRUMENT, AND CERTIFICATE REQUIREMENTS

91.201　**[Reserved]**

91.203　**CIVIL AIRCRAFT: CERTIFICATIONS REQUIRED**

(a)　Except as provided in §91.715, no person may operate a civil aircraft unless it has within it the following:

(1)　An appropriate and current airworthiness certificate. Each U.S. airworthiness certificate used to comply with this subparagraph (except a special flight permit, a copy of the applicable operations specifications issued under §21.197(c) of this chapter, appropriate sections of the air carrier manual required by Parts 121 and 135 of this chapter containing that portion of the operations specifications issued under §21.197(c), or an authorization under §91.611), must have on it the registration number assigned to the aircraft under Part 47 of this chapter. However, the airworthiness certificate need not have on it an assigned special identification number before 10 days after that number is first affixed to the aircraft. A revised airworthiness certificate having on it an assigned special identification number, that has been affixed to an aircraft, may only be obtained upon application to an FAA Flight Standards district office.

(2)　An effective U.S. registration certificate issued to its owner or, for operation within the United States, the second duplicate copy (pink) of the Aircraft Registration Application as provided for in §47.31(b), or a registration certificate issued under the laws of a foreign country.

(b)　No person may operate a civil aircraft unless the airworthiness certificate required by paragraph (a) of this section or a special flight authorization issued under §91.715 is displayed at the cabin or cockpit entrance so that it is legible to passengers or crew.

(c)　No person may operate an aircraft with a fuel tank installed within the passenger compartment or a baggage compartment unless the installation was accomplished pursuant to Part 43 of this chapter, and a copy of FAA Form 337 authorizing that installation is on board the aircraft.

(d)　No person may operate a civil airplane (domestic or foreign) into or out of an airport in the United States unless it complies with the fuel venting and exhaust emissions requirements of Part 34 of this chapter.

91.205　**POWERED CIVIL AIRCRAFT WITH STANDARD CATEGORY U.S. AIRWORTHINESS CERTIFICATES: INSTRUMENT AND EQUIPMENT REQUIREMENTS**

(a)　*General.* Except as provided in paragraphs (c)(3) and (e) of this section, no person may operate a powered civil aircraft with a standard category U.S. airworthiness certificate in any operation described in paragraphs (b) through (f) of this section unless that aircraft contains the instruments and equipment specified in those paragraphs (or FAA-approved equivalents) for that type of operation, and those instruments and items of equipment are in operable condition.

(b)　*Visual flight rules (day).* For VFR flight during the day, the following instruments and equipment are required:

(1)　Airspeed indicator.
(2)　Altimeter.
(3)　Magnetic direction indicator.
(4)　Tachometer for each engine.
(5)　Oil pressure gauge for each engine using pressure system.
(6)　Temperature gauge for each liquid-cooled engine.
(7)　Oil temperature gauge for each air-cooled engine.
(8)　Manifold pressure gauge for each altitude engine.
(9)　Fuel gauge indicating the quantity of fuel in each tank.

(10) Landing gear position indicator, if the aircraft has a retractable landing gear.

(11) For small civil airplanes certificated after March 11, 1996, in accordance with Part 23 of this chapter, an approved aviation red or aviation white anticollision light system. In the event of failure of any light of the anticollision light system, operation of the aircraft may continue to a location where repairs or replacement can be made.

(12) If the aircraft is operated for hire over water and beyond power-off gliding distance from shore, approved flotation gear readily available to each occupant, and at least one pyrotechnic signaling device. As used in this section, "shore" means that area of the land adjacent to the water which is above the high water mark and excludes land areas which are intermittently under water.

(13) An approved safety belt with an approved metal-to-metal latching device for each occupant 2 years of age or older.

(14) For small civil airplanes manufactured after July 18, 1978, an approved shoulder harness for each front seat. The shoulder harness must be designed to protect the occupant from serious head injury when the occupant experiences the ultimate inertia forces specified in §23.561(b)(2) of this chapter. Each shoulder harness installed at a flight crewmember station must permit the crewmember, when seated and with the safety belt and shoulder harness fastened, to perform all functions necessary for flight operations. For purposes of this paragraph —

(i) The date of manufacture of an airplane is the date the inspection acceptance records reflect that the airplane is complete and meets the FAA-approved type design data; and

(ii) A front seat is a seat located at a flight crewmember station or any seat located alongside such a seat.

(15) An emergency locator transmitter, if required by §91.207.

(16) For normal, utility, and acrobatic category airplanes with a seating configuration, excluding pilot seats, of 9 or less, manufactured after December 12, 1986, a shoulder harness for —

(i) Each front seat that meets the requirements of §23.785(g) and (h) of this chapter in effect on December 12, 1985;

(ii) Each additional seat that meets the requirements of §23.785(g) of this chapter in effect on December 12, 1985.

(17) For rotorcraft manufactured after September 16, 1992, a shoulder harness for each seat that meets the requirements of §27.2 or §29.2 of this chapter in effect on September 16, 1991.

(c) *Visual flight rules (night).* For VFR flight at night, the following instruments and equipment are required:

(1) Instruments and equipment specified in paragraph (b) of this section.

(2) Approved position lights.

(3) An approved aviation red or aviation white anticollision light system on all U.S.-registered civil aircraft. Anticollision light systems initially installed after August 11, 1971, on aircraft for which a type certificate was issued or applied for before August 11, 1971, must at least meet the anticollision light standards of Part 23, 25, 27, or 29, as applicable, that were in effect on August 10, 1971, except that the color may be either aviation red or aviation white. In the event of failure of any light of the anti-collision light system, operations with the aircraft may be continued to a stop where repairs or replacement can be made.

(4) If the aircraft is operated for hire, one electric landing light.

(5) An adequate source of electrical energy for all installed electrical and radio equipment.

(6) One spare set of fuses, or three spare fuses of each kind required, that are accessible to the pilot in flight.

(d) *Instrument flight rules.* For IFR flight, the following instruments and equipment are required:

(1) Instruments and equipment specified in paragraph (b) of this section, and, for night flight, instruments and equipment specified in paragraph (c) of this section.

(2) Two-way radio communications system and navigational equipment appropriate to the ground facilities to be used.

Ⓐ *Amend #248 eff 3-11-96*

(3)   Gyroscopic rate-of-turn indicator, except on the following aircraft:
 (i)   Airplanes with a third attitude instrument system usable through flight attitudes of 360 degrees of pitch and roll and installed in accordance with the instrument requirements prescribed in §121.305(j) of this chapter; and
 (ii) Rotorcraft with a third attitude instrument system usable through flight attitudes of ±80 degrees of pitch and ±120 degrees of roll and installed in accordance with §29.1303(g) of this chapter.
(4)   Slip-skid indicator.
(5)   Sensitive altimeter adjustable for barometric pressure.
(6)   A clock displaying hours, minutes, and seconds with a sweep-second pointer or digital presentation.
(7)   Generator or alternator of adequate capacity.
(8)   Gyroscopic pitch and bank indicator (artificial horizon).
(9)   Gyroscopic direction indicator (directional gyro or equivalent.)

(e) *Flight at and above 24,000 feet MSL (FL 240).* If VOR navigational equipment is required under paragraph (d)(2) of this section, no person may operate a U.S.-registered civil aircraft within the 50 states and the District of Columbia at or above FL 240 unless that aircraft is equipped with approved distance measuring equipment (DME). When DME required by this paragraph fails at and above FL 240, the pilot in command of the aircraft shall notify ATC immediately, and then may continue operations at and above FL 240 to the next airport of intended landing at which repairs or replacement of the equipment can be made.

(f) *Category II operations.* The requirements for Category II operations are the instruments and equipment specified in—
(1)   Paragraph (d) of this section; and
(2)   Appendix A to this part.

(g) *Category III operations.* The instruments and equipment required for Category III operations are specified in paragraph (d) of this section.

(h) *Exclusions.* Paragraphs (f) and (g) of this section do not apply to operations conducted by a holder of a certificate issued under part 121 or part 135 of this chapter.

91.207   EMERGENCY LOCATOR TRANSMITTERS

(a) Except as provided in paragraphs (e) and (f) of this section, no person may operate a U.S.-registered civil airplane unless —
(1)   There is attached to the airplane an approved automatic type emergency locator transmitter that is in operable condition for the following operations, except that after June 21, 1995, an emergency locator transmitter that meets the requirements of TSO-C91 may not be used for new installations.
 (i)   Those operations governed by the supplemental air carrier and commercial operator rules of Parts 121 and 125;
 (ii) Charter flights governed by the domestic and flag air carrier rules of Part 121 of this chapter; and
 (iii) Operations governed by Part 135 of this chapter; or
(2)   For operations other than those specified in paragraph (a)(1) of this section, there must be attached to the airplane an approved personal type or an approved automatic type emergency locator transmitter that is in operable condition, except that after June 21, 1995, an emergency locator transmitter that meets the requirements of TSO-C91 may not be used for new installations.

(b) Each emergency locator transmitter required by paragraph (a) of this section must be attached to the airplane in such a manner that the probability of damage to the transmitter in the event of crash impact is minimized. Fixed and deployable automatic type transmitters must be attached to the airplane as far aft as practicable.

(c) Batteries used in the emergency locator transmitters required by paragraphs (a) and (b) of this section must be replaced (or recharged, if the battery is rechargeable) —
(1)   When the transmitter has been in use for more than 1 cumulative hour; or
(2)   When 50 percent of their useful life (or, for rechargeable batteries, 50 percent of their useful life of charge) has expired, as established by the transmitter manufacturer under its approval.
The new expiration date for replacing (or recharging) the battery must be legibly marked on the outside of the transmitter and entered in the aircraft maintenance record. Paragraph (c)(2) of this section does not apply to batteries (such as water-activated batteries) that are essentially unaffected during probable storage intervals.

Ⓐ *Amend #251 eff 8-1-96*

(d)   Each emergency locator transmitter required by paragraph (a) of this section must be inspected within 12 calendar months after the last inspection for —
    (1)   Proper installation;
    (2)   Battery corrosion;
    (3)   Operation of the controls and crash sensor; and
    (4)   The presence of a sufficient signal radiated from its antenna.

(e)   Notwithstanding paragraph (a) of this section, a person may —
    (1)   Ferry a newly acquired airplane from the place where possession of it was taken to a place where the emergency locator transmitter is to be installed; and
    (2)   Ferry an airplane with an inoperative emergency locator transmitter from a place where repairs or replacements cannot be made to a place where they can be made.

No person other than required crewmembers may be carried aboard an airplane being ferried under paragraph (e) of this section.

(f)   Paragraph (a) of this section does not apply to —
    (1)   Turbojet-powered aircraft;
    (2)   Aircraft while engaged in scheduled flights by scheduled air carriers;
    (3)   Aircraft while engaged in training operations conducted entirely within a 50-nautical mile radius of the airport from which such local flight operations began;
    (4)   Aircraft while engaged in flight operations incident to design and testing;
    (5)   New aircraft while engaged in flight operations incident to their manufacture, preparation, and delivery;
    (6)   Aircraft while engaged in flight operations incident to the aerial application of chemicals and other substances for agricultural purposes;
    (7)   Aircraft certificated by the Administrator for research and development purposes;
    (8)   Aircraft while used for showing compliance with regulations, crew training, exhibition, air racing, or market surveys;
    (9)   Aircraft equipped to carry not more than one person; and
    (10) An aircraft during any period for which the transmitter has been temporarily removed for inspection, repair, modification, or replacement, subject to the following:
       (i)   No person may operate the aircraft unless the aircraft records contain an entry which includes the date of initial removal, the make, model, serial number, and reason for removing the transmitter, and a placard located in view of the pilot to show "ELT not installed."
       (ii) No person may operate the aircraft more than 90 days after the ELT is initially removed from the aircraft.

91.209   AIRCRAFT LIGHTS

No person may:
(a)   During the period from sunset to sunrise (or, in Alaska, during the period a prominent unlighted object cannot be seen from a distance of 3 statute miles or the sun is more than 6 degrees below the horizon) —
    (1)   Operate an aircraft unless it has lighted position lights;
    (2)   Park or move an aircraft in, or in dangerous proximity to, a night flight operations area of an airport unless the aircraft —
       (i)   Is clearly illuminated;
       (ii) Has lighted position lights; or
       (iii) Is in an area that is marked by obstruction lights.
    (3)   Anchor an aircraft unless the aircraft —
       (i)   Has lighted anchor lights; or
       (ii) Is in an area where anchor lights are not required on vessels; or
(b)   Operate an aircraft that is equipped with an anticollision light system, unless it has lighted anticollision lights. However, the anticollision lights need not be lighted when the pilot in command determines that, because of operating conditions, it would be in the interest of safety to turn the lights off.

91.211   SUPPLEMENTAL OXYGEN

(a)   *General.* No person may operate a civil aircraft of U.S. registry —
  (1)   At cabin pressure altitudes above 12,500 feet (MSL) up to and including 14,000 feet (MSL) unless the required minimum flight crew is provided with and uses supplemental oxygen for that part of the flight at those altitudes that is of more than 30 minutes duration;
  (2)   At cabin pressure altitudes above 14,000 feet (MSL) unless the required minimum flight crew is provided with and uses supplemental oxygen during the entire flight time at those altitudes; and
  (3)   At cabin pressure altitudes above 15,000 feet (MSL) unless each occupant of the aircraft is provided with supplemental oxygen.

(b)   *Pressurized cabin aircraft.*
  (1)   No person may operate a civil aircraft of U.S. registry with a pressurized cabin —
    (i)   At flight altitudes above flight level 250 unless at least a 10- minute supply of supplemental oxygen, in addition to any oxygen required to satisfy paragraph (a) of this section, is available for each occupant of the aircraft for use in the event that a descent is necessitated by loss of cabin pressurization; and
    (ii)   At flight altitudes above flight level 350 unless one pilot at the controls of the airplane is wearing and using an oxygen mask that is secured and sealed and that either supplies oxygen at all times or automatically supplies oxygen whenever the cabin pressure altitude of the airplane exceeds 14,000 feet (MSL), except that the one pilot need not wear and use an oxygen mask while at or below flight level 410 if there are two pilots at the controls and each pilot has a quick-donning type of oxygen mask that can be placed on the face with one hand from the ready position within 5 seconds, supplying oxygen and properly secured and sealed.
  (2)   Notwithstanding paragraph (b)(1)(ii) of this section, if for any reason at any time it is necessary for one pilot to leave the controls of the aircraft when operating at flight altitudes above flight level 350, the remaining pilot at the controls shall put on and use an oxygen mask until the other pilot has returned to that crewmember's station.

91.213   INOPERATIVE INSTRUMENTS AND EQUIPMENT

(a)   Except as provided in paragraph (d) of this section, no person may take off an aircraft with inoperative instruments or equipment installed unless the following conditions are met:
  (1)   An approved Minimum Equipment List exists for that aircraft.
  (2)   The aircraft has within it a letter of authorization, issued by the FAA Flight Standards district office having jurisdiction over the area in which the operator is located, authorizing operation of the aircraft under the Minimum Equipment List. The letter of authorization may be obtained by written request of the airworthiness certificate holder. The Minimum Equipment List and the letter of authorization constitute a supplemental type certificate for the aircraft.
  (3)   The approved Minimum Equipment List must —
    (i)   Be prepared in accordance with the limitations specified in paragraph (b) of this section; and
    (ii)   Provide for the operation of the aircraft with the instruments and equipment in an inoperable condition.
  (4)   The aircraft records available to the pilot must include an entry describing the inoperable instruments and equipment.
  (5)   The aircraft is operated under all applicable conditions and limitations contained in the Minimum Equipment List and the letter authorizing the use of the list.

(b)   The following instruments and equipment may not be included in a Minimum Equipment List:

    (1)   Instruments and equipment that are either specifically or otherwise required by the airworthiness requirements under which the aircraft is type certificated and which are essential for safe operations under all operating conditions.

    (2)   Instruments and equipment required by an airworthiness directive to be in operable condition unless the airworthiness directive provides otherwise.

    (3)   Instruments and equipment required for specific operations by this part.

(c)   A person authorized to use an approved Minimum Equipment List issued for a specific aircraft under part 121, 125, or 135 of this chapter shall use that Minimum Equipment List in connection with operations conducted with that aircraft under this part without additional approval requirements.

(d)   Except for operations conducted in accordance with paragraphs (a) or (c) of this section, a person may takeoff an aircraft in operations conducted under this part with inoperative instruments and equipment without an approved Minimum Equipment List provided —

    (1)   The flight operation is conducted in a —

        (i)   Rotorcraft, nonturbine-powered airplane, glider, or lighter-than- air aircraft for which a master Minimum Equipment List has not been developed; or

        (ii)   Small rotorcraft, nonturbine-powered small airplane, glider, or lighter-than-air aircraft for which a Master Minimum Equipment List has been developed; and

    (2)   The inoperative instruments and equipment are not —

        (i)   Part of the VFR-day type certification instruments and equipment prescribed in the applicable airworthiness regulations under which the aircraft was type certificated;

        (ii)   Indicated as required on the aircraft's equipment list, or on the Kinds of Operations Equipment List for the kind of flight operation being conducted;

        (iii)   Required by §91.205 or any other rule of this part for the specific kind of flight operation being conducted; or

        (iv)   Required to be operational by an airworthiness directive; and

    (3)   The inoperative instruments and equipment are —

        (i)   Removed from the aircraft, the cockpit control placarded, and the maintenance recorded in accordance with *§43.9 of this chapter; or

        (ii)   Deactivated and placarded "Inoperative." If deactivation of the inoperative instrument or equipment involves maintenance, it must be accomplished and recorded in accordance with *part 43 of this chapter; and

    (4)   A determination is made by a pilot, who is certificated and appropriately rated under part 61 of this chapter, or by a person, who is certificated and appropriately rated to perform maintenance on the aircraft, that the inoperative instrument or equipment does not constitute a hazard to the aircraft.

    An aircraft with inoperative instruments or equipment as provided in paragraph (d) of this section is considered to be in a properly altered condition acceptable to the Administrator.

(e)   Notwithstanding any other provision of this section, an aircraft with inoperable instruments or equipment may be operated under a special flight permit issued in accordance with *§§21.197 and *21.199 of this chapter.

*(Not published herein — Ed.)

91.215   **ATC TRANSPONDER AND ALTITUDE REPORTING EQUIPMENT AND USE**

(a)   *All airspace: U.S.-registered civil aircraft.* For operations not conducted under part 121, 127, or 135 of this chapter, ATC transponder equipment installed must meet the performance and environmental requirements of any class of *TSO-C74b (Mode A) or any class of *TSO-C74c (Mode A with altitude reporting capability) as appropriate, or the appropriate class of *TSO-C112 (Mode S).

(b)   *All airspace:* Unless otherwise authorized or directed by ATC, no person may operate an aircraft in the airspace described in paragraphs (b)(1) through (b)(5) of this section, unless that aircraft is equipped with an operable coded radar beacon transponder having either Mode 3/A 4096 code capability, replying to Mode 3/A interrogations with the code specified by ATC, or a Mode S capability, replying to Mode 3/A interrogations with the code specified by ATC and intermode and Mode S interrogations in accordance with the applicable provisions specified in *TSO C-112, and that aircraft is equipped with automatic pressure altitude reporting equipment having a Mode C capability that automatically replies to Mode C interrogations by transmitting pressure altitude information in 100-foot increments. This requirement applies —

(1)   *All aircraft.* In Class A, Class B, and Class C airspace areas;

(2)   *All aircraft.* In all airspace within 30 nautical miles of an airport listed in appendix D, section 1 of this part from the surface upward to 10,000 feet MSL;

(3)   Notwithstanding paragraph (b)(2) of this section, any aircraft which was not originally certificated with an engine-driven electrical system or which has not subsequently been certified with such a system installed, balloon or glider may conduct operations in the airspace within 30 nautical miles of an airport listed in appendix D, section 1 of this part provided such operations are conducted —

     (i)   Outside any Class A, Class B, or Class C airspace area; and

     (ii)   Below the altitude of the ceiling of a Class B or Class C airspace area designated for an airport or 10,000 feet MSL, whichever is lower; and

Amend #227
eff 9-16-93

(4)   All aircraft in all airspace above the ceiling and within the lateral boundaries of a Class B or Class C airspace area designated for an airport upward to 10,000 feet MSL; and

(5)   All aircraft except any aircraft which was not originally certificated with an engine-driven electrical system or which has not subsequently been certified with such a system installed, balloon, or glider —

     (i)   In all airspace of the 48 contiguous states and the District of Columbia at and above 10,000 feet MSL, excluding the airspace at and below 2,500 feet above the surface; and

     (ii)   In the airspace from the surface to 10,000 feet MSL within a 10-nautical mile radius of any airport listed in appendix D, section 2 of this part, excluding the airspace below 1,200 feet outside of the lateral boundaries of the surface area of the airspace designated for that airport.

*(Not published herein.)

(c) *Transponder-on operation.* While in the airspace as specified in paragraph (b) of this section or in all controlled airspace, each person operating an aircraft equipped with an operable ATC transponder maintained in accordance with §91.413 of this part shall operate the transponder, including Mode C equipment if installed, and shall reply on the appropriate code or as assigned by ATC.

(d) *ATC authorized deviations.* Requests for ATC authorized deviations must be made to the ATC facility having jurisdiction over the concerned airspace within the time periods specified as follows:

(1) For operation of an aircraft with an operating transponder but without operating automatic pressure altitude reporting equipment having a Mode C capability, the request may be made at any time.

(2) For operation of an aircraft with an inoperative transponder to the airport of ultimate destination, including any intermediate stops, or to proceed to a place where suitable repairs can be made or both, the request may be made at any time.

(3) For operation of an aircraft that is not equipped with a transponder, the request must be made at least one hour before the proposed operation.

91.217   DATA CORRESPONDENCE BETWEEN AUTOMATICALLY REPORTED PRESSURE ALTITUDE DATA AND THE PILOT'S ALTITUDE REFERENCE

No person may operate any automatic pressure altitude reporting equipment associated with a radar beacon transponder —

(a) When deactivation of that equipment is directed by ATC;

(b) Unless, as installed, that equipment was tested and calibrated to transmit altitude data corresponding within 125 feet (on a 95 percent probability basis) of the indicated or calibrated datum of the altimeter normally used to maintain flight altitude, with that altimeter referenced to 29.92 inches of mercury for altitudes from sea level to the maximum operating altitude of the aircraft; or

(c) Unless the altimeters and digitizers in that equipment meet the standards in *TSO-C10b and *TSO-C88, respectively.

91.219   ALTITUDE ALERTING SYSTEM OR DEVICE: TURBOJET-POWERED CIVIL AIRPLANES

(a) Except as provided in paragraph (d) of this section, no person may operate a turbojet-powered U.S.-registered civil airplane unless that airplane is equipped with an approved altitude alerting system or device that is in operable condition and meets the requirements of paragraph (b) of this section.

(b) Each altitude alerting system or device required by paragraph (a) of this section must be able to —

(1) Alert the pilot —

(i) Upon approaching a preselected altitude in either ascent or descent, by a sequence of both aural and visual signals in sufficient time to establish level flight at that preselected altitude; or

(ii) Upon approaching a preselected altitude in either ascent or descent, by a sequence of visual signals in sufficient time to establish level flight at that preselected altitude, and when deviating above and below that preselected altitude, by an aural signal;

(2) Provide the required signals from sea level to the highest operating altitude approved for the airplane in which it is installed;

*(Not published herein.)

    (3)   Preselect altitudes in increments that are commensurate with the altitudes at which the aircraft is operated;

    (4)   Be tested without special equipment to determine proper operation of the alerting signals; and

    (5)   Accept necessary barometric pressure settings if the system or device operates on barometric pressure.

However, for operations below 3,000 feet AGL, the system or device need only provide one signal, either visual or aural, to comply with this paragraph. A radio altimeter may be included to provide the signal if the operator has an approved procedure for its use to determine DH or MDA, as appropriate,

(c)   Each operator to which this section applies must establish and assign procedures for the use of the altitude alerting system or device and each flight crewmember must comply with those procedures assigned to him.

(d)   Paragraph (a) of this section does not apply to any operation of an airplane that has an experimental certificate or to the operation of any airplane for the following purposes:

    (1)   Ferrying a newly acquired airplane from the place where possession of it was taken to a place where the altitude alerting system or device is to be installed.

    (2)   Continuing a flight as originally planned, if the altitude alerting system or device becomes inoperative after the airplane has taken off; however, the flight may not depart from a place where repair or replacement can be made.

    (3)   Ferrying an airplane with any inoperative altitude alerting system or device from a place where repairs or replacements cannot be made to a place where it can be made.

    (4)   Conducting an airworthiness flight test of the airplane.

    (5)   Ferrying an airplane to a place outside the United States for the purpose of registering it in a foreign country.

    (6)   Conducting a sales demonstration of the operation of the airplane.

    (7)   Training foreign flight crews in the operation of the airplane before ferrying it to a place outside the United States for the purpose of registering it in a foreign country.

91.221   TRAFFIC ALERT AND COLLISION AVOIDANCE SYSTEM EQUIPMENT AND USE

(a)   *All airspace: U.S.-registered civil aircraft.* Any traffic alert and collision avoidance system installed in a U.S.-registered civil aircraft must be approved by the Administrator.

(b)   *Traffic alert and collision avoidance system, operation required.* Each person operating an aircraft equipped with an operable traffic alert and collision avoidance system shall have that system on and operating.

91.223 — 91.299 [Reserved]

INTENTIONALLY

LEFT

BLANK

SUBPART D — SPECIAL FLIGHT OPERATIONS

91.301   [Reserved]

91.303   **AEROBATIC FLIGHT**

No person may operate an aircraft in aerobatic flight —
(a)   Over any congested area of a city, town, or settlement;
(b)   Over an open air assembly of persons;
(c)   Within the lateral boundaries of the surface areas of Class B, Class C, Class D, or Class E airspace designated for an airport;
(d)   Within 4 nautical miles of the center line of any Federal airway;
(e)   Below an altitude of 1,500 feet above the surface; or
(f)   When flight visibility is less than three statute miles.
For the purposes of this section, aerobatic flight means an intentional maneuver involving an abrupt change in an aircraft's attitude, an abnormal attitude, or abnormal acceleration, not necessary for normal flight.

Amend #227
eff 9-16-93

91.305   **FLIGHT TEST AREAS**

No person may flight test an aircraft except over open water, or sparsely populated areas, having light air traffic.

91.307   **PARACHUTES AND PARACHUTING**

(a)   No pilot of a civil aircraft may allow a parachute that is available for emergency use to be carried in that aircraft unless it is an approved type and —
(1)   If a chair type (canopy in back), it has been packed by a certificated and appropriately rated parachute rigger within the preceding 120 days; or
(2)   If any other type, it has been packed by a certificated and appropriately rated parachute rigger —
(i)   Within the preceding 120 days, if its canopy, shrouds, and harness are composed exclusively of nylon, rayon, or other similar synthetic fiber or materials that are substantially resistant to damage from mold, mildew, or other fungi and other rotting agents propagated in a moist environment; or
(ii)   Within the preceding 60 days, if any part of the parachute is composed of silk, pongee, or other natural fiber, or materials not specified in paragraph (a)(2)(i) of this section.
(b)   Except in an emergency, no pilot in command may allow, and no person may make, a parachute jump from an aircraft within the United States except in accordance with *Part 105.
(c)   Unless each occupant of the aircraft is wearing an approved parachute, no pilot of a civil aircraft, carrying any person (other than a crewmember) may execute any intentional maneuver that exceeds —
(1)   A bank of 60 degrees relative to the horizon; or
(2)   A nose-up or nose-down attitude of 30 degrees relative to the horizon.
(d)   Paragraph (c) of this section does not apply to —
(1)   Flight tests for pilot certification or rating; or
(2)   Spins and other flight maneuvers required by the regulations for any certificate or rating when given by —
(i)   A certificated flight instructor; or
(ii)   An airline transport pilot instructing in accordance with §61.169 of this chapter.

*(Not published herein.)

(e) For the purposes of this section, "approved parachute" means —

    (1) A parachute manufactured under a type certificate or a technical standard order (C-23 series); or

    (2) A personnel-carrying military parachute identified by an NAF, AAF, or AN drawing number, an AAF order number, or any other military designation or specification number.

91.309   TOWING: GLIDERS

(a) No person may operate a civil aircraft towing a glider unless —

    (1) The pilot in command of the towing aircraft is qualified under §61.69 of this chapter.

    (2) The towing aircraft is equipped with a tow-hitch of a kind, and installed in a manner, that is approved by the Administrator.

    (3) The towline used has a breaking strength not less than 80 percent of the maximum certificated operating weight of the glider and not more than twice this operating weight. However, the towline used may have a breaking strength more than twice the maximum certificated operating weight of the glider if —

        (i) A safety link is installed at the point of attachment of the towline to the glider with a breaking strength not less than 80 percent of the maximum certificated operating weight of the glider and not greater than twice this operating weight.

        (ii) A safety link is installed at the point of attachment of the towline to the towing aircraft with a breaking strength greater, but not more than 25 percent greater, than that of the safety link at the towed glider end of the towline and not greater than twice the maximum certificated operating weight of the glider.

    (4) Before conducting any towing operation within the lateral boundaries of the surface areas of Class B, Class C, Class D, or Class E airspace designated for an airport, or before making each towing flight within such controlled airspace if required by ATC, the pilot in command notifies the control tower. If a control tower does not exist or is not in operation, the pilot in command must notify the FAA flight service station serving that controlled airspace before conducting any towing operations in that airspace; and

    (5) The pilots of the towing aircraft and the glider have agreed upon a general course of action, including takeoff and release signals, airspeeds, and emergency procedures for each pilot.

(b) No pilot of a civil aircraft may intentionally release a towline, after release of a glider, in a manner so as to endanger the life or property of another.

Amend #227
eff 9-16-93

91.311   TOWING: OTHER THAN UNDER §91.309.

No pilot of a civil aircraft may tow anything with that aircraft (other than under §91.309) except in accordance with the terms of a certificate of waiver issued by the Administrator.

91.313   RESTRICTED CATEGORY CIVIL AIRCRAFT: OPERATING LIMITATIONS

(a) No person may operate a restricted category civil aircraft —

    (1) For other than the special purpose for which it is certificated; or

    (2) In an operation other than one necessary to accomplish the work activity directly associated with that special purpose.

(b) For the purpose of paragraph (a) of this section, operating a restricted category civil aircraft to provide flight crewmember training in a special purpose operation for which the aircraft is certificated is considered to be an operation for that special purpose.

(c)   No person may operate a restricted category civil aircraft carrying persons or property for compensation or hire. For the purposes of this paragraph, a special purpose operation involving the carriage of persons or material necessary to accomplish that operation, such as crop dusting, seeding, spraying, and banner towing (including the carrying of required persons or material to the location of that operation), and operation for the purpose of providing flight crewmember training in a special purpose operation, are not considered to be the carriage of persons or property for compensation or hire.

(d)   No person may be carried on a restricted category civil aircraft unless that person —
(1)   Is a flight crewmember;
(2)   Is a flight crewmember trainee;
(3)   Performs an essential function in connection with a special purpose operation for which the aircraft is certificated; or
(4)   Is necessary to accomplish the work activity directly associated with that special purpose.

(e)   Except when operating in accordance with the terms and conditions of a certificate of waiver or special operating limitations issued by the Administrator, no person may operate a restricted category civil aircraft within the United States —
(1)   Over a densely populated area;
(2)   In a congested airway; or
(3)   Near a busy airport where passenger transport operations are conducted.

(f)   This section does not apply to nonpassenger-carrying civil rotorcraft external-load operations conducted under *Part 133 of this chapter.

(g)   No person may operate a small restricted-category civil airplane manufactured after July 18, 1978, unless an approved shoulder harness is installed for each front seat. The shoulder harness must be designed to protect each occupant from serious head injury when the occupant experiences the ultimate inertia forces specified in *§23.561 (b)(2) of this chapter. The shoulder harness installation at each flight crewmember station must permit the crewmember, when seated and with his safety belt and shoulder harness fastened, to perform all functions necessary for flight operations. For purposes of this paragraph —
(1)   The date of manufacture of an airplane is the date the inspection acceptance records reflect that the airplane is complete and meets the FAA-approved type design data; and
(2)   A front seat is a seat located at a flight crewmember station or any seat located alongside such a seat.

91.315   LIMITED CATEGORY CIVIL AIRCRAFT: OPERATING LIMITATIONS

No person may operate a limited category civil aircraft carrying persons or property for compensation or hire.

91.317   PROVISIONALLY CERTIFICATED CIVIL AIRCRAFT: OPERATING LIMITATIONS

(a)   No person may operate a provisionally certificated civil aircraft unless that person is eligible for a provisional airworthiness certificate under *§21.213 of this chapter.

(b)   No person may operate a provisionally certificated civil aircraft outside the United States unless that person has specific authority to do so from the Administrator and each foreign country involved.

(c)   Unless otherwise authorized by the Director, Flight Standards Service, no person may operate a provisionally certificated civil aircraft in air transportation.

*(Not published herein — Ed.)

(d)   Unless otherwise authorized by the Administrator, no person may operate a provisionally certificated civil aircraft except —

    (1)   In direct conjunction with the type or supplemental type certification of that aircraft;

    (2)   For training flight crews, including simulated air carrier operations;

    (3)   Demonstration flight by the manufacturer for prospective purchasers;

    (4)   Market surveys by the manufacturer;

    (5)   Flight checking of instruments, accessories, and equipment, that do not affect the basic airworthiness of the aircraft; or

    (6)   Service testing of the aircraft.

(e)   Each person operating a provisionally certificated civil aircraft shall operate within the prescribed limitations displayed in the aircraft or set forth in the provisional aircraft flight manual or other appropriate document. However, when operating in direct conjunction with the type or supplemental type certification of the aircraft, that person shall operate under the experimental aircraft limitations of *§21.191 of this chapter and when flight testing, shall operate under the requirements of §91.305 of this part.

(f)   Each person operating a provisionally certificated civil aircraft shall establish approved procedures for —

    (1)   The use and guidance of flight and ground personnel in operating under this section; and

    (2)   Operating in and out of airports where takeoffs or approaches over populated areas are necessary. No person may operate that aircraft except in compliance with the approved procedures.

(g)   Each person operating a provisionally certificated civil aircraft shall ensure that each flight crewmember is properly certificated and has adequate knowledge of, and familiarity with, the aircraft and procedures to be used by that crewmember.

(h)   Each person operating a provisionally certificated civil aircraft shall maintain it as required by applicable regulations and as may be specially prescribed by the Administrator.

(i)   Whenever the manufacturer, or the Administrator, determines that a change in design, construction, or operation is necessary to ensure safe operation, no person may operate a provisionally certificated civil aircraft until that change has been made and approved. *Section 21.99 of this chapter applies to operations under this section.

(j)   Each person operating a provisionally certificated civil aircraft —

    (1)   May carry in that aircraft only persons who have a proper interest in the operations allowed by this section or who are specifically authorized by both the manufacturer and the Administrator; and

    (2)   Shall advise each person carried that the aircraft is provisionally certificated.

(k)   The Administrator may prescribe additional limitations or procedures that the Administrator considers necessary, including limitations on the number of persons who may be carried in the aircraft.

(Approved by the Office of Management and Budget under OMB control number 2120-0005)

91.319   AIRCRAFT HAVING EXPERIMENTAL CERTIFICATES: OPERATING LIMITATIONS

(a)   No person may operate an aircraft that has an experimental certificate —

    (1)   For other than the purpose for which the certificate was issued; or

    (2)   Carrying persons or property for compensation or hire.

(b)   No person may operate an aircraft that has an experimental certificate outside of an area assigned by the Administrator until it is shown that —

    (1)   The aircraft is controllable throughout its normal range of speeds and throughout all the maneuvers to be executed; and

    (2)   The aircraft has no hazardous operating characteristics or design features.

*(Not published herein — Ed.)

(c) Unless otherwise authorized by the Administrator in special operating limitations, no person may operate an aircraft that has an experimental certificate over a densely populated area or in a congested airway. The Administrator may issue special operating limitations for particular aircraft to permit takeoffs and landings to be conducted over a densely populated area or in a congested airway, in accordance with terms and conditions specified in the authorization in the interest of safety in air commerce.

(d) Each person operating an aircraft that has an experimental certificate shall —
    (1) Advise each person carried of the experimental nature of the aircraft;
    (2) Operate under VFR, day only, unless otherwise specifically authorized by the Administrator; and
    (3) Notify the control tower of the experimental nature of the aircraft when operating the aircraft into or out of airports with operating control towers.

(e) The Administrator may prescribe additional limitations that the Administrator considers necessary, including limitations on the persons that may be carried in the aircraft.

91.321   CARRIAGE OF CANDIDATES IN FEDERAL ELECTIONS

(a) An aircraft operator, other than one operating an aircraft under the rules of part 121, 125, or 135 of this chapter, may receive payment for the carriage of a candidate in a Federal election, an agent of the candidate, or a person traveling on the behalf of the candidate, if —
    (1) That operator's primary business is not as an air carrier or commercial operator;
    (2) The carriage is conducted under the rules of part 91; and
    (3) The payment for the carriage is required, and does not exceed the amount required to be paid, by regulations of the Federal Election Commission *(11 CFR *et seq.*).

(b) For the purposes of this section, the terms "candidate" and "election" have the same meaning as that set forth in the regulations of the Federal Election Commission.

91.323   INCREASED MAXIMUM CERTIFICATED WEIGHTS FOR CERTAIN AIRPLANES OPERATED IN ALASKA

(a) Notwithstanding any other provision of the Federal Aviation Regulations, the Administrator will approve, as provided in this section, an increase in the maximum certificated weight of an airplane type certificated under *Aeronautics Bulletin No. 7-A of the U.S. Department of Commerce dated January 1, 1931, as amended, or under the normal category of *part 4a of the former Civil Air Regulations (14 CFR Part 4a, 1964 ed.), if that airplane is operated in the State of Alaska by —
    (1) An air taxi operator or other air carrier; or
    (2) The U.S. Department of Interior in conducting its game and fish law enforcement activities or its management, fire detection, and fire suppression activities concerning public lands.

(b) The maximum certificated weight approved under this section may not exceed —
    (1) 12,500 pounds;
    (2) 115 percent of the maximum weight listed in the FAA aircraft specifications;
    (3) The weight at which the airplane meets the positive maneuvering load factor requirement for the normal category specified in *§23.337 of this chapter; or
    (4) The weight at which the airplane meets the climb performance requirements under which it was type certificated.

(c) In determining the maximum certificated weight, the Administrator considers the structural soundness of the airplane and the terrain to be traversed.

(d) The maximum certificated weight determined under this section is added to the airplane's operation limitations and is identified as the maximum weight authorized for operations within the State of Alaska.

*(Not published herein.)

91.325   PRIMARY CATEGORY AIRCRAFT: OPERATING LIMITATIONS

(a)   No person may operate a primary category aircraft carrying persons or property for compensation or hire.

Amend #230
eff 12-31-92

(b)   No person may operate a primary category aircraft that is maintained by the pilot-owner under an approved special inspection and maintenance program except—

(1)   The pilot-owner; or

(2)   A designee of the pilot-owner, provided that the pilot-owner does not receive compensation for the use of the aircraft.

91.327 — 91.399 [Reserved]

SUBPART E — MAINTENANCE, PREVENTIVE MAINTENANCE, AND ALTERATIONS

91.401 APPLICABILITY

(a) This subpart prescribes rules governing the maintenance, preventive maintenance, and alterations of U.S.-registered civil aircraft operating within or outside the United States.

(b) Sections 91.405, 91.409, 91.411, 91.417, and 91.419 of this subpart do not apply to an aircraft maintained in accordance with a continuous airworthiness maintenance program as provided in part 121, *127, 129, or §135.411(a)(2) of this chapter.

(c) Sections 91.405 and 91.409 of this part do not apply to an airplane inspected in accordance with part 125 of this chapter.

91.403 GENERAL

(a) The owner or operator of an aircraft is primarily responsible for maintaining that aircraft in an airworthy condition, including compliance with *part 39 of this chapter.

(b) No person may perform maintenance, preventive maintenance, or alterations on an aircraft other than as prescribed in this subpart and other applicable regulations, including *part 43 of this chapter.

(c) No person may operate an aircraft for which a manufacturer's maintenance manual or instructions for continued airworthiness has been issued that contains an airworthiness limitations section unless the mandatory replacement times, inspection intervals, and related procedures specified in that section or alternative inspection intervals and related procedures set forth in an operations specification approved by the Administrator under part 121, *127, or 135 of this chapter or in accordance with an inspection program approved under §91.409(e) have been complied with.

91.405 MAINTENANCE REQUIRED

Each owner or operator of an aircraft —
(a) Shall have that aircraft inspected as prescribed in subpart E of this part and shall between required inspections, except as provided in paragraph (c) of this section, have discrepancies repaired as prescribed in *part 43 of this chapter;

(b) Shall ensure that maintenance personnel make appropriate entries in the aircraft maintenance records indicating the aircraft has been approved for return to service;

(c) Shall have any inoperative instrument or item of equipment, permitted to be inoperative by §91.213(d)(2) of this part, repaired, replaced, removed, or inspected at the next required inspection; and

(d) When listed discrepancies include inoperative instruments or equipment, shall ensure that a placard has been installed as required by *§43.11 of this chapter.

91.407 OPERATION AFTER MAINTENANCE, PREVENTIVE MAINTENANCE, REBUILDING, OR ALTERATION

(a) No person may operate any aircraft that has undergone maintenance, preventive maintenance, rebuilding, or alteration unless —
(1) It has been approved for return to service by a person authorized under *§43.7 of this chapter; and
(2) The maintenance record entry required by *§43.9 or *§43.11, as applicable, of this chapter has been made.

*(Not published herein — Ed.)

(b) No person may carry any person (other than crewmembers) in an aircraft that has been maintained, rebuilt, or altered in a manner that may have appreciably changed its flight characteristics or substantially affected its operation in flight until an appropriately rated pilot with at least a private pilot certificate flies the aircraft, makes an operational check of the maintenance performed or alteration made, and logs the flight in the aircraft records.

(c) The aircraft does not have to be flown as required by paragraph (b) of this section if, prior to flight, ground tests, inspections, or both show conclusively that the maintenance, preventive maintenance, rebuilding, or alteration has not appreciably changed the flight characteristics or substantially affected the flight operation of the aircraft.

(Approved by the Office of Management and Budget under OMB control number 2120-0005)

91.409   INSPECTIONS

(a) Except as provided in paragraph (c) of this section, no person may operate an aircraft unless, within the preceding 12 calendar months, it has had —

    (1) An annual inspection in accordance with *part 43 of this chapter and has been approved for return to service by a person authorized by *§43.7 of this chapter; or

    (2) An inspection for the issuance of an airworthiness certificate in accordance with *part 21 of this chapter.

No inspection performed under paragraph (b) of this section may be substituted for any inspection required by this paragraph unless it is performed by a person authorized to perform annual inspections and is entered as an "annual" inspection in the required maintenance records.

(b) Except as provided in paragraph (c) of this section, no person may operate an aircraft carrying any person (other than a crewmember) for hire, and no person may give flight instruction for hire in an aircraft which that person provides, unless within the preceding 100 hours of time in service the aircraft has received an annual or 100-hour inspection and been approved for return to service in accordance with *part 43 of this chapter, or has received an inspection for the issuance of an airworthiness certificate in accordance with *part 21 of this chapter. The 100-hour limitation may be exceeded by not more than 10 hours while en route to reach a place where the inspection can be done. The excess time used to reach a place where the inspection can be done must be included in computing the next 100 hours of time in service.

(c) Paragraphs (a) and (b) of this section do not apply to—

    (1) An aircraft that carries a special flight permit, a current experimental certificate, or a provisional airworthiness certificate;

    (2) An aircraft inspected in accordance with an approved aircraft inspection program under part 125, *127, or 135 of this chapter and so identified by the registration number in the operations specifications of the certificate holder having the approved inspection program;

    (3) An aircraft subject to the requirements of paragraph (d) or (e) of this section; or

    (4) Turbine-powered rotorcraft when the operator elects to inspect that rotorcraft in accordance with paragraph (e) of this section.

(d) *Progressive inspection.* Each registered owner or operator of an aircraft desiring to use a progressive inspection program must submit a written request to the FAA Flight Standards district office having jurisdiction over the area in which the applicant is located, and shall provide —

    (1) A certificated mechanic holding an inspection authorization, a certificated airframe repair station, or the manufacturer of the aircraft to supervise or conduct the progressive inspection;

*(Not published herein — Ed.)

(2)   A current inspection procedures manual available and readily understandable to pilot and maintenance personnel containing, in detail —
    (i)   An explanation of the progressive inspection, including the
continuity of inspection responsibility, the making of reports, and
the keeping of records and technical reference material;
    (ii) An inspection schedule, specifying the intervals in hours or days
when routine and detailed inspections will be performed and
including instructions for exceeding an inspection interval by not
more than 10 hours while en route and for changing an inspection
interval because of service experience;
    (iii) Sample routine and detailed inspection forms and instructions for
their use; and
    (iv) Sample reports and records and instructions for their use;
(3)   Enough housing and equipment for necessary disassembly and proper
inspection of the aircraft; and
(4)   Appropriate current technical information for the aircraft.
The frequency and detail of the progressive inspection shall provide for
the complete inspection of the aircraft within each 12 calendar months
and be consistent with the manufacturer's recommendations, field service
experience, and the kind of operation in which the aircraft is engaged.
The progressive inspection schedule must ensure that the aircraft, at all
times, will be airworthy and will conform to all applicable FAA aircraft
specifications, type certificate data sheets, airworthiness directives, and
other approved data. If the progressive inspection is discontinued, the
owner or operator shall immediately notify the local FAA Flight Standards
district office, in writing, of the discontinuance. After the discontinuance,
the first annual inspection under §91.409(a)(1) is due within 12 calendar
months after the last complete inspection of the aircraft under the
progressive inspection. The 100-hour inspection under §91.409(b) is due
within 100 hours after that complete inspection. A complete inspection of
the aircraft, for the purpose of determining when the annual and 100-hour
inspections are due, requires a detailed inspection of the aircraft and all
its components in accordance with the progressive inspection. A routine
inspection of the aircraft and a detailed inspection of several components
is not considered to be a complete inspection.

(e)   *Large airplanes (to which part 125 is not applicable), turbojet multiengine
airplanes, turbopropeller-powered multiengine airplanes, and turbine-powered
rotorcraft.* No person may operate a large airplane, turbojet multiengine airplane,
turbopropeller-powered multiengine airplane, or turbine-powered rotorcraft unless
the replacement times for life-limited parts specified in the aircraft specifications,
type data sheets, or other documents approved by the Administrator are
complied with and the airplane or turbine-powered rotorcraft, including the
airframe, engines, propellers, rotors, appliances, survival equipment, and
emergency equipment, is inspected in accordance with an inspection program
selected under the provisions of paragraph (f) of this section, except that, the
owner or operator of a turbine-powered rotorcraft may elect to use the
inspection provisions of §91.409(a), (b), (c), or (d) in lieu of an inspection option
of §91.409(f).

(f)   *Selection of inspection program under paragraph (e) of this section.* The
registered owner or operator of each airplane or turbine-powered rotorcraft
described in paragraph (e) of this section must select, identify in the aircraft
maintenance records, and use one of the following programs for the inspection
of the aircraft:
(1)   A continuous airworthiness inspection program that is part of a continuous
airworthiness maintenance program currently in use by a person holding
an air carrier operating certificate or an operating certificate issued under
part 121, *127, or 135 of this chapter and operating that make and model
aircraft under part 121 of this chapter or operating that make and model
under part 135 of this chapter and maintaining it under §135.411(a)(2) of
this chapter.

---

*(Not published herein — Ed.)

    (2)   An approved aircraft inspection program approved under §135.419 of this chapter and currently in use by a person holding an operating certificate issued under part 135 of this chapter.

    (3)   An current inspection program recommended by the manufacturer.

    (4)   Any other inspection program established by the registered owner or operator of that airplane or turbine-powered rotorcraft and approved by the Administrator under paragraph (g) of this section. However, the Administrator may require revision to this inspection program in accordance with the provisions of §91.415.

Each operator shall include in the selected program the name and address of the person responsible for scheduling the inspections required by the program and make a copy of that program available to the person performing inspections on the aircraft and, upon request, to the Administrator.

(g)   *Inspection program approved under paragraph (e) of this section.* Each operator of an airplane or turbine-powered rotorcraft desiring to establish or change an approved inspection program under paragraph (f)(4) of this section must submit the program for approval to the local FAA Flight Standards district office having jurisdiction over the area in which the aircraft is based. The program must be in writing and include at least the following information:

    (1)   Instructions and procedures for the conduct of inspections for the particular make and model airplane or turbine-powered rotorcraft, including necessary tests and checks. The instructions and procedures must set forth in detail the parts and areas of the airframe, engines, propellers, rotors, and appliances, including survival and emergency equipment required to be inspected.

    (2)   A schedule for performing the inspections that must be performed under the program expressed in terms of the time in service, calendar time, number of system operations, or any combination of these.

(h)   *Changes from one inspection program to another.* When an operator changes from one inspection program under paragraph (f) of this section to another, the time in service, calendar times, or cycles of operation accumulated under the previous program must be applied in determining inspection due times under the new program.

(Approved by the Office of Management and Budget under OMB control number 2120-0005)

91.411   ALTIMETER SYSTEM AND ALTITUDE REPORTING EQUIPMENT TESTS AND INSPECTIONS

(a)   No person may operate an airplane, or helicopter, in controlled airspace under IFR unless —

    (1)   Within the preceding 24 calendar months, each static pressure system, each altimeter instrument, and each automatic pressure altitude reporting system has been tested and inspected and found to comply with *Appendix E of part 43 of this chapter;

    (2)   Except for the use of system drain and alternate static pressure valves, following any opening and closing of the static pressure system, that system has been tested and inspected and found to comply with paragraph (a), *Appendices E and F, of part 43 of this chapter; and

    (3)   Following installation or maintenance on the automatic pressure altitude reporting system of the ATC transponder where data correspondence error could be introduced, the integrated system has been tested, inspected, and found to comply with paragraph (c), *Appendix E, of part 43 of this chapter.

*(Not published herein — Ed.)

(b) The tests required by paragraph (a) of this section must be conducted by —
  (1) The manufacturer of the airplane, or helicopter, on which the tests and inspections are to be performed;
  (2) A certified repair station properly equipped to perform those functions and holding —
    (i) An instrument rating, Class I;
    (ii) A limited instrument rating appropriate to the make and model of appliance to be tested;
    (iii) A limited rating appropriate to the test to be performed;
    (iv) An airframe rating appropriate to the airplane, or helicopter, to be tested; or
    (v) A limited rating for a manufacturer issued for the appliance in accordance with *§145.101(b)(4) of this chapter; or
  (3) A certified mechanic with an airframe rating (static pressure system tests and inspections only).
(c) Altimeter and altitude reporting equipment approved under Technical Standard Orders are considered to be tested and inspected as of the date of their manufacture.
(d) No person may operate an airplane, or helicopter, in controlled airspace under IFR at an altitude above the maximum altitude at which all altimeters and the automatic altitude reporting system of that airplane, or helicopter, have been tested.

91.413   ATC TRANSPONDER TESTS AND INSPECTIONS

(a) No person may use an ATC transponder that is specified in §91.215(a), §121.345(c), *§127.123(b) or §135.143(c) of this chapter unless, within the preceding 24 calendar months, that ATC transponder has been tested and inspected and found to comply with *appendix F of part 43 of this chapter; and
(b) Following any installation or maintenance on an ATC transponder where data correspondence error could be introduced, the integrated system has been tested, inspected, and found to comply with *paragraph (c), appendix E, of part 43 of this chapter.
(c) The tests and inspections specified in this section must be conducted by —
  (1) A certified repair station properly equipped to perform those functions and holding —
    (i) A radio rating, Class III;
    (ii) A limited radio rating appropriate to the make and model transponder to be tested;
    (iii) A limited rating appropriate to the test to be performed;
    (iv) A limited rating for a manufacturer issued for the transponder in accordance with *§145.101(b)(4) of this chapter; or
  (2) A holder of a continuous airworthiness maintenance program as provided in part 121, *127, or §135.411(a)(2) of this chapter; or
  (3) The manufacturer of the aircraft on which the transponder to be tested is installed, if the transponder was installed by that manufacturer.

91.415   CHANGES TO AIRCRAFT INSPECTION PROGRAMS

(a) Whenever the Administrator finds that revisions to an approved aircraft inspection program under §91.409(f)(4) are necessary for the continued adequacy of the program, the owner or operator shall, after notification by the Administrator, make any changes in the program found to be necessary by the Administrator.
(b) The owner or operator may petition the Administrator to reconsider the notice to make any changes in a program in accordance with paragraph (a) of this section.

*(Not published herein — Ed.)

(c)   The petition must be filed with the FAA Flight Standards district office which requested the change to the program within 30 days after the certificate holder receives the notice.

(d)   Except in the case of an emergency requiring immediate action in the interest of safety, the filing of the petition stays the notice pending a decision by the Administrator.

91.417   MAINTENANCE RECORDS

(a)   Except for work performed in accordance with §§91.411 and 91.413, each registered owner or operator shall keep the following records for the periods specified in paragraph (b) of this section:

(1)   Records of the maintenance, preventive maintenance, and alteration, and records of the 100-hour, annual, progressive, and other required or approved inspections, as appropriate, for each aircraft (including the airframe) and each engine, propeller, rotor, and appliance of an aircraft. The records must include —

(i)   A description (or reference to data acceptable to the Administrator) of the work performed; and

(ii)   The date of completion of the work performed; and

(iii)   The signature and certificate number of the person approving the aircraft for return to service.

(2)   Records containing the following information:

(i)   The total time in service of the airframe, each engine, each propeller, and each rotor.

(ii)   The current status of life-limited parts of each airframe, engine, propeller, rotor, and appliance.

(iii)   The time since last overhaul of all items installed on the aircraft which are required to be overhauled on a specified time basis.

(iv)   The current inspection status of the aircraft, including the time since the last inspection required by the inspection program under which the aircraft and its appliances are maintained.

(v)   The current status of applicable airworthiness directives (AD) including, for each, the method of compliance, the AD number, and revision date. If the AD involves recurring action, the time and date when the next action is required.

(vi)   Copies of the forms prescribed by *§43.9(a) of this chapter for each major alteration to the airframe and currently installed engines, rotors, propellers, and appliances.

(b)   The owner or operator shall retain the following records for the periods prescribed:

(1)   The records specified in paragraph (a)(1) of this section shall be retained until the work is repeated or superseded by other work or for 1 year after the work is performed.

(2)   The records specified in paragraph (a)(2) of this section shall be retained and transferred with the aircraft at the time the aircraft is sold.

(3)   A list of defects furnished to a registered owner or operator under *§43.11 of this chapter shall be retained until the defects are repaired and the aircraft is approved for return to service.

(c)   The owner or operator shall make all maintenance records required to be kept by this section available for inspection by the Administrator or any authorized representative of the National Transportation Safety Board (NTSB). In addition, the owner or operator shall present Form 337 described in paragraph (d) of this section for inspection upon request of any law enforcement officer.

(d)   When a fuel tank is installed within the passenger compartment or a baggage compartment pursuant to *part 43 of this chapter, a copy of FAA Form 337 shall be kept on board the modified aircraft by the owner or operator.

(Approved by the Office of Management and Budget under OMB control number 2120-0005)

*(Not published herein — Ed.)

91.419   TRANSFER OF MAINTENANCE RECORDS

Any owner or operator who sells a U.S.-registered aircraft shall transfer to the purchaser, at the time of sale, the following records of that aircraft, in plain language form or in coded form at the election of the purchaser, if the coded form provides for the preservation and retrieval of information in a manner acceptable to the Administrator.

(a)   The records specified in §91.417(a)(2).

(b)   The records specified in §91.417(a)(1) which are not included in the records covered by paragraph (a) of this section, except that the purchaser may permit the seller to keep physical custody of such records. However, custody of records by the seller does not relieve the purchaser of the responsibility under §91.417(c), to make the records available for inspection by the Administrator or any authorized representative of the National Transportation Safety Board (NTSB).

91.421   REBUILT ENGINE MAINTENANCE RECORDS

(a)   The owner or operator may use a new maintenance record, without previous operating history, for an aircraft engine rebuilt by the manufacturer or by an agency approved by the manufacturer.

(b)   Each manufacturer or agency that grants zero time to an engine rebuilt by it shall enter in the new record —
(1)   A signed statement of the date the engine was rebuilt;
(2)   Each change made as required by airworthiness directives; and
(3)   Each change made in compliance with manufacturer's service bulletins, if the entry is specifically requested in that bulletin.

(c)   For the purposes of this section, a rebuilt engine is a used engine that has been completely disassembled, inspected, repaired as necessary, reassembled, tested, and approved in the same manner and to the same tolerances and limits as a new engine with either new or used parts. However, all parts used in it must conform to the production drawing tolerances and limits for new parts or be of approved oversize or undersized dimensions for a new engine.

91.423 — 91.499 [Reserved]

INTENTIONALLY

LEFT

BLANK

SUBPART F — LARGE AND TURBINE-POWERED MULTIENGINE AIRPLANES

91.501   **APPLICABILITY**

(a)   This subpart prescribes operating rules, in addition to those prescribed in other subparts of this part, governing the operation of large and of turbojet-powered multiengine civil airplanes of U.S. registry. The operating rules in this subpart do not apply to those airplanes when they are required to be operated under parts 121, 125, 129, 135, and *137 of this chapter. (Section 91.409 prescribes an inspection program for large and for turbine-powered (turbojet and turboprop) multiengine airplanes of U.S. registry when they are operated under this part or parts *129 or *137.)

(b)   Operations that may be conducted under the rules in this subpart instead of those in parts 121, 129, 135, and *137 of this chapter when common carriage is not involved, include —

     (1)   Ferry or training flights;

     (2)   Aerial work operations such as aerial photography or survey, or pipeline patrol, but not including fire fighting operations;

     (3)   Flights for the demonstration of an airplane to prospective customers when no charge is made except for those specified in paragraph (d) of this section;

     (4)   Flights conducted by the operator of an airplane for his personal transportation, or the transportation of his guests when no charge, assessment, or fee is made for the transportation;

     (5)   Carriage of officials, employees, guests, and property of a company on an airplane operated by that company, or the parent or a subsidiary of the company or a subsidiary of the parent, when the carriage is within the scope of, and incidental to, the business of the company (other than transportation by air) and no charge, assessment or fee is made for the carriage in excess of the cost of owning, operating, and maintaining the airplane, except that no charge of any kind may be made for the carriage of a guest of a company, when the carriage is not within the scope of, and incidental to, the business of that company.

     (6)   The carriage of company officials, employees, and guests of the company on an airplane operated under a time sharing, interchange, or joint ownership agreement as defined in paragraph (c) of this section;

     (7)   The carriage of property (other than mail) on an airplane operated by a person in the furtherance of a business or employment (other than transportation by air) when the carriage is within the scope of, and incidental to, that business or employment and no charge, assessment, or fee is made for the carriage other than those specified in paragraph (d) of this section;

     (8)   The carriage on an airplane of an athletic team, sports group, choral group, or similar group having a common purpose or objective when there is no charge, assessment, or fee of any kind made by any person for that carriage; and

     (9)   The carriage of persons on an airplane operated by a person in the furtherance of a business other than transportation by air for the purpose of selling them land, goods, or property, including franchises or distributorships, when the carriage is within the scope of, and incidental to, that business and no charge, assessment, or fee is made for that carriage.

(c)   As used in this section —

     (1)   A "time sharing agreement" means an arrangement whereby a person leases his airplane with flight crew to another person, and no charge is made for the flights conducted under that arrangement other than those specified in paragraph (d) of this section;

---

*(Not published herein — Ed.)

(2)   An "interchange agreement" means an arrangement whereby a person leases his airplane to another person in exchange for equal time, when needed, on the other person's airplane, and no charge, assessment, or fee is made, except that a charge may be made not to exceed the difference between the cost of owning, operating, and maintaining the two airplanes;

(3)   A "joint ownership agreement" means an arrangement whereby one of the registered joint owners of an airplane employs and furnishes the flight crew for that airplane and each of the registered joint owners pays a share of the charge specified in the agreement.

(d)   The following may be charged, as expenses of a specific flight, for transportation as authorized by paragraphs (b)(3) and (7) and (c)(1) of this section:

(1)   Fuel, oil, lubricants, and other additives.
(2)   Travel expenses of the crew, including food, lodging, and ground transportation.
(3)   Hangar and tie-down costs away from the aircraft's base of operations.
(4)   Insurance obtained for the specific flight.
(5)   Landing fees, airport taxes, and similar assessments.
(6)   Customs, foreign permit, and similar fees directly related to the flight.
(7)   In flight food and beverages.
(8)   Passenger ground transportation.
(9)   Flight planning and weather contract services.
(10) An additional charge equal to 100 percent of the expenses listed in paragraph (d)(1) of this section.

91.503   FLYING EQUIPMENT AND OPERATING INFORMATION

(a)   The pilot in command of an airplane shall ensure that the following flying equipment and aeronautical charts and data, in current and appropriate form, are accessible for each flight at the pilot station of the airplane:

(1)   A flashlight having at least two size "D" cells, or the equivalent, that is in good working order.
(2)   A cockpit checklist containing the procedures required by paragraph (b) of this section.
(3)   Pertinent aeronautical charts.
(4)   For IFR, VFR over-the-top, or night operations, each pertinent navigational en route, terminal area, and approach and letdown chart.
(5)   In the case of multiengine airplanes, one-engine inoperative climb performance data.

(b)   Each cockpit checklist must contain the following procedures and shall be used by the flight crewmembers when operating the airplane:

(1)   Before starting engines.
(2)   Before takeoff.
(3)   Cruise.
(4)   Before landing.
(5)   After landing.
(6)   Stopping engines.
(7)   Emergencies.

(c)   Each emergency cockpit checklist procedure required by paragraph (b)(7) of this section must contain the following procedures, as appropriate:

(1)   Emergency operation of fuel, hydraulic, electrical, and mechanical systems.
(2)   Emergency operation of instruments and controls.
(3)   Engine inoperative procedures.
(4)   Any other procedures necessary for safety.

(d)   The equipment, charts, and data prescribed in this section shall be used by the pilot in command and other members of the flight crew, when pertinent.

91.505   FAMILIARITY WITH OPERATING LIMITATIONS AND EMERGENCY EQUIPMENT

(a)   Each pilot in command of an airplane shall, before beginning a flight, become familiar with the Airplane Flight Manual for that airplane, if one is required, and with any placards, listings, instrument markings, or any combination thereof, containing each operating limitation prescribed for that airplane by the Administrator, including those specified in §91.9(b).

(b)   Each required member of the crew shall, before beginning a flight, become familiar with the emergency equipment installed on the airplane to which that crewmember is assigned and with the procedures to be followed for the use of that equipment in an emergency situation.

91.507   EQUIPMENT REQUIREMENTS: OVER-THE-TOP, OR NIGHT VFR OPERATIONS

No person may operate an airplane over-the-top or at night under VFR unless that airplane is equipped with the instruments and equipment required for IFR operations under §91.205(d) and one electric landing light for night operations. Each required instrument and item of equipment must be in operable condition.

91.509   SURVIVAL EQUIPMENT FOR OVERWATER OPERATIONS

(a)   No person may take off an airplane for a flight over water more than 50 nautical miles from the nearest shore unless that airplane is equipped with a life preserver or an approved flotation means for each occupant of the airplane.

(b)   No person may take off an airplane for a flight over water more than 30 minutes flying time or 100 nautical miles from the nearest shore unless it has on board the following survival equipment:

    (1)   A life preserver, equipped with an approved survivor locator light, for each occupant of the airplane.

    (2)   Enough liferafts (each equipped with an approved survivor locator light) of a rated capacity and buoyancy to accommodate the occupants of the airplane.

    (3)   At least one pyrotechnic signaling device for each liferaft.

    (4)   One self-buoyant, water-resistant, portable emergency radio signaling device that is capable of transmission on the appropriate emergency frequency or frequencies and not dependent upon the airplane power supply.

    (5)   A lifeline stored in accordance with §25.1411(g) of this chapter.

(c)   The required liferafts, life preservers, and signaling devices must be installed in conspicuously marked locations and easily accessible in the event of a ditching without appreciable time for preparatory procedures.

(d)   A survival kit, appropriately equipped for the route to be flown, must be attached to each required liferaft.

(e)   As used in this section, the term shore means that area of the land adjacent to the water which is above the high water mark and excludes land areas which are intermittently under water.

91.511   RADIO EQUIPMENT FOR OVERWATER OPERATIONS

(a)   Except as provided in paragraphs (c), (d), and (f) of this section, no person may take off an airplane for a flight over water more than 30 minutes flying time or 100 nautical miles from the nearest shore unless it has at least the following operable equipment:

    (1)   Radio communication equipment appropriate to the facilities to be used and able to transmit to, and receive from, any place on the route, at least one surface facility:

        (i)   Two transmitters.

        (ii)   Two microphones.

        (iii)   Two headsets or one headset and one speaker.

        (iv)   Two independent receivers.

(2) Appropriate electronic navigational equipment consisting of at least two independent electronic navigation units capable of providing the pilot with the information necessary to navigate the airplane within the airspace assigned by air traffic control. However, a receiver that can receive both communications and required navigational signals may be used in place of a separate communications receiver and a separate navigational signal receiver or unit.

(b) For the purposes of paragraphs (a)(1)(iv) and (a)(2) of this section, a receiver or electronic navigation unit is independent if the function of any part of it does not depend on the functioning of any part of another receiver or electronic navigation unit.

(c) Notwithstanding the provisions of paragraph (a) of this section, a person may operate an airplane on which no passengers are carried from a place where repairs or replacement cannot be made to a place where they can be made, if not more than one of each of the dual items of radio communication and navigational equipment specified in paragraphs (a)(1)(i) through (iv) and (a)(2) of this section malfunctions or becomes inoperative.

(d) Notwithstanding the provisions of paragraph (a) of this section, when both VHF and HF communications equipment are required for the route and the airplane has two VHF transmitters and two VHF receivers for communications, only one HF transmitter and one HF receiver is required for communications.

(e) As used in this section, the term "shore" means that area of the land adjacent to the water which is above the high-water mark and excludes land areas which are intermittently under water.

(f) Notwithstanding the requirements in paragraph (a)(2) of this section, a person may operate in the Gulf of Mexico, the Caribbean Sea, and the Atlantic Ocean west of a line which extends from 44° 47' 00" N / 67° 00' 00" W to 39° 00' 00" N / 67° 00' 00" W to 38° 30' 00" N / 60° 00' 00" W south along the 60° 00' 00" W longitude line to the point where the line intersects with the northern coast of South America, when:

(1) A single long-range navigation system is installed, operational, and appropriate for the route; and

(2) Flight conditions and the aircraft's capabilities are such that no more than a 30-minute gap in two-way radio very high frequency communications is expected to exist.

91.513   EMERGENCY EQUIPMENT

(a) No person may operate an airplane unless it is equipped with the emergency equipment listed in this section:

(b) Each item of equipment —

(1) Must be inspected in accordance with §91.409 to ensure its continued serviceability and immediate readiness for its intended purposes;

(2) Must be readily accessible to the crew;

(3) Must clearly indicate its method of operation; and

(4) When carried in a compartment or container, must have that compartment or container marked as to contents and date of last inspection.

(c) Hand fire extinguishers must be provided for use in crew, passenger, and cargo compartments in accordance with the following:

(1) The type and quantity of extinguishing agent must be suitable for the kinds of fires likely to occur in the compartment where the extinguisher is intended to be used.

(2) At least one hand fire extinguisher must be provided and located on or near the flight deck in a place that is readily accessible to the flight crew.

(3) At least one hand fire extinguisher must be conveniently located in the passenger compartment of each airplane accommodating more than six but less than 31 passengers, and at least two hand fire extinguishers must be conveniently located in the passenger compartment of each airplane accommodating more than 30 passengers.

(4) Hand fire extinguishers must be installed and secured in such a manner that they will not interfere with the safe operation of the airplane or adversely affect the safety of the crew and passengers. They must be readily accessible and, unless the locations of the fire extinguishers are obvious, their stowage provisions must be properly identified.

(d) First aid kits for treatment of injuries likely to occur in flight or in minor accidents must be provided.

(e) Each airplane accommodating more than 19 passengers must be equipped with a crash axe.

Ⓐ *Amend #25 eff 2-26-96*

(f)   Each passenger-carrying airplane must have a portable battery-powered megaphone or megaphones readily accessible to the crewmember assigned to direct emergency evacuation, installed as follows:

    (1)   One megaphone on each airplane with a seating capacity of more than 60 but less than 100 passengers, at the most rearward location in the passenger cabin where it would be readily accessible to a normal flight attendant seat. However, the Administrator may grant a deviation from the requirements of this subparagraph if the Administrator finds that a different location would be more useful for evacuation of persons during an emergency.

    (2)   On each airplane with a seating capacity of 100 or more passengers, one megaphone installed at the forward end and one installed at the most rearward location where it would be readily accessible to a normal flight attendant seat.

91.515   FLIGHT ALTITUDE RULES

(a)   Notwithstanding §91.119, and except as provided in paragraph (b) of this section, no person may operate an airplane under VFR at less than —

    (1)   One thousand feet above the surface, or 1,000 feet from any mountain, hill, or other obstruction to flight, for day operations; and

    (2)   The altitudes prescribed in §91.177, for night operations.

(b)   This section does not apply —

    (1)   During takeoff or landing;

    (2)   When a different altitude is authorized by a waiver to this section under subpart J of this part; or

    (3)   When a flight is conducted under the special VFR weather minimums of §91.157 with an appropriate clearance from ATC.

91.517   PASSENGER INFORMATION

(a)   Except as provided in paragraph (b) of this section, no person may operate an airplane carrying passengers unless it is equipped with signs that are visible to passengers and flight attendants to notify them when smoking is prohibited and when safety belts must be fastened. The signs must be so constructed that the crew can turn them on and off. They must be turned on during airplane movement on the surface, for each takeoff, for each landing, and when otherwise considered to be necessary by the pilot in command.

(b)   The pilot in command of an airplane that is not required, in accordance with applicable aircraft and equipment requirements of this chapter, to be equipped as provided in paragraph (a) of this section shall ensure that the passengers are notified orally each time that it is necessary to fasten their safety belts and when smoking is prohibited.

Amend #231
eff 10-15-92

(c)   If passenger information signs are installed, no passenger or crewmember may smoke while any "no smoking" sign is lighted nor may any passenger or crewmember smoke in any lavatory.

(d)   Each passenger required by §91.107(a)(3) to occupy a seat or berth shall fasten his or her safety belt about him or her and keep it fastened while any "fasten seat belt" sign is lighted.

(e)   Each passenger shall comply with instructions given him or her by crewmembers regarding compliance with paragraphs (b), (c), and (d) of this section.

91.519   **PASSENGER BRIEFING**

(a)   Before each takeoff the pilot in command of an airplane carrying passengers shall ensure that all passengers have been orally briefed on —

    (1)   Smoking: Each passenger shall be briefed on when, where, and under what conditions smoking is prohibited. This briefing shall include a statement, as appropriate, that the Federal Aviation Regulations require passenger compliance with lighted passenger information signs and no smoking placards, prohibit smoking in lavatories, and require compliance with crewmember instructions with regard to these items;

Amend #231
eff 10-15-92

    (2)   Use of safety belts and shoulder harnesses: Each passenger shall be briefed on when, where, and under what conditions it is necessary to have his or her safety belt and, if installed, his or her shoulder harness fastened about him or her. This briefing shall include a statement, as appropriate, that Federal Aviation Regulations require passenger compliance with the lighted passenger sign and/or crewmember instructions with regard to these items;

    (3)   Location and means for opening the passenger entry door and emergency exits;

    (4)   Location of survival equipment;

    (5)   Ditching procedures and the use of flotation equipment required under §91.509 for a flight over water; and

    (6)   The normal and emergency use of oxygen equipment installed on the airplane.

(b)   The oral briefing required by paragraph (a) of this section shall be given by the pilot in command or a member of the crew, but need not be given when the pilot in command determines that the passengers are familiar with the contents of the briefing. It may be supplemented by printed cards for the use of each passenger containing —

    (1)   A diagram of, and methods of operating, the emergency exits; and

    (2)   Other instructions necessary for use of emergency equipment.

(c)   Each card used under paragraph (b) must be carried in convenient locations on the airplane for the use of each passenger and must contain information that is pertinent only to the type and model airplane on which it is used.

91.521   **SHOULDER HARNESS**

(a)   No person may operate a transport category airplane that was type certificated after January 1, 1958, unless it is equipped at each seat at a flight deck station with a combined safety belt and shoulder harness that meets the applicable requirements specified in *§25.785 of this chapter, except that —

    (1)   Shoulder harnesses and combined safety belt and shoulder harnesses that were approved and installed before March 6, 1980, may continue to be used; and

    (2)   Safety belt and shoulder harness restraint systems may be designed to the inertia load factors established under the certification basis of the airplane.

(b)   No person may operate a transport category airplane unless it is equipped at each required flight attendant seat in the passenger compartment with a combined safety belt and shoulder harness that meets the applicable requirements specified in *§25.785 of this chapter, except that —

    (1)   Shoulder harnesses and combined safety belt and shoulder harnesses that were approved and installed before March 6, 1980, may continue to be used; and

    (2)   Safety belt and shoulder harness restraint systems may be designed to the inertia load factors established under the certification basis of the airplane.

91.523   **CARRY-ON-BAGGAGE**

No pilot in command of an airplane having a seating capacity of more than 19 passengers may permit a passenger to stow his baggage aboard that airplane except —

(a)   In a suitable baggage or cargo storage compartment, or as provided in §91.525; or

(b)   Under a passenger seat in such a way that it will not slide forward under crash impacts severe enough to induce the ultimate inertia forces specified in *§25.561(b)(3) of this chapter, or the requirements of the regulations under which the airplane was type certificated. Restraining devices must also limit sideward motion of under-seat baggage and be designed to withstand crash impacts severe enough to induce sideward forces specified in *§25.561 (b)(3) of this chapter.

*(Not published herein.)

91.525   **CARRIAGE OF CARGO**

    (a)   No pilot in command may permit cargo to be carried in any airplane unless —
       (1)   It is carried in an approved cargo rack, bin, or compartment installed in the airplane;
       (2)   It is secured by means approved by the Administrator; or
       (3)   It is carried in accordance with each of the following:
          (i)   It is properly secured by a safety belt or other tiedown having enough strength to eliminate the possibility of shifting under all normally anticipated flight and ground conditions.
          (ii)   It is packaged or covered to avoid possible injury to passengers.
          (iii)   It does not impose any load on seats or on the floor structure that exceeds the load limitation for those components.
          (iv)   It is not located in a position that restricts the access to or use of any required emergency or regular exit, or the use of the aisle between the crew and the passenger compartment.
          (v)   It is not carried directly above seated passengers.
    (b)   When cargo is carried in cargo compartments that are designed to require the physical entry of a crewmember to extinguish any fire that may occur during flight, the cargo must be loaded so as to allow a crewmember to effectively reach all parts of the compartment with the contents of a hand fire extinguisher.

91.527   **OPERATING IN ICING CONDITIONS**

    (a)   No pilot may take off an airplane that has —
       (1)   Frost, snow, or ice adhering to any propeller, windshield, or powerplant installation or to an airspeed, altimeter, rate of climb, or flight attitude instrument system;
       (2)   Snow or ice adhering to the wings or stabilizing or control surfaces; or
       (3)   Any frost adhering to the wings or stabilizing or control surfaces, unless that frost has been polished to make it smooth.
    (b)   Except for an airplane that has ice protection provisions that meet the requirements in section 34 of Special Federal Aviation Regulation No. 23, or those for transport category airplane type certification, no pilot may fly —
       (1)   Under IFR into known or forecast moderate icing conditions; or
       (2)   Under VFR into known light or moderate icing conditions unless the aircraft has functioning de-icing or anti-icing equipment protecting each propeller, windshield, wing, stabilizing or control surface, and each airspeed, altimeter, rate of climb, or flight attitude instrument system.
    (c)   Except for an airplane that has ice protection provisions that meet the requirements in section 34 of Special Federal Aviation Regulation No. 23, or those for transport category airplane type certification, no pilot may fly an airplane into known or forecast severe icing conditions.
    (d)   If current weather reports and briefing information relied upon by the pilot in command indicate that the forecast icing conditions that would otherwise prohibit the flight will not be encountered during the flight because of changed weather conditions since the forecast, the restrictions in paragraphs (b) and (c) of this section based on forecast conditions do not apply.

91.529   **FLIGHT ENGINEER REQUIREMENTS**

    (a)   No person may operate the following airplanes without a flight crewmember holding a current flight engineer certificate:
       (1)   An airplane for which a type certificate was issued before January 2, 1964, having a maximum certificated takeoff weight of more than 80,000 pounds.
       (2)   An airplane type certificated after January 1, 1964, for which a flight engineer is required by the type certification requirements.
    (b)   No person may serve as a required flight engineer on an airplane unless, within the preceding 6 calendar months, that person has had at least 50 hours of flight time as a flight engineer on that type airplane or has been checked by the Administrator on that type airplane and is found to be familiar and competent with all essential current information and operating procedures.

91.531   SECOND IN COMMAND REQUIREMENTS

(a)   Except as provided in paragraph (b) of this section, no person may operate the following airplanes without a pilot who is designated as second in command of that airplane;

(1)   A large airplane, except that a person may operate an airplane certificated under SFAR 41 without a pilot who is designated as second in command if that airplane is certificated for operation with one pilot.

(2)   A turbojet-powered multiengine airplane for which two pilots are required under the type certification requirements for that airplane.

(3)   A commuter category airplane, except that a person may operate a commuter category airplane notwithstanding paragraph (a)(1) of this section, that has a passenger seating configuration, excluding pilot seats, of nine or less without a pilot who is designated as second in command if that airplane is type certificated for operations with one pilot.

(b)   The Administrator may issue a letter of authorization for the operation of an airplane without compliance with the requirements of paragraph (a) of this section if that airplane is designed for and type certificated with only one pilot station. The authorization contains any conditions that the Administrator finds necessary for safe operation.

(c)   No person may designate a pilot to serve as second in command, nor may any pilot serve as second in command, of an airplane required under this section to have two pilots unless that pilot meets the qualifications for second in command prescribed in §61.55 of this chapter.

91.533   FLIGHT ATTENDANT REQUIREMENTS

(a)   No person may operate an airplane unless at least the following number of flight attendants are on board the airplane:

(1)   For airplanes having more than 19 but less than 51 passengers on board, one flight attendant.

(2)   For airplanes having more than 50 but less than 101 passengers on board, two flight attendants.

(3)   For airplanes having more than 100 passengers on board, two flight attendants plus one additional flight attendant for each unit (or part of a unit) of 50 passengers above 100.

(b)   No person may serve as a flight attendant on an airplane when required by paragraph (a) of this section unless that person has demonstrated to the pilot in command familiarity with the necessary functions to be performed in an emergency or a situation requiring emergency evacuation and is capable of using the emergency equipment installed on that airplane.

91.535   STOWAGE OF FOOD, BEVERAGE, AND PASSENGER SERVICE EQUIPMENT DURING AIRCRAFT MOVEMENT ON THE SURFACE, TAKEOFF, AND LANDING

(a)   No operator may move an aircraft on the surface, take off, or land when any food, beverage, or tableware furnished by the operator is located at any passenger seat.

(b)   No operator may move an aircraft on the surface, take off, or land unless each food and beverage tray and seat back tray table is secured in its stowed position.

(c)   No operator may permit an aircraft to move on the surface, take off, or land unless each passenger serving cart is secured in its stowed position.

(d)   No operator may permit an aircraft to move on the surface, take off, or land unless each movie screen that extends into the aisle is stowed.

(e)   Each passenger shall comply with instructions given by a crewmember with regard to compliance with this section.

91.537 — 91.599 [Reserved]

SUBPART G — ADDITIONAL EQUIPMENT AND OPERATING REQUIREMENTS FOR LARGE AND TRANSPORT CATEGORY AIRCRAFT

91.601   APPLICABILITY

This subpart applies to operation of large and transport category U.S.-registered civil aircraft.

91.603   AURAL SPEED WARNING DEVICE

No person may operate a transport category airplane in air commerce unless that airplane is equipped with an aural speed warning device that complies with *§25.1303 (c)(1).

91.605   TRANSPORT CATEGORY CIVIL AIRPLANE WEIGHT LIMITATIONS

(a)   No person may take off any transport category airplane (other than a turbine-engine-powered airplane certificated after September 30, 1958) unless —
  (1)   The takeoff weight does not exceed the authorized maximum takeoff weight for the elevation of the airport of takeoff;
  (2)   The elevation of the airport of takeoff is within the altitude range for which maximum takeoff weights have been determined;
  (3)   Normal consumption of fuel and oil in flight to the airport of intended landing will leave a weight on arrival not in excess of the authorized maximum landing weight for the elevation of that airport; and
  (4)   The elevations of the airport of intended landing and of all specified alternate airports are within the altitude range for which maximum landing weights have been determined.

(b)   No person may operate a turbine-engine-powered transport category airplane certificated after September 30, 1958, contrary to the Airplane Flight Manual, or take off that airplane unless —
  (1)   The takeoff weight does not exceed the takeoff weight specified in the Airplane Flight Manual for the elevation of the airport and for the ambient temperature existing at the time of takeoff;
  (2)   Normal consumption of fuel and oil in flight to the airport of intended landing and to the alternate airports will leave a weight on arrival not in excess of the landing weight specified in the Airplane Flight Manual for the elevation of each of the airports involved and for the ambient temperatures expected at the time of landing;
  (3)   The takeoff weight does not exceed the weight shown in the Airplane Flight Manual to correspond with the minimum distances required for takeoff considering the elevation of the airport, the runway to be used, the effective runway gradient, and the ambient temperature and wind component existing at the time of takeoff; and
  (4)   Where the takeoff distance includes a clearway, the clearway distance is not greater than one-half of —
    (i)   The takeoff run, in the case of airplanes certificated after September 30, 1958, and before August 30, 1959; or
    (ii)   The runway length, in the case of airplanes certificated after August 29, 1959.

(c)   No person may take off a turbine-engine-powered transport category airplane certificated after August 29, 1959, unless, in addition to the requirements of paragraph (b) of this section —
  (1)   The accelerate-stop distance is no greater than the length of the runway plus the length of the stopway (if present); and
  (2)   The takeoff distance is no greater than the length of the runway plus the length of the clearway (if present); and
  (3)   The takeoff run is no greater than the length of the runway.

---

*(Not published herein — Ed.)

91.607   EMERGENCY EXITS FOR AIRPLANES CARRYING PASSENGERS FOR HIRE

(a)   Notwithstanding any other provision of this chapter, no person may operate a large airplane (type certificated under the Civil Air Regulations effective before April 9, 1957) in passenger-carrying operations for hire, with more than the number of occupants —

    (1)   Allowed under Civil Air Regulations *§4b. 362(a), (b), and (c) as in effect on December 20, 1951; or

    (2)   Approved under Special Civil Air Regulations *SR-387, *SR-389, *SR-389A, or *SR-389B, or under this section as in effect.

However, an airplane type listed in the following table may be operated with up to the listed number of occupants (including crewmembers) and the corresponding number of exits (including emergency exits and doors) approved for the emergency exit of passengers or with an occupant-exit configuration approved under paragraph (b) or (c) of this section.

Airplane type	Maximum number of occupants including all crewmembers	Corresponding number of exits authorized for passenger use
B-307	61	4
B-377	96	9
C-46	67	4
CV-240	53	6
CV-340 and CV-440	53	6
DC-3	35	4
DC-3 (Super)	39	5
DC-4	86	5
DC-6	87	7
DC-6B	112	11
L-18	17	3
L-049, L-649, L-749	87	7
L-1049 series	96	9
M-202	53	6
M-404	53	7
Viscount 700 series	53	7

(b)   Occupants in addition to those authorized under paragraph (a) of this section may be carried as follows:

    (1)   For each additional floor-level exit at least 24 inches wide by 48 inches high, with an unobstructed 20-inch-wide access aisleway between the exit and the main passenger aisle, 12 additional occupants.

    (2)   For each additional window exit located over a wing that meets the requirements of the airworthiness standards under which the airplane was type certificated or that is large enough to inscribe an ellipse 19 x 26 inches: eight additional occupants.

    (3)   For each additional window exit that is not located over a wing but that otherwise complies with paragraph (b)(2) of this section, five additional occupants.

*(Not published herein — Ed.)

(4) For each airplane having a ratio (as computed from the table in paragraph (a) of this section) of maximum number of occupants to number of exits greater than 14:1, and for each airplane that does not have at least one full-size, door-type exit in the side of the fuselage in the rear part of the cabin, the first additional exit must be a floor-level exit that complies with paragraph (b)(1) of this section and must be located in the rear part of the cabin on the opposite side of the fuselage from the main entrance door. However, no person may operate an airplane under this section carrying more than 115 occupants unless there is such an exit on each side of the fuselage in the rear part of the cabin.

(c) No person may eliminate any approved exit except in accordance with the following:

(1) The previously authorized maximum number of occupants must be reduced by the same number of additional occupants authorized for that exit under this section.

(2) Exits must be eliminated in accordance with the following priority schedule: First, non-over-wing window exits; second, over-wing window exits; third, floor-level exits located in the forward part of the cabin; fourth, floor-level exits located in the rear of the cabin.

(3) At least one exit must be retained on each side of the fuselage regardless of the number of occupants.

(4) No person may remove any exit that would result in a ratio of maximum number of occupants to approved exits greater than 14:1.

(d) This section does not relieve any person operating under part 121 of this chapter from complying with §121.291.

91.609   FLIGHT RECORDERS AND COCKPIT VOICE RECORDERS

(a) No holder of an air carrier operating certificate or an operating certificate may conduct any operation under this part with an aircraft listed in the holder's operations specifications or current list of aircraft used in air transportation unless that aircraft complies with any applicable flight recorder and cockpit voice recorder requirements of the part under which its certificate is issued except that the operator may —

(1) Ferry an aircraft with an inoperative flight recorder or cockpit voice recorder from a place where repair or replacement cannot be made to a place where they can be made;

(2) Continue a flight as originally planned, if the flight recorder or cockpit voice recorder becomes inoperative after the aircraft has taken off;

(3) Conduct an airworthiness flight test during which the flight recorder or cockpit voice recorder is turned off to test it or to test any communications or electrical equipment installed in the aircraft; or

(4) Ferry a newly acquired aircraft from the place where possession of it is taken to a place where the flight recorder or cockpit voice recorder is to be installed.

(b) Notwithstanding paragraphs (c) and (e) of this section, an operator other than the holder of an air carrier or a commercial operator certificate may —

(1) Ferry an aircraft with an inoperative flight recorder or cockpit voice recorder from a place where repair or replacement cannot be made to a place where they can be made;

(2) Continue a flight as originally planned if the flight recorder or cockpit voice recorder becomes inoperative after the aircraft has taken off;

(3) Conduct an airworthiness flight test during which the flight recorder or cockpit voice recorder is turned off to test it or to test any communications or electrical equipment installed in the aircraft;

(4) Ferry a newly acquired aircraft from a place where possession of it was taken to a place where the flight recorder or cockpit voice recorder is to be installed; or

(5) Operate an aircraft:

(i) For not more than 15 days while the flight recorder and/or cockpit voice recorder is inoperative and/or removed for repair provided that the aircraft maintenance records contain an entry that indicates the date of failure, and a placard is located in view of the pilot to show that the flight recorder or cockpit voice recorder is inoperative.

Amend #228
eff 5-5-92

Amend #228
eff 5-5-92

(ii) For not more than an additional 15 days, provided that the requirements in paragraph (b)(5)(i) are met and that a certificated pilot or a certificated person authorized to return an aircraft to service under *§43.7 of this chapter, certifies in the aircraft maintenance records that additional time is required to complete repairs or obtain a replacement unit.

(c) No person may operate a U.S. civil registered, multiengine, turbine-powered airplane or rotorcraft having a passenger seating configuration, excluding any pilot seats of 10 or more that has been manufactured after October 11, 1991, unless it is equipped with one or more approved flight recorders that utilize a digital method of recording and storing data and a method of readily retrieving that data from the storage medium, that are capable of recording the data specified in appendix E to this part, for an airplane, or appendix F to this part, for a rotorcraft, of this part within the range, accuracy, and recording interval specified, and that are capable of retaining no less than 8 hours of aircraft operation.

(d) Whenever a flight recorder, required by this section, is installed, it must be operated continuously from the instant the airplane begins the takeoff roll or the rotorcraft begins lift-off until the airplane has completed the landing roll or the rotorcraft has landed at its destination.

(e) Unless otherwise authorized by the Administrator, after October 11, 1991, no person may operate a U.S. civil registered multiengine, turbine-powered airplane or rotorcraft having a passenger seating configuration of six passengers or more and for which two pilots are required by type certification or operating rule unless it is equipped with an approved cockpit voice recorder that:

(1) Is installed in compliance with *§23.1457(a) (1) and (2), (b), (c), (d), (e), (f), and (g); *§25.1457(a) (1) and (2), (b), (c), (d), (e), (f), and (g); *§27.1457(a) (1) and (2), (b), (c), (d), (e), (f), and (g); or *§29.1457(a) (1) and (2), (b), (c), (d), (e), (f), and (g) of this chapter, as applicable; and

(2) Is operated continuously from the use of the check list before the flight to completion of the final checklist at the end of the flight.

(f) In complying with this section, an approved cockpit voice recorder having an erasure feature may be used, so that at any time during the operation of the recorder, information recorded more than 15 minutes earlier may be erased or otherwise obliterated.

(g) In the event of an accident or occurrence requiring immediate notification to the National Transportation Safety Board under part 830 of its regulations that results in the termination of the flight, any operator who has installed approved flight recorders and approved cockpit voice recorders shall keep the recorded information for at least 60 days or, if requested by the Administrator or the Board, for a longer period. Information obtained from the record is used to assist in determining the cause of accidents or occurrences in connection with the investigation under part 830. The Administrator does not use the cockpit voice recorder record in any civil penalty or certificate action.

91.611   AUTHORIZATION FOR FERRY FLIGHT WITH ONE ENGINE INOPERATIVE

(a) *General.* The holder of an air carrier operating certificate or an operating certificate issued under part 125 may conduct a ferry flight of a four-engine airplane or a turbine-engine-powered airplane equipped with three engines, with one engine inoperative, to a base for the purpose of repairing that engine subject to the following:

(1) The airplane model has been test flown and found satisfactory for safe flight in accordance with paragraph (b) or (c) of this section, as appropriate. However, each operator who before November 19, 1966 has shown that a model of airplane with an engine inoperative is satisfactory for safe flight by a test flight conducted in accordance with performance data contained in the applicable Airplane Flight Manual under paragraph (a)(2) of this section need not repeat the test flight for that model.

*(Not published herein)

(2) The approved Airplane Flight Manual contains the following performance data and the flight is conducted in accordance with that data:
    (i) Maximum weight.
    (ii) Center of gravity limits.
    (iii) Configuration of the inoperative propeller (if applicable).
    (iv) Runway length for takeoff (including temperature accountability).
    (v) Altitude range.
    (vi) Certificate limitations.
    (vii) Ranges of operational limits.
    (viii) Performance information.
    (ix) Operating procedures.

(3) The operator has FAA approved procedures for the safe operation of the airplane, including specific requirements for —
    (i) Limiting the operating weight on any ferry flight to the minimum necessary for the flight plus the necessary reserve fuel load;
    (ii) A limitation that takeoffs must be made from dry runways unless, based on a showing of actual operating takeoff techniques on wet runways with one engine inoperative, takeoffs with full controllability from wet runways have been approved for the specific model aircraft and included in the Airplane Flight Manual;
    (iii) Operations from airports where the runways may require a takeoff or approach over populated areas; and
    (iv) Inspection procedures for determining the operating condition of the operative engines.

(4) No person may take off an airplane under this section if —
    (i) The initial climb is over thickly populated areas; or
    (ii) Weather conditions at the takeoff or destination airport are less than those required for VFR flight.

(5) Persons other than required flight crewmembers shall not be carried during the flight.

(6) No person may use a flight crewmember for flight under this section unless that crewmember is thoroughly familiar with the operating procedures for one-engine inoperative ferry flight contained in the certificate holder's manual and the limitations and performance information in the Airplane Flight Manual.

(b) *Flight tests; reciprocating-engine-powered airplanes.* The airplane performance of a reciprocating-engine-powered airplane with one engine inoperative must be determined by flight test as follows:

(1) A speed not less than $1.3V_{S1}$ must be chosen at which the airplane may be controlled satisfactorily in a climb with the critical engine inoperative (with its propeller removed or in a configuration desired by the operator and with all other engines operating at the maximum power determined in paragraph (b)(3) of this section.

(2) The distance required to accelerate to the speed listed in paragraph (b)(1) of this section and to climb to 50 feet must be determined with —
    (i) The landing gear extended;
    (ii) The critical engine inoperative and its propeller removed or in a configuration desired by the operator; and
    (iii) The other engines operating at not more than maximum power established under paragraph (b)(3) of this section.

(3) The takeoff, flight, and landing procedures, such as the approximate trim settings, method of power application, maximum power, and speed must be established.

(4) The performance must be determined at a maximum weight not greater than the weight that allows a rate of climb of at least 400 feet per minute in the en route configuration set forth in *§25.67(d) of this chapter in effect on January 31, 1977, at an altitude of 5,000 feet.

(5) The performance must be determined using temperature accountability for the takeoff field length, computed in accordance with *§25.61 of this chapter in effect on January 31, 1977.

*(Not published herein — Ed.)

(c) *Flight tests: Turbine-engine-powered airplanes.* The airplane performance of a turbine-engine-powered airplane with one engine inoperative must be determined by flight tests, including at least three takeoff tests in accordance with the following:

(1) Takeoff speeds V_R and V_2, not less than the corresponding speeds under which the airplane was type certificated under *§25.107 of this chapter, must be chosen at which the airplane may be controlled satisfactorily with the critical engine inoperative (with its propeller removed or in a configuration desired by the operator, if applicable) and with all other engines operating at not more than the power selected for type certification as set forth in *§25.101 of this chapter.

(2) The minimum takeoff field length must be the horizontal distance required to accelerate and climb to the 35-foot height at V_2 speed (including any additional speed increment obtained in the tests) multiplied by 115 percent, and determined with —

(i) The landing gear extended;

(ii) The critical engine inoperative and its propeller removed or in a configuration desired by the operator (if applicable); and

(iii) The other engine operating at not more than the power selected for type certification as set forth in *§25.101 of this chapter.

(3) The takeoff, flight, and landing procedures such as the approximate trim setting, method of power application, maximum power, and speed must be established. The airplane must be satisfactorily controllable during the entire takeoff run when operated according to these procedures.

(4) The performance must be determined at a maximum weight not greater than the weight determined under *§25.121(c) of this chapter but with —

(i) The actual steady gradient of the final takeoff climb requirement not less than 1.2 percent at the end of the takeoff path with two critical engines inoperative; and

(ii) The climb speed not less than the two-engine inoperative trim speed for the actual steady gradient of the final takeoff climb prescribed by paragraph (c)(4)(i) of this section.

(5) The airplane must be satisfactorily controllable in a climb with two critical engines inoperative. Climb performance may be shown by calculations based on, and equal in accuracy to, the results of testing.

(6) The performance must be determined using temperature accountability for takeoff distance and final takeoff climb computed in accordance with *§25.101 of this chapter.

For the purposes of paragraphs (c)(4) and (5), "two critical engines" means two adjacent engines on one side of an airplane with four engines, and the center engine and one outboard engine on an airplane with three engines.

91.613 MATERIALS FOR COMPARTMENT INTERIORS

No person may operate an airplane that conforms to an amended or supplemental type certificate issued in accordance with *SFAR No. 41 for a maximum certificated takeoff weight in excess of 12,500 pounds unless within 1 year after issuance of the initial airworthiness certificate under that SFAR the airplane meets the compartment interior requirements set forth in *§25.853(a), (b), (b-1), (b-2), and (b-3) of this chapter in effect on September 26, 1978.

91.615 — 91.699 [Reserved]

*(Not published herein — Ed.)

SUBPART H — FOREIGN AIRCRAFT OPERATIONS AND OPERATIONS OF U.S.—REGISTERED CIVIL AIRCRAFT OUTSIDE OF THE UNITED STATES

91.701   APPLICABILITY

This subpart applies to the operations of civil aircraft of U.S. registry outside of the United States and the operations of foreign civil aircraft within the United States.

91.703   OPERATIONS OF CIVIL AIRCRAFT OF U.S. REGISTRY OUTSIDE OF THE UNITED STATES

(a)   Each person operating a civil aircraft of U.S. registry outside of the United States shall —

     (1)   When over the high seas, comply with annex 2 (Rules of the Air) to the Convention on International Civil aviation and with §§91.117(c), 91.127, 91.129, and 91.131;

Amend #227
eff 9-16-93

     (2)   When within a foreign country, comply with the regulations relating to the flight and maneuver of aircraft there in force;

     (3)   Except for §§91.307(b), 91.309, 91.323, and 91.711, comply with this part so far as it is not inconsistent with applicable regulations of the foreign country where the aircraft is operated or annex 2 of the Convention on International Civil Aviation; and

     (4)   When over the North Atlantic within airspace designated as Minimum Navigation Performance Specifications airspace, comply with § 91.705.

(b)   Annex 2 to the Convention on International Civil Aviation, Eighth Edition—July 1986, with amendments through Amendment 28 effective November 1987, to which reference is made in this part, is incorporated into this part and made a part hereof as provided in *5 U.S.C. 552 and pursuant to *1 CFR part 51, annex 2 (including a complete historic file of changes thereto) is available for public inspection at the Rules Docket, AGC—10, Federal Aviation Administration, 800 Independence Avenue SW, Washington, DC 20591. In addition, Annex 2 may be purchased from the International Civil Aviation Organization (Attention: Distribution Officer), P. O. Box 400, Succursale, Place de L'Aviation Internationale, 1000 Sherbrooke Street West, Montreal, Quebec, Canada H3A 2R2.

91.705   OPERATIONS WITHIN THE NORTH ATLANTIC MINIMUM NAVIGATION PERFORMANCE SPECIFICATIONS AIRSPACE

No person may operate a civil aircraft of U.S. registry in North Atlantic (NAT) airspace designated as Minimum Navigation Performance Specifications (MNPS) airspace unless —

(a)   The aircraft has approved navigation performance capability which complies with the requirements of Appendix C to this part; and

(b)   The operator is authorized by the Administrator to perform such operations.

(c)   The Administrator authorizes deviations from the requirements of this section in accordance with Section 3 of appendix C to this part.

91.707   FLIGHTS BETWEEN MEXICO OR CANADA AND THE UNITED STATES

Unless otherwise authorized by ATC, no person may operate a civil aircraft between Mexico or Canada and the United States without filing an IFR or VFR flight plan, as appropriate.

*(Not published herein.)

91.709   OPERATIONS TO CUBA

No person may operate a civil aircraft from the United States to Cuba unless —

(a)   Departure is from an international airport of entry designated in *§6.13 of the Air Commerce Regulations of the Bureau of Customs (19 CFR 6.13); and

(b)   In the case of departure from any of the 48 contiguous States or the District of Columbia, the pilot in command of the aircraft has filed —

    (1)   A DVFR or IFR flight plan as prescribed in *§99.11 or *99.13 of this chapter; and

    (2)   A written statement, within 1 hour before departure, with the Office of Immigration and Naturalization Service at the airport of departure, containing —

        (i)   All information in the flight plan;

        (ii)   The name of each occupant of the aircraft;

        (iii)   The number of occupants of the aircraft; and

        (iv)   A description of the cargo, if any.

This section does not apply to the operation of aircraft by a scheduled air carrier over routes authorized in operations specifications issued by the Administrator.

91.711   SPECIAL RULES FOR FOREIGN CIVIL AIRCRAFT

(a)   *General.* In addition to the other applicable regulations of this part, each person operating a foreign civil aircraft within the United States shall comply with this section.

(b)   *VFR.* No person may conduct VFR operations which require two-way radio communications under this part unless at least one crewmember of that aircraft is able to conduct two-way radio communications in the English language and is on duty during that operation.

(c)   *IFR.* No person may operate a foreign civil aircraft under IFR unless —

    (1)   That aircraft is equipped with —

Amend #227
eff 9-16-93

        (i)   Radio equipment allowing two-way radio communication with ATC when it is operated in controlled airspace; and

        (ii)   Radio navigational equipment appropriate to the navigational facilities to be used;

    (2)   Each person piloting the aircraft —

        (i)   Holds a current United States instrument rating or is authorized by his foreign airman certificate to pilot under IFR; and

        (ii)   Is thoroughly familiar with the United States en route, holding, and letdown procedures; and

    (3)   At least one crewmember of that aircraft is able to conduct two-way radiotelephone communications in the English language and that crewmember is on duty while the aircraft is approaching, operating within, or leaving the United States.

(d)   *Over water.* Each person operating a foreign civil aircraft over water off the shores of the United States shall give flight notification or file a flight plan in accordance with the Supplementary Procedure for the ICAO region concerned.

(e)   *Flight at and above FL 240.* If VOR navigational equipment is required under paragraph (c)(1)(ii) of this section, no person may operate a foreign civil aircraft within the 50 states and the District of Columbia at or above FL 240, unless the aircraft is equipped with distance measuring equipment (DME) capable of receiving and indicating distance information from the VORTAC facilities to be used. When DME required by this paragraph fails at and above FL 240, the pilot in command of the aircraft shall notify ATC immediately and may then continue operations at and above FL 240 to the next airport of intended landing at which repairs or replacement of the equipment can be made. However, paragraph (e) of this section does not apply to foreign civil aircraft that are not equipped with DME when operated for the following purposes and if ATC is notified prior to each takeoff:

*(Not published herein.)

(1) Ferry flights to and from a place in the United States where repairs or alterations are to be made.
(2) Ferry flights to a new country of registry.
(3) Flight of a new aircraft of U.S. manufacture for the purpose of —
(i) Flight testing the aircraft;
(ii) Training foreign flight crews in the operation of the aircraft; or
(iii) Ferrying the aircraft for export delivery outside the United States.
(4) Ferry, demonstration, and test flight of an aircraft brought to the United States for the purpose of demonstration or testing the whole or any part thereof.

91.713 OPERATION OF CIVIL AIRCRAFT OF CUBAN REGISTRY

No person may operate a civil aircraft of Cuban registry except in controlled airspace and in accordance with air traffic clearance or air traffic control instructions that may require use of specific airways or routes and landings at specific airports.

91.715 SPECIAL FLIGHT AUTHORIZATIONS FOR FOREIGN CIVIL AIRCRAFT

(a) Foreign civil aircraft may be operated without airworthiness certificates required under §91.203 if a special flight authorization for that operation is issued under this section. Application for a special flight authorization must be made to the Flight Standards Division Manager or Aircraft Certification Directorate Manager of the FAA region in which the applicant is located or to the region within which the U.S. point of entry is located. However, in the case of an aircraft to be operated in the U.S. for the purpose of demonstration at an air show, the application may be made to the Flight Standards Division Manager or Aircraft Certification Directorate Manager of the FAA region in which the air show is located.
(b) The Administrator may issue a special flight authorization for a foreign civil aircraft subject to any conditions and limitations that the Administrator considers necessary for safe operation in the U.S. airspace.
(c) No person may operate a foreign civil aircraft under a special flight authorization unless that operation also complies with *part 375 of the Special Regulations of the Department of Transportation (14 CFR 375).

(Approved by the Office of Management and Budget under OMB control number 2120-0005)

91.717 — 91.799 Reserved

*(Not published herein — Ed.)

INTENTIONALLY

LEFT

BLANK

SUBPART I — OPERATING NOISE LIMITS

91.801   APPLICABILITY: RELATION TO *PART 36

(a) This subpart prescribes operating noise limits and related requirements that apply, as follows, to the operation of civil aircraft in the United States

  (1) Sections 91.803, 91.805, 91.807, 91.809, and 91.811 apply to civil subsonic turbojet airplanes with maximum weights of more than 75,000 pounds and —

    (i) If U.S. registered, that have standard airworthiness certificates; or

    (ii) If foreign registered, that would be required by this chapter to have a U.S. standard airworthiness certificate in order to conduct the operations intended for the airplane were it registered in the United States. Those sections apply to operations to or from airports in the United States under this part and parts 121, 125, 129, and 135 of this chapter.

  (2) Section 91.813 applies to U.S. operators of civil subsonic turbojet airplanes covered by this subpart. That section applies to operators operating to or from airports in the United States under this part and parts 121, 125, and 135, but not to those operating under part 129 of this chapter.

  (3) Sections 91.803 and 91.819, and 91.821 apply to U.S. registered civil supersonic airplanes having standard airworthiness certificates and to foreign-registered civil supersonic airplanes that, if registered in the United States, would be required by this chapter to have U.S. standard airworthiness certificates in order to conduct the operations intended for the airplane. Those sections apply to operations under this part and under parts 121, 125, 129, and 135 of this chapter.

(b) Unless otherwise specified, as used in this subpart *"part 36" refers to 14 CFR *part 36, including the noise levels under appendix C of that part, notwithstanding the provisions of that part excepting certain airplanes from the specified noise requirements. For purposes of this subpart, the various stages of noise levels, the terms used to describe airplanes with respect to those levels, and the terms "subsonic airplane" and "supersonic airplane" have the meanings specified under *part 36 of this chapter. For purposes of this subpart, for subsonic airplanes operated in foreign air commerce in the United States, the Administrator may accept compliance with the noise requirements under *annex 16 of the International Civil Aviation Organization when those requirements have been shown to be substantially compatible with, and achieve results equivalent to those achievable under *part 36 for that airplane. Determinations made under these provisions are subject to the limitations of *§36.5 of this chapter as if those noise levels were *part 36 noise levels.

Amend #225
eff 9-25-91

(c) Sections 91.851 through 91.875 of this subpart prescribe operating noise limits and related requirements that apply to any civil subsonic turbojet airplane with a maximum certificated weight of more than 75,000 pounds operating to or from an airport in the 48 contiguous United States and the District of Columbia under this part, part 121, 125, 129, or 135 of this chapter on and after September 25, 1991.

91.803   PART 125 OPERATORS: DESIGNATION OF APPLICABLE REGULATIONS

For airplanes covered by this subpart and operated under part 125 of this chapter, the following regulations apply as specified:

(a) For each airplane operation to which requirements prescribed under this subpart applied before November 29, 1980, those requirements of this subpart continue to apply.

(b) For each subsonic airplane operation to which requirements prescribed under this subpart did not apply before November 29, 1980, because the airplane was not operated in the United States under this part or part 121, 129, or 135 of this chapter, the requirements prescribed under §§91.805, 91.809, 91.811, and 91.813 of this subpart apply.

*(Not published herein)

(c) For each supersonic airplane operation to which requirements prescribed under this subpart did not apply before November 29, 1980, because the airplane was not operated in the United States under this part or Part 121, 129, or 135 of this chapter, the requirements of §§91.819 and 91.821 of this subpart apply.

(d) For each airplane required to operate under part 125 for which a deviation under that part is approved to operate, in whole or in part, under this part or parts 121, 129, or 135 of this chapter, notwithstanding the approval, the requirements prescribed under paragraphs (a), (b), and (c) of this section continue to apply.

91.805 FINAL COMPLIANCE: SUBSONIC AIRPLANES

Except as provided in §§91.809 and 91.811, on and after January 1, 1985, no person may operate to or from an airport in the United States any subsonic airplane covered by this subpart unless that airplane has been shown to comply with Stage 2 or Stage 3 noise levels under *part 36 of this chapter.

91.807 PHASED COMPLIANCE UNDER PARTS 121, 125 and 135: SUBSONIC AIRPLANES

(a) *General.* Each person operating airplanes under Part 121, 125, or 135 of this chapter, as prescribed under §91.803 of this subpart, regardless of the state of registry of the airplane, shall comply with this section with respect to subsonic airplanes covered by this subpart.

(b) *Compliance schedule.* Except for airplanes shown to be operated in foreign air commerce under paragraph (c) of this section or covered by an exemption (including those issued under §91.811), airplanes operated by U.S. operators in air commerce in the United States must be shown to comply with Stage 2 or Stage 3 noise levels under *part 36 of this chapter, in accordance with the following schedule, or they may not be operated to or from airports in the United States:

(1) By January 1, 1981 —
  (i) At least one quarter of the airplanes that have four engines with no bypass ratio or with a bypass ratio less than two; and
  (ii) At least half of the airplanes powered by engines with any other bypass ratio or by another number of engines.

(2) By January 1, 1983 —
  (i) At least one-half of the airplanes that have four engines with no bypass ratio or with a bypass ratio less than two; and
  (ii) All airplanes powered by engines with any other bypass ratio or by another number of engines.

(c) *Apportionment of airplanes.* For purposes of paragraph (b) of this section, a person operating airplanes engaged in domestic and foreign air commerce in the United States may elect not to comply with the phased schedule with respect to that portion of the airplanes operated by that person shown, under an approved method of apportionment, to be engaged in foreign air commerce in the United States.

91.809 REPLACEMENT AIRPLANES

A Stage 1 airplane may be operated after the otherwise applicable compliance dates prescribed under §§91.805 and 91.807 if, under an approved plan, a replacement airplane has been ordered by the operator under a binding contract as follows:

(a) For replacement of an airplane powered by two engines, until January 1, 1986, but not after the date specified in the plan, if the contract is entered into by January 1, 1983, and specifies delivery before January 1, 1986, of a replacement airplane which has been shown to comply with Stage 3 noise levels under *part 36 of this chapter.

*(Not published herein)

(b) For replacement of an airplane powered by three engines, until January 1, 1985, but not after the date specified in the plan, if the contract is entered into by January 1, 1983, and specifies delivery before January 1, 1985, of a replacement airplane which has been shown to comply with Stage 3 noise levels under *part 36 of this chapter.

(c) For replacement of any other airplane, until January 1, 1985, but not after the date specified in the plan, if the contract specifies delivery before January 1, 1985, of a replacement airplane which —
 (1) Has been shown to comply with Stage 2 or Stage 3 noise levels under *part 36 of this chapter prior to issuance of an original standard airworthiness certificate; or
 (2) Has been shown to comply with Stage 3 noise levels under *part 36 of this chapter prior to issuance of a standard airworthiness certificate other than original issue.

(d) Each operator of a Stage 1 airplane for which approval of a replacement plan is requested under this section shall submit to the Director, Office of Environment and Energy, an application constituting the proposed replacement plan (or revised Plan) that contains the information specified under this paragraph and which is certified (under penalty of *18 U.S.C. 1001) as true and correct. Each application for approval must provide information corresponding to that specified in the contract, upon which the FAA may rely in considering its approval, as follows:
 (1) Name and address of the applicant.
 (2) Aircraft type and model and registration number for each airplane to be replaced under the plan.
 (3) Aircraft type and model of each replacement airplane.
 (4) Scheduled dates of delivery and introduction into service of each replacement airplane.
 (5) Names and addresses of the parties to the contract and any other persons who may effectively cancel the contract or otherwise control the performance of any party.
 (6) Information specifying the anticipated disposition of the airplanes to be replaced.
 (7) A statement that the contract represents a legally enforceable, mutual agreement for delivery of an eligible replacement airplane.
 (8) Any other information or documentation requested by the Director, Office of Environment and Energy, reasonably necessary to determine whether the plan should be approved.

91.811 SERVICE TO SMALL COMMUNITIES EXEMPTION: TWO-ENGINE, SUBSONIC AIRPLANES

(a) A Stage 1 airplane powered by two engines may be operated after the compliance dates prescribed under §§91.805, 91.807, and 91.809, when, with respect to that airplane, the Administrator issues an exemption to the operator from the noise level requirements under this subpart. Each exemption issued under this section terminates on the earliest of the following dates:
 (1) For an exempted airplane sold, or otherwise disposed of, to another person on or after January 1, 1983, on the date of delivery to that person;
 (2) For an exempted airplane with a seating configuration of 100 passenger seats or less, on January 1, 1988.
 (3) For an exempted airplane with a seating configuration of more than 100 passenger seats, on January 1, 1985.

(b) For purpose of this section, the seating configuration of an airplane is governed by that shown to exist on December 1, 1979, or an earlier date established for that airplane by the Administrator.

*(Not published herein — Ed.)

91.813   COMPLIANCE PLANS AND STATUS: U.S. OPERATORS OF SUBSONIC AIRPLANES

(a) Each U.S. operator of a civil subsonic airplane covered by this subpart (regardless of the state of registry) shall submit to the Director, Office of Environment and Energy, in accordance with this section, the operator's current compliance status and plan for achieving and maintaining compliance with the applicable noise level requirements of this subpart. If appropriate, an operator may substitute for the required plan a notice, certified as true (under penalty of *18 U.S.C. 1001) by that operator, that no change in the plan or status of any airplane affected by the plan has occurred since the date of the plan most recently submitted under this section.

(b) Each compliance plan, including each revised plan, must contain the information specified under paragraph (c) of this section for each airplane covered by this section that is operated by the operator. Unless otherwise approved by the Administrator, compliance plans must provide the required plan and status information as it exists on the date 30 days before the date specified for submission of the plan. Plans must be certified by the operator as true and complete (under penalty of *18 U.S.C. 1001) and be submitted for each airplane covered by this section on or before 90 days after initially commencing operation of airplanes covered by this section, whichever is later, and thereafter —

(1) Thirty days after any change in the operator's fleet or compliance planning decisions that has a separate or cumulative effect on 10 percent or more of the airplanes in either class of airplanes covered by §91.807(b); and

(2) Thirty days after each compliance date applicable to that airplane under this subpart, and annually thereafter through 1985, or until any later date for that airplane prescribed under this subpart, on the anniversary of that submission date, to show continuous compliance with this subpart.

(c) Each compliance plan submitted under this section must identify the operator and include information regarding the compliance plan and status for each airplane covered by the plan as follows:

(1) Name and address of the airplane operator.

(2) Name and telephone number of the person designated by the operator to be responsible for the preparation of the compliance plan and its submission.

(3) The total number of airplanes covered by this section and in each of the following classes and subclasses:

  (i) For airplanes engaged in domestic air commerce —

    (A) Airplanes powered by four turbojet engines with no bypass ratio or with a bypass ratio less than two.

    (B) Airplanes powered by engines with any other bypass ratio or by another number of engines; and

    (C) Airplanes covered by an exemption issued under §91.811 of this subpart.

  (ii) For airplanes engaged in foreign air commerce under an approved apportionment plan —

    (A) Airplanes powered by four turbojet engines with no bypass ratio or with a bypass ratio less than two;

    (B) Airplanes powered by engines with any other bypass ratio or by another number of engines; and

    (C) Airplanes covered by an exemption issued under §91.811 of this subpart.

(4) For each airplane covered by this section —

  (i) Aircraft type and model;

  (ii) Aircraft registration number;

  (iii) Aircraft manufacturer serial number;

  (iv) Aircraft powerplant make and model;

  (v) Aircraft year of manufacture;

*(Not published herein — Ed.)

(vi)   Whether *part 36 noise level compliance has been shown, "Yes/No";

(vii)   The appropriate code prescribed under paragraph (c)(5) of this section which indicates the acoustical technology installed, or to be installed, on the airplane;

(viii)   For airplanes on which acoustical technology has been or will be applied, following the appropriate code entry, the actual or scheduled month and year of installation on the airplane;

(ix)   For DC-8 and B-707 airplanes operated in domestic U.S. air commerce which have been or will be retired from service in the United States without replacement between January 24, 1977, and January 1, 1985, the appropriate code prescribed under paragraph (c)(5) of this section followed by the actual or scheduled month and year of retirement of the airplane from service;

(x)   For DC-8 and B-707 airplanes operated in foreign air commerce in the United States which have been or will be retired from service in the United States without replacement between April 14, 1980, and January 1, 1985, the appropriate code prescribed under paragraph (c)(5) of this section followed by the actual or scheduled month and year of retirement of the airplane from service;

(xi)   For airplanes covered by an approved replacement plan under §91.807(c) of this subpart, the appropriate code prescribed under paragraph (c)(5) of this section followed by the scheduled month and year for replacement of the airplane;

(xii)   For airplanes designated as "engaged in foreign commerce" in accordance with an approved method of apportionment under §91.807(c) of this subpart, the appropriate code prescribed under paragraph (c)(5) of this section;

(xiii)   For airplanes covered by an exemption issued to the operator granting relief from noise level requirements of this subpart, the appropriate code prescribed under paragraph (c)(5) of this section followed by the actual or scheduled month and year of expiration of the exemption and the appropriate code and applicable dates which indicate the compliance strategy planned or implemented for the airplane.

(xiv)   For all airplanes covered by this section, the number of spare shipsets of acoustical components needed for continuous compliance and the number available on demand to the operator in support of those airplanes; and

(xv)   For airplanes for which none of the other codes prescribed under paragraph (c)(5) of this section describes either the technology applied or to be applied to the airplane in accordance with the certification requirements under *parts 21 and 36 of this chapter, or the compliance strategy or methodology following the code "OTH," enter the date of any certificate action and attach an addendum to the plan explaining the nature and the extent of the certificated technology, strategy, or methodology employed, with reference to the type certificate documentation.

---

*(Not published herein — Ed.)

(5) TABLE OF ACOUSTICAL TECHNOLOGY/STRATEGY CODES

Code	Airplane type/ model	Certificated technology
A	B-707-120B; B-707-320B/C; B-720B	Quiet nacelles + 1-ring.
B	B-727-100.............	Double wall fan duct treatment.
C	B-727-200.............	Double wall fan duct treatment (pre-January 1977 installations and amended type certificate).
D	B-727-200; B-737-100; B-737-200	Quiet nacelles + double wall fan duct treatment
E	B-747-100 (pre-December 1971); B-747-200 (pre-December 1971).....................	Fixed lip inlets + sound absorbing material treatment.
F	DC-8.....................	New extended inlet and bullet with treatment + fan duct treatment areas.
G	DC-9.....................	P-36 sound absorbing material treatment kit.
H	BAC-111-200.......	Silencer kit (BAC Acoustic Report 522).
I	BAC-111-400.......	Silencer kit (BAC Acoustic Report 598).
J	B-707; DC-8..........	Reengined with high bypass ratio turbojet engines + quiet nacelles (if certificated under stage 3 noise level requirements).

REP-   For airplanes covered by an approved replacement plan under §91.807(c) of this subpart.

EFC-   For airplanes designated as "engaged in foreign commerce" in accordance with an approved method of apportionment under §91.811 of this subpart.

RET-   For DC-8 and B-707 airplanes operated in domestic U.S. air commerce and retired from service in the United States without replacement between January 24, 1977, and January 1, 1985.

RFC-   For DC-8 and B-707 airplanes operated by U.S. operators in foreign air commerce in the United States and retired from service in the United States without replacement between April 14, 1980, and January 1, 1985.

EXD-   For airplanes exempted from showing compliance with the noise level requirements of this subpart.

OTH-   For airplanes for which no other prescribed code describes either the certificated technology applied or to be applied to the airplane, or the compliance strategy or methodology. (An addendum must explain the nature and extent of technology, strategy, or methodology and reference the type certificate documentation.)

91.815   **AGRICULTURAL AND FIRE FIGHTING AIRPLANES: NOISE OPERATING LIMITATIONS**

(a) This section applies to propeller-driven, small airplanes having standard airworthiness certificates that are designed for "agricultural aircraft operations" (as defined in *§137.3 of this chapter, as effective on January 1, 1966) or for dispensing fire fighting materials.

(b) If the Airplane Flight Manual, or other approved manual material, information, markings, or placards for the airplane indicate that the airplane has not been shown to comply with the noise limits under *part 36 of this chapter, no person may operate that airplane, except —

   (1) To the extent necessary to accomplish the work activity directly associated with the purpose for which it is designed;

   (2) To provide flight crewmember training in the special purpose operation for which the airplane is designed; and

   (3) To conduct "nondispensing aerial work operations" in accordance with the requirements under *§137.29(c) of this chapter.

91.817   **CIVIL AIRCRAFT SONIC BOOM**

(a) No person may operate a civil aircraft in the United States at a true flight Mach number greater than 1 except in compliance with conditions and limitations in an authorization to exceed Mach 1 issued to the operator under appendix B of this part.

(b) In addition, no person may operate a civil aircraft for which the maximum operating limit speed M_{mo} exceeds a Mach number of 1, to or from an airport in the United States, unless —

   (1) Information available to the flight crew includes flight limitations that ensure that flights entering or leaving the Unites States will not cause a sonic boom to reach the surface within the United States; and

   (2) The operator complies with the flight limitations prescribed in paragraph (b)(1) of this section or complies with conditions and limitations in an authorization to exceed Mach 1 issued under appendix B of this part.

91.819   **CIVIL SUPERSONIC AIRPLANES THAT DO NOT COMPLY WITH *PART 36**

(a) *Applicability.* This section applies to civil supersonic airplanes that have not been shown to comply with the Stage 2 noise limits of *Part 36 in effect on October 13, 1977, using applicable trade-off provisions, and that are operated in the United States after July 31, 1978.

(b) *Airport use.* Except in an emergency, the following apply to each person who operates a civil supersonic airplane to or from an airport in the United States:

   (1) Regardless of whether a type design change approval is applied for under *part 21 of this chapter, no person may land or take off an airplane covered by this section for which the type design is changed, after July 31, 1978, in a manner constituting an "acoustical change" under *§21.93, unless the acoustical change requirements of *part 36 are complied with.

   (2) No flight may be scheduled, or otherwise planned, for takeoff or landing after 10 p.m. and before 7 a.m. local time.

91.821   **CIVIL SUPERSONIC AIRPLANES: NOISE LIMITS**

Except for Concorde airplanes having flight time before January 1, 1980, no person may operate in the United States a civil supersonic airplane that does not comply with the Stage 2 noise limits of *part 36 in effect on October 13, 1977, using applicable trade-off provisions.

91.823 — 91.850 [Reserved]

*(Not published herein)

91.851   **Definitions**

For the purposes of §§ 91.851 through 91.875 of this subpart:

Contiguous United States means the area encompassed by the 48 contiguous United States and the District of Columbia.

Fleet means those civil subsonic turbojet airplanes with a maximum certificated weight of more than 75,000 pounds that are listed on an operator's operations specifications as eligible for operation in the contiguous United States.

Import means a change in ownership of an airplane from a non-U.S. person to a U.S. person when the airplane is brought into the United States for operation.

Operations specifications means an enumeration of airplanes by type, model, series, and serial number operated by the operator or foreign air carrier on a given day, regardless of how or whether such airplanes are formally listed or designated by the operator.

Owner means any person that has indicia of ownership sufficient to register the airplane in the United States pursuant to *part 47 of this chapter.

New entrant means an air carrier or foreign air carrier that, on or before November 5, 1990, did not conduct operations under part 121, 125, 129, or 135 of this chapter using an airplane covered by this subpart to or from any airport in the contiguous United States, but that initiates such operation after that date.

Stage 2 noise levels mean the requirements for Stage 2 noise levels as defined in *part 36 of this chapter in effect on November 5, 1990.

Stage 3 noise levels mean the requirements for Stage 3 noise levels as defined in *part 36 of this chapter in effect on November 5, 1990.

Stage 2 airplane means a civil subsonic turbojet airplane with a maximum certificated weight of 75,000 pounds or more that complies with Stage 2 noise levels as defined in *part 36 of this chapter.

Stage 3 airplane means a civil subsonic turbojet airplane with a maximum certificated weight of 75,000 pounds or more that complies with Stage 3 noise levels as defined in *part 36 of this chapter.

91.853   **FINAL COMPLIANCE: CIVIL SUBSONIC AIRPLANES**

Except as provided in § 91.873, after December 31, 1999, no person shall operate to or from any airport in the contiguous United States any airplane subject to § 91.801(c) of this subpart, unless that airplane has been shown to comply with Stage 3 noise levels.

91.855   **ENTRY AND NONADDITION RULE**

No person may operate any airplane subject to § 91.801(c) of this subpart to or from an airport in the contiguous United States unless one or more of the following apply:

(a)   The airplane complies with Stage 3 noise levels.

(b)   The airplane complies with Stage 2 noise levels and was owned by a U.S. person on and since November 5, 1990. Stage 2 airplanes that meet these criteria and are leased to foreign airlines are also subject to the return provisions of paragraph (e) of this section.

(c)   The airplane complies with Stage 2 noise levels, is owned by a non-U.S. person, and is the subject of a binding lease to a U.S. person effective before and on September 25, 1991. Any such airplane may be operated for the term of the lease in effect on that date, and any extensions thereof provided for in that lease.

(d)   The airplane complies with Stage 2 noise levels and is operated by a foreign air carrier.

(e)   The airplane complies with Stage 2 noise levels and is operated by a foreign operator other than for the purpose of foreign air commerce.

(f)   The airplane complies with Stage 2 noise levels and—

     (1)   On November 5, 1990, was owned by:

         (i)   A corporation, trust, or partnership organized under the laws of the United States or any State (including individual States, territories, possessions, and the District of Columbia);

         (ii)   An individual who is a citizen of the United States; or

         (iii)   An entity owned or controlled by a corporation, trust, partnership, or individual described in paragraph (f)(1)(i) or (ii) of this section; and

Amend #225
eff 9-25-91

*(Not published herein)

(2)   Enters into the United States not later than 6 months after the expiration of a lease agreement (including any extensions thereof) between an owner described in paragraph (f)(1) of this section and a foreign airline.

(g)   The airplane complies with Stage 2 noise levels and was purchased by the importer under a written contract executed before November 5, 1990.

(h)   Any Stage 2 airplane described in this section is eligible for operation in the contiguous United States only as provided under § 91.865 or 91.867.

91.857   AIRPLANES IMPORTED TO POINTS OUTSIDE THE CONTIGUOUS UNITED STATES

An operator of a Stage 2 airplane that was imported into a noncontiguous State, territory, or possession of the United States on or after November 5, 1990, shall:

(a)   Include in its operations specifications a statement that such airplane may not be used to provide air transportation to or from any airport in the contiguous United States.

(b)   Obtain a special flight authorization to operate that airplane into the contiguous United States for the purpose of maintenance. The special flight authorization must include a statement indicating that this regulation is the basis for the authorization.

91.859   MODIFICATION TO MEET STAGE 3 NOISE LEVELS

For an airplane subject to § 91.801(c) of this subpart and otherwise prohibited from operation to or from an airport in the contiguous United States by § 91.855, any person may apply for a special flight authorization for that airplane to operate in the contiguous United States for the purpose of obtaining modification to meet Stage 3 noise levels.

91.861   BASE LEVEL

(a)   U.S. Operators. The base level of a U.S. operator is equal to the number of owned or leased Stage 2 airplanes subject to § 91.801(c) of this subpart that were listed on that operator's operations specifications for operations to or from airports in the contiguous United States on any one day selected by the operator during the period January 1, 1990, through July 1, 1991, plus or minus adjustments made pursuant to paragraphs (a)(1) and (2).

     (1)   The base level of a U.S. operator shall be increased by a number equal to the total of the following—

         (i)   The number of Stage 2 airplanes returned to service in the United States pursuant to § 91.855(f);

         (ii)   The number of Stage 2 airplanes purchased pursuant to § 91.855(g); and

         (iii)   Any U.S. operator base level acquired with a Stage 2 airplane transferred from another person under § 91.863.

     (2)   The base level of a U.S. operator shall be decreased by the amount of U.S. operator base level transferred with the corresponding number of Stage 2 airplanes to another person under § 91.863.

Amend #225
eff 9-25-91   (b)   Foreign air carriers. The base level of a foreign air carrier is equal to the number of owned or leased Stage 2 airplanes that were listed on that carrier's U.S. operations specifications on any one day during the period January 1, 1990, through July 1, 1991, plus or minus any adjustments to the base levels made pursuant to paragraphs (b)(1) and (2).

     (1)   The base level of a foreign air carrier shall be increased by the amount of foreign air carrier base level acquired with a Stage 2 airplane from another person under § 91.863.

     (2)   The base level of a foreign air carrier shall be decreased by the amount of foreign air carrier base level transferred with a Stage 2 airplane to another person under § 91.863.

(c)   New entrants do not have a base level.

91.863 TRANSFERS OF STAGE 2 AIRPLANES WITH BASE LEVEL

(a) Stage 2 airplanes may be transferred with or without the corresponding amount of base level. Base level may not be transferred without the corresponding number of Stage 2 airplanes.

(b) No portion of a U.S. operator's base level established under § 91.861 (a) may be used for operations by a foreign air carrier. No portion of a foreign air carrier's base level established under § 91.861(b) may be used for operations by a U.S. operator.

(c) Whenever a transfer of Stage 2 airplanes with base level occurs, the transferring and acquiring parties shall, within 10 days, jointly submit written notification of the transfer to the FAA, Office of Environment and Energy. Such notification shall state:

   (1) The names of the transferring and acquiring parties;

   (2) The name, address, and telephone number of the individual responsible for submitting the notification on behalf of the transferring and acquiring parties;

   (3) The total number of Stage 2 airplanes transferred, listed by airplane type, model, series, and serial number;

   (4) The corresponding amount of base level transferred and whether it is U.S. operator or foreign air carrier base level; and

   (5) The effective date of the transaction.

(d) If, taken as a whole, a transaction or series of transactions made pursuant to this section does not produce an increase or decrease in the number of Stage 2 airplanes for either the acquiring or transferring operator, such transaction or series of transactions may not be used to establish compliance with the requirements of § 91.865.

91.865 PHASED COMPLIANCE FOR OPERATORS WITH BASE LEVEL

Except as provided in paragraph (a) of this section, each operator that operates an airplane under part 91, 121, 125, 129, or 135 of this chapter, regardless of the national registry of the airplane, shall comply with paragraph (b) or (d) of this section at each interim compliance date with regard to its subsonic airplane fleet covered by § 91.801(c) of this subpart.

(a) This section does not apply to new entrants covered by § 91.867 or to foreign operators not engaged in foreign air commerce.

(b) Each operator that chooses to comply with this paragraph pursuant to any interim compliance requirement shall reduce the number of Stage 2 airplanes it operates that are eligible for operation in the contiguous United States to a maximum of:

   (1) After December 31, 1994, 75 percent of the base level held by the operator;

   (2) After December 31, 1996, 50 percent of the base level held by the operator;

   (3) After December 31, 1998, 25 percent of the base level held by the operator.

(c) Except as provided under § 91.871, the number of Stage 2 airplanes that must be reduced at each compliance date contained in paragraph (b) of this section shall be determined by reference to the amount of base level held by the operator on that compliance date as calculated under § 91.861.

(d) Each operator that chooses to comply with this paragraph pursuant to any interim compliance requirement shall operate a fleet that consists of:

   (1) After December 31, 1994, not less than 55 percent Stage 3 airplanes;

   (2) After December 31, 1996, not less than 65 percent Stage 3 airplanes;

   (3) After December 31, 1998, not less than 75 percent Stage 3 airplanes.

(e) Calculations resulting in fractions may be rounded to permit the continued operation of the next whole number of Stage 2 airplanes.

91.867 PHASED COMPLIANCE FOR NEW ENTRANTS

(a) New entrant U.S. air carriers.

   (1) A new entrant initiating operations under part 121, 125, or 135 of this chapter on or before December 31, 1994, may initiate service without regard to the percentage of its fleet composed of Stage 3 airplanes.

   (2) After December 31, 1994, at least 25 percent of the fleet of a new entrant must comply with Stage 3 noise levels.

(3) After December 31, 1996, at least 50 percent of the fleet of a new entrant must comply with Stage 3 noise levels.
(4) After December 31, 1998, at least 75 percent of the fleet of a new entrant must comply with Stage 3 noise levels.
(b) New entrant foreign air carriers.
   (1) A new entrant foreign air carrier initiating part 129 operations on or before December 31, 1994, may initiate service without regard to the percentage of its fleet composed of Stage 3 airplanes.
   (2) After December 31, 1994, at least 25 percent of the fleet on U.S. operations specifications of a new entrant foreign air carrier must comply with Stage 3 noise levels.
   (3) After December 31, 1996, at least 50 percent of the fleet on U.S. operations specifications of a new entrant foreign air carrier must comply with Stage 3 noise levels.
   (4) After December 31, 1998, at least 75 percent of the fleet on U.S. operations specifications of a new entrant foreign air carrier must comply with Stage 3 noise levels.
(c) Calculations resulting in fractions may be rounded to permit the continued operation of the next whole number of Stage 2 airplanes.

91.869   CARRY-FORWARD COMPLIANCE

(a) Any operator that exceeds the requirements of paragraph (b) of § 91.865 of this part on or before December 31, 1994, or on or before December 31, 1996, may claim a credit that may be applied at a subsequent interim compliance date.

Amend #225
eff 9-25-91 (b) Any operator that eliminates or modifies more Stage 2 airplanes pursuant to § 91.865(b) than required as of December 31, 1994, or December 31, 1996, may count the number of additional Stage 2 airplanes reduced as a credit toward—
   (1) The number of Stage 2 airplanes it would otherwise be required to reduce following a subsequent interim compliance date specified in § 91.865(b); or
   (2) The number of Stage 3 airplanes it would otherwise be required to operate in its fleet following a subsequent interim compliance date to meet the percentage requirements specified in § 91.865(d).

91.871   WAIVERS FROM INTERIM COMPLIANCE REQUIREMENTS

(a) Any U.S. operator or foreign air carrier subject to the requirements of §§ 91.865 or 91.867 of this subpart may request a waiver from any individual compliance requirement.
(b) Applications must be filed with the Secretary of Transportation at least 120 days prior to the compliance date from which the waiver is requested.
(c) Applicants must show that a grant of waiver would be in the public interest, and must include in its application its plans and activities for modifying its fleet, including evidence of good faith efforts to comply with the requirements of § 91.865 or § 91.867. The application should contain all information the applicant considers relevant, including, as appropriate, the following:
   (1) The applicant's balance sheet and cash flow positions;
   (2) The composition of the applicant's current fleet; and
   (3) The applicant's delivery position with respect to new airplanes or noise-abatement equipment.
(d) Waivers will be granted only upon a showing by the applicant that compliance with the requirements of §§ 91.865 or 91.867 at a particular interim compliance date is financially onerous, physically impossible, or technologically infeasible, or that it would have an adverse effect on competition or on service to small communities.
(e) The conditions of any waiver granted under this section shall be determined by the circumstances presented in the application, but in no case may the term extend beyond the next interim compliance date.
(f) A summary of any request for a waiver under this section will be published in the Federal Register, and public comment will be invited. Unless the Secretary finds that circumstances require otherwise, the public comment period will be at least 14 days.

91.873   WAIVERS FROM FINAL COMPLIANCE

(a)   A U.S. air carrier may apply for a waiver from the prohibition contained in § 91.853 for its remaining Stage 2 airplanes, provided that, by July 1, 1999, at least 85 percent of the airplanes used by the carrier to provide service to or from an airport in the contiguous United States will comply with the Stage 3 noise levels.

(b)   An application for the waiver described in paragraph (a) of this section must be filed with the Secretary of Transportation no later than January 1, 1999. Such application must include a plan with firm orders for replacing or modifying all airplanes to comply with Stage 3 noise levels at the earliest practicable time.

(c)   To be eligible to apply for the waiver under this section, a new entrant U.S. air carrier must initiate service no later than January 1, 1999, and must comply fully with all provisions of this section.

(d)   The Secretary may grant a waiver under this section if the Secretary finds that granting such waiver is in the public interest. In making such a finding, the Secretary shall include consideration of the effect of granting such waiver on competition in the air carrier industry and the effect on small community air service, and any other information submitted by the applicant that the Secretary considers relevant.

(e)   The term of any waiver granted under this section shall be determined by the circumstances presented in the application, but in no case will the waiver permit the operation of any Stage 2 airplane covered by this subchapter in the contiguous United States after December 31, 2003.

(f)   A summary of any request for a waiver under this section will be published in the Federal Register, and public comment will be invited. Unless the secretary finds that circumstances require otherwise, the public comment period will be at least 14 days.

Amend #225
eff 9-25-91

91.875   ANNUAL PROGRESS REPORTS

(a)   Each operator subject to § 91.865 or § 91.867 of this chapter shall submit an annual report to the FAA, Office of Environment and Energy, on the progress it has made toward complying with the requirements of that section. Such reports shall be submitted no later than 45 days after the end of a calendar year. All progress reports must provide the information through the end of the calendar year, be certified by the operator as true and complete (under penalty of *18 U.S.C. 1001), and include the following information:

(1)   The name and address of the operator;

(2)   The name, title, and telephone number of the person designated by the operator to be responsible for ensuring the accuracy of the information in the report;

(3)   The operator's progress during the reporting period toward compliance with the requirements of § 91.853, § 91.865 or § 91.867. For airplanes on U.S. operations specifications, each operator shall identify the airplanes by type, model, series, and serial number.

(i)   Each Stage 2 airplane added or removed from operation or U.S. operations specifications (grouped separately by those airplanes acquired with and without base level);

(ii)   Each Stage 2 airplane modified to Stage 3 noise levels (identifying the manufacturer and model of noise abatement retrofit equipment;

(iii)   Each Stage 3 airplane on U.S. operations specifications as of the last day of the reporting period; and

(iv)   For each Stage 2 airplane transferred or acquired, the name and address of the recipient or transferor; and, if base level was transferred, the person to or from whom base level was transferred or acquired pursuant to Section 91.863 along with the effective date of each base level transaction, and the type of base level transferred or acquired.

(b)   Each operator subject to § 91.865 or § 91.867 of this chapter shall submit an initial progress report covering the period from January 1, 1990, through December 31, 1991, and provide:

(1)   For each operator subject to § 91.865:

(i)   The date used to establish its base level pursuant to § 91.861(a); and

*(Not published herein)

        (ii)   a list of those Stage 2 airplanes (by type, model, series and serial number) in its base level, including adjustments made pursuant to § 91.861 after the date its base level was established.

  (2)   For each U.S. operator:

        (i)   A plan to meet the compliance schedules in § 91.865 or § 91.867 and the final compliance date of § 91.853, including the schedule for delivery of replacement Stage 3 airplanes or the installation of noise abatement retrofit equipment; and

        (ii)   A separate list (by type, model, series, and serial number) of those airplanes included in the operator's base level, pursuant to § 91.861(a)(1)(i) and (ii), under the categories "returned" or "purchased," along with the date each was added to its operations specifications.

(c)   Each operator subject to § 91.865 or § 91.867 of this chapter shall submit subsequent annual progress reports covering the calendar year preceding the report and including any changes in the information provided in paragraphs (a) and (b) of this section; including the use of any carry-forward credits pursuant to § 91.869.

Amend #225
eff 9-25-91

(d)   An operator may request, in any report, that specific planning data be considered proprietary.

(e)   If an operator's actions during any reporting period cause it to achieve compliance with § 91.853, the report should include a statement to that effect. Further progress reports are not required unless there is any change in the information reported pursuant to paragraph (a) of this section.

(f)   For each U.S. operator subject to § 91.865, progress reports submitted for calendar years 1994, 1996, and 1998, shall also state how the operator achieved compliance with the requirements of that section, i.e.—

  (1)   By reducing the number of Stage 2 airplanes in its fleet to no more than the maximum permitted percentage of its base level under § 91.865(b), or

  (2)   By operating a fleet that consists of at least the minimum required percentage of Stage 3 airplanes under § 91.865(d).

91.876 — 91.899 [Reserved]

INTENTIONALLY

LEFT

BLANK

SUBPART J — WAIVERS

91.901   **[Reserved]**

91.903   **POLICY AND PROCEDURES**

(a)   The Administrator may issue a certificate of waiver authorizing the operation of aircraft in deviation from any rule listed in this subpart if the Administrator finds that the proposed operation can be safely conducted under the terms of that certificate of waiver.

(b)   An application for a certificate of waiver under this part is made on a form and in a manner prescribed by the Administrator and may be submitted to any FAA office.

(c)   A certificate of waiver is effective as specified in that certificate of waiver.

91.905   **LIST OF RULES SUBJECT TO WAIVERS**

Sec.

91.107	Use of safety belts.
91.111	Operating near other aircraft.
91.113	Right-of-way rules: Except water operations.
91.115	Right-of-way rules: Water operations.
91.117	Aircraft speed.
91.119	Minimum safe altitudes: General.
91.121	Altimeter settings.
91.123	Compliance with ATC clearances and instructions.
91.125	ATC light signals.
91.126	Operating on or in the vicinity of an airport in Class G airspace.
91.127	Operating on or in the vicinity of an airport in Class E airspace.
91.129	Operations in Class D airspace.
91.130	Operations in Class C airspace.
91.131	Operations in Class B airspace.
91.133	Restricted and prohibited areas.
91.135	Operations in Class A airspace.
91.137	Temporary flight restrictions.
91.141	Flight restrictions in the proximity of the Presidential and other parties.
91.143	Flight limitation in the proximity of space flight operations.
91.153	VFR flight plan: Information required.
91.155	Basic VFR weather minimums.
91.157	Special VFR weather minimums.
91.159	VFR cruising altitude or flight level.
91.169	IFR flight plan: Information required.
91.173	ATC clearance and flight plan required.
91.175	Takeoff and landing under IFR.
91.177	Minimum altitudes for IFR operations.
91.179	IFR cruising altitude or flight level.
91.181	Course to be flown.
91.183	IFR radio communications.
91.185	IFR operations: Two-way radio communications failure.
91.187	Operation under IFR in controlled airspace: Malfunction reports.
91.209	Aircraft lights.
91.303	Aerobatic flights.
91.305	Flight test areas.
91.311	Towing: Other than under §91.309.
91.313(e)	Restricted category civil aircraft: Operating limitations.
91.515	Flight altitude rules.
91.705	Operations within the North Atlantic Minimum Navigation Performance Specifications Airspace.
91.707	Flights between Mexico or Canada and the United States.
91.713	Operation of civil aircraft of Cuban registry.

91.907 — 91.999   [Reserved]

Amend #227
eff 9-16-93

INTENTIONALLY

LEFT

BLANK

APPENDIX C
OPERATIONS IN THE NORTH ATLANTIC (NAT)
MINIMUM NAVIGATION PERFORMANCE SPECIFICATIONS (MNPS) AIRSPACE

Section 1.

NAT MNPS airspace is that volume of airspace between FL 275 and FL 400 extending between latitude 27 degrees north and the North Pole, bounded in the east by the eastern boundaries of control areas Santa Maria Oceanic, Shanwick Oceanic, and Reykjavik Oceanic and in the west by the western boundary of Reykjavik Oceanic Control Area, the western boundary of Gander Oceanic Control Area, and the western boundary of New York Oceanic Control Area, excluding the areas west of 60 degrees west and south of 38 degrees 30 minutes north.

Section 2.

The navigation performance capability required for aircraft to be operated in the airspace defined in section 1 of this appendix is as follows:
(a) The standard deviation of lateral track errors shall be less than 6.3 NM (11.7 Km). Standard deviation is a statistical measure of data about a mean value. The mean is zero nautical miles. The overall form of data is such that the plus and minus 1 standard deviation about the mean encompasses approximately 68 percent of the data and plus or minus 2 deviations encompasses approximately 95 percent.
(b) The proportion of the total flight time spent by aircraft 30 NM (55.6 Km) or more off the cleared track shall be less than 5.3×10^{-4} (less than 1 hour in 1,887 flight hours.)
(c) The proportion of the total flight time spent by aircraft between 50 NM and 70 NM (92.6 Km and 129.6 Km) off the cleared track shall be less than 13×10^{-5} (less than 1 hour in 7,693 flight hours).

Section 3.

Air traffic control (ATC) may authorize an aircraft operator to deviate from the requirements of §91.705 for a specific flight if, at the time of flight plan filing for that flight, ATC determines that the aircraft may be provided appropriate separation and that the flight will not interfere with, or impose a burden upon, the operations of other aircraft which meet the requirements of §91.705.

APPENDIX D
AIRPORTS/LOCATIONS: SPECIAL OPERATING RESTRICTIONS

Section 1.

Locations at which the requirements of §91.215(b)(2) apply.
The requirements of §91.215(b)(2) apply below 10,000 feet MSL within a 30-nautical-mile radius of each location in the following list:

Atlanta, GA (The William B. Hartsfield Atlanta International Airport)

Baltimore, MD (Baltimore Washington International Airport)

Boston, MA (General Edward Lawrence Logan International Airport)

Chantilly, VA (Washington Dulles International Airport)

Charlotte, NC (Charlotte/Douglas International Airport)

Chicago, IL (Chicago-O'Hare International Airport)

Cleveland, OH (Cleveland-Hopkins International Airport)

Dallas, TX (Dallas/Fort Worth Regional Airport)

Denver, CO (Denver International Airport)

Detroit, MI (Metropolitan Wayne County Airport)

Honolulu, HI (Honolulu International Airport)

Houston, TX (Houston Intercontinental Airport)

Kansas City, KS (Mid-Continent International Airport)

Las Vegas, NV (McCarran International Airport)

Los Angeles, CA (Los Angeles International Airport)

Memphis, TN (Memphis International Airport)

Miami, FL (Miami International Airport)

Minneapolis, MN (Minneapolis-St. Paul International Airport)

Newark, NJ (Newark International Airport)

New Orleans, LA (New Orleans International Airport-Moisant Field)

New York, NY (John F. Kennedy International Airport)

New York, NY (LaGuardia Airport)

Orlando, FL (Orlando International Airport)

Philadelphia, PA (Philadelphia International Airport)

Phoenix, AZ (Phoenix Sky Harbor International Airport)

Pittsburgh, PA (Greater Pittsburgh International Airport)

St. Louis, MO (Lambert-St. Louis International Airport)

Salt Lake City, UT (Salt Lake City International Airport)

San Diego, CA (San Diego International Airport)

San Francisco, CA (San Francisco International Airport)

Seattle, WA (Seattle-Tacoma International Airport)

Tampa, FL (Tampa International Airport)

Washington, DC (Washington National Airport)

→ Amend #237
Amend #238
eff 5-15-94

Section 2.

Airports at which the requirements of §91.215(b)(5)(ii) apply.
The requirements of §91.215(b)(5)(ii) apply to operations in the vicinity of each of the following airports:

Billings, MT (Logan International Airport)

Section 3.

Locations at which fixed-wing Special VFR operations are prohibited.
The Special VFR weather minimums of §91.157 do not apply to the following airports:

Atlanta, GA (The William B. Hartsfield Atlanta International Airport)
Baltimore, MD (Baltimore/Washington International Airport)
Boston, MA (General Edward Lawrence Logan International Airport)
Buffalo, NY (Greater Buffalo International Airport)
Chicago, IL (Chicago-O'Hare International Airport)
Cleveland, OH (Cleveland-Hopkins International Airport)
Columbus, OH (Port Columbus International Airport)
Covington, KY (Greater Cincinnati International Airport)
Dallas, TX (Dallas/Fort Worth Regional Airport)
Dallas, TX (Love Field)
Denver, CO (Denver International Airport)
Amend #237
Amend #238 Detroit, MI (Metropolitan Wayne County
eff 5-15-94   Airport)
Honolulu, HI (Honolulu International Airport)
Houston, TX (Houston Intercontinental Airport)
Indianapolis, IN (Indianapolis International Airport)

Los Angeles, CA (Los Angeles International Airport)
Louisville, KY (Standiford Field)
Memphis, TN (Memphis International Airport)
Miami, FL (Miami International Airport)
Minneapolis, MN (Minneapolis-St. Paul International Airport)
Newark, NJ (Newark International Airport)
New Orleans, LA (New Orleans International Airport-Moisant Field)
New York, NY (John F. Kennedy International Airport)
New York, NY (LaGuardia Airport)
Philadelphia, PA (Philadelphia International Airport)
Pittsburgh, PA (Greater Pittsburgh International Airport)
Portland, OR (Portland International Airport)
San Francisco, CA (San Francisco International Airport)
Seattle, WA (Seattle-Tacoma International Airport)
St. Louis, MO (Lambert-St. Louis International Airport)
Tampa, FL (Tampa International Airport)
Washington, DC (Washington National Airport)

Section 4.

Locations at which solo student pilot activity is not permitted.
Pursuant to §91.131(b)(2), solo student pilot operations are not permitted at any of the following airports.

Atlanta, GA (The William B. Hartsfield Atlanta International Airport)
Boston, MA (General Edward Lawrence Logan International Airport)
Chicago, IL (Chicago-O'Hare International Airport)
Dallas, TX (Dallas/Fort Worth Regional Airport)
Los Angeles, CA (Los Angeles International Airport)

Miami, FL (Miami International Airport)
Newark, NJ (Newark International Airport)
New York, NY (John F. Kennedy International Airport)
New York, NY (LaGuardia Airport)
San Francisco, CA (San Francisco International Airport)
Washington, DC (Washington National Airport)
Andrews Air Force Base, MD

INTENTIONALLY

LEFT

BLANK

FEDERAL AVIATION REGULATIONS

PART 119 — CERTIFICATION: AIR CARRIERS AND COMMERCIAL OPERATORS

This part contains amendment #2 effective 15 July 1996.

TABLE OF CONTENTS

SUBPART A — GENERAL

SUBPART B — APPLICABILITY OF OPERATING REQUIREMENTS TO DIFFERENT KINDS OF OPERATIONS UNDER PART 121, 125 AND 135 OF THIS CHAPTER

SUBPART C — CERTIFICATION, OPERATIONS SPECIFICATIONS, AND CERTAIN OTHER REQUIREMENTS FOR OPERATIONS CONDUCTED UNDER PART 121 OR PART 135 OF THIS CHAPTER

INTENTIONALLY

LEFT

BLANK

DERIVATION TABLE FOR PART 119

New section	Based on
Subpart A:	
119.1(a)	New language
119.1(b)	SFAR 38-2, Section 1(a)
119.1(c)	New language
119.1(d)	New language
119.1(e)	New language
119.2	New language
119.3	SFAR 38-2, Section 6 and new language
119.5(a)	SFAR 38-2, Section 2(a)
119.5(b)	SFAR 38-2, Section 2(b)
119.5(c)	New language
119.5(d)	SFAR 38-2, Section 1(a)(3)
119.5(e)	SFAR 38-2, Section 1(a)(3)
119.5(f)	SFAR 38-2, Section 1(b)
119.5(g)	SFAR 38-2, Section 1(c), 121.4, 135.7
119.5(h)	SFAR 38-2, Flush paragraph following Section 1(a)(3) and new language
119.5(i)	121.27(a)(1), 121.51(a)(1), 135.13(a)(3)
119.5(j)	135.33
119.7(a)	SFAR 38-2, Section 3
119.7(b)	121.23, 121.43
119.9(a)	135.29
119.9(b)	New language
Subpart B:	
119.21(a)	SFAR 38-2, Section 4(a), 121.3
119.21(b)	SFAR 38-2, Section 4(b)
119.21(c)	New language
119.23(a)	SFAR 38-2, Section 5(a)
119.23(b)	SFAR 38-2, Section 5(b)
119.25(a)	SFAR 38-2, Section 4(c), 5(c) and (d), and new language
119.25(b)	SFAR 38-2, Section 4(c), 5(c) and (d), and new language
Subpart C:	
119.31	SFAR 38-2, Section 1(c), 2(a) and (b), 121.3, and 135.5
119.33(a)	SFAR 38-2, Section 1(c), 2(a) and (b), 3, 121.3, 135.5, 135.13(a)
119.33(b)	SFAR 38-2, Section 1(c), 2(a) and (b), 3, 121.3, 135.5, 135.13(a)
119.33(c)	SFAR 38-2, Section 1(c), 2(a) and (b), 3, 121.3, 135.5, 135.13(a)
119.35(a)	121.26, 121.47(a), 135.11(a)
119.35(b)	121.26, 121.47(a), 135.11(a)

DERIVATION TABLE FOR PART 119 (cont)

New section	Based on
Subpart A:	
119.35(c)	121.47(a)
119.35(d)	121.47(b)
119.35(e)	121.47(c)
119.35(f)	121.47(d)
119.35(g)	121.48
119.35(h)	121.49
119.37(a)	121.25(a), 121.45(a), 135.11(b)(1), and new language
119.37(b)	121.25(a), 121.45(a), 135.11(b)(1), and new language
119.37(c)	121.25(a), 121.45(a), 135.11(b)(1), and new language
119.37(d)	121.25(a), 121.45(a), 135.11(b)(1), and new language
119.37(e)	121.25(a), 121.45(a), 135.11(b)(1), and new language
119.39(a)	121.27(a)(2), 121.51(a)(3), 135.11(b)(1)
119.39(b)	121.27(a)(2), 121.51, 135.13(a)(2) and (b)
119.41(a)	121.77(a), 135.15(a)
119.41(b)	New language
119.41(c)	121.77(b), 135.15(b)
119.41(d)	121.77(c), 135.15(d)
119.43(a)	121.75(b), 135.63(a)(2)
119.43(b)	121.75(b), 135.63(a)(2)
119.47(a)	135.27(a)
119.47(b)	121.83, 135.27(b)
119.49(a)	121.5, 121.25(b), 121.45(b), 135.11(b), and new language
119.49(b)	121.45(b), 135.11(b)(1), and new language
119.49(c)	135.11(b)(1) and new language
119.51(a)	121.79(a), 135.17(a)
119.51(b)	121.79(b), 135.17(d)
119.51(c)	121.79(c), 135.17(b), and new language
119.51(d)	121.79(d), 135.17(c) and (d)
119.51(e)	121.79(b), 135.17(c) and (d)
119.53(a)	121.6(a)
119.53(b)	New language
119.53(c)	121.6(b)
119.53(d)	121.5(c)
119.53(e)	New language
119.53(f)	New language
119.55(a)	121.57(a) and (b)
119.55(b)	121.57(a) and (b)

DERIVATION TABLE FOR PART 119 (cont)

New section	Based on
Subpart A:	
119.55(c)	121.57(a) and (b)
119.55(d)	121.57(a) and (b)
119.55(e)	121.57(a) and (b)
119.57(a)	121.57(c)
119.57(b)	New language
119.59(a)	121.81(a), 135.73, and new language
119.59(b)	121.73, 121.81(a), 135.63(a), 135.73, and new language
119.59(c)	121.81(a)
119.59(d)	New language
119.59(e)	New language
119.59(f)	New language
119.61(a)	121.29(a), 121.53(a), (c), and (d), 135.9(a)
119.61(b)	121.29(a), 121.53(c), and new language
119.61(c)	135.35
119.63(a)	New language
119.63(b)	New language
119.65(a)	121.59(a)
119.65(b)	121.59(b)
119.65(c)	121.59(b)
119.65(d)	121.61 and new language
119.65(e)	121.59(c)
119.67(a)	121.61(a) and new language
119.67(b)	121.61(b) and new language
119.67(c)	121.61(c), 135.39(c), and new language
119.67(d)	121.61(d) and new language
119.67(e)	121.61(b), 135.39(d)
119.69(a)	135.37(a)
119.69(b)	121.59(b), 135.37(b)
119.69(c)	121.59(b)
119.69(d)	135.39 and new language
119.69(e)	121.59, 135.37(c)
119.71(a)	135.39(a)(1) and new language
119.71(b)	135.39(a)(2) and new language
119.71(c)	135.39(b)(1) and new language
119.71(d)	135.39(b)(2) and new language
119.71(e)	135.39(c) and new language
119.71(f)	135.39(d) and new language

INTENTIONALLY

LEFT

BLANK

SUBPART A — GENERAL

119.1 APPLICABILITY

(a) This part applies to each person operating or intending to operate civil aircraft—

   (1) As an air carrier or commercial operator, or both, in air commerce; or

   (2) When common carriage is not involved, in operations of U.S.-registered civil airplanes with a seat configuration of 20 or more passengers, or a maximum payload capacity of 6,000 pounds or more.

(b) This part prescribes—

   (1) The types of air operator certificates issued by the Federal Aviation Administration, including air carrier certificates and operating certificates;

   (2) The certification requirements an operator must meet in order to obtain and hold a certificate authorizing operations under Part 121, 125, or 135 of this chapter and operations specifications for each kind of operation to be conducted and each class and size of aircraft to be operated under Part 121 or 135 of this chapter;

   (3) The requirements an operator must meet to conduct operations under Part 121, 125, or 135 of this chapter and in operating each class and size of aircraft authorized in its operations specifications;

   (4) Requirements affecting wet leasing of aircraft and other arrangements for transportation by air;

   (5) Requirements for obtaining deviation authority to perform operations under a military contract and obtaining deviation authority to perform an emergency operation; and

   (6) Requirements for management personnel for operations conducted under Part 121 or Part 135 of this chapter.

(c) Persons subject to this part must comply with the other requirements of this chapter, except where those requirements are modified by or where additional requirements are imposed by Part 119, 121, 125, or 135 of this chapter.

(d) This part does not govern operations conducted under Part 129, 133, 137, or 139 of this chapter.

(e) Except for operations when common carriage is not involved conducted with airplanes having a passenger-seat configuration of 20 seats or more, excluding any required crewmember seat, or a payload capacity of 6,000 pounds or more, this part does not apply to—

   (1) Student instruction;

   (2) Nonstop sightseeing flights conducted with aircraft having a passenger seat configuration of 30 or fewer, excluding each crewmember seat, and a payload capacity of 7,500 pounds or less, that begin and end at the same airport, and are conducted within a 25 statute mile radius of that airport; however, for nonstop sightseeing flights for compensation or hire conducted in the vicinity of the Grand Canyon National Park, Arizona, the requirements of SFAR 50-2 of this part and SFAR 38-2 of 14 CFR Part 121 or 14 CFR Part 119, as applicable, apply;

   (3) Ferry or training flights;

   (4) Aerial work operations, including—

     (i) Crop dusting, seeding, spraying, and bird chasing;

     (ii) Banner towing;

     (iii) Aerial photography or survey;

     (iv) Fire fighting;

     (v) Helicopter operations in construction or repair work (but it does apply to transportation to and from the site of operations); and

     (vi) Powerline or pipeline patrol;

   (5) Sightseeing flights conducted in hot air balloons;

   (6) Nonstop flights conducted within a 25 statute mile radius of the airport of takeoff carrying persons for the purpose of intentional parachute jumps;

   (7) Helicopter flights conducted within a 25 statute mile radius of the airport of takeoff if—

     (i) Not more than two passengers are carried in the helicopter in addition to the required flightcrew;

     (ii) Each flight is made under day VFR conditions;

     (iii) The helicopter used is certificated in the standard category and complies with the 100-hour inspection requirements of Part 91 of this chapter;

     (iv) The operator notifies the FAA Flight Standards District Office responsible for the geographic area concerned at least 72 hours before each flight and furnishes any essential information that the office requests;

     (v) The number of flights does not exceed a total of six in any calendar year;

     (vi) Each flight has been approved by the Administrator; and

     (vii) Cargo is not carried in or on the helicopter;

   (8) Operations conducted under Part 133 of this chapter or 375 of this title;

   (9) Emergency mail service conducted under 49 U.S.C. 41906; or

  (10) Operations conducted under the provisions of §91.321 of this chapter.

119.2 COMPLIANCE WITH 14 CFR PART 119 OR SFAR 38-2 OF 14 CFR PART 121

(a) Each certificate holder that before January 19, 1996, was issued an air carrier certificate or operating certificate and operations specifications under the requirements of Part 121, Part 135, or SFAR 38-2 of Parts 121 and 135 of this chapter shall continue to comply with SFAR 38-2 of Parts 121 and 135 until March 20, 1997, or until the date on which the certificate holder is issued operations specifications in accordance with Part 119, whichever occurs first. In addition, persons conducting operations under SFAR 38-2 of parts 121 and 135 of this chapter shall continue to comply with the applicable requirements of §§121.6, 121.57, 121.59, 121.61, 121.71 through 121.83, 135.5, 135.11(c), 135.15, 135.17, 135.27, 135.29, 135.33, 135.35, 135.37, and 135.39 of this chapter as in effect on January 18, 1996, until March 20, 1997, or until the date on which the certificate holder is issued operations specifications in accordance with part 119, whichever occurs first. If a certificate holder is issued operation specifications in accordance with Part 119 before March 20, 1997, then, notwithstanding all provisions in SFAR 38-2 of Parts 121 and 135 of this chapter, such certificate holder shall comply with the provisions of Part 119. A copy of these regulations may be obtained from the Federal Aviation Administration, Office of Rulemaking (ARM), 800 Independence Ave., SW., Washington, DC 20591, or by phone (202)267-9677.

(b) Each person who on or after January 19, 1996, applies for or obtains an initial air carrier certificate or operating certificate and operations specifications to conduct operations under Part 121 or 135 of this chapter shall comply with this part notwithstanding all provisions of SFAR 38-2 of Parts 121 and 135 of this chapter.

119.3 DEFINITIONS

For the purpose of subchapter G of this chapter, the term—

All-cargo operation means any operation for compensation or hire that is other than a passenger-carrying operation or, if passengers are carried, they are only those specified in §§121.583(a) or 135.85 of this chapter.

Certificate-holding district office means the Flight Standards District Office that has responsibility for administering the certificate and is charged with the overall inspection of the certificate holder's operations.

Commuter operation means any scheduled operation conducted by any person operating one of the following types of aircraft with a frequency of operations of at least five round trips per week on at least one route between two or more points according to the published flight schedules:

(1) Airplanes, other than turbojet powered airplanes, having a maximum passenger-seat configuration of 9 seats or less, excluding each crewmember seat, and a maximum payload capacity of 7,500 pounds or less; or

(2) Rotorcraft.

Direct air carrier means a person who provides or offers to provide air transportation and who has control over the operational functions performed in providing that transportation.

Domestic operation means any scheduled operation conducted by any person operating any airplane described in paragraph (1) of this definition at locations described in paragraph (2) of this definition:

(1) Airplanes:
   (i) Turbojet-powered airplanes;
   (ii) Airplanes having a passenger-seat configuration of more than 9 passenger seats, excluding each crewmember seat; or
   (iii) Airplanes having a payload capacity of more than 7,500 pounds.

(2) Locations:
   (i) Between any points within the 48 contiguous States of the United States or the District of Columbia; or
   (ii) Operations solely within the 48 contiguous States of the United States or the District of Columbia; or
   (iii) Operations entirely within any State, territory, or possession of the United States; or
   (iv) When specifically authorized by the Administrator, operations between any point within the 48 contiguous States of the United States or the District of Columbia and any specifically authorized point located outside the 48 contiguous States of the United States or the District of Columbia.

Empty weight means the weight of the airframe, engines, propellers, rotors, and fixed equipment. Empty weight excludes the weight of the crew and payload, but includes the weight of all fixed ballast, unusable fuel supply, undrainable oil, total quantity of engine coolant, and total quantity of hydraulic fluid.

Flag operation means any scheduled operation conducted by any person operating any airplane described in paragraph (1) of this definition at the locations described in paragraph (2) of this definition:

(1) Airplanes:
   (i) Turbojet-powered airplanes;
   (ii) Airplanes having a passenger-seat configuration of more than 9 passenger seats, excluding each crewmember seat; or
   (iii) Airplanes having a payload capacity of more than 7,500 pounds.

Ⓐ *Amend #2 Eff 7-15-96*

(2) Locations:
  (i) Between any point within the State of Alaska or the State of Hawaii or any territory or possession of the United States and any point outside the State of Alaska or the State of Hawaii or any territory or possession of the United States, respectively; or
  (ii) Between any point within the 48 contiguous States of the United States or the District of Columbia and any point outside the 48 contiguous States of the United States and the District of Columbia.
  (iii) Between any point outside the U.S. and another point outside the U.S.

Justifiable aircraft equipment means any equipment necessary for the operation of the aircraft. It does not include equipment or ballast specifically installed, permanently or otherwise, for the purpose of altering the empty weight of an aircraft to meet the maximum payload capacity.

Kind of operation means one of the various operations a certificate holder is authorized to conduct, as specified in its operations specifications, i.e., domestic, flag, supplemental, commuter, or on-demand operations.

Maximum payload capacity means:
(1) For an aircraft for which a maximum zero fuel weight is prescribed in FAA technical specifications, the maximum zero fuel weight, less empty weight, less all justifiable aircraft equipment, and less the operating load (consisting of minimum flightcrew, foods and beverages, and supplies and equipment related to foods and beverages, but not including disposable fuel or oil).
(2) For all other aircraft, the maximum certificated takeoff weight of an aircraft, less the empty weight, less all justifiable aircraft equipment, and less the operating load (consisting of minimum fuel load, oil, and flightcrew). The allowance for the weight of the crew, oil, and fuel is as follows:
  (i) Crew—for each crewmember required by the Federal Aviation Regulations—
    (A) For male flight crewmembers—180 pounds.
    (B) For female flight crewmembers—140 pounds.
    (C) For male flight attendants—180 pounds.
    (D) For female flight attendants—130 pounds.
    (E) For flight attendants not identified by gender—140 pounds.
  (ii) Oil—350 pounds or the oil capacity as specified on the Type Certificate Data Sheet.
  (iii) Fuel—the minimum weight of fuel required by the applicable Federal Aviation Regulations for a flight between domestic points 174 nautical miles apart under VFR weather conditions that does not involve extended overwater operations.

Maximum zero fuel weight means the maximum permissible weight of an aircraft with no disposable fuel or oil. The zero fuel weight figure may be found in either the aircraft type certificate data sheet, the approved Aircraft Flight Manual, or both.

Noncommon carriage means an aircraft operation for compensation or hire that does not involve a holding out to others.

On-demand operation means any operation for compensation or hire that is one of the following:
(1) Passenger-carrying operations in which the departure time, departure location, and arrival location are specifically negotiated with the customer or the customer's representative that are any of the following types of operations:
  (i) Common carriage operations conducted with airplanes, including turbojet-powered airplanes, having a passenger-seat configuration of 30 seats or fewer, excluding each crewmember seat, and a payload capacity of 7,500 pounds or less, except that operations using a specific airplane that is also used in domestic or flag operations and that is so listed in the operations specifications as required by §119.49(a)(4) for those operations are considered supplemental operations;
  (ii) Noncommon or private carriage operations conducted with airplanes having a passenger-seat configuration of less than 20 seats, excluding each crewmember seat, or a payload capacity of less than 6,000 pounds; or
  (iii) Any rotorcraft operation.
(2) Scheduled passenger-carrying operations conducted with one of the following types of aircraft with a frequency of operations of less than five round trips per week on at least one route between two or more points according to the published flight schedules:
  (i) Airplanes, other than turbojet powered airplanes, having a maximum passenger-seat configuration of 9 seats or less, excluding each crewmember seat, and a maximum payload capacity of 7,500 pounds or less; or
  (ii) Rotorcraft.
(3) All-cargo operations conducted with airplanes having a payload capacity of 7,500 pounds or less, or with rotorcraft.

Passenger-carrying operation means any aircraft operation carrying any person, unless the only persons on the aircraft are those identified in §§121.583(a) or 135.85 of this chapter, as applicable. An aircraft used in a passenger-carrying operation may also carry cargo or mail in addition to passengers.

Principal base of operations means the primary operating location of a certificate holder as established by the certificate holder.

Provisional airport means an airport approved by the Administrator for use by a certificate holder for the purpose of providing service to a community when the regular airport used by the certificate holder is not available.

Regular airport means an airport used by a certificate holder in scheduled operations and listed in its operations specifications.

Scheduled operation means any common carriage passenger-carrying operation for compensation or hire conducted by an air carrier or commercial operator for which the certificate holder or its representative offers in advance the departure location, departure time, and arrival location. It does not include any operation that is a charter operation for which the certificate holder or its representative offers in advance the departure location, departure time, and arrival location. It does not include any operation that is a charter operation.

Supplemental operation means any common carriage operation for compensation or hire conducted with any airplane described in paragraph (1) of this definition that is a type of operation described in paragraph (2) of this definition:
  (1) Airplanes:
    (i) Airplanes having a passenger-seat configuration of more than 30 seats, excluding each crewmember seat;
    (ii) Airplanes having a payload capacity of more than 7,500 pounds; or
    (iii) Each propeller-powered airplane having a passenger-seat configuration of more than 9 seats and less than 31 seats, excluding each crewmember seat, that is also used in domestic or flag operations and that is so listed in the operations specifications as required by §119.49(a)(4) for those operations; or
    (iv) Each turbojet powered airplane having a passenger seat configuration of 1 or more and less than 31 seats, excluding each crewmember seat, that is also used in domestic or flag operations and that is so listed in the operations specifications as required by §119.49(a)(4) for those operations.
  (2) Types of operation:
    (i) Passenger-carrying operations for which the departure time, departure location, and arrival location are specifically negotiated with the customer or the customer's representative; or
    (ii) All-cargo operations.

Wet lease means any leasing arrangement whereby a person agrees to provide an entire aircraft and at least one crewmember. A wet lease does not include a code-sharing arrangement.

When common carriage is not involved or *operations not involving common carriage* means any of the following:
  (1) Noncommon carriage.
  (2) Operations in which persons or cargo are transported without compensation or hire.
  (3) Operations not involving the transportation of persons or cargo.
  (4) Private carriage.

119.5 CERTIFICATIONS, AUTHORIZATIONS, AND PROHIBITIONS

(a) A person authorized by the Administrator to conduct operations as a direct air carrier will be issued an Air Carrier Certificate.

(b) A person who is not authorized to conduct direct air carrier operations, but who is authorized by the Administrator to conduct operations as a U.S. commercial operator, will be issued an Operating Certificate.

(c) A person who is not authorized to conduct direct air carrier operations, but who is authorized by the Administrator to conduct operations when common carriage is not involved as an operator of U.S.-registered civil airplanes with a seat configuration of 20 or more passengers, or a maximum payload capacity of 6,000 pounds or more, will be issued an Operating Certificate.

(d) A person authorized to engage in common carriage under Part 121 or Part 135 of this chapter, or both, shall be issued only one certificate authorizing such common carriage, regardless of the kind of operation or the class or size of aircraft to be operated.

(e) A person authorized to engage in noncommon or private carriage under Part 125 or Part 135 of this chapter, or both, shall be issued only one certificate authorizing such carriage, regardless of the kind of operation or the class or size of aircraft to be operated.

(f) A person conducting operations under more than one paragraph of §§119.21, 119.23, or 119.25 shall conduct those operations in compliance with—
  (1) The requirements specified in each paragraph of those sections for the kind of operation conducted under that paragraph; and
  (2) The appropriate authorizations, limitations, and procedures specified in the operations specifications for each kind of operation.

(g) No person may operate as a direct air carrier or as a commercial operator without, or in violation of, an appropriate certificate and appropriate operations specifications. No person may operate as a direct air carrier or as a commercial operator in violation of any deviation or exemption authority, if issued to that person or that person's representative.

(h) A person holding an Operating Certificate authorizing noncommon or private carriage operations shall not conduct any operations in common carriage. A person holding an Air Carrier Certificate or Operating Certificate authorizing common carriage operations shall not conduct any operations in noncommon carriage.

(i) No person may operate as a direct air carrier without holding appropriate economic authority from the Department of Transportation.

(j) A certificate holder under this part may not operate aircraft under Part 121 or Part 135 of this chapter in a geographical area unless its operations specifications specifically authorize the certificate holder to operate in that area.

Ⓐ *Amend #2 Eff 7-15-96*

119.7 OPERATIONS SPECIFICATIONS

(a) Each certificate holder's operations specifications must contain—

    (1) The authorizations, limitations, and certain procedures under which each kind of operation, if applicable, is to be conducted; and

    (2) Certain other procedures under which each class and size of aircraft is to be operated.

(b) Except for operations specifications paragraphs identifying authorized kinds of operations, operations specifications are not a part of a certificate.

119.9 USE OF BUSINESS NAMES

(a) A certificate holder under this part may not operate an aircraft under Part 121 or Part 135 of this chapter using a business name other than a business name appearing in the certificate holder's operations specifications.

(b) Unless otherwise authorized by the Assistant Administrator for Civil Aviation Security, no person may operate an aircraft under Part 121 or Part 135 of this chapter unless the name of the certificate holder who is operating the aircraft is legibly displayed on the aircraft and is clearly visible and readable from the outside of the aircraft to a person standing on the ground at any time except during flight time. The means of displaying the name on the aircraft and its readability must be acceptable to the Administrator.

INTENTIONALLY

LEFT

BLANK

SUBPART B - APPLICABILITY OF OPERATING REQUIREMENTS TO DIFFERENT KINDS OF OPERATIONS UNDER PART 121, 125, AND 135 OF THIS CHAPTER

119.21 COMMERCIAL OPERATORS ENGAGED IN INTRASTATE COMMON CARRIAGE AND DIRECT AIR CARRIERS

(a) Each person who conducts airplane operations as a commercial operator engaged in intrastate common carriage of persons or property for compensation or hire in air commerce or as a direct air carrier, shall comply with the certification and operations specifications requirements in Subpart C of this part, and shall conduct its:

(1) Domestic operations in accordance with the applicable requirements of Part 121 of this chapter, and shall be issued operations specifications for those operations in accordance with those requirements. However, based on a showing of safety in air commerce, the Administrator may permit persons who conduct domestic operations between any point located within Alaska's Aleutian Islands chain and any point in the State of Alaska to comply with the requirements applicable to flag operations contained in Subpart U of Part 121 of this chapter.

(2) Flag operations in accordance with the applicable requirements of Part 121 of this chapter, and shall be issued operations specifications for those operations in accordance with those requirements.

(3) Supplemental operations in accordance with the applicable requirements of Part 121 of this chapter, and shall be issued operations specifications for those operations in accordance with those requirements. However, based on a determination of safety in air commerce, the Administrator may authorize or require those operations to be conducted under paragraph (a)(1) or (a)(2) of this section:

(i) Passenger-carrying operations which are conducted between points that are also served by the certificate holder's domestic or flag operations.

(ii) All-cargo operations which are conducted regularly and frequently between the same two points.

(4) Commuter operations in accordance with the applicable requirements of Part 135 of this chapter, and shall be issued operations specifications for those operations in accordance with those requirements.

(5) On-demand operations in accordance with the applicable requirements of Part 135 of this chapter, and shall be issued operations specifications for those operations in accordance with those requirements.

(b) Persons who are subject to the requirements of paragraph (a)(4) of this section may conduct those operations in accordance with the requirements of paragraph (a)(1) or (a)(2) of this section, provided they obtain authorization from the Administrator.

(c) Persons who are subject to the requirements of paragraph (a)(5) of this section may conduct those operations in accordance with the requirements of paragraph (a)(3) of this section, provided they obtain authorization from the Administrator.

119.23 OPERATORS ENGAGED IN PASSENGER-CARRYING OPERATIONS, CARGO OPERATIONS, OR BOTH WITH AIR PLANES WHEN COMMON CARRIAGE IS NOT INVOLVED

(a) Each person who conducts operations when common carriage is not involved with airplanes having a passenger-seat configuration of 20 seats or more, excluding each crewmember seat, or a payload capacity of 6,000 pounds or more, shall, unless deviation authority is issued—

(1) Comply with the certification and operations specifications requirements of Part 125 of this chapter;

(2) Conduct its operations with those airplanes in accordance with the requirements of Part 125 of this chapter; and

(3) Be issued operations specifications in accordance with those requirements.

(b) Each person who conducts noncommon carriage (except as provided in §91.501(b) of this chapter) or private carriage operations for compensation or hire with airplanes having a passenger-seat configuration of less than 20 seats, excluding each crewmember seat, and a payload capacity of less than 6,000 pounds shall—

(1) Comply with the certification and operations specifications requirements in Subpart C of this part;

(2) Conduct those operations in accordance with the requirements of Part 135 of this chapter, except for those requirements applicable only to commuter operations; and

(3) Be issued operations specifications in accordance with those requirements.

119.25 ROTORCRAFT OPERATIONS: DIRECT AIR CARRIERS AND COMMERCIAL OPERATORS

Each person who conducts rotorcraft operations for compensation or hire must comply with the certification and operations specifications requirements of Subpart C of this part, and shall conduct its:

(a) Commuter operations in accordance with the applicable requirements of Part 135 of this chapter, and shall be issued operations specifications for those operations in accordance with those requirements.

(b) On-demand operations in accordance with the applicable requirements of Part 135 of this chapter, and shall be issued operations specifications for those operations in accordance with those requirements.

SUBPART C — CERTIFICATION, OPERATIONS SPECIFICATIONS, AND CERTAIN OTHER REQUIREMENTS FOR OPERATIONS CONDUCTED UNDER PART 121 OR PART 135 OF THIS CHAPTER

119.31 APPLICABILITY

This subpart sets out certification requirements and prescribes the content of operations specifications and certain other requirements for operations conducted under Part 121 or Part 135 of this chapter.

119.33 GENERAL REQUIREMENTS

(a) A person may not operate as a direct air carrier unless that person—
  (1) Is a citizen of the United States;
  (2) Obtains an Air Carrier Certificate; and
  (3) Obtains operations specifications that prescribe the authorizations, limitations, and procedures under which each kind of operation must be conducted.

(b) A person other than a direct air carrier may not conduct any commercial passenger or cargo aircraft operation for compensation or hire under Part 121 or Part 135 of this chapter unless that person—
  (1) Is a citizen of the United States;
  (2) Obtains an Operating Certificate; and
  (3) Obtains operations specifications that prescribe the authorizations, limitations, and procedures under which each kind of operation must be conducted.

(c) Each applicant for a certificate under this part and each applicant for operations specifications authorizing a new kind of operation that is subject to §121.163 or §135.145 of this chapter shall conduct proving tests as authorized by the Administrator during the application process for authority to conduct operations under Part 121 or Part 135 of this chapter. All proving tests must be conducted in a manner acceptable to the Administrator. All proving tests must be conducted under the appropriate operating and maintenance requirements of Part 121 or 135 of this chapter that would apply if the applicant were fully certificated. The Administrator will issue a letter of authorization to each person stating the various authorities under which the proving tests shall be conducted.

119.35 CERTIFICATE APPLICATION

(a) A person applying to the Administrator for an Air Carrier Certificate or Operating Certificate under this part (applicant) must submit an application—
(1) In a form and manner prescribed by the Administrator; and
(2) Containing any information the Administrator requires the applicant to submit.

(b) Each applicant must submit the application to the Administrator at least 90 days before the date of intended operation.

(c) Each applicant for the original issue of an operating certificate for the purpose of conducting intrastate common carriage operations under Part 121 or Part 135 of this chapter must submit an application in a form and manner prescribed by the Administrator to the Flight Standards District Office in whose area the applicant proposes to establish or has established his or her principal operations base of operations.

(d) Each application submitted under paragraph (c) of this section must contain a signed statement showing the following:
  (1) For corporate applicants:
    (i) The name and address of each stockholder who owns 5 percent or more of the total voting stock of the corporation, and if that stockholder is not the sole beneficial owner of the stock, the name and address of each beneficial owner. An individual is considered to own the stock owned, directly or indirectly, by or for his or her spouse, children, grandchildren, or parents.
    (ii) The name and address of each director and each officer and each person employed or who will be employed in a management position described in §§119.65 and 119.69, as applicable.
    (iii) The name and address of each person directly or indirectly controlling or controlled by the applicant and each person under direct or indirect control with the applicant.
  (2) For non-corporate applicants:
    (i) The name and address of each person having a financial interest therein in the non-corporate applicant and the nature and extent of that interest.
    (ii) The name and address of each person employed or who will be employed in a management position described in §§119.65 and 119.69, as applicable.

(e) In addition, each applicant for the original issue of an operating certificate under paragraph (c) of this section must submit with the application a signed statement showing—
(1) The financial information listed in paragraph (h) of this section; and
(2) The nature and scope of its intended operation, including the name and address of each person, if any, with whom the applicant has a contract to provide

services as a commercial operator and the scope, nature, date, and duration of each of those contracts.

(f) Each applicant for, or holder of, a certificate issued under paragraph (c) of this section, shall notify the Administrator within 10 days after—

(1) A change in any of the persons, or the names and addresses of any of the persons, submitted to the Administrator under paragraph (d)(1) or (d)(2) of this section; or

(2) A change in the financial information submitted to the Administrator under paragraph (g) of this section that occurs while the application for the issue is pending before the FAA and that would make the applicant's financial situation substantially less favorable than originally reported.

(g) Each applicant for the original issue of an operating certificate under paragraph (c) of this section must submit the following financial information:

(1) A balance sheet that shows assets, liabilities, and net worth, as of a date not more than 60 days before the date of application.

(2) An itemization of liabilities more than 60 days past due on the balance sheet date, if any, showing each creditor's name and address, a description of the liability, and the amount and due date of the liability.

(3) An itemization of claims in litigation, if any, against the applicant as of the date of application showing each claimant's name and address and a description and the amount of the claim.

(4) A detailed projection of the proposed operation covering 6 complete months after the month in which the certificate is expected to be issued including—

(i) Estimated amount and source of both operating and nonoperating revenue, including identification of its existing and anticipated income producing contracts and estimated revenue per mile or hour of operation by aircraft type;

(ii) Estimated amount of operating and nonoperating expenses by expense objective classification; and

(iii) Estimated net profit or loss for the period.

(5) An estimate of the cash that will be needed for the proposed operations during the first 6 months after the month in which the certificate is expected to be issued, including—

(i) Acquisition of property and equipment (explain);

(ii) Retirement of debt (explain);

(iii) Additional working capital (explain);

(iv) Operating losses other than depreciation and amortization (explain); and

(v) Other (explain).

(6) An estimate of the cash that will be available during the first 6 months after the month in which the certificate is expected to be issued, from—

(i) Sale of property or flight equipment (explain);

(ii) New debt (explain);

(iii) New equity (explain);

(iv) Working capital reduction (explain);

(v) Operations (profits) (explain);

(vi) Depreciation and amortization (explain); and

(vii) Other (explain).

(7) A schedule of insurance coverage in effect on the balance sheet date showing insurance companies; policy numbers; types, amounts, and period of coverage; and special conditions, exclusions, and limitations.

(8) Any other financial information that the Administrator requires to enable him to determine that the applicant has sufficient financial resources to conduct his or her operations with the degree of safety required in the public interest.

(h) Each financial statement containing financial information required by paragraph (g) of this section must be based on accounts prepared and maintained on an accrual basis in accordance with generally accepted accounting principles applied on a consistent basis, and must contain the name and address of the applicant's public accounting firm, if any. Information submitted must be signed by an officer, owner, or partner of the applicant or certificate holder.

119.37 CONTENTS OF AN AIR CARRIER CERTIFICATE OR OPERATING CERTIFICATE

The Air Carrier Certificate or Operating Certificate includes—

(a) The certificate holder's name;

(b) The location of the certificate holder's principal base of operations;

(c) The certificate number;

(d) The certificate's effective date; and

(e) The name or the designator of the certificate-holding district office.

119.39 ISSUING OR DENYING A CERTIFICATE

(a) An applicant may be issued an Air Carrier Certificate or Operating Certificate if, after investigation, the Administrator finds that the applicant—

Ⓐ *Amend #60 eff 2-26-96.*

(1) Meets the applicable requirements of this part;

(2) Holds the economic authority applicable to the kinds of operations to be conducted, issued by the Department of Transportation, if required; and

(3) Is properly and adequately equipped in accordance with the requirements of this chapter and is able to conduct a safe operation under appropriate provisions of Part 121 or Part 135 of this chapter and operations specifications issued under this part.

(b) An application for a certificate may be denied if the Administrator finds that—

(1) The applicant is not properly or adequately equipped or is not able to conduct safe operations under this subchapter;

(2) The applicant previously held an Air Carrier Certificate or Operating Certificate which was revoked;

(3) The applicant intends to or fills a key management position listed in §119.65(a) or §119.69(a), as applicable, with an individual who exercised control over or who held the same or a similar position with a certificate holder whose certificate was revoked, or is in the process of being revoked, and that individual materially contributed to the circumstances causing revocation or causing the revocation process;

(4) An individual who will have control over or have a substantial ownership interest in the applicant, had the same or similar control or interest in a certificate holder whose certificate was revoked, or is in the process of being revoked, and that individual materially contributed to the circumstances causing revocation or causing the revocation process; or

(5) In the case of an applicant for an Operating Certificate for intrastate common carriage, that for financial reasons the applicant is not able to conduct a safe operation.

119.41 AMENDING A CERTIFICATE

(a) The Administrator may amend any certificate issued under this part if—

(1) The Administrator determines, under 49 U.S.C. 44709 and Part 13 of this chapter, that safety in air commerce and the public interest requires the amendment; or

(2) The certificate holder applies for the amendment and the certificate-holding district office determines that safety in air commerce and the public interest allows the amendment.

(b) When the Administrator proposes to issue an order amending, suspending, or revoking all or part of any certificate, the procedure in §13.19 of this chapter applies.

(c) When the certificate holder applies for an amendment of its certificate, the following procedure applies:

(1) The certificate holder must file an application to amend its certificate with the certificate-holding district office at least 15 days before the date proposed by the applicant for the amendment to become effective, unless the administrator approves filing within a shorter period; and

(2) The application must be submitted to the certificate-holding district office in the form and manner prescribed by the Administrator.

(d) When a certificate holder seeks reconsideration of a decision from the certificate-holding district office concerning amendments of a certificate, the following procedure applies:

(1) The petition for reconsideration must be made within 30 days after the certificate holder receives the notice of denial; and

(2) The certificate holder must petition for reconsideration to the Director, Flight Standards Service.

119.43 CERTIFICATE HOLDER'S DUTY TO MAINTAIN OPERATIONS SPECIFICATIONS

(a) Each certificate holder shall maintain a complete and separate set of its operations specifications at its principal base of operations.

(b) Each certificate holder shall insert pertinent excerpts of its operations specifications, or references thereto, in its manual and shall—

(1) Clearly identify each such excerpt as a part of its operations specifications; and

(2) State that compliance with each operations specifications requirement is mandatory.

(c) Each certificate holder shall keep each of its employees and other persons used in its operations informed of the provisions of its operations specifications that apply to that employee's or person's duties and responsibilities.

119.45 [Reserved]

119.47 MAINTAINING A PRINCIPAL BASE OF OPERATIONS, MAIN OPERATIONS BASE, AND MAIN MAINTENANCE BASE; CHANGE OF ADDRESS

(a) Each certificate holder must maintain a principal base of operations. Each certificate holder may also establish a main operations base and a main maintenance base which may be located at either the same location as the principal base of operations or at separate locations.

(b) At least 30 days before it proposes to establish or change the location of its principal base of operations, its main operations base, or its main maintenance base, a certificate holder must provide written notification to its certificate-holding district office.

119.49   CONTENTS OF OPERATIONS SPECIFICATIONS

(a) Each certificate holder conducting domestic, flag, or commuter operations must obtain operations specifications containing all of the following:

(1) The specific location of the certificate holder's principal base of operations and, if different, the address that shall serve as the primary point of contact for correspondence between the FAA and the certificate holder and the name and mailing address of the certificate holder's agent for service.

(2) Other business names under which the certificate holder may operate.

(3) Reference to the economic authority issued by the Department of Transportation, if required.

(4) Type of aircraft, registration markings, and serial numbers of each aircraft authorized for use, each regular and alternate airport to be used in scheduled operations, and, except for commuter operations, each provisional and refueling airport.

(i) Subject to the approval of the Administrator with regard to form and content, the certificate holder may incorporate by reference the items listed in paragraph (a)(4) of this section into the certificate holder's operations specifications by maintaining a current listing of those items and by referring to the specific list in the applicable paragraph of the operations specifications.

(ii) The certificate holder may not conduct any operation using any aircraft or airport not listed.

(5) Kinds of operations authorized.

(6) Authorization and limitations for routes and areas of operations.

(7) Airport limitations.

(8) Time limitations, or standards for determining time limitations, for overhauling,

inspecting, and checking airframes, engines, propellers, rotors, appliances, and emergency equipment.

(9) Authorization for the method of controlling weight and balance of aircraft.

(10) Interline equipment interchange requirements, if relevant.

(11) Aircraft wet lease information required by §119.53(c).

(12) Any authorized deviation and exemption granted from any requirement of this chapter.

(13) Any other item the Administrator determines is necessary.

(b) Each certificate holder conducting supplemental operations must obtain operations specifications containing all of the following:

(1) The specific location of the certificate holder's principal base of operations and, if different, the address that shall serve as the primary point of contact for correspondence between the FAA and the certificate holder and the name and mailing address of the certificate holder's agent for service.

(2) Other business names under which the certificate holder may operate.

(3) Reference to the economic authority issued by the Department of Transportation, if required.

(4) Type of aircraft, registration markings, and serial number of each aircraft authorized for use.

(i) Subject to the approval of the Administrator with regard to form and content, the certificate holder may incorporate by reference the items listed in paragraph (b)(4) of this section into the certificate holder's operations specifications by maintaining a current listing of those items and by referring to the specific list in the applicable paragraph of the operations specifications.

(ii) The certificate holder may not conduct any operation using any aircraft not listed.

(5) Kinds of operations authorized.

(6) Authorization and limitations for routes and areas of operations.

(7) Special airport authorizations and limitations.

(8) Time limitations, or standards for determining time limitations, for overhauling, inspecting, and checking airframes, engines, propellers, appliances, and emergency equipment.

(9) Authorization for the method of controlling weight and balance of aircraft.

(10) Aircraft wet lease information required by §119.53(c).

(11) Any authorization or requirement to conduct supplemental operations as provided by §119.21(a)(3)(i) or (ii).

(12) Any authorized deviation or exemption from any requirement of this chapter.

(13) Any other item the Administrator determines is necessary.

(c) Each certificate holder conducting on-demand operations must obtain operations specifications containing all of the following:

(1) The specific location of the certificate holder's principal base of operations and, if different, the address that shall serve as the primary point of contact for correspondence between the FAA and the name and mailing address of the certificate holder's agent for service.

(2) Other business names under which the certificate holder may operate.

(3) Reference to the economic authority issued by the Department of Transportation, if required.

(4) Kind and area of operations authorized.

(5) Category and class of aircraft that may be used in those operations.

(6) Type of aircraft, registration markings, and serial number of each aircraft that is subject to an airworthiness maintenance program required by §135.411(a)(2) of this chapter.

    (i) Subject to the approval of the Administrator with regard to form and content, the certificate holder may incorporate by reference the items listed in paragraph (c)(6) of this section into the certificate holder's operations specifications by maintaining a current listing of those items and by referring to the specific list in the applicable paragraph of the operations specifications.

    (ii) The certificate holder may not conduct any operation using any aircraft not listed.

(7) Registration markings of each aircraft that is to be inspected under an approved aircraft inspection program under §135.419 of this chapter.

(8) Time limitations or standards for determining time limitations, for overhauls, inspections, and checks for airframes, engines, propellers, rotors, appliances, and emergency equipment of aircraft that are subject to an airworthiness maintenance program required by §135.411(a)(2) of this chapter.

(9) Additional maintenance items required by the Administrator under §135.421 of this chapter.

(10) Aircraft wet lease information required by §119.53(c).

(11) Any authorized deviation or exemption from any requirement of this chapter.

(12) Any other item the Administrator determines is necessary.

119.51   AMENDING OPERATIONS SPECIFICATIONS

(a) The Administrator may amend any operations specifications issued under this part if—

(1) The Administrator determines that safety in air commerce and the public interest require the amendment; or

(2) The certificate holder applies for the amendment, and the Administrator determines that safety in air commerce and the public interest allows the amendment.

(b) Except as provided in paragraph (e) of this section, when the Administrator initiates an amendment to a certificate holder's operations specifications, the following procedure applies:

(1) The certificate-holding district office notifies the certificate holder in writing of the proposed amendment.

(2) The certificate-holding district office sets a reasonable period (but not less than 7 days) within which the certificate holder may submit written information, views, and arguments on the amendment.

(3) After considering all material presented, the certificate-holding district office notifies the certificate holder of—

    (i) The adoption of the proposed amendment;

    (ii) The partial adoption of the proposed amendment; or

    (iii) The withdrawal of the proposed amendment.

(4) If the certificate-holding district office issues an amendment to the operations specifications, it becomes effective not less than 30 days after the certificate holder receives notice of it unless—

    (i) The certificate-holding district office finds under paragraph (e) of this section that there is an emergency requiring immediate action with respect to safety in air commerce; or

    (ii) The certificate holder petitions for reconsideration of the amendment under paragraph (d) of this section.

(c) When the certificate holder applies for an amendment to its operations specifications, the following procedure applies:

(1) The certificate holder must file an application to amend its operations specifications—

    (i) At least 90 days before the date proposed by the applicant for the amendment to become effective, unless a shorter time is approved, in cases of mergers; acquisitions of airline operational assets that require an additional showing of safety (e.g., proving tests); changes in the kind of operation as defined in §119.3; resumption of operations following a suspension of operations as a result of bankruptcy actions; or the initial introduction of aircraft not before proven for use in air carrier or commercial operator operations.

    (ii) At least 15 days before the date proposed by the applicant for the amendment to become effective in all other cases.

(2) The application must be submitted to the certificate-holding district office in a form and manner prescribed by the Administrator.

(3) After considering all material presented, the certificate-holding district office notifies the certificate holder of—

    (i) The adoption of the applied for amendment;

    (ii) The partial adoption of the applied for amendment; or

    (iii) The denial of the applied for amendment. The certificate holder may petition for reconsideration of a denial under paragraph (d) of this section.

(4) If the certificate-holding district office approves the amendment, following coordination with the certificate holder regarding its implementation, the amendment is effective on the date the Administrator approves it.

(d) When a certificate holder seeks reconsideration of a decision from the certificate-holding district office concerning the amendment of operations specifications, the following procedure applies:

(1) The certificate holder must petition for reconsideration of that decision within 30 days of the date that the certificate holder receives a notice of denial of the amendment to its operations specifications, or of the date it receives notice of an FAA-initiated amendment to its operations specifications, whichever circumstance applies.

(2) The certificate holder must address its petition to the Director, Flight Standards Service.

(3) A petition for reconsideration, if filed within the 30-day period, suspends the effectiveness of any amendment issued by the certificate-holding district office unless the certificate-holding district office has found, under paragraph (e) of this section, that an emergency exists requiring immediate action with respect to safety in air transportation or air commerce.

(4) If a petition for reconsideration is not filed within 30 days, the procedures of paragraph (c) of this section apply.

(e) If the certificate-holding district office finds that an emergency exists requiring immediate action with respect to safety in air commerce or air transportation that makes the procedures set out in this section impracticable or contrary to the public interest:

(1) The certificate-holding district office amends the operations specifications and makes the amendment effective on the day the certificate holder receives notice of it.

(2) In the notice to the certificate holder, the certificate-holding district office articulates the reasons for its finding that an emergency exists requiring immediate action with respect to safety in air transportation or air commerce or that makes it impracticable or contrary to the public interest to stay the effectiveness of the amendment.

119.53 WET LEASING OF AIRCRAFT AND OTHER ARRANGEMENTS FOR TRANSPORTATION BY AIR

(a) Unless otherwise authorized by the Administrator, prior to conducting operations involving a wet lease, each certificate holder under this part authorized to conduct common carriage operations under this subchapter shall provide the Administrator with a copy of the wet lease to be executed which would lease the aircraft to any other person engaged in common carriage operations under this subchapter, including foreign air carriers, or to any other foreign person engaged in common carriage wholly outside the United States.

(b) No certificate holder under this part may wet lease from a foreign air carrier or any other foreign person or any person not authorized to engage in common carriage.

(c) Upon receiving a copy of a wet lease, the Administrator determines which party to the agreement has operational control of the aircraft and issues amendments to the operations specifications of each party to the agreement, as needed. The lessor must provide the following information to be incorporated into the operations specifications of both parties, as needed.

(1) The names of the parties to the agreement and the duration thereof.

(2) The nationality and registration markings of each aircraft involved in the agreement.

   (3) The kind of operation (e.g., domestic, flag, supplemental, commuter, or on-demand).

   (4) The airports or areas of operation.

   (5) A statement specifying the party deemed to have operational control and the times, airports, or areas under which such operational control is exercised.

(d) In making the determination of paragraph (c) of this section, the Administrator will consider the following:

   (1) Crewmembers and training.

   (2) Airworthiness and performance of maintenance.

   (3) Dispatch.

   (4) Servicing the aircraft.

   (5) Scheduling.

   (6) Any other factor the Administrator considers relevant.

(e) Other arrangements for transportation by air: Except as provided in paragraph (f) of this section, a certificate holder under this part operating under Part 121 or 135 of this chapter may not conduct any operation for another certificate holder under this part or a foreign air carrier under Part 129 of this chapter or a foreign person engaged in common carriage wholly outside the United States unless it holds applicable Department of Transportation economic authority, if required, and is authorized under its operations specifications to conduct the same kinds of operations (as defined in §119.3). The certificate holder conducting the substitute operation must conduct that operation in accordance with the same operations authority held by the certificate holder arranging for the substitute operation. These substitute operations must be conducted between airports for which the substitute certificate holder holds authority for scheduled operations or within areas of operations for which the substitute certificate holder has authority for supplemental or on-demand operations.

(f) A certificate holder under this part may, if authorized by the Department of Transportation under §380.3 of this title and the Administrator in the case of interstate commuter, interstate domestic, and flag operations, or the Administrator in the case of scheduled intrastate common carriage operations, conduct one or more flights for passengers who are stranded because of the cancellation of their scheduled flights. These flights must be conducted under the rules of Part 121 or Part 135 of this chapter applicable to supplemental or on-demand operations.

119.55 OBTAINING DEVIATION AUTHORITY TO PERFORM OPERATIONS UNDER A U.S. MILITARY CONTRACT

(a) The Administrator may authorize a certificate holder that is authorized to conduct supplemental or on-demand operations to deviate from the applicable requirements of this part, Part 121, or Part 135 of this chapter in order to perform operations under a U.S. military contract.

(b) A certificate holder that has a contract with the U.S. Department of Defense's Air Mobility Command (AMC) must submit a request for deviation authority to AMC. AMC will review the requests, then forward the carriers' consolidated requests, along with AMC's recommendations, to the FAA for review and action.

(c) The Administrator may authorize a deviation to perform operations under a U.S. military contract under the following conditions—

   (1) The Department of Defense certifies to the Administrator that the operation is essential to the national defense;

   (2) The Department of Defense further certifies that the certificate holder cannot perform the operation without deviation authority;

   (3) The certificate holder will perform the operation under a contract or subcontract for the benefit of a U.S. armed service; and

   (4) The Administrator finds that the deviation is based on grounds other than economic advantage either to the certificate holder or to the United States.

(d) In the case where the Administrator authorizes a deviation under this section, the Administrator will issue an appropriate amendment to the certificate holder's operations specifications.

(e) The Administrator may, at any time, terminate any grant of deviation authority issued under this section.

119.57 OBTAINING DEVIATION AUTHORITY TO PERFORM AN EMERGENCY OPERATION

(a) In emergency conditions, the Administrator may authorize deviations if—

   (1) Those conditions necessitate the transportation of persons or supplies for the protection of life or property; and

   (2) The Administrator finds that a deviation is necessary for the expeditious conduct of the operations.

(b) When the Administrator authorizes deviations for operations under emergency conditions—

   (1) The Administrator will issue an appropriate amendment to the certificate holder's operations specifications; or

(2) If the nature of the emergency does not permit timely amendment of the operations specifications—
   (i) The Administrator may authorize the deviation orally; and
   (ii) The certificate holder shall provide documentation describing the nature of the emergency to the certificate-holding district office within 24 hours after completing the operation.

119.59 CONDUCTING TESTS AND INSPECT-IONS

(a) At any time or place, the Administrator may conduct an inspection or test to determine whether a certificate holder under this part is complying with title 49 of the United States Code, applicable regulations, the certificate, or the certificate holder's operations specifications.

(b) The certificate holder must—
   (1) Make available to the Administrator at the certificate holder's principal base of operations—
     (i) The certificate holder's Air Carrier Certificate or the certificate holder's Operating Certificate and the certificate holder's operations specifications; and
     (ii) A current listing that will include the location and persons responsible for each record, document, and report required to be kept by the certificate holder under title 49 of the United States Code applicable to the operation of the certificate holder.
   (2) Allow the Administrator to make any test or inspection to determine compliance respecting any matter stated in paragraph (a) of this section.

(c) Each employee of, or person used by, the certificate holder who is responsible for maintaining the certificate holder's records must make those records available to the Administrator.

(d) The Administrator may determine a certificate holder's continued eligibility to hold its certificate and/or operations specifications on any grounds listed in paragraph (a) of this section, or any other appropriate grounds.

(e) Failure by any certificate holder to make available to the Administrator upon request, the certificate, operations specifications, or any required record, document, or report is grounds for suspension of all or any part of the certificate holder's certificate and operations specifications.

(f) In the case of operators conducting intrastate common carriage operations, these inspections and tests include inspections and tests of financial books and records.

119.61 DURATION AND SURRENDER OF CERTIFICATE AND OPERATIONS SPECIFICATIONS

(a) An Air Carrier Certificate or Operating Certificate issued under this part is effective until—
   (1) The certificate holder surrenders it to the Administrator; or
   (2) The Administrator suspends, revokes, or otherwise terminates the certificate.

(b) Operations specifications issued under this part, Part 121, or Part 135 of this chapter are effective unless—
   (1) The Administrator suspends, revokes, or otherwise terminates the certificate;
   (2) The operations specifications are amended as provided in §119.51;
   (3) The certificate holder does not conduct a kind of operation for more than the time specified in §119.63 and fails to follow the procedures of §119.63 upon resuming that kind of operation; or
   (4) The Administrator suspends or revokes the operations specifications for a kind of operation.

(c) Within 30 days after a certificate holder terminates operations under Part 135 of this chapter, the operating certificate and operations specifications must be surrendered by the certificate holder to the certificate-holding district office.

119.63 RECENCY OF OPERATION

(a) Except as provided in paragraph (b) of this section, no certificate holder may conduct a kind of operation for which it holds authority in its operations specifications unless the certificate holder has conducted that kind of operation within the preceding number of consecutive calendar days specified in this paragraph:
   (1) For domestic, flag, or commuter operations—30 days.
   (2) For supplemental or on-demand operations—90 days, except that if the certificate holder has authority to conduct domestic, flag, or commuter operations, and has conducted domestic, flag or commuter operations within the previous 30 days, this paragraph does not apply.

(b) If a certificate holder does not conduct a kind of operation for which it is authorized in its operations specifications within the number of calendar days specified in paragraph (a) of this section, it shall not conduct such kind of operation unless—
   (1) It advises the Administrator at least 5 consecutive calendar days before resumption of that kind of operation; and

➡ Ⓐ

(2) It makes itself available and accessible during the 5 consecutive calendar day period in the event that the FAA decides to conduct a full inspection re-examination to determine whether the certificate holder remains properly and adequately equipped and able to conduct a safe operation.

119.65 MANAGEMENT PERSONNEL REQUIRED FOR OPERATIONS CONDUCTED UNDER PART 121 OF THIS CHAPTER

(a) Each certificate holder must have sufficient qualified management and technical personnel to ensure the highest degree of safety in its operations. The certificate holder must have qualified personnel serving full-time in the following or equivalent positions:
(1) Director of Safety.
(2) Director of Operations.
(3) Chief Pilot.
(4) Director of Maintenance.
(5) Chief Inspector.

(b) The Administrator may approve positions or numbers of positions other than those listed in paragraph (a) of this section for a particular operation if the certificate holder shows that it can perform the operation with the highest degree of safety under the direction of fewer or different categories of management personnel due to—
(1) The kind of operation involved;
(2) The number and type of airplanes used; and
(3) The area of operations.

(c) The title of the positions required under paragraph (a) of this section or the title and number of equivalent positions approved under paragraph (b) of this section shall be set forth in the certificate holder's operations specifications.

(d) The individuals who serve in the positions required or approved under paragraph (a) or (b) of this section and anyone in a position to exercise control over operations conducted under the operating certificate must—
(1) Be qualified through training, experience, and expertise;
(2) To the extent of their responsibilities, have a full understanding of the following materials with respect to the certificate holder's operation—
(i) Aviation safety standards and safe operating practices;
(ii) 14 CFR Chapter I (Federal Aviation Regulations);
(iii) The certificate holder's operations specifications;
(iv) All appropriate maintenance and airworthiness requirements of this chapter (e.g., Parts 1, 21, 23, 25, 43, 45, 47, 65, 91, and 121 of this chapter); and
(v) The manual required by §121.133 of this chapter; and

(3) Discharge their duties to meet applicable legal requirements and to maintain safe operations.

(e) Each certificate holder must:
(1) State in the general policy provisions of the manual required by §121.133 of this chapter, the duties, responsibilities, and authority of personnel required under paragraph (a) of this section;
(2) List in the manual the names and business addresses of the individuals assigned to those positions; and
(3) Notify the certificate-holding district office within 10 days of any change in personnel or any vacancy in any position listed.

119.67 MANAGEMENT PERSONNEL: QUALIFICATIONS FOR OPERATIONS CONDUCTED UNDER PART 121 OF THIS CHAPTER

(a) To serve as Director of Operations under §119.65(a) a person must—
(1) Hold an airline transport pilot certificate;
(2) Have at least 3 years supervisory or managerial experience within the last 6 years in a position that exercised operational control over any operations conducted with large airplanes under Part 121 or Part 135 of this chapter, or if the certificate holder uses only small airplanes in its operations, the experience may be obtained in large or small airplanes; and
(3) In the case of a person becoming a Director of Operations—
(i) For the first time ever, have at least 3 years experience, within the past 6 years, as pilot in command of a large airplane operated under Part 121 or Part 135 of this chapter, if the certificate holder operates large airplanes. If the certificate holder uses only small airplanes in its operation, the experience may be obtained in either large or small airplanes.
(ii) In the case of a person with previous experience as a Director of Operations, have at least 3 years experience as pilot in command of a large airplane operated under Part 121 or Part 135 of this chapter, if the certificate holder operates large airplanes. If the certificate holder uses only small airplanes in its operation, the experience may be obtained in either large or small airplanes.

(b) To serve as Chief Pilot under §119.65(a) a person must hold an airline transport pilot certificate with appropriate ratings for at least one of the airplanes used in the certificate holder's operation and:

(1) In the case of a person becoming a Chief Pilot for the first time ever, have at least 3 years experience, within the past 6 years, as pilot in command of a large airplane operated under Part 121 or Part 135 of this chapter, if the certificate holder operates large airplanes. If the certificate holder uses only small airplanes in its operation, the experience may be obtained in either large or small airplanes.

(2) In the case of a person with previous experience as a Chief Pilot, have at least 3 years experience, as pilot in command of a large airplane operated under Part 121 or Part 135 of this chapter, if the certificate holder operates large airplanes. If the certificate holder uses only small airplanes in its operation, the experience may be obtained in either large or small airplanes.

(c) To serve as Director of Maintenance under §119.65(a) a person must—

(1) Hold a mechanic certificate with airframe and powerplant ratings;

(2) Have 1 year of experience in a position responsible for returning airplanes to service;

(3) Have at least 1 year of experience in a supervisory capacity under either paragraph (c)(4)(i) or (c)(4)(ii) of this section maintaining the same category and class of airplane as the certificate holder uses; and

(4) Have 3 years experience within the past 6 years in one or a combination of the following—

(i) Maintaining large airplanes with 10 or more passenger seats, including at the time of appointment as Director of Maintenance, experience in maintaining the same category and class of airplane as the certificate holder uses; or

(ii) Repairing airplanes in a certificated airframe repair station that is rated to maintain airplanes in the same category and class of airplane as the certificate holder uses.

(d) To serve as Chief Inspector under §119.65(a) a person must—

(1) Hold a mechanic certificate with both airframe and powerplant ratings, and have held these ratings for at least 3 years;

(2) Have at least 3 years of maintenance experience on different types of large airplanes with 10 or more passenger seats with an air carrier or certificated repair station, 1 year of which must have been as maintenance inspector; and

(3) Have at least 1 year in a supervisory capacity maintaining the same category and class of aircraft as the certificate holder uses.

Ⓐ

(e) A certificate holder may request a deviation to employ a person who does not meet the appropriate airman, managerial, or supervisory experience requirements of this section if the Manager of the Air Transportation Division or the Manager of the Aircraft Maintenance Division of the FAA Flight Standards Service finds that the person has comparable experience, and can effectively perform the functions associated with the position in accordance with the Federal Aviation Regulations and the procedures outlined in the certificate holder's manual. Grants of deviation under this paragraph may be granted after consideration of the size and scope of the operation and the qualifications of the intended personnel. The Administrator may, at any time, terminate any grant of deviation authority issued under this paragraph.

119.69 MANAGEMENT PERSONNEL REQUIRED FOR OPERATIONS CONDUCTED UNDER PART 135 OF THIS CHAPTER

(a) Each certificate holder must have sufficient qualified management and technical personnel to ensure the safety of its operations. Except for a certificate holder using only one pilot in its operations, the certificate holder must have qualified personnel serving in the following or equivalent positions:

(1) Director of Operations.
(2) Chief Pilot.
(3) Director of Maintenance.

(b) The Administrator may approve positions or numbers of positions other than those listed in paragraph (a) of this section for a particular operation if the certificate holder shows that it can perform the operation with the highest degree of safety under the direction of fewer or different categories of management personnel due to—

(1) The kind of operation involved;
(2) The number and type of aircraft used; and
(3) The area of operations.

(c) The title of the positions required under paragraph (a) of this section or the title and number of equivalent positions approved under paragraph (b) of this section shall be set forth in the certificate holder's operations specifications.

(d) The individuals who serve in the positions required or approved under paragraph (a) or (b) of this section and anyone in a position to exercise control over operations conducted under the operating certificate must—

(1) Be qualified through training, experience, and expertise;

(2) To the extent of their responsibilities, have a full understanding of the following material with respect to the certificate holder's operation—

(i) Aviation safety standards and safe operating practices;

Ⓐ *Amend #60 eff 2-26-96.*

(ii) 14 CFR Chapter I (Federal Aviation Regulations);

(iii) The certificate holder's operations specifications;

(iv) All appropriate maintenance and airworthiness requirements of this chapter (e.g., Parts 1, 21, 23, 25, 43, 45, 47, 65, 91, and 135 of this chapter); and

(v) The manual required by §135.21 of this chapter; and

(3) Discharge their duties to meet applicable legal requirements and to maintain safe operations.

(e) Each certificate holder must—

(1) State in the general policy provisions of the manual required by §135.21 of this chapter, the duties, responsibilities, and authority of personnel required or approved under paragraph (a) or (b), respectively, of this section;

(2) List in the manual the names and business addresses of the individuals assigned to those positions; and

(3) Notify the certificate-holding district office within 10 days of any change in personnel or any vacancy in any position listed.

119.71 MANAGEMENT PERSONNEL: QUALIFICATIONS FOR OPERATIONS CONDUCTED UNDER PART 135 OF THIS CHAPTER

(a) To serve as Director of Operations under §119.69(a) for a certificate holder conducting any operations for which the pilot in command is required to hold an airline transport pilot certificate a person must hold an airline transport pilot certificate and either:

(1) Have at least 3 years supervisory or managerial experience within the last 6 years in a position that exercised operational control over any operations conducted under Part 121 or Part 135 of this chapter; or

(2) In the case of a person becoming Director of Operations—

(i) For the first time ever, have at least 3 years experience, within the past 6 years, as pilot in command of an aircraft operated under Part 121 or Part 135 of this chapter.

(ii) In the case of a person with previous experience as a Director of Operations, have at least 3 years experience, as pilot in command of an aircraft operated under Part 121 or Part 135 of this chapter.

(b) To serve as Director of Operations under §119.69(a) for a certificate holder that only conducts operations for which the pilot in command is required to hold a commercial pilot certificate, a person must hold at least a commercial pilot certificate with an instrument rating and either:

(1) Have at least 3 years supervisory or managerial experience within the last 6 years in a position that exercised operational control over any operations conducted under Part 121 or Part 135 of this chapter; or

(2) In the case of a person becoming Director of Operations—

(i) For the first time ever, have at least 3 years experience, within the past 6 years, as pilot in command of an aircraft operated under Part 121 or Part 135 of this chapter.

(ii) In the case of a person with previous experience as a Director of Operations, have at least 3 years experience as pilot in command of an aircraft operated under Part 121 or Part 135 of this chapter.

(c) To serve as Chief Pilot under §119.69(a) for a certificate holder conducting any operation for which the pilot in command is required to hold an airline transport pilot certificate a person must hold an airline transport pilot certificate with appropriate ratings and be qualified to serve as pilot in command in at least one aircraft used in the certificate holder's operation and:

(1) In the case of a person becoming a Chief Pilot for the first time ever, have at least 3 years experience, within the past 6 years, as pilot in command of an aircraft operated under Part 121 or Part 135 of this chapter.

(2) In the case of a person with previous experience as a Chief Pilot, have at least 3 years experience as pilot in command of an aircraft operated under Part 121 or Part 135 of this chapter.

(d) To serve as Chief Pilot under §119.69(a) for a certificate holder that only conducts operations for which the pilot in command is required to hold a commercial pilot certificate, a person must hold at least a commercial pilot certificate with an instrument rating and be qualified to serve as pilot in command in at least one aircraft used in the certificate holder's operation and:

(1) In the case of a person becoming a Chief Pilot for the first time ever, have at least 3 years experience, within the past 6 years, as pilot in command of an aircraft operated under Part 121 or Part 135 of this chapter.

(2) In the case of a person with previous experience as a Chief Pilot, have at least 3 years experience as pilot in command of an aircraft operated under Part 121 or Part 135 of this chapter.

(e) To serve as Director of Maintenance under §119.69(a) a person must hold a mechanic certificate with airframe and powerplant ratings and either:

(1) Have 3 years of experience within the past 3 years maintaining aircraft as a certificated mechanic, including, at the time of appointment as Director of Maintenance, experience in maintaining the same category and class of aircraft as the certificate holder uses; or

(2) Have 3 years of experience within the past 3 years repairing aircraft in a certificated airframe repair station, including 1 year in the capacity of approving aircraft for return to service.

(f) A certificate holder may request a deviation to employ a person who does not meet the appropriate airman, managerial, or supervisory experience requirements of this section if the Manager of the Air Transportation Division or the Manager of the Aircraft Maintenance Division of the FAA Flight Standards Service finds that the person has comparable experience, and can effectively perform the functions associated with the position in accordance with 14 CFR Chapter I and the procedures outlined in the certificate holder's manual. Grants of deviation under this paragraph may be granted after consideration of the size and scope of the operation and the qualifications of the intended personnel. The Administrator may, at any time, terminate any grant of deviation authority issued under this paragraph.

FEDERAL AVIATION REGULATIONS

PART 135—OPERATING REQUIREMENTS: COMMUTER AND ON-DEMAND OPERATIONS

This part contains all effective amendments through #65. This revision incorporates amendment #63 effective 1 August 1996, amendment #64 effective 17 June 1996 and amendment #65 effective 15 July 1996. Amendment #62 not yet effective.

TABLE OF CONTENTS

SUBPART A — GENERAL

SUBPART B — FLIGHT OPERATIONS

TABLE OF CONTENTS

SUBPART B — FLIGHT OPERATIONS (cont)

SUBPART C — AIRCRAFT AND EQUIPMENT

SUBPART D — VFR/IFR OPERATING LIMITATIONS AND WEATHER REQUIREMENTS

TABLE OF CONTENTS

SUBPART D — VFR/IFR OPERATING LIMITATIONS
AND WEATHER REQUIREMENTS (cont)

SUBPART E — FLIGHT CREWMEMBER REQUIREMENTS

SUBPART F — FLIGHT CREWMEMBER FLIGHT TIME LIMITATIONS
AND REST REQUIREMENTS

SUBPART G — CREWMEMBER TESTING REQUIREMENTS

SUBPART H — TRAINING

TABLE OF CONTENTS

SUBPART H — TRAINING (cont)

TABLE OF CONTENTS

SUBPART J — MAINTENANCE, PREVENTIVE MAINTENANCE, AND ALTERATIONS (cont)

INTENTIONALLY

LEFT

BLANK

DISTRIBUTION TABLE FOR PART 135

Section	Replaced By
Part 135:	
135.5	119.31; 119.33(a), (b), and (c)
135.7	119.5(g)
135.9(a)	119.61(a)
135.11(a)	119.35(a) and (b)
135.11(b)	119.49(a)
135.11(b)(1)	119.37(a), (b), (c), (d), (e), (f), and (g); 119.39(a); 119.49(b) and (c)
135.13(a)	119.33(a), (b), and (c)
135.13(a)(2)	119.39(b)
135.13(a)(3)	119.5(i)
135.13(b)	119.39(b)
135.15(a)	119.41(a)
135.15(b)	119.41(b)
135.15(d)	119.41(d)
135.17(a)	119.51(a)
135.17(b)	119.51(c)
135.17(c)	119.51(d) and (e)
135.17(d)	119.51(b), (d), and (e)
135.19	119.58
135.27(a)	119.47(a)
135.27(b)	119.47(b)
135.29	119.9(a)
135.31	119.5
135.33	119.5(j)
135.35	119.61(c)
135.37(a)	119.69(a)
135.37(b)	119.69(b)
135.37(c)	119.69(e)
135.39	119.69(d)
135.39(a)(1)	119.71(a)
135.39(a)(2)	119.71(b)
135.39(b)(1)	119.71(c)
135.39(b)(2)	119.71(d)
135.39(c)	119.67(c); 119.71(e)
135.39(d)	119.67(e); 119.71(f)
135.63(a)	119.59(b)
135.63(a)(2)	119.43(a) and (b)
135.73	119.59(a) and (b)
135.81	119.49(d)

COMPARABLE SECTIONS IN PARTS 121 AND 135

This table shows the comparable sections in Parts 121 and 135. Affected commuters, however, must comply with all sections in Part 121 that are applicable to their operations, not just the ones listed in this table.

Subject	Section 135	Section 121
Subparts E and F—Approval of Routes: Domestic, Flag, and Supplemental Operations	135.213	121.97, .99, .101, .107
Subpart G—Manual Requirements —Contents and personnel . . . . —Airplane flight manual	135.21, .23	121.133, .135, .137 121.141
Subpart I—Airplane Performance Operating Limitations	135.365-.387	121.175-.197

COMPARABLE SECTIONS IN PARTS 121 AND 135 (cont)

Subject	Section 135	Section 121
Subpart J—Special Airworthiness Requirements		121.217
—Internal doors	135.87	121.285
—Cargo carried in the passenger compartment	135 App. A	121.289
—Landing gear aural warning device		121.191
—Emergency evacuation and ditching demonstration		
—New special airworthiness requirements (retrofit) and requirements applicable to future manufactured airplanes		121.293(a) (new)
—Ditching emergency exits		121.293(b) (new)
—Takeoff warning system		
Subpart K—Instrument and Equipment Requirements:		
—Third attitude indicator		
—Lavatory fire protection	135.149, .163 (a),(h)	121.305(j)
—Emergency equipment inspection		121.308
—Hand-held fire extinguishers	135.177(b)	121.309(b)
—First aid kits and medical kits	135.155	121.309(c)
—Crash ax	135.177(a)(1)	121.309(d)
—Emergency evacuation lighting and marking requirements	135.177(a)(2) 135.178(c)-(h)	121.309(e) 121.310(c)-(h)
—Seatbacks		
—Seatbelt and shoulder harnesses on the flight deck	135.117	121.311(e), (f)
—Interior materials and passenger seat cushion flammability	135.169(a)	121.312(b)
—Miscellaneous equipment		121.313(c), (f), (g)
—Cockpit and door keys		121.313(f) 121.587
—Cargo and baggage compartments		
—Fuel tank access covers		121.314, .221
—Passenger information		121.316
—Instruments and equipment for operations at night	135.127	121.317, .323
—Oxygen requirements		
—Portable oxygen for flight attendants	135.157	121.327-.335, .333(d)
—Protective breathing equipment (PBE)		121.337
—Additional life rafts for extended underwater operations	135.167	121.339
—Flotation devices		
—Pitot heat indication system		121.340
—Radio equipment	135.158	121.342
—Emergency equipment for operations over uninhabited terrain	135.161 135.177, .178	121.354-.351
—TCAS		121.353
—Flight data recorders	135.180	
—Airborne weather radar	135.152(a), (b)	121.356
—Cockpit voice recorders	135.173, .175	121.343
—Low-altitude windshear systems	135.151	121.357
—Ground proximity warning system (GPWS)	135.153	121.359 121.358
Subpart L—Maintenance, Preventive Maintenance, and Alterations:		
—Applicability	135.411(a)(2)	121.361
—Responsibility for Airworthiness	135.413	121.363
—Maintenance, preventive maintenance, and alteration organization	135.423, .425	121.365, .367
—Manual requirements	135.427	121.369
—Required inspection personnel	135.429	121.371
—Continuing analysis and surveillance	135.431	121.373
—Maintenance and preventive maintenance training programs	135.433	121.375

COMPARABLE SECTIONS IN PARTS 121 AND 135 (cont)

Subject	Section 135	Section 121
Subpart L—Maintenance, Preventive Maintenance, and Alterations (cont):		
—Maintenance and preventive maintenance personnel duty time limitations	. . . .	121.377
—Certificate requirements	135.435	121.378
—Authority to perform and approve maintenance, preventive maintenance, and alterations	135.437	121.379
—Maintenance recording requirements	135.439(a)(2)	121.380(a)(2)
—Transfer of maintenance records	135.441	121.380a
Subpart M—Airman and Crewmember Requirements:		
—Flight attendant complement	135.107	121.391
—Flight attendants being seated during movement on the surface	135.128(a)	121.391(d)
—Flight attendants or other qualified personnel at the gate	. . . .	121.391(e), .417, .393 (new)
Subpart N and O—Training Program and Crewmember Requirements	. . . .	121.400-.459
Subpart P—Aircraft Dispatcher Qualifications and Duty Time Limitations: Domestic and Flag Air Carriers	. . . .	121.461-.467
Subparts Q, R, and S—Flight Time Limitations and Rest Requirements: Domestic, Flag, and Supplemental Operations	135.261-.273	121.470-.525
Subpart T—Flight Operations:		
—Operational control	135.77, .79	121.533, .535, .537
—Admission to the flight deck	135.75	121.547
—Emergency procedures	135.69, .19	121.551, .553, .557, .559, .565 (new)
—Passenger information	135.117, .127	121.571(a), .533, .573, .585
—Oxygen for medical use by passengers	135.91(d)	121.574
—Alcoholic beverages	135.121	121.575
—Retention of items of mass	135.87, .122	121.577
—Cabin ozone concentration	. . . .	121.578(b)
—Minimum altitudes for use of autopilot	135.93	121.579
—Forward observer's seat	135.75	121.581
—Authority to refuse transportation	135.23(q)	121.586
—Carry-on baggage	135.87	121.589
—Airports	135.229, .217	121.590, .617(a)
Subpart U—Dispatching and Flight Release Rules:		
—Flight release authority	. . . .	121.597
—Dispatch or flight release under VFR	135.211	121.611
—Operations in icing conditions	135.227, .341, .345 . . .	121.629
—Fuel reserves	135.209, .223	121.639, .641, .643, .645
Subpart V—Records and Reports		
—Maintenance log: Airplane	135.65(c), .415(a)	121.701(a), .703(a), (e)
—Mechanical interruption summary report	135.417	121.705(b)
—Alteration and repair reports	135.439(a)(2)	121.707
—Airworthiness release or airplane log entry	135.443	121.709
—Other recordkeeping requirements	. . . .	121.711, .713, .715

INTENTIONALLY

LEFT

BLANK

SUBPART A — GENERAL

135.1 APPLICABILITY

(a) This part prescribes rules governing—
  (1) The commuter or on-demand operations of each person who holds or is required to hold an Air Carrier Certificate or Operating Certificate under Part 119 of this chapter.
  (2) Each person employed or used by a certificate holder conducting operations under this part including the maintenance, preventative maintenance and alteration of an aircraft.
  (3) The transportation of mail by aircraft conducted under a postal service contract awarded under 39 U.S.C. 5402c.
  (4) Each person who applies for provisional approval of an Advanced Qualification Program curriculum, curriculum segment, or portion of a curriculum segment under SFAR No. 58 of 14 CFR Part 121 and each person employed or used by an air carrier or commercial operator under this part to perform training, qualification, or evaluation functions under an Advanced Qualification Program under SFAR No. 58 of 14 CFR Part 121.
  (5) Nonstop sightseeing flights for compensation or hire that begin and end at the same airport, and are conducted within a 25 statute mile radius of that airport; however, except for operations subject to SFAR 50-2, these operations, when conducted for compensation or hire, must comply only with §§135.249, 135.251, 135.253, 135.255, and 135.353.
  (6) Each person who is on board an aircraft being operated under this part.
  (7) Each person who is an applicant for an Air Carrier Certificate or an Operating Certificate under 119 of this chapter, when conducting proving tests.
(b) [Reserved]
(c) For the purpose of §§135.249, 135.251, 135.253, 135.255, and 135.353, *operator* means any person or entity conducting non-stop sightseeing flights for compensation or hire in an airplane or rotorcraft that begin and end at the same airport and are conducted within a 25 statute mile radius of that airport.
(d) Notwithstanding the provisions of this part and Appendices I and J to Part 121 of this chapter, an operator who does not hold a Part 121 or Part 135 certificate is permitted to use a person who is otherwise authorized to perform aircraft maintenance or preventive maintenance duties and who is not subject to FAA-approved anti-drug and alcohol misuse prevention programs to perform—

  (1) Aircraft maintenance or preventive maintenance on the operator's aircraft if the operator would otherwise be required to transport the aircraft more than 50 nautical miles further than the repair point closest to operator's principal place of operation to obtain these services; or
  (2) Emergency repairs on the operator's aircraft if the aircraft cannot be safely operated to a location where an employee subject to FAA-approved programs can perform the repairs.

135.2 COMPLIANCE SCHEDULE FOR OPERATORS THAT TRANSITION TO PART 121 OF THIS CHAPTER; CERTAIN NEW ENTRANT OPERATORS

(a) *Applicability*. This section applies to the following:
  (1) Each certificate holder that was issued an Air Carrier or Operating Certificate and operations specifications under the requirements of Part 135 of this chapter or under SFAR No. 38-2 of 14 CFR Part 121 before January 19, 1996, and that conducts scheduled passenger-carrying operations with:
    (i) Nontransport category turbopropeller powered airplanes type certificated after December 31, 1964, that have a passenger seat configuration of 10-19 seats;
    (ii) Transport category turbopropeller powered airplanes that have a passenger seat configuration of 20-30 seats; or
    (iii) Turbojet engine powered airplanes having a passenger seat configuration of 1-30 seats.
  (2) Each person who, after January 19, 1996, applies for or obtains an initial air carrier or operating certificate and operations specifications to conduct scheduled passenger-carrying operations in the kinds of airplanes described in paragraphs (a)(1)(i), (a)(1)(ii), or paragraph (a)(1)(iii) of this section.
(b) *Obtaining operations specifications*. A certificate holder described in paragraph (a)(1) of this section may not, after March 20, 1997, operate an airplane described in paragraphs (a)(1)(i), (a)(1)(ii), or (a)(1)(iii) of this section in scheduled passenger-carrying operations, unless it obtains operations specifications to conduct its scheduled operations under Part 121 of this chapter on or before March 20, 1997.

(c) *Regular or accelerated compliance.* Except as provided in paragraphs (d) and (e) of this section, each certificate holder described in paragraph (a)(1) of this section shall comply with each applicable requirement of Part 121 of this chapter on and after March 20, 1997, or on and after the date on which the certificate holder is issued operations specifications under this part, whichever occurs first. Except as provided in paragraphs (d) and (e) of this section, each person described in paragraph (a)(2) of this section shall comply with each applicable requirement of Part 121 of this chapter on and after the date on which that person is issued a certificate and operations specifications under Part 121 of this chapter.

(d) *Delayed compliance dates.* Unless paragraph (e) of this section specifies an earlier compliance date, no certificate holder that is covered by paragraph (a) of this section may operate an airplane in 14 CFR Part 121 operations on or after a date listed in this paragraph unless that airplane meets the applicable requirement of this paragraph:

   (1) *Nontransport category turbopropeller powered airplanes type certificated after December 31, 1964, that have a passenger seating configuration of 10-19 seats.* No certificate holder may operate under this part an airplane that is described in paragraph (a)(1)(i) of this section on or after a date listed in paragraph (d)(1) of this section unless that airplane meets the applicable requirement listed in paragraph (d)(1) of this section:

     (i) December 22, 1997:

       (A) Section 121.289, Landing gear aural warning.

       (B) Section 121.308, Lavatory fire protection.

       (C) Section 121.310(e), Emergency exit handle illumination.

       (D) Section 121.337(b)(8), Protective breathing equipment.

       (E) Section 121.340, Emergency flotation means.

     (ii) December 20, 1999: Section 121.342, Pitot heat indication system.

     (iii) December 20, 2010:

       (A) For airplanes described in §121.157(f), the Airplane Performance Operating Limitations in §§121.189 through 121.197.

       (B) Section 121.161(b), Ditching approval.

       (C) Section 121.305(j), Third attitude indicator.

       (D) Section 121.312(c), Passenger seat cushion flammability.

   (2) *Transport category turbopropeller powered airplanes that have a passenger seat configuration of 20-30 seats.* No certificate holder may operate under this part an airplane that is described in paragraph (a)(1)(ii) of this section on or after a date listed in paragraph (d)(2) of this section unless that airplane meets the applicable requirement listed in this paragraph (d)(2) of this section:

     (i) December 22, 1997:

       (A) Section 121.308, Lavatory fire protection.

       (B) Section 121.337(b)(8) and (9), Protective breathing equipment.

       (C) Section 121.340, Emergency flotation means.

     (ii) December 20, 2010: Section 121.305(j), Third attitude indicator.

(e) *Newly manufactured airplanes.* No certificate holder that is described in paragraph (a) of this section may operate under Part 121 of this chapter an airplane manufactured on or after a date listed in this paragraph (e) unless that airplane meets the applicable requirement listed in this paragraph (e).

   (1) For nontransport category turbopropeller powered airplanes type certificated after December 31, 1964, that have a passenger seat configuration of 10-19 seats:

     (i) Manufactured on or after March 20, 1997:

       (A) Section 121.305(j), Third attitude indicator.

       (B) Section 121.311(f), Safety belts and shoulder harnesses.

     (ii) Manufactured on or after December 22, 1997: Section 121.317(a), Fasten seat belt light.

     (iii) Manufactured on or after December 20, 1999: Section 121.293, Takeoff warning system.

   (2) For transport category turbopropeller powered airplanes that have a passenger seat configuration of 20-30 seats manufactured on or after March 20, 1997: Section 121.305(j), Third attitude indicator.

(f) *New type certification requirements.* No person may operate an airplane for which the application for a type certificate was filed after March 29, 1995, in 14 CFR Part 121 operations unless that airplane is type certificated under Part 25 of this chapter.

🅐 *Amend #65 eff 7-15-96.*

(g) *Transition plan.* Before March 19, 1996, each certificate holder described in paragraph (a)(1) of this section must submit to the FAA a transition plan (containing a calendar of events) for moving from conducting its scheduled operations under the commuter requirements of Part 135 of this chapter to the requirements for domestic or flag operations under Part 121 of this chapter. Each transition plan must contain details on the following:

(1) Plans for obtaining new operations specifications authorizing domestic or flag operations;

(2) Plans for being in compliance with the applicable requirements of Part 121 of this chapter on or before March 20, 1997; and

(3) Plans for complying with the compliance date schedules contained in paragraphs (d) and (e) of this section.

(h) *Continuing requirements.* Until each certificate holder that is covered by paragraph (a) of this section meets the specific compliance dates listed in paragraphs (d) and (e) of this section, the certificate holder shall comply with the applicable airplane and equipment requirements of Part 135 of this chapter.

(i) *Delayed pilot age limitation.* (1) Notwithstanding §121.383(c) of this chapter, and except as provided in paragraph (i)(2) of this section, a certificate holder covered by paragraph (a)(1) of this section may use the services of a person as a pilot after that person has reached his or her 60th birthday, until December 20, 1999. Notwithstanding §121.383(c) of this chapter, and except as provided in paragraph (i)(2) of this section, a person may serve as a pilot for a certificate holder covered by paragraph (a)(1) of this section after that person has reached his or her 60th birthday, until December 20, 1999.

(2) Paragraph (i)(1) applies only to persons who were employed as pilots by a certificate holder covered by paragraph (a)(1) of this section on or before March 20, 1997.

135.3 RULES APPLICABLE TO OPERATIONS SUBJECT TO THIS PART

(a) Each person operating an aircraft in operations under this part shall—

(1) While operating inside the United States, comply with the applicable rules of this chapter; and

(2) While operating outside the United States, comply with Annex 2, Rules of the Air, to the Convention on International Civil Aviation or the regulations of any foreign country, whichever applies, and with any rules of Parts 61 and 91 of this chapter

and this part that are more restrictive than that Annex or those regulations and that can be complied with without violating that Annex or those regulations. Annex 2 is incorporated by reference in §91.703(b) of this chapter.

(b) After March 19, 1997, each certificate holder that conducts commuter operations under this part with airplanes in which two pilots are required by the type certification rules of this chapter shall comply with subparts N and O of Part 121 of this chapter instead of the requirements of subparts E, G, and H of this part. Each affected certificate holder must submit to the Administrator and obtain approval of a transition plan (containing a calendar of events) for moving from its present Part 135 training, checking, testing, and qualification requirements to the requirements of Part 121 of this chapter. Each transition plan must be submitted by March 19, 1996, and must contain details on how the certificate holder plans to be in compliance with subparts N and O of Part 121 on or before March 19, 1997.

(c) If authorized by the Administrator upon application, each certificate holder that conducts operations under this part to which paragraph (b) of this section does not apply, may comply with the applicable sections of subparts N and O of Part 121 instead of the requirements of subparts E, G, and H of this part, except that those authorized certificate holders may choose to comply with the operating experience requirements of §135.244, instead of the requirements of §121.434 of this chapter.

135.7 APPLICABILITY OF RULES TO UNAUTHORIZED OPERATORS

The rules in this part which apply to a person certificated under Part 119 of this Chapter also apply to a person who engages in any operation governed by this part without an appropriate certificate and operations specifications required by Part 119 of this Chapter.

135.12 PREVIOUSLY TRAINED CREW-MEMBERS

A certificate holder may use a crewmember who received the certificate holder's training in accordance with subparts E, G, and H of this part before March 19, 1997 without complying with initial training and qualification requirements of subparts N and O of Part 121 of this chapter. The crewmember must comply with the applicable recurrent training requirements of Part 121 of this chapter.

Ⓐ *Amend #65 eff 7-15-96.*

135.19 EMERGENCY OPERATIONS

(a) In an emergency involving the safety of persons or property, the certificate holder may deviate from the rules of this part relating to aircraft and equipment and weather minimums to the extent required to meet that emergency.

(b) In an emergency involving the safety of persons or property, the pilot in command may deviate from the rules of this part to the extent required to meet that emergency.

(c) Each person who, under the authority of this section, deviates from a rule of this part shall, within 10 days, excluding Saturdays, Sundays, and Federal holidays, after the deviation, send to the FAA Flight Standards District Office charged with the overall inspection of the certificate holder a complete report of the aircraft operation involved, including a description of the deviation and reasons for it.

135.21 MANUAL REQUIREMENTS

(a) Each certificate holder, other than one who uses only one pilot in the certificate holder's operations, shall prepare and keep current a manual setting forth the certificate holder's procedures and policies acceptable to the Administrator. This manual must be used by the certificate holder's flight, ground, and maintenance personnel in conducting its operations. However, the Administrator may authorize a deviation from this paragraph if the Administrator finds that, because of the limited size of the operation, all or part of the manual is not necessary for guidance of flight, ground, or maintenance personnel.

(b) Each certificate holder shall maintain at least one copy of the manual at its principal base of operations.

(c) The manual must not be contrary to any applicable Federal regulations, foreign regulation applicable to the certificate holder's operations in foreign countries, or the certificate holder's operating certificate or operations specifications.

(d) A copy of the manual, or appropriate portions of the manual (and changes and additions) shall be made available to maintenance and ground operations personnel by the certificate holder and furnished to—
  (1) Its flight crewmembers; and
  (2) Representatives of the Administrator assigned to the certificate holder.

(e) Each employee of the certificate holder to whom a manual or appropriate portions of it are furnished under paragraph (d)(1) of this section shall keep it up to date with the changes and additions furnished to them.

(f) Except as provided in paragraph (g) of this section, each certificate holder shall carry appropriate parts of the manual on each aircraft when away from the principal base of operations. The appropriate parts must be available for use by ground or flight personnel.

(g) If a certificate holder conducts aircraft inspections or maintenance at specified stations where it keeps the approved inspection program manual, it is not required to carry the manual aboard the aircraft enroute to those stations.

135.23 MANUAL CONTENTS

Each manual shall have the date of the last revision on each revised page. The manual must include—

(a) The name of each management person required under §119.69(a) of this chapter who is authorized to act for the certificate holder, the person's assigned area of responsibility, the person's duties, responsibilities, and authority, and the name and title of each person authorized to exercise operational control under §135.77;

(b) Procedures for ensuring compliance with aircraft weight and balance limitations and, for multiengine aircraft, for determining compliance with §135.185;

(c) Copies of the certificate holder's operations specifications or appropriate extracted information, including area of operations authorized, category and class of aircraft authorized, crew complements, and types of operations authorized;

(d) Procedures for complying with accident notifications requirements;

(e) Procedures for ensuring that the pilot in command knows that required airworthiness inspections have been made and that the aircraft has been approved for return to service in compliance with applicable maintenance requirements;

(f) Procedures for reporting and recording mechanical irregularities that come to the attention of the pilot in command before, during, and after completion of a flight;

(g) Procedures to be followed by the pilot in command for determining that mechanical irregularities or defects reported for previous flights have been corrected or that correction has been deferred;

(h) Procedures to be followed by the pilot in command to obtain maintenance, preventive maintenance, and servicing of the aircraft at a place where previous arrangements have not been made by the operator, when the pilot is authorized to so act for the operator;

(i) Procedures under §135.179 for the release for, or continuation of, flight if any item of equipment required for the particular type of operation becomes inoperative or unserviceable enroute;

(j) Procedures for refueling aircraft, eliminating fuel contamination, protecting from fire (including electrostatic protection), and supervising and protecting passengers during refueling;

(k) Procedures to be followed by the pilot in command in the briefing under §135.117;

(l) Flight locating procedures, when applicable;

(m) Procedures for ensuring compliance with emergency procedures, including a list of the functions assigned each category of required crewmembers in connection with an emergency and emergency evacuation duties under §135.123;

(n) Enroute qualification procedures for pilots, when applicable;

(o) The approved aircraft inspection program, when applicable;

(p) Procedures and instructions to enable personnel to recognize hazardous materials, as defined in Title 49 CFR, and if these materials are to be carried, stored, or handled, procedures and instruction for—

  (1) Accepting shipment of hazardous material required by Title 49 CFR, to assure proper packaging, marking, labeling, shipping documents, compatibility of articles, and instructions on their loading, storage, and handling;

  (2) Notification and reporting hazardous material incidents as required by Title 49 CFR; and

  (3) Notification of the pilot in command when there are hazardous materials aboard, as required by Title 49 CFR;

(q) Procedures for the evacuation of persons who may need the assistance of another person to move expeditiously to an exit if an emergency occurs; and

(r) Other procedures and policy instructions regarding the certificate holder's operations, that are issued by the certificate holder.

135.25 AIRCRAFT REQUIREMENTS

(a) Except as provided in paragraph (d) of this section, no certificate holder may operate an aircraft under this part unless that aircraft—

  (1) Is registered as a civil aircraft of the United States and carries an appropriate and current airworthiness certificate issued under this chapter; and

  (2) Is in an airworthy condition and meets the applicable airworthiness requirements of this chapter, including those relating to identification and equipment.

(b) Each certificate holder must have the exclusive use of at least one aircraft that meets the requirements for at least one kind of operation authorized in the certificate holder's operations specifications. In addition, for each kind of operation for which the certificate holder does not have the exclusive use of an aircraft, the certificate holder must have available for use under a written agreement (including arrangements for performing required maintenance) at least one aircraft that meets the requirements for that kind of operation. However, this paragraph does not prohibit the operator from using or authorizing the use of the aircraft for other than air taxi or commercial operations and does not require the certificate holder to have exclusive use of all aircraft that the certificate holder uses.

(c) For the purposes of paragraph (b) of this section, a person has exclusive use of an aircraft if that person has the sole possession, control, and use of it for flight, as owner, or has a written agreement (including arrangements for performing required maintenance), in effect when the aircraft is operated, giving the person that possession, control, and use for at least 6 consecutive months.

(d) A certificate holder may operate in common carriage, and for the carriage of mail, a civil aircraft which is leased or chartered to it without crew and is registered in a country which is a party to the Convention on International Civil Aviation if—

  (1) The aircraft carries an appropriate airworthiness certificate issued by the country of registration and meets the registration and identification requirements of that country;

  (2) The aircraft is of a type design which is approved under a U.S. type certificate and complies with all of the requirements of this chapter (14 CFR Chapter 1) that would be applicable to that aircraft were it registered in the United States, including the requirements which must be met for issuance of a U.S. standard airworthiness certificate (including type design conformity, condition for safe operation, and the noise, fuel venting, and engine emission requirements of this chapter), except that a U.S. registration certificate and a U.S. standard airworthiness certificate will not be issued for the aircraft;

  (3) The aircraft is operated by a U.S. certificated airmen employed by the certificate holder; and

  (4) The certificate holder files a copy of the aircraft lease or charter agreement with the FAA Aircraft Registry, Department of Transportation, 6400 South MacArthur Boulevard, Oklahoma City, Oklahoma (Mailing address: P.O. Box 25504, Oklahoma City, Oklahoma 73125).

135.41 CARRIAGE OF NARCOTIC DRUGS, MARIJUANA, AND DEPRESSANT OR STIMULANT DRUGS OR SUBSTANCES

If the holder of a certificate operating under this part allows any aircraft owned or leased by that holder to be engaged in any operation that the certificate holder knows to be in violation of §91.19(a) of this chapter, that operation is a basis for suspending or revoking the certificate.

135.43 CREWMEMBER CERTIFICATES: INTERNATIONAL OPERATIONS:

(a) This section describes the certificates that were issued to United States citizens who were employed by air carriers at the time of issuance as flight crewmembers on United States registered aircraft engaged in international air commerce. The purpose of the certificate is to facilitate the entry and clearance of those crewmembers into ICAO contracting states. They were issued under Annex 9, as amended, to the Convention on International Civil Aviation.

(b) The holder of a certificate issued under this section, or the air carrier by whom the holder is employed, shall surrender the certificate for cancellation at the nearest FAA Flight Standards District Office at the termination of the holder's employment with that air carrier.

(c) The holder of a certificate issued under this section, or the certificate holder by whom the holder is employed, shall surrender the certificate for cancellation at the nearest certificate-holding district office or submit it for cancellation to the Airmen Certification Branch, AAC-260, P.O. Box 25082, Oklahoma City, Oklahoma 73125, at the termination of the holder's employment with that certificate holder.

PAGES 135-13 thru 135-18 RESERVED FOR EXPANSION

Ⓐ *Amend #65 eff 7-15-96.*

SUBPART B — FLIGHT OPERATIONS

135.61 GENERAL

This subpart prescribes rules, in addition to those in Part 91 of this chapter, that apply to operations under this part.

135.63 RECORDKEEPING REQUIREMENTS

(a) Each certificate holder shall keep at its principal business office or at other places approved by the Administrator, and shall make available for inspection by the Administrator the following—
 (1) The certificate holder's operating certificate;
 (2) The certificate holder's operations specifications;
 (3) A current list of the aircraft used or available for use in operations under this part and the operations for which each is equipped;
 (4) An individual record of each pilot used in operations under this part, including the following information:
  (i) The full name of the pilot.
  (ii) The pilot certificate (by type and number) and ratings that the pilot holds.
  (iii) The pilot's aeronautical experience in sufficient detail to determine the pilot's qualifications to pilot aircraft in operations under this part.
  (iv) The pilot's current duties and the date of the pilot's assignment to those duties.
  (v) The effective date and class of the medical certificate that the pilot holds.
  (vi) The date and result of each of the initial and recurrent competency tests and proficiency and route checks required by this part and the type of aircraft flown during that test or check.
  (vii) The pilot's flight time in sufficient detail to determine compliance with the flight time limitations of this part.
  (viii) The pilot's check pilot authorization, if any.
  (ix) Any action taken concerning the pilot's release from employment for physical or professional disqualification.

  (x) The date of the completion of the initial phase and each recurrent phase of the training required by this part; and
 (5) An individual record for each flight attendant who is required under this part, maintained in sufficient detail to determine compliance with the applicable portions of §135.273 of this part.
(b) Each certificate holder must keep each record required by paragraph (a)(3) of this section for at least 6 months, and must keep each record required by paragraphs (a)(4) and (a)(5) of this section for at least 12 months.
(c) For multiengine aircraft, each certificate holder is responsible for the preparation and accuracy of a load manifest in duplicate containing information concerning the loading of the aircraft. The manifest must be prepared before each takeoff and must include—
 (1) The number of passengers;
 (2) The total weight of the loaded aircraft;
 (3) The maximum allowable takeoff weight for that flight;
 (4) The center of gravity limits;
 (5) The center of gravity of the loaded aircraft, except that the actual center of gravity need not be computed if the aircraft is loaded according to a loading schedule or other approved method that ensures that the center of gravity of the loaded aircraft is within approved limits. In those cases, an entry shall be made on the manifest indicating that the center of gravity is within limits according to a loading schedule or other approved method;
 (6) The registration number of the aircraft or flight number;
 (7) The origin and destination; and
 (8) Identification of crewmembers and their crew position assignments.
(d) The pilot in command of an aircraft for which a load manifest must be prepared shall carry a copy of the completed load manifest in the aircraft to its destination. The certificate holder shall keep copies of completed load manifests for at least 30 days at its principal operations base, or at another location used by it and approved by the Administrator.

135.64 RETENTION OF CONTRACTS AND AMENDMENTS: COMMERCIAL OPERATORS WHO CONDUCT INTRASTATE OPERATIONS FOR COMPENSATION OR HIRE

(a) Each commercial operator who conducts intrastate operations for compensation or hire shall keep a copy of each written contract under which it provides services as a commercial operator for a period of at least one year after the date of execution of the contract. In the case of an oral contract, it shall keep a memorandum stating its elements, and of any amendments to it, for a period of at least one year after the execution of that contract or change.

(b) Each commercial operator who conducts intrastate operations for compensation or hire shall submit a financial report for the first 6 months of each fiscal year and another financial report for each complete fiscal year. If that person's operating certificate is suspended for more than 29 days, that person shall submit a financial report as of the last day of the month in which the suspension is terminated. The report required to be submitted by this section shall be submitted within 60 days of the last day of the period covered by the report and must include—

(1) A balance sheet that shows assets, liabilities, and net worth on the last day of the reporting period;

A (2) The information required by §119.35(g)(2), (g)(7), and (g)(8) of this chapter;

(3) An itemization of claims in litigation against the applicant, if any, as of the last day of the period covered by the report;

(4) A profit and loss statement with the separation of items relating to the applicant's commercial operator activities from his other business activities, if any; and

(5) A list of each contract that gave rise to operating income on the profit and loss statement, including the names and addresses of the contracting parties and the nature, scope, date, and duration of each contract.

135.65 REPORTING MECHANICAL IRREGULARITIES

(a) Each certificate holder shall provide an aircraft maintenance log to be carried on board each aircraft for recording or deferring mechanical irregularities and their correction.

(b) The pilot in command shall enter or have entered in the aircraft maintenance log each mechanical irregularity that comes to the pilot's attention during flight time. Before each flight, the pilot in command shall, if the pilot does not already know, determine the status of each irregularity entered in the maintenance log at the end of the preceding flight.

(c) Each person who takes corrective action or defers action concerning a reported or observed failure or malfunction of an airframe, powerplant, propeller, rotor, or appliance, shall record the action taken in the aircraft maintenance log under the applicable maintenance requirements of this chapter.

(d) Each certificate holder shall establish a procedure for keeping copies of the aircraft maintenance log required by this section in the aircraft for access by appropriate personnel and shall include that procedure in the manual required by §135.21.

135.67 REPORTING POTENTIALLY HAZARDOUS METEOROLOGICAL CONDITIONS AND IRREGULARITIES OF COMMUNICATIONS OR NAVIGATION FACILITIES

Whenever a pilot encounters a potentially hazardous meteorological condition or an irregularity in a ground communications or navigational facility in flight, the knowledge of which the pilot considers essential to the safety of other flights, the pilot shall notify an appropriate ground radio station as soon as practicable.

135.69 RESTRICTION OR SUSPENSION OF OPERATIONS: CONTINUATION OF FLIGHT IN AN EMERGENCY

(a) During operations under this part, if a certificate holder or pilot in command knows of conditions, including airport and runway conditions, that are a hazard to safe operations, the certificate holder or pilot in command, as the case may be, shall restrict or suspend operations as necessary until those conditions are corrected.

(b) No pilot in command may allow a flight to continue toward any airport of intended landing under the conditions set forth in paragraph (a) of this section, unless in the opinion of the pilot in command, the conditions that are a hazard to safe operations may reasonably be expected to be corrected by the estimated time of arrival or, unless there is no safer procedure. In the latter event, the continuation toward that airport is an emergency situation under §135.19.

135.71 AIRWORTHINESS CHECK

The pilot in command may not begin a flight unless the pilot determines that the airworthiness inspections required by §91.409 of this chapter, or §135.419, whichever is applicable, have been made.

A *Amend #65 eff 7-15-96.*

135.73 INSPECTIONS AND TESTS

Each certificate holder and each person employed by the certificate holder shall allow the Administrator, at any time or place, to make inspections or test (including en route inspections) to determine the holder's compliance with the Federal Aviation Act of 1958, applicable regulations, and the certificate holder's operating certificate, and operations specifications.

135.75 INSPECTORS CREDENTIALS: ADMISSIONS TO PILOT'S COMPARTMENT: FORWARD OBSERVER'S SEAT

(a)   Whenever, in performing the duties of conducting an inspection, an FAA inspector presents an Aviation Safety Inspector credential, FAA Form 110A, to the pilot in command of an aircraft operated by the certificate holder, the inspector must be given free and uninterrupted access to the pilot's compartment of that aircraft. However, this paragraph does not limit the emergency authority of the pilot in command to exclude any person from the pilot's compartment in the interest of safety.

(b)   A forward observer's seat on the flight deck, or forward passenger seat with headset or speaker must be provided for use by the Administrator while conducting enroute inspections. The suitability of the location of the seat and the headset or speaker for use in conducting enroute inspections is determined by the Administrator.

135.77 RESPONSIBILITY FOR OPERATIONAL CONTROL

Each certificate holder is responsible for operational control and shall list, in the manual required by §135.21, the name and title of each person authorized by it to exercise operational control.

135.79 FLIGHT LOCATING REQUIREMENTS

(a)   Each certificate holder must have procedures established for locating each flight, for which an FAA flight plan is not filed, that—
   (1)   Provide the certificate holder with at least the information required to be included in a VFR flight plan;
   (2)   Provide for timely notification of an FAA facility or search and rescue facility, if an aircraft is overdue or missing; and
   (3)   Provide the certificate holder with the location, date, and estimated time for reestablishing radio or telephone communications, if the flight will operate in an area where communications cannot be maintained.

(b)   Flight locating information shall be retained at the certificate holder's principal place of business, or at other places designated by the certificate holder in the flight locating procedures, until the completion of the flight.

(c)   Each certificate holder shall furnish the representative of the Administrator assigned to it with a copy of its flight locating procedures and any changes or additions, unless those procedures are included in a manual required under this part.

135.81 INFORMING PERSONNEL OF OPERATIONAL INFORMATION AND APPROPRIATE CHANGES

Each certificate holder shall inform each person in its employment of the operations specifications that apply to that person's duties and responsibilities and shall make available to each pilot in the certificate holder's employ the following materials in current form:

(a)   Airman's Information Manual (Alaska Supplement in Alaska and Pacific Chart Supplement in Pacific-Asia Regions) or a commercial publication that contains the same information.

(b)   This part and Part 91 of this chapter.

(c)   Aircraft Equipment Manuals, and Aircraft Flight Manual or equivalent.

(d)   For foreign operations, the International Flight Information Manual or a commercial publication that contains the same information concerning the pertinent operational and entry requirements of the foreign country or countries involved.

135.83 OPERATING INFORMATION REQUIRED

(a) The operator of an aircraft must provide the following materials, in current and appropriate form, accessible to the pilot at the pilot station, and the pilot shall use them:
(1) A cockpit checklist.
(2) For multiengine aircraft or for aircraft with retractable landing gear, an emergency cockpit checklist containing the procedures required by paragraph (c) of this section, as appropriate.
(3) Pertinent aeronautical charts.
(4) For IFR operations, each pertinent navigational enroute, terminal area, and approach and letdown chart.
(5) For multiengine aircraft, one-engine-inoperative climb peformance data and if the aircraft s approved for use in IFR or over-the-top operations, that data must be sufficient to enable the pilot to determine compliance with §135.181(a)(2).

(b) Each cockpit checklist required by paragraph (a)(1) of this section must contain the following procedures:
(1) Before starting engines;
(2) Before takeoff;
(3) Cruise;
(4) Before landing;
(5) After landing;
(6) Stopping engines.

(c) Each emergency cockpit checklist required by paragraph (a)(2) of this section must contain the following procedures, as appropriate:
(1) Emergency operation of fuel, hydraulic, electrical, and mechanical systems.
(2) Emergency operation of instruments and controls.
(3) Engine inoperative procedures.
(4) Any other emergency procedures necessary for safety.

135.85 CARRIAGE OF PERSONS WITHOUT COMPLIANCE WITH THE PASSENGER-CARRYING PROVISIONS OF THIS PART

The following persons may be carried aboard an aircraft without complying with the passenger-carrying requirements of this part:
(a) A crewmember or other employee of the certificate holder.
(b) A person necessary for the safe handling of animals on the aircraft.
(c) A person necessary for the safe handling of hazardous materials (as defined in Subchapter C of *Title 49 CFR).
(d) A person performing duty as a security or honor guard accompanying a shipment made by or under the authority of the U.S. Government.
(e) A military courier or a military route supervisor carried by a military cargo contract air carrier or commercial operator in operations under a military cargo contract, if that carriage is specifically authorized by the appropriate military service.
(f) An authorized representative of the Administrator conducting an enroute inspection.
(g) A person, authorized by the Administrator, who is performing a duty connected with a cargo operation of the certificate holder.

135.87 CARRIAGE OF CARGO INCLUDING CARRY-ON BAGGAGE

No person may carry cargo, including carry-on baggage, in or on any aircraft unless—
(a) It is carried in an approved cargo rack, bin, or compartment installed in or on the aircraft;
(b) It is secured by an approved means; or

(*Not published herein—Ed.)

(c) It is carried in accordance with each of the following:
  (1) For cargo, it is properly secured by a safety belt or other tie-down having enough strength to eliminate the possibility of shifting under all normally anticipated flight and ground conditions, or for carry-on baggage, it is restrained so as to prevent its movement during air turbulence.
  (2) It is packaged or covered to avoid possible injury to occupants.
  (3) It does not impose any load on seats or on the floor structure that exceeds the load limitation for those components.
  (4) It is not located in a position that obstructs the access to, or use of, any required emergency or regular exit, or the use of the aisle between the crew and the passenger compartment, or located in a position that obscures any passenger's view of the "seat belt" sign, "no smoking" sign, or any required exit sign, unless an auxiliary sign or other approved means for proper notification of the passengers is provided.
  (5) It is not carried directly above seated occupants.
  (6) It is stowed in compliance with this section for takeoff and landing.
  (7) For cargo only operations, paragraph (c)(4) of this section does not apply if the cargo is loaded so that at least one emergency or regular exit is available to provide all occupants of the aircraft a means of unobstructed exit from the aircraft if an emergency occurs.
(d) Each passenger seat under which baggage is stowed shall be fitted with a means to prevent articles of baggage stowed under it from sliding under crash impacts severe enough to induce the ultimate inertia forces specified in the emergency landing condition regulations under which the aircraft was type certificated.
(e) When cargo is carried in cargo compartments that are designed to require the physical entry of a crewmember to extinguish any fire that may occur during flight, the cargo must be loaded so as to allow a crewmember to effectively reach all parts of the compartment with the contents of a hand fire extinguisher.

135.89 PILOT REQUIREMENTS: USE OF OXYGEN

(a) *Unpressurized aircraft.* Each pilot of an unpressurized aircraft shall use oxygen continuously when flying—
  (1) At altitudes above 10,000 feet through 12,000 feet MSL for that part of the flight at those altitudes that is of more than 30 minutes duration; and
  (2) Above 12,000 feet MSL.
(b) *Pressurized aircraft.*
  (1) Whenever a pressurized aircraft is operated with the cabin pressure altitude more than 10,000 feet MSL, each pilot shall comply with paragraph (a) of this section.
  (2) Whenever a pressurized aircraft is operated at altitudes above 25,000 feet through 35,000 feet MSL, unless each pilot has an approved quick-donning type oxygen mask—
    (i) At least one pilot at the controls shall wear, secured and sealed, an oxygen mask that either supplies oxygen at all times or automatically supplies oxygen whenever the cabin pressure altitude exceeds 12,000 feet MSL; and
    (ii) During that flight, each other pilot on flight deck duty shall have an oxygen mask, connected to an oxygen supply, located so as to allow immediate placing of the mask on the pilot's face sealed and secured for use.
  (3) Whenever a pressurized aircraft is operated at altitudes above 35,000 feet MSL, at least one pilot at the controls shall wear, secured and sealed, an oxygen mask required by paragraph (2)(i) of this paragraph.
  (4) If one pilot leaves a pilot duty station of an aircraft when operating at altitudes above 25,000 feet MSL, the remaining pilot at the controls shall put on and use an approved oxygen mask until the other pilot returns to the pilot duty station of the aircraft.

135.91   OXYGEN FOR MEDICAL USE BY PASSENGERS

(a)   Except as provided in paragraphs (d) and (e) of this section, no certificate holder may allow the carriage or operation of equipment for the storage, generation or dispensing of medical oxygen unless the unit to be carried is constructed so that all valves, fittings, and gauges are protected from damage during that carriage or operation and unless the following conditions are met—

    (1)   The equipment must be—

        (i)   Of an approved type or in conformity with the manufacturing, packaging, marking, labeling, and maintenance requirements of Title 49 CFR Parts 171, 172, and 173, except §173.24(a)(1);

        (ii)   When owned by the certificate holder, maintained under the certificate holders approved maintenance program;

        (iii)   Free of flammable contaminants on all exterior surfaces; and

        (iv)   Appropriately secured.

    (2)   When the oxygen is stored in the form of a liquid, the equipment must have been under the certificate holder's approved maintenance program since its purchase new or since the storage container was last purged.

    (3)   When the oxygen is stored in the form of a compressed gas as defined in Title 49 CFR §173.300(a)—

        (i)   When owned by the certificate holder, it must be maintained under its approved maintenance program; and

        (ii)   The pressure in any oxygen cylinder must not exceed the rated cylinder pressure.

    (4)   The pilot in command must be advised when the equipment is on board, and when it is intended to be used.

    (5)   The equipment must be stowed, and each person using the equipment must be seated, so as not to restrict access to or use of any required emergency or regular exit, or of the aisle in the passenger compartment.

(b)   No person may smoke and no certificate holder may allow any person to smoke within 10 feet of oxygen storage and dispensing equipment carried under paragraph (a) of this section.

(c)   No certificate holder may allow any person other than a person trained in the use of medical oxygen equipment to connect or disconnect oxygen bottles or any other ancillary component while any passenger is aboard the aircraft.

(d)   Paragraph (a)(1)(i) of this section does not apply when that equipment is furnished by a professional or medical emergency service for use on board an aircraft in a medical emergency when no other practical means of transportation (including any other properly equipped certificate holder) is reasonably available and the person carried under the medical emergency is accompanied by a person trained in the use of medical oxygen.

(e)   Each certificate holder who, under the authority of paragraph (d) of this section, deviates from paragraph (a)(1)(i) if this section under a medical emergency shall, within 10 days, excluding Saturdays, Sundays, and Federal holidays, after the deviation, send to the certificate-holding district office a complete report of the operation involved, including a description of the deviation and the reasons for it.

135.93   AUTOPILOT: MINIMUM ALTITUDES FOR USE

(a)   Except as provided in paragraphs (b), (c), and (d) of this section, no person may use an autopilot at an altitude above the terrain which is less than 500 feet or less than twice the maximum altitude loss specified in the approved Aircraft Flight Manual or equivalent for a malfunction of the autopilot, whichever is higher.

Ⓐ *Amend #60 eff 2-26-96*

(b) When using an instrument approach facility other than ILS, no person may use an autopilot at an altitude above the terrain that is less than 50 feet below the approved minimum descent altitude for that procedure, or less than twice the maximum loss specified in the approved Airplane Flight Manual or equivalent for a malfunction of the autopilot under approach conditions, whichever is higher.

(c) For ILS approaches, when reported weather conditions are less than the basic weather conditions in §91.155 of this chapter, no person may use an autopilot with an approach coupler at an altitude above the terrain that is less than 50 feet above the terrain, or the maximum altitude loss specified in the approved Airplane Flight Manual or equivalent for the malfunction of the autopilot with approach coupler, whichever is higher.

(d) Without regard to paragraphs (a), (b), or (c) of this section, the Administrator may issue operations specifications to allow the use, to touchdown, of an approved flight control guidance system with automatic capability, if —

    (1) The system does not contain any altitude loss (above zero) specified in the approved Aircraft Flight Manual or equivalent for malfunction of the autopilot with approach coupler; and

    (2) The Administrator finds that the use of the system to touchdown will not otherwise adversely affect the safety standards of this section.

(e) This section does not apply to operations conducted in rotorcraft.

135.95 AIRMEN: LIMITATIONS ON USE OF SERVICES

No certificate holder may use the services of any person as an airman unless the person performing those services —

(a) Holds an appropriate and current airman certificate; and

(b) Is qualified, under this chapter, for the operation for which the person is to be used.

135.97 AIRCRAFT AND FACILITIES FOR RECENT FLIGHT EXPERIENCE

Each certificate holder shall provide aircraft and facilities to enable each of its pilots to maintain and demonstrate the pilot's ability to conduct all operations for which the pilot is authorized.

135.99 COMPOSITION OF FLIGHT CREW

(a) No certificate holder may operate an aircraft with less than the minimum flight crew specified in the aircraft operating limitations or the Aircraft Flight Manual for that aircraft and required by this part for the kind of operation being conducted.

(b) No certificate holder may operate an aircraft without a second in command if that aircraft has a passenger seating configuration, excluding any pilot seat, of ten seats or more.

135.100 FLIGHT CREWMEMBER DUTIES

(a) No certificate holder shall require, nor may any flight crewmember perform, any duties during a critical phase of flight except those duties required for the safe operation of the aircraft. Duties such as company required calls made for such nonsafety related purposes as ordering galley supplies and confirming passenger connections, announcements made to passengers promoting the air carrier or pointing out sights of interest, and filling out company payroll and related records are not required for the safe operation of the aircraft.

(b) No flight crewmember may engage in, nor may any pilot in command permit, any activity during a critical phase of flight which could distract any flight crewmember from the performance of his or her duties or which could interfere in any way with the proper conduct of those duties. Activities such as eating meals, engaging in nonessential conversations within the cockpit and nonessential communications between the cabin and cockpit crews, and reading publications not related to the proper conduct of the flight are not required for the safe operation of the aircraft.

(c) For the purposes of this section, critical phases of flight includes all ground operations involving taxi, takeoff and landing, and all other flight operations conducted below 10,000 feet, except cruise flight.

135.101   SECOND IN COMMAND REQUIRED IN IFR CONDITIONS

Except as provided in §§135.103 and 135.105, no person may operate an aircraft carrying passengers in IFR conditions, unless there is a second in command in the aircraft.

135.103   EXCEPTION TO SECOND IN COMMAND REQUIREMENT: IFR OPERATIONS

The pilot in command of an aircraft carrying passengers may conduct IFR operations without a second in command under the following conditions:

(a)   A takeoff may be conducted under IFR conditions if the weather reports or forecasts, or any combination of them, indicate that the weather along the planned route of flight allows flight under VFR within 15 minutes flying time, at normal cruise speed, from the takeoff airport.

(b)   Enroute IFR may be conducted if unforecast weather conditions below the VFR minimums of this chapter are encountered on a flight that was planned to be conducted under VFR.

(c)   An IFR approach may be conducted if, upon arrival at the destination airport, unforecast weather conditions do not allow an approach to be completed under VFR.

(d)   When IFR operations are conducted under this section:

     (1)   The aircraft must be properly equipped for IFR operations under this part.

     (2)   The pilot must be authorized to conduct IFR operations under this part.

     (3)   The flight must be conducted in accordance with an ATC IFR clearance.

IFR operations without a second in command may not be conducted under this section in an aircraft requiring a second in command under §135.99.

135.105   EXCEPTION TO SECOND IN COMMAND REQUIREMENT: APPROVAL FOR USE OF AUTOPILOT SYSTEM

(a)   Except as provided in §§135.99 and 135.111, unless two pilots are required by this chapter for operations under VFR, a person may operate an aircraft without a second in command, if it is equipped with an operative approved autopilot system and the use of that system is authorized by appropriate operations specifications.

🅐 No certificate holder may use any person, nor may any person serve, as a pilot in command under this section of an aircraft operated in a commuter operation, as defined in Part 119 of this Chapter, unless that person has at least 100 hours pilot in command flight time in the make and model of aircraft to be flown and has met all other applicable requirements of this part.

(b)   The certificate holder may apply for an amendment of its operations specifications to authorize the use of an autopilot system in place of a second in command.

(c)   The Administrator issues an amendment to the operations specifications authorizing the use of an autopilot system, in place of a second in command, if —

     (1)   The autopilot is capable of operating the aircraft controls to maintain flight and maneuver it about the three axes; and

     (2)   The certificate holder shows, to the satisfaction of the Administrator, that operations using the autopilot system can be conducted safely and in compliance with this part.

The amendment contains any conditions or limitations on the use of the autopilot system that the Administrator determines are needed in the interest of safety.

135.107   FLIGHT ATTENDANT CREWMEMBER REQUIREMENT

No certificate holder may operate an aircraft that has a passenger seating configuration, excluding any pilot seat, of more than 19 unless there is a flight attendant crewmember on board the aircraft.

🅐 *Amend #58 eff 1-19-96.*

135.109 PILOT IN COMMAND OR SECOND IN COMMAND: DESIGNATION REQUIRED

(a) Each certificate holder shall designate a—
(1) Pilot in command for each flight; and
(2) Second in command for each flight requiring two pilots.
(b) The pilot in command, as designated by the certificate holder, shall remain the pilot in command at all times during that flight.

135.111 SECOND IN COMMAND REQUIRED IN CATEGORY II OPERATIONS

No person may operate an aircraft in a Category II operation unless there is a second in command of the aircraft.

135.113 PASSENGER OCCUPANCY OF PILOT SEAT

No certificate holder may operate an aircraft type certificated after October 15, 1971, that has a passenger seating configuration, excluding any pilot seat, of more than eight seats if any person other than the pilot in command, a second in command, a company check airman, or an authorized representative of the Administrator, the National Transportation Safety Board, or the United States Postal Service occupies a pilot seat.

135.115 MANIPULATION OF CONTROLS

No pilot in command may allow any person to manipulate the flight controls of an aircraft during flight conducted under this part, nor may any person manipulate the controls during such flight unless that person is—
(a) A pilot employed by the certificate holder and qualified in the aircraft; or
(b) An authorized safety representative of the Administrator who has the permission of the pilot in command, is qualified in the aircraft, and is checking flight operations.

135.117 BRIEFING OF PASSENGERS BEFORE FLIGHT

(a) Before each takeoff each pilot in command of an aircraft carrying passengers shall ensure that all passengers have been orally briefed on—
(1) *Smoking.* Each passenger shall be briefed on when, where, and under what conditions smoking is prohibited (including, but not limited to, any applicable requirements of *part 252, of this title). This briefing shall include a statement that the Federal Aviation Regulations require passenger compliance with the lighted passenger information signs (if such signs are required), posted placards, areas designated for safety purposes as no smoking areas, and crewmember instructions with regard to these items. The briefing shall also include a statement (if the aircraft is equipped with a lavatory) that Federal law prohibits: tampering with, disabling, or destroying any smoke detector installed in an aircraft lavatory; smoking in lavatories; and, when applicable, smoking in passenger compartments.
(2) The use of safety belts, including instructions on how to fasten and unfasten the safety belts. Each passenger shall be briefed on when, where, and under what conditions the safety belt must be fastened about that passenger. This briefing shall include a statement that the Federal Aviation Regulations require passenger compliance with lighted passenger information signs and crewmember instructions concerning the use of safety belts.
(3) The placement of seat backs in an upright position before takeoff and landing;
(4) Location and means for opening the passenger entry door and emergency exits;
(5) Location of survival equipment;
(6) If the flight involves extended overwater operation, ditching procedures and the use of required flotation equipment;
(7) If the flight involves operations above 12,000 feet MSL, the normal and emergency use of oxygen; and
(8) Location and operation of fire extinguishers.

Amend #44
eff 10-15-92

*(Not published herein)

(b)   Before each takeoff the pilot in command shall ensure that each person who may need the assistance of another person to move expeditiously to an exit if an emergency occurs and that person's attendant, if any, has received a briefing as to the procedures to be followed if an evacuation occurs. This paragraph does not apply to a person who has been given a briefing before a previous leg of a flight in the same aircraft.

(c)   The oral briefing required by paragraph (a) of this section shall be given by the pilot in command or a crewmember.

(d)   Notwithstanding the provisions of paragraph (c) of this section, for aircraft certificated to carry 19 passengers or less, the oral briefing required by paragraph (a) of this section shall be given by the pilot in command, a crewmember, or other qualified person designated by the certificate holder and approved by the Administrator.

(e)   The oral briefing required by paragraph (a) shall be supplemented by printed cards which must be carried in the aircraft in locations convenient for the use of each passenger. The cards must—

(1)   Be appropriate for the aircraft on which they are to be used;

(2)   Contain a diagram of, and method of operating, the emergency exits; and

(3)   Contain other instructions necessary for the use of emergency equipment on board the aircraft.

(f)   The briefing required by paragraph (a) may be delivered by means of an approved recording playback device that is audible to each passenger under normal noise levels.

135.119   PROHIBITION AGAINST CARRIAGE OF WEAPONS

No person may, while on board an aircraft being operated by a certificate holder, carry on or about that person a deadly or dangerous weapon, either concealed or unconcealed. This section does not apply to—

(a)   Officials or employees of a municipality or a State, or of the United States, who are authorized to carry arms; or

(b)   Crewmembers and other persons authorized by the certificate holder to carry arms.

135.121   ALCOHOLIC BEVERAGES

(a)   No person may drink any alcoholic beverage aboard an aircraft unless the certificate holder operating the aircraft has served that beverage.

(b)   No certificate holder may serve any alcoholic beverage to any person aboard its aircraft if that person appears to be intoxicated.

(c)   No certificate holder may allow any person to board any of its aircraft if that person appears to be intoxicated.

135.122   STOWAGE OF FOOD, BEVERAGE, AND PASSENGER SERVICE EQUIPMENT DURING AIRCRAFT MOVEMENT ON THE SURFACE, TAKEOFF, AND LANDING

(a)   No certificate holder may move an aircraft on the surface, take off, or land when any food, beverage, or tableware furnished by the certificate holder is located at any passenger seat.

Amend #44
eff 10-15-92

(b)   No certificate holder may move an aircraft on the surface, take off, or land unless each food and beverage tray and seat back tray table is secured in its stowed position.

(c)   No certificate holder may permit an aircraft to move on the surface, take off, or land unless each passenger serving cart is secured in its stowed position.

(d)   Each passenger shall comply with instructions given by a crewmember with regard to compliance with this section.

---

*(Not published herein)

135.123   EMERGENCY AND EMERGENCY EVACUATION DUTIES

(a)   Each certificate holder shall assign to each required crewmember for each type of aircraft as appropriate, the necessary functions to be performed in an emergency or in a situation requiring emergency evacuation. The certificate holder shall ensure that those functions can be practicably accomplished, and will meet any reasonably anticipated emergency including incapacitation of individual crewmembers or their inability to reach the passenger cabin because of shifting cargo in combination cargo-passenger aircraft.

(b)   The certificate holder shall describe in the manual required under §135.21 the functions of each category of required crewmembers assigned under paragraph (a) of this section.

135.125   AIRPLANE SECURITY

Certificate holders conducting operations under this part shall comply with applicable security requirements in Part 108 of this chapter.

135.127   PASSENGER INFORMATION

(a)   No person may conduct a scheduled flight segment on which smoking is prohibited unless the "No Smoking" passenger information signs are lighted during the entire flight segment, or one or more "No Smoking" placards meeting the requirements of §25.1541 are posted during the entire flight segment. If both the lighted signs and the placards are used, the signs must remain lighted during the entire flight segment. Smoking is prohibited on scheduled flight segments:

(1)   Between any two points within Puerto Rico, the United States Virgin Islands, the District of Columbia, or any State of the United States (other than Alaska or Hawaii) or between any two points in any one of the above-mentioned jurisdictions (other than Alaska or Hawaii);

(2)   Within the State of Alaska or within the State of Hawaii; or

(3)   Scheduled in the current Worldwide or North American Edition of the *Official Airline Guide* or 6 hours or less in duration and between any point listed in paragraph (a)(1) of this section and any point in Alaska or Hawaii, or between any point in Alaska and any point in Hawaii.

(b)   No person may smoke while a "No Smoking" sign is lighted or while "No Smoking" placards are posted, except that the pilot in command may authorize smoking on the flight deck (if it is physically separated from the passenger compartment) except during any movement of an aircraft on the surface, takeoff, and landing.

(c)   No person may smoke in any aircraft lavatory.

(d)   No person may operate an aircraft with a lavatory equipped with a smoke detector unless there is in that lavatory a sign or placard which reads: "Federal law provides for a penalty of up to $2,000 for tampering with the smoke detector installed in this lavatory."

(e)   No person may tamper with, disable, or destroy any smoke detector installed in any aircraft lavatory.

(f)   On flight segments other than those described in paragraph (a) of this section, the "No Smoking" sign required by §135.177(a)(3) of this part must be turned on during any movement of the aircraft on the surface, for each takeoff or landing, and at any other time considered necessary by the pilot in command.

(g)   The passenger information requirements prescribed in §91.517(b) and (d) of this chapter are in addition to the requirements prescribed in this section.

(h)   Each passenger shall comply with instructions given him or her by crewmembers regarding compliance with paragraphs (b), (c), and (e) of this section.

Ⓐ *Amend #60 eff 2-26-96.*

135.128   USE OF SAFETY BELTS AND CHILD RESTRAINT SYSTEMS

(a)   Except as provided in this paragraph, each person on board an aircraft operated under this part shall occupy an approved seat or berth with a separate safety belt properly secured about him or her during movement on the surface, takeoff, and landing. For seaplane and float equipped rotorcraft operations during movement on the surface, the person pushing off the seaplane or rotorcraft from the dock and the person mooring the seaplane or rotorcraft at the dock are excepted from the preceding seating and safety belt requirements. A safety belt provided for the occupant of a seat may not be used by more than one person who has reached his or her second birthday. Notwithstanding the preceding requirements, a child may:

(1)   Be held by an adult who is occupying an approved seat or berth if that child has not reached his or her second birthday; or

(2)   Notwithstanding any other requirement of this chapter, occupy an approved child restraint system furnished by the certificate holder or one of the persons described in paragraph (a)(2)(i) of this section, provided:

(i)   The child is accompanied by a parent, guardian, or attendant designated by the child's parent or guardian to attend to the safety of the child during the flight;

(ii)   The approved child restraint system bears one or more labels as follows:

(A)   Seats manufactured to U.S. standards between January 1, 1981, and February 25, 1985, must bear the label: "This child restraint system conforms to all applicable Federal motor vehicle safety standards." Vest- and harness-type child restraint systems manufactured before February 26, 1985, bearing such a label are not approved for the purposes of this section;

(B)   Seats manufactured to U.S. standards on or after February 26, 1985, must bear two labels:

(1)   "This child restraint system conforms to all applicable Federal motor vehicle safety standards"; and

(2)   "THIS RESTRAINT IS CERTIFIED FOR USE IN MOTOR VE-HICLES AND AIRCRAFT" in red lettering;

(C)   Seats that do not qualify under paragraphs (a)(2)(ii)(A) and (a)(2)(ii)(B) of this section must bear either a label showing approval of a foreign government or a label showing that the seat was manufactured under the standards of the United Nations; and

(iii)   The certificate holder complies with the following requirements:

(A)   The restraint system must be properly secured to an approved forward-facing seat or berth;

(B)   The child must be properly secured in the restraint system and must not exceed the specified weight limit for the restraint system; and

(C)   The restraint system must bear the appropriate label(s).

(b)   No certificate holder may prohibit a child, if requested by the child's parent, guardian, or designated attendant from occupying a child restraint system furnished by the child's parent, guardian, or designated attendant, provided the child holds a ticket for an approved seat or berth, or such seat or berth is otherwise made available by the certificate holder for the child's use, and the requirements contained in paragraphs (a)(2)(i) through (a)(2)(iii) of this section are met. This section does not prohibit the certificate holder from providing child restraint systems or, consistent with safe operating practices, determining the most appropriate passenger seat location for the child restraint system.

135.129   EXIT SEATING

(a)   (1)   *Applicability.* This section applies to all certificate holders operating under this part, except for on-demand operations with aircraft having 19 or fewer passenger seats and commuter operations with aircraft having 9 or fewer passenger seats.

(2) *Duty to make determination of suitability.* Each certificate holder shall determine, to the extent necessary to perform the applicable functions of paragraph (d) of this section, the suitability of each person it permits to occupy an exit seat. For the purpose of this section —
   (i) *Exit seat means* —
      (A) Each seat having direct access to an exit; and
      (B) Each seat in a row of seats through which passengers would have to pass to gain access to an exit, from the first seat inboard of the exit to the first aisle inboard of the exit.
   (ii) A passenger seat having *direct access* means a seat from which a passenger can proceed directly to the exit without entering an aisle or passing around an obstruction.

(3) *Persons designated to make determination.* Each certificate holder shall make the passenger exit seating determinations required by this paragraph in a non-discriminatory manner consistent with the requirements of this section, by persons designated in the certificate holder's required operations manual.

(4) *Submission of designation for approval.* Each certificate holder shall designate the exit seats for each passenger seating configuration in its fleet in accordance with the definitions in this paragraph and submit those designations for approval as part of the procedures required to be submitted for approval under paragraphs (n) and (p) of this section.

(b) No certificate holder may seat a person in a seat affected by this section if the certificate holder determines that it is likely that the person would be unable to perform one or more of the applicable functions listed in paragraph (d) of this section because —

(1) The person lacks sufficient mobility, strength, or dexterity in both arms and hands, and both legs:
   (i) To reach upward, sideways, and downward to the location of emergency exit and exit-slide operating mechanisms;
   (ii) To grasp and push, pull, turn, or otherwise manipulate those mechanisms;
   (iii) To push, shove, pull, or otherwise open emergency exits;
   (iv) To lift out, hold, deposit on nearby seats, or maneuver over the seatbacks to the next row objects the size and weight of over-wing window exit doors;
   (v) To remove obstructions of size and weight similar over-wing exit doors;
   (vi) To reach the emergency exit expeditiously;
   (vii) To maintain balance while removing obstructions;
   (viii) To exit expeditiously;
   (ix) To stabilize an escape slide after deployment; or
   (x) To assist others in getting off an escape slide;

(2) The person is less than 15 years of age or lacks the capacity to perform one or more of the applicable functions listed in paragraph (d) of this section without the assistance of an adult companion, parent, or other relative;

(3) The person lacks the ability to read and understand instructions required by this section and related to emergency evacuation provided by the certificate holder in printed or graphic form or the ability to understand oral crew commands.

(4) The person lacks sufficient visual capacity to perform one or more of the applicable functions in paragraph (d) of this section without the assistance of visual aids beyond contact lenses or eyeglasses;

(5) The person lacks sufficient aural capacity to hear and understand instructions shouted by flight attendants, without assistance beyond a hearing aid;

(6) The person lacks the ability adequately to impart information orally to other passengers; or,

(7) The person has:
   (i) A condition or responsibilities, such as caring for small children, that might prevent the person from performing one or more of the applicable functions listed in paragraph (d) of this section; or
   (ii) A condition that might cause the person harm if he or she performs one or more of the applicable functions listed in paragraph (d) of this section.

(c) Each passenger shall comply with instructions given by a crewmember or other authorized employee of the certificate holder implementing exit seating restrictions established in accordance with this section.

(d)   Each certificate holder shall include on passenger information cards, presented in the language in which briefings and oral commands are given by the crew, at each exit seat affected by this section, information that, in the event of an emergency in which a crewmember is not available to assist, a passenger occupying an exit seat may use if called upon to perform the following functions:

    (1)   Locate the emergency exit;

    (2)   Recognize the emergency exit opening mechanism;

    (3)   Comprehend the instructions for operating the emergency exit;

    (4)   Operate the emergency exit;

    (5)   Assess whether opening the emergency exit will increase the hazards to which passengers may be exposed;

    (6)   Follow oral directions and hand signals given by a crewmember;

    (7)   Stow or secure the emergency exit door so that it will not impede use of the exit;

    (8)   Assess the condition of an escape slide, activate the slide, and stabilize the slide after deployment to assist others in getting off the slide;

    (9)   Pass expeditiously through the emergency exit; and

    (10)   Assess, select, and follow a safe path away from the emergency exit.

(e)   Each certificate holder shall include on passenger information cards, at each exit seat—

    (1)   In the primary language in which emergency commands are given by the crew, the selection criteria set forth in paragraph (b) of this section, and a request that a passenger identify himself or herself to allow reseating if he or she—

       (i)   Cannot meet the selection criteria set forth in paragraph (b) of this section;

       (ii)   Has a nondiscernible condition that will prevent him or her from performing the applicable functions listed in paragraph (d) of this section;

       (iii)   May suffer bodily harm as the result of performing one or more of those functions; or

       (iv)   Does not wish to perform those functions; and,

    (2)   In each language used by the certificate holder for passenger information cards, a request that a passenger identify himself or herself to allow reseating if he or she lacks the ability to read, speak, or understand the language or the graphic form in which instructions required by this section and related to emergency evacuations are provided by the certificate holder, or the ability to understand the specified language in which crew commands will be given in an emergency;

    (3)   May suffer bodily harm as the result of performing one or more of those functions; or,

    (4)   Does not wish to perform those functions.

A certificate holder shall not require the passenger to disclose his or her reason for needing reseating.

(f)   Each certificate holder shall make available for inspection by the public at all passenger loading gates and ticket counters at each airport where it conducts passenger operations, written procedures established for making determinations in regard to exit row seating.

(g)   No certificate holder may allow taxi or pushback unless at least one required crewmember has verified that no exit seat is occupied by a person the crewmember determines is likely to be unable to perform the applicable functions listed in paragraph (d) of this section.

(h)   Each certificate holder shall include in its passenger briefings a reference to the passenger information cards, required by paragraphs (d) and (e), the selection criteria set forth in paragraph (b), and the functions to be performed, set forth in paragraph (d) of this section.

(i)   Each certificate holder shall include in its passenger briefings a request that a passenger identify himself or herself to allow reseating if he or she —

    (1)   Cannot meet the selection criteria set forth in paragraph (b) of this section;

    (2)   Has a nondiscernible condition that will prevent him or her from performing the applicable functions listed in paragraph (d) of this section;

    (3)   May suffer bodily harm as the result of performing one or more of those functions; or,

    (4)   Does not wish to perform those functions.

A certificate holder shall not require the passenger to disclose his or her reason for needing reseating.

(j)   [Reserved]

(k)   In the event a certificate holder determines in accordance with this section that it is likely that a passenger assigned to an exit seat would be unable to perform the functions listed in paragraph (d) of this section or a passenger requests a non-exit seat, the certificate holder shall expeditiously relocate the passenger to a non-exit seat.

(l)   In the event of full booking in the non-exit seats and if necessary to accommodate a passenger being relocated from an exit seat, the certificate holder shall move a passenger who is willing and able to assume the evacuation functions that may be required, to an exit seat.

(m)   A certificate holder may deny transportation to any passenger under this section only because —

    (1)   The passenger refuses to comply with instructions given by a crewmember or other authorized employee of the certificate holder implementing exit seating restrictions established in accordance with this section, or

    (2)   The only seat that will physically accommodate the person's handicap is an exit seat.

(n)   In order to comply with this section certificate holders shall —

    (1)   Establish procedures that address:

       (i)   The criteria listed in paragraph (b) of this section;

       (ii)   The functions listed in paragraph (d) of this section;

       (iii)   The requirements for airport information, passenger information cards, crewmember verification of appropriate seating in exit seats, passenger briefings, seat assignments, and denial of transportation as set forth in this section;

       (iv)   How to resolve disputes arising from implementation of this section, including identification of the certificate holder employee on the airport to whom complaints should be addressed for resolution; and,

    (2)   Submit their procedures for preliminary review and approval to the principal operations inspectors assigned to them at the certificate-holding district office.

(o)   Certificate holders shall assign seats prior to boarding consistent with the criteria listed in paragraph (b) and the functions listed in paragraph (d) of this section, to the maximum extent feasible.

(p)   The procedures required by paragraph (n) of this section will not become effective until final approval is granted by the Director, Flight Standards Service, Washington, DC. Approval will be based solely upon the safety aspects of the certificate holder's procedures.

Ⓐ *Amend #60 eff 2-26-96.*

INTENTIONALLY

LEFT

BLANK

SUBPART C — AIRCRAFT AND EQUIPMENT

135.141   APPLICABILITY

This subpart prescribes aircraft and equipment requirements for operations under this part. The requirements of this subpart are in addition to the aircraft and equipment requirements of Part 91 of this chapter. However, this part does not require the duplication of any equipment required by this chapter.

135.143   GENERAL REQUIREMENTS

(a)   No person may operate an aircraft under this part unless that aircraft and its equipment meet the applicable regulations of this chapter.

(b)   Except as provided in §135.179, no person may operate an aircraft under this part unless the required instruments and equipment in it have been approved and are in an operable condition.

(c)   ATC transponder equipment installed within the time periods indicated below must meet the performance and environmental requirements of the following TSO's

    (1)   *Through January 1, 1992:*

       (i)   Any class of TSO-C74b or any class of TSO-C74c as appropriate, provided that the equipment was manufactured before January 1, 1990; or

       (ii)   The appropriate class of TSO-C112 (Mode S).

    (2)   *After January 1, 1992:* The appropriate class of TSO-C112 (Mode S). For purposes of paragraph (c)(2) of this section, "installation" does not include —

       (i)   Temporary installation of TSO-C74b or TSO-C74c substitute equipment, as appropriate, during maintenance of the permanent equipment;

       (ii)   Reinstallation of equipment after temporary removal for maintenance; or

       (iii)   For fleet operations, installation of equipment in a fleet aircraft after removal of the equipment for maintenance from another aircraft in the same operator's fleet.

135.145   AIRCRAFT PROVING TESTS

(a)   No certificate holder may operate a turbojet airplane, or an aircraft for which two pilots are required by this chapter for operations under VFR, if it has not previously proved that aircraft or an aircraft of the same make and similar design in any operation under this part unless, in addition to the aircraft certification tests, at least 25 hours of proving tests acceptable to the Administrator have been flown by that certificate holder including —

    (1)   Five hours of night time, if night flights are to be authorized;

    (2)   Five instrument approach procedures under simulated or actual instrument weather conditions, if IFR flights are to be authorized; and

    (3)   Entry into a representative number of enroute airports as determined by the Administrator.

(b)   No certificate holder may carry passengers in an aircraft during proving tests, except those needed to make the tests and those designated by the Administrator to observe the tests. However, pilot flight training may be conducted during the proving tests.

(c)   For the purposes of paragraph (a) of this section, an aircraft is not considered to be of similar design if an alteration includes —

    (1)   The installation of powerplants other than those of a type similar to those with which it is certificated; or

    (2)   Alterations to the aircraft or its components that materially affect flight characteristics.

(d)   The Administrator may authorize deviations from this section if the Administrator finds that special circumstances make full compliance with this section unnecessary.

135.147   DUAL CONTROLS REQUIRED

No person may operate an aircraft in operations requiring two pilots unless it is equipped with functioning dual controls. However, if the aircraft type certification operating limitations do not require two pilots, a throwover control wheel may be used in place of two control wheels.

135.149   EQUIPMENT REQUIREMENTS: GENERAL

No person may operate an aircraft unless it is equipped with —
(a)   A sensitive altimeter that is adjustable for barometric pressure;
(b)   Heating or deicing equipment for each carburetor or, for a pressure carburetor, an alternate air source;
(c)   For turbojet airplanes, in addition to two gyroscopic bank-and-pitch indicators (artificial horizons) for use at the pilot stations, a third indicator that is installed in accordance with the instrument requirements prescribed in §121.305(j) of this chapter.

▶ Amend #38 eff 11-26-90 ◀

   (1)   Is powered from a source independent of the aircraft's electrical generating system;
   (2)   Continues reliable operation for at least 30 minutes after total failure of the aircraft's electrical generating system;
   (3)   Operates independently of any other attitude indicating system;
   (4)   Is operative without selection after total failure of the aircraft's electrical generating system;
   (5)   Is located on the instrument panel in a position that will make it plainly visible to, and usable by, any pilot at the pilot's station; and
   (6)   Is appropriately lighted during all phases of operation;
(d)   Reserved.
(e)   For turbine powered aircraft, any other equipment as the Administrator may require.

135.150   PUBLIC ADDRESS AND CREWMEMBER INTERPHONE SYSTEMS

No person may operate an aircraft having a passenger seating configuration, excluding any pilot seat, of more than 19 unless it is equipped with —
(a)   A public address system which —
   (1)   Is capable of operation independent of the crewmember interphone system required by paragraph (b) of this section, except for handsets, headsets, microphones, selector switches, and signaling devices;
   (2)   Is approved in accordance with §*21.305 of this chapter;
   (3)   Is accessible for immediate use from each of two flight crewmember stations in the pilot compartment;
   (4)   For each required floor-level passenger emergency exit which has an adjacent flight attendant seat, has a microphone which is readily accessible to the seated flight attendant, except that one microphone may serve more than one exit, provided the proximity of the exits allows unassisted verbal communication between seated flight attendants;
   (5)   Is capable of operation within 10 seconds by a flight attendant at each of those stations in the passenger compartment from which its use is accessible;
   (6)   Is audible at all passenger seats, lavatories, and flight attendant seats and work stations; and
   (7)   For transport category airplanes manufactured on or after [insert a date one year after the effective date of this amendment], meets the requirements of §*25.1423 of this chapter.
(b)   A crewmember interphone system which —
   (1)   Is capable of operation independent of the public address system required by paragraph (a) of this section, except for handsets, headsets, microphones, selector switches, and signaling devices;
   (2)   Is approved in accordance with §*21.305 of this chapter;
   (3)   Provides a means of two-way communication between the pilot compartment and —
      (i)   Each passenger compartment; and
      (ii)   Each galley located on other than the main passenger deck level;
   (4)   Is accessible for immediate use from each of two flight crewmember stations in the pilot compartment;

*(Not published herein — Ed.)

(5)   Is accessible for use from at least one normal flight attendant station in each passenger compartment;

(6)   Is capable of operation within 10 seconds by a flight attendant at each of those stations in each passenger compartment from which its use is accessible; and

(7)   For large turbojet-powered airplanes —

     (i)   Is accessible for use at enough flight attendant stations so that all floor-level emergency exits (or entryways to those exits in the case of exits located within galleys) in each passenger compartment are observable from one or more of those stations so equipped;

     (ii)   Has an alerting system incorporating aural or visual signals for use by flight crewmembers to alert flight attendants and for use by flight attendants to alert flight crewmembers;

     (iii)   For the alerting system required by paragraph (b)(7)(ii) of this section, has a means for the recipient of a call to determine whether it is a normal call or an emergency call; and

     (iv)   When the airplane is on the ground, provides a means of two-way communication between ground personnel and either of at least two flight crewmembers in the pilot compartment. The interphone system station for use by ground personnel must be so located that personnel using the system may avoid visible detection from within the airplane.

135.151   COCKPIT VOICE RECORDERS

(a)   No person may operate a multiengine, turbine-powered airplane or rotorcraft having a passenger seating configuration of six or more and for which two pilots are required by certification or operating rules unless it is equipped with an approved cockpit voice recorder that:

     (1)   Is installed in compliance with §23.1457(a)(1) and (2), (b), (c), (d), (e), (f), and (g); §25.1457(a)(1) and (2), (b), (c), (d), (e), (f), and (g); §27.1457(a)(1) and (2), (b), (c), (d), (e), (f), and (g); §29.1457(a)(1) and (2), (b), (c), (d), (e), (f), and (g) of this chapter, as applicable; and

     (2)   Is operated continuously from the use of the check list before the flight to completion of the final check list at the end of the flight.

(b)   No person may operate a multiengine, turbine-powered airplane or rotorcraft having a passenger seating configuration of 20 or more seats unless it is equipped with an approved cockpit voice recorder that —

     (1)   Is installed in compliance with §23.1457, §25.1457, §27.1457 or §29.1457 of this chapter, as applicable; and

     (2)   Is operated continuously from the use of the check list before the flight to completion of the final check list at the end of the flight.

(c)   In the event of an accident, or occurrence requiring immediate notification of the National Transportation Safety Board which results in termination of the flight, the certificate holder shall keep the recorded information for at least 60 days or, if requested by the Administrator or the Board, for a longer period. Information obtained from the record may be used to assist in determining the cause of accidents or occurrences in connection with investigations. The Administrator does not use the record in any civil penalty or certificate action.

(d)   For those aircraft equipped to record the uninterrupted audio signals received by a boom or a mask microphone the flight crewmembers are required to use the boom microphone below 18,000 feet mean sea level. No person may operate a large turbine engine powered airplane manufactured after October 11, 1991, or on which a cockpit voice recorder has been installed after October 11, 1991, unless it is equipped to record the uninterrupted audio signal received by a boom or mask microphone in accordance with §25.1457(c)(5) of this chapter.

(e)   In complying with this section, an approved cockpit voice recorder having an erasure feature may be used, so that during the operation of the recorder, information:

     (1)   Recorded in accordance with paragraph (a) of this section and recorded more than 15 minutes earlier; or

     (2)   Recorded in accordance with paragraph (b) of this section and recorded more than 30 minutes earlier; may be erased or otherwise obliterated.

Ⓐ *Amend #60 eff 2-26-96.*

135.152   FLIGHT RECORDERS

(a)   No person may operate a multiengine, turbine-powered airplane or rotorcraft having a passenger seating configuration, excluding any pilot seat, of 10 to 19 seats, that is brought onto the U.S. register after October 11, 1991, unless it is equipped with one or more approved flight recorders that utilize a digital method of recording and storing data, and a method of readily retrieving that data from the storage medium. The parameters specified in Appendix B or C, as applicable, of this part must be recorded within the range, accuracy, resolution, and recording intervals as specified. The recorder shall retain no less than 8 hours of aircraft operation.

(b)   After October 11, 1991, no person may operate a multiengine, turbine-powered airplane having a passenger seating configuration of 20 to 30 seats or a multiengine, turbine-powered rotorcraft having a passenger seating configuration of 20 or more seats unless it is equipped with one or more approved flight recorders that utilize a digital method of recording and storing data, and a method of readily retrieving that data from the storage medium. The parameters in Appendix D or E of this part, as applicable, that are set forth below, must be recorded within the ranges, accuracies, resolutions, and sampling intervals as specified.

(1)   Except as provided in paragraph (b)(3) of this section for aircraft type certificated before October 1, 1969, the following parameters must be recorded:

(i)   Time;
(ii)   Altitude;
(iii)   Airspeed;
(iv)   Vertical acceleration;
(v)   Heading;
(vi)   Time of each radio transmission to or from air traffic control;
(vii)   Pitch attitude;
(viii) Roll attitude;
(ix)   Longitudinal acceleration;
(x)   Control column or pitch control surface position; and
(xi)   Thrust of each engine.

(2)   Except as provided in paragraph (b)(3) of this section for aircraft type certificated after September 30, 1969, the following parameters must be recorded:

(i)   Time;
(ii)   Altitude;
(iii)   Airspeed;
(iv)   Vertical acceleration;
(v)   Heading;
(vi)   Time of each radio transmission either to or from air traffic control;
(vii)   Pitch attitude
(viii) Roll attitude;
(ix)   Longitudinal acceleration;
(x)   Pitch trim position;
(xi)   Control column or pitch control surface position;
(xii)   Control wheel or lateral control surface position;
(xiii) Rudder pedal or yaw control surface position;
(xiv) Thrust of each engine;
(xv)   Position of each thrust reverser;
(xvi) Trailing edge flap or cockpit flap control position; and
(xvii) Leading edge flap or cockpit flap control position.

(3)   For aircraft manufactured after October 11, 1991, all of the parameters listed in Appendix D or E of this part, as applicable, must be recorded.

(c)   Whenever a flight recorder required by this section is installed, it must be operated continuously from the instant the airplane begins the takeoff roll or the rotorcraft begins the lift-off until the airplane has completed the landing roll or the rotorcraft has landed at its destination.

(d)   Except as provided in paragraph (c) of this section, and except for recorded data erased as authorized in this paragraph, each certificate holder shall keep the recorded data prescribed in paragraph (a) of this section until the aircraft has been operating for at least 8 hours of the operating time specified in paragraph (c) of this section. In addition, each certificate holder shall keep the recorded data prescribed in paragraph (b) of this section for an airplane until the airplane has been operating for at least 25 hours, and for a rotorcraft until the rotorcraft has been operating for at least 10 hours, of the operating time specified in paragraph (c) of this section. A total of 1 hour of recorded data may be erased for the purpose of testing the flight recorder or the flight recorder system. Any erasure made in accordance with this paragraph must be of the oldest recorded data accumulated at the time of testing. Except as provided in paragraph (c) of this section, no record need be kept more than 60 days.

(e)   In the event of an accident or occurrence that requires the immediate notification of the National Transportation Safety Board under 49 CFR Part 830 of its regulations and that results in termination of the flight, the certificate holder shall remove the recording media from the aircraft and keep the recorded data required by paragraphs (a) and (b) of this section for at least 60 days or for a longer period upon request of the Board or the Administrator.

(f)   Each flight recorder required by this section must be installed in accordance with the requirements of §§23.1459, 25.1459, 27.1459, or 29.1459, as appropriate, of this chapter. The correlation required by paragraph (c) of §§23.1459, 25.1459, 27.1459, or 29.1459, as appropriate, of this chapter need be established only on one aircraft of a group of aircraft:

(1)   That are of the same type:

(2)   On which the flight recorder models and their installations are the same; and

(3)   On which there are no differences in the type design with respect to the installation of the first pilot's instruments associated with the flight recorder. The most recent instrument calibration, including the recording medium from which this calibration is derived, and the recorder correlation must be retained by the certificate holder.

(g)   Each flight recorder required by this section that records the data specified in paragraphs (a) and (b) of this section must have an approved device to assist in locating that recorder under water.

INTENTIONALLY

LEFT

BLANK

135.153   **GROUND PROXIMITY WARNING SYSTEM**

(a)   Except as provided in paragraph (b) of this section, no person may operate a turbine-powered airplane having a passenger seating configuration, excluding any pilot seat, of 10 seats or more, unless it is equipped with an approved ground proximity warning system.

(b)   Any airplane equipped before April 20, 1992, with an alternative system that conveys warnings of excessive closure rates with the terrain and any deviations below glide slope by visual and audible means may continue to be operated with that system until April 20, 1996, provided that—

     (1)   The system must have been approved by the Administrator;

     (2)   The system must have a means of alerting the pilot when a malfunction occurs in the system; and

     (3)   Procedures must have been established by the certificate holder to ensure that the performance of the system can be appropriately monitored.

(c)   For a system required by this section, the Airplane Flight Manual shall contain—

     (1)   Appropriate procedures for—

         (i)   The use of the equipment;

         (ii)   Proper flight crew action with respect to the equipment; and

         (iii)   Deactivation for planned abnormal and emergency conditions; and

     (2)   An outline of all input sources that must be operating.

(d)   No person may deactivate a system required by this section except under procedures in the Airplane Flight Manual.

(e)   Whenever a system required by this section is deactivated, an entry shall be made in the airplane maintenance record that includes the date and time of deactivation.

135.155   **FIRE EXTINGUISHERS: PASSENGER-CARRYING AIRCRAFT**

No person may operate an aircraft carrying passengers unless it is equipped with hand fire extinguishers of an approved type for use in crew and passenger compartments as follows —

(a)   The type and quantity of extinguishing agent must be suitable for all the kinds of fires likely to occur;

(b)   At least one hand fire extinguisher must be provided and conveniently located on the flight deck for use by the flight crew; and

(c)   At least one hand fire extinguisher must be conveniently located in the passenger compartment of each aircraft having a passenger seating configuration, excluding any pilot seat, of at least 10 seats but less than 31 seats.

135.157   **OXYGEN EQUIPMENT REQUIREMENTS**

(a)   *Unpressurized aircraft.* No person may operate an unpressurized aircraft at altitudes prescribed in this section unless it is equipped with enough oxygen dispensers and oxygen to supply the pilots under §135.89(a) and to supply, when flying —

     (1)   At altitudes above 10,000 feet through 15,000 feet MSL, oxygen to at least 10 percent of the occupants of the aircraft, other than the pilots, for that part of the flight at those altitudes that is of more than 30 minutes duration; and

     (2)   Above 15,000 feet MSL, oxygen to each occupant of the aircraft other than the pilots.

(b) *Pressurized aircraft.* No person may operate a pressurized aircraft —
   (1) At altitudes above 25,000 feet MSL, unless at least a 10-minute supply of supplemental oxygen is available for each occupant of the aircraft, other than the pilots, for use when a descent is necessary due to loss of cabin pressurization; and
   (2) Unless it is equipped with enough oxygen dispensers and oxygen to comply with paragraph (a) of this section whenever the cabin pressure altitude exceeds 10,000 feet MSL and, if the cabin pressurization fails, to comply with §135.89(a) or to provide a 2-hour supply for each pilot, whichever is greater, and to supply when flying —
      (i) At altitudes above 10,000 feet through 15,000 feet MSL, oxygen to at least 10 percent of the occupants of the aircraft, other than the pilots, for that part of the flight at those altitudes that is of more than 30 minutes duration; and
      (ii) Above 15,000 feet MSL, oxygen to each occupant of the aircraft, other than the pilots, for one hour unless, at all times during flight above that altitude, the aircraft can safely descend to 15,000 feet MSL within four minutes, in which case only a 30-minute supply is required.

(c) The equipment required by this section must have a means —
   (1) To enable the pilots to readily determine, in flight, the amount of oxygen available in each source of supply and whether the oxygen is being delivered to the dispensing units; or
   (2) In the case of individual dispensing units, to enable each user to make those determinations with respect to that person's oxygen supply and delivery; and
   (3) To allow the pilots to use undiluted oxygen at their discretion at altitudes above 25,000 feet MSL.

135.158   PITOT HEAT INDICATION SYSTEMS

(a) Except as provided in paragraph (b) of this section, after April 12, 1981, no person may operate a transport category airplane equipped with a flight instrument pitot heating system unless the airplane is also equipped with an operable pitot heat indication system that complies with §25.1326 of this chapter in effect on April 12, 1978.

(b) A certificate holder may obtain an extension of the April 12, 1981, compliance date specified in paragraph (a) of this section, but not beyond April 12, 1983, from the Director, Flight Standards Service if the certificate holder —
   (1) Shows that due to circumstances beyond its control it cannot comply by the specified compliance date; and
   (2) Submits by the specified compliance date a schedule for compliance, acceptable to the Director, indicating that compliance will be achieved at the earliest practicable date.

135.159   EQUIPMENT REQUIREMENTS: CARRYING PASSENGERS UNDER VFR AT NIGHT OR UNDER VFR OVER-THE-TOP CONDITIONS

No person may operate an aircraft carrying passengers under VFR at night or under VFR over-the-top, unless it is equipped with —

(a) A gyroscopic rate-of-turn indicator except on the following aircraft:
   (1) Airplanes with a third attitude instrument system usable through flight attitudes of 360 degrees of pitch-and-roll and installed in accordance with the instrument requirements prescribed in §121.305(j) of this chapter.
   (2) Helicopters with a third attitude instrument system usable through flight attitudes of ±80 degrees of pitch and ±120 degrees of roll and installed in accordance with §29.1303(g) of this chapter.
   (3) Helicopters with a maximum certificated takeoff weight of 6,000 pounds or less.

(b) A slip skid indicator.

(c) A gyroscopic bank-and-pitch indicator.

(d) A gyroscopic direction indicator.

(e) A generator or generators able to supply all probable combinations of continuous in-flight electrical loads for required equipment and for recharging the battery.

(f)   For night flights —
    (1)   An anticollision light system;
    (2)   Instrument lights to make all instruments, switches, and gauges easily readable, the direct rays of which are shielded from the pilots' eyes; and
    (3)   A flashlight having at least two size "D" cells or equivalent.

(g)   For the purpose of paragraph (e) of this section, a continuous in-flight electrical load includes one that draws current continuously during flight, such as radio equipment and electrically driven instruments and lights, but does not include occasional intermittent loads.

(h)   Notwithstanding provisions of paragraphs (b), (c), and (d), helicopters having a maximum certificated takeoff weight of 6,000 pounds or less may be operated until January 6, 1988, under visual flight rules at night without a slip skid indicator, a gyroscopic bank-and-pitch indicator, or a gyroscopic direction indicator.

135.161   RADIO AND NAVIGATIONAL EQUIPMENT: CARRYING PASSENGERS UNDER VFR AT NIGHT OR UNDER VFR OVER-THE-TOP

(a)   No person may operate an aircraft carrying passengers under VFR at night, or under VFR over-the-top, unless it has two-way radio communications equipment able, at least in flight, to transmit to, and receive from, ground facilities 25 miles away.

(b)   No person may operate an aircraft carrying passengers under VFR over-the- top unless it has radio navigational equipment able to receive radio signals from the ground facilities to be used.

(c)   No person may operate an airplane carrying passengers under VFR at night unless it has radio navigational equipment able to receive radio signals from the ground facilities to be used.

135.163   EQUIPMENT REQUIREMENTS: AIRCRAFT CARRYING PASSENGERS UNDER IFR

No person may operate an aircraft under IFR, carrying passengers, unless it has —

(a)   A vertical speed indicator

(b)   A free-air temperature indicator;

(c)   A heated pitot tube for each airspeed indicator;

(d)   A power failure warning device or vacuum indicator to show the power available for gyroscopic instruments from each power source;

(e)   An alternate source of static pressure for the altimeter and the airspeed and vertical speed indicators;

(f)   For a single-engine aircraft, a generator or generators able to supply all probable combinations of continuous in-flight electrical loads for required equipment and for recharging the battery;

(g)   For multiengine aircraft, at least two generators each of which is on a separate engine, of which any combination of one-half of the total number are rated sufficiently to supply the electrical loads of all required instruments and equipment necessary for safe emergency operations of the aircraft except that for multiengine helicopters, the two required generators may be mounted on the main rotor drive train; and

(h)   Two independent sources of energy (with means of selecting either), of which at least one is an engine-driven pump or generator, each of which is able to drive all gyroscopic instruments and installed so that failure of one instrument or source does not interfere with the energy supply to the remaining instruments or the other energy source, unless, for single-engine aircraft, the rate-of-turn indicator has a source of energy separate from the bank and pitch and direction indicators. For the purpose of this paragraph, for multiengine aircraft, each engine-driven source of energy must be on a different engine.

(i)   For the purpose of paragraph (f) of this section, a continuous in-flight electrical load includes one that draws current continuously during flight such as radio equipment, electrically driven instruments, and lights, but does not include occasional intermittent loads.

135.165 RADIO AND NAVIGATION EQUIPMENT: EXTENDED OVERWATER OR IFR OPERATIONS

(a) No person may operate a turbojet airplane having a passenger seating configuration, excluding any pilot seat, of 10 seats or more, or a multi-engine airplane in a commuter operation, as defined in Part 119 of this Chapter, under IFR or in extended overwater operations unless it has at least the following radio communications and navigational equipment appropriate to the facilities to be used which are capable of transmitting to, and receiving from, at any place on the route to be flown, at least one ground facility:

    (1) Two transmitters, (2)
    (2) Two microphones,
    (3) Two headsets or one headset and one speaker,
    (4) A marker beacon receiver,
    (5) Two independent receivers for navigation, and
    (6) Two independent receivers for communications.

(b) No person may operate an aircraft other than that specified in paragraph (a) of this section, under IFR or in extended overwater operations unless it has at least the following radio communication and navigational equipment appropriate to the facilities to be used and which are capable of transmitting to, and receiving from, at any place on the route, at least one ground facility:

    (1) A transmitter,
    (2) Two microphones,
    (3) Two headsets or one headset and one speaker,
    (4) A marker beacon receiver,
    (5) Two independent receivers for navigation,
    (6) Two independent receivers for communications, and
    (7) For extended overwater operations only, an additional transmitter.

(c) For the purpose of paragraphs (a)(5), (a)(6), (b)(5), and (b)(6) of this section, a receiver is independent if the function of any part of it does not depend on the functioning of any part of another receiver. However, a receiver that can receive both communications and navigational signals may be used in place of a separate communications receiver and separate navigational signal receiver.

(d) Notwithstanding the requirements of paragraph (a) and (b) of this section, installation and use of a single long-range navigation system and a single long-range communication system, for extended overwater operations, may be authorized by the Administrator and approved in the certificate holder's operations specifications. The following are among the operational factors the Administrator may consider in granting an authorization:

    (1) The ability of the flightcrew to reliably fix the position of the airplane within the degree of accuracy required by ATC,
    (2) The length of the route being flown, and
    (3) The duration of the very high frequency communications gap.

135.167 EMERGENCY EQUIPMENT: EXTENDED OVERWATER OPERATIONS

(a) No person may operate an aircraft in extended overwater operations unless it carries, installed in conspicuously marked locations easily accessible to the occupants if a ditching occurs, the following equipment:

    (1) An approved life preserver equipped with an approved survivor locator light for each occupant of the aircraft. The life preserver must be easily accessible to each seated occupant.
    (2) Enough approved liferafts of a rated capacity and buoyancy to accommodate the occupants of the aircraft.

(b) Each liferaft required by paragraph (a) of this section must be equipped with or contain at least the following:

    (1) One approved survivor locator light.
    (2) One approved pyrotechnic signaling device.

Ⓐ *Amend #61 eff 2-26-96.*

(3)   Either—
     (i)   One survival kit, appropriately equipped for the route to be flown; or
     (ii)   One canopy (for sail, sunshade, or rain catcher);
     (iii)   One radar reflector;
     (iv)   One liferaft repair kit;
     (v)   One bailing bucket;
     (vi)   One signaling mirror;
     (vii)   One police whistle;
     (viii) One raft knife;
     (ix)   One CO_2 bottle for emergency inflation;
     (x)   One inflation pump;
     (xi)   Two oars;
     (xii)   One 75-foot retaining line;
     (xiii) One magnetic compass;
     (xiv) One dye marker;
     (xv)   One flashlight having at least two size "D" cells or equivalent;
     (xvi) A 2-day supply of emergency food rations supplying at least 1,000 calories per day for each person;
     (xvii) For each two persons the raft is rated to carry, two pints of water or one sea water desalting kit;
     (xviii) One fishing kit; and
     (xix) One book on survival appropriate for the area in which the aircraft is operated.

(c)   No person may operate an airplane in extended overwater operations unless there is attached to one of the life rafts required by paragraph (a) of this section, an approved survival type emergency locator transmitter. Batteries used in this transmitter must be replaced (or recharged, if the batteries are rechargeable) when the transmitter has been in use for more than 1 cumulative hour, or, when 50 percent of their useful life (or for rechargeable batteries, 50 percent of their useful life of charge) has expired, as established by the transmitter manufacturer under its approval. The new expiration date for replacing (or recharging) the battery must be legibly marked on the outside of the transmitter. The battery useful life (or useful life of charge) requirements of this paragraph do not apply to batteries (such as water-activated batteries) that are essentially unaffected during probable storage intervals.

135.169   ADDITIONAL AIRWORTHINESS REQUIREMENTS

(a)   Except for commuter category airplanes, no person may operate a large airplane unless it meets the additional airworthiness requirements of §§121.213 through 121.283 and 121.307 of this chapter.

(b)   No person may operate a reciprocating-engine or turbopropeller-powered small airplane that has a passenger seating configuration, excluding pilot seats, of 10 seats or more unless it is type certificated —
    (1)   In the transport category;
    (2)   Before July 1, 1970, in the normal category and meets special conditions issued by the Administrator for airplanes intended for use in operations under this part;
    (3)   Before July 19, 1970, in the normal category and meets the additional airworthiness standards in Special Federal Aviation Regulation No. 23;
    (4)   In the normal category and meets the additional airworthiness standards in Appendix A;
    (5)   In the normal category and complies with section 1.(a) of Special Federal Aviation Regulation No. 41;
    (6)   In the normal category and complies with section 1. (b) of Special Federal Aviation Regulation No. 41; or
    (7)   In the commuter category.

(c)   No person may operate a small airplane with a passenger seating configuration, excluding any pilot seat, of 10 seats or more, with a seating configuration greater than the maximum seating configuration used in that type of airplane in operations under this part before August 19, 1977. This paragraph does not apply to —
    (1)   An airplane that is type certificated in the transport category; or
    (2)   An airplane that complies with —
      (i)   Appendix A of this part provided that its passenger seating configuration, excluding pilot seats, does not exceed 19 seats; or
      (ii)   Special Federal Aviation Regulation No. 41.

(d)   Cargo or baggage compartments:

(1)   After March 20, 1991, each Class C or D compartment, as defined in §25.857 of Part 25 of this chapter, greater than 200 cubic feet in volume in a transport category airplane type certificated after January 1, 1958, must have ceiling and sidewall panels which are constructed of:

(i)   Glass fiber reinforced resin;

(ii)   Materials which meet the test requirements of Part 25, Appendix F, Part III of this chapter; or

(iii)   In the case of liner installations approved prior to March 20, 1989, aluminum.

(2)   For compliance with this paragraph, the term "liner" includes any design feature, such as a joint or fastener, which would affect the capability of the liner to safely contain a fire.

135.170   MATERIALS FOR COMPARTMENT INTERIORS

(a)   No person may operate an airplane that conforms to an amended or supplemental type certificate issued in accordance with SFAR No. 41 for a maximum certificated takeoff weight in excess of 12,500 pounds unless within one year after issuance of the initial airworthiness certificate under that SFAR, the airplane meets the compartment interior requirements set forth in § 25.853(a) in effect March 6, 1995 (formerly § 25.853 (a), (b), (b-1), (b-2), and (b-3) of this chapter in effect on September 26, 1978.)

(b)   Except for commuter category airplanes and airplanes certificated under Special Federal Aviation Regulation No. 41, no person may operate a large airplane unless it meets the following additional airworthiness requirements:

(1)   Except for those materials covered by paragraph (b)(2) of this section, all materials in each compartment used by the crewmembers or passengers must meet the requirements of § 25.853 of this chapter in effect as follows or later amendment thereto:

(i)   Except as provided in paragraph (b)(1)(iv) of this section, each airplane with a passenger capacity of 20 or more and manufactured after August 19, 1988, but prior to August 20, 1990, must comply with the heat release rate testing provisions of § 25.853(d) in effect March 6, 1995 (formerly § 25.853 (a-1) in effect on August 20, 1986), except that the total heat release over the first 2 minutes of sample exposure rate must not exceed 100 kilowatt minutes per square meter and the peak heat release rate must not exceed 100 kilowatts per square meter.

(ii)   Each airplane with a passenger capacity of 20 or more and manufactured after August 19, 1990, must comply with the heat release rate and smoke testing provisions of § 25.853(d) in effect March 6, 1995 (formerly § 25.853 (a-1) in effect on September 26, 1988).

(iii)   Except as provided in paragraph (b)(1)(v) or (vi) of this section, each airplane for which the application for type certificate was filed prior to May 1, 1972, must comply with the provisions of § 25.853 in effect April 30, 1972, regardless of the passenger capacity, if there is a substantially complete replacement of the cabin interior after April 30, 1972.

(iv)   Except as provided in paragraph (b)(1)(v) or (vi) of this section, each airplane for which the application for type certificate was filed after May 1, 1972, must comply with the material requirements under which the airplane was type certificated regardless of the passenger capacity if there is a substantially complete replacement of the cabin interior after that date.

(v)   Except as provided in paragraph (b)(1)(vi) of this section, each airplane that was type certificated after January 1, 1958, must comply with the heat release rate testing provisions of § 25.853(d) in effect March 6, 1995 (formerly § 25.853(a-1) in effect on August 20, 1986), if there is a substantially complete replacement of the cabin interior components identified in that paragraph on or after that date, except that the total heat release over the first 2 minutes of sample exposure rate shall not exceed 100 kilowatt-minutes per square meter and the peak heat release rate shall not exceed 100 kilowatts per square meter.

(vi)   Each airplane that was type certificated after January 1, 1958, must comply with the heat release rate and smoke testing provisions of § 25.853(d) in effect March 6, 1995 (formerly § 25.853(a-1) in effect on August 20, 1986), if there is a substantially complete replacement of the cabin interior components identified in that paragraph after August 19, 1990.

(vii)   Contrary provisions of this section notwithstanding, the Manager of the Transport Airplane Directorate, Aircraft Certification Service, Federal Aviation Administration, may authorize deviation from the requirements of paragraph (b)(1)(i), (b)(1)(ii), (b)(1)(v), or (b)(1)(vi) of this section for specific components of the cabin interior that do not meet applicable flammability and smoke emission requirements, if the determination is made that special circumstances exist that make compliance impractical. Such grants of deviation will be limited to those airplanes manufactured within 1 year after the applicable date specified in this section and those airplanes in which the interior is replaced within 1 year of that date. A request for such grant of deviation must include a thorough and accurate analysis of each component subject to §25.583(d) in effect March 6, 1995 (formerly §25.853 (a-1) in effect on August 20, 1986), the steps being taken to achieve compliance, and for the few components for which timely compliance will not be achieved, credible reasons for such noncompliance.

(viii)   Contrary provisions of this section notwithstanding, galley carts and standard galley containers that do not meet the flammability and smoke emission requirements of §25.853(d) in effect March 6, 1995 (formerly §25.853(a-1) in effect on August 20, 1986), may be used in airplanes that must meet the requirements of paragraph (b)(1)(i), (b)(1)(ii), (b)(1)(iv) or (b)(1)(vi) of this section provided the galley carts or standard containers were manufactured prior to March 6, 1995.

(2)   For airplanes type certificated after January 1, 1958, seat cushions, except those on flight crewmember seats, in any compartment occupied by crew or passengers must comply with the requirements pertaining to fire protection of seat cushions in §25.853(c) effective November 26, 1984.

135.171 SHOULDER HARNESS INSTALLATION AT FLIGHT CREWMEMBER STATIONS

(a)   No person may operate a turbojet aircraft or an aircraft having a passenger seating configuration, excluding any pilot seat, of 10 seats or more unless it is equipped with an approved shoulder harness installed for each flight crewmember station.

(b)   Each flight crewmember occupying a station equipped with a shoulder harness must fasten the shoulder harness during takeoff and landing, except that the shoulder harness may be unfastened if the crewmember cannot perform the required duties with the shoulder harness fastened.

135.173 AIRBORNE THUNDERSTORM DETECTION EQUIPMENT REQUIREMENTS

(a)   No person may operate an aircraft that has a passenger seating configuration, excluding any pilot seat, of 10 seats or more in passenger-carrying operations, except a helicopter operating under day VFR conditions, unless the aircraft is equipped with either approved thunderstorm detection equipment or approved airborne weather radar equipment.

(b)   No person may operate a helicopter that has a passenger seating configuration, excluding any pilot seat, of 10 seats or more in passenger-carrying operations, under night VFR when current weather reports indicate that thunderstorms or other potentially hazardous weather conditions that can be detected with airborne thunderstorm detection equipment may reasonably be expected along the route to be flown, unless the helicopter is equipped with either approved thunderstorm detection equipment or approved airborne weather radar equipment.

(c)   No person may begin a flight under IFR or night VFR conditions when current weather reports indicate that thunderstorms or other potentially hazardous weather conditions that can be detected with airborne thunderstorm detection equipment, required by paragraph (a) or (b) of this section, may reasonably be expected along the route to be flown, unless the airborne thunderstorm detection equipment is in satisfactory operating condition.

(d)   If the airborne thunderstorm detection equipment becomes inoperative en route, the aircraft must be operated under the instructions and procedures specified for that event in the manual required by §135.21.

(e)   This section does not apply to aircraft used solely within the State of Hawaii, within the State of Alaska, within that part of Canada west of longitude 130 degrees W, between latitude 70 degrees N, and latitude 53 degrees N, or during any training, test, or ferry flight.

(f)   Without regard to any other provision of this part, an alternate electrical power supply is not required for airborne thunderstorm detection equipment.

Ⓐ *Amend #60 eff 2-26-96.*

INTENTIONALLY

LEFT

BLANK

135.175   AIRBORNE WEATHER RADAR EQUIPMENT REQUIREMENTS

(a) No person may operate a large, transport category aircraft in passenger-carrying operations unless approved airborne weather radar equipment is installed in the aircraft.

(b) No person may begin a flight under IFR or night VFR conditions when current weather reports indicate that thunderstorms, or other potentially hazardous weather conditions that can be detected with airborne weather radar equipment, may reasonably be expected along the route to be flown, unless the airborne weather radar equipment required by paragraph (a) of this section is in satisfactory operating condition.

(c) If the airborne weather radar equipment becomes inoperative enroute, the aircraft must be operated under the instructions and procedures specified for that event in the manual required by §135.21.

(d) This section does not apply to aircraft used solely within the State of Hawaii, within the State of Alaska, within that part of Canada west of longitude 130 degrees W, between latitude 70 degrees N, and latitude 53 degrees N, or during any training test, or ferry flight.

(e) Without regard to any other provision of this part, an alternate electrical power supply is not required for airborne weather radar equipment.

135.177   EMERGENCY EQUIPMENT REQUIREMENTS FOR AIRCRAFT HAVING A PASSENGER SEATING CONFIGURATION OF MORE THAN 19 PASSENGERS

(a) No person may operate an aircraft having a passenger seating configuration, excluding any pilot seat, of more than 19 seats unless it is equipped with the following emergency equipment:

 (1) One approved first aid kit for treatment of injuries likely to occur in flight or in a minor accident, which meets the following specifications and requirements:

  (i) Each first aid kit must be dust and moisture proof, and contain only materials that either meet Federal Specifications GGK- 319a, as revised, or as approved by the Administrator.

  (ii) Required first aid kits must be readily accessible to the cabin flight attendants.

  (iii) Except as provided in paragraph (a)(1)(iv) of this section, at time of takeoff, each first aid kit must contain at least the following or other contents approved by the Administrator:

Amend #53
eff 12-2-94

Contents:	Quantity
Adhesive bandage compressors, 1 in	16
Antiseptic swabs	20
Ammonia inhalants	10
Bandage compressors, 4 in	8
Triangular bandage compressors, 40 in	5
Arm splint, noninflatable	1
Leg splint, noninflatable	1
Roller bandage, 4 in	4
Adhesive tape, 1-in standard roll	2
Bandage scissors	1
Protective latex gloves or equivalent nonpermeable gloves	[1]1

[1]Pair.

  (iv) Protective latex gloves or equivalent nonpermeable gloves may be placed in the first aid kit or in a location that is readily accessible to crewmembers.

 (2) A crash axe carried so as to be accessible to the crew but inaccessible to passengers during normal operations.

 (3) Signs that are visible to all occupants to notify them when smoking is prohibited and when safety belts must be fastened. The signs must be constructed so that they can be turned on during any movement of the aircraft on the surface, for each takeoff or landing, and at other times considered necessary by the pilot in command. "No smoking" signs shall be turned on when required by §135.127.

(b) Each item of equipment must be inspected regularly under inspection periods established in the operations specifications to ensure its condition for continued serviceability and immediate readiness to perform its intended emergency purposes.

135.178   ADDITIONAL EMERGENCY EQUIPMENT

No person may operate an airplane having a passenger seating configuration of more than 19 seats, unless it has the additional emergency equipment specified in paragraphs (a) through (l) of this section.

(a)   *Means for emergency evacuation.* Each passenger-carrying landplane emergency exit (other than over-the-wing) that is more than 6 feet from the ground, with the airplane on the ground and the landing gear extended, must have an approved means to assist the occupants in descending to the ground. The assisting means for a floor-level emergency exit must meet the requirements of §25.809(f)(1) of this chapter in effect on April 30, 1972, except that, for any airplane for which the application for the type certificate was filed after that date, it must meet the requirements under which the airplane was type certificated. An assisting means that deploys automatically must be armed during taxiing, takeoffs, and landings; however, the Administrator may grant a deviation from the requirement of automatic deployment if he finds that the design of the exit makes compliance impractical, if the assisting means automatically erects upon deployment and, with respect to required emergency exits, if an emergency evacuation demonstration is conducted in accordance with §121.291(a) of this chapter. This paragraph does not apply to the rear window emergency exit of Douglas DC-3 airplanes operated with fewer than 36 occupants, including crewmembers, and fewer than five exits authorized for passenger use.

(b)   *Interior emergency exit marking.* The following must be complied with for each passenger-carrying airplane:

(1)   Each passenger emergency exit, its means of access, and its means of opening must be conspicuously marked. The identity and location of each passenger emergency exit must be recognizable from a distance equal to the width of the cabin. The location of each passenger emergency exit must be indicated by a sign visible to occupants approaching along the main passenger aisle. There must be a locating sign—

(i)   Above the aisle near each over-the-wing passenger emergency exit, or at another ceiling location if it is more practical because of low headroom;

(ii)   Next to each floor level passenger emergency exit, except that one sign may serve two such exits if they both can be seen readily from that sign; and

(iii)   On each bulkhead or divider that prevents fore and aft vision along the passenger cabin, to indicate emergency exits beyond and obscured by it, except that if this is not possible, the sign may be placed at another appropriate location.

(2)   Each passenger emergency exit marking and each locating sign must meet the following:

(i)   For an airplane for which the application for the type certificate was filed prior to May 1, 1972, each passenger emergency exit marking and each locating sign must be manufactured to meet the requirement of §25.812(b) of this chapter in effect on April 30, 1972. On these airplanes, no sign may continue to be used if its luminescence (brightness) decreases to below 100 microlamberts. The colors may be reversed if it increases the emergency illumination of the passenger compartment. However, the Administrator may authorize deviation from the 2-inch background requirements if he finds that special circumstances exist that make compliance impractical and that the proposed deviation provides an equivalent level of safety.

(ii)   For an airplane for which the application for the type certificate was filed on or after May 1, 1972, each passenger emergency exit marking and each locating sign must be manufactured to meet the interior emergency exit marking requirements under which the airplane was type certificated. On these airplanes, no sign may continue to be used if its luminescence (brightness) decreases to below 250 microlamberts.

(c) *Lighting for interior emergency exit markings.* Each passenger-carrying airplane must have an emergency lighting system, independent of the main lighting system; however, sources of general cabin illumination may be common to both the emergency and the main lighting systems if the power supply to the emergency lighting system is independent of the power supply to the main lighting system. The emergency lighting system must—

(1) Illuminate each passenger exit marking and locating sign;

(2) Provide enough general lighting in the passenger cabin so that the average illumination when measured at 40-inch intervals at seat armrest height, on the centerline of the main passenger aisle, is at least 0.05 foot-candles; and

(3) For airplanes type certificated after January 1, 1958, include floor proximity emergency escape path marking which meets the requirements of §25.812(e) of this chapter in effect on November 26, 1984.

(d) *Emergency light operation.* Except for lights forming part of emergency lighting subsystems provided in compliance with §25.812(h) of this chapter (as prescribed in paragraph (h) of this section) that serve no more than one assist means, are independent of the airplane's main emergency lighting systems, and are automatically activated when the assist means is deployed, each light required by paragraphs (c) and (h) of this section must;

(1) Be operable manually both from the flightcrew station and from a point in the passenger compartment that is readily accessible to a normal flight attendant seat;

(2) Have a means to prevent inadvertent operation of the manual controls;

(3) When armed or turned on at either station, remain lighted or become lighted upon interruption of the airplane's normal electric power.

(4) Be armed or turned on during taxiing, takeoff, and landing. In showing compliance with this paragraph a transverse vertical separation of the fuselage need not be considered;

(5) Provide the required level of illumination for at least 10 minutes at the critical ambient conditions after emergency landing; and

(6) Have a cockpit control device that has an "on," "off," and "armed" position.

(e) *Emergency exit operating handles.*

(1) For a passenger-carrying airplane for which the application for the type certificate was filed prior to May 1, 1972, the location of each passenger emergency exit operating handle, and instructions for opening the exit, must be shown by a marking on or near the exit that is readable from a distance of 30 inches. In addition, for each Type I and Type II emergency exit with a locking mechanism released by rotary motion of the handle, the instructions for opening must be shown by—

(i) A red arrow with a shaft at least three-fourths inch wide and a head twice the width of the shaft, extending along at least 70° of arc at a radius approximately equal to three-fourths of the handle length; and

(ii) The word "open" in red letters 1 inch high placed horizontally near the head of the arrow.

(2) For a passenger-carrying airplane for which the application for the type certificate was filed on or after May 1, 1972, the location of each passenger emergency exit operating handle and instructions for opening the exit must be shown in accordance with the requirements under which the airplane was type certificated. On these airplanes, no operating handle or operating handle cover may continue to be used if its luminescence (brightness) decreases to below 100 microlamberts.

(f) *Emergency exit access.* Access to emergency exits must be provided as follows for each passenger-carrying airplane;

(1) Each passageway between individual passenger areas, or leading to a Type I or Type II emergency exit, must be unobstructed and at least 20 inches wide.

(2) There must be enough space next to each Type I or Type II emergency exit to allow a crewmember to assist in the evacuation of passengers without reducing the unobstructed width of the passageway below that required in paragraph (f)(1) of this section; however, the Administrator may authorize deviation from this requirement for an airplane certificated under the provisions of part 4b of the Civil Air Regulations in effect before December 20, 1951, if he finds that special circumstances exist that provide an equivalent level of safety.

    (3)   There must be access from the main aisle to each Type III and Type IV exit. The access from the aisle to these exits must not be obstructed by seats, berths, or other protrusions in a manner that would reduce the effectiveness of the exit. In addition, for a transport category airplane type certificated after January 1, 1958, there must be placards installed in accordance with §25.813(c)(3) of this chapter for each Type III exit after December 3, 1992.

    (4)   If it is necessary to pass through a passageway between passenger compartments to reach any required emergency exit from any seat in the passenger cabin, the passageway must not be obstructed. Curtains may, however, be used if they allow free entry through the passageway.

    (5)   No door may be installed in any partition between passenger compartments.

    (6)   If it is necessary to pass through a doorway separating the passenger cabin from other areas to reach a required emergency exit from any passenger seat, the door must have a means to latch it in the open position, and the door must be latched open during each takeoff and landing. The latching means must be able to withstand the loads imposed upon it when the door is subjected to the ultimate inertia forces, relative to the surrounding structure, listed in §25.561(b) of this chapter.

(g) *Exterior exit markings.* Each passenger emergency exit and the means of opening that exit from the outside must be marked on the outside of the airplane. There must be a 2-inch colored band outlining each passenger emergency exit on the side of the fuselage. Each outside marking, including the band, must be readily distinguishable from the surrounding fuselage area by contrast in color. The markings must comply with the following:

    (1)   If the reflectance of the darker color is 15 percent or less, the reflectance of the lighter color must be at least 45 percent.

    (2)   If the reflectance of the darker color is greater than 15 percent, at least a 30 percent difference between its reflectance and the reflectance of the lighter color must be provided.

    (3)   Exits that are not in the side of the fuselage must have the external means of opening and applicable instructions marked conspicuously in red or, if red is inconspicuous against the background color, in bright chrome yellow and, when the opening means for such an exit is located on only one side of the fuselage, a conspicuous marking to that effect must be provided on the other side. "Reflectance" is the ratio of the luminous flux reflected by a body to the luminous flux it receives.

(h) *Exterior emergency lighting and escape route.*

    (1)   Each passenger-carrying airplane must be equipped with exterior lighting that meets the following requirements:

        (i)   For an airplane for which the application for the type certificate was filed prior to May 1, 1972, the requirements of §25.812(f) and (g) of this chapter in effect on April 30, 1972.

        (ii)   For an airplane for which the application for the type certificate was filed on or after May 1, 1972, the exterior emergency lighting requirements under which the airplane was type certificated.

    (2)   Each passenger-carrying airplane must be equipped with a slip-resistant escape route that meets the following requirements:

        (i)   For an airplane for which the application for the type certificate was filed prior to May 1, 1972, the requirements of §25.803(e) of this chapter in effect on April 30, 1972.

        (ii)   For an airplane for which the application for the type certificate was filed on or after May 1, 1972, the slip-resistant escape route requirements under which the airplane was type certificated.

(i) *Floor level exits.* Each floor level door or exit in the side of the fuselage (other than those leading into a cargo or baggage compartment that is not accessible from the passenger cabin) that is 44 or more inches high and 20 or more inches wide, but not wider than 48 inches, each passenger ventral exit (except the ventral exits on Martin 404 and Convair 240 airplanes), and each tail cone exit, must meet the requirements of this section for floor level emergency exits. However, the Administrator may grant a deviation from this paragraph if he finds that circumstances make full compliance impractical and that an acceptable level of safety has been achieved.

(j) *Additional emergency exits.* Approved emergency exits in the passenger compartments that are in excess of the minimum number of required emergency exits must meet all of the applicable provisions of this section, except paragraphs (f)(1), (2), and (3) of this section, and must be readily accessible.

(k) On each large passenger-carrying turbojet-powered airplane, each ventral exit and tailcone exit must be—
  (1) Designed and constructed so that it cannot be opened during flight; and
  (2) Marked with a placard readable from a distance of 30 inches and installed at a conspicuous location near the means of opening the exit, stating that the exit has been designed and constructed so that it cannot be opened during flight.
(l) *Portable lights.* No person may operate a passenger-carrying airplane unless it is equipped with flashlight stowage provisions accessible from each flight attendant seat.

135.179   INOPERABLE INSTRUMENTS AND EQUIPMENT

(a) No person may take off an aircraft with inoperable instruments or equipment installed unless the following conditions are met:
  (1) An approved Minimum Equipment List exists for that aircraft.
  (2) The certificate-holding district office has issued the certificate holder operations specifications authorizing operations in accordance with an approved Minimum Equipment List. The flight crew shall have direct access at all times prior to flight to all of the information contained in the approved Minimum Equipment List through printed or other means approved by the Administrator in the certificate holders operations specifications. An approved Minimum Equipment List, as authorized by the operations specifications, constitutes an approved change to the type design without requiring recertification.
  (3) The approved Minimum Equipment List must:
    (i) Be prepared in accordance with the limitations specified in paragraph (b) of this section.
    (ii) Provide for the operation of the aircraft with certain instruments and equipment in an inoperable condition.
  (4) Records identifying the inoperable instruments and equipment and the information required by paragraph (a)(3)(ii) of this section must be available to the pilot.
  (5) The aircraft is operated under all applicable conditions and limitations contained in the Minimum Equipment List and the operations specifications authorizing use of the Minimum Equipment List.
(b) The following instruments and equipment may not be included in the Minimum Equipment List:
  (1) Instruments and equipment that are either specifically or otherwise required by the airworthiness requirements under which the airplane is type certificated and which are essential for safe operations under all operating conditions.
  (2) Instruments and equipment required by an airworthiness directive to be in operable conditions unless the airworthiness directive provides otherwise.
  (3) Instruments and equipment required for specific operations by this part.
(c) Notwithstanding paragraphs (b)(1) and (b)(3) of this section, an aircraft with inoperable instruments or equipment may be operated under a special flight permit under §§21.197 and 21.199 of this chapter.

135.180   TRAFFIC ALERT AND COLLISION AVOIDANCE SYSTEM

(a) Unless otherwise authorized by the Administrator, after December 31, 1995, no person may operate a turbine powered airplane that has a passenger seat configuration, excluding any pilot seat, of 10 to 30 seats unless it is equipped with an approved traffic alert and collision avoidance system. If a TCAS II system is installed, it must be capable of coordinating with TCAS units that meet TSO C-119.
(b) The airplane flight manual required by §135.21 of this part shall contain the following information on the TCAS I system required by this section:
  (1) Appropriate procedures for—
    (i) The use of the equipment; and
    (ii) Proper flightcrew action with respect to the equipment operation.
  (2) An outline of all input sources that must be operating for the TCAS to function properly.

135.181   **PERFORMANCE REQUIREMENTS: AIRCRAFT OPERATED OVER-THE-TOP OR IN IFR CONDITIONS**

(a)   Except as provided in paragraphs (b) and (c) of this section, no person may—

    (1)   Operate a single-engine aircraft carrying passengers over-the-top or in IFR conditions; or

    (2)   Operate a multiengine aircraft carrying passengers over-the-top or in IFR conditions at a weight that will not allow it to climb, with the critical engine inoperative, at least 50 feet a minute when operating at the MEAs of the route to be flown or 5,000 feet MSL, whichever is higher.

(b)   Notwithstanding the restrictions in paragraph (a)(2) of this section, multiengine helicopters carrying passengers offshore may conduct such operations in over-the-top or in IFR conditions at a weight that will allow the helicopter to climb at least 50 feet per minute with the critical engine inoperative when operating at the MEA of the route to be flown or 1,500 feet MSL, whichever is higher.

(c)   Without regard to paragraph (a) of this section—

    (1)   If the latest weather reports or forecasts, or any combination of them, indicate that the weather along the planned route (including takeoff and landing) allows flight under VFR under the ceiling (if a ceiling exists) and that the weather is forecast to remain so until at least 1 hour after the estimated time of arrival at the destination, a person may operate an aircraft over-the-top; or

    (2)   If the latest weather reports or forecasts, or any combination of them, indicate that the weather along the planned route allows flight under VFR under the ceiling (if a ceiling exists) beginning at a point no more than 15 minutes flying time at normal cruise speed from the departure airport, a person may—

        (i)   Take off from the departure airport in IFR conditions and fly in IFR conditions to a point no more than 15 minutes flying time at normal cruise speed from that airport;

        (ii)   Operate an aircraft in IFR conditions if unforecast weather conditions are encountered while enroute on a flight planned to be conducted under VFR; and

        (iii)   Make an IFR approach at the destination airport if unforecast weather conditions are encountered at the airport that do not allow an approach to be completed under VFR.

(d)   Without regard to paragraph (a) of this section, a person may operate an aircraft over-the-top under conditions allowing—

    (1)   For multiengine aircraft, descent or continuance of the flight under VFR if its critical engine fails; or

    (2)   For single-engine aircraft, descent under VFR if its engine fails.

135.183   **PERFORMANCE REQUIREMENTS: LAND AIRCRAFT OPERATED OVER WATER**

No person may operate a land aircraft carrying passengers over water unless—

(a)   It is operated at an altitude that allows it to reach land in the case of engine failure;

(b)   It is necessary for takeoff or landing;

(c)   It is a multiengine aircraft operated at a weight that will allow it to climb, with the critical engine inoperative, at least 50 feet a minute, at an altitude of 1,000 feet above the surface; or

(d)   It is a helicopter equipped with helicopter flotation devices.

135.185   **EMPTY WEIGHT AND CENTER OF GRAVITY: CURRENCY REQUIREMENT**

(a)   No person may operate a multiengine aircraft unless the current empty weight and center of gravity are calculated from values established by actual weighing of the aircraft within the preceding 36 calendar months.

(b)   Paragraph (a) of this section does not apply to—

    (1)   Aircraft issued an original airworthiness certificate within the preceding 36 calendar months; and

    (2)   Aircraft operated under a weight and balance system approved in the operations specifications of the certificate holder.

SUBPART D — VFR/IFR OPERATING LIMITATIONS AND WEATHER REQUIREMENTS

135.201 APPLICABILITY

This subpart prescribes the operating limitations for VFR/IFR flight operations and associated weather requirements for operations under this part.

135.203 VFR: MINIMUM ALTITUDES

Except when necessary for takeoff and landing, no person may operate under VFR—
(a) An airplane—
 (1) During the day, below 500 feet above the surface or less than 500 feet horizontally from any obstacle; or
 (2) At night, at an altitude less than 1,000 feet above the highest obstacle within a horizontal distance of 5 miles from the course intended to be flown or, in designated mountainous terrain, less than 2,000 feet above the highest obstacle within a horizontal distance of 5 miles from the course intended to be flown; or
(b) A helicopter over a congested area at an altitude less than 300 feet above the surface.

135.205 VFR: VISIBILITY REQUIREMENTS

(a) No person may operate an airplane under VFR in uncontrolled airspace when the ceiling is less than 1,000 feet unless flight visibility is at least 2 miles.
(b) No person may operate a helicopter under VFR in Class G airspace at an altitude of 1,200 feet or less above the surface or within the lateral boundaries of the surface areas of Class B, Class C, Class D, or Class E airspace designated for an airport unless the visibility is at least—
 (1) During the day–1/2 mile; or
 (2) At night–1 mile.

135.207 VFR: HELICOPTER SURFACE REFERENCE REQUIREMENTS

No person may operate a helicopter under VFR unless that person has visual surface reference or, at night, visual surface light reference, sufficient to safely control the helicopter.

135.209 VFR: FUEL SUPPLY

(a) No person may begin a flight operation in an airplane under VFR unless, considering wind and forecast weather conditions, it has enough fuel to fly to the first point of intended landing and, assuming normal cruising fuel consumption—
 (1) During the day, to fly after that for at least 30 minutes; or

 (2) At night, to fly after that for at least 45 minutes.
(b) No person may begin a flight operation in a helicopter under VFR unless, considering wind and forecast weather conditions, it has enough fuel to fly to the first point of intended landing and, assuming normal cruising fuel consumption, to fly after that for at least 20 minutes.

135.211 VFR: OVER-THE-TOP CARRYING PASSENGERS: OPERATING LIMITATIONS

Subject to any additional limitations in §135.181, no person may operate an aircraft under VFR over-the-top carrying passengers, unless—
(a) Weather reports or forecasts, or any combination of them, indicate that the weather at the intended point of termination of over-the-top flight—
 (1) Allows descent to beneath the ceiling under VFR and is forecast to remain so until at least 1 hour after the estimated time of arrival at that point; or
 (2) Allows an IFR approach and landing with flight clear of the clouds until reaching the prescribed initial approach altitude over the final approach facility, unless the approach is made with the use of radar under §91.175(i) of this chapter; or
(b) It is operated under conditions allowing—
 (1) For multiengine aircraft, descent or continuation of the flight under VFR if its critical engine fails; or
 (2) For single-engine aircraft, descent under VFR if its engine fails.

135.213 WEATHER REPORTS AND FORECASTS

(a) Whenever a person operating an aircraft under this part is required to use a weather report or forecast, that person shall use that of the U.S. National Weather Service, a source approved by the U.S. National Weather Service, or a source approved by the Administrator. However, for operations under VFR, the pilot in command may, if such a report is not available, use weather information based on that pilot's own observations or on those of other persons competent to supply appropriate observations.
(b) For the purposes of paragraph (a) of this section, weather observations made and furnished to pilots to conduct IFR operations at an airport must be taken at the airport where those IFR operations are conducted, unless the Administrator issues operations specifications allowing the use of weather observations taken

at a location not at the airport where the IFR operations are conducted. The Administrator issues such operations specifications when, after investigation by the U.S. National Weather Service and the certificate-holding district office, it is found that the standards of safety for that operation would allow the deviation from this paragraph for a particular operation for which an air carrier operating certificate or operating certificate has been issued.

135.215   IFR: OPERATING LIMITATIONS

(a) Except as provided in paragraphs (b), (c), and (d) of this section, no person may operate an aircraft under IFR outside of controlled airspace or at any airport that does not have an approved standard instrument approach procedure.

(b) The Administrator may issue operations specifications to the certificate holder to allow it to operate under IFR over routes outside controlled airspace if—

   (1) The certificate holder shows the Administrator that the flight crew is able to navigate, without visual reference to the ground, over an intended track without deviating more than 5 degrees or 5 miles, whichever is less, from that track; and

   (2) The Administrator determines that the proposed operations can be conducted safely.

(c) A person may operate an aircraft under IFR outside of controlled airspace if the certificate holder has been approved for the operations and that operation is necessary to—

   (1) Conduct an instrument approach to an airport for which there is in use a current approved standard or special instrument approach procedure; or

   (2) Climb into controlled airspace during an approved missed approach procedure; or

   (3) Make an IFR departure from an airport having an approved instrument approach procedure.

(d) The Administrator may issue operations specifications to the certificate holder to allow it to depart at an airport that does not have an approved standard instrument approach procedure when the Administrator determines that it is necessary to make an IFR departure from that airport and that the proposed operations can be conducted safely. The approval to operate at that airport does not include an approval to make an IFR approach to that airport.

135.217   IFR: TAKEOFF LIMITATIONS

No person may takeoff an aircraft under IFR from an airport where weather conditions are at or above take off minimums but are below authorized IFR landing minimums unless there is an alternate airport within 1 hour's flying time (at normal cruising speed, in still air) of the airport of departure.

135.219   IFR: DESTINATION AIRPORT WEATHER MINIMUMS

No person may take off an aircraft under IFR or begin an IFR or over-the-top operation unless the latest weather reports or forecasts, or any combination of them, indicate that weather conditions at the estimated time of arrival at the next airport of intended landing will be at or above authorized IFR landing minimums.

135.221   IFR: ALTERNATE AIRPORT WEATHER MINIMUMS

No person may designate an alternate airport unless the weather reports or forecasts, or any combination of them, indicate that the weather conditions will be at or above authorized alternate airport landing minimums for that airport at the estimated time of arrival.

135.223   IFR: ALTERNATE AIRPORT REQUIREMENTS

(a) Except as provided in paragraph (b) of this section, no person may operate an aircraft in IFR conditions unless it carries enough fuel (considering weather reports or forecasts or any combination of them) to—

   (1) Complete the flight to the first airport of intended landing;

   (2) Fly from that airport to the alternate airport; and

   (3) Fly after that for 45 minutes at normal cruising speed or, for helicopters, fly after that for 30 minutes at normal cruising speed.

(b) Paragraph (a)(2) of this section does not apply if Part 97 of this chapter prescribes a standard instrument approach procedure for the first airport of intended landing and, for at least one hour before and after the estimated time of arrival, the appropriate weather reports or forecasts, or any combination of them, indicate that—

   (1) The ceiling will be at least 1,500 feet above the lowest circling approach MDA; or

   (2) If a circling instrument approach is not authorized for the airport, the ceiling will be at least 1,500 feet above the lowest published minimum or 2,000 feet above the airport elevation, whichever is higher; and

   (3) Visibility for that airport is forecast to be at least three miles, or two miles more than the lower applicable visibility minimums, whichever is the greater, for the instrument approach procedure to be used at the destination airport.

A *Amend #60 eff 2-26-96.*

135.225 IFR: TAKEOFF, APPROACH AND LANDING MINIMUMS

(a) No pilot may begin an instrument approach procedure to an airport unless—
  (1) That airport has a weather reporting facility operated by the U.S. National Weather Service, a source approved by U.S. National Weather Service, or a source approved by the Administrator; and
  (2) The latest weather report issued by that weather reporting facility indicates that weather conditions are at or above the authorized IFR landing minimums for that airport.

(b) No pilot may begin the final approach segment of an instrument approach procedure to an airport unless the latest weather reported by the facility described in paragraph (a)(1) of this section indicates that weather conditions are at or above the authorized IFR landing minimums for that procedure.

(c) If a pilot has begun the final approach segment of an instrument approach to an airport under paragraph (b) of this section and a later weather report indicating below minimum conditions is received after the aircraft is—
  (1) On an ILS final approach and has passed the final approach fix; or
  (2) On an ASR or PAR final approach and has been turned over to the final approach controller; or
  (3) On a final approach using a VOR, NDB, or comparable approach procedure; and the aircraft—
    (i) Has passed the appropriate facility or final approach fix; or
    (ii) Where a final approach fix is not specified, has completed the procedure turn and is established inbound toward the airport on the final approach course within the distance prescribed in the procedure;
  the approach may be continued and a landing made if the pilot finds, upon reaching the authorized MDA or DH, that actual weather conditions are at least equal to the minimums prescribed for the procedure.

(d) The MDA or DH and visibility landing minimums prescribed in Part 97 of this chapter or in the operator's operations specifications are increased by 100 feet and 1/2 mile respectively, but not to exceed the ceiling and visibility minimums for that airport when used as an alternate airport, for each pilot in command of a turbine-powered airplane who has not served at least 100 hours as pilot in command in that type of airplane.

(e) Each pilot making an IFR takeoff or approach and landing at a military or foreign airport shall comply with applicable instrument approach procedures and weather minimums prescribed by the authority having jurisdiction over that airport. In addition, no pilot may, at that airport—
  (1) Take off under IFR when the visibility is less than 1 mile; or
  (2) Make an instrument approach when the visibility is less than 1/2 mile.

(f) If takeoff minimums are specified in Part 97 of this chapter for the takeoff airport, no pilot may take off an aircraft under IFR when the weather conditions reported by the facility described in paragraph (a)(1) of this section are less than the takeoff minimums specified for the takeoff airport in Part 97 or in the certificate holder's operations specifications.

(g) Except as provided in paragraph (h) of this section, if takeoff minimums are not prescribed in Part 97 of this chapter for the takeoff airport, no pilot may take off an aircraft under IFR when the weather conditions reported by the facility described in paragraph (a)(1) of this section are less than that prescribed in Part 91 of this chapter or in the certificate holder's operations specifications.

(h) At airports where straight-in instrument approach procedures are authorized, a pilot may take off an aircraft under IFR when the weather conditions reported by the facility described in paragraph (a)(1) of this section are equal to or better than the lowest straight-in landing minimums, unless otherwise restricted, if—
  (1) The wind direction and velocity at the time of takeoff are such that a straight-in instrument approach can be made to the runway served by the instrument approach;
  (2) The associated ground facilities upon which the landing minimums are predicated and the related airborne equipment are in normal operation; and
  (3) The certificate holder has been approved for such operations.

135.227 ICING CONDITIONS: OPERATING LIMITATIONS

(a) No pilot may take off an aircraft that has frost, ice, or snow adhering to any rotor blade, propeller, windshield, wing, stabilizing or control surface, to a powerplant installation, or to an airspeed, altimeter, rate of climb, or flight attitude instrument system, except under the following conditions:
  (1) Takeoffs may be made with frost adhering to the wings, or stabilizing or control surfaces, if the frost has been polished to make it smooth.
  (2) Takeoffs may be made with frost under the wing in the area of the fuel tanks if authorized by the Administrator.

(b) No certificate holder may authorize an airplane to take off and no pilot may take off an airplane any time conditions are such that frost, ice, or snow may reasonably be expected to adhere to the airplane unless the pilot has completed all applicable training as required by §135.341 and unless one of the following requirements is met:

  (1) A pretakeoff contamination check, that has been established by the certificate holder and approved by the Administrator for the specific airplane type, has been completed within 5 minutes prior to beginning takeoff. A pretakeoff contamination check is a check to make sure the wings and control surfaces are free of frost, ice, or snow.

  (2) The certificate holder has an approved alternative procedure and under that procedure the airplane is determined to be free of frost, ice, or snow.

  (3) The certificate holder has an approved deicing/anti-icing program that complies with §121.629(c) of this chapter and the takeoff complies with that program.

(c) Except for an airplane that has ice protection provisions that meet §34 of Appendix A, or those for transport category airplane type certification, no pilot may fly—

  (1) Under IFR into known or forecast light or moderate icing conditions; or

  (2) Under VFR into known light or moderate icing conditions; unless the aircraft has functioning deicing or anti-icing equipment protecting each rotor blade, propeller, windshield, wing, stabilizing or control surface, and each airspeed, altimeter, rate of climb or flight attitude instrument system.

(d) No pilot may fly a helicopter under IFR into known or forecast icing conditions or under VFR into known icing conditions unless it has been type certificated and appropriately equipped for operations in icing conditions.

(e) Except for an airplane that has ice protection provisions that meet §34 of Appendix A, or those for transport category airplane type certification, no pilot may fly an aircraft into known or forecast severe icing conditions.

(f) If current weather reports and briefing information relied upon by the pilot in command indicate that the forecast icing condition that would otherwise prohibit the flight will not be encountered during the flight because of changed weather conditions since the forecast, the restrictions in paragraphs (c), (d) and (e) of this section based on forecast conditions do not apply.

135.229 AIRPORT REQUIREMENTS

(a) No certificate holder may use any airport unless it is adequate for the proposed operation, considering such items as size, surface, obstructions, and lighting.

(b) No pilot of an aircraft carrying passengers at night may take off from, or land on, an airport unless—

  (1) That pilot has determined the wind direction from an illuminated wind direction indicator or local ground communications or, in the case of takeoff, that pilot's personal observations; and

  (2) The limits of the area to be used for landing or takeoff are clearly shown—

    (i) For airplanes, by boundary or runway marker lights;

    (ii) For helicopters, by boundary or runway marker lights or reflective material.

(c) For the purpose of paragraph (b) of this section, if the area to be used for takeoff or landing is marked by flare pots or lanterns, their use must be approved by the Administrator.

PAGE 135-45 AND 135-46 RESERVED FOR EXPANSION.

SUBPART E — FLIGHT CREWMEMBER REQUIREMENTS

135.241   APPLICABILITY

➤
Ⓐ   Except as provided in §135.3, this subpart prescribes the flight crewmember requirements for operations under this part.

135.243   PILOT IN COMMAND QUALIFICATIONS

(a)   No certificate holder may use a person, nor may any person serve, as pilot in command in passenger-carrying operations—

    (1)   Of a turbojet airplane, of an airplane having a passenger-seat configuration, excluding each crewmember seat, of 10 seats or more, or a multiengine airplane in a commuter operation as defined in Part 119 of this Chapter, unless that person holds an airline transport pilot certificate with appropriate category and class ratings and, if required, an appropriate type rating for that airplane.

    (2)   Of a helicopter in a scheduled interstate air transportation operation by an air carrier within the 48 contiguous states unless that person holds an airline transport pilot certificate, appropriate type ratings, and an instrument rating.

(b)   Except as provided in paragraph (a) of this section, no certificate holder may use a person, nor may any person serve, as pilot in command of an aircraft under VFR unless that person—

    (1)   Holds at least a commercial pilot certificate with appropriate category and class ratings and, if required, an appropriate type rating for that aircraft; and

    (2)   Has had at least 500 hours of flight time as a pilot, including at least 100 hours of cross-country flight time, at least 25 hours of which were at night; and

    (3)   For an airplane, holds an instrument rating or an airline transport pilot certificate with an airplane category rating; or

    (4)   For helicopter operations conducted VFR over-the-top, holds a helicopter instrument rating, or an airline transport pilot certificate with a category and class rating for that aircraft, not limited to VFR.

(c)   Except as provided in paragraph (a) of this section, no certificate holder may use a person, nor may any person serve, as pilot in command of an aircraft under IFR unless that person—

    (1)   Holds at least a commercial pilot certificate with appropriate category and class ratings and, if required, an appropriate type rating for that aircraft; and

    (2)   Has had at least 1,200 hours of flight time as a pilot, including 500 hours of cross country flight time, 100 hours of night flight time, and 75 hours of actual or simulated instrument time at least 50 hours of which were in actual flight; and

    (3)   For an airplane, holds an instrument rating or an airline transport pilot certificate with an airplane category rating; or

    (4)   For a helicopter, holds a helicopter instrument rating, or an airline transport pilot certificate with a category and class rating for that aircraft, not limited to VFR.

(d)   Paragraph (b)(3) of this section does not apply when—

    (1)   The aircraft used is a single reciprocating-engine-powered airplane;

    (2)   The certificate holder does not conduct any operation pursuant to a published flight schedule which specifies five or more round trips a week between two or more points and places between which the round trips are performed, and does not transport mail by air under a contract or contracts with the United States Postal Service having total amount estimated at the beginning of any semiannual reporting period (January 1 - June 30: July 1 - December 31) to be in excess of $20,000 over the 12 months commencing with the beginning of the reporting period;

Ⓐ *Amend #57 eff 3-19-96.*

(3)   The area, as specified in the certificate holder's operations specifications, is an isolated area, as determined by the Flight Standards district office, if it is shown that—

    (i)   The primary means of navigation in the area is by pilotage, since radio navigational aids are largely ineffective; and

    (ii)   The primary means of transportation in the area is by air;

(4)   Each flight is conducted under day VFR with a ceiling of not less than 1,000 feet and visibility not less than 3 statute miles;

(5)   Weather reports or forecasts, or any combination of them, indicate that for the period commencing with the planned departure and ending 30 minutes after the planned arrival at the destination the flight may be conducted under VFR with a ceiling of not less than 1,000 feet and visibility of not less than 3 statute miles, except that if weather reports and forecasts are not available, the pilot in command may use that pilot's observations or those of other persons competent to supply weather observations if those observations indicate the flight may be conducted under VFR with the ceiling and visibility required in this paragraph;

(6)   The distance of each flight from the certificate holder's base of operation to destination does not exceed 250 nautical miles for a pilot who holds a commercial pilot certificate with an airplane rating without an instrument rating, provided the pilot's certificate does not contain any limitation to the contrary; and

(7)   The areas to be flown are approved by the certificate-holding FAA Flight Standards district office and are listed in the certificate holder's operations specifications.

135.244   OPERATING EXPERIENCE

(a)   No certificate holder may use any person, nor may any person serve, as a pilot in command of an aircraft operated in a commuter operation, as defined in Part 119 of this Chapter, in passenger-carrying operations, unless that person has completed, prior to designation as pilot in command, on that make and basic model aircraft and in that crewmember position, the following operating experience in each make and basic model of aircraft to be flown:

(1)   Aircraft, single engine—10 hours.

(2)   Aircraft multiengine, reciprocating engine-powered—15 hours.

(3)   Aircraft multiengine, turbine engine-powered—20 hours.

(4)   Airplane, turbojet-powered—25 hours.

(b)   In acquiring the operating experience, each person must comply with the following:

(1)   The operating experience must be acquired after satisfactory completion of the appropriate ground and flight training for the aircraft and crewmember position. Approved provisions for the operating experience must be included in the certificate holder's training program.

(2)   The experience must be acquired in flight during commuter passenger- carrying operations under this Part. However, in the case of an aircraft not previously used by the certificate holder in operations under this Part, operating experience acquired in the aircraft during proving flights or ferry flights may be used to meet this requirement.

(3)   Each person must acquire the operating experience while performing the duties of a pilot in command under the supervision of a qualified check pilot.

(4)   The hours of operating experience may be reduced to not less than 50 percent of the hours required by this section by the substitution of one additional takeoff and landing for each hour of flight.

135.245　SECOND IN COMMAND QUALIFICATIONS

(a) Except as provided in paragraph (b), no certificate holder may use any person, nor may any person serve, as second in command of an aircraft unless that person holds at least a commercial pilot certificate with appropriate category and class ratings and an instrument rating. For flight under IFR, that person must meet the recent instrument experience requirements of Part 61 of this chapter.

(b) A second in command of a helicopter operated under VFR, other than over-the-top, must have at least a commercial pilot certificate with an appropriate aircraft category and class rating.

135.247　PILOT QUALIFICATIONS: RECENT EXPERIENCE

(a) No certificate holder may use any person, nor may any person serve, as pilot in command of an aircraft carrying passengers unless, within the preceding 90 days, that person has—
   (1) Made three takeoffs and three landings as the sole manipulator of the flight controls in an aircraft of the same category and class and, if a type rating is required, of the same type in which that person is to serve; or
   (2) For operation during the period beginning 1 hour after sunset and ending 1 hour before sunrise (as published in the Air Almanac), made three takeoffs and three landings during that period as the sole manipulator of the flight controls in an aircraft of the same category and class and, if a type rating is required, of the same type in which that person is to serve.
   A person who complies with paragraph (a)(2) of this paragraph need not comply with paragraph (a)(1) of this paragraph.

(b) For the purpose of paragraph (a) of this section, if the aircraft is a tailwheel airplane, each takeoff must be made in a tailwheel airplane and each landing must be made to a full stop in a tailwheel airplane.

135.249　USE OF PROHIBITED DRUGS

(a) This section applies to persons who perform a function listed in Appendix I to Part 121 of this chapter for a certificate holder or an operator. For the purpose of this section, a person who performs such a function pursuant to a contract with the certificate holder or the operator is considered to be performing that function for the certificate holder or the operator.

(b) No certificate holder or operator may knowingly use any person to perform, nor may any person perform for a certificate holder or an operator, either directly or by contract, any function listed in Appendix I to Part 121 of this chapter while that person has a prohibited drug, as defined in that appendix, in his or her system.

(c) No certificate holder or operator shall knowingly use any person to perform, nor shall any person perform for a certificate holder or operator, either directly or by contract, any safety-sensitive function if the person has a verified positive drug test result on or has refused to submit to a drug test required by Appendix I to Part 121 of this chapter and the person has not met the requirements of Appendix I to Part 121 of this chapter for returning to the performance of safety-sensitive duties.

135.251　TESTING FOR PROHIBITED DRUGS

(a) Each certificate holder or operator shall test each of its employees who performs a function listed in Appendix I to Part 121 of this chapter in accordance with that appendix.

(b) No certificate holder or operator may use any contractor to perform a function listed in Appendix I to Part 121 of this chapter unless that contractor tests each employee performing such a function for the certificate holder or operator in accordance with that appendix.

135.253 MISUSE OF ALCOHOL

(a) This section applies to employees who perform a function listed in Appendix J to Part 121 of this chapter for a certificate holder or operator (*covered employees*). For the purpose of this section, a person who meets the definition of covered employee in Appendix J is considered to be performing the function for the certificate holder or operator.

(b) *Alcohol concentration.* No covered employee shall report for duty or remain on duty requiring the performance of safety-sensitive functions while having an alcohol concentration of 0.04 or greater. No certificate holder or operator having actual knowledge that an employee has an alcohol concentration of 0.04 or greater shall permit the employee to perform or continue to perform safety-sensitive functions.

(c) *On-duty use.* No covered employee shall use alcohol while performing safety-sensitive functions. No certificate holder or operator having actual knowledge that a covered employee is using alcohol while performing safety-sensitive functions shall permit the employee to perform or continue to perform safety-sensitive functions.

(d) *Pre-duty use.*

  (1) No covered employee shall perform flight crewmember or flight attendant duties within 8 hours after using alcohol. No certificate holder or operator having actual knowledge that such an employee has used alcohol within 8 hours shall permit the employee to perform or continue to perform the specified duties.

  (2) No covered employee shall perform safety-sensitive duties other than those specified in paragraph (d)(1) of this section within 4 hours after using alcohol. No certificate holder or operator having actual knowledge that such an employee has used alcohol within 4 hours shall permit the employee to perform or continue to perform safety-sensitive functions.

(e) *Use following an accident.* No covered employee who has actual knowledge of an accident involving an aircraft for which he or she performed a safety-sensitive function at or near the time of the accident shall use alcohol for 8 hours following the accident, unless he or she has been given a post-accident test under Appendix J of Part 121 of this chapter, or the employer has determined that the employee's performance could not have contributed to the accident.

(f) *Refusal to submit to a required alcohol test.* No covered employee shall refuse to submit to a post-accident, random, reasonable suspicion, or follow-up alcohol test required under Appendix J to Part 121 of this chapter. No operator or certificate holder shall permit a covered employee who refuses to submit to such a test to perform or continue to perform safety-sensitive functions.

135.255 TESTING FOR ALCOHOL

(a) Each certificate holder and operator must establish an alcohol misuse prevention program in accordance with the provisions of Appendix J to Part 121 of this chapter.

(b) No certificate holder or operator shall use any person who meets the definition of "covered employee" in Appendix J to Part 121 to perform a safety-sensitive function listed in that appendix unless such person is subject to testing for alcohol misuse in accordance with the provisions of Appendix J.

**SUBPART F — FLIGHT CREWMEMBER FLIGHT TIME LIMITATIONS
AND REST REQUIREMENTS**

135.261   APPLICABILITY

Sections 135.263 through 135.273 of this part prescribe flight time limitations, duty period limitations, and rest requirements for operations conducted under this part as follows:
(a) Section 135.263 applies to all operations under this subpart.
(b) Section 135.265 applies to:
   (1) Scheduled passenger-carrying operations except those conducted solely within the state of Alaska. "Scheduled passenger-carrying operations" means passenger-carrying operations that are conducted in accordance with a published schedule which covers at least five round trips per week on at least one route between two or more points, includes dates or times (or both), and is openly advertised or otherwise made readily available to the general public, and
   (2) Any other operation under this part, if the operator elects to comply with §135.265 and obtains an appropriate operations specification amendment.
(c) Sections 135.267 and 135.269 apply to any operation that is not a scheduled passenger-carrying operation and to any operation conducted solely within the State of Alaska, unless the operator elects to comply with §135.265 as authorized under paragraph (b)(2) of this section.
(d) Section 135.271 contains special daily flight time limits for operations conducted under the helicopter emergency medical evacuation service (HEMES).
(e) Section 135.273 prescribes duty period limitations and rest requirements for flight attendants in all operations conducted under this part.

135.263   FLIGHT TIME LIMITATIONS AND REST REQUIREMENTS: ALL CERTIFICATE HOLDERS

(a) A certificate holder may assign a flight crewmember and a flight crewmember may accept an assignment for flight time only when the applicable requirements of §§135.263 through 135.271 are met.
(b) No certificate holder may assign any flight crewmember to any duty with the certificate holder during any required rest period.
(c) Time spent in transportation, not local in character, that a certificate holder requires of a flight crewmember and provides to transport the crewmember to an airport at which he is to serve on a flight as a crewmember, or from an airport at which he was relieved from duty to return to his home station, is not considered part of a rest period.

(d) A flight crewmember is not considered to be assigned flight time in excess of flight time limitations if the flights to which he is assigned normally terminate within the limitations, but due to circumstances beyond the control of the certificate holder or flight crewmember (such as adverse weather conditions), are not at the time of departure expected to reach their destination within the planned flight time.

135.265   FLIGHT TIME LIMITATIONS AND REST REQUIREMENTS: SCHEDULED OPERATIONS

(a) No certificate holder may schedule any flight crewmember, and no flight crewmember may accept an assignment, for flight time in scheduled operations or in other commercial flying if that crewmember's total flight time in all commercial flying will exceed—
   (1) 1,200 hours in any calendar year.
   (2) 120 hours in any calendar month.
   (3) 34 hours in any 7 consecutive days.
   (4) 8 hours during any 24 consecutive hours for a flight crew consisting of one pilot.
   (5) 8 hours between required rest periods for a flight crew consisting of two pilots qualified under this part for the operation being conducted.
(b) Except as provided in paragraph (c) of this section, no certificate holder may schedule a flight crewmember, and no flight crewmember may accept an assignment, for flight time during the 24 consecutive hours preceding the scheduled completion of any flight segment without a scheduled rest period during that 24 hours of at least the following:
   (1) 9 consecutive hours of rest for less than 8 hours of scheduled flight time.
   (2) 10 consecutive hours of rest for 8 or more but less than 9 hours of scheduled flight time.
   (3) 11 consecutive hours of rest for 9 or more hours of scheduled flight time.
(c) A certificate holder may schedule a flight crewmember for less than the rest required in paragraph (b) of this section or may reduce a scheduled rest under the following conditions:
   (1) A rest required under paragraph (b)(1) of this section may be scheduled for or reduced to a minimum of 8 hours if the flight crewmember is given a rest period of at least 10 hours that must begin no later than 24 hours after the commencement of the reduced rest period.
   (2) A rest required under paragraph (b)(2) of this section may be scheduled for or reduced to a minimum of 8 hours if the flight crewmember is given a rest period of at least 11 hours that must begin no later than 24 hours after the commencement of the reduced rest period.

(3) A rest required under paragraph (b)(3) of this section may be scheduled for or reduced to a minimum of 9 hours if the flight crewmember is given a rest period of at least 12 hours that must begin no later than 24 hours after the commence-ment of the reduced rest period.

(d) Each certificate holder shall relieve each flight crewmember engaged in scheduled air transportation from all further duty for at least 24 consecutive hours during any 7 consecutive days.

135.267 FLIGHT TIME LIMITATIONS AND REST REQUIREMENTS: UNSCHEDULED ONE- AND TWO-PILOT CREWS

(a) No certificate holder may assign any flight crewmember, and no flight crewmember may accept an assignment, for flight time as a member of a one- or two-pilot crew if that crewmember's total flight time in all commercial flying will exceed—
   (1) 500 hours in any calendar quarter.
   (2) 800 hours in any two consecutive calendar quarters.
   (3) 1,400 hours in any calendar year.
(b) Except as provided in paragraph (c) of this section, during any 24 consecutive hours the total flight time of the assigned flight when added to any other commercial flying by that flight crewmember may not exceed—
   (1) 8 hours for a flight crew consisting of one pilot; or
   (2) 10 hours for a flight crew consisting of two pilots qualified under this Part for the operation being conducted.
(c) A flight crewmember's flight time may exceed the flight time limits of paragraph (b) of this section if the assigned flight time occurs during a regularly assigned duty period of no more than 14 hours and—
   (1) If this duty period is immediately preceded by and followed by a required rest period of at least 10 consecutive hours of rest;
   (2) If flight time is assigned during this period, that total flight time when added to any other commercial flying by the flight crewmember may not exceed—
      (i) 8 hours for a flight crew consisting of one pilot; or
      (ii) 10 hours for a flight crew consisting of two pilots; and
   (3) If the combined duty and rest periods equal 24 hours.
(d) Each assignment under paragraph (b) of this section must provide for at least 10 consecutive hours of rest during the 24-hour period that precedes the planned completion time of the assignment.

(e) When a flight crewmember has exceeded the daily flight time limitations in this section, because of circumstances beyond the control of the certificate holder or flight crewmember (such as adverse weather conditions), that flight crewmember must have a rest period before being assigned or accepting an assignment for flight time of at least—
   (1) 11 consecutive hours of rest if the flight time limitation is exceeded by not more than 30 minutes.
   (2) 12 consecutive hours of rest if the flight time limitation is exceeded by more than 30 minutes, but not more than 60 minutes; and
   (3) 16 consecutive hours of rest if the flight time limitation is exceeded by more than 60 minutes.
(f) The certificate holder must provide each flight crewmember at least 13 rest periods of at least 24 consecutive hours each in each calendar quarter.

135.269 FLIGHT TIME LIMITATIONS AND REST REQUIREMENTS: UNSCHEDULED THREE- AND FOUR-PILOT CREWS

(a) No certificate holder may assign any flight crewmember, and no flight crewmember may accept an assignment for flight time as a member of a three- or four-pilot crew if that crewmember's total flight time in all commercial flying will exceed—
   (1) 500 hours in any calendar quarter.
   (2) 800 hours in any two consecutive calendar quarters.
   (3) 1,400 hours in any calendar year.
(b) No certificate holder may assign any pilot to a crew of three or four pilots, unless that assignment provides—
   (1) At least 10 consecutive hours of rest immediately preceding the assignment;
   (2) No more than 8 hours of flight deck duty in any 24 consecutive hours;
   (3) No more than 18 duty hours for a three-pilot crew or 20 duty hours for a four-pilot crew in any 24 consecutive hours;
   (4) No more than 12 hours aloft for a three-pilot crew or 16 hours aloft for a four-pilot crew during the maximum duty hours specified in paragraph (b)(3) of this section;
   (5) Adequate sleeping facilities on the aircraft for the relief pilot;
   (6) Upon completion of the assignment, a rest period of at least 12 hours;
   (7) For a three-pilot crew, a crew which consists of at least the following:
      (i) A pilot in command (PIC) who meets the applicable flight crewmember requirements of Subpart E of Part 135;

Amend #60 eff 2-26-96.

(ii) A PIC who meets the applicable flight crewmember requirements of Subpart E of Part 135, except those prescribed in §§135.244 and 135.247; and

(iii) A second in command (SIC) who meets the SIC qualifications of §135.245.

(8) For a four-pilot crew, at least three pilots who meet the conditions of paragraph (b)(7) of this section; plus a fourth pilot who meets the SIC qualifications of §135.245.

(c) When a flight crewmember has exceeded the daily flight deck duty limitation in this section by more than 60 minutes; because of circumstances beyond the control of the certificate holder or flight crewmember, that flight crewmember must have a rest period before the next duty period of at least 16 consecutive hours.

(d) A certificate holder must provide each flight crewmember at least 13 rest periods of at least 24 consecutive hours each in each calendar quarter.

135.271 HELICOPTER HOSPITAL EMERGENCY MEDICAL EVACUATION SERVICE (HEMES)

(a) No certificate holder may assign any flight crewmember, and no flight crewmember may accept an assignment for flight time if that crewmember's total flight time in all commercial flight will exceed—
(1) 500 hours in any calendar quarter.
(2) 800 hours in any two consecutive calendar quarters.
(3) 1,400 hours in any calendar year.

(b) No certificate holder may assign a helicopter flight crewmember, and no flight crewmember may accept an assignment, for hospital emergency medical evacuation service helicopter operations unless that assignment provides for at least 10 consecutive hours of rest immediately preceding reporting to the hospital for availability for flight time.

(c) No flight crewmember may accrue more than 8 hours of flight time during any 24-consecutive hour period of a HEMES assignment, unless an emergency medical evacuation operation is prolonged. Each flight crewmember who exceeds the daily 8 hour flight time limitation in this paragraph must be relieved of the HEMES assignment immediately upon the completion of that emergency medical evacuation operation and must be given a rest period in compliance with paragraph (h) of this section.

(d) Each flight crewmember must receive at least 8 consecutive hours of rest during any 24 consecutive hour period of a HEMES assignment. A flight crewmember must be relieved of the HEMES assignment if he or she has not or cannot receive at least 8 consecutive hours of rest during any 24 consecutive hour period of a HEMES assignment.

(e) A HEMES assignment may not exceed 72 consecutive hours at the hospital.

(f) An adequate place of rest must be provided at, or in close proximity to, the hospital at which the HEMES assignment is being performed.

(g) No certificate holder may assign any other duties to a flight crewmember during a HEMES assignment.

(h) Each pilot must be given a rest period upon completion of the HEMES assignment and prior to being assigned any further duty with the certificate holder of—
(1) At least 12 consecutive hours for an assignment of less than 48 hours.
(2) At least 16 consecutive hours for an assignment of more than 48 hours.
(i) The certificate holder must provide each flight crewmember at least 13 rest periods of at least 24 consecutive hours each in each calendar quarter.

135.273 DUTY PERIOD LIMITATIONS AND REST TIME REQUIREMENTS

(a) For purposes of this section—
Calendar day means the period of elapsed time, using Coordinated Universal Time or local time, that begins at midnight and ends 24 hours later at the next midnight.
Duty period means the period of elapsed time between reporting for an assignment involving flight time and release from that assignment by the certificate holder. The time is calculated using either Coordinated Universal Time or local time to reflect the total elapsed time.
Flight attendant means an individual, other than a flight crewmember, who is assigned by the certificate holder, in accordance with the required minimum crew complement under the certificate holder's operations specifications or in addition to that minimum complement, to duty in an aircraft during flight time and whose duties include but are not necessarily limited to cabin safety-related responsibilities.
Rest period means the period free of all responsibility for work or duty should the occasion arise.

(b) Except as provided in paragraph (c) of this section, a certificate holder may assign a duty period to a flight attendant only when the applicable duty period limitations and rest requirements of this paragraph are met.
(1) Except as provided in paragraphs (b)(4), (b)(5), and (b)(6) of this section, no certificate holder may assign a flight attendant to a scheduled duty period of more than 14 hours.
(2) Except as provided in paragraph (b)(3) of this section, a flight attendant scheduled to a duty period of 14 hours or less as provided under paragraph (b)(1) of this section must be given a scheduled rest period of at least 9 consecutive hours. This rest period must occur between the completion of the scheduled duty period and the commencement of the subsequent duty period.

(3) The rest period required under paragraph (b)(2) of this section may be scheduled or reduced to 8 consecutive hours if the flight attendant is provided a subsequent rest period of at least 10 consecutive hours; this subsequent rest period must be scheduled to begin no later than 24 hours after the beginning of the reduced rest period and must occur between the completion of the scheduled duty period and the com-mencement of the subsequent duty period.

(4) A certificate holder may assign a flight attendant to a scheduled duty period of more than 14 hours, but no more than 16 hours, if the certificate holder has assigned to the flight or flights in that duty period at least one flight attendant in addition to the minimum flight attendant complement required for the flight or flights in that duty period under the certificate holder's operations specifications.

(5) A certificate holder may assign a flight attendant to a scheduled duty period of more than 16 hours, but no more than 18 hours, if the certificate holder has assigned to the flight or flights in that duty period at least two flight attendants in addition to the minimum flight attendant complement required for the flight or flights in that duty period under the certificate holder's operations specifications.

(6) A certificate holder may assign a flight attendant to a scheduled duty period of more than 18 hours, but no more than 20 hours, if the scheduled duty period includes one or more flights that land or take off outside the 48 contiguous states and the District of Columbia, and if the certificate holder has assigned to the flight or flights in that duty period at least three flight attendants in addition to the minimum flight attendant complement required for the flight or flights in that duty period under the certificate holder's operations specifications.

(7) Except as provided in paragraph (b)(8) of this section, a flight attendant scheduled to a duty period of more than 14 hours but no more than 20 hours, as provided in paragraphs (b)(4), (b)(5), and (b)(6) of this section, must be given a scheduled rest period of at least 12 consecutive hours. This rest period must occur between the completion of the scheduled duty period and the commencement of the subsequent duty period.

(8) The rest period required under paragraph (b)(7) of this section may be scheduled or reduced to 10 consecutive hours if the flight attendant is provided a subsequent rest period of at least 14 consecutive hours; this subsequent rest period must be scheduled to begin no later than 24 hours after the beginning of the reduced rest period and must occur between the completion of the scheduled duty period and the commencement of the subsequent duty period.

(9) Notwithstanding paragraphs (b)(4), (b)(5), and (b)(6) of this section, if a certificate holder elects to reduce the rest period to 10 hours as authorized by paragraph (b)(8) of this section, the certificate holder may not schedule a flight attendant for a duty period of more than 14 hours during the 24-hour period commencing after the beginning of the reduced rest period.

(10) No certificate holder may assign a flight attendant any duty period with the certificate holder unless the flight attendant has had at least the mini-mum rest required under this section.

(11) No certificate holder may assign a flight attendant to perform any duty with the certificate holder during any required rest period.

(12) Time spent in transportation, not local in character, that a certificate holder requires of a flight attendant and provides to transport the flight attendant to an airport at which that flight attendant is to serve on a flight as a crewmember, or from an airport at which the flight attendant was relieved from duty to return to the flight attendant's home station, is not considered part of a rest period.

(13) Each certificate holder must relieve each flight attendant engaged in air transportation from all further duty for at least 24 consecutive hours during any 7 consecutive calendar days.

(14) A flight attendant is not considered to be scheduled for duty in excess of duty period limitations if the flights to which the flight attendant is assigned are scheduled and normally terminate within the limitations but due to circumstances beyond the control of the certificate holder (such as adverse weather conditions) are not at the time of departure expected to reach their destination within the scheduled time.

(c) Notwithstanding paragraph (b) of this section, a certificate holder may apply the flight crewmember flight time and duty limitations and rest requirements of this part to flight attendants for all operations conducted under this part provided that—

(1) The certificate holder establishes written procedures that—

    (i) Apply to all flight attendants used in the certificate holder's operation;

(ii) Include the flight crewmember requirements contained in Subpart F of this part, as appropriate to the operation being conducted, except that rest facilities on board the aircraft are not required; and

(iii) Include provisions to add one flight attendant to the minimum flight attendant complement for each flight crewmember who is in excess of the minimum number required in the aircraft type certificate data sheet and who is assigned to the aircraft under the provisions of Subpart F of this part, as applicable.

(iv) Are approved by the Administrator and described or referenced in the certificate holder's operations specifications; and

Ⓐ

(2) Whenever the Administrator finds that revisions are necessary for the continued adequacy of duty period limitation and rest requirement procedures that are required by paragraph (c)(1) of this section and that had been granted final approval, the certificate holder must, after notification by the Administrator, make any changes in the procedures that are found necessary by the Administrator. Within 30 days after the certificate holder receives such notice, it may file a petition to reconsider the notice with the certificate-holding district office. The filing of a petition to reconsider stays the notice, pending decision by the Administrator. However, if the Administrator finds that there is an emergency that requires immediate action in the interest of safety, the Administrator may, upon a statement of the reasons, require a change effective without stay.

Ⓐ *Amend #60 eff 2-26-96.*

INTENTIONALLY

LEFT

BLANK

SUBPART G — CREWMEMBER TESTING REQUIREMENTS

135.291   **APPLICABILITY**

Except as provided in Sec. 135.3, this subpart—

(a) Prescribes the tests and checks required for pilot and flight attendant crewmembers and for the approval of check pilots in operations under this part; and

(b) Permits training center personnel authorized under part 142 of this chapter who meet the requirements of §§135.337 and 135.339 to provide training, testing, and checking under contract or other arrangement to those persons subject to the requirements of this subpart.

135.293   **INITIAL AND RECURRENT PILOT TESTING REQUIREMENTS**

(a) No certificate holder may use a pilot, nor may any person serve as pilot, unless, since the beginning of the 12th calendar month before that service, that pilot has passed a written or oral test, given by the Administrator or an authorized check pilot, on that pilot's knowledge in the following areas—

  (1) The appropriate provisions of Parts 61, 91, and 135 of this chapter and the operations specifications and the manual of the certificate holder;

  (2) For each type of aircraft to be flown by the pilot, the aircraft powerplant, major components and systems, major appliances, performance and operating limitations, standard and emergency operating procedures, and the contents of the approved Aircraft Flight Manual or equivalent, as applicable;

  (3) For each type of aircraft to be flown by the pilot, the method of determining compliance with weight and balance limitations for takeoff, landing and enroute operations;

  (4) Navigation and use of air navigation aids appropriate to the operation or pilot authorization, including, when applicable, instrument approach facilities and procedures;

  (5) Air traffic control procedures, including IFR procedures when applicable;

  (6) Meteorology in general, including the principles of frontal systems, icing, fog, thunderstorms, and windshear, and if appropriate for the operation of the certificate holder, high altitude weather;

(7) Procedures for —

  (i) Recognizing and avoiding severe weather situations;

  (ii) Escaping from severe weather situations, in case of inadvertent encounters, including low-altitude windshear (except that rotorcraft pilots are not required to be tested on escaping from low-altitude windshear); and

  (iii) Operating in or near thunderstorms (including best penetrating altitudes), turbulent air (including clear air turbulence), icing, hail, and other potentially hazardous meteorological conditions; and

(8) New equipment, procedures, or techniques, as appropriate.

(b) No certificate holder may use a pilot, nor may any person serve as pilot, in any aircraft unless, since the beginning of the 12th calendar month before that service, that pilot has passed a competency check given by the Administrator or an authorized check pilot in that class of aircraft, if single-engine airplane other than turbojet, or that type of aircraft, if helicopter, multiengine airplane, or turbojet airplane, to determine the pilot's competence in practical skills and techniques in that aircraft or class of aircraft. The extent of the competency check shall be determined by the Administrator or authorized check pilot conducting the competency check. The competency check may include any of the maneuvers and the procedures currently required for the original issuance of the particular pilot certificate required for the operations authorized and appropriate to the category, class and type of aircraft involved. For the purposes of this paragraph, type, as to an airplane, means any one of a group of airplanes determined by the Administrator to have a similar means of propulsion, the same manufacturer, and no significantly different handling or flight characteristics. For the purposes of this paragraph, type, as to a helicopter, means a basic make and model.

(c) The instrument proficiency check required by §135.297 may be substituted for the competency check required by this section for the type of aircraft used in the check.

Ⓐ *Amend #63 eff 8-1-96.*

(d) For the purposes of this part, competent performance of a procedure or maneuver by a person to be used as a pilot requires that the pilot be the obvious master of the aircraft, with the successful outcome of the maneuver never in doubt.

(e) The Administrator or authorized check pilot certifies the competency of each pilot who passes the knowledge or flight check in the certificate holder's pilot records.

(f) Portions of a required competency check may be given in an aircraft simulator or other appropriate training device, if approved by the Administrator.

135.295 INITIAL AND RECURRENT FLIGHT ATTENDANT CREWMEMBER TESTING REQUIREMENTS

No certificate holder may use a flight attendant crewmembers, nor may any person serve as a flight attendant crewmember unless, since the beginning of the 12th calendar month before that service, the certificate holder has determined by appropriate initial and recurrent testing that the person is knowledgeable and competent in the following areas as appropriate to assigned duties and responsibilities—

(a) Authority of the pilot in command;

(b) Passenger handling, including procedures to be followed in handling deranged persons or other persons whose conduct might jeopardize safety;

(c) Crewmember assignments, functions, and responsibilities during ditching and evacuation of persons who may need the assistance of another person to move expeditiously to an exit in an emergency;

(d) Briefing of passengers;

(e) Location and operation of portable fire extinguishers and other items of emergency equipment;

(f) Proper use of cabin equipment and controls;

(g) Location and operation of passenger oxygen equipment;

(h) Location and operation of all normal and emergency exits, including evacuation chutes and escape ropes; and

(i) Seating of persons who may need assistance of another person to move rapidly to an exit in an emergency as prescribed by the certificate holder's operations manual.

135.297 PILOT IN COMMAND: INSTRUMENT PROFICIENCY CHECK REQUIRE- MENTS

(a) No certificate holder may use a pilot, nor may any person serve, as a pilot in command of an aircraft under IFR unless, since the beginning of the sixth calendar month before that service, that pilot has passed an instrument proficiency check under this section administered by the Administrator or an authorized check pilot.

(b) No pilot may use any type of precision instrument approach procedure under IFR unless, since the beginning of the sixth calendar month before that use, the pilot has satisfactorily demonstrated that type of approach procedure. No pilot may use any type of nonprecision approach procedure under IFR unless, since the beginning of the sixth calendar month before that use, the pilot has satisfactorily demonstrated either that type approach procedure or any other two different types of nonprecision approach procedures. The instrument approach procedure or procedures must include at least one straight-in approach, one circling approach, and one missed approach. Each type of approach procedure demonstrated must be conducted to published minimums for that procedure.

(c) The instrument proficiency check required by paragraph (a) of this section consists of an oral or written equipment test and a flight check under simulated or actual IFR conditions. The equipment test includes questions on emergency procedures, engine operation, fuel and lubrication systems, power settings, stall speeds, best engine-out speed, propeller and supercharger operations, and hydraulic, mechanical, and electrical systems, as appropriate. The flight check includes navigation by instruments, recovery from simulated emergencies, and standard instrument approaches involving navigational facilities which that pilot is to be authorized to use. Each pilot taking the instrument proficiency check must show that standard of competence required by §135.293(d).

    (1)   The instrument proficiency check must—
       (i)   For a pilot in command of an airplane under §135.243(a), include the procedures and maneuvers for an airline transport pilot certificate in the particular type of airplane, if appropriate; and
       (ii)   For a pilot in command of an airplane or helicopter under §135.243(c), include the procedures and maneuvers for a commercial pilot certificate with an instrument rating and, if required, for the appropriate type rating.
    (2)   The instrument proficiency check must be given by an authorized check airman or by the Administrator.
(d)   If the pilot in command is assigned to pilot only one type of aircraft, that pilot must take the instrument proficiency check required by paragraph (a) of this section in that type of aircraft.
(e)   If the pilot in command is assigned to pilot more than one type of aircraft, that pilot must take the instrument proficiency check required by paragraph (a) of this section in each type of aircraft to which that pilot is assigned, in rotation, but not more than one flight check during each period described in paragraph (a) of this section.
(f)   If the pilot in command is assigned to pilot both single-engine and multiengine aircraft, that pilot must initially take the instrument proficiency check required by paragraph (a) of this section in a multiengine aircraft, and each succeeding check alternately in single-engine and multiengine aircraft, but not more than one flight check during each period described in paragraph (a) of this section. Portions of a required flight check may be given in an aircraft simulator or other appropriate training device, if approved by the Administrator.
(g)   If the pilot in command is authorized to use an autopilot system in place of a second in command, that pilot must show, during the required instrument proficiency check, that the pilot is able (without a second in command) both with and without using the autopilot to—
    (1)   Conduct instrument operations competently; and
    (2)   Properly conduct air-ground communications and comply with complex air traffic control instructions.
    (3)   Each pilot taking the autopilot check must show that, while using the autopilot, the airplane can be operated as proficiently as it would be if a second in command were present to handle air-ground communications and air traffic control instructions. The autopilot check need only be demonstrated once every 12 calendar months during the instrument proficiency check required under paragraph (a) of this section.

135.299   PILOT IN COMMAND: LINE CHECKS: ROUTES AND AIRPORTS

(a)   No certificate holder may use a pilot, nor may any person serve, as a pilot in command of a flight unless, since the beginning of the 12th calendar month before that service, that pilot has passed a flight check in one of the types of aircraft which that pilot is to fly. The flight check shall—
    (1)   Be given by an approved check pilot or by the Administrator;
    (2)   Consist of at least one flight over one route segment; and
    (3)   Include takeoffs and landings at one or more representative airports. In addition to the requirements of this paragraph, for a pilot authorized to conduct IFR operations, at least one flight shall be flown over a civil airway, an approved off-airway route, or a portion of either of them.
(b)   The pilot who conducts the check shall determine whether the pilot being checked satisfactorily performs the duties and responsibilities of a pilot in command in operations under this part, and shall so certify in the pilot training record.
(c)   Each certificate holder shall establish in the manual required by §135.21 a procedure which will ensure that each pilot who has not flown over a route and into an airport within the preceding 90 days will, before beginning the flight become familiar with all available information required for the safe operation of that flight.

135.301 CREWMEMBER: TESTS AND CHECKS, GRACE PROVISIONS, TRAINING TO ACCEPTED STANDARDS

(a) If a crewmember who is required to take a test or a flight check under this part, completes the test or flight check in the calendar month before or after the calendar month in which it is required, that crewmember is considered to have completed the test or check in the calendar month in which it is required.

(b) If a pilot being checked under this subpart fails any of the required maneuvers, the person giving the check may give additional training to the pilot during the course of the check. In addition to repeating the maneuvers failed, the person giving the check may require the pilot being checked to repeat any other maneuvers that are necessary to determine the pilot's proficiency. If the pilot being checked is unable to demonstrate satisfactory performance to the person conducting the check, the certificate holder may not use the pilot, nor may the pilot serve, as a flight crewmember in operations under this part until the pilot has satisfactorily completed the check.

Amend #44
eff 10-15-92

SUBPART H — TRAINING

135.321 APPLICABILITY AND TERMS USED

(a) Except as provided in §135.3, this subpart prescribes the requirements applicable to—

(1) A certificate holder under this part which contracts with, or otherwise arranges to use the services of a training center certificated under part 142 to perform training, testing, and checking functions;

A
(2) Each certificate holder for establishing and maintaining an approved training program for crewmembers, check airmen and instructors, and other operations personnel employed or used by that certificate holder; and

(3) Each certificate holder for the qualification, approval, and use of aircraft simulators and flight training devices in the conduct of the program.

(b) For the purposes of this subpart, the following terms and definitions apply:

(1) *Initial training.* The training required for crewmembers who have not qualified and served in the same capacity on an aircraft.

(2) *Transition training.* The training required for crewmembers who have qualified and served in the same capacity on another aircraft.

(3) *Upgrade training.* The training required for crewmembers who have qualified and served as second in command on a particular aircraft type, before they serve as pilot in command on that aircraft.

(4) *Differences training.* The training required for crewmembers who have qualified and served on a particular type aircraft, when the Administrator finds differences training is necessary before a crewmember serves in the same capacity on a particular variation of that aircraft.

(5) *Recurrent training.* The training required for crewmembers to remain adequately trained and currently proficient for each aircraft crewmember position, and type of operation in which the crewmember serves.

(6) *In flight.* The maneuvers, procedures, or functions that must be conducted in the aircraft.

(7) *Training center.* An organization governed by the applicable requirements of part 142 of this chapter that provides training, testing, and checking under contract or other arrangement to certificate holders subject to the requirements of this part.

A
(8) *Requalification training.* The training required for crewmembers previously trained and qualified, but who have become unqualified due to not having met within the required period the—

(i) Recurrent pilot testing requirements of §135.293;

(ii) Instrument proficiency check requirements of §135.297; or

(iii) Line checks required by §135.299.

135.323 TRAINING PROGRAM: GENERAL

(a) Each certificate holder required to have a training program under §135.341 shall:

(1) Establish, obtain the appropriate initial and final approval of, and provide a training program that meets this subpart and that ensures that each crewmember, flight instructor, check airman, and each person assigned duties for the carriage and handling of hazardous materials (as defined in 49 CFR 171.8) is adequately trained to perform their assigned duties.

(2) Provide adequate ground and flight training facilities and properly qualified ground instructors for the training required by this subpart.

(3) Provide and keep current for each aircraft type used and, if applicable, the particular variations within the aircraft type, appropriate training material, examinations, forms, instructions, and procedures for use in conducting the training and checks required by this subpart.

(4) Provide enough flight instructors, check airmen, and simulator instructors to conduct required flight training and flight checks, and simulator training courses allowed under this subpart.

(b) Whenever a crewmember who is required to take recurrent training under this subpart completes the training in the calendar month before, or the calendar month after, the month in which that training is required, the crewmember is considered to have completed it in the calendar month in which it was required.

(c) Each instructor, supervisor, or check airman who is responsible for a particular ground training subject, segment of flight training, course of training, flight check, or competence check under this part shall certify as to the proficiency and knowledge of the crewmember, flight instructor, or check airman concerned upon completion of that training or check. The certification shall be made a part of the crewmember's record. When the certification required by this paragraph is made by an entry in a computerized recordkeeping system, the certifying instructor, supervisor, or check airman, must be identified with that entry. However, the signature of the certifying instructor, supervisor, or check airman, is not required for computerized entries.

(d) Training subjects that apply to more than one aircraft or crewmember position and that have been satisfactorily completed during previous training while employed by the certificate holder for another aircraft or another crewmember position, need not be repeated during subsequent training other than recurrent training.

(e) Aircraft simulators and other training devices may be used in the certificate holder's training program if approved by the Administrator.

A *Amend #63 eff 8-1-96*

135.324 TRAINING PROGRAM: SPECIAL RULE

(a) Other than the certificate holder, only another certificate holder certificated under this part or a training center certificated under part 142 of this chapter is eligible under this subpart to provide training, testing, and checking under contract or other arrangement to those persons subject to the requirements of this subpart.

(b) A certificate holder may contract with, or otherwise arrange to use the services of, a training center certificated under part 142 of this chapter to provide training, testing, and checking required by this part only if the training center—

(1) Holds applicable training specifications issued under part 142 of this chapter;

(2) Has facilities, training equipment, and courseware meeting the applicable requirements of part 142 of this chapter;

(3) Has approved curriculums, curriculum segments, and portions of curriculum segments applicable for use in training courses required by this subpart; and

(4) Has sufficient instructor and check airmen qualified under the applicable requirements of §§135.337 or 135.339 to provide training, testing, and checking to persons subject to the requirements of this subpart.

135.325 TRAINING PROGRAM AND REVISION: INITIAL AND FINAL APPROVAL

(a) To obtain initial and final approval of a training program, or a revision to an approved training program, each certificate holder must submit to the Administrator—

(1) An outline of the proposed or revised curriculum, that provides enough information for a preliminary evaluation of the proposed training program or revision; and

(2) Additional relevant information that may be requested by the Administrator.

(b) If the proposed training program or revision complies with this subpart, the Administrator grants initial approval in writing after which the certificate holder may conduct the training under that program. The Administrator then evaluates the effectiveness of the training program and advises the certificate holder of deficiencies, if any, that must be corrected.

(c) The Administrator grants final approval of the proposed training program or revision if the certificate holder shows that the training conducted under the initial approval in paragraph (b) of this section ensures that each person who successfully completes the training is adequately trained to perform that person's assigned duties.

(d) Whenever the Administrator finds that revisions are necessary for the continued adequacy of a training program that has been granted final approval, the certificate holder shall, after notification by the Administrator,

make any changes in the program that are found necessary by the Administrator. Within 30 days after the certificate holder receives the notice, it may file a petition to reconsider the notice with the Administrator. The filing of a petition to reconsider stays the notice pending a decision by the Administrator. However, if the Administrator finds that there is an emergency that requires immediate action in the interest of safety, the Administrator may, upon a statement of the reasons, require a change effective without stay.

135.327 TRAINING PROGRAM: CURRICULUM

(a) Each certificate holder must prepare and keep current a written training program curriculum for each type of aircraft for each crewmember required for that type aircraft. The curriculum must include ground and flight training required by this subpart.

(b) Each training program curriculum must include the following:

(1) A list of principal ground training subjects, including emergency training subjects, that are provided.

(2) A list of all the training devices, mockups, systems trainers, procedures trainers, or other training aids that the certificate holder will use.

(3) Detailed descriptions or pictorial displays of the approved normal, abnormal, and emergency maneuvers, procedures and functions that will be performed during each flight training phase or flight check, indicating those maneuvers, procedures and functions that are to be performed during the inflight portions of flight training and flight checks.

135.329 CREWMEMBER TRAINING REQUIREMENTS

(a) Each certificate holder must include in its training program the following initial and transition ground training as appropriate to the particular assignment of the crewmember:

(1) Basic indoctrination ground training for newly hired crewmembers including instruction in at least the—

(i) Duties and responsibilities of crewmembers as applicable;

(ii) Appropriate provisions of this chapter;

(iii) Contents of the certificate holder's operating certificate and operations specifications (not required for flight attendants); and

(iv) Appropriate portions of the certificate holder's operating manual.

(2) The initial and transition ground training in §§135.345 and 135.349, as applicable.

(3) Emergency training in §135.331

(b) Each training program must provide the initial and transition flight training in §135.347, as applicable.

(c) Each training program must provide recurrent ground and flight training in §135.351.

Ⓐ *Amend #63 eff 8-1-96*

(d) Upgrade training in §§135.345 and 135.347 for a particular type aircraft may be included in the training program for crewmembers who have qualified and served as second in command on that aircraft.

(e) In addition to initial, transition, upgrade and recurrent training, each training program must provide ground and flight training, instruction, and practice necessary to ensure that each crewmember—

(1) Remains adequately trained and currently proficient for each aircraft, crewmember position, and type of operation in which the crewmember serves; and

(2) Qualifies in new equipment, facilities, procedures, and techniques, including modifications to aircraft.

135.331 CREWMEMBER EMERGENCY TRAINING

(a) Each training program must provide emergency training under this section for each aircraft type, model, and configuration, each crewmember, and each kind of operation conducted, as appropriate for each crewmember and the certificate holder.

(b) Emergency training must provide the following:

(1) Instruction in emergency assignments and procedures, including coordination among crewmembers.

(2) Individual instruction in the location, function, and operation of emergency equipment including—

(i) Equipment used in ditching and evacuation;

(ii) First aid equipment and its proper use; and

(iii) Portable fire extinguishers, with emphasis on the type of extinguisher to be used on different classes of fires.

(3) Instruction in the handling of emergency situations including—

(i) Rapid decompression;

(ii) Fire in flight or on the surface and smoke control procedures with emphasis on electrical equipment and related circuit breakers found in cabin areas;

(iii) Ditching and evacuation;

(iv) Illness, injury, or other abnormal situations involving passengers or crewmembers; and

(v) Hijacking and other unusual situations.

(4) Review of the certificate holder's previous aircraft accidents and incidents involving actual emergency situations.

(c) Each crewmember must perform at least the following emergency drills, using the proper emergency equipment and procedures, unless the Administrator finds that, for a particular drill, the crewmember can be adequately trained by demonstration:

(1) Ditching, if applicable.

(2) Emergency evacuation.

(3) Fire extinguishing and smoke control.

(4) Operation and use of emergency exits, including deployment and use of evacuation chutes, if applicable.

(5) Use of crew and passenger oxygen.

(6) Removal of life rafts from the aircraft, inflation of the life rafts, use of life lines, and boarding of passengers and crew, if applicable.

(7) Donning and inflation of life vests and the use of other individual flotation devices, if applicable.

(d) Crewmembers who serve in operations above 25,000 feet must receive instruction in the following:

(1) Respiration.

(2) Hypoxia.

(3) Duration of consciousness without supplemental oxygen at altitude.

(4) Gas expansion.

(5) Gas bubble formation.

(6) Physical phenomena and incidents of decompression.

135.333 TRAINING REQUIREMENTS: HANDLING AND CARRIAGE OF HAZARDOUS MATERIALS

(a) Except as provided in paragraph (d) of this section, no certificate holder may use any person to perform, and no person may perform, any assigned duties and responsibilities for the handling or carriage of hazardous materials (as defined in *49 CFR 171.8), unless within the preceding 12 calendar months that person has satisfactorily completed initial or recurrent training in an appropriate training program established by the certificate holder, which includes instruction regarding—

(1) The proper shipper certification, packaging, marking, labeling, and documentation for hazardous materials; and

(2) The compatibility, loading, storage, and handling characteristics of hazardous materials.

(b) Each certificate holder shall maintain a record of the satisfactory completion of the initial and recurrent training given to crewmembers and ground personnel who perform assigned duties and responsibilities for the handling and carriage of hazardous materials.

(c) Each certificate holder that elects not to accept hazardous materials shall ensure that each crewmember is adequately trained to recognize those items classified as hazardous materials.

(d) If a certificate holder operates into or out of airports at which trained employees or contract personnel are not available, it may use persons not meeting the requirements of paragraphs (a) and (b) of this section to load, offload, or otherwise handle hazardous materials if these persons are supervised by a crewmember who is qualified under paragraphs (a) and (b) of this section.

135.335 APPROVAL OF AIRCRAFT SIMULATORS AND OTHER TRAINING DEVICES

(a) Training courses using aircraft simulators and other training devices may be included in the certificate holder's training program if approved by the Administrator.

(b) Each aircraft simulator and other training device that is used in a training course or in checks required under this subpart must meet the following requirements:

(1) It must be specifically approved for—
   (i) The certificate holder; and
   (ii) The particular maneuver, procedure, or crewmember function involved.

(2) It must maintain the performance, functional and other characteristics that are required for approval.

(3) Additionally, for aircraft simulators, it must be—
   (i) Approved for the type aircraft and, if applicable, the particular variation within type for which the training or check is being conducted; and
   (ii) Modified to conform with any modification to the aircraft being simulated that changes the performance, functional, or other characteristics required for approval.

(c) A particular aircraft simulator or other training device may be used by more than one certificate holder.

(d) In granting initial and final approval of training programs or revisions to them, the Administrator considers the training devices, methods, and procedures listed in the certificate holder's curriculum under §135.327.

135.337 QUALIFICATIONS: CHECK AIRMEN (AIRCRAFT) AND CHECK AIRMEN (SIMULATOR)

(a) For the purposes of this section and §135.339:

(1) A check airman (aircraft) is a person who is qualified to conduct flight checks in an aircraft, in a flight simulator, or in a flight training device for a particular type aircraft.

(2) A check airman (simulator) is a person who is qualified to conduct flight checks, but only in a flight simulator, in a flight training device, or both, for a particular type aircraft.

(3) Check airmen (aircraft) and check airmen (simulator) are those check airmen who perform the functions described in §§135.321 and 135.323(a)(4) and (c).

(b) No certificate holder may use a person, nor may any person serve as a check airman (aircraft) in a training program established under this subpart unless, with respecxt to the aircraft type involved, that person—

(1) Holds the airman certificates and ratings required to serve as a pilot in command in operations under this part;

(2) Has satisfactorily completed the training phases for the aircraft, including recurrent training, that are required to serve as a pilot in command in operations under this part;

(3) Has satisfactorily completed the proficiency or competency checks required to serve as a pilot in command in operations under this part;

(4) Has satisfactorily completed the applicable training requirements of §135.339;

(5) Holds a Class III medical certificate unless serving as a required crewmember, in which case holds a Class I or Class II medical certificate as appropriate;

(6) Has satisfied the recency of experience requirements of §135.247; and

(7) Has been approved by the Administrator for the check airman duties involved; and

(c) No certificate holder may use a person, nor may any person serve as a check airman (simulator) in a training program established under this subpart unless, with respect to the aircraft type involved, that person meets the provisions of paragraph (b) of this section, or —

(1) Holds the applicable airman certificates and ratings, except medical certificate, required to serve as a pilot in command in operations under this part;

(2) Has satisfactorily completed the appropriate training phases for the aircraft, including recurrent training, that are required to serve as a pilot in command in operations under this part;

(3) Has satisfactorily completed the appropriate proficiency or competency checks that are required to serve as a pilot in command in operations under this part;

(4) Has satisfactorily completed the applicable training requirements of §135.339; and

(5) Has been approved by the Administrator for the check airman (simulator) duties involved.

(d) Completion of the requirements in paragraphs (b)(2), (3), and (4) or (c)(2), (3), and (4) of this section, as applicable, shall be entered in the individual's training record maintained by the certificate holder.

(e) An airman who does not hold a medical certificate may function as flight instructor in an aircraft if functioning as a non-required crewmember, but may not serve as flightcrew members in operations under this part.

A *Amend #63 eff 8-1-96*

(f) A flight instructor (simulator) must accomplish the following —
  (1) Fly at least two flight segments as a required crewmember for the type, class, or category aircraft involved within the 12-month period preceding the performance of any flight instructor duty in a flight simulator; or
  (2) Satisfactorily complete an approved line-observation program within the period prescribed by that program and that must precede the performance of any check airman duty in a flight simulator.

(g) The flight segments or line-observation program required in paragraph (f) of this section are considered to be completed in the month required if completed in the calendar month before or the calendar month after the month in which they are due.

135.338 QUALIFICATIONS: FLIGHT INSTRUCTORS (AIRCRAFT) AND FLIGHT INSTRUCTORS (SIMULATOR)

(a) For the purposes of this section and §135.339:
  (1) A flight instructor (aircraft) is a person who is qualified to conduct flight checks in an aircraft, in a flight simulator, or in a flight training device for a particular type aircraft.
  (2) A flight instructor (simulator) is a person who is qualified to conduct flight checks, but only in a flight simulator, in a flight training device, or both, for a particular type aircraft.
  (3) Flight instructors (aircraft) and flight instructors (simulator) are those instructors who perform the functions described in §§135.321 and 135.323(a)(4) and (c).

(b) No certificate holder may use a person, nor may any person serve as a flight instructor (aircraft) in a training program established under this subpart unless, with respect to the type, class, or category aircraft involved, that person—
  (1) Holds the airman certificates and ratings required to serve as a pilot in command in operations under this part;
  (2) Has satisfactorily completed the training phases for the aircraft, including recurrent training, that are required to serve as a pilot in command in operations under this part;
  (3) Has satisfactorily completed the proficiency or competency checks required to serve as a pilot in command in operations under this part;
  (4) Has satisfactorily completed the applicable training requirements of §135.340;
  (5) Holds a Class III medical certificate; and
  (6) Has satisfied the recency of experience requirements of §135.247.

(c) No certificate holder may use a person, nor may any person serve as a flight instructor (simulator) in a training program established under this subpart unless, with respect to the type, class, or category aircraft involved, that person meets the provisions of paragraph (b) of this section, or —
  (1) Holds the applicable airman certificates and ratings, except medical certificate, required to serve as a pilot in command in operations under this part, except before February 19, 1997 that person need not hold a type rating for the type, class, or category of aircraft involved.
  (2) Has satisfactorily completed the appropriate training phases for the aircraft, including recurrent training, that are required to serve as a pilot in command in operations under this part;
  (3) Has satisfactorily completed the appropriate proficiency or competency checks that are required to serve as a pilot in command in operations under this part; and
  (4) Has satisfactorily completed the applicable training requirements of §135.340.

(d) Completion of the requirements in paragraphs (b)(2), (3), and (4) or (c)(2), (3), and (4) of this section, as applicable, shall be entered in the individual's training record maintained by the certificate holder.

(e) An airman who does not hold a medical certificate may function as a flight instructor in an aircraft if functioning as a non-required crewmember, but may not serve as flightcrew member in operations under this part.

(f) A flight instructor (simulator) must accomplish the following —
  (1) Fly at least two flight segments as a required crewmember for the type, class, or category aircraft involved within the 12-month period preceding the performance of any flight instructor duty in a flight simulator; or
  (2) Satisfactorily complete an approved line-observation program within the period prescribed by that program and that must precede the performance of any check airman duty in a flight simulator.

(g) The flight segments or line-observation program required in paragraph (f) of this section are considered completed in the month required if completed in the calendar month before, or in the calendar month after the month in which they are due.

135.339 INITIAL AND TRANSITION TRAINING AND CHECKING: CHECK AIRMEN (AIRCRAFT), CHECK AIRMEN (SIMULATOR)

(a) No certificate holder may use a person, nor may any person serve as a check airman unless —

(1) That person has satisfactorily completed initial or transition check airman training; and

(2) Within the preceding 24 calendar months, that person satisfactorily conducts a proficiency or competency check under the observation of an FAA inspector or an aircrew designated examiner employed by the operator. The observation check may be accomplished in part or in full in an aircraft, in a flight simulator, or in a flight training device. This paragraph applies after February 19, 1997.

(b) The observation check required by paragraph (a)(2) of this section is considered to have been completed in the month required if completed in the calendar month before or the calendar month after the month in which it is due.

(c) The initial ground training for check airmen must include the following:

(1) Check airman duties, functions, and responsibilities.

(2) The applicable Code of Federal Regulations and the certificate holder's policies and procedures.

(3) The applicable methods, procedures, and techniques for conducting the required checks.

(4) Proper evaluation of pilot performance including the detection of —

(i) Improper and insufficient training; and

(ii) Personal characteristics that could adversely affect safety.

(5) The corrective action in the case of unsatisfactory checks.

(6) The approved methods, procedures, and limitations for performing the required normal, abnormal, and emergency procedures in the aircraft.

(d) The transition ground training for check airmen must include the approved methods, procedures, and limitations for performing the required normal, abnormal, and emergency procedures applicable to the aircraft to which the check airman is in transition.

(e) The initial and transition flight training for check airmen (aircraft) must include the following:

(1) The safety measures for emergency situations that are likely to develop during a check;

(2) The potential results of improper, untimely, or nonexecution of safety measures during a check;

(3) Training and practice in conducting flight checks from the left and right pilot seats in the required normal, abnormal, and emergency procedures to ensure competence to conduct the pilot flight checks required by this part; and

(4) The safety measures to be taken from either pilot seat for emergency situations that are likely to develop during checking.

(f) The requirements of paragraph (e) of this section may be accomplished in flight or in full or in part in flight, in a flight simulator, or in a flight training device, as appropriate.

(g) The initial and transition flight training for check airmen (simulator) must include the following:

(1) Training and practice in conducting flight checks in the required normal, abnormal, and emergency procedures to ensure competence to conduct the flight checks required by this part. This training and practice must be accomplished in a flight simulator or in a flight training device.

(2) Training in the operation of flight simulators, flight training devices, or both, to ensure competence to conduct the flight checks required by this part.

135.340 INITIAL AND TRANSITION TRAINING AND CHECKING: FLIGHT INSTRUCTORS (AIRCRAFT), FLIGHT INSTRUCTORS (SIMULATOR)

(a) No certificate holder may use a person, nor may any person serve as a flight instructor unless —

(1) That person has satisfactorily completed initial or transition flight instructor training; and

(2) Within the preceding 24 calendar months, that person satisfactorily conducts instruction under the observation of an FAA inspector, an operator check airman, or aircrew designated examiner employed by the operator. The observation check may be accomplished in part or in full in an aircraft, in a flight simulator, or in a flight training device. This paragraph applies after February 19, 1997.

(b) The observation check required by paragraph (a)(2) of this section is considered to have been completed in the month required if completed in the calendar month before or the calendar month after, the month in which it is due.

(c) The initial ground training for flight instructors must include the following:

(1) Flight instructor duties, functions, and responsibilities.

(2) The applicable Code of Federal Regulations and the certificate holder's policies and procedures.

(3) The applicable methods, procedures, and techniques for conducting flight instruction.

(4) Proper evaluation of student performance including the detection of —

(i) Improper and insufficient training; and

(ii) Personal characteristics that could adversely affect safety.

(5) The corrective action in the case of unsatisfactory training progress.

(6) The approved methods, procedures, and limitations for performing the required normal, abnormal, and emergency procedures in the aircraft.

Ⓐ *Amend #64 eff 6-17-96*

(7) Except for holders of a flight instructor certificate —
   (i) The fundamental principles of the teaching-learning process:
   (ii) Teaching methods and procedures: and
   (iii) The instructor-student relationship.

(d) The transition ground training for flight instructors must include the approved methods, procedures, and limitations for performing the required normal, abnormal, and emergency procedures applicable to the type, class, or category aircraft to which the flight instructor is in transition.

(e) The initial and transition flight training for flight instructors (aircraft) must include the following —
   (1) The safety measures for emergency situations that are likely to develop during instruction;
   (2) The potential results of improper or untimely safety measures during instruction;
   (3) Training and practice from the left and right pilot seats in the required normal, abnormal, and emergency maneuvers to ensure competence to conduct the flight instruction required by this part; and
   (4) The safety measures to be taken from the left or right pilot seat for emergency situations that are likely to develop during instruction.

(f) The requirements of paragraph (e) of this section may be accomplished in full or in part in flight, in a flight simulator, or in a flight training device, as appropriate.

(g) The initial and transition flight training for a flight instructor (simulator) must include the following:
   (1) Training and practice in the required normal, abnormal, and emergency procedures to ensure competence to conduct the flight instruction required by this part. These maneuvers and procedures must be accomplished in full or in part in a flight simulator or in a flight training device.
   (2) Training in the operation of flight simulators, flight training devices, or both, to ensure competence to conduct the flight instruction required by this part.

135.341 PILOT AND FLIGHT ATTENDANT CREWMEMBER TRAINING PROGRAMS

(a) Each certificate holder, other than one who uses only one pilot in the certificate holder's operation, shall establish and maintain an approved pilot training program, and each certificate holder who uses a flight attendant crewmember shall establish and maintain an approved flight attendant training program, that is appropriate to the operations to which each pilot and flight attendant is to be

assigned, and will ensure that they are adequately trained to meet the applicable knowledge and practical testing requirements of §§135.293 through 135.301. However, the Administrator may authorize a deviation from this section if the Administrator finds that, because of the limited size and scope of the operation, safety will allow a deviation from these requirements.

(b) Each certificate holder required to have a training program by paragraph (a) of this section shall include in that program ground and flight training curriculums for —
   (1) Initial training;
   (2) Transition training;
   (3) Upgrade training;
   (4) Differences training; and
   (5) Recurrent training.

(c) Each certificate holder required to have a training program by paragraph (a) of this section shall provide current and appropriate study materials for use by each required pilot and flight attendant.

(d) The certificate holder shall furnish copies of the pilot and flight attendant crewmember training program, and all changes and additions, to the assigned representative of the Administrator. If the certificate holder uses training facilities of other persons, a copy of those training programs or appropriate portions used for those facilities shall also be funished. Curricula that follow FAA published curricula may be cited by reference in the copy of the training program furnished to the representative of the Administrator and need not be furnished with the program.

135.343 CREWMEMBER INITIAL AND RECURRENT TRAINING REQUIRE- MENTS

No certificate holder may use a person, nor may any person serve, as a crewmember in operations under this part unless that crewmember has completed the appropriate initial or recurrent training phase of the training program appropriate to the type of operation in which the crewmember is to serve since the beginning of the 12th calendar month before that service. This section does not apply to a certificate holder who uses only one pilot in the certificate holder's operation.

135.345 PILOTS: INITIAL, TRANSITIONS, AND UPGRADE GROUND TRAINING

Initial, transition, and upgrade ground training for pilots must include instruction in at least the following, as applicable to their duties:
(a) General subjects —
   (1) The certificate holder's flight locating procedures;
   (2) Principles and methods for determining weight and balance, and runway limitations for takeoff and landing;
   (3) Enough meteorology to ensure a practical knowledge of weather phenomena, including the principles of frontal systems, icing, fog,

Ⓐ *Amend #64 eff 6-17-96*

thunderstorms, windshear and, if appropriate, high altitude weather situations;

(4) Air traffic control systems, procedures, and phraseology;

(5) Navigation and the use of navigational aids, including instrument approach procedures;

(6) Normal and emergency communication procedures;

(7) Visual cues before and during descent below DH or MDA; and

(8) Other instructions necessary to ensure the pilot's competence.

(b) For each aircraft type —

(1) A general description;

(2) Performance characteristics;

(3) Engines and propellers;

(4) Major components;

(5) Major aircraft systems (i.e., flight controls, electrical, and hydraulic,) other systems, as appropriate, principles of normal, abnormal, and emergency operations, appropriate procedures and limitations;

(6) Knowledge and procedures for —

(i) Recognizing and avoiding severe weather situations;

(ii) Escaping from severe weather situations, in case of inadvertent encounters, including low-altitude windshear (except that rotorcraft pilots are not required to be trained in escaping from low-altitude windshear);

(iii) Operating in or near thunderstorms (including best penetrating altitudes), turbulent air (including clear air turbulence), icing, hail, and other potentially hazardous meteorological conditions; and

(iv) Operating airplanes during ground icing conditions, (i.e., any time conditions are such that frost, ice, or snow may reasonably be expected to adhere to the airplane), if the certificate holder expects to authorize takeoffs in ground icing conditions, including:

(A) The use of holdover times when using deicing/anti-icing fluids;

(B) Airplane deicing/anti-icing procedures, including inspection and check procedures and responsibilities;

(C) Communications;

(D) Airplane surface contamination (i.e., adherence of frost, ice, or snow) and critical area identification, and knowledge of how contamination adversely affects airplane performance and flight characteristics;

(E) Types and characteristics of deicing/anti-icing fluids, if used by the certificate holder;

(F) Cold weather preflight inspection procedures;

(G) Techniques for recognizing contamination on the airplane;

(7) Operating limitations;

(8) Fuel consumption and cruise control;

(9) Flight planning;

(10) Each normal and emergency procedure; and

(11) The approved Aircraft Flight Manual, or equivalent.

135.347 PILOTS: INITIAL, TRANSITION, UPGRADE, AND DIFFERENCES FLIGHT TRAINING

(a) Initial, transition, upgrade, and differences training for pilots must include flight and practice in each of the maneuvers and procedures in the approved training program curriculum.

(b) The maneuvers and procedures required by paragraph (a) of this section must be performed in flight, except to the extent that certain maneuvers and procedures may be performed in an aircraft simulator, or an appropriate training device, as allowed by this subpart.

(c) If the certificate holder's approved training program includes a course of training using an aircraft simulator or other training device, each pilot must successfully complete —

(1) Training and practice in the simulator or training device in at least the maneuvers and procedures in this subpart that are capable of being performed in the aircraft simulator or training device; and

(2) A flight check in the aircraft or a check in the simulator or training device to the level of proficiency of a pilot in command or second in command, as applicable, in at least the maneuvers and procedures that are capable of being performed in an aircraft simulator or training device.

135.349 FLIGHT ATTENDANTS: INITIAL AND TRANSITION GROUND TRAINING

Initial and transition ground training for flight attendants must include instruction in at least the following —

(a) General subjects —

(1) The authority of the pilot in command; and

(2) Passenger handling, including procedures to be followed in handling deranged persons or other persons whose conduct might jeopardize safety.

(b) For each aircraft type —

(1) A general description of the aircraft emphasizing physical characteristics that may have a bearing on ditching, evacuation, and inflight emergency procedures and on other related duties;

(2) The use of both the public address system and the means of communicating with other flight crewmembers, including emergency means in the case of attempted hijacking or other unusual situations; and

(3) Proper use of electrical galley equipment and the controls for cabin heat and ventilation.

Ⓐ *Amend #64 eff 6-17-96*

135.351 RECURRENT TRAINING

(a) Each certificate holder must ensure that each crewmember receives recurrent training and is adequately trained and currently proficient for the type aircraft and crewmember position involved.

(b) Recurrent ground training for crewmembers must include at least the following:

   (1) A quiz or other review to determine the crewmember's knowledge of the aircraft and crewmember position involved.

   (2) Instruction as necessary in the subjects required for initial ground training by this subpart, as appropriate, including low-altitude windshear training and training on operating during ground icing conditions, as prescribed in §135.341 and described in §135.345, and emergency training.

(c) Recurrent flight training for pilots must include, at least, flight training in the maneuvers or procedures in this subpart, except that satisfactory completion of the check required by §135.293 within the preceding 12 calendar months may be substituted for recurrent flight training.

135.353 PROHIBITED DRUGS

(a) Each certificate holder or operator shall provide each employee performing a function listed in Appendix I to Part 121 of this chapter and his or her supervisor with the training specified in that appendix.

(b) No certificate holder or operator may use any contractor to perform a function specified in Appendix I to Part 121 of this chapter unless that contractor provides each of its employees performing that function for the certificate holder or the operator and his or her supervisor with the training specified in that appendix.

INTENTIONALLY

LEFT

BLANK

SUBPART I — AIRPLANE PERFORMANCE OPERATING LIMITATIONS

135.361   APPLICABILITY

(a)   This subpart prescribes airplane performance operating limitations applicable to the operation of the categories of airplanes listed in §135.363 when operated under this part.

(b)   For the purpose of this subpart, "effective length of the runway," for landing means the distance from the point at which the obstruction clearance plane associated with the approach end of the runway intersects the centerline of the runway to the far end of the runway.

(c)   For the purpose of this subpart, "obstruction clearance plane" means a plane sloping upward from the runway at a slope of 1:20 to the horizontal, and tangent to or clearing all obstructions within a specified area surrounding the runway as shown in a profile view of that area. In the plan view, the centerline of the specified area coincides with the centerline of the runway, beginning at the point where the obstruction clearance plane intersects the centerline of the runway and proceeding to a point at least 1,500 feet from the beginning point. After that the centerline coincides with the takeoff path over the ground for the runway (in the case of takeoffs) or with the instrument approach counterpart (for landings), or, where the applicable one of these paths has not been established, it proceeds consistent with turns of at least 4,000-foot radius until a point is reached beyond which the obstruction clearance plane clears all obstructions. This area extends laterally 200 feet on each side of the centerline at the point where the obstruction clearance plane intersects the runway and continues at this width to the end of the runway; then it increases uniformly to 500 feet on each side of the centerline at a point 1,500 feet from the intersection of the obstruction clearance plane with the runway; after that it extends laterally 500 feet on each side of the centerline.

135.363   GENERAL

(a)   Each certificate holder operating a reciprocating engine powered large transport category airplane shall comply with §§135.365 through 135.377.

(b)   Each certificate holder operating a turbine engine powered large transport category airplane shall comply with §§135.379 through 135.387, except that when it operates a turbo-propeller-powered large transport category airplane certificated after August 29, 1959, but previously type certificated with the same number of reciprocating engines, it may comply with §§135.365 through 135.377.

(c)   Each certificate holder operating a large nontransport category airplane shall comply with §§135.389 through 135.395 and any determination of compliance must be based only on approved performance data. For the purpose of this subpart, a large nontransport category airplane is an airplane that was type certificated before July 1, 1942.

(d)   Each certificate holder operating a small transport category airplane shall comply with §135.397.

(e)   Each certificate holder operating a small nontransport category airplane shall comply with §135.399.

(f)   The performance data in the Airplane Flight Manual applies in determining compliance with §§135.365 through 135.387. Where conditions are different from those on which the performance data is based, compliance is determined by interpolation or by computing the effects of change in the specific variables, if the results of the interpolation or computations are substantially as accurate as the results of direct tests.

(g)   No person may take off a reciprocating engine powered large transport category airplane at a weight that is more than the allowable weight for the runway being used (determined under the runway takeoff limitations of the transport category operating rules of this subpart) after taking into account the temperature operating correction factors in *§4a.749a-T or §4b.117 of the Civil Air Regulations in effect on January 31, 1965, and in the applicable Airplane Flight Manual.

(h)   The Administrator may authorize in the operations specifications deviations from this subpart if special circumstances make a literal observance of a requirement unnecessary for safety.

(i)   The 10-mile width specified in §§135.369 through 135.373 may be reduced to 5 miles, for not more than 20 miles, when operating under VFR or where navigation facilities furnish reliable and accurate identification of high ground and obstructions located outside of 5 miles, but within 10 miles, on each side of the intended track.

Amend #21
eff 2-17-87

(j)   Each certificate holder operating a commuter category airplane shall comply with §135.398.

135.365   LARGE TRANSPORT CATEGORY AIRPLANES: RECIPROCATING ENGINE POWERED: WEIGHT LIMITATIONS

(a)   No person may take off a reciprocating engine powered large transport category airplane from an airport located at an elevation outside of the range for which maximum takeoff weights have been determined for that airplane.

(b)   No person may take off a reciprocating engine powered large transport category airplane for an airport of intended destination that is located at an elevation outside of the range for which maximum landing weights have been determined for that airplane.

(c)   No person may specify, or have specified, an alternate airport that is located at an elevation outside of the range for which maximum landing weights have been determined for the reciprocating engine powered large transport category airplane concerned.

(d)   No person may take off a reciprocating engine powered large transport category airplane at a weight more than the maximum authorized takeoff weight for the elevation of the airport.

(e)   No person may take off a reciprocating engine powered large transport category airplane if its weight on arrival at the airport of destination will be more than maximum authorized landing weight for the elevation of that airport, allowing for normal consumption of fuel and oil enroute.

135.367   LARGE TRANSPORT CATEGORY AIRPLANES: RECIPROCATING ENGINE POWERED: TAKEOFF LIMITATIONS

(a)   No person operating a reciprocating engine powered large transport category airplane may take off that airplane unless it is possible —
(1)   To stop the airplane safely on the runway, as shown by the accelerate-stop distance data, at any time during takeoff until reaching critical engine failure speed;
(2)   If the critical engine fails at any time after the airplane reaches critical-engine failure speed V_1, to continue the takeoff and reach a height of 50 feet, as indicated by the takeoff path data, before passing over the end of the runway; and
(3)   To clear all obstacles either by at least 50 feet vertically (as shown by the takeoff path data) or 200 feet horizontally within the airport boundaries and 300 feet horizontally beyond the boundaries, without banking before reaching a height of 50 feet (as shown by the takeoff path data) and after that without banking more than 15 degrees.

(b)   In applying this section, corrections must be made for any runway gradient. To allow for wind effect, takeoff data based on still air may be corrected by taking into account not more than 50 percent of any reported headwind component and not less than 150 percent of any reported tailwind component.

(*Not published herein — Ed.)

135.369   LARGE TRANSPORT CATEGORY AIRPLANES: RECIPROCATING ENGINE POWERED: ENROUTE LIMITATIONS: ALL ENGINES OPERATING

(a)   No person operating a reciprocating engine powered large transport category airplane may take off that airplane at a weight, allowing for normal consumption of fuel and oil, that does not allow a rate of climb (in feet per minute), with all engines operating, of at least 6.90 V_{SO} (that is, the number of feet per minute obtained by multiplying the number of knots by 6.90) at an altitude of at least 1,000 feet above the highest ground or obstruction within ten miles of each side of the intended track.

(b)   This section does not apply to large transport category airplanes certificated under *Part 4a of the Civil Air Regulations.

135.371   LARGE TRANSPORT CATEGORY AIRPLANES: RECIPROCATING ENGINE POWERED: ENROUTE LIMITATIONS: ONE ENGINE INOPERATIVE

(a)   Except as provided in paragraph (b) of this section, no person operating a reciprocating engine powered large transport category airplane may take off that airplane at a weight, allowing for normal consumption of fuel and oil, that does not allow a rate of climb (in feet per minute), with one engine inoperative, of at least $(0.079-0.106/N)$ V_{SO}^2 (where N is the number of engines installed and V_{SO} is expressed in knots) at an altitude of at least 1,000 feet above the highest ground or obstruction within 10 miles of each side of the intended track. However, for the purposes of this paragraph the rate of climb for transport category airplanes certificated under *Part 4a of the Civil Air Regulations is 0.026 V_{SO}^2.

(b)   In place of the requirements of paragraph (a) of this section, a person, may, under an approved procedure, operate a reciprocating engine powered large transport category airplane at an all-engines-operating altitude that allows the airplane to continue, after an engine failure, to an alternate airport where a landing can be made under §135.377, allowing for normal consumption of fuel and oil. After the assumed failure, the flight path must clear the ground and any obstruction within five miles on each side of the intended track by at least 2,000 feet.

(c)   If an approved procedure under paragraph (b) of this section is used, the certificate holder shall comply with the following:

(1)   The rate of climb (as prescribed in the Airplane Flight Manual for the appropriate weight and altitude) used in calculating the airplane's flight path shall be diminished by an amount in feet per minute, equal to $(0.079-0.106/N)$ V_{SO}^2 (where N is the number of engines installed and V_{SO} is expressed in knots) for airplanes certificated under *Part 25 of this chapter and by 0.026 V_{SO}^2 for airplanes certificated under *Part 4a for the Civil Air Regulations.

(2)   The all-engines-operating altitude shall be sufficient so that in the event the critical engine becomes inoperative at any point along the route, the flight will be able to proceed to a predetermined alternate airport by use of this procedure. In determining the takeoff weight, the airplane is assumed to pass over the critical obstruction following engine failure at a point no closer to the critical obstruction than the nearest approved radio navigational fix, unless the Administrator approves a procedure established on a different basis upon finding that adequate operational safeguards exist.

(3)   The airplane must meet the provisions of paragraph (a) of this section at 1,000 feet above the airport used as an alternate in this procedure.

(4)   The procedure must include an approved method of accounting for winds and temperatures that would otherwise adversely affect the flight path.

(*Not published herein—Ed.)

    (5)   In complying with this procedure, fuel jettisoning is allowed if the certificate holder shows that it has an adequate training program, that proper instructions are given to the flight crew, and all other precautions are taken to ensure a safe procedure.

    (6)   The certificate holder and the pilot in command shall jointly elect an alternate airport for which the appropriate weather reports or forecasts, or any combination of them, indicate that weather conditions will be at or above the alternate weather minimum specified in the certificate holder's operations specifications for that airport when the flight arrives.

135.373   *PART 25 TRANSPORT CATEGORY AIRPLANES WITH FOUR OR MORE ENGINES: RECIPROCATING ENGINE POWERED: ENROUTE LIMITATIONS: TWO ENGINES INOPERATIVE

(a)   No person may operate an airplane certificated under *Part 25 and having four or more engines unless —

    (1)   There is no place along the intended track that is more than 90 minutes (with all engines operating at cruising power) from an airport that meets §135.377; or

    (2)   It is operated at a weight allowing the airplane, with the two critical engines inoperative, to climb at $0.013 \ V_{SO}^2$ feet per minute (that is, the number of feet per minute obtained by multiplying the number of knots squared by 0.013) at an altitude of 1,000 feet above the highest ground or obstruction within 10 miles on each side of the intended track, or at an altitude of 5,000 feet, whichever is higher.

(b)   For the purposes of paragraph (a)(2) of this section, it is assumed that —

    (1)   The two engines fail at the point that is most critical with respect to the takeoff weight;

    (2)   Consumption of fuel and oil is normal with all engines operating up to the point where the two engines fail with two engines operating beyond that point;

    (3)   Where the engines are assumed to fail at an altitude above the prescribed minimum altitude, compliance with the prescribed rate of climb at the prescribed minimum altitude need not be shown during the descent from the cruising altitude to the prescribed minimum altitude, if those requirements can be met once the prescribed minimum altitude is reached, and assuming descent to be along a net flight path and the rate of descent to be $0.013 \ V_{SO}^2$ greater than the rate in the approved performance data; and

    (4)   If fuel jettisoning is provided, the airplane's weight at the point where the two engines fail is considered to be not less than that which would include enough fuel to proceed to an airport meeting §135.377 and to arrive at an altitude of at least 1,000 feet directly over that airport.

135.375   **LARGE TRANSPORT CATEGORY AIRPLANES: RECIPROCATING ENGINE POWERED: LANDING LIMITATIONS: DESTINATION AIRPORTS**

(a)   Except as provided in paragraph (b) of this section, no person operating a reciprocating engine powered large transport category airplane may take off that airplane, unless its weight on arrival, allowing for normal consumption of fuel and oil in flight, would allow a full stop landing at the intended destination within 60 percent of the effective length of each runway described below from a point 50 feet directly above the intersection of the obstruction clearance plane and the runway. For the purposes of determining the allowable landing weight at the destination airport the following is assumed:

    (1)   The airplane is landed on the most favorable runway and in the most favorable direction in still air.

(*Not published herein-Ed.)

(2)   The airplane is landed on the most suitable runway considering the probable wind velocity and direction (forecast for the expected time of arrival), the ground handling characteristics of the type of airplane, and other conditions such as landing aids and terrain, and allowing for the effect of the landing path and roll of not more than 50 percent of the headwind component or not less than 150 percent of the tailwind component.

(b)   An airplane that would be prohibited from being taken off because it could not meet paragraph (a)(2) of this section may be taken off if an alternate airport is selected that meets all of this section except that the airplane can accomplish a full stop landing within 70 percent of the effective length of the runway.

135.377   LARGE TRANSPORT CATEGORY AIRPLANES: RECIPROCATING ENGINE POWERED: LANDING LIMITATIONS: ALTERNATE AIRPORTS

No person may list an airport as an alternate airport in a flight plan unless the airplane (at the weight anticipated at the time of arrival at the airport), based on the assumptions in §135.375(a)(1) and (2), can be brought to a full stop landing within 70 percent of the effective length of the runway.

135.379   LARGE TRANSPORT CATEGORY AIRPLANES: TURBINE ENGINE POWERED: TAKEOFF LIMITATIONS

(a)   No person operating a turbine engine powered large transport category airplane may take off that airplane at a weight greater than that listed in the Airplane Flight Manual for the elevation of the airport and for the ambient temperature existing at takeoff.

(b)   No person operating a turbine engine powered large transport category airplane certificated after August 26, 1957, but before August 30, 1959 (SR422, 422A), may take off that airplane at a weight greater than that listed in the Airplane Flight Manual for the minimum distance required for takeoff. In the case of an airplane certificated after September 30, 1958 (SR422A, 422B), the takeoff distance may include a clearway distance but the clearway distance included may not be greater than one-half of the takeoff run.

(c)   No person operating a turbine engine powered large transport category airplane certificated after August 29, 1959 (SR422B), may take off that airplane at a weight greater than that listed in the Airplane Flight manual at which compliance with the following may be shown:

(1)   The accelerate-stop distance, as defined in *§25.109 of this chapter, must not exceed the length of the runway plus the length of any stopway.

(2)   The takeoff distance must not exceed the length of the runway plus the length of any clearway except that the length of any clearway included must not be greater than one-half the length of the runway.

(3)   The takeoff run must not be greater than the length of the runway.

(d)   No person operating a turbine engine powered large transport category airplane may takeoff that airplane at a weight greater than that listed in the Airplane Flight Manual —

(1)   For an airplane certificated after August 26, 1957, but before October 1, 1958 (SR422), that allows a takeoff path that clears all obstacles either by at least (35 + 0.01 D) feet vertically (D is the distance along the intended flight path from the end of the runway in feet), or by at least 200 feet horizontally within the airport boundaries and by at least 300 feet horizontally after passing the boundaries; or

(2)   For an airplane certificated after September 30, 1958 (SR422A, 422B), that allows a net takeoff flight path that clears all obstacles either by a height of at least 35 feet vertically, or by at least 200 feet horizontally within the airport boundaries and by at least 300 feet horizontally after passing the boundaries.

(*Not published herein—Ed.)

(e) In determining maximum weights, minimum distances and flight paths under paragraphs (a) through (d) of this section, correction must be made for the runway to be used, the elevation of the airport, the effective runway gradient, and the ambient temperature and wind component at the time of takeoff.

(f) For the purposes of this section, it is assumed that the airplane is not banked before reaching a height of 50 feet, as shown by the takeoff path or net takeoff flight path data (as appropriate) in the Airplane Flight Manual, and after that the maximum bank is not more than 15 degrees.

(g) For the purposes of this section, the terms, "takeoff distance," "takeoff run," "net takeoff flight path," have the same meanings as set forth in the rules under which the airplane was certificated.

135.381 LARGE TRANSPORT CATEGORY AIRPLANES: TURBINE ENGINE POWERED: ENROUTE LIMITATIONS: ONE ENGINE INOPERATIVE

(a) No person operating a turbine engine powered large transport category airplane may take off that airplane at a weight, allowing for normal consumption of fuel and oil, that is greater than that which (under the approved, one engine inoperative, enroute net flight path data in the Airplane Flight Manual for that airplane) will allow compliance with subparagraph (1) or (2) of this paragraph, based on the ambient temperatures expected en route.

(1) There is a positive slope at an altitude of at least 1,000 feet above all terrain and obstructions within five statute miles on each side of the intended track, and, in addition, if that airplane was certificated after August 29, 1958 (SR422B), there is a positive slope at 1,500 feet above the airport where the airplane is assumed to land after an engine fails.

(2) The net flight path allows the airplane to continue flight from the cruising altitude to an airport where a landing can be made under §135.387 clearing all terrain and obstructions within five statute miles of the intended track by at least 2,000 feet vertically and with a positive slope at 1,000 feet above the airport where the airplane lands after an engine fails, or, if that airplane was certificated after September 30, 1958 (SR422A, 422B), with a positive slope at 1,500 feet above the airport where the airplane lands after an engine fails.

(b) For the purpose of paragraph (a)(2) of this section, it is assumed that —

(1) The engine fails at the most critical point enroute;

(2) The airplane passes over the critical obstruction, after engine failure at a point that is no closer to the obstruction than the approved radio navigation fix, unless the Administrator authorizes a different procedure based on adequate operational safeguards;

(3) An approved method is used to allow for adverse winds;

(4) Fuel jettisoning will be allowed if the certificate holder shows that the crew is properly instructed, that the training program is adequate, and that all other precautions are taken to ensure a safe procedure;

(5) The alternate airport is selected and meets the prescribed weather minimums; and

(6) The consumption of fuel and oil after engine failure is the same as the consumption that is allowed for in the approved net flight path data in the Airplane Flight Manual.

135.383   **LARGE TRANSPORT CATEGORY AIRPLANES: TURBINE ENGINE POWERED: ENROUTE LIMITATIONS: TWO ENGINES INOPERATIVE**

(a)   Airplanes certificated after August 26, 1957, but before October 1, 1958 (SR422). No person may operate a turbine engine powered large transport category airplane along an intended route unless that person complies with either of the following:

    (1)   There is no place along the intended track that is more than 90 minutes (with all engines operating at cruising power) from an airport that meets §135.387.

    (2)   Its weight, according to the two-engine-inoperative, enroute, net flight path data in the Airplane Flight Manual, allows the airplane to fly from the point where the two engines are assumed to fail simultaneously to an airport that meets §135.387, with a net flight path (considering the ambient temperature anticipated along the track) having a positive slope at an altitude of at least 1,000 feet above all terrain and obstructions within five statute miles on each side of the intended track, or at an altitude of 5,000 feet, whichever is higher.

    For the purposes of paragraph (2) of this paragraph, it is assumed that the two engines fail at the most critical point enroute, that if fuel jettisoning is provided, the airplane's weight at the point where the engines fail includes enough fuel to continue to the airport and to arrive at an altitude of at least 1,000 feet directly over the airport, and that the fuel and oil consumption after engine failure is the same as the consumption allowed for in the net flight path data in the Airplane Flight Manual.

(b)   Airplanes certificated after September 30, 1958, but before August 30, 1959 (SR422A). No person may operate a turbine engine powered large transport category airplane along an intended route unless that person complies with either of the following:

    (1)   There is no place along the intended track that is more than 90 minutes (with all engines operating at cruising power) from an airport that meets §135.387.

    (2)   Its weight, according to the two-engine-inoperative, enroute, net flight path data in the Airplane Flight Manual allows the airplane to fly from the point where the two engines are assumed to fail simultaneously to an airport that meets §135.387 with a net flight path (considering the ambient temperatures anticipated along the track) having a positive slope at an altitude for at least 1,000 feet above all terrain and obstructions within five statute miles on each side of the intended track, or at an altitude of 2,000 feet, whichever is higher.

    For the purpose of paragraph (2) of this paragraph, it is assumed that the two engines fail at the most critical point enroute, that the airplane's weight at the point where the engines fail includes enough fuel to continue to the airport, to arrive at an altitude of at least 1,500 feet directly over the airport, and after that to fly for 15 minutes at cruise power or thrust, or both, and that the consumption of fuel and oil after engine failure is the same as the consumption allowed for in the net flight path data in the Airplane Flight Manual.

(c)   Aircraft certificated after August 29, 1959 (SR422B). No person may operate a turbine engine powered large transport category airplane along an intended route unless that person complies with either of the following:

    (1)   There is no place along the intended track that is more than 90 minutes (with all engines operating at cruising power) from an airport that meets §135.387.

(2)   Its weight, according to the two-engine-inoperative, enroute, net flight path data in the Airplane Flight Manual, allows the airplane to fly from the point where the two engines are assumed to fail simultaneously to an airport that meets §135.387, with the net flight path (considering the ambient temperatures anticipated along the track) clearing vertically by at least 2,000 feet all terrain and obstructions within five statute miles on each side of the intended track. For the purposes of this paragraph, it is assumed that —

(i)   The two engines fail at the most critical point enroute;

(ii)   The net flight path has a positive slope at 1,500 feet above the airport where the landing is assumed to be made after the engines fail;

(iii) Fuel jettisoning will be approved if the certificate holder shows that the crew is properly instructed, that the training program is adequate, and that all other precautions are taken to ensure a safe procedure;

(iv) The airplane's weight at the point where the two engines are assumed to fail provides enough fuel to continue to the airport, to arrive at an altitude of at least 1,500 feet directly over the airport, and after that to fly for 15 minutes at cruise power or thrust, or both; and

(v)   The consumption of fuel and oil after the engines fail is the same as the consumption that is allowed for in the net flight path data in the Airplane Flight Manual.

135.385 LARGE TRANSPORT CATEGORY AIRPLANES: TURBINE ENGINE POWERED: LANDING LIMITATIONS: DESTINATION AIRPORTS

(a)   No person operating a turbine engine powered large transport category airplane may take off that airplane at a weight that (allowing for normal consumption of fuel and oil in flight to the destination or alternate airport) the weight of the airplane on arrival would exceed the landing weight in the Airplane Flight Manual for the elevation of the destination or alternate airport and the ambient temperature anticipated at the time of landing.

(b)   Except as provided in paragraph (c), (d), or (e) of this section, no person operating a turbine engine powered large transport category airplane may take off that airplane unless its weight on arrival, allowing for normal consumption of fuel and oil in flight (in accordance with the landing distance in the Airplane Flight Manual for the elevation of the destination airport and the wind conditions anticipated there at the time of landing), would allow a full stop landing at the intended destination airport within 60 percent of the effective length of each runway described below from a point 50 feet above the intersection of the obstruction clearance plane and the runway. For the purpose of determining the allowable landing weight at the destination airport the following is assumed:

(1)   The airplane is landed on the most favorable runway and in the most favorable direction, in still air.

(2)   The airplane is landed on the most suitable runway considering the probable wind velocity and direction and the ground handling characteristics of the airplane, and considering the other conditions such as landing aids and terrain.

(c)   A turbopropeller powered airplane that would be prohibited from being taken off because it could not meet paragraph (b)(2) of this section, may be taken off if an alternate airport is selected that meets all of this section except that the airplane can accomplish a full stop landing within 70 percent of the effective length of the runway.

(d) Unless, based on a showing of actual operating landing techniques on wet runways, a shorter landing distance (but never less than that required by paragraph (b) of this section) has been approved for a specific type and model airplane and included in the Airplane Flight Manual, no person may take off a turbojet airplane when the appropriate weather reports or forecasts, or any combination of them, indicate that the runways at the destination airport may be wet or slippery at the estimated time of arrival unless the effective runway length at the destination airport is at least 115 percent of the runway length required under paragraph (b) of this section.

(e) A turbojet airplane that would be prohibited from being taken off because it could not meet paragraph (b)(2) of this section may be taken off if an alternate airport is selected that meets all of paragraph (b) of this section.

135.387   LARGE TRANSPORT CATEGORY AIRPLANES: TURBINE ENGINE POWERED: LANDING LIMITATIONS: ALTERNATE AIRPORTS

No person may select an airport as an alternate airport for a turbine engine powered large transport category airplane unless (based on the assumptions in §135.385(b)) that airplane, at the weight anticipated at the time of arrival, can be brought to a full stop landing within 70 percent of the effective length of the runway for turbopropeller-powered airplanes and 60 percent of the effective length of the runway for turbojet airplanes, from a point 50 feet above the intersection of the obstruction clearance plane and the runway.

135.389   LARGE NONTRANSPORT CATEGORY AIRPLANES: TAKEOFF LIMITATIONS

(a) No person operating a large nontransport category airplane may take off that airplane at a weight greater than the weight that would allow the airplane to be brought to a safe stop within the effective length of the runway, from any point during the takeoff before reaching 105 percent of minimum control speed (the minimum speed at which an airplane can be safely controlled in flight after an engine becomes inoperative) or 115 percent of the power off stalling speed in the takeoff configuration, whichever is greater.

(b) For the purposes of this section —
(1) It may be assumed that takeoff power is used on all engines during the acceleration;
(2) Not more than 50 percent of the reported headwind component, or not less than 150 percent of the reported tailwind component, may be taken into account;
(3) The average runway gradient (the difference between the elevations of the endpoints of the runway divided by the total length) must be considered if it is more than one-half of one percent;
(4) It is assumed that the airplane is operating in standard atmosphere; and
(5) For takeoff, "effective length of the runway" means the distance from the end of the runway at which the takeoff is started to a point at which the obstruction clearance plane associated with the other end of the runway intersects the runway centerline.

135.391   LARGE NONTRANSPORT CATEGORY AIRPLANES: ENROUTE LIMITATIONS: ONE ENGINE INOPERATIVE

(a) Except as provided in paragraph (b) of this section, no person operating a large nontransport category airplane may take off that airplane at a weight that does not allow a rate of climb of at least 50 feet a minute, with the critical engine inoperative, at an altitude of at least 1,000 feet above the highest obstruction within five miles on each side of the intended track, or 5,000 feet, whichever is higher.

(b)   Without regard to paragraph (a) of this section, if the Administrator finds that safe operations are not impaired, a person may operate the airplane at an altitude that allows the airplane, in case of engine failure, to clear all obstructions within five miles on each side of the intended track by 1,000 feet. If this procedure is used, the rate of descent for the appropriate weight and altitude is assumed to be 50 feet a minute greater than the rate in the approved performance data. Before approving such a procedure, the Administrator considers the following for the route, route segment, or area concerned:

      (1)   The reliability of wind and weather forecasting.

      (2)   The location and kinds of navigation aids.

      (3)   The prevailing weather conditions, particularly the frequency and amount of turbulence normally encountered.

      (4)   Terrain features.

      (5)   Air traffic problems.

      (6)   Any other operational factors that affect the operations.

(c)   For the purposes of this section, it is assumed that —

      (1)   The critical engine is inoperative;

      (2)   The propeller of the inoperative engine is in the minimum drag position;

      (3)   The wing flaps and landing gear are in the most favorable position;

      (4)   The operating engines are operating at the maximum continuous power available;

      (5)   The airplane is operating in standard atmosphere; and

      (6)   The weight of the airplane is progressively reduced by the anticipated consumption of fuel and oil.

135.393   LARGE NONTRANSPORT CATEGORY AIRPLANES: LANDING LIMITATIONS: DESTINATION AIRPORTS

(a)   No person operating a large nontransport category airplane may take off that airplane at a weight that —

      (1)   Allowing for anticipated consumption of fuel and oil, is greater than the weight that would allow a full stop landing within 60 percent of the effective length of the most suitable runway at the destination airport; and

      (2)   Is greater than the weight allowable if the landing is to be made on the runway —

           (i)   With the greatest effective length in still air; and

           (ii)   Required by the probable wind, taking into account not more than 50 percent of the headwind component or not less than 150 percent of the tailwind component.

(b)   For the purpose of this section, it is assumed that —

      (1)   The airplane passes directly over the intersection of the obstruction clearance plane and the runway at a height of 50 feet in a steady gliding approach at a true indicated airspeed of at least 1.3 V_{SO};

      (2)   The landing does not require exceptional pilot skill; and

      (3)   The airplane is operating in standard atmosphere.

135.395   LARGE NONTRANSPORT CATEGORY AIRPLANES: LANDING LIMITATIONS: ALTERNATE AIRPORTS

No person may select an airport as an alternate airport for a large nontransport category airplane unless that airplane (at the weight anticipated at the time of arrival), based on the assumptions in §135.393(b), can be brought to a full stop landing within 70 percent of the effective length of the runway.

135.397   **SMALL TRANSPORT CATEGORY AIRPLANE PERFORMANCE OPERATING LIMITATIONS**

(a)   No person may operate a reciprocating engine powered small transport category airplane unless that person complies with the weight limitations in §135.365, the takeoff limitations in §135.367 (except paragraph (a)(3)), and the landing limitations in §§135.375 and 135.377.

(b)   No person may operate a turbine engine powered small transport category airplane unless that person complies with the takeoff limitations in §135.379 (except paragraphs (d) and (f) and the landing limitations in §§135.385 and 135.387.

135.398   **COMMUTER CATEGORY AIRPLANES PERFORMANCE OPERATING LIMITATIONS**

(a)   No person may operate a commuter category airplane unless that person complies with the takeoff weight limitations in the approved Airplane Flight Manual.

Amend #21
eff 2-17-87

(b)   No person may take off an airplane type certificated in the commuter category at a weight greater than that listed in the Airplane Flight Manual that allows a net takeoff flight path that clears all obstacles either by a height of at least 35 feet vertically, or at least 200 feet horizontally within the airport boundaries and by at least 300 feet horizontally after passing the boundaries.

(c)   No person may operate a commuter category airplane unless that person complies with the landing limitations prescribed in §§135.385 and 135.387 of this Part. For purposes of this paragraph, §§135.385 and 135.387 are applicable to all commuter category airplanes notwithstanding their stated applicability to turbine-engine-powered large transport category airplanes.

(d)   In determining maximum weights, minimum distances and flight paths under paragraphs (a) through (c) of this section, correction must be made for the runway to be used, the elevation of the airport, the effective runway gradient, and ambient temperature, and wind component at the time of takeoff.

(e)   For the purposes of this section, the assumption is that the airplane is not banked before reaching a height of 50 feet as shown by the net takeoff flight path data in the Airplane Flight Manual and thereafter the maximum bank is not more than 15 degrees.

135.399   **SMALL NONTRANSPORT CATEGORY AIRPLANE PERFORMANCE OPERATING LIMITATIONS**

(a)   No person may operate a reciprocating engine or turbopropeller-powered small airplane that is certificated under §135.169 (b)(2), (3), (4), (5), or (6) unless that person complies with the takeoff weight limitations in the approved Airplane Flight Manual or equivalent for operations under this part, and, if the airplane is certificated under §135.169 (b)(4) or (5) with the landing weight limitations in the Approved Airplane Flight Manual or equivalent for operations under this part.

(b)   No person may operate an airplane that is certificated under §135.169 (b)(6) unless that person complies with the landing limitations prescribed in §§135.385 and 135.387 of this part. For purposes of this paragraph, §§135.385 and 135.387 are applicable to reciprocating and turbopropeller-powered small airplanes notwithstanding their stated applicability to turbine engine powered large transport category airplanes.

INTENTIONALLY

LEFT

BLANK

SUBPART J — MAINTENANCE, PREVENTIVE MAINTENANCE, AND ALTERATIONS

135.411   APPLICABILITY

(a)   This subpart prescribes rules in addition to those in other parts of this chapter for the maintenance, preventive maintenance, and alterations for each certificate holder as follows:

(1)   Aircraft that are type certificated for a passenger seating configuration, excluding any pilot seat, of nine seats or less, shall be maintained under Parts 91 and *43 of this chapter and §§135.415, 135.417, and 135.421. An approved aircraft inspection program may be used under §135.419.

(2)   Aircraft that are type certificated for a passenger seating configuration, excluding any pilot seat, of ten seats or more, shall be maintained under a maintenance program in §§135.415, 135.417, 135.423 through 135.443.

(b)   A certificate holder who is not otherwise required, may elect to maintain its aircraft under paragraph (a)(2) of this section.

135.413   RESPONSIBILITY FOR AIRWORTHINESS

(a)   Each certificate holder is primarily responsible for the airworthiness of its aircraft, including airframes, aircraft engines, propellers, rotors, appliances, and parts, and shall have its aircraft maintained under this chapter, and shall have defects repaired between required maintenance under *Part 43 of this chapter.

(b)   Each certificate holder who maintains its aircraft under §135.411(a)(2) shall —

(1)   Perform the maintenance, preventive maintenance, and alteration of its aircraft, including airframe, aircraft engines, propellers, rotors, appliances, emergency equipment and parts, under its manual and this chapter; or

(2)   Make arrangements with another person for the performance of maintenance, preventive maintenance, or alteration. However, the certificate holder shall ensure that any maintenance, preventive maintenance, or alteration that is performed by another person is performed under the certificate holder's manual and this chapter

135.415   MECHANICAL RELIABILITY REPORTS

(a)   Each certificate holder shall report the occurrence or detection of each failure, malfunction, or defect in an aircraft concerning —

(1)   Fires during flight and whether the related fire-warning system functioned properly;

(2)   Fires during flight not protected by related fire-warning system;

(3)   False fire-warning during flight;

(4)   An exhaust system that causes damage during flight to the engine, adjacent structure, equipment, or components;

(5)   An aircraft component that causes accumulation or circulation of smoke, vapor, or toxic or noxious fumes in the crew compartment or passenger cabin during flight;

(6)   Engine shutdown during flight because of flameout;

(7)   Engine shutdown during flight when external damage to the engine or aircraft structure occurs;

(8)   Engine shutdown during flight due to foreign object ingestion or icing;

(9)   Shutdown of more than one engine during flight;

(10) A propeller feathering system or ability of the system to control overspeed during flight;

(11) A fuel or fuel-dumping system that affects fuel flow or causes hazardous leakage during flight;

(12) An unwanted landing gear extension or retraction or opening or closing of landing gear doors during flight.

(*Not published herein—Ed.)

       (13)   Brake system components that result in loss of brake actuating force when the aircraft is in motion on the ground;

       (14)   Aircraft structure that requires major repair;

       (15)   Cracks, permanent deformation, or corrosion of aircraft structures, if more than the maximum acceptable to the manufacturer or the FAA; and

       (16)   Aircraft components or systems that result in taking emergency actions during flight (except action to shut-down an engine).

(b)   For the purpose of this section, "during flight" means the period from the moment the aircraft leaves the surface of the earth on takeoff until it touches down on landing.

(c)   In addition to the reports required by paragraph (a) of this section, each certificate holder shall report any other failure, malfunction, or defect in an aircraft that occurs or is detected at any time if, in its opinion, the failure, malfunction, or defect has endangered or may endanger the safe operation of the aircraft.

(d)   Each certificate holder shall send each report required by this section, in writing, covering each 24-hour period beginning at 0900 hours local time of each day and ending at 0900 hours local time on the next day to the FAA Flight Standards District Office charged with the overall inspection of the certificate holder. Each report of occurrences during a 24-hour period must be mailed or delivered to that office within the next 72 hours. However, a report that is due on Saturday or Sunday may be mailed or delivered on the following Monday and one that is due on a holiday may be mailed or deliverd on the next work day. For aircraft operated in areas where mail is not collected, reports may be mailed or delivered within 72 hours after the aircraft returns to a point where the mail is collected.

(e)   The certificate holder shall transmit the reports required by this section on a form and in a manner prescribed by the Administrator, and shall include as much of the following as is available:

       (1)   The type and identification number of the aircraft.

       (2)   The name of the operator.

       (3)   The date.

       (4)   The nature of the failure, malfunction, or defect.

       (5)   Identification of the part and system involved, including available information pertaining to type designation of the major component and time since last overhaul, if known.

       (6)   Apparent cause of the failure, malfunction or defect (e.g., wear, crack, design deficiency, or personnel error).

       (7)   Other pertinent information necessary for more complete identification, determination of seriousness, or corrective action.

(f)   A certificate holder that is also the holder of a type certificate (including a supplemental type certificate), a Parts Manufacturer Approval, or a Technical Standard Order Authorization, or that is the licensee of a type certificate need not report a failure, malfunction, or defect under this section if the failure, malfunction, or defect has been reported by it under *§21.3 or *§37.17 of this chapter or under the accident reporting provisions of Part 830 of the regulations of the National Transportation Safety Board.

(g)   No person may withhold a report required by this section even though all information required by this section is not available.

(h)   When the certificate holder gets additional information, including information from the manufacturer or other agency, concerning a report required by this section, it shall expeditiously submit it as a supplement to the first report and reference the date and place of submission of the first report.

(*Not published herein—Ed.)

135.417   **MECHANICAL INTERRUPTION SUMMARY REPORT**

Each certificate holder shall mail or deliver, before the end of the 10th day of the following month, a summary report of the following occurrences in multiengine aircraft for the preceding month to the certificate-holding district office:

(a)   Each interruption to a flight, unscheduled change of aircraft en route, or unscheduled stop or diversion from a route, caused by known or suspected mechanical difficulties or malfunctions that are not required to be reported under §135.415.

(b)   The number of propeller featherings in flight, listed by type of propeller and engine and aircraft on which it was installed. Propeller featherings for training, demonstration, or flight check purposes need not be reported.

135.419   **APPROVED AIRCRAFT INSPECTION PROGRAM**

(a)   Whenever the Administrator finds that the aircraft inspections required or allowed under Part 91 of this chapter are not adequate to meet this part, or upon application by a certificate holder, the Administrator may amend the certificate holder's operations specifications under §135.17, to require or allow an approved aircraft inspection program for any make and model aircraft of which the certificate holder has the exclusive use of at least one aircraft (as defined in §135.25(b)).

(b)   A certificate holder who applies for an amendment of its operations specifications to allow an approved aircraft inspection program must submit that program with its application for approval by the Administrator.

(c)   Each certificate holder who is required by its operations specifications to have an approved aircraft inspection program shall submit a program for approval by the Administrator within 30 days of the amendment of its operations specifications or within any other period that the Administrator may prescribe in the operations specifications.

(d)   The aircraft inspection program submitted for approval by the Administrator must contain the following:

    (1)   Instructions and procedures for the conduct of aircraft inspections (which must include necessary tests and checks), setting forth in detail the parts and areas of the airframe, engines, propellers, rotors, and appliances, including emergency equipment that must be inspected.

    (2)   A schedule for the performance of the aircraft inspections under paragraph (1) of this paragraph expressed in terms of the time in service, calendar time, number of system operations or any combination of these.

    (3)   Instructions and procedures for recording discrepancies found during inspections and correction or deferral of discrepancies including form and disposition of records.

(e)   After approval, the certificate holder shall include the approved aircraft inspection program in the manual required by §135.21.

(f)   Whenever the Administrator finds that revisions to an approved aircraft inspection program are necessary for the continued adequacy of the program, the certificate holder shall, after notification by the Administrator, make any changes in the program found by the Administrator to be necessary. The certificate holder may petition the Administrator to reconsider the notice to make any changes in a program. The petition must be filed with the representatives of the Administrator assigned to it within 30 days after the certificate holder receives the notice. Except in the case of an emergency requiring immediate action in the interest of safety, the filing of the petition stays the notice pending a decision by the Administrator.

(g)   Each certificate holder who has an approved aircraft inspection program shall have each aircraft that is subject to the program inspected in accordance with the program.

(h)   The registration number of each aircraft that is subject to an approved aircraft inspection program must be included in the operations specifications of the certificate holder.

Ⓐ *Amend #60 eff 2-26-96.*

135.421 ADDITIONAL MAINTENANCE REQUIREMENTS

(a) Each certificate holder who operates an aircraft type certificated for a passenger seating configuration, excluding any pilot seat, of nine seats or less, must comply with the manufacturer's recommended maintenance programs, or a program approved by the Administrator, for each aircraft engine, propeller, rotor, and each item of emergency equipment required by this chapter.

(b) For the purpose of this section, a manufacturer's maintenance program is one which is contained in the maintenance manual or maintenance instructions set forth by the manufacturer as required by this chapter for the aircraft, aircraft engine, propeller, rotor or item of emergency equipment.

135.423 MAINTENANCE, PREVENTIVE MAINTENANCE, AND ALTERATION ORGANIZATION

(a) Each certificate holder that performs any of its maintenance (other than required inspections), preventive maintenance, or alterations, and each person with whom it arranges for the performance of that work, must have an organization adequate to perform the work.

(b) Each certificate holder that performs any inspections required by its manual under §135.427(b)(2) or (3), (in this subpart referred to as "required inspections"), and each person with whom it arranges for the performance of that work, must have an organization adequate to perform that work.

(c) Each person performing required inspections in addition to other maintenance, preventive maintenance, or alterations, shall organize the performance of those functions so as to separate the required inspection functions from the other maintenance, preventive maintenance, and alteration functions. The separation shall be below the level of administrative control at which overall responsibility for the required inspection functions and other maintenance, preventive maintenance, and alteration functions is exercised.

135.425 MAINTENANCE, PREVENTIVE MAINTENANCE, AND ALTERATION PROGAMS

Each certificate holder shall have an inspection program and a program covering other maintenance, preventive maintenance, and alterations, that ensures that —

(a) Maintenance, preventive maintenance, and alterations performed by it, or by other persons, are performed under the certificate holder's manual;

(b) Competent personnel and adequate facilities and equipment are provided for the proper performance of maintenance, preventive maintenance, and alterations; and

(c) Each aircraft released to service is airworthy and has been properly maintained for operations under this part.

135.427 MANUAL REQUIREMENTS

(a) Each certificate holder shall put in its manual the chart or description of the certificate holder's organization required by §135.423 and a list of persons with whom it has arranged for the performance of any of its required inspections, other maintenance, preventive maintenance, or alterations, including a general description of that work.

(b) Each certificate holder shall put in its manual the programs required by §135.425 that must be followed in performing maintenance, preventive maintenance, and alterations of that certificate holder's aircraft, including airframes, aircraft engines, propellers, rotors, appliances, emergency equipment, and parts, and must include at least the following:

(1) The method of performing routine and nonroutine maintenance (other than required inspections), preventive maintenance, and alterations.

(2) A designation of the items of maintenance and alteration that must be inspected (required inspections) including at least those that could result in a failure, malfunction, or defect endangering the safe operations of the aircraft, if not performed properly or if improper parts or materials are used.

(3) The method of performing required inspections and a designation by occupational title of personnel authorized to perform each required inspection.

(4) Procedures for the reinspection of work performed under previous required inspection findings ("buy-back procedures").

(5) Procedures, standards, and limits necessary for required inspections and acceptance or rejection of the items required to be inspected and for periodic inspection and calibration of precisions tools, measuring devices, and test equipment.

(6) Procedures to ensure that all required inspections are performed.

(7) Instructions to prevent any person who performs any item of work from performing any required inspection of that work.

(8) Instructions and procedures to prevent any decision of an inspector regarding any required inspection from being countermanded by persons other than supervisory personnel of the inspection unit, or a person at the level of administrative control that has overall responsibility for the management of both the required inspection functions and the other maintenance, preventive maintenance, and alterations functions.

(9) Procedures to ensure that required inspections, other maintenance, preventive maintenance, and alterations that are not completed as a result of work interruptions are properly completed before the aircraft is released to service.

(c) Each certificate holder shall put in its manual a suitable system (which may include a coded system) that provides for the retention of the following information —

(1) A description (or reference to data acceptable to the Administrator) of the work performed;

(2) The name of the person performing the work if the work is performed by a person outside the organization of the certificate holder; and

(3) The name or other positive identification of the individual approving the work.

135.429   REQUIRED INSPECTION PERSONNEL

(a) No person may use any person to perform required inspections unless the person performing the inspection is appropriately certificated, properly trained, qualified, and authorized to do so.

(b) No person may allow any person to perform a required inspection unless, at the time, the person performing that inspection is under the supervision and control of an inspection unit.

(c) No person may perform a required inspection if that person performed the item of work required to be inspected.

(d) In the case of rotorcraft that operate in remote areas or sites, the Administrator may approve procedures for the performance of required inspection items by a pilot when no other qualified person is available, provided—

(1) The pilot is employed by the certificate holder;

(2) It can be shown to the satisfaction of the Administrator that each pilot authorized to perform required inspections is properly trained and qualified;

(3) The required inspection is a result of a mechanical interruption and is not a part of a certificate holder's continuous airworthiness maintenance program;

(4) Each item is inspected after each flight until the item has been inspected by an appropriately certificated mechanic other than the one who originally performed the item of work; and

(5) Each item of work that is a required inspection item that is part of the flight control system shall be flight tested and reinspected before the aircraft is approved for return to service.

(e)   Each certificate holder shall maintain, or shall determine that each person with whom it arranges to perform its required inspections maintains, a current listing of persons who have been trained, qualified, and authorized to conduct required inspections. The persons must be identified by name, occupational title and the inspections that they are authorized to perform. The certificate holder (or person with whom it arranges to perform its required inspections) shall give written information to each person so authorized, describing the extent of that person's responsibilities, authorities, and inspectional limitations. The list shall be made available for inspection by the Administrator upon request.

135.431   CONTINUING ANALYSIS AND SURVEILLANCE

(a)   Each certificate holder shall establish and maintain a system for the continuing analysis and surveillance of the performance and effectiveness of its inspection program and the program covering other maintenance, preventive maintenance, and alterations and for the correction of any deficiency in those programs, regardless of whether those programs are carried out by the certificate holder or by another person.

(b)   Whenever the Administrator finds that either or both of the programs described in paragraph (a) of this section does not contain adequate procedures and standards to meet this part, the certificate holder shall, after notification by the Administrator, make changes in those programs requested by the Administrator.

(c)   A certificate holder may petition the Administrator to reconsider the notice to make a change in a program. The petition must be filed with the certificate-holding district office within 30 days after the certificate holder receives the notice. Except in the case of an emergency requiring immediate action in the interest of safety, the filing of the petition stays the notice pending a decision by the Administrator.

Ⓐ

135.433   MAINTENANCE AND PREVENTIVE MAINTENANCE TRAINING PROGRAM

Each certificate holder or a person performing maintenance or preventive maintenance functions for it shall have a training program to ensure that each person (including inspection personnel) who determines the adequacy of work done is fully informed about procedures and techniques and new equipment in use and is competent to perform that person's duties.

135.435   CERTIFICATE REQUIREMENTS

(a)   Except for maintenance, preventive maintenance, alterations, and required inspections performed by repair stations certificated under the provisions of Subpart C of Part 145 of this chapter, each person who is directly in charge of maintenance, preventive maintenance, or alterations, and each person performing required inspections must hold an appropriate airman certificate.

(b)   For the purpose of this section, a person "directly in charge" is each person assigned to a position in which that person is responsible for the work of a shop or station that performs maintenance, preventive maintenance, alterations, or other functions affecting airworthiness. A person who is "directly in charge" need not physically observe and direct each worker constantly but must be available for consultation and decision on matters requiring instruction or decision from higher authority than that of the person performing the work.

135.437   AUTHORITY TO PERFORM AND APPROVE MAINTENANCE, PREVENTIVE MAINTENANCE, AND ALTERATIONS

(a)   A certificate holder may perform, or make arrangements with other persons to perform, maintenance, preventive maintenance, and alterations as provided in its maintenance manual. In addition, a certificate holder may perform these functions for another certificate holder as provided in the maintenance manual of the other certificate holder.

(b)   A certificate holder may approve any airframe, aircraft engine, propeller, rotor, or appliance for return to service after maintenance, preventive maintenance, or alterations that are performed under paragraph (a) of this section. However, in the case of a major repair or alteration, the work must have been done in accordance with technical data approved by the Administrator.

Ⓐ *Amend #60 eff 2-26-96.*

135.439   **MAINTENANCE RECORDING REQUIREMENTS**

(a)   Each certificate holder shall keep (using the system specified in the manual required in §135.427(1) the following records for the periods specified in paragraph (b) of this section:

     (1)   All the records necessary to show that all requirements for the issuance of an airworthiness release under §135.443 have been met.

     (2)   Records containing the following information:

         (i)   The total time in service of the airframe, engine, propeller, and rotor.

         (ii)   The current status of life-limited parts of each airframe, engine, propeller, rotor, and appliance.

         (iii)   The time since last overhaul of each item installed on the aircraft which are required to be overhauled on a specified time basis.

         (iv)   The identification of the current inspection status of the aircraft including the time since the last inspections required by the inspection program under which the aircraft and its appliances are maintained.

         (v)   The current status of applicable airworthiness directives, including the date and methods of compliance, and, if the airworthiness directive involves recurring action, the time and date when the next action is required.

         (vi)   A list of current major alterations and repairs to each airframe, engine, propeller, rotor, and appliance.

(b)   Each certificate holder shall retain the records required to be kept by this section for the following periods:

     (1)   Except for the records of the last complete overhaul of each airframe, engine, propeller, rotor, and appliance the records specified in paragraph (a)(1) of this section shall be retained until the work is repeated or superseded by other work or for one year after the work is performed.

     (2)   The records of the last complete overhaul of each airframe, engine, propeller, rotor, and appliance shall be retained until the work is superseded by work of equivalent scope and detail.

     (3)   The records specified in paragraph (a)(2) of this section shall be retained and transferred with the aircraft at the time the aircraft is sold.

(c)   The certificate holder shall make all maintenance records required to be kept by this section available for inspection by the Administrator or any representative of the National Transportation Safety Board.

135.441   **TRANSFER OF MAINTENANCE RECORDS**

Each certificate holder who sells a United States registered aircraft shall transfer to the purchaser, at the time of the sale, the following records of that aircraft, in plain language form or in coded form which provides for the preservation and retrieval of information in a manner acceptable to the Administrator:

(a)   The records specified in §135.439(a)(2).

(b)   The records specified in §135.439(a)(1) which are not included in the records covered by paragraph (a) of this section, except that the purchaser may allow the seller to keep physical custody of such record. However, custody of records by the seller does not relieve the purchaser of its responsibility under §135.439(c) to make the records available for inspection by the Administrator or any representative of the National Transportation Safety Board.

135.443   AIRWORTHINESS RELEASE OR AIRCRAFT MAINTENANCE LOG ENTRY

(a)   No certificate holder may operate an aircraft after maintenance, preventive maintenance, or alternations are performed on the aircraft unless the certificate holder prepares, or causes the person with whom the certificate holder arranges for the performance of the maintenance, preventive maintenance, or alternations, to prepare —

     (1)   An airworthiness release; or

     (2)   An appropriate entry in the aircraft maintenance log.

(b)   The airworthiness release or log entry required by paragraph (a) of this section must —

     (1)   Be prepared in accordance with the procedure in the certificate holder's manual;

     (2)   Include a certification that —

         (i)   The work was performed in accordance with the requirements of the certificate holder's manual;

         (ii)   All items required to be inspected were inspected by an authorized person who determined that the work was satisfactorily completed;

         (iii)   No known condition exists that would make the aircraft unairworthy;

         (iv)   So far as the work performed is concerned, the aircraft is in condition for safe operation; and

     (3)   Be signed by an authorized certificated mechanic or repairman, except that a certificated repairman may sign the release or entry only for the work for which that person is employed and for which that person is certificated.

Amend #29
eff 12-22-88

Notwithstanding paragraph (b)(3) of this section, after maintenance, preventive maintenance, or alterations performed by a repair station certificated under the provisions of *Subpart C of Part 145, the airworthiness release or log entry required by paragraph (a) of this section may be signed by a person authorized by that repair station.

(c)   Instead of restating each of the conditions of the certification required by paragraph (b) of this section, the certificate holder may state in its manual that the signature of an authorized certificated mechanic or repairman constitutes that certification.

(*Not published herein — Ed.)

FEDERAL AVIATION REGULATIONS

PART 141 — PILOT SCHOOLS

➤ This part contains all effective amendments through #7 effective 1 August 1996. Amendment #6 (not published herein).

TABLE OF CONTENTS

SUBPART A — GENERAL

SUBPART B — PERSONNEL, AIRCRAFT, AND FACILITIES REQUIREMENTS

SUBPART C — TRAINING COURSE OUTLINE AND CURRICULUM

SUBPART D — EXAMINING AUTHORITY

TABLE OF CONTENTS

SUBPART E — OPERATING RULES

SUBPART F — RECORDS

SUBPART A — GENERAL

141.1 APPLICABILITY

This Part prescribes the requirements for issuing pilot school certificates, provisional pilot school certificates, and associated ratings and the general operating rules for the holders of those certificates and ratings.

141.3 CERTIFICATE REQUIRED

No person may operate as a certificated pilot school without, or in violation of, a pilot school certificate or provisional pilot school certificate issued under this Part.

141.5 PILOT SCHOOL CERTIFICATE

An applicant is issued a pilot school certificate with associated ratings for that certificate if —
(a) It meets the pertinent requirements of Subparts A through C of this Part; and
(b) Within the 24 months before the date of application, it has trained and recommended for pilot certification and rating tests, at least 10 applicants for pilot certificates and ratings and at least 8 of 10 most recent graduates tested by an FAA inspector or designated pilot examiner, passed that test the first time.

141.7 PROVISIONAL PILOT SCHOOL CERTIFICATE

An applicant is issued a provisional pilot school certificate with associated ratings if it meets the pertinent requirements of Subparts A through C of this Part, but does not meet the recent training activity requirement specified in §141.5(b).

141.9 EXAMINING AUTHORITY

An applicant is issued an examining authority for its pilot school certificate if it meets the requirements of Subpart D of this Part.

141.11 PILOT SCHOOL RATINGS

Associated ratings are issued with a pilot school certificate or a provisional pilot school certificate, specifying each of the following courses that the school is authorized to conduct:
(a) *Certification courses.*
  (1) Private pilot.
  (2) Private test course.
  (3) Instrument rating.
  (4) Commercial pilot.
  (5) Commercial test course.
  (6) Additional aircraft rating.
(b) *Pilot ground school course.*
  (1) Pilot ground school.
(c) *Test preparation courses.*
  (1) Flight instructor certification.
  (2) Additional flight instructor rating.
  (3) Additional instrument rating.
  (4) Airline transport pilot certification.
  (5) Pilot refresher course.
  (6) Agricultural aircraft operations course.
  (7) Rotorcraft external load operations course.

141.13 APPLICATION FOR ISSUANCE, AMENDMENT, OR RENEWAL

(a) Application for an original certificate and rating, for an additional rating, or for the renewal of a certificate under this Part is made on a form and in a manner prescribed by the Administrator.
(b) An application for the issuance or amendment of a certificate or rating must be accompanied by three copies of the proposed training course outline for each course for which approval is sought.

141.15   LOCATION OF FACILITIES

Neither a pilot school certificate nor a provisional pilot school certificate is issued for a school having a base or other facilities located outside the United States unless the Administrator finds that the location of the base or facilities at that place is needed for the training of students who are citizens of the United States.

141.17   DURATION OF CERTIFICATES

(a)   Unless sooner surrendered, suspended, or revoked, a pilot school certificate or a provisional pilot school certificate expires —
  (1)   At the end of the twenty-fourth month after the month in which it was issued or renewed; or
  (2)   Except as provided in paragraph (b) of this section, on the date that any change in ownership of the school or the facilities upon which its certification is based occurs; or
  (3)   Upon notice by the Administrator that the school has failed for more than 60 days to maintain the facilities, aircraft, and personnel required for at least one of its approved courses.
(b)   A change in the ownership of a certificated pilot school or provisional pilot school does not terminate that certificate if within 30 days after the date that any change in ownership of the school occurs, application is made for an appropriate amendment to the certificate and no change in the facilities, instructor, personnel or training course is involved.
(c)   An examining authority issued to the holder of a pilot school certificate expires on the date that the pilot school certificate expires, or is surrendered, suspended, or revoked.

141.18   CARRIAGE OF NARCOTIC DRUGS, MARIHUANA AND DEPRESSANT OR STIMULANT DRUGS OR SUBSTANCES

If the holder of a certificate issued under this Part permits any aircraft owned or leased by that holder to be engaged in any operation that the certificate holder knows to be in violation of §91.19(a) of this chapter, that operation is a basis for suspending or revoking the certificate.

141.19   DISPLAY OF CERTIFICATE

(a)   Each holder of a pilot school certificate or a provisional pilot school certificate shall display that certificate at a place in the school that is normally accessible to the public and is not obscured.
(b)   A certificate shall be made available for inspection upon request by the Administrator, or an authorized representative of the National Transportation Safety Board, or of any Federal, State, or local law enforcement officer.

141.21   INSPECTIONS

Each holder of a certificate issued under this Part shall allow the Administrator to inspect its personnel, facilities, equipment, and records to determine its compliance with the Federal Aviation Act of 1958, and the Federal Aviation Regulations, and its eligibility to hold its certificate.

141.23   ADVERTISING LIMITATIONS

(a)   The holder of a pilot school certificate or a provisional pilot school certificate may not make any statement relating to its certification and ratings which is false or designed to mislead any person contemplating enrollment in that school.
(b)   The holder of a pilot school certificate or a provisional pilot school certificate may not advertise that the school is certificated unless it clearly differentiates between courses that have been approved and those that have not.
(c)   The holder of a pilot school certificate or a provisional pilot school certificate —
  (1)   That has relocated its school shall promptly remove from the premises it has vacated all signs indicating that the school was certificated by the Administrator; or
  (2)   Whose certificate has expired, or has been surrendered, suspended, or revoked shall promptly remove all indication (including signs), wherever located, that the school is certificated by the Administrator.

141.25   BUSINESS OFFICE AND OPERATIONS BASE

(a)   Each holder of a pilot school or a provisional pilot school certificate shall maintain a principal business office with a mailing address in the name shown on its certificate. The business office shall have facilities and equipment that are adequate to maintain the required school files and records and to operate the business of the school. The office may not be shared with, or used by, another pilot school.

(b)   Each certificate holder shall, before changing the location of its business office or base of operations, notify the FAA Flight Standards District Office having jurisdiction over the area of the new location. The notice shall be submitted in writing at least 30 days before the change. For a change in the holder's base of operations, the notice shall be accompanied by any amendments needed for the holder's approved training course outline.

(c)   No certificate holder may conduct training at an operations base other than the one specified in its certificate, until —
   (1)   The base has been inspected and approved by the FAA Flight Standards District Office having jurisdiction over the school for use by the certificate holder; and
   (2)   The course of training and any needed amendments thereto have been approved for training at that base.

141.26   TRAINING AGREEMENTS

A training center certificated under part 142 of this chapter may provide the training, testing, and checking for pilot schools certificated under part 141 of this chapter and is considered to meet the requirements of part 141 provided—

(a)   There is a training agreement between the certificated training center and the pilot school;

(b)   The training, testing, and checking provided by the certificated training center is approved and conducted under part 142;

(c)   The pilot school certificated under part 141 obtains the Administrator's approval for a training course outline that includes the training, testing, and checking to be conducted under part 141 and the training, testing, and checking to be conducted under part 142 of this chapter; and

(d)   Upon completion of the training, testing, and checking conducted under part 142 of this chapter, a copy of each student's training record is forwarded to the part 141 school and becomes part of the student's permanent record.

141.27   RENEWAL OF CERTIFICATES AND RATINGS

(a)   *Pilot school certificates.* The holder of a pilot school certificate may apply for a renewal of the certificate not less than 30 days before the certificate expires. If the school meets the requirements of this Part for the issuance of the certificate, its certificate is renewed for 24 months.

(b)   *Pilot school ratings.* Each pilot school rating on a pilot school certificate may be renewed with that certificate for another 24 months if the Administrator finds that the school meets the requirements prescribed in this Part for the issuance of the rating.

(c)   *Provisional pilot school certificates.*
   (1)   A provisional pilot school certificate and any ratings on that certificate may not be renewed. However, the holder of that certificate may apply for a pilot school certificate with appropriate ratings not less than 30 days before the provisional certificate expires. The school is issued a pilot school certificate with appropriate ratings, if it meets the appropriate requirements of this Part.
   (2)   The holder of a provisional pilot school certificate may not reapply for a provisional pilot school certificate for at least 180 days after the date of its expiration.

141.29   (Reserved)

Ⓐ *Amend #7 eff 8-1-96.*

SUBPART B — PERSONNEL, AIRCRAFT, AND FACILITIES REQUIREMENTS

141.31 APPLICABILITY

This subpart prescribes the personnel and aircraft requirements for a pilot school or a provisional pilot school certificate. It also prescribes the facilities an applicant must have available to him on a continuous use basis to hold a pilot school or provisional pilot school certificate. As used in this subpart, a person has the continuous use of a facility, including an airport, if it has the use of the facility when needed as the owner, or under a written agreement giving it that use for at least 6 calendar months from the date of the application for the initial certificate or a renewal of that certificate.

141.33 PERSONNEL

(a) An applicant for a pilot school or provisional pilot school certificate must show that —
  (1) It has adequate personnel and authorized instructors, including a chief instructor for each course of training, who are qualified and competent to perform the duties to which they are assigned;
  (2) Each dispatcher, aircraft handler, line crewman, and serviceman to be used has been instructed in the procedures and responsibilities of his employment. (Qualified operations personnel may serve in more than one capacity with a pilot school or provisional pilot school); and
  (3) Each instructor to be used for ground or flight instruction holds a flight or ground instructor certificate, as appropriate, with ratings for the course of instruction and any aircraft used in that course.
(b) An applicant for a pilot school or a provisional pilot school certificate shall designate a chief instructor for each course of training who meets the requirements of a §141.35 of this Part. Where necessary, the applicant shall also designate at least one instructor to assist the chief instructor and serve for the chief instructor in his absence. A chief instructor or his assistant may be designated to serve in that capacity for more than one approved course but not for more than one school.

141.35 CHIEF INSTRUCTOR QUALIFICATIONS

(a) To be eligible for a designation as a chief flight instructor for a course of training, a person must meet the following requirements:
  (1) He must pass —
    (i) An oral test on this Part and on Parts 61 and 91 of this chapter and on the training standards and objectives of the course for which he is designated; and
    (ii) A flight test on the flight procedures and maneuvers appropriate to that course.
  (2) He must meet the applicable requirements of paragraphs (b), (c), and (d) of this section. However, a chief flight instructor or an assistant chief flight instructor for a course of training for gliders, free balloons or airships is only required to have 40 percent of the hours required in paragraphs (b) and (c) of this section.
(b) For a course of training leading to the issuance of a private pilot certificate or rating, a chief flight instructor or an assistant chief flight instructor must have —
  (1) At least a commercial pilot certificate and a flight instructor certificate, each with a rating for the category and class of aircraft used in the course;
  (2) At least 1,000 hours as pilot in command;
  (3) Primary flight instruction experience, acquired as either a certificated flight instructor or an instructor in a military pilot primary flight training program, or a combination thereof, consisting of at least —
    (i) Two years and a total of 500 flight hours;
    (ii) 1,000 flight hours; and
  (4) Within the year preceding designation, at least 100 hours of flight instruction as a certificated flight instructor in the category of aircraft used in the course.

(c) For a course of training leading to the issuance of an instrument rating or a rating with instrument privileges, a chief flight instructor must have —
   (1) At least a commercial pilot or airline transport pilot certificate and a valid flight instructor certificate, each with an appropriate instrument rating;
   (2) At least 100 hours of flight time under actual or simulated instrument conditions;
   (3) At least 1,000 hours as pilot in command;
   (4) Instrument flight instructor experience, acquired as either a certificated instrument flight instructor or an instructor in a military pilot basic or instrument flight training program, or a combination thereof; consisting of at least —
      (i) Two years and a total of 250 flight hours; or
      (ii) 400 flight hours.
(d) For a course of training other than those that lead to the issuance of a private pilot certificate or rating, or an instrument rating or a rating with instrument privileges, a chief flight instructor must have —
   (1) At least a commercial pilot or airline transport pilot certificate and a valid flight instructor certificate, each with a rating for the category and class of aircraft used in the course of training and, for a course of training using airplanes or airships, an instrument rating on the instructor's commercial pilot certificate;
   (2) At least 2,000 hours as pilot in command;
   (3) Flight instruction experience, acquired as either a certificated flight instructor or an instructor in a military pilot primary or basic flight training program or a combination thereof, consisting of at least —
      (i) Three years and a total of 1,000 flight hours; or
      (ii) 1,500 flight hours.
(e) To be eligible for designation as a chief instructor for a ground school course, a person must have 1 year of experience as a ground school instructor in a certificated pilot school.

141.36 ASSISTANT CHIEF INSTRUCTOR QUALIFICATIONS

(a) To be eligible for a designation as an assistant chief flight instructor for a course of training, a person must meet the following requirements:
   (1) Possess a commercial pilot or airline transport pilot certificate and a valid flight instructor certificate,
   (2) Meet the pilot-in-command recent flight experience requirements of §61.57 of this chapter,
   (3) Pass an oral test on teaching methods, applicable provisions of the Airman's Information Manual, Parts 61, 91, and 141 of this chapter, and the objectives and approved course completion standards of the course for which the person seeks to obtain designation,
   (4) Pass a flight test on the flight procedures and maneuvers appropriate to that course, and
   (5) Meet the applicable requirements of paragraphs (b), (c), and (d) of this section. However, an assistant chief flight instructor for a course of training for gliders, free balloons, or airships is only required to have 40 percent of the hours required in paragraphs (b) and (c) of this section.
(b) For a course of training leading to the issuance of a private pilot certificate or rating, an assistant chief flight instructor must have—
   (1) At least a commercial pilot or airline transport pilot certificate and a valid flight instructor certificate, each with a rating for the category and class of aircraft used in the course;
   (2) At least 500 hours as pilot in command;
   (3) Primary flight instruction experience, acquired as either a certificated flight instructor or an instructor in a military pilot primary flight training program, or a combination thereof, consisting of at least—
      (i) One year and a total of 250 flight hours; or
      (ii) 500 flight hours.

(c) For a course of training leading to the issuance of an instrument rating or a rating with instrument privileges, an assistant chief flight instructor must have—

    (1) At least a commercial pilot or airline transport pilot certificate and a valid flight instructor certificate, each with an appropriate instrument rating;

    (2) At least 50 hours of flight time under actual or simulated instrument conditions;

    (3) At least 500 hours as pilot in command;

    (4) Instrument flight instructor experience, acquired as either a certificated instrument flight instructor or an instructor in a military pilot basic or instrument flight training program, or a combination thereof, consisting of at least—

        (i) One year and a total of 125 flight hours; or

        (ii) 200 flight hours.

(d) For a course of training other than those that lead to the issuance of a private pilot certificate or rating, or an instrument rating or a rating with instrument privileges, an assistant chief flight instructor must have—

    (1) At least a commercial pilot or airline transport pilot certificate and a valid flight instructor certificate, each with a rating for the category and class of aircraft used in the course of training and, for a course of training using airplanes or airships, an instrument rating on the instructor's commercial pilot certificate;

    (2) At least 1,000 hours as pilot in command;

    (3) Flight instruction experience, acquired as either a certificated flight instructor or an instructor in a military pilot primary or basic flight training program or a combination thereof, consisting of at least—

        (i) One and one half years and a total of 500 flight hours; or

        (ii) 750 flight hours.

(e) To be eligible for a designation as an assistant chief instructor for a ground school course, a person must have one year of experience as a ground school instructor in a certificated pilot school.

141.37   AIRPORTS

(a) An applicant for a pilot school certificate or a provisional pilot school certificate must show that it has continuous use of each airport at which training flights originate.

(b) Each airport used for airplanes and gliders must have at least one runway or takeoff area that allows training aircraft to make a normal takeoff or landing at full gross weight —

    (1) Under calm wind (not more than five miles per hour) conditions and temperatures equal to the mean high temperature for the hottest month of the year in the operating area;

    (2) Clearing all obstacles in the takeoff flight path by at least 50 feet;

    (3) With the powerplant operation and landing gear and flap operation, if applicable, recommended by the manufacturer; and

    (4) With smooth transition from liftoff to the best rate of climb speed without exceptional piloting skills or techniques.

(c) Each airport must have a wind direction indicator that is visible from the ends of each runway at ground level.

(d) Each airport must have a traffic direction indicator when the airport has no operating control tower and UNICOM advisories are not available.

(e) Each airport used for night training flights must have permanent runway lights.

141.39   AIRCRAFT

An applicant for a pilot school or provisional pilot school certificate must show that each aircraft used by that school for flight instruction and solo flights meets the following requirements:

(a) It must be registered as a civil aircraft of the United States.

(b) Except for aircraft used for flight instruction and solo flights in course of training for agricultural aircraft operations, external load operations and similar aerial work operations, it must be certificated in the standard airworthiness category.

(c) It must be maintained and inspected in accordance with the requirements of Part 91 of this chapter that apply to aircraft used to give flight instruction for hire.

(d) For use in flight instruction, it must be at least a two-place aircraft having engine power controls and flight controls that are easily reached and that operate in a normal manner from both pilot stations.

(e) For use in IFR enroute operations and instrument approaches, it must be equipped and maintained for IFR operations. However, for instruction in the control and precision maneuvering of an aircraft by reference to instruments, the aircraft may be equipped as provided in the approved course of training.

141.41 GROUND TRAINERS AND TRAINING AIDS

An applicant for a pilot school or a provisional pilot school certificate must show that its ground trainers, and training aids and equipment meet the following requirements:

(a) *Pilot ground trainers.*
  (1) Each pilot ground trainer used to obtain the maximum flight training credit allowed for ground trainers in an approved pilot training course curriculum must have —
    (i) An enclosed pilot's station or cockpit which accommodates one or more flight crewmembers;
    (ii) Controls to simulate the rotation of the trainer about three axes;
    (iii) The minimum instrumentation and equipment required for powered aircraft in §91.205 of this chapter, for the type of flight operations simulated;
    (iv) For VFR instruction, a means for simulating visual flight conditions, including motion of the trainer, or projections, or models operated by the flight controls; and
    (v) For IFR instruction, a means for recording the flight path simulated by the trainer.
  (2) Pilot ground trainers other than those covered under paragraph (a)(1) of this section must have —
    (i) An enclosed pilots's station or cockpit, which accommodates one or more flight crewmembers;
    (ii) Controls to simulate the rotation of the trainer about three axes; and
    (iii) The minimum instrumentation and equipment required for powered aircraft in §91.205 of this chapter, for the type of flight operations simulated.

(b) *Training aids and equipment.* Each training aid, including any audiovisuals, mockup, chart, or aircraft component listed in the approved training course outline must be accurate and appropriate to the course for which it is used.

141.43 PILOT BRIEFING AREAS

(a) An applicant for a pilot school or provisional pilot school certificate must show that it has the continuous use of a briefing area located at each airport at which training flights originate, that is —
  (1) Adequate to shelter students waiting to engage in their training flights;
  (2) Arranged and equipped for the conduct of pilot briefings; and
  (3) For a school with an instrument or commercial pilot course rating, equipped with private landline or telephone communication to the nearest FAA Flight Service Station, except that this communication equipment is not required if the briefing area and the flight service station are located on the same airport and are readily accessible to each other.

(b) A briefing area required by paragraph (a) of this section may not be used by the applicant if it is available for use by any other pilot school during the period it is required for use by the applicant.

141.45 GROUND TRAINING FACILITIES

An applicant for a pilot school or provisional pilot school certificate must show that each room, training booth, or other space used for instructional purposes is heated, lighted, and ventilated to conform to local building, sanitation, and health codes. In addition, the training facility must be so located that the students in that facility are not distracted by the instruction conducted in other rooms, or by flight and maintenance operations on the airport.

SUBPART C — TRAINING COURSE OUTLINE AND CURRICULUM

141.51 APPLICABILITY

This subpart prescribes the curriculum and course outline requirements for the issuance of a pilot school or provisional pilot school certificate and ratings.

141.53 TRAINING COURSE OUTLINE: GENERAL

(a) *General.* An applicant for a pilot school or provisional pilot school certificate must obtain the Administrator's approval of the outline of each training course for which certification and rating is sought.

(b) *Application.* An application for the approval of an initial or amended training course outline is made in triplicate to the FAA Flight Standards District Office having jurisdiction over the area in which the operations base of the applicant is located. It must be made at least 30 days before any training under that course, or any amendment thereto, is scheduled to begin. An application for an amendment to an approved training course must be accompanied by three copies of the pages in the course outline for which an amendment is requested.

141.55 TRAINING COURSE OUTLINE: CONTENTS

(a) *General.* The outline for each course of training for which approval is requested must meet the minimum curriculum for that course prescribed in the appropriate appendix of this Part, and contain the following information:

(1) A description of each room used for ground training, including its size and the maximum number of students that may be instructed in the room at one time.

(2) A description of each type of audiovisual aid, projector, tape recorder, mockup, aircraft component and other special training aid used for ground training.

(3) A description of each pilot ground trainer used for instruction.

(4) A listing of the airports at which training flights originate and a description of the facilities, including pilot briefing areas that are available for use by the students and operating personnel at each of those airports.

(5) A description of the type of aircraft including any special equipment, used for each phase of instruction.

(6) The minimum qualifications and ratings for each instructor used for ground or flight training.

(b) *Training syllabus.* In addition to the items specified in paragraph (a) of this section, the course outline must include a training syllabus for each course of training that includes at least the following information:

(1) The pilot certificate and ratings, if any; the medical certificate, if necessary; and the training, pilot experience and knowledge, required for enrollment in the course.

(2) A description of each lesson, including its objectives and standards and the measurable unit of student accomplishment or learning to be derived from the lesson or course.

(3) The stage of training (including the standards therefor) normally accomplished within each training period of not more than 90 days.

(4) A description of the tests and checks used to measure a student's accomplishment for each stage of training.

141.57 SPECIAL CURRICULA

An applicant for a pilot school or provisional pilot school certificate may apply for approval to conduct a special course of pilot training for which a curriculum is not prescribed in the appendixes to this Part, if it shows that the special course of pilot training contains features which can be expected to achieve a level of pilot competency equivalent to that achieved by the curriculum prescribed in the appendixes to this Part or the requirements of Part 61 of this chapter.

SUBPART D — EXAMINING AUTHORITY

141.61 APPLICABILITY

This subpart prescribes the requirements for the issuance of an examining authority to the holder of a pilot school certificate and the privileges and limitations of that authority.

141.63 APPLICATION AND QUALIFICATION

(a) Application for an examining authority is made on a form and in a manner prescribed by the Administrator.

(b) To be eligible for an examining authority an applicant must hold a pilot school certificate. In addition, the applicant must snow that —

(1) It has actively conducted a certificated pilot school for at least 24 months before the date of application; and

(2) Within the 24 months before the date of application for the examining authority, at least 10 students were graduated from the course for which the authority is requested, and at least 9 of the most recent 10 graduates of that course, who were given an interim or final test by an FAA inspector or a designated pilot examiner, passed that test the first time.

141.65 PRIVILEGES

The holder of an examining authority may recommend graduates of the school's approved certification courses for pilot certificates and ratings except flight instructor certificates, airline transport pilot certificates and ratings, and turbojet type ratings, without taking the FAA flight or written test, or both, in accordance with the provisions of this subpart.

141.67 LIMITATIONS AND REPORTS

(a) The holder of an examining authority may not recommend any person for the issuance of a pilot certificate or rating without taking the FAA written or flight test unless that person has —

(1) Been enrolled by the holder of the examining authority in its approved course of training for the particular pilot certificate or rating recommended; and

(2) Satisfactorily completed all of that course of training at its school.

(b) Each final written or flight test given by the holder of an examining authority to a person who has completed the approved course of training must be at least equal in scope, depth, and difficulty to the comparable written or flight test prescribed by the Administrator under Part 61 of this chapter.

(c) A final ground school written test may not be given by the holder of an examining authority to a student enrolled in its approved course of training unless the test has been approved by the FAA Flight Standards District Office having jurisdiction over the area in which the holder of the examining authority is located. In addition, an approved test may not be given by the holder of an examining authority when —

(1) It knows or has reason to believe that the test has been compromised; or

(2) It has been notified that the Flight Standards District Office knows or has reason to believe that the test has been compromised.

(d) The holder of an examining authority shall submit to the FAA Flight Standards District Office a copy of the appropriate training record for each person recommended by it for a pilot certificate or rating.

INTENTIONALLY

LEFT

BLANK

SUBPART E — OPERATING RULES

141.71   APPLICABILITY

This subpart prescribes the operating rules that are applicable to a pilot school or provisional pilot school certificated under the provisions of this part.

141.73   PRIVILEGES

(a)   The holder of a pilot school or a provisional pilot school certificate may advertise and conduct approved pilot training courses in accordance with the certificate and ratings that it holds.

(b)   A certificate pilot school holding an examining authority for a certification course may recommend each graduate of that course for the issuance of a pilot certificate and rating appropriate to that course without the necessity of taking an FAA written or flight test from an FAA inspector or designated pilot examiner.

141.75   AIRCRAFT REQUIREMENTS

(a)   A pretakeoff and prelanding checklist, and the operator's handbook for the aircraft (if one is furnished by the manufacturer) or copies of the handbook if furnished to each student using the aircraft, must be carried on each aircraft used for flight instruction and solo flights.

(b)   Each aircraft used for flight instruction and solo flight must have a standard airworthiness certificate, except that an aircraft certificated in the restricted category may be used for flight training and solo flights conducted under special courses for agricultural aircraft operation, external load operations, and similar aerial work operations if its use for training is not prohibited by the operating limitations for the aircraft.

141.77   LIMITATIONS

(a)   The holder of a pilot school or a provisional pilot school certificate may not issue a graduation certificate to a student, nor may a certificate pilot school recommend a student for a pilot certificate or rating, unless the student has completed the training therefor specified in the school's course of training and passed the required final tests.

(b)   The holder of a pilot school or a provisional pilot school certificate may not graduate a student from a course of training unless he has completed all of the curriculum requirements of that course. A student may be credited, but not for more than one-half of the curriculum requirements, with previous pilot experience and knowledge, based upon an appropriate flight check or test by the school. Course credits may be transferred from one certificated school to another. The receiving school shall determine the amount to be transferred, based on a flight check or written test, or both, of the student. Credit for training and instruction received in another school may not be given unless—

(1)   The other school holds a certificate issued under this part and certifies to the kind and amount of training and to the result of each stage and final test given to that student;

(2)   The training and instruction was conducted by the other school in accordance with that school's approved training course; and

(3)   The student was enrolled in the other school's approved training course before he received the instruction and training.

141.79   FLIGHT INSTRUCTION

(a)   No person other than a flight instructor who has the ratings and the minimum qualifications specified in the approved training course outline may give a student flight instruction under an approved course of training.

(b)   No student pilot may be authorized to start a solo practice flight from an airport until the flight has been approved by an authorized flight instructor who is present at that airport.

┌ Amend #5
└ eff 4-13-94

(c) Each chief flight instructor must complete at least once each 12 months, an approved flight instructor refresher course consisting of ground or flight instruction, or both.

(d) Each flight instructor for an approved course of training must satisfactorily accomplish a flight check given to him by the designated chief flight instructor for the school by whom he is employed. He must also satisfactorily accomplish this flight check each 12 months from the month in which the initial check is given. In addition, he must satisfactorily accomplish a flight check in each type of aircraft in which he gives instruction.

(e) An instructor may not be used in an approved course of training until he has been briefed in regard to the objectives and standards of the course by the designated chief instructor or his assistant.

141.81   GROUND TRAINING

(a) Except as provided in paragraph (b) of this section, each instructor used for ground training in an approved course of training must hold a flight or ground instructor certificate with an appropriate rating for the course of training.

(b) A person who does not meet the requirements of paragraph (a) of this section may be used for ground training in an approved course of training if —
  (1) The chief instructor for that course of training finds him qualified to give that instruction; and
  (2) The instruction is given under the direct supervision of the chief instructor or the assistant chief instructor who is present at the base when the instruction is given.

(c) An instructor may not be used in an approved course of training until he has been briefed in regard to the objectives and standards of that course by the designated chief instructor or his assistant.

141.83   QUALITY OF INSTRUCTION

(a) Each holder of a pilot school or provisional pilot school certificate must comply with the approved course of training and must provide training and instruction of such quality that at least 8 out of the 10 students or graduates of that school most recently tested by an FAA inspector or designated pilot examiner, passed on their first attempt either of the following tests:
  (1) A test for a pilot certificate or rating, or for an operating privilege appropriate to the course from which the student graduated; or
  (2) A test given to a student to determine his competence and knowledge of a completed stage of the training course in which he is enrolled.

(b) The failure of a certificated pilot school or provisional pilot school to maintain the quality of instruction specified in paragraph (a) of this section is considered to be the basis for the suspension or revocation of the certificate held by that school.

(c) The holder of a pilot school or provisional pilot school certificate shall allow the Administrator to make any test, flight check, or examination of its students to determine compliance with its approved course of training and the quality of its instruction and training. A flight check conducted under the provisions of this paragraph is based upon the standards prescribed in the school's approved course of training. However, if the student has completed a course of training for a pilot certificate or rating, the flight test is based upon the standards prescribed in Part 61 of this chapter.

141.85   CHIEF INSTRUCTOR RESPONSIBILITIES

(a) Each person designated as a chief instructor for a certificated pilot school or provisional pilot school shall be responsible for —
  (1) Certifying training records, graduation certificates, stage and final test reports, and student recommendations;
  (2) Conducting an initial proficiency check of each instructor before he is used in an approved course of instruction and, thereafter, at least once each 12 months from the month in which the initial check was conducted;
  (3) Conducting each stage or final test given to a student enrolled in an approved course of instruction; and
  (4) Maintaining training techniques, procedures, and standards for the school that are acceptable to the Administrator.

Amend #4
Eff 4-15-91

(b)   The chief instructor or his designated assistant chief instructor shall be available at the pilot school or, if away from the premises, by telephone, radio, or other electronic means during the time that instruction is given for an approved course of training.

141.87   CHANGE OF CHIEF INSTRUCTOR

(a)   The holder of a pilot school or provisional pilot school certificate shall immediately notify in writing the FAA Flight Standards District Office having jurisdiction over the area in which the school is located, of any change in its designation of a chief instructor of an approved training course.

(b)   The holder of a pilot school or provisional pilot school certificate may, after providing the notification required in paragraph (a) of this section and pending the designation and approval of another chief instructor, conduct training or instruction without a chief instructor for that course of training for a period of not more than 60 days. However, during that time each stage or final test of a student enrolled in that approved course of training must be given by an FAA inspector, or a designated pilot examiner.

141.89   MAINTENANCE OF PERSONNEL, FACILITIES, AND EQUIPMENT

The holder of a pilot school or provisional pilot school certificate may not give instruction or training to a student who is enrolled in an approved course of training unless —

(a)   Each airport, aircraft, and facility necessary for that instruction or training meets the standards specified in the holder's approved training course outline and the appropriate requirements of this Part; and

(b)   Except as provided in §141.87, each instructor or chief instructor meets the qualifications specified in the holder's approved course of training and the appropriate requirements of this Part.

141.91   SATELLITE BASES

The holder of a pilot school or provisional pilot school certificate may conduct ground or flight training and instruction in an approved course of training at a base other than its main operations base if —

(a)   An assistant chief instructor is designated for each satellite base, and that assistant chief instructor shall be available at the satellite pilot school or, if away from the premises, by telephone, radio, or other electronic means during the time that instruction is given for an approved course of training;

Amend #4
Eff 4-15-91

(b)   The airport, facilities, and personnel used at the satellite base meet the appropriate requirements of Subpart B of this Part and its approved training course outline;

(c)   The instructors are under the direct supervision of the chief flight instructor or assistant chief flight instructor for the appropriate training course, who is readily available for consultation in accordance with § 141.85(b); and

(d)   The FAA Flight Standards District Office having jurisdiction over the area in which the school is located is notified in writing if training or instruction is conducted there for more than seven consecutive days.

141.93   ENROLLMENT

(a)   The holder of a pilot school or a provisional pilot school certificate shall furnish each student, at the time he is enrolled in each approved training course, with the following:

  (1)   A certificate of enrollment containing —
    (i)   The name of the course in which he is enrolled; and
    (ii)   The date of that enrollment.
  (2)   A copy of the training syllabus required under §141.55(b).
  (3)   A copy of the safety procedures and practices developed by the school covering the use of its facilities and the operation of its aircraft, including instructions on the following:
    (i)   The weather minimums required by the school for dual and solo flights.
    (ii)   The procedures for starting and taxiing aircraft on the ramp.
    (iii)   Fire precautions and procedures.
    (iv)   Redispatch procedures after unprogrammed landings, on and off airports.

       (v)   Aircraft discrepancies and write offs.
       (vi)   Securing of aircraft when not in use.
       (vii)   Fuel reserves necessary for local and cross-country flights.
       (viii) Avoidance of other aircraft in flight and on the ground.
       (ix)   Minimum altitude limitations and simulated emergency landing instructions.
       (x)   Description and use of assigned practice areas.

(b)   The holder of a pilot school or provisional pilot school certificate shall, within 5 days after the date of enrollment, forward a copy of each certificate of enrollment required by paragraph (a)(1) of this section to the FAA Flight Standards District Office having jurisdiction over the area in which the school is located.

141.95   GRADUATION CERTIFICATE

(a)   The holder of a pilot school or provisional pilot school certificate shall issue a graduation certificate to each student who completes its approved course of training.

(b)   The certificate shall be issued to the student upon his completion of the course of training and contain at least the following information:

   (1)   The name of the school and the number of the school certificate.
   (2)   The name of the graduate to whom it was issued.
   (3)   The course of training for which it was issued.
   (4)   The date of graduation.
   (5)   A statement that the student has satisfactorily completed each required stage of the approved course of training including the tests for those stages.
   (6)   A certification of the information contained in the certification by the chief instructor for that course of training.
   (7)   A statement showing the cross-country training the student received in the course of training.

SUBPART F — RECORDS

141.101   TRAINING RECORDS

(a)   Each holder of a pilot school or provisional pilot school certificate shall establish and maintain a current and accurate record of the participation and accomplishment of each student enrolled in an approved course of training conducted by the school (the student's logbook is not acceptable for this record). The record shall include —

   (1)   The date the student was enrolled:
   (2)   A chronological log of the student's attendance, subjects, and flight operations covered in his training and instruction, and the names and grades of any tests taken by the student; and
   (3)   The date the student graduated, terminated his training, or transferred to another school.

(b)   Whenever a student graduates, terminates his training, or transfers to another school, his record shali be certified to that effect by the chief instructor.

(c)   The holder of a certificate for a pilot school or a provisional pilot school shall retain each student record required by this section for at least 1 year from the date that the student graduates from the course to which the record pertains, terminates his enrollment in that course, or transfers to another school.

(d)   The holder of a certificate for a pilot school or a provisional pilot school shall, upon request of a student, make a copy of his record available to him.

APPENDIX A — PRIVATE PILOT CERTIFICATION COURSE (AIRPLANES)

1. *Applicability.* This Appendix prescribes the minimum curriculum for a private pilot certification course (airplanes) required by § 141.55.
2. *Ground training.* The course must consist of at least 35 hours of ground training in the following subjects:
   (a) The Federal Aviation Regulations applicable to private pilot privileges, limitations, and flight operations; the rules of the National Transportation Safety Board pertaining to accident reporting; the use of the Airman's Information Manual; and the FAA Advisory Circular System.
   (b) VFR navigation using pilotage, dead reckoning, and radio aids.
   (c) The recognition of critical weather situations from the ground and in flight and the procurement and use of aeronautical weather reports and forecasts.
   (d) The safe and efficient operation of airplanes, including high density airport operations, collision avoidance precautions, and radio communication procedures.

Amend #4
Eff 4-15-91 ➤ (e) Stall awareness, spin entry, spins, and spin recovery techniques.

3. *Flight training.*
   (a) The course must consist of at least 35 hours of the flight training listed in this section and section 4 of this Appendix. Instruction in a pilot ground trainer that meets the requirements of § 141.41(a)(1) may be credited for not more than 5 of the required 35 hours of flight time. Instruction in a pilot ground trainer that meets the requirement of § 141.41(a)(2) may be credited for not more than 2.5 hours of the required 35 hours of flight time.
   (b) Each training flight must include a preflight briefing and a postflight critique of the student by the instructor assigned to that flight.
   (c) Flight training must consist of at least 20 hours of instruction in the following subjects:
      (1) Preflight operations, including weight and balance determination, line inspection, starting and runups, and airplane servicing.
      (2) Airport and traffic pattern operations, including operations at controlled airports, radio communications, and collision avoidance precautions.
      (3) Flight maneuvering by reference to ground objects.

Amend #4
Eff 4-15-91
      (4) Flight at slow airspeeds with realistic distractions, recognition of and recovery from stalls entered from straight flight and from turns.
      (5) Normal and crosswind takeoffs and landings.
      (6) Control and maneuvering an airplane solely by reference to instruments, including emergency descents and climbs using radio aids or radar directives.
      (7) Cross-country flying using pilotage, dead reckoning, and radio aids including a two-hour dual flight at least part of which must be on Federal airways.
      (8) Maximum performance takeoffs and landings.
      (9) Night flying, including 5 takeoffs and landings as sole manipulator of the controls, and VFR navigation.
      (10) Emergency operations, including simulated aircraft and equipment malfunctions, lost procedures, and emergency go-arounds.

4. *Solo flights.* The course must provide at least 15 hours of solo flights, including—
   (a) *Solo practice.* Directed solo practice on all VFR flight operations for which flight instruction is required (except simulated emergencies) to develop proficiency, resourcefulness, and self-reliance.
   (b) *Cross-country flights.*
      (1) Ten hours of cross-country flights, each flight with a landing at a point more than 50 nautical miles from the original departure point. One flight must be of at least 300 nautical miles with landings at a minimum of three points, one of which is at least 100 nautical miles from the original departure point.
      (2) If a pilot school or a provisional pilot school shows that it is located on an island from which cross-country flights cannot be accomplished without flying over water more than 10 nautical miles from the nearest shoreline, it need not include cross-country flights under subparagraph (1) of this paragraph. However, if other airports that permit civil operations are available to which a flight may be made without flying over water more than 10 nautical miles from the nearest shoreline, the school must include in its course, two round trip solo flights between those airports that are farthest apart, including a landing at each airport on both flights.

5. *Stage and final tests.*
    (a) Each student enrolled in a private pilot certification course must satisfactorily accomplish the stage and final tests prescribed in this section. The written tests may not be credited for more than 3 hours of the 35 hours of required ground training, and the flight tests may not be credited for more than 4 hours of the 35 hours of required flight training.
    (b) Each student must satisfactorily accomplish a written examination at the completion of each stage of training specified in the approved training syllabus for the private pilot certification course and a final test at the conclusion of that course.
    (c) Each student must satisfactorily accomplish a flight test at the completion of the first solo flight and at the completion of the first solo cross-country flight and at the conclusion of that course.

APPENDIX B — PRIVATE TEST COURSE (AIRPLANES)

1. *Applicability.* This Appendix prescribes the minimum curriculum for a private test course (airplanes) required by § 141.55.
2. *Experience.* For enrollment as a student in a private test course (airplanes) an applicant must—
    (a) Have logged at least 30 hours of flight time as a pilot; and
    (b) Have such experience and flight training that upon completion of his approved private test course (airplanes) he will meet the aeronautical experience requirements prescribed in Part 61 of this chapter for a private pilot certificate.
3. *Ground training.* The course must consist of at least 35 hours of ground training in the subjects listed in § 2 of Appendix A of this Part.
4. *Flight training.*
    (a) The course must consist of a total of at least 10 hours of flight instruction in the subjects listed in § 3 (c) of Appendix A of this Part.
    (b) Each training flight must include a preflight briefing and a postflight critique of the student by the instructor assigned to that flight.
5. *Stage and final tests.* Each student enrolled in the course must satisfactorily accomplish the final tests prescribed in § 5 of Appendix A of this Part. Written tests may not be credited for more than 3 hours of the required 35 hours of ground training, and the flight tests may not be credited for more than 2 hours of the required 10 hours of flight training.

APPENDIX C — INSTRUMENT RATING COURSE (AIRPLANES)

1. *Applicability.* This Appendix prescribes the minimum curriculum for training course for an Instrument Rating Course (airplanes) required by §141.55.
2. *Ground-training.* The course must consist of at least 30 hours of ground training instruction in the followng subjects:
   (a) The Federal Aviation Regulations that apply to flight under IFR conditions, the IFR air traffic system and procedures, and the provisions of the Airman's Information Manual pertinent to IFR flights.
   (b) Dead reckoning appropriate to IFR navigation, IFR navigation by radio aids using the VOR, ADF, and ILS systems, and the use of IFR charts and instrument approach procedures charts.
   (c) The procurement and use of aviation weather reports and forecasts, and the elements of forecasting weather trends on the basis of that information and personal observation of weather conditions.
   (d) The function, use, and limitations of flight instruments required for IFR flights, including transponders, radar and radio aids to navigation.
3. *Flight training.* The course must consist of at least 35 hours of instrument flight instruction given by an appropriately rated flight instructor, covering the operations listed in paragraphs (a) through (d) of this section. Instruction given by an authorized instructor in a pilot ground trainer which meets the requirements of §141.41(a)(1) may be credited for not more than 15 hours of the required flight instruction. Instruction in a pilot ground trainer that meets the requirements of §141.41(a)(2) may be credited for not more than 7.5 of the required 35 hours of flight time.
   (a) Control and accurate maneuvering of an airplane solely by reference to flight instruments.
   (b) IFR navigation by the use of VOR and ADF systems, including time, speed and distance computations and compliance with air traffic control instructions and procedures.
   (c) Instrument approaches to published minimums using the VOR, ADF and ILS systems (instruction in the use of the ILS glide slope may be given in an instrument ground trainer or with an airborne ILS simulator).
   (d) Cross-country flying in simulated or actual IFR conditions, on Federal airways or as routed by ATC, including one such trip of at least 250 nautical miles including VOR, ADF, and ILS approaches at different airports.
   (e) Emergency procedures appropriate to the maneuvering of an airplane solely by reference to flight instruments.
4. *Stage and final tests.*
   (a) Each student must satisfactorily accomplish a written test at the completion of each stage of training specified in the approved training syllabus for the instrument rating course. In addition, he must satisfactorily accomplish a final written test at the conclusion of that course. The written tests may not be credited for more than 5 hours of the 30 hours of required ground training.
   (b) Each student must satisfactorily accomplish a flight stage test at the completion of each operation listed in paragraphs (a), (b), and (c) of section 3 of this Appendix. In addition, he must satisfactorily accomplish a final flight test at the completion of the course. The stage and final tests may not be credited for more than 5 hours of the required 35 hours of flight training.

APPENDIX D — COMMERCIAL PILOT CERTIFICATION COURSE (AIRPLANES)

1. *Applicability.* This Appendix prescribes the minimum curriculum for a commercial pilot certification course (airplanes) required by §141.55.

2. *Ground training.* The course must consist of at least 100 hours of ground training instruction in the following subjects:

    (a) The ground training subjects prescribed in section 2 of Appendix A of this Part for a private pilot certification course, except the private pilot privileges and limitations of paragraph (a) of that section.

    (b) The ground training subjects prescribed in section 2 of Appendix C of this Part 141 for an Instrument Rating Course.

    (c) The Federal Aviation Regulations covering the privileges, limitations, and operations of a commercial pilot, and the operations for which an air taxi/commercial operator, agricultural aircraft operator, and external load operator certificate, waiver, or exemption is required.

    (d) Basic aerodynamics, and the principles of flight which apply to airplanes.

    (e) The safe and efficient operation of airplanes, including inspection and certification requirements, operating limitations, high altitude operations and physiological considerations, loading computations, the significance of the use of airplane performance speeds, the computations involved in runway and obstacle clearance and crosswind component considerations, and cruise control.

3. *Flight training.*

    (a) *General.* The course must consist of at least 190 hours of the flight training and instruction prescribed in this section. Instruction in a pilot ground trainer that meets the requirements of §141.41(a)(1) may be credited for not more than 40 hours of the required 190 hours of flight time. Instruction in a pilot ground trainer that meets the requirements of §141.41(a)(2) may be credited for not more than 20 hours of the required 190 hours of flight time.

    (b) *Flight instruction.* The course must consist of at least 75 hours of instruction in the operations listed in subparagraphs (1) through (6) of this paragraph. Instruction in a pilot ground trainer that meets the requirements of §141.41(a)(1) may be credited for not more than 20 hours of the required 75 hours. Instruction in a pilot ground trainer that meets the requirements of §141.41(a)(2) may be credited for not more than 10 hours of the required 75 hours.

        (1) The pilot operations for the Private Pilot Course prescribed in §3 of Appendix A of this Part.

        (2) The IFR operations for the Instrument Rating Course prescribed in §3 of Appendix C of this Part.

        (3) Ten hours of flight instruction in an airplane with retractable gear, flaps, a controllable propeller, and powered by at least 180 hp. engine.

        (4) Night flying, including a cross-country night flight with a landing at a point more than 100 miles from the point of departure.

        (5) Normal and maximum performance takeoffs and landings using precision approaches and prescribed airplane performance speeds, including operations at maximum authorized takeoff weight.

        (6) Emergency procedures appropriate to VFR and IFR flight and to the operation of complex airplane systems.

    (c) *Solo practice.* The course must consist of at least 100 hours of the flights listed in subparagraphs (1) through (4) of this paragraph. Flight time as pilot in command of an airplane carrying only those persons who are pilots assigned by the school to specific flight crew duties on the flight may be credited for not more than 50 hours of that requirement.

        (1) Directed solo practice on each VFR operation for which flight instruction is required (except simulated emergencies).

        (2) At least 40 hours of solo cross-country flights, each flight with a landing at a point more than 50 nautical miles from the original departure point. One flight must have landings at a minimum of three points, one of which is at least 150 nautical miles from the original departure point if the flight is conducted in Hawaii, or at least 250 nautical miles from the original departure point if it is conducted elsewhere.

- (3) At least 5 hours of pilot in command time in an airplane described in paragraph (b)(3) of this section, including not less than 10 takeoffs and 10 landings to a full stop.
- (4) At least 5 hours of night flight, including at least 10 takeoffs and 10 landings to a full stop.

4. *Stage and final tests.*
  - (a) *Written examinations.* Each student enrolled in the course must satisfactorily accomplish a written test upon the completion of each stage of training specified in the approved training syllabus for the commercial pilot certification course. In addition, he must satisfactorily accomplish a final stage test at the completion of all of that course. The stage and final tests may be credited for not more than 6 hours of the required 100 hours of ground training.
  - (b) *Flight tests.* Each student enrolled in a commercial pilot certification course (airplanes) must satisfactorily accomplish a stage flight test at the completion of each of the stages listed in subparagraphs (1), (2), (3), (4), and (5), of this paragraph. In addition, he must satisfactorily accomplish a final test at the completion of all of those stages. The stage and final tests may not be credited for more than 10 hours of the required 190 hours of flight training.
    - (1) Solo.
    - (2) Cross-country.
    - (3) High performance airplane operations.
    - (4) IFR operations.
    - (5) Commercial Pilot Course test, VFR and IFR.

APPENDIX E — COMMERCIAL TEST COURSE (AIRPLANES)

1. *Applicability*. This Appendix prescribes the minimum curriculum for a commercial test course (airplanes) required by § 141.55.
2. *Experience*. For enrollment as a student in a commercial test course (airplanes) an applicant must—
   (a) Hold a valid private pilot certificate;
   (b) Hold a valid instrument rating, or be enrolled in an approved instrument rating course; and
   (c) Have such experience and flight training that upon completion of his approved commercial test course he will meet the aeronautical experience requirements prescribed in Part 61 of this chapter for a commercial pilot certificate.
3. *Ground training*. The course must consist of at least 50 hours of ground training instruction in the following subjects:
   (a) A review of the ground training subjects prescribed in § 2 of Appendix A of this Part 141 for a private pilot certification.
   (b) A review of the ground training subjects prescribed in § 2 of Appendix C of this Part 141 for an instrument rating course.
   (c) The Federal Aviation Regulations covering the privileges, limitations, and operations of a commericial pilot, and the operations for which an air taxi/commercial operator, agricultural aircraft operator, and external load operator certificate, waiver or exemption is required.
   (d) Basic aerodynamics, and the principles of flight that apply to airplanes.
   (e) The safe and efficient operation of airplanes, including inspection and certification requirements, operating limitations, high altitude operations and physiological considerations, loading computations, the significance and use of airplane performance speeds, and computations involved in runway and obstacles clearance and crosswind component considerations.
4. *Flight training*.
   (a) *General*. The course must consist of at least 25 hours of flight training prescribed in this section. Instruction in a pilot ground trainer that meets the requirements of § 141.41(a)(1) may be credited for not more than 20 percent of the total number of hours of flight time. Instruction in a pilot ground trainer that meets the requirements of § 141.41(a)(2) may be credited for not more than 10 percent of the total number of hours of flight time.
   (b) *Flight instruction*. The course must consist of at least 20 hours of flight instruction in the subjects listed in subparagraphs (1) through (3) of this paragraph. Instruction in a ground trainer that meets the requirements of § 141.41(a)(1) may be credited for not more than 4 hours of the required 20 hours. Instruction in a ground trainer that meets the requirements of § 141.41(a)(2) may be credited for not more than 2 hours of the required 20 hours.
       (1) A review of the VFR operations prescribed in § 3 of Appendix A of this Part for a private course.
       (2) A review of the IFR operations prescribed in § 3 of Appendix C of this Part for an instrument rating course.
       (3) A review of the VFR operations prescribed in § 3(b)(3) through (6) of Appendix D of this Part for a commercial pilot certification course.
   (c) *Directed solo practice*. If the course includes directed solo practice necessary to develop the flight proficiency of each student, the practice may not exceed a ratio of 3 hours of directed solo practice for each hour of the flight instruction required by the school's approved course outline.
5. *Stage and final tests*.
   (a) *Written tests*. Each student enrolled in the course must satisfactorily accomplish a stage test upon the completion of each stage of training specified in the approved training syllabus for the commercial test course. In addition, he must satisfactorily accomplish a final test at the conclusion of that course. The stage and final tests may not be credited for more than 4 hours of the required 50 hours of ground training.

(b) *Flight tests.* Each student enrolled in the course must satisfactorily accomplish a final test at the completion of the course. However, if the approved course of training exceeds 35 hours he must be given a test at an appropriate stage prior to completion of 35 hours of flight training. The flight tests may not be credited for more than 3 of the required hours of flight training.

(c) *Total flight experience.* The approved training course outline must specify the minimum number of hours of flight instruction and directed solo practice (if any) that is provided for each student under the requirements of paragraphs (b) and (c) of § 4 of this Appendix. The total number of hours of all flight training given to a student under this section and the minimum experience required for enrollment under § 2 of this Appendix must meet the minimum aeronautical experience requirements of § 61.129 of this chapter for the issuance of a commercial pilot certificate.

APPENDIX F — ROTORCRAFT, GLIDERS, LIGHTER-THAN-AIR AIRCRAFT AND AIRCRAFT RATING COURSES

A. *Applicability.* This Appendix prescribes the minimum curriculum for a pilot certification course for a rotorcraft, glider, lighter-than-air aircraft, or aircraft rating, required by § 141.55.

B. *General Requirements.* The course must be comparable in scope, depth, and detail with the curriculum prescribed in Appendices A through D of this Part for a pilot certification course (airplanes) with the same rating. Each course must provide ground and flight training covering the aeronautical knowledge and skill items required by Part 61 of this chapter for the certificate or rating concerned. In addition, each course must meet the appropriate requirements of this Appendix.

C. *Rotorcraft.*

   I. *Kinds of rotorcraft pilot certification courses.* An approved rotorcraft pilot certification course includes—

     (a) A helicopter or gyroplane course—private pilots;

     (b) A helicopter or gyroplane course—commercial pilots; and

     (c) An instrument rating—helicopter.

   II. *Helicopter or gyroplane course: Private pilots.*

     (a) A private pilot certification course for helicopter or gyroplanes must consist of at least the following:

       (1) Ground training—35 hours.

       (2) Flight training—35 hours, including the following:

         (i) Flight instruction—20 hours.

         (ii) Solo practice—10 hours, including a flight with landings at three points, each of which is more than 25 nautical miles from the other two points.

     (b) Stage and final tests may be credited for not more than 3 hours of the 35 hours of ground training, and for not more than 4 hours of the 35 hours of flight training required by paragraphs (a)(1) and (a)(2) of this section.

   III. *Helicopter or gyroplane course—commercial pilots.*

     (a) A commercial pilot certification course of training for helicopters or gyroplanes must consist of at least the following:

       (1) Ground training—65 hours.

       (2) Flight training—150 hours of flight training at least 50 hours of which must be in helicopters or gyroplanes.

       The flight training must include the following:

         (i) Flight instruction—50 hours.

         (ii) Directed solo—100 hours (including a cross-country flight with landings at three points, each of which is more than 50 nautical miles from the other two points).

     (b) Stage and final tests may be credited for not more than 5 hours of the required 65 hours of ground training, and for not more than 7 hours of the required 150 hours of flight training prescribed in paragraphs (a)(1) and (a)(2) of this section.

   IV. *Instrument rating—helicopter course.*

     (a) An instrument rating—helicopter course of training must consist of at least the following:

       (1) Ground training—35 hours.

       (2) Instrument flight training—35 hours. Instrument instruction in a pilot ground trainer that meets the requirements of § 141.41(a)(1) may be credited for not more than 10 hours of the required 35 hours of flight training. Instruction in a ground trainer that meets the requirements of § 141.41(a)(2) may be credited for not more than 5 hours of the required 35 hours. The instrument flight instruction must include a 100-mile simulated or actual IFR cross-country flight, and 25 hours of flight instruction.

       (3) Stage and final tests may be credited for not more than 5 hours of the 35 hours of required ground training, and not more than 5 hours of the 35 hours of instrument training.

D. *Gliders.*
  I.   *Kinds of glider pilot certification courses.* An approved glider certification course includes—
    (a)   A glider course—private pilot; and
    (b)   A glider course—commercial pilots.
  II.   *Glider course: Private pilot.* A private pilot certification course for gliders must consist of at least the following:
    (a)   Ground training—15 hours.
    (b)   Flight training—8 hours (including 35 flights if ground tows are used or 20 flights if aero tows are used). The flight training must include the following:
      (1)   Flight instruction—2 hours (including 20 flights if ground tows are used or 15 flights if aero tows are used).
      (2)   Directed solo—5 hours (including at least 15 flights if ground tows are used or 5 flights if aero tows are used).
    (c)   Stage and flight tests may be credited for not more than one hour of the 15 hours of ground training, and for not more than one-half hour of the 2 hours of flight instruction required by paragraphs (a)(1) and (a)(2) of this section.
  III.   *Glider course: Commercial pilot.*
    (a)   An approved commercial pilot certification course for gliders must consist of at least the following:
      (1)   Ground training—25 hours.
      (2)   Flight training—20 hours of flight time in gliders (consisting of at least 50 flights,) including the following:
        (i)   Flight instruction—8 hours.
        (ii)   Directed solo—10 hours.
    (b)   Stage and final tests may be credited for not more than 2 hours of the 25 hours of ground training, and for not more than 2 hours of the 20 hours of flight training required by paragraphs (a)(1) and (a)(2) of this section.

E.   *Lighter-than-air aircraft.*
  I.   *Kinds of lighter-than-air pilot certification courses.* An approved lighter-than-air pilot certification course includes—
    (a)   An airship course—private pilot;
    (b)   A free balloon course—private pilot;
    (c)   An airship course—commercial pilot; and
    (d)   A free balloon course—commercial pilot.
  II.   *Airship—private pilot.*
    (a)   A private pilot certification course for an airship must consist of at least the following:
      (1)   Ground training—35 hours.
      (2)   Flight training—50 hours (45 hours must be in airships), including the following:
        (i)   Flight instruction—20 hours in airships.
        (ii)   Directed solo, or performing the functions of a pilot in command of an airship for which more than one pilot is required—10 hours.
    (b)   Stage and final tests may be credited for not more than 5 hours of the 35 hours of ground training, and not more than 5 hours of the 50 hours of flight training required by paragraphs (a)(1) and (a)(2) of this section.
  III.   *Free balloon course; private pilot.*
    (a)   A private pilot course for a free balloon must consist of at least the following:
      (1)   Ground training—10 hours.
      (2)   Flight training—6 free flights, including—
        (i)   Two flights of one hour duration each if a gas balloon is used, or of 30 minutes duration if a hot air balloon is used;
        (ii)   At least one solo flight; and
        (iii)   One ascent under control to 5,000 feet above the point of takeoff if a gas balloon is used, or 3,000 feet above the point of takeoff if a hot air balloon is used.
    (b)   The written and stage checks may be credited for not more than one hour of the ground training, and not more than one of the 6 flights required by paragraph (a)(1) and (a)(2) of this section.

IV. *Airship course—Commercial pilot.*
    (a)   A commercial pilot course for an airship must consist of at least the following:
        (1) Ground training—100 hours.
        (2) Flight training—190 hours in airships as follows:
            (i) Flight instruction—80 hours, including 30 hours instrument time.
            (ii) 100 hours of solo time, or flight time performing the functions of a pilot in command in an airship that requires more than one pilot, including 10 hours of cross-country flying and 10 hours of night flying.
    (b)   Stage and final tests may be credited for not more than 6 hours of the 100 hours of ground training, and not more than 10 hours of the 190 hours of flight training required by paragraphs (a)(1) and (a)(2), respectively, of this section.

V. *Free balloon course; Commercial pilot.*
    (a)   A commercial pilot certification course for free balloons must consist of at least the following:
        (1) Ground training—20 hours.
        (2) Flight training—8 free flights, including—
            (i) 2 flights of more than 2 hours duration if a gas balloon is used, or 2 flights of more than 1 hour duration if a hot air balloon is used;
            (ii) 1 ascent under control to more than 10,000 feet above the takeoff point if a gas balloon is used, or to more than 5,000 feet above the takeoff point if a hot air balloon is used; and
           (iii) 2 solo flights.
    (b)   Stage and final tests may be credited for not more than 2 hours of 20 hours of ground training, and not more than one of the flights required by paragraph (a)(1) and (a)(2), respectively, of this section.

F. *Aircraft rating course.*
   I. *Kinds of aircraft rating courses.* An approved aircraft rating course includes—
     (a)   An aircraft category rating;
     (b)   An aircraft class rating; and
     (c)   An aircraft type rating;
   II. *Aircraft category rating.* An aircraft category rating course must include at least the ground training and flight instruction required by Part 61 of this chapter for the issuance of a category rating with a category rating appropriate to the course. However, the Administrator may approve a lesser number of hours of ground training, or flight instruction, or both, if the course provides for the use of special training aids, such as ground procedures, trainers, systems mockups, and audiovisual training materials, or requires appropriate aeronautical experience of the students as a prerequisite for enrollment in the course.
   III. *Aircraft class rating.* An aircraft class rating course must include at least the flight instruction required by Part 61 of this chapter for the issuance of a pilot certificate wth a class rating appropriate to the course.
   IV. *Aircraft type rating.*
     (a)   An aircraft type rating course must include at least 10 hours of ground training on the aircraft systems, performance, operation, and loading. In addition, it must include at least 10 hours of flight instruction. Instruction in a pilot ground trainer that meets the requirements of § 141.41(a)(1) may be credited for not more than 5 of the 10 hours of required flight instruction. Instruction in a pilot ground trainer that meets the requirements of § 141.41(a)(2) may be credited for not more than 2.5 of the 10 hours of required flight instruction.
     (b)   For airplanes that require type ratings, the aircraft type rating course must include ground and flight training on the maneuvers and procedures of Part 61, Appendix A that is appropriate to the airplane for which a type rating is sought.

Amend #4
Eff 4-15-91

APPENDIX G — PILOT GROUND SCHOOL COURSE

1. *Applicability.* This Appendix prescribes the minimum curriculum for a pilot ground school course required by § 141.55.
2. *General requirements.* An approved course of training for a pilot ground school course must contain the instruction necessary to provide each student with adequate knowledge of those subjects needed to safely exercise the privileges of the pilot certificate sought.
3. *Ground training instruction.* A pilot ground school course must include at least the subjects and the number of hours of ground training specified in the ground training section of the curriculum prescribed in the Appendices to this Part for the certification or test preparation course to which the ground school course is directed.
4. *Stage and final tests.* Each student must pass a written test at the completion of each stage of training specified in the approved training syllabus for each ground training course in which he is enrolled. In addition, he must pass a final written test at the completion of the course. The stage and final tests may be credited towards the total ground training time required for each certification and test preparation course as provided in the curriculum prescribed in the Appendices to this Part for that course.

APPENDIX H — TEST PREPARATION COURSES

1. *Applicability.* This Appendix prescribes the minmum curriculum required under § 141.55 of this Part 141 for each test preparation course listed in § 141.11
2. *General requirements.*
   (a) A test preparation course is eligible for approval if the Administrator determines that it is adequate for a student enrolled in that course, upon graduation, to safely exercise the privileges of the certificate, rating, or authority for which the course is conducted.
   (b) Each course for a test preparation must be equivalent in scope, depth, and detail with the curriculum for the corresponding test course prescribed in Appendices A, B, C, and D of this Part 141. However, the number of hours of ground training and flight training included in the course must meet the curriculum prescribed in this Appendix. (The minimums prescribed in this Appendix for each test preparation course are based upon the amount of training that is required for students who meet the total flight experience requirements prescribed in Part 61 of this chapter at the time of enrollment.)
   (c) Minimum experience, knowledge, or skill, requirements necessary as a prerequisite for enrollment are prescribed in the appropriate test preparation course contained in this Appendix.
3. *Flight instructor certification course.*
   (a) An approved course of training for a flight instructor certification course must contain at least the following:
      (1) *Ground training*—40 hours.
      (2) *Instructor training*—25 hours, including—
         (i) 10 hours of flight instruction in the analysis and performance of flight training maneuvers, which for students enrolled in a flight instructor airplane certification course and a flight instructor glider certification course includes the satisfactory demonstration of stall awareness, spin entry, spins, and spin recovery techniques in an aircraft of the appropriate category that is certificated for spins; and
         (ii) 5 hours of practice ground instruction; and
         (iii) 10 hours of practice flight instruction (with the instructor in the aircraft).
   (b) *Credit for previous training or experience*: A student may be credited with the following training and experience acquired before his enrollment in the course.
      (1) Satisfactory completion of two years of study on the principles of education in a college or university may be credited for 20 hours of the required 40 hours of ground training prescribed in paragraph (a)(1) of this section.
      (2) One year of experience as a full-time instructor in an institution of secondary or advanced education may be credited for 5 hours of the required practice ground instruction prescribed in paragraph (a)(2) of this section.
   (c) *Prerequisite for enrollment.* To be eligible for enrollment each student must hold—
      (1) A commercial pilot certificate;
      (2) A rating for the aircraft used in the course; and
      (3) An instrument rating for enrollment in an airplane instructor rating course.
4. *Additional flight instructor rating courses.*
   (a) An approved course of training for an additional flight instructor rating course must consist of at least the following:
      (1) *Ground training*—20 hours.
      (2) *Instructor training (with an instructor in the aircraft).* 20 hours including —
         (i) 10 hours or 10 flights in a glider in the case of a glider instructor rating course, performing analysis of flight training maneuvers, which in the case of an airplane instructor rating course and a glider instructor rating course includes the satisfactory demonstration of stall awareness, spin entry, spins, and spin recovery techniques in an aircraft of the appropriate category that is certificated for spins; and
         (ii) 10 hours of practice flight instruction, or, in the case of glider instructor rating course, 10 flights in a glider.

Amend #4
Eff 4-15-91

5. *Additional instrument rating course (airplane or helicopter).*
    (a) An approved training course for an additional instrument rating course must include at least the following:
        (1) *Ground training*—15 hours.
        (2) *Flight instruction*—15 hours.
    (b) *Prerequisites for enrollment.* To be eligible for enrollment each student must hold a valid pilot certificate with an instrument rating, and an aircraft rating for the aircraft used in the course.
6. *Airline transport pilot test course.*
    (a) An approved training course for an airline transport pilot test course must include at least the following:
        (1) *Ground training*—40 hours.
        (2) *Flight instruction*—25 hours, including at least 15 hours of instrument flight instruction.
        (3) In airplanes that require type ratings, the course must include ground and flight training on the maneuvers and procedures of Part 61, Appendix A that are appropriate to the airplane for which a type rating is sought.
    (b) *Prerequisites for enrollment.* To be eligible for enrollment each student must—
        (1) Hold a commercial pilot certificate with an instrument rating and a rating for the aircraft used in the course; and
        (2) Meet the experience requirements of Part 61 of this chapter for the issuance of an airline transport pilot certificate.
7. *Pilot certificate, aircraft or instrument rating refresher course.*
    (a) An approved refresher training course for a pilot certificate, aircraft rating, or an instrument rating must contain at least the following:
        (1) *Ground training*—4 hours.
        (2) *Flight instruction*—6 hours, which may include not more than 2 hours of directed solo or pilot in command practice.
    (b) *Prerequisites for enrollment.* To be eligible for enrollment each student must hold a valid pilot certificate with ratings appropriate to the refresher course.
8. *Agricultural aircraft operations course.*
    (a) An approved training course for pilots of agricultural aircraft must include at least the following:
        (1) *Ground training*—25 hours, including at least 15 hours on the handling of agricultural and industrial chemicals.
        (2) *Flight instruction*—15 hours, which may include not more than 5 hours of directed solo practice.
    (b) *Prerequisite for enrollment.* To be eligible for enrollment each student must hold a valid commercial pilot certificate with a rating for the aircraft used in the course.
9. *Rotorcraft external-load operations course.*
    (a) An approved training course for pilots of a rotorcraft with an external-load must contain at least the following:
        (1) *Ground training*—10 hours.
        (2) *Flight instruction*—15 hours.
    (b) *Prerequisite for enrollment.* To be eligible for enrollment each student must hold a valid commercial pilot certificate with a rating for the rotorcraft used in the course.

Amend #4
Eff 4-15-91

INTENTIONALLY

LEFT

BLANK

HAZARDOUS MATERIAL REGULATION (HMR) 175

This section contains a summary of HMR 175. It does not contain a reprint of that regulation.

HMR 175 governs the carriage of hazardous and magnetized materials onboard civil aircraft in the United States, as well as civil aircraft of U.S. registry anywhere in air commerce. This regulation does not specifically identify each item classified as hazardous. Instead, it references other Department of Transportation regulations governing their shipment.

Dangerous articles regulated by HMR 175 fall into the following general classes.

1. Explosives
2. Flammable and combustible liquids and solids, including paint removers, liquid flavoring extracts, rubber cement, paints and varnishes, alcohol, matches, and charcoal
3. Oxidizing materials, such as nitrates, that readily yield oxygen to stimulate combustion
4. Corrosive liquids and solids, including battery acid, some cleaning compounds and rust removing or prevention compounds
5. Compressed gases, including most household sprays
6. Poisons, such as pesticides, roach powder and motor-fuel antiknock compound
7. Etiological agents, including medical and diagnostic supplies such as serums, specimens, and vaccines
8. Radioactive materials

These general classes cover thousands of items, including many common household products. The types of items listed either require special handling, must be packaged in a specific manner, can be carried only in limited quantities, or are totally prohibited from transport by air.

Items commonly carried by the uninformed pilot include aerosol spray cans and other pressurized containers, such as filled scuba tanks, which can explode at high altitudes in an unpressurized aircraft. Medicinal and toilet articles in this category, however, are exempt from the regulation when carried by a crew member or passenger, provided they do not exceed specific small quantities. Even the carriage of survival items, such as fire extinguishers, oxygen tanks, matches, lighter fluid, signal flares, and small arms ammunition are regulated, unless they are carried in small quantities or are specially packaged.

Final responsibility for compliance with these rules is placed on the pilot in command. Since severe penalties are imposed for noncompliance, you should familiarize yourself with the general requirements of HMR 175 and make certain that no hazardous materials are carried in your aircraft unless properly packed and loaded. Included in this responsibility are requirements for visual inspection of the product for container damage or leakage. Compatibility with other products, persons, or living animals, as well as the potential for contamination of food, are listed among pilot responsibilities. If you are in doubt as to what you may carry in the aircraft, contact the local Flight Standards District Office for guidance.

INTENTIONALLY

LEFT

BLANK

NATIONAL TRANSPORTATION SAFETY BOARD

**PART 830 — RULES PERTAINING TO THE NOTIFICATION AND REPORTING
OF AIRCRAFT ACCIDENTS OR INCIDENTS AND OVERDUE AIRCRAFT,
AND PRESERVATION OF AIRCRAFT WRECKAGE, MAIL, CARGO, AND RECORDS**

Revised 6 September 1995.

TABLE OF CONTENTS

SUBPART A — GENERAL

**SUBPART B — INITIAL NOTIFICATION OF AIRCRAFT
ACCIDENTS, INCIDENTS, AND OVERDUE AIRCRAFT**

**SUBPART C — PRESERVATION OF AIRCRAFT WRECKAGE, MAIL
CARGO, AND RECORDS**

**SUBPART D — REPORTING OF AIRCRAFT ACCIDENTS, INCIDENTS,
AND OVERDUE AIRCRAFT**

INTENTIONALLY

LEFT

BLANK

SUBPART A — GENERAL

830.1 APPLICABILITY

This part contains rules pertaining to:
(a) Initial notification and later reporting of aircraft incidents and accidents and certain other occurrences in the operation of aircraft, wherever they occur, when they involve civil aircraft of the United States; when they involve certain public aircraft, as specified in this part, wherever they occur; and when they involve foreign civil aircraft where the events occur in the United States, its territories, or its possessions.
(b) Preservation of aircraft wreckage, mail, cargo, and records involving all civil and certain public aircraft accidents, as specified in this part, in the United States and its territories or possessions.

830.2 DEFINITIONS

As used in this part the following words or phrases are defined as follows:

"Aircraft accident" means an occurrence associated with the operation of an aircraft which takes place between the time any person boards the aircraft with the intention of flight and all such persons have disembarked, and in which any person suffers death or serious injury, or in which the aircraft receives substantial damage.

"Civil aircraft" means any aircraft other than a public aircraft.

"Fatal injury" means any injury which results in death within 30 days of the accident.

"Incident" means an occurrence other than an accident, associated with the operation of an aircraft, which affects or could affect the safety of operations.

"Operator" means any person who causes or authorizes the operation of an aircraft, such as the owner, lessee, or bailee of an aircraft.

"Public aircraft" means an aircraft used only for the United States Government, or an aircraft owned and operated (except for commercial purposes) or exclusively leased for at least 90 continuous days by a government other than the United States Government, including a State, the District of Columbia, a territory or possession of the United States, or a political subdivision of that government. "Public aircraft" does not include a government-owned aircraft transporting property for commerical purposes and does not include a government-owned aircraft transporting passengers other than: transporting (for other than commerical purposes) crewmembers or other persons aboard the aircraft whose presence is required to perform, or is associated with the performance of, a governmental function such as firefighting, search and rescue, law enforcement, aeronautical research, or biological or geological resource management; or transporting (for other than commercial purposes) persons aboard the aircraft if the aircraft is operated by the Armed Forces or an intelligence agency of the United States. Notwithstanding any limitation relating to use of the aircraft for commercial purposes, an aircraft shall be considered to be a public aircraft without regard to whether it is operated by a unit of government on behalf of another unit of government pursuant to a cost reimbursement agreement, if the unit of government on whose behalf the operation is conducted certifies to the Administrator of the Federal Aviation Administration that the operation was necessary to respond to a significant and imminent threat to life or property (including natural resources) and that no service by a private operator was reasonably available to meet the threat.

"Serious injury" means any injury which: (1) requires hospitalization for more than 48 hours, commencing within 7 days from the date the injury was received; (2) results in a fracture of any bone (except simple fractures of fingers, toes, or nose); (3) causes severe hemorrhages, nerve, muscle, or tendon damage; (4) involves any internal organ; or (5) involves second- or third-degree burns, or any burns affecting more than 5 percent of the body surface.

"Substantial damage" means damage or failure which adversely affects the structural strength, performance, or flight characteristics of the aircraft, and which would normally require major repair or replacement of the affected component. Engine failure or damage limited to an engine if only one engine fails or is damaged, bent fairings or cowling, dented skin, small punctured holes in the skin or fabric, ground damage to rotor or propeller blades, and damage to landing gear, wheels, tires, flaps, engine accessories, brakes, or wingtips are not considered "substantial damage" for the purpose of this part.

Ⓐ *Eff 9/6/95*

SUBPART B — INITIAL NOTIFICATION OF AIRCRAFT ACCIDENTS, INCIDENTS, AND OVERDUE AIRCRAFT

830.5   IMMEDIATE NOTIFICATION

⌐ The operator of any civil aircraft, or any public aircraft not operated by the Armed Forces or an intelligence agency of the United States, or any **A** foreign aircraft shall immediately, and by the most expeditious means available, notify the nearest National Transportation Safety Board (Board) field ⌐ office[1] when:

(a) An aircraft accident or any of the following listed incidents occur:

    (1) Flight control system malfunction or failure;

    (2) Inability of any required flight crewmember to perform his normal flight duties as a result of injury or illness;

    (3) Failure of structural components of a turbine engine excluding compressor and turbine blades and vanes;

    (4) In-flight fire; or

    (5) Aircraft collide in flight.

    (6) Damage to property, other than the aircraft, estimated to exceed $25,000 for repair (including materials and labor) or fair market value in the event of total loss, whichever is less.

    (7) For large multiengine aircraft (more than 12,500 pounds maximum certificated takeoff weight):

      (i) In-flight failure of electrical systems which requires the sustained use of an emergency bus powered by a back-up source such as a battery, auxiliary power unit, or air-driven generator to retain flight control or essential instruments;

      (ii) In-flight failure of hydraulic systems that results in sustained reliance on the sole remaining hydraulic or mechanical system for movement of flight control surfaces;

      (iii) Sustained loss of the power or thrust produced by two or more engines; and

      (iv) An evacuation of an aircraft in which an emergency egress system is utilized.

(b) An aircraft is overdue and is believed to have been involved in an accident.

830.6   INFORMATION TO BE GIVEN IN NOTIFICATION

The notification required in §830.5 shall contain the following information, if available:

(a) Type, nationality, and registration marks of the aircraft;

(b) Name of owner, and operator of the aircraft;

(c) Name of the pilot-in-command;

(d) Date and time of the accident;

(e) Last point of departure and point of intended landing of the aircraft;

(f) Position of the aircraft with reference to some easily defined geographical point;

(g) Number of persons aboard, number killed, and number seriously injured;

(h) Nature of the accident, the weather and the extent of damage to the aircraft, so far as is known; and

(i) A description of any explosives, radioactive materials, or other dangerous articles carried.

A *Eff 9/6/95*

[1] The Board field offices are listed under U.S. Government in the telephone directories of the following cities: Anchorage, AK, Atlanta, GA, West Chicago, IL, Denver, CO, Arlington, TX, Gardena (Los Angeles), CA, Miami, FL, Parsippany, NJ (metropolitan New York, NY), Seattle, WA, and Washington, DC.

SUBPART C — PRESERVATION OF AIRCRAFT WRECKAGE, MAIL, CARGO, AND RECORDS

830.10 PRESERVATION OF AIRCRAFT WRECKAGE, MAIL, CARGO, AND RECORDS

(a) The operator of an aircraft involved in an accident or incident for which notification must be given is responsible for preserving, to the extent possible, any aircraft wreckage, cargo, and mail aboard the aircraft, and all records, including all recording mediums of flight, maintenance, and voice recorders, pertaining to the operation and maintenance of the aircraft and to the airmen until the Board takes custody thereof or a release is granted pursuant to §831.12(b).

(b) Prior to the time the Board or its authorized representative takes custody of aircraft wreckage, mail, or cargo, such wreckage, mail, or cargo may not be disturbed or moved except to the extent necessary:

(1) To remove persons injured or trapped;
(2) To protect the wreckage from further damage; or
(3) To protect the public from injury.

(c) Where it is necessary to move aircraft wreckage, mail or cargo, sketches, descriptive notes, and photographs shall be made, if possible, of the original position and condition of the wreckage and any significant impact marks.

(d) The operator of an aircraft involved in an accident or incident shall retain all records, reports, internal documents and memoranda dealing with the accident or incident, until authorized by the Board to the contrary.

SUBPART D — REPORTING OF AIRCRAFT ACCIDENTS, INCIDENTS, AND OVERDUE AIRCRAFT

830.15 REPORTS AND STATEMENTS TO BE FILED

A

(a) *Reports.* The operator of a civil, public (as specified in §830.5), or foreign aircraft shall file a report on Board Form 6120.½ (OMB No. 3147-0001)[2] within 10 days after an accident, or after 7 days if an overdue aircraft is still missing. A report on an incident for which immediate notification is required by §830.5(a) shall be filed only as requested by an authorized representative of the Board.

(b) *Crewmember statement.* Each crewmember, if physically able at the time the report is submitted, shall attach a statement setting forth the facts, conditions, and circumstances relating to the accident or incident as they appear to him. If the crewmember is incapacitated, he shall submit the statement as soon as he is physically able.

(c) *Where to file the reports.* The operator of an aircraft shall file any report with the field office of the Board nearest the accident or incident.

A *Eff 9/6/95*

[2] Forms are available from the Board field offices (see footnote 1), from Board headquarters in Washington, DC, and from the Federal Aviation Administration Flight Standards District Offices.

EXERCISES

E

FAR EXERCISES

SECTION

A

PRIVATE PILOT

FAR PART 1

1. The Federal Aviation Administrator or any person to whom he has delegated his authority in the matter concerned is referred to throughout the FARs as the _____.

2. From the following list, select the terms that pertain to "category" with respect to aircraft certification.

   A. Utility   D. Multiengine
   B. Balloon   E. Transport
   C. Acrobatic   F. Landplane

3. The time that an aircraft first moves under its own power for the purpose of flight until it comes to rest at the next point of landing is _____ _____.

4. The average forward horizontal distance at which prominent unlighted objects may be seen and identified by day and prominent lighted objects may be seen and identified by night is known as

   1. ground visibility.
   2. flight visibility.
   3. runway visual value.
   4. runway visual range.

5. "Night" is defined as the time from

   1. sunset to sunrise.
   2. one hour before sunset to one hour before sunrise.
   3. one-half hour after sunset to one-half hour after sunrise.
   4. the end of evening civil twilight to the beginning of morning civil twilight as published in the American Air Almanac, converted to local time.

FAR PART 61

1. [61.5] What document(s) is/are required to be in your personal possession when you are acting as pilot in command of an aircraft?

   1. A pilot logbook with appropriate endorsements
   2. An appropriate pilot certificate, medical certificate, and logbook
   3. A certificate showing satisfactory completion of a flight review
   4. A current pilot certificate and an appropriate current medical certificate

2. [61.6] The four aircraft category ratings that are placed on pilot certificates are

   _____, _____, _____, and _____-_____.

3. [61.31] What is required before you act as pilot in command of an airplane with more than 200 h.p. if you logged no pilot-in-command time in a high-performance airplane prior to November 1, 1973?

   1. An FAA flight test in the airplane
   2. 15 hours of instruction in the airplane
   3. Three solo takeoffs and landings within the previous 90 days
   4. Receipt of flight instruction in an airplane that has more than 200 h.p.

4. [61.57] As a private pilot, you may not act as pilot in command of an aircraft carrying passengers unless you have made at least three takeoffs and landings in an aircraft of the same _____ and _____ within the preceding _____ days.

[61.23] **Use the accompanying table to answer questions 5 through 7. Fill in the expiration dates of the various medical certificates by specifying the month, day, and year, such as "1/31, one year later."**

Type Certificate	Date Issued	Usage	Expiration Date
5. First-class	7/12/_____	Airline transport pilot Commercial pilot Private pilot Student pilot	_____ _____ _____ _____ _____ _____
6. Second-class	11/1/_____	Commercial pilot Private pilot Student pilot	_____ _____ _____ _____ _____
7. Third-class	2/28/_____	Private pilot Student pilot	_____ _____ _____ _____

8. [61.57] Assume that you are a private pilot acting as pilot in command of an aircraft carrying passengers at night. Within the preceding 90 days, you must have made at least three

 1. touch-and-goes at night in any aircraft.
 2. touch-and-goes at night in an aircraft of the same category and class.
 3. takeoffs and three full-stop landings in an aircraft of the same class.
 4. takeoffs and three full-stop landings in an aircraft of the same category and class at night.

9. [61.57] Assume you are making a flight carrying passengers, and official sunset will occur at 1900 local time. If you do not meet the recent flight experience requirements for night flight, you must be on the ground not later than

 1. 1900.
 2. 1930.
 3. 2000.
 4. 2030.

10. [61.56] To act as pilot in command of an aircraft, you must have either a logbook endorsement showing the satisfactory completion of a flight review or the completion of a pilot proficiency check within the preceding

 1. 6 calendar months.
 2. 12 calendar months.
 3. 24 calendar months.
 4. 36 calendar months.

11. [61.60] If you change your permanent mailing address and wish to continue to exercise the privileges of your pilot certificate, you must notify the FAA of the change within

 _____ _____ .

12. [61.83] _____(True, False) Before your first solo as a student pilot, you must hold at least a current third-class medical certificate.

13. [61.87] Before solo, you must receive the required ground and flight instruction and demonstrate to an authorized instructor that you

 1. have satisfactory knowledge to pass the FAA Private Pilot Airmen Knowledge Test.
 2. are familiar with the flight rules of FAR Part 91 that pertain to student solo flights.
 3. can divert to an alternate airport if you are unable to return to the home base airport.
 4. know all of the emergency procedures that are included in the POH of the aircraft you are using.

14. [61.89] _____(True, False) A student pilot may act as the pilot in command of an aircraft carrying passengers, provided the instructor has endorsed the student pilot certificate for solo flight.

15. [61.118] In relation to operating expenses and compensation while you are acting as pilot in command, the regulations specify that as a private pilot you may

 1. not share operating expenses with passengers.
 2. share the operating expenses with passengers.
 3. share the operating expenses with passengers and receive compensation from them for pilot services.
 4. share operating expenses plus be compensated for the time involved if the pilot meets the flight-time requirements for a commercial pilot certificate.

16. [61.118] What exception, if any, allows you as a private pilot to act as pilot in command of an aircraft carrying paying passengers?

 1. There is no exception
 2. If the passengers pay for the operating expenses
 3. If a donation for the flight is made to a charitable organization
 4. If the flight is made with a 50 n.m. radius of the airport of origination

FAR PART 91

1. [91.3] Assume an in-flight emergency occurs which requires immediate action. As the pilot in command, you may
   1. not deviate from any FARs.
   2. not deviate from FARs unless permission is obtained from ATC.
   3. deviate from FARs to the extent required to meet that emergency.
   4. deviate from FARs to the extent required to meet the emergency but must then submit a written report to the Administrator within 24 hours.

2. [91.3] The final authority as to the operation of an aircraft is the

   _____ _____

   _____ .

3. [91.7] Who is responsible for determining if the aircraft is airworthy?
   1. The owner of the aircraft
   2. The company operating the aircraft
   3. The pilot in command of the aircraft
   4. A certificated aircraft maintenance inspector

4. [91.9, 91.203] From the following list, select the certificates and documents that FARs require you to carry aboard an aircraft during flight.
   A. Operating limitations
   B. Registration certificate
   C. Return to service endorsement
   D. Airworthiness certificate
   E. Aircraft maintenance records
   F. Restricted radiotelephone operator permit
   G. Record of next required maintenance

5. [91.17] You may not act as pilot in command of an aircraft while under the influence of alcohol or while
   1. under stress.
   2. taking any prescription drug.
   3. under the care of a physician.
   4. using any drug that affects your faculties contrary to safety.

6. [91.17] No person may act as a crewmember of a civil aircraft within eight hours after the consumption of any alcoholic beverage or while having alcohol in the blood which is
   1. detectable.
   2. .04% by weight or more.
   3. .05% by volume or more.
   4. .09% by weight or more.

7. [91.17] When may a pilot allow a person who is obviously under the influence of alcohol or drugs to be carried in the aircraft?
   1. Never
   2. Only if there are two pilots aboard the aircraft
   3. If the person does not have access to the cockpit or pilot's compartment
   4. Only in an emergency or if the person is a medical patient under proper care

8. [91.103] Regulations require that, prior to each flight under VFR, the pilot in command must
   1. preflight the airplane.
   2. check for any known traffic delays.
   3. become familiar with all available information concerning that flight.
   4. calculate the weight and balance to determine if the CG is within limits.

9. [91.103] For flights not in the vicinity of an airport, in addition to considering the weather and the amount of fuel required for the flight, you must also
   1. file a flight plan.
   2. designate an alternate airport.
   3. ensure that all navigation equipment in the aircraft is operational.
   4. consider an alternate course of action if the flight cannot be completed as planned.

10. [91.103] Before beginning a flight, as pilot in command, you must

    1. check the accuracy of the ELT.
    2. check to see that each flight instrument is operational.
    3. file a flight plan for all night flights.
    4. determine the runway lengths at the airports you intend to use and calculate the airplane's takeoff and landing distances.

11. [91.105] As pilot in command, when are you required to wear your seat belt?

    1. During flight
    2. During takeoff and landing
    3. When flying through turbulent conditions
    4. During takeoff and landing and in turbulent conditions

12. [91.107] Regarding passengers, the pilot in command must ensure that all passengers are briefed on the use of seatbelts and notified that they must be fastened

    1. at all times.
    2. during takeoff and landing.
    3. when flying through turbulent conditions.
    4. during takeoff and landing and in turbulent conditions.

13. [91.113] While on base leg in an airport traffic pattern, you sight another airplane on a two-mile final. The airplane that has the right-of-way is the one

    1. that is the least maneuverable.
    2. which is closest to the landing threshold.
    3. on final approach, regardless of altitude.
    4. you are flying, provided you are at the lowest altitude.

14. [91.113] Arrange the choices on the right in order of priority with regard to right-of-way over other aircraft.

    1. _____   A. Glider
    2. _____   B. Airship
    3. _____   C. Aircraft in distress
    4. _____   D. Airplane or helicopter
    5. _____   E. Balloon

15. [91.117] What is the maximum indicated airspeed for flights at or below 2,500 feet AGL within four nautical miles of the primary airport of a Class C or D airspace area?

    1. 156 knots (180 m.p.h.)
    2. 200 knots (230 m.p.h.)
    3. 230 knots (265 m.p.h.)
    4. 265 knots (305 m.p.h.)

16. [91.117] The maximum authorized airspeed for flight beneath the lateral limits of a Class B airspace area, or in a VFR corridor designated through a Class B airspace area is

    1. 156 knots.
    2. 180 knots.
    3. 200 knots.
    4. 250 knots.

17. [91.117] The maximum indicated airspeed for flight below 10,000 feet MSL, unless otherwise authorized or required by ATC, is

    1. 156 knots.
    2. 180 knots.
    3. 200 knots.
    4. 250 knots.

18. [91.119] Except when necessary for takeoff and landing, when you are flying over congested areas you must maintain an altitude of at least

    1. 1,000 feet from any obstacle.
    2. 1,500 feet above any obstacle.
    3. 1,000 feet vertically and 1,000 feet horizontally from the nearest obstacle.
    4. 1,000 feet above the highest obstacle within a horizontal radius of 2,000 feet of the aircraft.

19. [91.121] During a cross-country flight at an altitude below 18,000 feet, you should set the altimeter to

1. 29.92 when operating at an altitude of more than 10,000 feet AGL.
2. the setting of a station along the route and within 100 n.m. of the aircraft.
3. the departure airport elevation, and reset it to the destination airport setting at the midpoint of the flight.
4. the departure airport elevation, a station at the midpoint of the flight, and finally to the destination airport setting when you are within 10 n.m. of the airport.

20. [91.123] When may ATC request a detailed report of an emergency, even though a rule has not been violated?

1. Anytime an emergency occurs
2. When priority has been given
3. When the incident occurs in controlled airspace
4. Only when an accident results from the emergency

21. [91.123] What action, if any, may be required if you deviate from an ATC instruction during an emergency and are given priority over other air traffic?

1. No action is required.
2. File a report with the FAA Administrator within 48 hours.
3. File a report with the chief of the ATC facility within 48 hours.
4. File a detailed report within 48 hours with the manager of the air traffic control facility only if requested.

[91.125] For questions 22 through 27, complete the appropriate pilot action for each of the different ATC light signals.

Color and Type	Aircraft on Surface	Aircraft in Flight
22. Steady red		
23. Steady green		
24. Flashing red		
25. Flashing green		
26. Flashing white		
27. Alternating red and green		

28. [91.127, 91.129] You must comply with any departure procedures established by the FAA at

1. controlled airports only.
2. uncontrolled airports only.
3. any airport, whether it is controlled or uncontrolled.
4. airports with published instrument approach procedures when the tower is in operation.

29. [91.151] The fuel requirement for flight under VFR during daylight hours requires that you carry enough fuel to fly to the first point of intended landing and to fly after that, at normal cruise speed, for _____ minutes.

30. [91.151] For VFR flight at night, you must carry enough fuel to fly to the first point of intended landing and, at normal cruise speed, fly for at least another _____ minutes.

31. [91.153] What is not required information for your VFR flight plan?

1. Cruising altitude
2. Type of aircraft
3. Names of the passengers
4. Any information that the pilot in command believes is necessary for ATC purposes

[91.155] For questions 32 through 34, complete the following table for minimum flight visibility and distance from clouds.

Altitude	Visibility	Cloud Separation
32. 1,200 feet or less above the surface (regardless of MSL altitude) Within controlled airspace:	_____ statute mile(s)	_____ feet below _____ feet above _____ feet horizontal
Outside controlled airspace: (except as provided in FAR 91.155(b) Day Night	_____ statute mile(s) _____ statute mile(s)	_____ _____ feet below _____ feet above _____ feet horizontal
33. More than 1,200 feet above the surface but less than 10,000 feet MSL Within controlled airspace:	_____ statute mile(s)	_____ feet below _____ feet above _____ feet horizontal
Outside controlled airspace: Day Night	_____ statute mile(s) _____ statute mile(s)	_____ feet below _____ feet above _____ feet horizontal
34. More than 1,200 feet above the surface and at or above 10,000 feet MSL	_____ statute mile(s)	_____ feet below _____ feet above _____ mile(s) horizontal
Class B airspace areas: (altitudes as charted)	_____ statute mile(s)	_____

35. [91.157] You may not operate an airplane within controlled airspace at night under special VFR unless

1. a certified flight instructor is on board.
2. the flight visibility is at least 3 miles.
3. the flight can be conducted 500 feet below the clouds.
4. you have a current instrument rating and the airplane is equipped for instrument flight.

36. [91.157] A special VFR clearance authorizes you to enter the lateral boundaries of Class B, C, D, or E airspace designated for an airport when the

1. ceiling is less than 1,000 feet and the visibility is less than 1 mile.
2. visibility is at least 1 mile and the aircraft remains clear of clouds.
3. flight can remain clear of clouds with no restriction on visibility.
4. the flight can maintain 1 mile visibility at an altitude no lower than the cloud base, provided this altitude is at least 1,000 feet AGL.

37. [91.159] Compliance with the VFR cruising altitudes is required

1. at any altitude.
2. above 3,000 feet AGL.
3. above 5,000 feet AGL.
4. above 10,000 feet MSL.

38. [91.203] From the list of required certificates or documents specified in the regulations, the one that must be displayed at the cabin or cockpit entrance and within view of passengers or crew is the

_____ _____ .

39. [91.207] _____(True, False) The installation of an emergency locator transmitter is not required on training aircraft flown within a 50 n.m. radius of the airport where the training flight originated.

40. [91.207] The nonrechargeable batteries in an ELT are required to be replaced

1. annually.
2. every 24 months.
3. during each 100 hour or annual inspection.
4. after 1 hour of cumulative use or when 50% of the useful life has expired.

41. [91.209] Aircraft position lights are required to be illuminated from

1. sunset to sunrise.
2. 1 hour before sunset to 1 hour after sunrise.
3. 30 minutes after sunset to 30 minutes before sunrise.
4. 1 hour after sunset to 1 hour before sunrise.

42. [91.211] Assume that you are planning to cruise at a cabin pressure altitude of 13,500 feet MSL for 1 hour and 45 minutes. For how long are you required to use supplemental oxygen?

1. 1 hour
2. 1 hour and 15 minutes
3. 1 hour and 30 minutes
4. 1 hour and 45 minutes

43. [91.211] All occupants of an aircraft must be provided with supplemental oxygen if the flight will be above a cabin pressure altitude of

1. 10,000 feet MSL.
2. 12,500 feet MSL.
3. 14,000 feet MSL.
4. 15,000 feet MSL.

44. [91.215] _____(True, False) If an altitude-encoding, transponder-equipped aircraft is flown in uncontrolled airspace, the Mode C function need not be turned on when the aircraft is below the floor of a Class B airspace area.

45. [91.303] _____(True, False) Aerobatic flight is prohibited within four nautical miles of the centerline of any Federal airway.

46. [91.303] Aerobatic flight is not allowed

1. within 5 miles of any airport.
2. within 2,000 feet of the surface.
3. when the flight visibility is less than 5 s.m.
4. over any congested area of a city, town, or settlement.

47. [91.303] What is the minimum flight visibility and lowest altitude that is permitted for aerobatic flight?

1. 3 miles and 1,500 feet
2. 5 miles and 1,000 feet
3. 7 miles and 1,000 feet above the highest obstacle within 5 miles
4. 10 miles and 1,500 feet above the highest obstacle within 5 miles

48. [91.307] Except for certain provisions, you are required to wear a parachute if any intentional maneuver exceeds _____ of bank or _____ nose-up or nose-down attitude.

49. [91.313] Restricted category civil aircraft are normally prohibited from flight
    1. within Class D airspace.
    2. within 20 n.m. of Class B airspace areas.
    3. over densely populated areas.
    4. under instrument flight rules.

50. [91.405] The responsibility for ensuring that an aircraft is maintained in an airworthy condition is primarily that of the
    1. maintenance shop.
    2. owner or operator of the aircraft.
    3. the pilot in command of the aircraft.
    4. certified mechanic who signs the aircraft maintenance records.

51. [91.407] If an alteration or repair substantially affects an aircraft's operation in flight, that aircraft must be test flown by an appropriately rated pilot and approved for return to service prior to being operated
    1. by a private pilot.
    2. with passengers aboard.
    3. for compensation or hire.
    4. away from the vicinity of the airport.

52. [91.409] Completion of an annual inspection and the return of the aircraft to service should always be indicated by
    1. an entry in the maintenance records.
    2. completion of an alteration and repair form.
    3. issuance of a new airworthiness certificate.
    4. issuance of an aircraft registration certificate.

53. [91.409] If an aircraft receives an annual inspection on September 20 of this year, the next annual inspection will be due no later than
    1. September 30 of next year.
    2. September 20 of next year.
    3. 100 flight hours following the last annual inspection.
    4. 12 calendar months after the date shown on the registration certificate.

54. [91.417] What record or documents shall the owner or operator of an aircraft keep to show compliance with an applicable airworthiness directive?
    1. The aircraft maintenance records
    2. Airworthiness and registration certificate
    3. Aircraft flight manual and owner's handbook
    4. Airworthiness certificate and owner's handbook

NTSB PART 830

1. [830.2] According to NTSB Part 830, an aircraft accident is an occurrence associated with the operation of an aircraft for the purpose of flight which results in
    1. serious injury to any person or substantial damage to the aircraft.
    2. injury to any person or property, regardless of the extent involved.
    3. injury to any person or damage to the aircraft in excess of $300.
    4. an injury to any person which requires hospitalization or damage to the aircraft which would require repairs.

2. [830.5] If an aircraft is involved in an accident which results in substantial damage to the aircraft but no injuries to the occupants, the nearest NTSB field office should be notified
    1. immediately.
    2. within 48 hours.
    3. within 7 days.
    4. within 10 days.

3. [830.5] What incident would necessitate an immediate notification to the nearest NTSB office?

   1. An in-flight fire
   2. An in-flight radio failure
   3. Ground damage to the propeller blades
   4. An in-flight loss of VOR receiver capability

4. [830.5] Select the incident that requires immediate notification to the nearest NTSB field office?

   1. A near miss
   2. An in-flight radio failure
   3. An in-flight generator or alternator failure
   4. An overdue aircraft that is believed to be involved in an accident

5. [830.5] _____(True, False) The inability of a required flight crewmember to perform normal flight duties due to in-flight injury or illness is a requirement for immediate notification of the NTSB.

6. [830.5] Immediate notification to the NTSB is also required when damage to property other than the aircraft is estimated to exceed _____.

7. [830.15] The operator of an aircraft that has been involved in an accident is required to file an accident report within _____ days.

8. [830.15] Within what time frame, if any, is the operator of an aircraft that has been involved in an incident required to submit a report to the nearest field office of the NTSB?

   1. Immediately
   2. Within 48 hours
   3. Within 7 days
   4. Immediately, if requested to do so

FAR PART 1

1. According to FAR Part 1, a "ceiling" is defined as the height above the earth's surface of the lowest layer of clouds or obscuring phenomena that is reported as "broken," "overcast," or "obscured" and not classified as

   1. scattered.
   2. thin or partial.
   3. partially scattered.
   4. a surface-based obscuration.

2. From the cockpit of an aircraft in flight, the average forward horizontal distance at which prominent unlighted objects may be seen and identified by day and prominent lighted objects may be seen and identified at night is the definition of
   _____ _____ .

3. With respect to the operation of an aircraft on a VFR flight plan, flight above an overcast is known as

   1. VFR.
   2. VFR-on-top.
   3. IFR-on-top.
   4. VFR over-the-top.

4. "Night" is defined as the time from

   1. sunset to sunrise.
   2. one hour before sunset to one hour before sunrise.
   3. one-half hour after sunset to one-half hour after sunrise.
   4. the end of evening civil twilight to the beginning of morning civil twilight as published in the American Air Almanac, converted to local time.

FAR PART 61

1. [61.5] Under what condition must the pilot in command of a civil aircraft have at least an instrument rating?

   1. When operating above a solid overcast
   2. When operating in the continental control area
   3. For a flight in VFR conditions while on an IFR flight plan
   4. For any flight above 1,200 feet AGL when the visibility is less than three miles

2. [61.5] As pilot in command of a civil aircraft, you must have an instrument rating when you are operating an aircraft

   1. by reference to the flight instruments in controlled airspace.
   2. below FL180 while simulating flight in instrument conditions.
   3. solely by reference to the flight instruments, regardless of the weather conditions.
   4. under instrument flight rules, or in weather conditions less than the minimum for VFR flight.

3. [61.6] _____(True, False) The term "single-engine land" refers to an airplane class rating.

4. [61.51] When you enter the condition of flight time in your logbook as "simulated instrument conditions," what additional information must you also enter?
   1. The number and type of instrument approaches completed, along with the route of flight
   2. The place and type of each instrument approach completed and the name of your safety pilot
   3. The name and pilot certificate number of your safety pilot and the type of approaches completed
   4. Number, type, and place of the instrument approaches completed, and the name and pilot certificate number of your flight instructor

5. [61.51] For operations conducted on an instrument flight plan, you may enter in your logbook as actual instrument time only the time
   1. from liftoff to touchdown.
   2. you were flying in IFR weather conditions.
   3. that the aircraft was not controlled by reference to the ground.
   4. you controlled the aircraft solely by reference to the flight instruments.

6. [61.53] _____(True, False) You may not act as pilot in command of an aircraft while you have a known medical deficiency or an increase of a deficiency that would make you unable to meet the requirements of your current medical certificate.

7. [61.57] If your required recent IFR experience lapses, how much time do you have to reestablish your currency before you must pass an instrument competency check in order to act as pilot in command under IFR?
   1. 90 days
   2. 6 calendar months
   3. 12 calendar months
   4. 24 calendar months

8. [61.57] To be current for IFR, the minimum instrument time required within the last six calendar months is _____ hours, at least _____ hours of which must be in the category of aircraft to be flown.

9. [61.129] As a commercial pilot, what limitations are imposed on you if you do not have an instrument rating?
   1. You are limited to private pilot privileges at night.
   2. You may only carry passengers or property for hire on cross-country night flights within 50 nautical miles.
   3. The carrying of passengers for hire on cross-country flights is limited to 50 nautical miles for night flights, but is not limited for day flights.
   4. You may only carry passengers for hire on cross-country flights limited to 50 nautical miles, and you may not carry passengers for hire at night.

10. [61.129] A certificated commercial pilot who carries passengers for hire on a local flight at night _____ (is, is not) required to have an instrument rating.

FAR PART 91

1. [91.3] Who is responsible for determining that the altimeter system and other required inspections have been completed and that they meet the FAR requirements for a particular instrument flight?
   1. Owner
   2. Operator
   3. Pilot in command
   4. An FAA-certificated mechanic

2. [91.7] If your aircraft develops a condition in flight which makes it unairworthy, you are required to

   _____ _____

   _____ .

3. [91.17] You may not act as pilot in command or as a required pilot flight crewmember if your blood alcohol level, by weight, is _____% or more.

4. [91.17] Regulations also prohibit you from flying as a required crewmember within how many hours after you have consumed any alcoholic beverage?
   1. 8
   2. 16
   3. 24
   4. 48

5. [91.103] Before beginning a VFR flight, you must become familiar with all available information concerning that flight. For an IFR flight, what additional items must you accomplish?
   1. Familiarize yourself with all of the instrument approaches at your destination airport.
   2. List an alternate airport and compute the takeoff and landing distances at your intended destination.
   3. List an alternate airport on your flight plan and familiarize yourself with the instrument approaches to that airport.
   4. Alternatives available if the planned flight cannot be completed.

6. [91.113] _____(True, False) Upon entering VFR conditions while on an IFR flight plan, ATC is still responsible for your separation from other air traffic.

7. [91.113] On an IFR flight plan, when are you required to see and avoid other aircraft?
   1. Only when you are advised by ATC
   2. At all times when you are not in radar contact with ATC
   3. When weather conditions permit, regardless of whether you are operating under IFR or VFR
   4. During takeoff and landing and until established on airways, if you are not in radar contact with ATC

8. [91.113] Which aircraft has the right-of-way over all other air traffic?
   1. Glider
   2. Balloon
   3. Aircraft in distress
   4. Aircraft on final approach

9. [91.121] When you are at or above FL180 in U.S. airspace, you are required to set your altimeter to _____ in. Hg.

10. [91.121] If you are departing from an airport where you cannot obtain an altimeter setting, you should set your altimeter to
    1. zero.
    2. 29.92 in. Hg.
    3. the airport elevation.
    4. the current airport barometric pressure, if known.

11. [91.123] While on an IFR flight, you have an emergency that causes you to deviate from an ATC clearance. According to regulations, what action must you take?
    1. Squawk 7700.
    2. Notify ATC of the deviation as soon as possible.
    3. Request an amended clearance or cancel your IFR flight plan.
    4. Submit a detailed report of the deviation to the chief of the ATC facility within 48 hours.

12. [91.129] If you have canceled your IFR flight plan 10 miles from your controlled airport destination, when are you required to establish communications with the control tower?

1. When advised by the ARTCC
2. Immediately after you cancel the flight plan
3. Anytime prior to entering Class D airspace
4. At least five miles from the center of the airport

13. [91.130] You may not operate an aircraft within Class C airspace unless

1. the aircraft is equipped with a VOR receiver.
2. you possess at least a private pilot certificate.
3. the aircraft has a basic 4096-code transponder.
4. you establish and maintain two-way radio communications with ATC.

14. [91.131] For IFR operations in Class B airspace, what equipment is required in addition to a VOR receiver and two-way radio communications?

1. Standby VOR, communications receiver, and DME
2. An operable transponder with Mode C capability
3. Standby communications receiver, DME, and a transponder
4. Another VOR, communications receiver, and a transponder

15. [91.131] _____ (True, False) In Class B airspace, a 4096-code transponder with automatic altitude reporting equipment is not required.

16. [91.135] Regulations require an instrument rating for flight in VFR weather conditions when you are flying

1. into an ADIZ.
2. in Class B airspace.
3. in Class A airspace.
4. through military operations areas.

17. [91.135] VFR-on-top operations are prohibited in

1. Class D airspace.
2. in Class B airspace.
3. all controlled airspace.
4. in Class A airspace.

18. [91.135] An IFR clearance is required during VFR weather conditions when you are

1. practicing instrument approaches.
2. operating in Class A airspace.
3. operating in Class E airspace above 14,500 feet.
4. operating in an ADIZ.

19. [91.155] What minimum flight visibility and distance from clouds are required during a VFR-on-top flight at 12,500 feet MSL (more than 1,200 feet AGL) in controlled airspace?

1. Five miles visibility and 2,000 feet from, 1,000 feet above, and 500 feet below any clouds
2. Five miles visibility and one mile from, 1,000 feet above, and 1,000 feet below any clouds
3. Three miles visibility and 2,000 feet from, 1,000 feet above, and 500 feet below any clouds
4. Three miles visibility and one mile from, 1,000 feet above, and 1,000 feet below any clouds

20. [91.155] What is the minimum flight visibility and distance from clouds required for you to operate under VFR in controlled airspace at less than 1,200 feet AGL?

1. Three miles visibility and clear of clouds
2. One mile flight visibility and clear of clouds
3. One mile visibility and 2,000 feet from, 1,000 feet above, and 1,000 feet below clouds
4. Three miles visibility and 2,000 feet from, 1,000 feet above, and 500 feet below clouds

21. [91.157] What is the minimum flight visibility and distance from clouds required for a special VFR clearance?

   1. One mile flight visibility and clear of clouds
   2. Three miles flight visibility and clear of clouds
   3. One mile flight visibility, 2,000 feet from, 1,000 feet above, and 1,000 feet below clouds
   4. Three miles flight visibility, 2,000 feet from, 1,000 feet above, and 1,000 feet below clouds

22. [91.159, 91.179] When you are flying with a VFR-on-top clearance, your cruising altitude is based on

   1. true course.
   2. true heading.
   3. magnetic course.
   4. magnetic heading.

23. [91.159, 91.179] Below 18,000 feet MSL, what cruising altitudes would be appropriate for a westbound VFR-on-top flight?

   1. Odd thousand-foot altitudes
   2. Even thousand-foot altitudes
   3. Odd thousand-foot altitudes plus 500 feet, but not one below the MEA
   4. Even thousand-foot altitudes plus 500 feet, but not one below the MEA

24. [91.167, 91.169] An alternate airport is not required for an IFR flight if a ceiling of at least 2,000 feet and a visibility of three miles is forecast for the destination airport at your _____ plus or minus _____ hour(s).

25. [91.167] Assume you are on a flight in IFR conditions and the airport where you intend to land is forecast at your ETA to have a 1,500-foot ceiling and three miles visibility. The minimum fuel required in this situation is enough to fly to your destination and then fly

   1. for another 45 minutes at normal cruise speed.
   2. thereafter for 30 minutes at normal cruise speed.
   3. to your alternate airport, and thereafter for 30 minutes at normal cruise speed.
   4. to your alternate airport, and thereafter for 45 minutes at normal cruise speed.

Refer to the accompanying terminal aerodrome forecast for question 26.

```
TAF
KMEM 091135Z 091212 15005KT 5SM HZ
BKN060
    FM1600 VRB04KT P6SM SKC
```

26. [91.169] _____(True, False) The terminal aerodrome forecast for your arrival (ETA 1700Z) at Memphis Airport indicates that an alternate airport is not required on your IFR flight plan.

27. [91.169] Assume an airport with a precision approach procedure has standard alternate minimums. To qualify as an alternate airport, the minimum forecast conditions at your ETA must be no lower than a ceiling of _____ feet and visibility of _____ _____ miles.

28. [91.169] If an airport with a nonprecision approach has standard alternate minimums, the forecast conditions at your ETA must indicate a ceiling of at least _____ feet and visibility of _____ _____ miles or more.

29. [91.169] For an airport without approved instrument approach procedures to qualify as an alternate, the minimum ceiling and visibility forecast for your ETA must

    1. be at least 2,000 feet and three miles.
    2. allow descent from the MEA, approach, and landing under basic VFR.
    3. be at least 2,000 feet and three miles from two hours before until two hours after your ETA.
    4. be at least 1,000 feet above the highest obstacle and three miles from two hours before until two hours after your ETA.

30. [91.171] For use in IFR conditions, VOR equipment must be operationally checked every _____.

31. [91.171] What type of entry must be made in the aircraft logbook or other permanent record by a pilot who has made a VOR operational check?

    1. The date, place, bearing error, and signature
    2. The date, place, satisfactory or unsatisfactory check, and signature
    3. The date, frequency used, and bearing reading of VOR or VOT, along with the tach reading and signature
    4. The date, frequency of VOR or VOT, number of flight hours since the last operational check, and signature

32. [91.171] If you are making an airborne VOR operational check, what is the maximum allowable tolerance between the two indicators of a dual VOR system?

    1. Four degrees between the indicated bearings to a VOR
    2. Six degrees between the indicated bearings to a VOR
    3. Plus or minus four degrees when set to identical radials of a VOR
    4. Plus or minus six degrees when set to identical radials of a VOR

33. [91.171] If you are flying directly over an airborne VOR checkpoint, what is the maximum tolerance for the VOR indication when the CDI is centered?

    1. Within four degrees of the designated radial with a TO indication
    2. Within six degrees of the designated radial with a TO indication
    3. Plus or minus four degrees of the designated radial with a FROM indication
    4. Plus or minus six degrees of the designated radial

34. [91.173] If you are departing an airport located outside of controlled airspace during IFR conditions, you must file an IFR flight plan and receive a clearance before entering _____.

35. [91.173] Filing an IFR flight plan is required before you enter which types of airspace?

    1. Any airspace where the visibility is less than one mile.
    2. Class E airspace with IFR weather conditions and Class A airspace.
    3. Any airspace above 700 feet AGL, if the visibility is less than one mile.
    4. In Class A through E airspace areas, and all other airspace, if the visibility is less than one mile.

36. [91.175] If, during an ILS approach in IFR conditions, the approach lights are not visible upon your arrival at the DH, you are required to execute a missed approach unless you have at least _____ of the other required visual cues in sight.

37. [91.177] When no other minimum altitude is prescribed, the minimum IFR altitude over the highest obstacle in designated mountainous areas is _____ feet.

38. [91.183] The pilot in command of an aircraft on an IFR flight plan in controlled airspace is required to report

   1. entering VFR conditions.
   2. changing heading onto a new airway.
   3. any unforecast weather conditions encountered.
   4. passing designated checkpoints while under radar control.

39. [91.185] Assume you enter a holding pattern at a fix that is not the same as the approach fix and receive an EFC time of 1530. If you experience complete two-way communications failure at 1520, what procedure should you follow to execute the approach to a landing?

   1. Depart the holding fix at the EFC time and complete the approach.
   2. Depart the holding fix at the EFC time, or earlier, if your flight planned ETA is before the EFC.
   3. Depart the holding fix to arrive at the approach fix at the EFC and complete the approach.
   4. Depart the holding fix to arrive about two minutes ahead of the EFC, enter a holding pattern at the final fix, and adjust the pattern to leave the fix inbound at the EFC.

40. [91.185] What altitude and route should you use if you are flying in IFR weather conditions and have two-way radio communications failure?

   1. Fly the most direct route to your destination, maintaining the highest of last assigned altitude or MEA.
   2. Descend to the MEA, and, if clear of clouds, proceed to the nearest appropriate airport. If not clear of clouds, maintain the highest of the MEAs along the clearance route.
   3. Fly direct to an area that has been forecast to have VFR conditions. Fly at an altitude that is at least 1,000 feet above the highest obstacles along the route.
   4. Continue on the route specified in your clearance. Fly an altitude that is the highest of: the last assigned altitude, the altitude ATC has informed you to expect, or the MEA.

41. [91.187] Assume your aircraft is equipped with two VOR receivers, the No. 1 receiver has VOR/LOC/GS capability, and the No. 2 has only VOR. What action, if any, should you take if your No. 1 VOR receiver malfunctions while you are operating in controlled airspace under IFR?

   1. Report the malfunction immediately to ATC.
   2. Continue the flight as cleared; no report is required.
   3. Continue the approach and request a VOR or NDB approach.
   4. Report the malfunction to ATC if you do not have ADF for backup.

42. [91.203] Select the documents that are normally required to be in the airplane for flight.

   A. Airframe logbooks
   B. Proof of insurance
   C. Registration certificate
   D. Aircraft engine logbooks
   E. Airworthiness certificate

43. [91.205] According to regulations, the three flight instruments required for any VFR or IFR flight are the _____, _____ indicator, and the _____ _____ indicator.

44. [91.205] What minimum navigation equipment is required for IFR flight?

   1. VOR/LOC receiver, transponder, and DME
   2. Nav equipment compatible with the enroute ground facilities
   3. Navigational equipment appropriate to the facilities to be used
   4. VOR receiver, ADF receiver, and an altitude encoding transponder

45. [91.205] Approved DME is required within the 50 states and the District of Columbia for U.S.-registered civil aircraft operated at or above _____ feet MSL.

46. [91.205] What should you do if you are operating in an area requiring DME and your DME fails?

1. Request an altitude below FL240 and continue to your destination.
2. Advise ATC of the failure and land at the nearest available airport where repairs can be made.
3. Notify ATC that it will be necessary for you to receive radar vectors to your destination airport.
4. Notify ATC of the failure and continue to your next airport of intended landing where repairs can be made.

47. [91.205] What aircraft equipment is required for flight under IFR?

1. Radar altimeter
2. Dual VOR system
3. Flight director system
4. Gyroscopic direction indicator

For questions 48 through 51, match the required minimum equipment with the specified flight operation. Each flight operation may have more than one answer.

48. [91.205] _____ VFR (night)

49. [91.205] _____ IFR (day)

50. [91.205] _____ IFR (night)

51. [91.131] _____ Class B airspace (day)

A. Position lights and anticollision lights
B. Flotation gear for each occupant and a pyrotechnic signaling device
C. Slip-skid indicator, sensitive adjustable altimeter, rate-of-turn indicator, clock, attitude indicator, and heading indicator
D. Radio capable of communicating with ATC, appropriate radio navigation equipment, and a transponder with Mode C

52. [91.207] ELT batteries must be replaced or recharged after one cumulative hour of use or

1. after three years.
2. when the shelf life of the battery has expired.
3. after the manufacturer's recommended replacement date.
4. when one half of the useful life of the battery has expired.

53. [91.209] Aircraft position lights must be illuminated from

1. sunrise to sunset.
2. sunset to sunrise.
3. one hour after sunset to one hour after sunrise.
4. one hour before sunset to one hour before sunrise.

54. [91.211] Supplemental oxygen must be available for each occupant of an aircraft above a cabin pressure altitude of _____ feet MSL.

55. [91.211] If you fly an unpressurized aircraft above 12,500 feet MSL, but at not more than 14,000 feet MSL, for a period of 2 hours and 20 minutes, how long are you required to use supplemental oxygen during the flight?

1. 1 hour and 20 minutes
2. 1 hour and 50 minutes
3. 2 hours and 20 minutes
4. Supplemental oxygen is not required at these altitudes

56. [91.215] Excluding the airspace at and below 2,500 feet AGL, transponders with altitude encoding capability are required in controlled airspace above _____ feet _____ effective July 1, 1989.

57. [91.215] If your aircraft is equipped with an operational transponder, regulations specifically require that it must be turned on while flying within _____ _____ .

58. [91.215] If you need to fly through Class B airspace, how far in advance must you contact the controlling ATC facility for permission to deviate from the transponder equipment requirement?

1. One hour before the proposed flight.
2. 8 hours before the proposed flight.
3. 24 hours before the proposed flight.
4. Aircraft without transponders are not allowed in Class B airspace areas.

59. [91.403] The person who is primarily responsible for maintaining an aircraft in an airworthy condition is the _____ or _____.

60. [91.411] IFR flight in controlled airspace is prohibited unless, within the previous 24 calendar months, the

1. static system has been tested and inspected.
2. flight instruments have been tested and inspected.
3. communications radios have been tested and inspected.
4. aircraft has received a new airworthiness certificate.

61. [91.413] In order for a transponder to be used in controlled airspace, it must be inspected by a certificated repair station within the previous _____

_____ _____.

NTSB PART 830

1. [830.2] According to NTSB Part 830, an aircraft accident is an occurrence associated with the operation of an aircraft for the purpose of flight which results in

1. serious injury to any person or substantial damage to the aircraft.
2. injury to any person or property, regardless of the extent involved.
3. injury to any person or damage to the aircraft in excess of $3,000.
4. an injury requiring hospitalization of any person or damage to the aircraft which would render it unairworthy.

2. [830.5] If an aircraft is involved in an occurrence which results in substantial damage to the aircraft but no injuries to the occupants, the nearest NTSB field office should be notified

1. immediately.
2. within 48 hours.
3. within 7 days.
4. within 10 days.

3. [830.5] Of the following incidents, which would require an immediate notification to the nearest NTSB field office?

1. In-flight fire
2. In-flight radio failure
3. Ground damage to the propeller blades
4. In-flight loss of VOR receiver capability

4. [830.5] Select the situation that requires immediate notification of the nearest NTSB field office?

1. Near miss
2. In-flight radio failure
3. In-flight generator or alternator failure
4. Damage to property, other than the aircraft, estimated to exceed $25,000

5. [830.15] The operator of an aircraft that has been involved in an accident is required to file a written accident report within _____ days.

6. [830.15] The operator of an aircraft that has been involved in an incident is required to submit a report to the nearest field office of the NTSB

1. immediately.
2. within 48 hours.
3. within 7 days.
4. immediately, if requested to do so.

COMMERCIAL PILOT

FAR PART 1

1. _____(True, False) "Operate," with respect to an aircraft, means to use, cause to be used, or authorize use of an aircraft.

2. A person who, for compensation or hire, engages in the carriage by aircraft in air commerce of persons or property, other than as an air carrier, is defined as a(n) _____ _____ .

3. The terms lighter-than-air, airplane, rotorcraft, and glider, when used with respect to certification of airmen, are aircraft _____ .

4. If you are exercising "operational control" over an aircraft, you are
   1. flying for compensation or hire.
   2. acting as the sole manipulator of the aircraft controls.
   3. causing the aircraft to be used, or authorizing its use.
   4. exercising authority over initiating, conducting, or terminating a flight.

FAR PART 61

1. [61.5] _____(True, False) Your commercial pilot certificate is not required to be in your personal possession when you are acting as pilot in command, unless you are carrying passengers or cargo for compensation or hire.

2. [61.6] Single-engine land, multi-engine land, single-engine sea, and multi-engine sea are examples of aircraft _____ ratings.

3. [61.19] _____(True, False) A commercial pilot certificate expires at the end of the 12th month after it was issued.

4. [61.23] If you have a second-class medical certificate that was issued on September 12, you are permitted to exercise commercial pilot privileges until _____ , one year later.

5. [61.31] To act as pilot in command of an aircraft with a maximum certificated takeoff weight of more than 12,500 pounds, you must hold a(n) _____ _____ for that aircraft.

6. [61.31] If a pilot has not logged pilot-in-command time in a high-performance aircraft prior to November 1, 1973, requirements to operate such an aircraft include flight instruction in that aircraft and a(n) _____ _____ .

7. [61.51] _____(True, False) If you are copilot on an aircraft that requires two pilots, you can log all flight time as second in command while acting in that capacity.

8. [61.51] If you are exercising the privileges of a commercial certificate, you must have a reliable record of all flight time
   1. flown.
   2. with passengers on board.
   3. since commercial certification.
   4. necessary to meet the recent experience requirements.

9. [61.55] What items are required for you to act as second in command of a large aircraft under VFR?
   A. Private pilot certificate
   B. Commercial pilot certificate
   C. Airline transport pilot certificate
   D. Instrument rating
   E. Appropriate type rating
   F. Appropriate category and class ratings

10. [61.57] To act as pilot in command of an aircraft carrying passengers at night, you must have made at least three takeoffs and landings to a full stop in the same category and class of aircraft within the last _____ days.

11. [61.56] To act as pilot in command, you must have completed a flight review or proficiency check within the last _____ calendar months.

12. [61.60] To continue to use your airman certificate, you must notify the FAA Airman Certification Branch of any permanent address change within _____ days after moving.

13. [61.129] If you hold a commercial pilot certificate without an instrument rating, you are prohibited from carrying passengers for hire at night or on any cross-country flight of more than _____ miles.

FAR PART 91

1. [91.3] If you have to deviate from a rule in FAR Part 91 due to an emergency, a written report of the deviation should be submitted
   1. to the Administrator within 7 days.
   2. only if it is requested by the Administrator.
   3. within 10 days to the nearest Flight Standards District Office.
   4. immediately upon landing to the supervisor of the nearest ATC facility.

2. [91.7] The person who is solely responsible for determining that the aircraft is safe for flight is the
   1. owner.
   2. mechanic.
   3. pilot in command.
   4. commercial operator.

3. [91.23] You cannot operate a large U.S. aircraft under lease unless you have mailed a copy of the lease agreement to the FAA within _____ hours of its execution.

4. [91.103] As part of your preflight planning, you should identify alternate airports in the event that the flight cannot be completed if you are
   1. carrying passengers.
   2. flying at night.
   3. flying outside the vicinity of the airport.
   4. operating an aircraft for compensation or hire.

5. [91.105] Required flight crewmembers must keep their seatbelts fastened during all phases of flight while they are at their _____ _____ .

6. [91.107] _____(True, False) Although passengers should be notified to fasten their seatbelts during all air carrier and air taxi operations, this is only a recommended procedure for private operators.

7. [91.111] You are prohibited from conducting a formation flight
   1. under 1,500 feet AGL.
   2. under any circumstances.
   3. within controlled airspace.
   4. while carrying passengers for hire.

8. [91.113] _____(True, False) When you are overtaking another aircraft, you have the right-of-way over the slower aircraft.

9. [91.117] The maximum indicated airspeed permissible within four nautical miles of the primary airport of a Class C or D airspace area is _____ knots.

10. [91.119] The minimum safe altitude above a sparsely populated area is _____ feet; above a congested area it is _____ feet.

11. [91.123] If you are given priority handling by ATC due to an emergency, you are required to submit
    1. an NTSB report of the emergency within 24 hours.
    2. a written report to the nearest FSDO within 7 days.
    3. a report of the emergency to the Administrator within 10 days.
    4. a report of the emergency within 48 hours, if requested, to the manager of the ATC facility involved.

12. [91.135] Operations in what areas require that you possess an instrument rating while flying in VFR conditions?
    1. Restricted areas
    2. Class A airspace
    3. Class E airspace above 14,500 feet
    4. Air defense identification zone (ADIZ)

13. [91.151] For a night flight, you must carry enough fuel to fly to your intended destination, and then fly after that for at least _____ minutes.

For questions 14 through 17, fill in the missing information pertaining to an aircraft operating under day VFR.

		Airspace	Altitude	Flight Visibility	Distance from Clouds
14.	(91.155)	Uncontrolled	500 ft. AGL	_____	_____
	(91.155)	Class B	2,000 ft. AGL	_____	_____
15.	(91.155)	Controlled	1,000 ft. AGL	_____	_____ ft. below _____ ft. above _____ ft. horizontally
16.	(91.155)	Controlled	5,000 ft. AGL (below 10,000 ft. MSL)	_____	_____ ft. below _____ ft. above _____ ft. horizontally
17.	(91.155)	Controlled	12,500 ft. AGL	_____	_____ ft. below _____ ft. above _____ horizontally

18. [91.157] To legally operate in Class B, C, D, or E airspace, designated for an airport, with a special VFR clearance, you must remain clear of clouds, and the flight visibility must be at least _____ statue mile(s).

19. [91.157] In addition to the specified weather requirements, a special VFR clearance at night requires you to hold a(n) _____ _____, and the aircraft to be equipped for _____ flight.

20. [91.159] You are required to use VFR cruising altitudes when flying at more than 3,000 feet

    1. MSL based on true course.
    2. MSL based on true heading.
    3. AGL based on magnetic course.
    4. AGL based on magnetic heading.

21. [91.203] In addition to the operating limitations and weight and balance information, two additional documents required aboard the aircraft during flight are a current _____ certificate, and the _____ certificate.

22. [91.205] _____(True, False) For a private VFR flight at night, your aircraft must be equipped with both anticollision lights and a landing light.

23. [91.205] When you fly an airplane for hire over water, beyond power-off gliding distance from shore, required equipment includes at least one pyrotechnic signaling device and, for each occupant, approved _____ _____ .

24. [91.207] Rechargeable batteries for an ELT must be recharged before what percentage of their useful life is depleted?

    1. 40%
    2. 50%
    3. 60%
    4. 70%

25. [91.207] The maximum distance from an airport that an aircraft engaged in training operations can operate without an ELT is _____ miles.

26. [91.209] Aircraft position lights must be on from _____ until _____ .

27. [91.211] Continuous supplemental oxygen is required for flight crewmembers above a cabin pressure altitude of _____ feet and must be available for passengers above a cabin pressure altitude of _____ feet.

28. [91.215] Excluding the airspace at and below 2,500 feet AGL, an operable transponder equipped with Mode C capability is required for flight in all airspace at and above

    1. 10,000 feet MSL.
    2. 12,500 feet AGL.
    3. 14,500 feet MSL.
    4. 14,500 feet AGL.

29. [91.215] Required equipment for operating in all airspace within 30 n.m. of a Class B airspace primary airport, from the surface upward to 10,000 feet MSL, includes

    1. VOR receiver with DME.
    2. dual VOR receiver with DME.
    3. VOR, DME, and a 4096-code transponder.
    4. 4096-code transponder with altitude encoding capability (Mode C).

30. [91.303] Select the area(s) where aerobatic flight is prohibited.

    A. Over congested areas
    B. Within a Federal airway
    C. At altitudes less than 1,500 feet AGL
    D. In visibilities of less than three miles
    E. Over an open-air assembly of people

31. [91.311] _____ (True, False) A certificate of waiver issued by the Administrator is required before you can legally operate an aircraft towing a banner.

32. [91.313] Unless it is specifically authorized, you should not operate a restricted category aircraft within a
    1. Class A airspace.
    2. Class E airspace.
    3. Class G airspace.
    4. congested airway.

33. [91.315] Carriage of passengers for hire is
    1. authorized in an experimental aircraft.
    2. authorized in a restricted category aircraft.
    3. not authorized in a limited category aircraft.
    4. not authorized in a utility category aircraft.

34. [91.403, 91.405] _____ (True, False) The owner or operator is primarily responsible for determining when maintenance is to be performed on the aircraft, that all mandatory airworthiness directives are complied with, and that all of the appropriate entries are made in the maintenance records.

35. [91.407] If an aircraft's operation in flight has been substantially affected by alterations or repair, the aircraft documents must show that it has been test flown and approved for return to service by an appropriately rated pilot prior to being operated
    1. for training purposes.
    2. with passengers aboard.
    3. for compensation or hire.
    4. within controlled airspace.

36. [91.409] A record of an aircraft's last annual inspection can be found in the aircraft's required _____ records.

37. [91.409] An aircraft received a 100-hour inspection at 3,210 hours, which was 10 hours overdue. The next 100-hour inspection is due at _____ hours.

38. [91.413] Your ATC 4096-code transponder was last tested, inspected, and found to comply with regulations on May 1. The next inspection is due by
    1. May 1, one year later.
    2. May 31, one year later.
    3. May 1, two years later.
    4. May 31, two years later.

39. [91.417] _____ (True, False) Aircraft maintenance records must show the current status of life-limited parts for the airframe and engine only.

40. [91.417] Compliance with all airworthiness directives should be clearly indicated in the aircraft _____ _____ .

41. [91.421] _____ (True, False) A new maintenance record used for a rebuilt aircraft engine must include previous changes as required by airworthiness directives.

42. [91.421] The old maintenance records of an engine may be discarded after that engine is
    1. reconditioned.
    2. top overhauled.
    3. rebuilt by the manufacturer or agency approved by the manufacturer.
    4. overhauled by the manufacturer or repair station approved by the manufacturer.

FAR PART 119/135

1. [119.1] Select the operations which are governed by FAR Part 119.

   A. Student instruction for hire at an approved school
   B. As an air carrier or commercial operator, or both, in air commerce
   C. A real estate agent flying prospective clients for a potential sale
   D. When common carriage is not involved, in operations of U.S.-registered civil airplanes with a seat configuration of 20 or more passengers, or a maximum payload capacity of 6,000 pounds or more
   E. A commercial pilot who is an employee of a company, flying a company-rented aircraft
   F. A commercial pilot carrying parachute jumpers to a jump site within 25 miles of the airport
   G. Aerial operations for compensation, such as aerial photography, pipeline patrol, rescue, and crop dusting

2. [135.21] Who is responsible for keeping copies of the procedures and policies manual up-to-date with approved changes and additions?

   1. The aircraft owner
   2. Maintenance chief for the certificate holder
   3. The Air Taxi/Commercial technical representative
   4. Each employer of the certificate holder who is issued a manual

3. [135.23] _____(True, False) The operations inspections and surveillance procedures handbook contains information that enables the pilot in command to determine if the return-to-service conditions have been met.

4. [119.5] The document which authorizes you to operate under FAR Part 119 in a specific geographic area is the _____ _____ .

5. [135.85] Which of the following persons may you carry aboard the aircraft without complying with the passenger-carrying requirements under FAR Part 135?

   1. Technical representative of an aircraft company
   2. Member of the U.S. diplomatic corps on an official courier mission
   3. Political candidate campaigning for election to a federal office
   4. Person who is necessary for the safe handling of animals on the aircraft

6. [135.87] _____(True, False) You can carry cargo within the passenger compartment if it has been secured with a seatbelt.

7. [135.87] In regard to rules governing cargo, all carry-on baggage must be

   1. less than 30 pounds in weight.
   2. stowed under the passenger's seat.
   3. secured with a seatbelt or tiedown device.
   4. restrained so that it cannot move during turbulence.

8. [135.89] State the minimum amount of time a flight crew operating under FAR Part 135 would be required to use supplemental oxygen for each of the following flights in an unpressurized aircraft.

   A. 9,500 feet for 2 hours at night
      _____ hours, _____ minutes
   B. 10,500 feet for 3 hours 15 minutes
      _____ hours, _____ minutes
   C. 11,000 feet for 1 hour 45 minutes
      _____ hours, _____ minutes
   D. 12,500 feet for 2 hours 45 minutes
      _____ hours, _____ minutes
   E. 13,500 feet for 3 hours
      _____ hours, _____ minutes

9. [135.93] Assume the aircraft flight manual specifies the maximum loss of altitude for malfunction of the autopilot under cruise conditions is 75 feet. The lowest altitude at which you may use the autopilot under cruise conditions is _____ feet AGL.

10. [135.99] Which of the following aircraft requires two crewmembers under FAR Part 135?

    1. All commuter aircraft
    2. All aircraft with more than 9 passenger seats
    3. All aircraft with more than 10 passenger seats
    4. All turbine-powered aircraft used in commuter service

11. [135.105] Assume you are the pilot in command of a commuter aircraft carrying passengers. What are the minimum experience requirements if the aircraft is equipped with an autopilot and you do not have a second in command?

    1. 50 hours and 10 landings in type
    2. 100 hours and 20 landings in type
    3. 100 hours as pilot in command in the make and model
    4. 200 hours as pilot in command in the category, class, and type

12. [135.107] Under FAR Part 135, the maximum number of passenger seats an aircraft can have without requiring a flight attendant is _____ .

13. [135.117] _____(True, False) The preflight passenger briefing conducted by a crewmember must be supplemented by printed cards for each passenger.

14. [135.149] According to FAR Part 135, a third gyroscopic pitch and bank indicator is required on all

    1. turbojet airplanes.
    2. turbine-powered aircraft.
    3. aircraft requiring a second in command.
    4. aircraft with a gross weight over 12,500 pounds.

15. [135.171] _____(True, False) Any aircraft that has a passenger seating configuration of 10 seats or more is required to have shoulder harnesses installed for all crewmember positions.

NTSB PART 830

1. [830.2] According to NTSB Part 830, an aircraft accident is an occurrence associated with the operation of an aircraft for the purpose of flight which results in

   1. serious injury to any person or substantial damage to the aircraft.
   2. injury to any person or property regardless of the extent involved.
   3. injury to any person or damage to the aircraft in excess of $3,000.
   4. an injury to any person requiring hospitalization or damage to the aircraft which would render it unairworthy.

2. [830.5] If an aircraft is involved in an accident which results in substantial damage to the aircraft, but no injuries to the occupants, the nearest NTSB field office should be notified

   1. immediately.
   2. within 48 hours.
   3. within 7 days.
   4. within 10 days.

3. [830.5] _____(True, False) Damage to property other than the aircraft that is in excess of $25,000 does not require immediate notification to the NTSB.

4. [830.5] Select the situation that requires immediate notification to the nearest NTSB field office?

   1. A near miss
   2. An in-flight radio failure
   3. An in-flight generator or alternator failure
   4. An aircraft that is overdue and is believed to be involved in an accident

5. [830.5] Assume a small fire was extinguished during flight, but it burned the insulation from a wire in the cockpit. What action is required by regulations?

   1. Land immediately
   2. Notify the NTSB if requested
   3. Notify the NTSB immediately
   4. No notification or report is required

6. [830.15] The operator of an aircraft that has been involved in an accident is required to file a written accident report within _____ days.

7. [830.15] The operator of an aircraft that has been involved in an incident is required to submit a report to the nearest field office of the NTSB

   1. immediately.
   2. within 48 hours.
   3. within 7 days.
   4. immediately, if requested to do so.

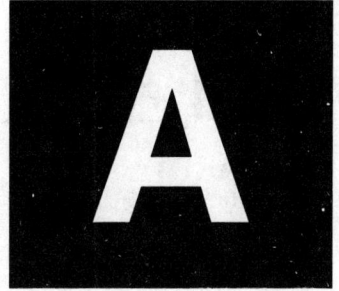

ANSWERS

A PRIVATE PILOT

FAR PART 1
1. Administrator
2. A, C, E
3. flight time
4. 2
5. 4

FAR PART 61
1. 4
2. airplane, rotorcraft, glider, lighter than air
3. 4
4. category, class, 90
5.-7. *Refer to illustration.*
8. 4
9. 3
10. 3
11. 30 days
12. True
13. 2
14. False
15. 2
16. 3

FAR PART 91
1. 3
2. pilot in command
3. 3
4. A, B, D
5. 4
6. 2
7. 4
8. 3
9. 4
10. 4
11. 1
12. 2
13. 3
14. 1. C
    2. E
    3. A
    4. B
    5. D
15. 2
16. 3
17. 4
18. 4
19. 2
20. 2
21. 4
22.-27. *Refer to illustration.*
28. 3
29. 30
30. 45
31. 3
32.-34. *Refer to illustration.*
35. 4

Type Certificate	Date Issued	Usage	Expiration Date
5. First-class	7/12/____	Airline transport pilot	1/31/6 months
		Commercial pilot	7/31/1 year
		Private pilot	7/31/2 years later - if 40 or over
			7/31/3 years later - if under 40
		Student pilot	7/31/2 years later - if 40 or over
			7/31/3 years later - if under 40
6. Second-class	11/1/____	Commercial pilot	11/30/1 year later
		Private pilot	11/30/2 years later - if 40 or over
			11/30/3 years later - if under 40
		Student pilot	11/30/2 years later - if 40 or over
			11/30/3 years later - if under 40
7. Third-class	2/28/____	Private pilot	2/28/2 years later - if 40 or over
			2/28/3 years later - if under 40
		Student pilot	2/28/2 years later - if 40 or over
			2/28/3 years later - if under 40

Color and Type	Aircraft on Surface	Aircraft in Flight
22. Steady red	Stop	Give way to other aircraft and continue circling
23. Steady green	Cleared for Takeoff	Cleared to land
24. Flashing red	Taxi clear of runway in use	Airport unsafe - do not land
25. Flashing green	Cleared to taxi	Return for landing (to be followed by steady green at the proper time)
26. Flashing white	Return to starting point on airport	N/A
27. Alternating red and green	Exercise extreme caution	Exercise Extreme Caution

Altitude	Visibility	Cloud Separation
32. 1,200 feet or less above the surface (regardless of MSL altitude) Within controlled airspace:	3 statute mile(s)	500 feet below 1,000 feet above 2,000 feet horizontal
Outside controlled airspace: (except as provided in FAR 91.155(b) Day Night	1 statute mile(s) 3 statute mile(s)	Clear of Clouds 500 feet below 1,000 feet above 2,000 feet horizontal
33. More than 1,200 feet above the surface but less than 10,000 feet MSL Within controlled airspace:	3 statute mile(s)	500 feet below 1,000 feet above 2,000 feet horizontal
Outside controlled airspace: Day Night	1 statute mile(s) 3 statute mile(s)	500 feet below 1,000 feet above 2,000 feet horizontal
34. More than 1,200 feet above the surface and at or above 10,000 feet MSL	5 statute mile(s)	1,000 feet below 1,000 feet above 1 mile(s) horizontal
Class B airspace areas: (altitudes as charted)	3 statute mile(s)	Clear of Clouds

36. 2
37. 2
38. airworthiness certificate
39. True
40. 4
41. 1
42. 2
43. 4
44. False
45. True

46. 4
47. 1
48. 60, 30
49. 3
50. 2
51. 2
52. 1
53. 1
54. 1

NTSB PART 830

1. 1
2. 1
3. 1
4. 4
5. True
6. $25,000
7. 10
8. 4

B INSTRUMENT RATING

FAR PART 1

1. 2
2. flight visibility
3. 4
4. 4

FAR PART 61

1. 3
2. 4
3. True
4. 2
5. 4
6. True
7. 2
8. six, three
9. 4
10. is

FAR PART 91

1. 3
2. discontinue the flight
3. .04
4. 1
5. 4
6. False

7. 3
8. 3
9. 29.92
10. 3
11. 2
12. 3
13. 4
14. 2
15. False
16. 3
17. 4
18. 2
19. 2
20. 4
21. 1
22. 3
23. 4
24. ETA, 1
25. 4
26. True
27. 600, 2 statute
28. 800, 2 statute
29. 2
30. 30 days
31. 1
32. 1

33. 4
34. controlled airspace
35. 2
36. one
37. 2,000
38. 3
39. 1
40. 4
41. 1
42. C, E
43. altimeter, airspeed, magnetic direction
44. 3
45. 24,000
46. 4
47. 4
48. A
49. C, D
50. A, C, D
51. D
52. 4
53. 2
54. 15,000
55. 2
56. 10,000, MSL
57. controlled airspace

58. 1
59. owner, operator
60. 1
61. 24 calendar months

NTSB PART 830
1. 1
2. 1
3. 1

4. 4
5. 10
6. 4

C COMMERCIAL PILOT

FAR PART 1
1. True
2. commercial operator
3. categories
4. 4

FAR PART 61
1. False
2. class
3. False
4. September 30
5. type rating
6. logbook endorsement
7. True
8. 4
9. A, F
10. 90
11. 24
12. 30
13. 50

FAR PART 91
1. 2
2. 3
3. 24
4. 3
5. crewmember stations
6. False
7. 4
8. False
9. 200

10. 500, 1,000
11. 4
12. 2
13. 45
14.-17. *Refer to illustration on page A-6*
18. 1
19. instrument rating, IFR (or instrument)
20. 3
21. airworthiness, registration
22. False
23. flotation gear
24. 2
25. 50
26. sunset, sunrise
27. 14,000, 15,000
28. 1
29. 4
30. A, B, C, D, E
31. True
32. 4
33. 3
34. True
35. 2
36. maintenance
37. 3300
38. 4
39. False
40. maintenance records
41. True
42. 3

FAR PART 119/135
1. B, D
2. 4
3. False
4. operations specifications
5. 4
6. True
7. 4
8. A. not required
   B. 2 hours, 45 minutes
   C. 1 hour, 15 minutes
   D. 2 hours, 45 minutes
   E. 3 hours
9. 500
10. 2
11. 3
12. 19
13. True
14. 1
15. True

NTSB PART 830
1. 1
2. 1
3. False
4. 4
5. 3
6. 10
7. 4

		Airspace	Altitude	Flight Visibility	Distance from Clouds
14.	(91.155)	Uncontrolled	500 ft. AGL	1	Clear of clouds
	(91.155)	Class B	2,000 ft. AGL	3	Clear of clouds
15.	(91.155)	Controlled	1,000 ft. AGL	3	500 ft. below 1,000 ft. above 2,000 ft. horizontally
16.	(91.155)	Controlled	5,000 ft. AGL (below 10,000 ft. MSL)	3	500 ft. below 1,000 ft. above 2,000 ft. horizontally
17.	(91.155)	Controlled	12,500 ft. AGL	5	1,000 ft. below 1,000 ft. above 1 mile horizontally

New! Aviation Weather Book

Our new text presents the most current, comprehensive information on aviation weather available. 410 information-packed pages, with over 300 full-color illustrations, presenting detailed material in an uncomplicated way. Whether you have ten, or ten thousand hours, you'll gain a new, better understanding of the environment you fly in.
Item Number JS319007 $44.95.

Instructor's Guide
Item Number JS415320 $20.95

Turbulence / A New Perspective For Pilots

The most comprehensive, understandable book available on aviation turbulence today. Helps pilots recognize the conditions that cause turbulence, so the effects can be avoided or minimized. The book provides answers to questions such as: What is turbulence? • What does it look like? • How long does it last? • What causes it? • Where is it found? • What are its indicators? • What are its typical dimensions and intensities?
Item Number JS319006 $24.95

Human Factors For General Aviation

Helps pilots analyze why accidents happen. This text covers: How to Identify Cockpit Design Problems • How Your Eyes and Ears Gather Information • What Factors Affect Your Decision Making • How To Use Cockpit Resources Effectively • Plus Much More.
Item Number JS319005 $36.95

FARs Explained (F.A.R.E.)

Jeppesen's F.A.R.E. has quickly become an industry standard. It helps answer the question, "I know what it says, but what does it mean?" These publications will save you time, money and frustration. Our standard FARs Explained includes FAR Parts 1, 61, 91, 141, and NTSB 830. And introducing our latest publication FARs Explained 135 includes FAR Parts 1 and 135. Each FARs Explained publication also includes: Plain language FARs • Easy to read and understand explanations to the FARs • Cross-references to other FARs to aid understanding • Actual case histories and FAA Chief Counsel Opinion excerpts. Order yours today!

FARs Explained 1, 61, 91, 141, and NTSB 830
Item Number JS319012 $28.50

FARs Explained 135
Item Number JS319013 $28.50

Airway Manual Accessories: Make The Best Even Better

Our complete line of accessories makes your Airway Manual Service even more useful. These distinctive items are designed specifically to protect and help organize your flight information.

You've got the best in navigation information. Our accessories help you get the most from it.

Airway Manual Accessory Pack-Efficiency in a package. Contains: Chartabs (Set of 3) • Approach Chart Protectors (Set of 10) • NavLog/Flight Plan Forms (Set of 50) • Multitabs (Set of 13) • Pilot Notes (Set of 25 Lined)
Item Number AM626046 $12.95

FlighTime Videos Make More Of Your Flight Time

The perfect supplement to Jeppesen's printed training materials. Professionally designed and produced, the FlighTime Video Series covers a wide variety of subjects. Each video is designed to refresh and enhance pilot knowledge. Effective for student and continuing education use.

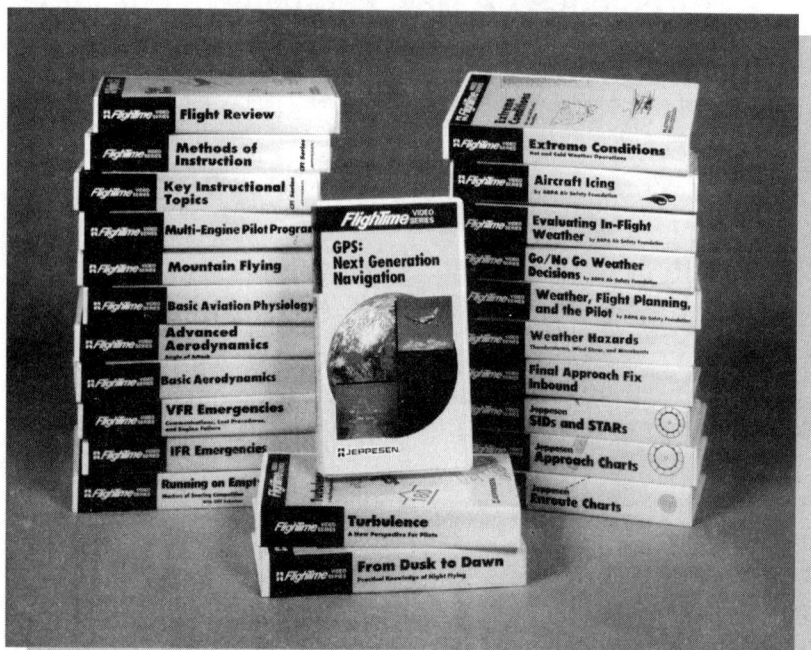

Global Positioning System: The Next Generation of Navigation
Our new video provides the latest information available on GPS' rapidly changing technology, tools, rules and procedures. You'll learn how to use GPS in VFR and IFR operations, and see how three different GPS approaches are flown. This fast paced, 50 minute video includes a 16 page GPS Reference Guide summarizing key requirements for GPS flight.
Item Number JS274010 $36.95

Turbulence, A New Perspective
Provides the latest, most comprehensive look at turbulence; where it can occur, how to avoid it and what to do if you encounter it. Perfect complement to the text, Turbulence. Available with or without the text.
Item Number JS302162 (VHS)W/Text $48.95
Item Number JS274007 (VHS)W/O Text $29.95

Get The Most Out of Your Jeppesen Char

Approach Charts Reviews the various types of information portrayed on approach charts and provides in-depth coverage which goes beyond the chart legend.
Item Number JS273268 (VHS) $36.95

Enroute Charts Enhances the usefulness of your Enroute Charts by thoroughly analyzing chart data to help you quickly and efficiently identify chart information.
Item Number JS273269 (VHS) $36.95

SIDs and STARs Presents the unique characteristics of SID and STAR charts so you can take advantage of these simplified procedures at busy terminal areas.
Item Number JS273270 (VHS) $29.95

Jeppesen Chart 3-Pak Includes the three videos listed above.
Item Number JS200251 (VHS) $97.95

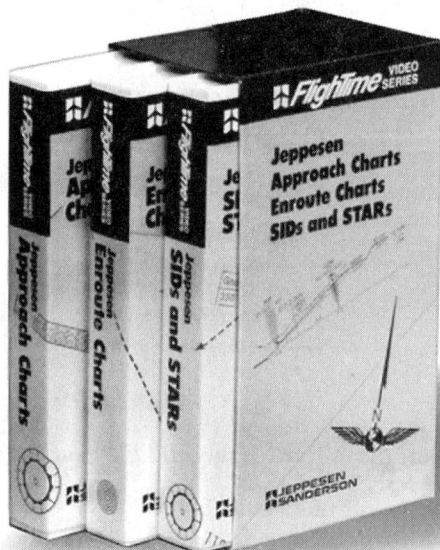

Test Preparation Software

Our new software helps you confidently prepare for the Private Pilot and Recreational Pilot Computer Tests. User friendly and highly flexible. You can study by subject or by FAA question, take a simulated FAA Computer Test and receive instant feedback. Designed to follow our Jeppesen manuals, the software includes explanations to questions, references and reprints of the FAA computerized testing supplements.

Private Pilot And Recreational Pilot Item Number JS200030 $29.95
Instrument Pilot Item Number JS200031 $34.95
Commercial Pilot Item Number JS200032 $39.95

Practical Test Standards

Jeppesen's FAA Practical Test Standards reprints are valuable training aids for instructors and students. New! Private Pilot Practical Test Study Guide carefully parallels the FAA Areas of Operation in the Private Practical Test Standards. Provides key questions, answers, explanations and references. Designed to coordinate with the knowledge and task portions of the PTS. Includes a complete reprint of the FAA PTS.

Item Number JS312404 $17.95

Private Pilot Single-Engine Land PTS
Item Number JS315125 $3.65

Private Pilot Multi-Engine Land PTS
Item Number JS315124 $7.95

Instrument Pilot PTS
Item Number JS316022 $3.10

Commercial Pilot Single-Engine Land PTS
Item Number JS319017 $3.65

Commercial Pilot Multi-Engine Land PTS
Item Number JS315631 $3.65

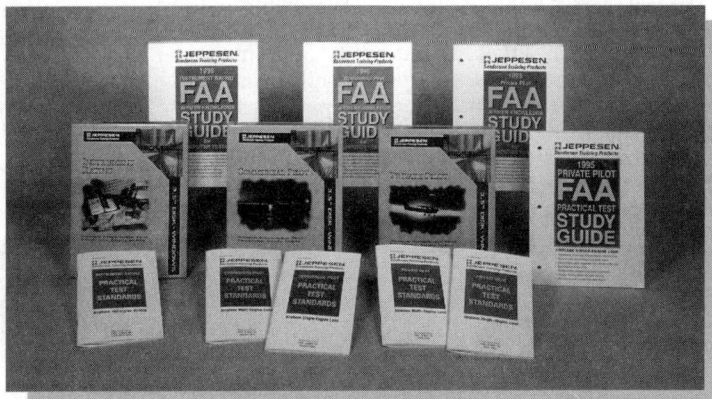

Airmen Knowledge Study Guides

Contain FAA airplane questions arranged in the same sequence as the chapters in our textbooks. Explanations are placed next to each question and include study references to the pages in our textbooks where the topic is covered.

Private Pilot
Item Number JS312400 $13.95

Instrument Rating
Item Number JS312401 $19.95

Commercial Pilot
Item Number JS312402 $16.95

New! Private Pilot Test Prep Video Set

No better way to prepare for the FAA Private Pilot Airmen Knowledge Computer Test. This comprehensive six-tape series covers all of the information on the test. It's a perfect complement to our Private Pilot Manual, Study Guide and the overall Jeppesen training system.

Private Pilot Airmen Knowledge Test Video Set With Study Guide
Item Number JS200020 (VHS) $169.00

Private Pilot Airmen Knowledge Test Video Set With Study
Guide Item Number JS200024 (PAL) $169.00

Private Pilot Airmen Knowledge Test Video Set Without Study
Guide Item Number JS200021 (VHS) $159.00

Private Pilot Airmen Knowledge Test Video Set Without Study
Guide Item Number JS200025 (PAL) $159.00

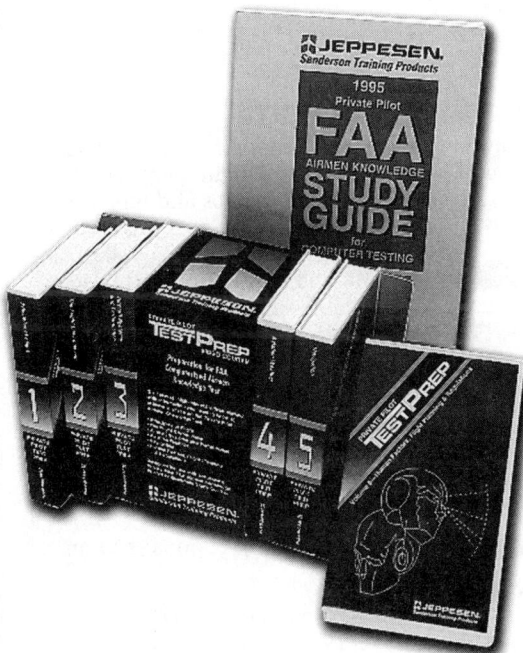

JEPPFAX: Weather By Fax

Instant Information, Worldwide

Regardless of your destination or route, *JeppFax*'s interactive weather by fax service gives you instant access to the latest weather maps and briefing. Any time night or day; 24 hours a day, seven days a week, 365 days a year.

The Latest Weather Only A Phone Call Away

All you need is a phone and a fax. No membership fees or subscription required. You choose the weather maps and text briefings that fit your needs: Real-time radar maps • Radar composite maps • Satellite images (infrared and visible) • Analysis maps • Surface and low level significant weather forecasts • High level significant weather forecasts • Wind and temperature forecast maps • Long-range prognosis maps • Spectral prognosis maps • National Weather Service DIFAX maps • Airport and route briefings specific to your flight.

The Price Is Right!

With JeppFax you get more than just weather, more than just price. You get the added value Jeppesen products and services are known for worldwide.

1 Panel Map or NWS DIFAX Map	$1.40
1 Panel Satellite or Real Time Radar	$1.80
2 Panel Map (2 Maps on 1 Page)	$2.15
2 Panel Map (Incl. 1 Sat or R-T Radar)	$2.60
2 Panel Map (Incl. 2 Sat and/or R-T Radar)	$3.00
Airport Briefing	$1.00
All Other Text Briefings	$1.65

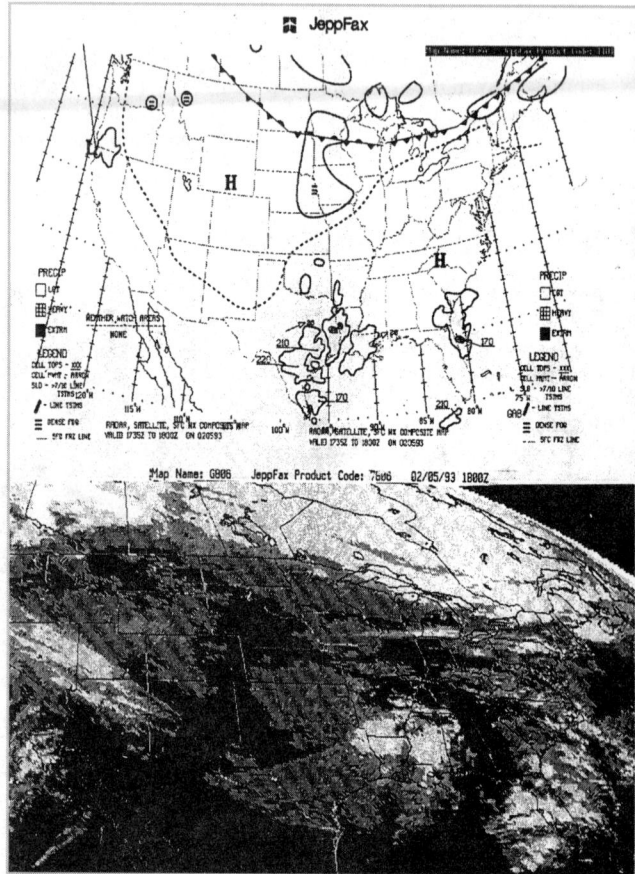

For immediate access to the JeppFax service using your credit card, call 1-800-677-5377. Or to obtain more information and a FREE product demo, call JeppFax sales at 1-800-621-5377.

New! Kneeboard

Our new kneeboard places information at your fingertips. It holds charts, flight computers/plotters, flashlight, pen, pilot notes and more. An elastic leg strap holds this unit comfortably in place with a Velcro closure. The metal clipboard (also available separately) contains valuable information for your VFR and IFR flight needs. An additional strap is included allowing you to use the clipboard independent of the kneeboard. You're really getting two products in one.

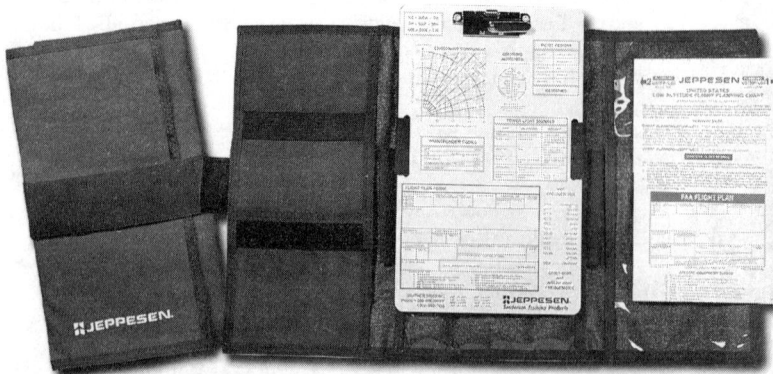

Kneeboard
Item Number JS626003 $34.95.

Clipboard
Item Number JS6260001 $14.95